The Viennese Concerted Mass
of the Early Classic Period

Studies in Musicology, No. 89

George J. Buelow, Series Editor

Professor of Music
Indiana University

Other Titles in This Series

The Viennese Concerted Mass
of the Early Classic Period

by
Bruce C. Mac Intyre

With a Foreword by Jens Peter Larsen

U·M·I Research Press

Ann Arbor / London

Produced and distributed by
UMI Research Press
an imprint of
University Microfilms, Inc.
Ann Arbor, Michigan 48106

Library of Congress Cataloging in Publication Data

Mac Intyre, Bruce Campbell.
 The Viennese concerted mass of the early Classic
period.

 (Studies in musicology ; no. 89)
 Revision of thesis (Ph.D.)—City University of
New York, 1984.
 Bibliography: p.
 Includes index.
 1. Mass (Music) 1. Series.
ML3088.M24 1986   783.2'1'0943613   85-20872
ISBN 0-8357-1673-2 (alk. paper)

In Memoriam

My Father
James Campbell Mac Intyre
(1908–1979)

Contents

"Dona" as a Finale to the Mass
Expressive Devices of the "Dona"
Summary

List of Illustrations

Figures

List of Abbreviations

A	Alto
app.	appendix
avg.	average
b.	born
B	Bass
bapt.	baptized
bc	basso continuo
Bsn	Bassoon
cat.	catalogue
Cl	Clarinet
Clno	Clarino
Clni	Clarini
conc.	concertato
d.	died
decept.	deceptive cadence
DTÖ	*Denkmäler der Tonkunst in Österreich*
EH	English horn
ex.	music example
fig.	figure
Fl	Flute
fl	gulden
Hn	Horn
Hob.	Hoboken, *Haydn Werkverzeichnis*
K.	Köchel
kr	kreuzer
m.	measure
M.	Mass no. in app. C
MDC	Maestro di cappella

MGG	*Die Musik in Geschichte und Gegenwart*
Ob	Oboe
Org	Organ
pl.	plate (no.)
Qty.	quantity
rev.	revised
rip.	ripieno
S	Soprano
T	Tenor
Tbn	Trombone
Timp	Timpani
Trombe	(low trumpet)
unis.	unisono
V (Vln)	Violin(s)
Vc (Vcllo)	Violoncello
Vlone	Violone
w/	with
V/I	V of I
V/V	V of V
c^1	middle C
c	C below middle C

Lowercase Roman numerals represent minor keys; uppercase numerals are major keys.

Manuscript sources are located by RISM sigla; see the introduction to appendix C.

Foreword

Our knowledge of the history of Western music is full of gaps. Oddly enough one of the most remarkable gaps concerns the development which took place around the middle of the eighteenth century. We all know about the giants of the late Baroque, Handel and Bach, who in our retrospective view have tended to count as almost the only representatives of the great period in music history that ended about 1750. We also know that a quite different, but equally outstanding period was forming about 1770 with two other great representatives: Haydn and Mozart. But we have only a rather vague notion of what happened between the end of the "late Baroque" and the forming of the "classical style." It is obvious that there is no direct connection between the Bach-Handel tradition and the Haydn-Mozart breakthrough. There is an intermediary generation between Bach-Handel and Haydn-Mozart, comprising a great many important people like the three composers born in 1714: Gluck, C. Ph. Em. Bach, and Jommelli. But even if they—and others—did pioneering work, they did not create a new general style. They were forerunners, besides being important composers in their own right. But it may seem as if the new style originated, not from the influence of single pioneering forerunners, but primarily from the merging of less prominent local stylistic traditions.

At the beginning of our century an argument came up about the origin of the classical symphony, especially the Viennese symphony tradition emanating from Haydn. It was Hugo Riemann who brought up the virtually forgotten Johann Stamitz as "the long-sought predecessor of Haydn." He was opposed by Guido Adler and his circle, who introduced a number of still less known Viennese forerunners of Haydn. The fight was cut off by World War I and was never really carried to an end. In the long run Stamitz—who is undoubtedly a greater composer than Monn, who was put up against him— was more or less generally accepted as the pioneer Riemann wanted him to be, even if his influence on Haydn has obviously been quite inferior. Haydn's point of departure was undoubtedly primarily the Viennese tradition, not the

"Mannheim School." But the vast material to be studied was only brought to light to a very limited degree and is still not generally available today, even if much progress has been made.

However, scarcely any other branch of preclassical music has been neglected as much as church music. There are several reasons for that. First of all, church music was meant to serve, to function as a secondary contribution to a divine service, not as a brilliant entertainment like the opera. And second, though undoubtedly much music has disappeared, there are still mountains of eighteenth-century church music by known and unknown composers left over in old music archives, which is slowly being registered today. To get this music ready for research, to find out about the true composer of many works, and about the often very difficult question of chronology may present enough problems before the music itself can be put to trial.

A special circumstance has delayed the study of church music from this period, including Haydn's Masses. The Viennese concerted Mass was regarded as too "worldly" for the church and was opposed in leading circles first some time in the late eighteenth century, then again in the nineteenth century by the Cecilian movement and even in the beginning of this century in the papal *motu proprio* (1903). A new beginning with Haydn was made by Carl M. Brand, whose comprehensive study of Haydn's Masses (1940) served as a point of departure and was followed by a critical edition of the Masses by the Haydn Society and later by the Joseph Haydn Institute from about 1950 and by recordings of the Masses, made possible by the new longplaying records from the same time. But then again the question had to come up: how did Haydn find his way to this kind of Mass? Again, there was no single composer serving as a model for Haydn, but a large Mass tradition surrounded him on all sides. He is reported to have once said about his development as a young composer that he learned more from hearing than from studying music, and he added: "But how much was there to hear in Vienna at that time?"

Bruce MacIntyre has taken upon himself the substantial task of expounding the world of the Viennese concerted Mass, from which Haydn found his way to a Mass tradition of his own, culminating in his six late Masses (1796–1802). He has done it with a rare predilection for completeness. He might perhaps have chosen one composer as his central figure, e.g., Haydn's (supposed) teacher, G. Reutter, Jr. (with "approximately 72 Masses"), or else a small number of composers from just before Haydn's start as a composer. But he chose to have as his basis for analysis a selection of no fewer than 72 Masses by 28 composers. The core of this large project is a very comprehensive analysis of the five single constituents of the Ordinarium Missae. Each of these, Kyrie, Gloria, etc., is dealt with in a separate chapter, based on examples from the basic group of 72 Masses. But this central investigation is embedded in an extensive general survey of the background of the central investigation, comprising music life in Vienna at the time in question (ca. 1740–83) and the conditions of church music, an elaborate survey of the elected composers, and chapters on instrumentation and scoring as well as on general form and style. And a supplementary closing part of the study furnishes a number of highly practical collocations concerning liturgical matters and more, comprising also a 100-page thematic catalogue of the 7 selected Masses.

One special feature should be stressed very strongly: the rich amount of music examples. Compared to the history of art or the history of literature, music history has a much tougher job in mastering the problem of relevant examples. They are normally more difficult to get at, take up much more space, and are perhaps not even readable to many users of the book. Since they are also rather expensive, they will often be found in a very limited number. The result of this is that the reader will have too little opportunity to get to know the music in question; he will get to know what the author tells him about it, but he does not get a personal impression of the music.

That is not true of Mac Intyre's book. He has given the reader such a wealth of examples that no detail of any importance is left without one or more relevant examples, giving the reader full opportunity to confirm the author's judgment—or to oppose it if he wants to.

Through the very richness of his book, and through its wealth of music examples, the author leads us to a very well-documented insight into this special world of church music, and at the same time he makes an important contribution to the widened understanding of the development of the Viennese classical style that has been under way a very long time and is undoubtedly coming closer in these years.

Jens Peter Larsen

Preface

When I first studied Haydn's early Masses for a special seminar at the City University of New York,[1] I was amazed at what little contemporary sacred music from mid-eighteenth-century Vienna was readily available for study. In addition, there were relatively few analyses of this repertoire and its milieu, undoubtedly because the more significant new forms of symphonic, chamber, and theatrical music had always attracted the attention of scholars. Thus, convinced that it was about time for musicians to become acquainted with the Masses by Haydn's and Mozart's contemporaries, I began the present study. I hope that some readers will be sufficiently inspired to investigate more closely one or more of the composers and works recommended here.

The principal research was carried out from 1978 to 1980 in Europe with the generous support of graduate research and travel stipends from the Deutscher Akademischer Austauschdienst (DAAD). At that time I resided in Cologne where I was fortunate to have the encouragement and guidance of Dr. Georg Feder and his colleagues at the Joseph Haydn-Institut. The resources of this institute and of the musicological institute at the University of Cologne were invaluable at the outset of the project. Three extended trips to archives in and near Vienna allowed me to personally search for, compare, and gather the primary sources. The RISM files in Kassel, Munich, and Vienna were kindly put at my disposal and were thus helpful in locating additional copies of the Masses. A most generous grant from the Martha Baird Rockefeller Fund for Music, Inc., underwrote my acquisition of microfilms and other needed materials and allowed me the luxury of working full-time on the project during the 1982–83 academic year.

I could describe at length the countless ways so many friends, colleagues, and institutions have aided me in this endeavor. But, considering the economies of space necessary for a work of this scope, I trust they shall understand my inability to name them all here.

However, I must mention a few persons who certainly went far beyond the call of duty. Barry S. Brook was a most helpful and patient advisor from start to finish. His suggestions and careful reading of my text were invaluable. I am also appreciative of others who later read and commented upon this work, including Allan Atlas, Stephen Bonta, Howard Brofsky, Floyd Grave, George Stauffer, Sherman Van Solkema, and Hermine Williams. In Vienna, Otto Biba of the Gesellschaft der Musikfreunde was especially generous in his sharing of ideas, scores, and tips related to this subject. Among other kindnesses, Professor Friedrich Wilhelm Riedel of the University of Mainz assisted me in pruning down my original list of composers and in gaining access to manuscripts at the Benedictine monastery of Göttweig. Last, but of course not least, my wife Mary Paul must be thanked for her excellent typing of the original manuscript as well as for her constant encouragement and support, especially at those times when the problems of this subject and its sources made me feel like throwing up my hands.

The present work is based on the research I completed in 1984 at the City University of New York. Several musical examples, charts, and notes have been shortened or deleted where they seemed redundant or unnecessary for the main topic under discussion. The scores of two complete masses (M. 6 and 19) included in the original work have been left out because I plan to publish them separately in the near future. My thanks also go out to Jens Peter Larsen, who has so graciously offered a few words of introduction.

Introduction

Aims

When we think of the concerted Mass of the Classic period in Vienna, invariably only the 29 complete settings by Haydn and Mozart come to mind. Certainly their works are accessible both in score and on records. However, by no means do Haydn and Mozart alone provide us with a complete picture of Vienna's Mass tradition. As the present study demonstrates, there were more than two dozen other composers actively writing significant and beautiful Masses in Vienna during the second half of the eighteenth century. Undoubtedly these were the contemporary settings to which Haydn and Mozart were exposed. Particularly, the Masses of Dittersdorf, Gassmann, Sonnleithner, Vaňhal, and even Reutter are deserving of more attention than they have heretofore received. After all, Vienna was a large, influential city whose church music was disseminated throughout Lower Austria, Czechoslovakia, and Hungary. The study of the works by these Viennese *Gross-* and *Kleinmeister* not only enhances our understanding of style and performance practices in Vienna but also provides a background that allows the settings by Haydn and Mozart to be observed with a proper historical perspective.

As a byproduct of this study, certain myths about church music practices of the day may be removed or qualified (e.g., how strictly the 1753–67 ban on trumpets and timpani was enforced). In addition, source data and stylistic traits of potential use for later authenticity studies have been presented. But most importantly, we become acquainted with several works which ought to be performed again.

Besides deepening our understanding of the Viennese concerted Mass, this study tries (with the help of the musical examples in the final six chapters) to make several of the composers more than obscure names occasionally encountered in old catalogues. As Adler once wrote, "Heilig achten wir die Geister, aber Namen sind uns Dunst."[1] Indeed, most of the 28 composers under investigation have been caught in a period of transition that has made them easily overshadowed by the two composers who transformed common practices into unique, more mature, and imaginatively designed statements. It is to be hoped that, through the following history, biographies, musical examples, and analyses comparing selected settings of the unchanging Mass text, these *Kleinmeister* and their milieu will come alive once more.

Definitions

Not long after Pius X sought to reform the music of the Catholic Church with his *motu proprio* of 1903 and the previous century's tide of Cecilianism began to ebb, Alfred Schnerich and Guido Adler began writing about the historical and musical significance of the Viennese Mass.[2] Since World War I, a few dissertations and articles have dealt separately with individual composers who were active in Vienna's sacred music at the middle of the eighteenth century.[3] Georg Reichert's 1935 dissertation "Zur Geschichte der Wiener Messenkomposition in der ersten Hälfte des 18. Jahrhunderts" remains an excellent study, a pathbreaker in the complex task of determining Mass output and authenticity as well as a model for the present study, which, in a sense, continues Reichert's account from the death of Fux (1741) up to the Josephine reforms of 1783.[4] In 1941 Carl Maria Brand published *Die Messen von Joseph Haydn,* a monograph remarkable for its scholarship as well as its appreciation of Vienna's sacred music heritage. Ernst Tittel's *Österreichische Kirchenmusik* (1961) includes a useful, detailed survey of Baroque and Classic sacred music in Vienna.

Like Reichert, I have concentrated upon concerted Masses for orchestra, chorus, and soloists. Seventy-two Masses by 28 composers were selected as a representative sample to be closely analyzed and compared.[5] All are settings of the complete Mass Ordinary; Requiems and *missae breves* of the Italo-Lutheran type (i.e., Kyrie-Gloria only) have not been considered.[6] In addition to the analyses of the Masses and the biographies of the composers, two chapters are devoted to the history and role of church music in eighteenth-century Vienna, including an extensive discussion of the liturgical context and the changing interpretations of "church style." These chapters provide background that is essential for understanding the nature and function of these Masses.

The subject matter has many problems and pitfalls that can be discouraging. First of all, the repertoire of concerted Masses at this time is vast and hence difficult to control. Originally all Masses by composers working within a 50-mile radius of Vienna were considered for this study. This approach was abandoned after a list of more than 65 composers resulted. Even by limiting ourselves to the city of Vienna, the 28 composers under study produced over 568 Mass settings (including a cappella as well as concerted ones).[7]

A second problem results from the fact that these Masses have very rarely been published. Because they were disseminated chiefly in manuscript copies (usually parts, rarely scores), conflicting attributions for the same Mass often arise, and dates of composition are seldom known.[8] Related problems are the different titles, versions, and orchestrations encountered for the same Mass in different sources. More studies of individual institutions and of individual composers, their handwritings, and their copyists are needed before all questions about alternate versions and instrumentations can begin to be answered satisfactorily. However, a short digression on the significance of Mass titles must be included here for purposes of clarification and definition.

In the literature about eighteenth-century Masses, we discover some contradictions (and confusion) in the meanings of the terms *missa solemnis* and *missa brevis*. These discrepancies arise from a combination of factors:

1. Lack of uniformity in the use and meaning of the terms during the eighteenth century
2. Differences between the liturgical and musical meanings
3. Various conflicting interpretations by recent analysts

The testimony of contemporary musical sources and lexicons can, however, shed some light on eighteenth-century definitions of *missa brevis* and *missa solemnis*. Such sources demonstrate that definitions from the nineteenth century cannot always be uniformly applied to the preceding century; this problem has arisen previously with terms such as the symphony, sonata, and divertimento. In the end, it seems best to avoid pigeonholing Masses into categories and, instead, to think of each work in terms of its own particular title, length, and scoring.

According to eighteenth-century rubrics, thematic catalogues, musical treatises, lexicons, and the musical manuscripts themselves, Masses were variously categorized according to the occasion, instrumentation, style, or length. In his "Rubriche Generali" of 1727, Kilian Reinhardt classified the polyphonic music used at the Imperial Hofmusikkapelle in Vienna according to three styles:

1. "in contrapunto" (a cappella style)
2. "mediocre" or "ordinarie" (middle style; the usual type of accompanied church music; in Fux's *stylus mixtus*)
3. "solenne" (solemn; for the most important occasions and feasts, usually with trumpets and timpani and of greater length)[9]

Thematic catalogues varied in how they classified Masses. For some collections Mass catalogues were arranged only by instrumentation. For instance, the *Catalogus Selectiorum Musicalium* that was assembled in 1751 for the Chorherrenstift in Herzogenburg divided Masses into *Missae solemnes cum clarinis et tympanis* and *Missae sine clarinis et tympanis*.[10] Other catalogues simply arranged the works by composer (e.g., at Lambach, 1768) or in order of acquisition (e.g., at Raigern, 1771). On the other hand, a catalogue assembled ca. 1785 or later for the Hofmusikkapelle separates Masses "in concerto" from Masses "in pieno," i.e., the concerted from the tutti ones.[11] Two inventories, from the Brothers of Mercy in Prague and Feldberg (Valtice), distinguish "Missae pastorales" from festive and ordinary Masses in their listings.[12] An 1857 catalogue for Vienna's Schottenstift lists Masses according to three categories: "vokal" (probably a cappella), "de Dominica" (ordinary Sundays), and "solemnis" (special feasts).[13] In sum, then, Masses in contemporary catalogues were classified and arranged differently from place to place, undoubtedly according to the circumstances and needs of the local choir director or institution.

Lexicons and treatises from the period also do not offer a uniform categorization of Masses. For example, Walther's *Musicalisches Lexicon* (1732) defines three Mass types, one based on length and two based on scoring:[14]

Messe brevi	—	short Masses
Messe concertate	—	Masses whose voices "concertiren (*solo* singen)" with the choruses intermingled
Messe da capella	—	Masses which are to be sung throughout by a full choir (i.e., "von starck besetzten Stimmen gesungen") and which usually include fugues, double counterpoint, and other artistically proper ornamentation

These types are probably equivalent to what we know today as the *missa brevis,* the concerted Mass, and the a cappella *(stile antico)* Mass. That Walther fails to give a definition of *missa solemnis* and *missa longa* perhaps indicates that such terms were not yet commonly used among musicians.

The most common title for the Viennese Masses under study was simply "Missa" or "Messe." This word, along with a key designation (e.g., "ex C" or "in C"), usually heads the title on the folder containing the manuscript parts. As Reichert points out, a variety of other descriptive words may also follow "Missa" in the title.[15] These include a Saint's name; a group designation; parts of the Litany of Loreto; a feast day or time of the church year; a quotation from the Bible, liturgy, or prayers; names of virtues; adjectival names; an open-ended general title; a stylistic character; or any peculiarity of the instrumentation. As already mentioned and as may be seen in the thematic catalogue (app. C), Mass titles varied from place to place and served primarily as local "labels" for the Masses. *Missa brevis* and *missa solemnis* actually appear seldom as titles in the sources. The following list shows the diversity of titles that indicate something about the length or occasion of a Mass:[16]

> *Missa alla capella (cappella)*
> *Missa brevis, brevior, brevissima, curta*
> *Missa de dominica, Missa dominicalis, Messe ordinäre, Missa mediocris*
> *Missa panem quotidianum, Missa usui quotidiano accomodata*
> *Missa minus solennis*
> *Missa solemnis vell de dominica*
> *Missa solennis, solemnis (sollemnis), solemnior, Sacrum solenne,*
>   *solemne, Fest-Messe*

Apparently there was no standard practice in the use of these titles. Again, Masses were named according to local usage. Composers' preference for using only the word "Missa" as a title and the discrepancies between titles in different sources support the view that the terms *missa brevis, missa solemnis, missa longa,* etc. were not used consistently during the eighteenth century.

Twentieth-century writers have increased the confusion by unjustifiably trying to make later characterizations of the Mass apply to eighteenth-century nomenclature. For example, in his discussion of Haydn's Masses, H.C. Robbins Landon writes that "there were, basically, three kinds of Mass": the "cantata" Mass, the less lengthy, "ordinary" kind of *missa solemnis* with or without trumpets and timpani, and the *missa brevis.*[17] In light of the preceding discussion this categorization seems historically unfounded and overly simple. What is more, Haydn's *Nicolaimesse* (Hob. XXII: 6), has elements of all three types. "Cantata" Mass is a convenient modern name for an extended, multi-movement, richly crafted *missa solemnis,* the most famous examples of which are Bach's *B-minor Mass* (BWV 232), Haydn's *St. Cecilia Mass* (Hob. XXII: 5), and Mozart's unfinished *Mass in C Minor* (K. 427).[18] Indeed the expression "missa cantata" never appears in any musical source and is misleading because the Masses lack cantata traits such as recitative-aria pairs, a continuous narrative, etc. A better name, as recently suggested to me by F.W. Riedel, is number Mass.

In his *MGG* article on the history of the Mass since 1600, Walter Senn carefully shows us the diversity of Mass types. However, his typology might lead one to think that these Mass genres were inflexible in meaning and use.[19] Later, in the second volume of Masses for the *Neue Ausgabe* of Mozart, Senn states categorically that the two chief types of Mass Ordinary settings ("Haupttypen des Ordinarium missae") are the *missa brevis* and *missa solemnis.* He admits, however, that the definition of these types is difficult because they are not of the same plane and that they differ essentially according to the degree of ceremony required.[20] Senn also describes a third, "Sonderform" of Mass, one that is both short and solemn. In manuscripts this "Zwischenform" is often entitled "Missa brevis et solemnis." Mozart's earliest example of this hybrid type is the so-called *Spatzen-Messe,* K. 220.[21]

Several other modern explanations of these Mass types could be cited.[22] In sum, though, a disturbing confusion results from the discrepancies between these various attempts at definition. As James Dack has correctly observed, hybrid types of Mass settings were "by no means uncommon" in eighteenth-century Vienna and "make rigid classification of 'missa solemnis', 'missa', and 'missa brevis' characteristics quite impossible."[23] Appropriately, he finds size to be the main determinant between the various Mass types, since the same formal procedures can be found in all types.[24]

Thus we shall consider these Masses not so much according to general types but rather as individual entities, as *missae* of varying lengths composed for certain occasions and performing forces. On the other hand, as Senn has pointed out, we cannot totally ignore the existence of Mass types since they sometimes explain the changes in a composer's style from one Mass to the next.[25] The crux of the problem lies in the fact that *Missa solemnis* was originally a liturgical not a musical designation. Nonetheless, the musical traits of the *missa brevis* and *missa solemnis* ought to be kept in mind. They are generally agreed to be the following:

Missa brevis
  1. Short Mass for ordinary Sundays or smaller churches (with elements of abbreviation such as fewer movements and polytextuality)
  2. Simple setting (mostly for chorus; few solos; "church trio" orchestra)

Missa solemnis (better: *Missa longa*)
  1. Elaborate, extensive setting of festive character (often including arias, solo ensembles, fugues, etc.); a "number Mass"
  2. Usually with trumpets and timpani (i.e., an expanded orchestra)

Several other distinctions could be cited, but then we would start finding exceptions. The chief musical differences are length and instrumentation, although we must always remain aware that hybrid forms existed. We must also be careful not to mix liturgical and musical uses of terms, an error easily made when the same or similar words are used in both areas.[26]

In sum, each Mass is best viewed separately in terms of its length, performing forces, and (if known) the occasion and place for which it was written. Mass titles are of secondary importance and should be interpreted carefully and not necessarily as indicators of style. In other words, the qualifiers following *Missa* in a title should be treated as adjectives just for *that* particular Mass in *that* particular source and not as standardized types of the eighteenth century. Furthermore, a title found in the sources is not necessarily the same title given a Mass by its composer.[27]

Composers Selected

The present study focuses upon 28 composers who worked in Vienna during the period 1741–83 and whose Masses were undoubtedly performed there (see fig. A). Composers who studied there but soon went elsewhere to write their Masses (e.g., Donberger and Zechner) have not been considered. Earlier composers whose Masses continued to be performed frequently (e.g., Palestrina, Ziani, Fux, Caldara, et al.) have also not been treated. Selection of the composers was based upon biographical research and study of Mass repertoires listed in eighteenth-century catalogues of church and monastery libraries, contemporary accounts of sacred music, and the extant music itself.

As figure A shows, the 28 composers represent approximately two generations. The elder generation, led by Hasse, Monn, Reutter, Tuma, and Wagenseil, primarily represents an older tradition that directly descends from late Baroque composers of Austria (e.g., Fux, Caldara) and Italy (e.g., A. Scarlatti, Porpora). Composers of the younger generation are more or less Joseph Haydn's contemporaries, the most progressive of whom (especially Albrechtsberger, Dittersdorf, Gassmann, Haydn, Sonnleithner, and Vaňhal) contributed to the development of the more concise, instrumentally varied, and symmetrically phrased Masses of the early Classic era. Marianne von Martínez is the only known female composer of Masses in Vienna at this time.

Surprising is the number of well-known Viennese composers who apparently wrote little church music or no Masses. Why, for instance, are there no known Masses by Franz Aspelmayr (1728–86), Wenzel Birck (1717/18–63), Christoph Willibald Gluck (1714–87), Gottlieb Muffat (1690–1770), Carlos d'Ordoñez (1734–86), Giuseppe Scarlatti (ca. 1718–77), Joseph Starzer (1726/27–87), or Joseph Antonín Štěpán (1726–97)? Obviously these composers were fully occupied producing other kinds of music, be it opera, ballet, organ, symphonic, or chamber music. Yet the fact remains that these composers restricted their output only to certain genres and did not write choral music for the church. As shall be seen, most of the present 28 composers were active in chamber, symphonic, and theater music as well as sacred music.

A few composers were not included among the 28 because of lack of information and the scarcity of sources. These men include Johann Habbegger (d. 1795), Pancrazio Huber (see Burney, *Musical Tours,* ed. Scholes, II, pp. 97, 124), and Johann Georg Joseph Spangler (1752–1802).

Figure A. Viennese Composers under Consideration

Elder Generation (born before ca. 1720)

Arbesser, Ferdinand (1719–94)	4	Masses
Bonno, Giuseppe (1711–88)	30	Masses
Carl, Anton (ca. 1717–84)	ca. 22	Masses
Hasse, J. A. (1699–1783)	10+	Masses
Holzbauer, Ignaz (1711–83)	ca. 36	Masses
Monn, Mathias Georg (1717–50)	ca. 6	Masses
Predieri, L. A. (1688–1767)	14+	Masses
Reutter, Jr., Georg von (1708–72)	ca. 72	Masses
Schmidt, Ferdinand (1693/94–1756)	14+	Masses
Seuche, Joseph (ca. 1702–90)	ca. 19	Masses
Strasser	ca. 17	Masses
Tuma, Franz (1704–74)	ca. 65	Masses
Wagenseil, Georg (1715–77)	ca. 18	Masses

Haydn and His Immediate Contemporaries (born after 1720)

Albrechtsberger, J. G. (1736–1809)	ca. 35	Masses
Boog, Johann Nepomuk (ca. 1724–64)	ca. 16	Masses
Dittersdorf, Karl (1739–99)	ca. 18	Masses
Friberth, Karl (1736–1816)	9	Masses
Gassmann, Florian (1729–74)	5	Masses
Grassl	ca. 14	Masses
Gsur, Tobias (ca. 1725–94)	ca. 7	Masses
Hofmann, Leopold (1738–93)	33	Masses
Kohaut, Carl (1726–84)	ca. 8	Masses
Krottendorfer, Joseph (1741–98)	ca. 10	Masses
Martínez, Marianne von (1744–1812)	4	Masses
Müller, Silverius (1745–1812)	ca. 2	Masses
Sonnleithner, Christoph (1734–86)	ca. 14	Masses
Vaňhal, Jan (1739–1813)	ca. 60	Masses
Ziegler, Joseph (1722–67)	ca. 6	Masses

Joseph Kainz (1738–1810), a talented Augustinian father who composed about 20, mostly short tutti (i.e., chorus only) Masses, was also not included.

Masses Selected

Seventy-two Masses by the 28 composers were selected to be the study sample ("M" numbers 1–72 in the thematic catalogue of the appendix). Choices were made from the author's ongoing thematic catalogues and from personal inspection of most of the sources.[28] The final selection was based upon the following five criteria:

1. *Authenticity.* There is no doubt about the authorship of each Mass. (For M. 20 and M. 59 we are sure only of the composers' last names.)
2. *Concerted Mass.* Only works for chorus, soloists, and orchestra were considered. A cappella and tutti (i.e., chorus only) Masses were not included because they seem not to have played a major role in stylistic changes during this period.
3. *Vienna 1741–83.* Evidence from contemporary performing materials, thematic catalogues, and the composers' biographies indicates that each Mass was probably written or performed in Vienna during this period.[29] With the exception of one Mass each by Holzbauer (M. 30; before 1739), Reutter (M. 49; 1734), and Vaňhal (M. 66; before 1797), all Masses can be dated between the death of Fux (1741) and the imposition of Joseph II's ecclesiastical regulations (1783). Most dates for the Masses are only *tempi ante quem* based on known performance dates; hence "before" often precedes the date of a Mass.
4. *Wide Dissemination.* Preference was given to Masses that were found in more than one archive.
5. *Variety in Type.* An attempt was made to achieve a reasonable balance of Masses with respect to tonality, instrumentation, length, and dates within the period chosen.

Using these five criteria, I came up with a fairly representative cross section of Mass composition in Vienna during this period. Half the Masses in the sample are *missae longae* (see fig. 5-1). Because of limitations of time and expense, only one manuscript copy of each Mass has been closely inspected for the musical analyses. (In the thematic catalogue these sources are marked by an asterisk.) Nonetheless, study and comparison of the 72 Masses in the sample and the resultant discovery of several superb settings have proven the wisdom in this remark by Oliver Strunk: "When you look for a needle in a haystack, perhaps you may turn it up by system, but often you find it simply by kicking the straws around."[30]

Part I

The Historical Background

Plate 1.   Vienna as Viewed from the Josephstadt in 1785
Faintly silhouetted against the skyline from left to right are the spires of the
Schotten-Kirche, Maria Stiegen, Minoriten, St. Peter's (low dome), St. Stephen's
(tallest), St. Michael's, and St. Augustine's.   Engraving by Karl Schütz
(Vienna: Artaria, 1785; Albertina, Vienna)

Die Residenstadt Wien, von der
Josephstadt anzusehen.

Vue de la Capitale de Vienne prise
du côté du Joseph Stadt.

1

Church Music in the Context of Musical Life in Eighteenth-Century Vienna

Church music played an important role in the everyday life and music of eighteenth-century Vienna. The "business" of providing adequate music for the city's numerous churches significantly affected not only the daily lives of the worshiping public but also the musical economy, the musical style (to a certain extent), and even the development of instrumental genres. This impact of the church and its music upon life in Vienna is all too easily underestimated by us today in our secularly oriented world.

In the eighteenth century Vienna was a staunchly Catholic city. The piety of its more than 100,000 residents closely reflected that of the *Hof,* or Imperial Court.[1] The number of church events where music was used to enhance the ceremony and strengthen the faith of believers seems unlimited. There were public Masses (*Ämter, Gottesdienste, Messen*), Vespers, litanies, miscellaneous devotions (*Andachten*), processions through the streets, and pilgrimages (*Wallfahrten*) to various churches near and far.[2] Most public holidays and festivals were religiously oriented and touched the lives of nearly all citizens. Since music was also a part of most of these celebrations, we can safely assert that the church maintained a preeminent position in the musical life of Vienna. It should not be surprising, then, when Burney remarks about Vienna of 1772 that "... there is scarce a church or convent in Vienna, which has not every morning its *mass in music:* that is, a great portion of the church service of the day, set in parts, and performed with voices, accompanied by at least three or four violins, a tenor and base, besides the organ...";[3] or when the Berlin book dealer and man of letters Friedrich Nicolai (1733–1811) writes of his visit to Vienna in 1781: "I heard much church music there, for still at that time Masses were constantly performed with music; and because the starting time for each church was different, I could certainly hear the music for three or four Masses on Sundays or holidays."[4] When we realize that in early 1783 there were over 40 houses of worship hiring singers and instrumentalists in Vienna and its suburbs, the significance of church music for the devout believer—as well as for the musicians of the day—becomes quite clear.[5]

Reports tell us how instrumentally accompanied music was used for diverse special occasions beyond those associated with the regular services for a Sunday or holiday. For instance, in 1773 Leopold Hofmann composed a *Festmesse* in honor of Joseph Hörl's election to the post of *Bürgermeister* of Vienna. It was probably first performed at St. Stephen's Cathedral, where Hofmann was Kapellmeister.[6] As both Burney and Nicolai observe, long religious processions were a common sight in Vienna, and music with instruments often accompanied them (see plate 2). Indeed Burney seemed quite amused:

> I was told by an Italian at Vienna, that the Austrians are extremely addicted to processions, *portatissimi alle processioni*. There were five or six of these processions this morning [Sunday, 6 September 1772]; and yet it is observed that they are much less frequent than formerly: however not a day passed, while I remained in this city, without one or more to some church or convent: but all this helps to teach the people to sing in different parts.

> The Emperor came from Laxemberg [*sic*] to attend the celebration of this festival [Sunday, 13 September 1772, celebrating the expulsion of the Turks], and walked in the procession, which set off from the Franciscan's church, and proceeded through the principal streets of the city to the Cathedral of St. Stephan, where *Te Deum* was sung, under the direction of M. Gasman, imperial *maestro di capella*.[7]

On Trinity Sunday in 1781 Nicolai witnessed a procession from St. Peter's in Vienna and was especially impressed with the chorus accompanied by cornetti (*Zinken*), two trombones, and two bassoons,[8] Much iconographic evidence exists for such musical accompaniment of these processions.[9]

Music was also part of more private church events such as memorial services for the dead (*Totengedächtnisse*), brotherhood services (*Bruderschaftsgottesdienste*), and pilgrimages (*Wallfahrten*) made to a certain church.[10] Probably the best known examples of music for a pilgrimage church are two of Joseph Haydn's early Masses, (Hoboken XXII: 5 and 8) both bearing the title *Missa Cellensis* which refers to the church of Mariazell. Many residents of Vienna (Haydn included) made the arduous, nearly 80-mile pilgrimage, often on foot, to this remarkable church.[11] Even the Emperor Francis I, husband of Maria Theresa, made regular pilgrimages to Hernals and Maria-Lanzendorf.[12]

Brotherhoods were significant supporters of church music in Vienna until their abolition by Emperor Joseph II in 1783. These "geistliche Bruderschaften" (Latin *sodalitas*), whose histories often extended back to the fourteenth century, were societies of laymen coming from the same profession or city of residence. They usually served a particular religious or charitable purpose.[13] Every Austrian church in a large city enjoyed the support of two or three, often five or six, brotherhoods. In Vienna alone there were some 216 brotherhoods when Joseph II abolished them and gave their wealth to the

Die Frohnleichnahms Prozession, über den Michaelerplatz aö 1780.

Plate 2. A Corpus Christi Procession Passing before St. Michael's
in 1780
Anonymous ink drawing
(Historische Blätter Wien III, 1750–82, blaue Nr. 24,
Albertina, Vienna)

poor in 1783. According to Hanslick, the purpose of these fellowships was twofold: (1) the maintenance of weekly communal devotions (*Andachten*), and (2) the honoring of a particular guardian saint by means of processions, big commemorative feasts (*Gedächtnisfeste*), etc. The better part of their activities consisted of aiding members who had become impoverished.[14] In Vienna these brotherhoods also supported the musical celebration of certain church feasts and contributed directly to church endowments for music.[15]

Two of the Viennese brotherhoods were made up of musicians. At St. Michael's there was the St. Nicholas Brotherhood or "Bruderschaft der Musiker unter dem Schutz des heiligen Niclas [*sic*]." Founded in 1288, this brotherhood was actually a musical guild (*Zunft*) to which all professional musicians of the archduchy had to belong.[16] The other musical brotherhood was the *Cäcilienbruderschaft* or "musikalische Kongregation" at St. Stephen's Cathedral. Better known of the two, this St. Cecilia Brotherhood was founded in 1725 under the benevolent protection of Emperor Charles VI. It was a free union of musicians whose purpose was "to promote and perform good church music."[17] According to Hanslick, this brotherhood was the more modern and free of the two musical societies: membership included not only musicians but also amateurs, and the imperial family was always numbered among its patrons.[18] The *Tonkünstler Societät* founded in 1771 was a secular society of musicians which also looked after the welfare of its members; it can be regarded as the successor to the St. Cecilia Brotherhood in 1783.

In 1779 Ogesser, a priest, published the following account of the St. Cecilia Brotherhood in his *Beschreibung der Metropolitan-Kirche zu St. Stephan in Wien:*

> This brotherhood was established for praising God and honoring His saints, especially St. Cecilia, and for improving souls. Because its founders were devout musicians and because they administer this brotherhood, it is named the *musikalische Kongregation,* whose first president was Prince Ludwig Pius von Savoyen. They celebrate their main feast on St. Cecilia's Day [22 November], when one hears the most excellent music (*die vortrefflichste Musik*) not only at the Vespers beginning after four o'clock the evening before but also at the High Mass and second Vespers on the feast day itself. On the following day there are obsequies for all deceased brothers and sisters in addition to 50 holy Masses for the dead and living colleagues. They cover all expenses with contributions which are made annually and upon joining.[19]

Thus the St. Cecilia Brotherhood gathered each year on November 22 for performances, at first in the Augustinerkirche and later in St. Stephen's Cathedral.[20] H. C. Robbins Landon reports that it also organized a Litany on the eve of St. Cecilia's Day. He also cites the following passage from the *Wiener Diarium* (no. 94) of 25 November 1767: "... the Musical Brotherhood this evening gave the Vespers in honour of the Feast of their patron, which falls on the Sunday. Monday morning this Feast will be celebrated by a solemn High Mass, during which various excellent musicians will be heard in arias and concertos."[21] Many Masses from this period bear the title *Missa Sanctae Caeciliae* or *Cäcilienmesse* because they may have been composed for or used on this brotherhood's patronal feast day. The *Wiener Diarium* of 1769 reports that a *Cäcilienmesse* by Albrechtsberger was performed on St. Cecilia's Day.[22] The statutes of the brotherhood apparently required that half the works for their services be German.[23] In any event, the brotherhood's promotion of fine church music seems beyond question.

The Jesuits played a vital role in training many of Vienna's—Austria's— finest musicians. Albrechtsberger, Aumann, Dittersdorf, Donberger, Gassmann, Michael Haydn, Christoph Sonnleithner, and Tuma are among their successful students. Several other musicians (e.g., Johann Nepomuk Boog and Karl Friberth) taught or performed in Vienna's Jesuit institutions.[24] The Jesuits were helpful to promising young musicians, as is demonstrated by their assistance to Leopold Mozart when he was trying to introduce his gifted son to the Viennese.[25] Accordingly, Leopold was quite upset in September 1773 when the Jesuit Order in Vienna was suppressed.

The outline which follows summarizes the ways in which both instrumental and vocal music were employed in Viennese churches during this period.[26]

I. Voices (and Instruments)
   A. Mass
      1. Ordinary (Kyrie, Gloria, Credo, Sanctus, Agnus Dei)
      2. Proper
         a) Introit (polyphonic, rarely with instruments and usually replaced by the prelude)
         b) Gradual (usually replaced by instrumental music)
         c) Alleluia (replaced by the Tract during Lent)
         d) Sequence (in the octave of Easter, Pentecost, and Corpus Christi)
         e) Offertory (sometimes replaced by a motet)
         f) Communion (performed *figural* at most only during Advent and Lent)
         g) Te Deum (for special occasions; after Mass)
   B. Requiem Mass
   C. Votive Masses (*Lobämter*)
   D. Divine Office (*Stunden-Offizium*), especially:
      1. Vespers
         a) Psalms
         b) Hymn
         c) Magnificat

        d) Marian antiphon (seasonal)

        e) Litany (seasonal)

        f) Te Deum (seasonal; after Vespers)

    E. Special Devotions (*Andachten, Totengedächtnisse*)

        1. Motets and arias sometimes included along with litanies

        2. "Sepolcro-Musik" (during Holy Week)

    F. Processions

    G. Special Services

        1. Brotherhood services (*Bruderschaftsgottesdienste*)

        2. Pilgrimage services (*Wallfahrtsgottesdienste*)

II. Instruments (without voices)

    A. Organ prelude and postlude

    B. Intrada for trumpets and timpani (replaces prelude and postlude on high feasts)

    C. Gradual music (organ piece, instrumental "epistle" sonata, concerto, symphony, etc. instead of the sung Gradual)

    D. Offertory music (an instrumental substitute, like Gradual music above)

    E. Communion music

Obviously the higher the feast, the more time and funds there were for additional music.

    Just how musically rich a High Mass could be at that time may be seen from the list of special music planned by the Sebastian Brotherhood for a Mass at the *Filialkirche* in Furth near Göttweig on Wednesday, 20 January 1773, the Feast of Saints Fabian and Sebastian:[27]

Mass Ordinary
    Karl Ditters von Dittersdorf: Mass in C (without Credo)
Gradual Music
    Robert Kimmerling: Symphony in C (first movement)
Offertory Music
    Joseph Haydn: "Super flumina" (motet, Hoboken XXIIIa: 7)

This program is made all the more impressive by the fact that all these pieces included trumpets and timpani; and that the service occurred in a small rural town some 36 miles west of Vienna. We have already seen how in 1767 the St. Cecilia Brotherhood in Vienna organized a High Mass that included arias and concertos. On 12 November 1768 Leopold Mozart wrote about the upcoming service planned for the dedication of the new church at Vienna's *Waisenhaus* (orphanage): "For this Feast Wolfgang has composed a solemn mass, an offertorium and a trumpet concerto for a boy, and has dedicated them to the orphanage. Presumably Wolfgang himself will conduct (*taktieren*) this music."[28] At St. Stephen's Cathedral on 8 September 1772 (Nativity of the B.V.M.) Charles Burney heard "several symphonies for instruments only" by Hofmann.[29]

Based on these accounts, churches should be considered among the earliest "concert halls" in Vienna. Ursprung is probably correct in saying there were "church concerts with liturgical accompaniment."[30] During the eighteenth century, concert music for church services became excessive—both in cost and liturgical propriety—and led to Joseph II's ecclesiastical restrictions beginning in 1783.

Church music was certainly an important part of the musical economy in Vienna. Although composers were still trying to keep the three musical styles (church, chamber, and theater) separate and distinct, musicians did not hesitate to work simultaneously in all three areas in order to make a living. For instance, there was nothing to stop the operatic tenor and composer Karl Friberth from holding choir directorships at seven Viennese churches in the early 1780s.[31] Multiple positions held simultaneously by the same person were accepted as a necessity in eighteenth-century Vienna, especially among church musicians. Georg von Reutter, Jr. (1708-72) provides perhaps the most striking example of this practice. From 1756 until his death, Reutter held what were probably the three top jobs in Viennese church music: *Hofkapellmeister,* Kapellmeister at St. Stephen's Cathedral, and Kapellmeister for that cathedral's *Gnadenbildkapelle.*

During the period preceding the imposition of church restrictions in 1783, the ecclesiastical institutions of Vienna provided many jobs for musicians.[32] Opportunities were plentiful for choir directors (*regentes chororum*), organists, singers, instrumentalists, substitute organists, and even organ blowers (*Kalkanten*). There were jobs not only at the principal places of public worship (e.g., St. Stephen's Cathedral and the parish churches) but also at the churches of the various religious orders (e.g., Benedictine, Carmelite, Dominican, Franciscan, Jesuit, Minorite, Piarist, et al.) and at the more private chapels of the emperor and nobility.[33]

Just how important the church was for Viennese musical life is seen in Karl Ditters von Dittersdorf's autobiography. In the late 1740s, when violinist and composer Joseph Ziegler became Dittersdorf's violin master at a Jesuit school in Vienna, the teacher advised the young boy to improve his sightreading and become a good orchestral player and "devourer of notes" by playing regularly in church choirs on Sundays and holidays.[34] Indeed, along with the theater and aristocratic houses, the church was a third and perhaps most secure source of jobs for Viennese musicians.[35]

Although the church provided musicians with many opportunities, it was not always the best-paying employer in Vienna. As Otto Biba has pointed out, unless a city church musician held a major post, he was obliged to accept other duties or give music lessons on the side to make ends meet.[36] Mozart's letters to his father in 1781 remind us again and again how very expensive it was to live in Vienna. In his later years Haydn spoke candidly to Griesinger about his brother's church music endeavors in Salzburg: "In church music the works of his brother Michael are first-rate, but it is only a shame that this field [of church music] is so badly paid, for one can earn more money with a bagpipe than with Offertories and Masses."[37] To appreciate the economic plight of church musicians, a short discussion of monetary matters in Vienna is appropriate.

It is important to keep in mind that eighteenth-century salary figures can be deceiving because of three principal factors: (1) account books and contracts did not always spell out all sources of income for a musician; (2) comparisons for different years are not always reliable because of price fluctuations induced by inflation, wars, crop failures, shortage of supplies, etc.; and (3) the cost of living varied geographically and according to class and rank (e.g., city versus rural, aristocratic versus bourgeois living). In addition to a cash salary a musician might also receive food or housing from his employer; extra income from supplemental work elsewhere; and unreported gifts, bonuses, and rewards for special services, especially from the nobility. Although some positions at court and in the military had fixed salaries, we cannot assume that a musician received the same compensation as his predecessor. Mozart, for example, received only 800 instead of 2,000 fl when he followed Gluck as *Hofkomponist* in 1787.[38] The researches of Alfred Pribram show us how salaries and prices in Austria changed from year to year and from place to place during this period.[39] Some local differences in currency and the rates of exchange also make income comparisons difficult. Nonetheless, with the above factors in mind, we can obtain a reasonable idea of the status of different salaries reported in contemporary sources.

What was generally considered a fair income in Vienna during the second half of the eighteenth century? The information from the sources varies from as low as 350 fl to as high as 1,000 fl per year. According to Roman Sandgruber, one late eighteenth-century traveler wrote that a single man of rank could live quite well on 350 fl per year in Vienna, whereas other authors of the day set 500 to 1,000 fl as the comfortable salary range.[40] Sandgruber concludes, however, that one could live "very comfortably" with 500 fl a year. Such a salary, of course, is well below that of the landed aristocracy whose incomes ran from 20,000 to 500,000 fl a year.[41]

Musicians saw things rather differently. As music director for Count Morzin in 1759, the then relatively unknown Haydn received an annual salary of only 200 fl, which Landon terms "a good sum" for musicians of that day.[42]

Mahling has found that annual salaries of orchestral musicians for the period ca. 1740–70 ranged from 200 to 500 fl, and that 250 to 300 fl per year could support a family of four.[43] Earnings of musicians were generally higher than those of servants (*Hausknechte, Diener*) who received only 60 to 140 fl per year.[44] In fact, when additional benefits are reckoned in, musicians often were better off than the "servants" historians usually consider them.[45]

On 11 April 1781 Mozart wrote from Vienna (where he had just arrived) that a prince was paying him only 400 fl, which the young composer damned as "a lousy salary."[46] A month later, in a letter dated 19 May, Mozart urged his father to come work in Vienna and added, "You can get four hundred gulden anywhere."[47] Mozart had a high opinion of his worth and great expectations about salaries and fees. Sadly, however, he and most musicians had to be content with whatever work and income came their way. Twelve hundred gulden must have been an excellent salary—indeed one worthy of a *Hofkapellmeister*—since Mozart asserted in a letter of 9 June 1781 that he would not work for the Salzburg archbishop any longer, even if the latter offered him a salary of 1,200 fl.[48] The following year (1782) the composer was earning possibly more than 500 fl just from giving lessons "which brings me in 18 ducats a month." He added that with one more pupil he would be earning 102 fl 24 kr per month; that would easily amount to more than 1,000 fl over a ten-month year. He wrote: "With this sum a man and his wife can manage in Vienna if they live quietly and in a retired way which we desire...."[49]

Vienna was always a very expensive place to live. Burney remarked in 1772 that "every thing is very dear at Vienna, and nothing more so than music, of which none is printed."[50] The Viennese prices for a few items of importance to musicians show what Burney was complaining about:[51]

Year	Item	Cost
1759	"Sei divertimenti da Cimbalo Scritti da Giuseppe Steffan" (printed music)	1 fl 30 kr
1759	Small apartment (2 rooms)	170 fl/year
1759	First floor of house (5 rooms)	225 fl/year
1740–83	Paper (*Konzeptpapier*)	1 fl 15 kr–2 fl/ream
1740–86	Higher quality paper (*Kanzleipapier*)	2–4 fl/ream

Suppose, for instance, some musician did have the "comfortable" salary of 500 fl, rented the above advertised first floor (225 fl), purchased 10 copies of music priced as above (15 fl), and used two reams of the most expensive writing paper (8 fl). This annual expenditure for rent, music, and paper would total 248 fl, or nearly one-half of that musician's salary! The economically tight situation was compounded by the fact that most city dwellers were spending at least 40 to 50 percent of their incomes on food alone.[52]

For church musicians in Vienna, salaries were generally low and seemed to vary widely from church to church and from post to post. When cutbacks fostered by Joseph II were begun in 1783, the court accountants (*Hofbuchhaltung*) made a census of parish, church, and cloister musical expenses. One product of this inventory was the "Verzeichnis über sämtliches Musick-Personal samt ihrer vorhin und dermaligen bezohenen Besoldung."[53] This index of music personnel shows that, for the period immediately preceding the cuts, the annual wages of the city's choir directors ranged from as low as 35 fl 10 kr to as high as 500 fl. Organists generally had lower salaries, ranging from 3 fl 21 kr to 339 fl 58 kr. Undoubtedly the lower end of these ranges represents part-time employees, who were either substitutes or "ringers" hired for special occasions. Actually most full-time choir directors seem to have earned at least 100 fl annually, organists at least 50 fl.

Since responsibilities could vary from church to church, a detailed comparison of these salaries yields limited results. However, the figures do reveal which institutions could afford to pay the most to their musicians.

Among *regentes chororum* in 1783 the three highest salaries went to Anton Carl (500 fl at St. Clara's, the Kirche im Bürgerspital), Johann Georg Albrechtsberger (444 fl 25 kr at St. Joseph's, the Karmeliterkirche), and Karl Friberth (411 fl 48 kr at the former Jesuitenkirche or Pfarrkirche am Hof). Despite their decent wages, all three of these directors—like most church musicians—held other jobs simultaneously; Albrechtsberger, for example, was also a *Hoforganist*. The average pay for some 28 choir directorships was about 200 fl, certainly below the "comfortable" 500 fl level. Their duties for this relatively small sum were often extensive and will be discussed in the next chapter. The lowest choir director wage in the *Verzeichnis* of 1783 was that of Karl Friberth (35 fl 10 kr at the Trattnerische Kapelle) who, as we have just seen, was receiving adequate income from his several other musical posts.

Most musicians hoped to obtain an appointment at the imperial *Hof.* There annual salaries were generous, up around 1,000 fl and higher—enough to tempt even a Mozart. For example, *Hofkapellmeister* Fux and Bonno were receiving 3,100 fl and 1,200 fl, respectively, at the time of their deaths (1741 and 1788, respectively), while *Vize-Hofkapellmeister* Reutter was making 1,200 fl when appointed in 1751.[54]

For organists in 1783 the three highest salaries went to a Xaver Flamm (339 fl 58 kr at St. Michael's), Andreas Henneberger (336 fl 45 kr at the Benedictine Schottenkirche), and Joseph Haida (112 fl 40 kr at Holy Trinity, the Pfarr bey den Trinitariern). The average yearly wage for some 28 organist positions in 1783 was about 70 fl, a salary more on a par with that for servants and one making additional employment a necessity. A few organists (e.g., Xaver Flamm and Andreas Henneberger) earned more than the *regens chori* of their respective churches. In the Esterházy archives Landon found a

Ein Theil der Leopoldstadt.   Une Partie de la Leopoldstadt.

Plate 3.   The Suburb Leopoldstadt, as Seen from the Walls of Vienna across the Danube Canal
From left to right the spires are St. Leopold's, the Karmeliter-Kirche, and Kirche der
Barmherzigen Brüder. Albrechtsberger and Eybler were among the more distinguished
choir directors of the Karmeliter-Kirche. Joseph Haydn conducted the orchestra of the
Barmherzigen Brüder during the 1750s. Engraving by Johann Ziegler
(Vienna: Artaria, 1780; Albertina, Vienna)

document that seems to indicate organists' salaries had been higher 10 years earlier. When searching Vienna for a new organist for Eisenstadt in 1773, Nicolaus Esterházy's Estates-Director informed the prince that "it will be difficult to get one under 400 to 500 fl."[55]

As with *regentes chororum* and Kapellmeister, the organists at the Hofmusikkapelle earned the highest emoluments among their colleagues. Available information shows that *Hoforganist* Gottlieb Muffat (1690-1770) earned 900 fl until economizing measures at court forced him in 1751 to accept only 600 fl per year.[56] The other *Hoforganisten* were receiving only 400 to 550 fl per year at mid-century.[57] These figures perhaps indicate that in 1773 Prince Esterházy's Estates-Director had looked no further than the Viennese court for a new organist.

To summarize and clarify the preceding discussion, figure 1-1 may prove helpful. It diagrams the known ranges (and averages) of individual annual salaries for choir directors and organists in Vienna during the third quarter of the eighteenth century. The chart summarizes several points. First, there seems to have been a rough hierarchy of salaries for these positions, a hierarchy making the musical jobs at the *Hof* most coveted. Secondly, *regentes chororum* tended to be more highly paid than organists. (Solo singers, whose incomes have not been discussed here, often commanded astronomical fees which put them in a far higher economic bracket than that of choir directors or organists.[58]) Thirdly, average salaries for choir directors and organists were so low that multiple jobs were a necessity to meet the high costs of the city. Certain musicians at the *Hof*, however, earned such good wages that they really did not need to work elsewhere. Lastly, Joseph Haydn's meteoric salary increases at Eisenstadt (on the far right side of the chart) provide contemporary testimony for his rank and success in Vienna.

In his description of Viennese church music in 1796, Schönfeld was quite perceptive about its dubious rewards: "Every parish church has its own personnel belonging to the *Kapelle,* and the pay is nothing special."[59] Comparison of the various wages also reveals that a musician's reputation seemed to have been a decisive factor in determining salary—along, of course, with the financial resources of the institution. Whether a church was in the center of Vienna or in its suburbs (at that time the villages outside the city walls) and what a musician's predecessor had earned little affected the salary assigned to him. His abilities and public recognition apparently came first in such salary decisions.

This chapter has attempted to portray the many ties between church music and overall musical life in Vienna during the second half of the eighteenth

Figure 1-1. Annual Salary Ranges per Institution for Choir
Directions and Organists in Vienna

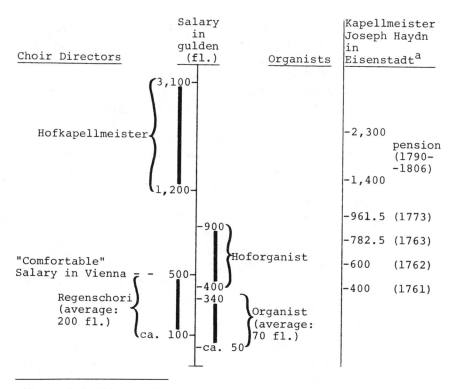

[a]The sources for Haydn's income were Landon, *Haydn: Chronicle and Works*, II, p. 748; V, pp. 348–49, and Sandgruber, "Wirtschaftsentwicklung," p. 79.

century. Sacred music had to have played an important part in the daily lives of most Viennese, what with voices and instruments being required for many services at dozens of churches on Sundays, holidays, and special occasions. Frequently music for instruments alone was also heard at these services. Along with opera houses and the aristocracy, the church remained a significant supporter of the musical economy in this expensive city. Despite low wages, numerous Viennese musicians and their families were supported by the churches' outlay for splendid music. Often holding several jobs simultaneously, a musician could make ends meet with a total annual income of about 500 gulden.

Whether Vienna's church music of this period had any influence upon other kinds of music remains debatable. The common view is that sacred music was always conservative and occasionally borrowed new elements from music outside the sanctuary. Nonetheless Burney did make the following provocative comment when he was in Vienna in 1772: "And it seems as if *the national music of a country was good or bad, in proportion to that of its church service....* "[60] Later analytical chapters should demonstrate how Vienna's composers were still contributing outstanding Masses to a church repertoire that was by no means flagging.

Josephinism of the 1780s and its concomitant series of reforms nearly dealt a deathblow to the church's active role in Vienna's (and Austria's) musical life. The 1783 "Verzeichnis" of Viennese music personnel shows that dozens upon dozens of musicians lost their church jobs that year because of the required cutbacks in expenditures. We can only imagine how many musicians had to find work elsewhere (several fled to the few remaining cloisters out in the country) or were compelled to learn a new trade.[61] In addition, the production of new concerted music for the church declined considerably during this decade as increased emphasis was put upon congregational singing.

Just the same, despite the economic problems shared by most Viennese church musicians, the importance of their diverse activities—as conductors, performers, and, most important here, composers—cannot be denied. In some cases their talents are confirmed by the high quality of their compositions. However, before discussing the composers and some of their concerted Masses, we must examine certain conditions of this period's church music.

2

The Conditions of Church Music in Vienna ca. 1740–83

Although the church played a major role in the musical life of Vienna, the state of church music at this time is generally viewed as having undergone a decline.[1] The less-than-optimum conditions were manifest in more ways than just the low salaries already discussed. Many organs were out of tune, musicians were overworked and inadequately rehearsed, and music often had to be hastily composed and inaccurately copied. The economic difficulties that began with Austria's wars of the 1740s and ended with the frugal policies of the "enlightened" Emperor Joseph II did not help. The present chapter will survey the conditions of church music, the important function of the *regens chori* or choir director, the liturgical requirements of the Mass in performance, and the changing meanings of "church style" during this era—all fundamental to the historical background of the composers and Masses under study.

General Conditions

Although he occasionally praised the music of Veinna's churches, Charles Burney found many organs improperly tuned during his visit of September 1772. About St. Stephen's he writes: "The great organ at the west end of this church has not been fit for use these forty years; there are three or four more organs of a smaller size in different parts of the church, which are used occasionally. That which I heard in the choir this morning is but a poor one, and as usual, was much out of tune; it was played, however, in a very masterly, though not a modern style."[2] This tuning problem is surprising, if not shocking, when we remember that most accompanied church music of the time used the organ as continuo and that the highly accomplished Leopold Hofmann was the recently appointed first Kapellmeister at the cathedral. Burney blames the church: "The church organs being almost always out of tune here, may be occasioned by the parsimony or negligence of the clergy, bishop, or superiors of a church or convent. . . . "[3] On 12 August 1773 Leopold Mozart wrote from Vienna that young Wolfgang had to play a violin concerto instead of an organ concerto because the organ at the Jesuit Fathers "was not good enough for an organ concerto."[4] Although not all churches had badly tuned organs (Burney praises the "well-toned" pipes at St. Michael's),[5] poorly tuned ones were common in Vienna and must have tainted many a service.

As we have already seen, Vienna's church musicians were kept very busy, accepting jobs wherever possible. Mozart writes: "In such a place [as Vienna] has not a man (who has not a kreuzer of assured income) enough to think about and to work at day and night?"[6] This hyperactivity was not always conducive to a fine performance in church. Not unlike today, rehearsal time was at a premium—probably limited to the few hours when all the musicians were available. Friedrich Nicolai perceptively recognized this problem in his 1781 criticism of the playing and singing in Viennese churches:

> In no church were the orchestras as good as in the two playhouses [i.e., Kärntnertortheater and Burgtheater]. Undoubtedly there were good musicians among them [i.e., the church orchestras], but they were not so well rehearsed [*zusammen eingespielt*]. Even in St. Stephen's I found the music not as good as I had imagined under the direction of Leopold Hofmann. Presumably this famous man is not to blame. In all churches the singing voices were not first rate; the best ones were only mediocre.[7]

Probably much of the music was read at sight; we need only recall Dittersdorf's autobiographical testimony that churches were excellent places for improving one's sightreading capabilities. Nonetheless, there were some good performances at church services, as even Burney would occasionally admit: "The first time I went to the cathedral of St. Stephen, I heard an excellent mass, in the true church style, very well performed; there were violins and violoncellos though it was not a festival."[8] We shall observe other positive remarks about church service performances in the biographical chapter that follows.

Vienna's churches provided musicians with not only numerous jobs but also several magnificent edifices within which to perform. Besides the towering cathedral of St. Stephen with its two separate *Kapellen* (*Haupt-* and *Gnadenbild-Kapellen*) and several organs, Gothic churches included St. Augustine's (Augustinerkirche; fourteenth century, with the *Loreto-* and *Totenbruderschaft-Kapellen*) and St. Michael's (Michaelerkirche; thirteenth century). Among the later structures were Johann Bernhard Fischer von Erlach's sumptuously Baroque Church of Saint Charles Borromeo (Karlskirche; completed outside the city walls in 1737), Johann Luka von Hildebrandt's St. Peter's Church (Peterskirche; finished in 1708), and the Universitätskirche (today's Jesuitenkirche; built 1627–31 with its ornate interior by Andrea Pozzo).[9] A separate study could be made of just the diverse performance conditions offered by the physical layouts of the various churches, for certainly the architectural as well as financial resources of a church affected the style of its music. Fortunately most of the churches are still standing today; locations of the more significant churches are shown in figure 2-1.

Figure 2-1. Significant Churches in Vienna during the Second Half
of the Eighteenth Century*

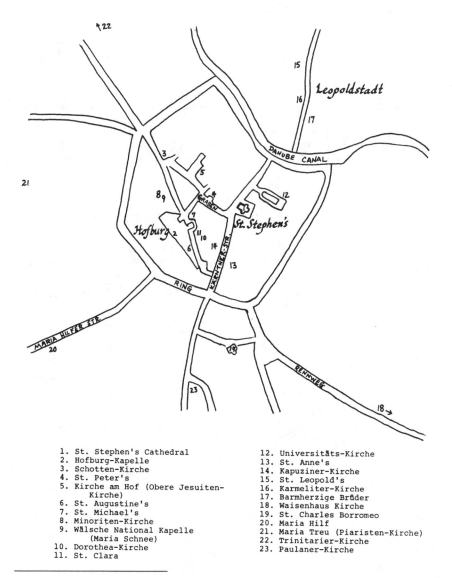

1. St. Stephen's Cathedral
2. Hofburg-Kapelle
3. Schotten-Kirche
4. St. Peter's
5. Kirche am Hof (Obere Jesuiten-
   Kirche)
6. St. Augustine's
7. St. Michael's
8. Minoriten-Kirche
9. Wälsche National Kapelle
   (Maria Schnee)
10. Dorothea-Kirche
11. St. Clara

12. Universitäts-Kirche
13. St. Anne's
14. Kapuziner-Kirche
15. St. Leopold's
16. Karmeliter-Kirche
17. Barmherzige Brüder
18. Waisenhaus Kirche
19. St. Charles Borromeo
20. Maria Hilf
21. Maria Treu (Piaristen-Kirche)
22. Trinitarier-Kirche
23. Paulaner-Kirche

---

* See appendix B for choirmasters and other names of these churches. For other churches see the map in Riedel, *Karl VI*, pp.
310-11.

Aside from the obvious influences coming from Italy (e.g., with Caldara and Predieri as well as Austrians who studied there), church musicians in Vienna were largely insulated from the styles and practices of other regions. In 1781 Nicolai found that "the choral singers [of Vienna], especially basses, do not shriek so forcefully (*nicht so gewaltig*) as in many cities of northern Germany."[10] In his *General History of Music* (1776–89) Charles Burney believed religion was a basic cause of this musical isolation.

> . . . but there seems an unwillingness in the Protestant states of Germany to allow due praise, even to the musical works and opinions of the Catholics. And, on the contrary, the Catholics appear equally unwilling to listen to the musical strains of the Protestants. Thus the compositions of the Bachs, Grauns, and Bendas are little known at Vienna; and at Berlin or Hamburg, those of Wagenseil, Hofmann, Ditters, Gluck, Haydn, Vanhal, and Pleyel, are not only less played and approved than at Vienna or Munich, but infinitely less than in France, Spain, Italy, or England.[11]

But the slow dissemination of church music (chiefly by manuscript copy) was probably a main reason why composers tended to be out of touch with music from distant places. Although Vienna was a growing cosmopolitan center in the eighteenth century, the musical perspective of its residents was formed mostly by the local cultural institutions (sacred and secular). In fact, throughout Europe the church repertoires almost always emphasized the compositions of local composers.[12]

Two basic conditions of church music at this time should be recognized. First, sacred music—like most types of music then—was still a ware, a commodity that was composed in the performance of a duty or the execution of a commission.[13] Indeed church music was *Gebrauchsmusik* in the best sense of the term. Secondly, the composer as "free creator," a type better associated with the following century, was exceedingly rare. One did not live from composing alone; composition was a sideline for musicians.[14] Practically all the composers of the present study had many other responsibilities beside providing new music for the church. The composers were also active as organists, choir directors, orchestra conductors, music teachers, instrumentalists, singers, copyists, or even servants. Jan Vanhal (1739–1813), who wrote over 40 Masses (among other things) but held no fixed job, was an exception among composers; some historians accordingly regard him as "one of the first independent artists."[15] Since many of the composers under study were also active choir directors, a survey of the requirements, obligations, and responsibilities of the eighteenth-century *regens chori* will show the conditions of Vienna's sacred music from another perspective.

The *Regens Chori*

In eighteenth-century Austria, *regens chori* (German *Regenschori* or *Chorregent*) was the most common designation for the choir director in a church or monastery. Other possible titles were *rector chori* (at St. Veit's in Krems), *praefectus chori* (St. Lambrecht), and *Chorpräfekt* (Gnadenkirche in Mariazell).[16] Although there was no rigid consistency in the use of these titles, the designation Kapellmeister (*maestro di cappella*) seems to have been reserved for only the highest and most esteemed musical posts at a court, city, or wherever there was a permanent orchestra and chorus.[17] A Kapellmeister tended to be more a music director than just a choir director. For example, according to the 1783 "Verzeichnis" of church music personnel in Vienna, all choir directors had the title *regens chori;* the exceptions were Kapellmeister Giuseppe Bonno (*Hofmusikkapelle*), Leopold Hofmann (St. Stephen's and St. Peter's), and Karl Friberth (Kapellmeister at six churches).[18] The terms *Kantor, precentor, Chormeister, Chorleiter,* and *Chordirigent* seem to have been seldom used, if at all.

The duties of a *regens chori* were numerous and far-flung. He was not simply a learned *Takt-Führer* (time-beater) as Walther's 1732 definition of *maestro di cappella* would lead us to believe.[19] A director's responsibilities could include all or some of the following:

1. Hiring, rehearsing, directing, and paying the musicians
2. Playing continuo or organ accompaniment for the choir
3. Selecting, acquiring, or copying the music to be performed
4. Composing, arranging, or rearranging the necessary music
5. Providing instruction in music or in other subjects
6. Supporting the choirboys
7. Fulfilling miscellaneous musical duties elsewhere in the city or court

Naturally the extent of these responsibilities varied from place to place, with rural directors usually having more wide-ranging duties than city directors. Just the same, a *regens chori* had to be a person of many talents, one ready to assume all kinds of additional work from music copying to opera directing. Several of the *regentes chororum* at Vienna's churches and cloisters also played or sang at the Imperial *Hof.*[20] The previous chapter has shown how economically necessary such multiple jobs were for most musicians in Vienna at that time. Until 1740, when Charles VI died and court opera performances ceased, the *Hofkapellmeister* was required to compose operas in addition to church and chamber music.[21] Indeed the choir director must have been a special character in every city since the famous comedian Josef Felix von Kurz (1717–84) presented his popular farce *Bernardon, der verrückte Regenschori* (Bernardon the Insane Choir Director) in Vienna in 1754.[22]

A *regens chori* had to be a capable administrator and musician, even if not always a first-rate composer. For example, it was the *regens chori* Tobias Gsur and not the orchestra leader Karl Huber who decided whether or not the young Dittersdorf could join the violin section at the Schottenkirche in Vienna.[23]

As we know from the famous 1761 example of Vice-Kapellmeister Joseph Haydn at Eisenstadt, a director's contract could be lengthy and specify every duty in great detail.[24] Georg von Reutter's sevenfold contract as *Hofkapellmeister* on 11 March 1751 stipulated that he had to provide for all church, table, and chamber music (including musicians' salaries) with the inadequate sum of 20,000 fl per year.[25] Usually a director's contract consisted of a series of instructions. The contract for Ferdinand Kämpfl, Jr. is typical of this format. On 31 December 1791 Kämpfl became organist and choir director of St. Veit's, the *Stadtpfarrkirche* in Krems (about 40 miles up the Danube from Vienna). His contract read:

Instruction
for choir director and organist
at the parish church in Krems

First, the present *regens chori* and organist should, along with a Christian life style, fulfill the church office established by the Lower Austrian government with the appropriate honor and obedience and, above all, accommodate the dean (*Dechant*) and parish priest (*Stadtpfarrer*) in the arrangement of their Masses.

Second: to diligently provide church music using the *Thurnermeister*, basses, and tenors listed below in such a way that he should not only acquire well-set music (*wohlgesetzte Musikalien*) from time to time but also see that this church music is augmented in both instrumental and vocal parts, filled more and more by those who enjoy the designated contributions of the *Altanische Stiftung* and who at the moment are *Thurnermeister* Zollner and tenor Fiby, so that:

Third: all High Feast Days of the Lord and of the B.V.M. as well as other normal (*gewöhnlichen*) days with a High Mass (*Hochamt*) will be provided with solemn choral music (*mit einer feyerlichen Chormusik*), but the High Mass on ordinary (*ordinari*) Sundays and holy days should last three-quarters of an hour.

Fourth: within eight days the present *regens chori* Kämpfl will submit to the church office an inventory of the musical instruments belonging to the parish church, and [he] will not permit these instruments to be used for any other purpose than Masses.

Fifth: the *regens chori* is required to continuously support three choirboys, namely an alto and two sopranos, and to annually provide the second soprano with clothes; the present *regens chori*-organist Ferd[inand] Kämpfl is to observe all these points exactly, otherwise the church office could make things unpleasant for him.

Sixth: for these his faithfully executed church duties and in addition to the fees (*Stollgebührenissen*) fixed for him and the three choirboys at memorial Masses, funeral Masses, and burials, the *regens-chori*-organist must collect an annual salary of 310 fl (paid and receipted quarterly), 100 fl for the care of the alto and 50 fl for clothing the second soprano, no less than 14 peck (*Metzen*) of grain (*Korn*) at the selling price, and, finally, 12 *Emmer* of wine must from the church cellar.[26]

A similar "instruction" two weeks later (13 January 1792) required Kämpfl to hold one rehearsal per week with the musicians. In Vienna, unlike Krems, the organist post and choir directorship at a church were usually not held by the same person.

No unusual marriage requirements are known for any *regens chori* in Vienna. However, certain stipulations or traditions of the kind so famous at Buxtehude's church in Lübeck may have existed. Why, for example, did Franz Joseph Altpart marry the widow of his predecessor (Kämpfl) on 10 April 1798 before becoming the new *regens chori* at St. Veit's in Krems?[27] Although not formally written into the regulations or contracts of a church, such marriages "of convenience" did take care of several potential problems. First, the former director's widow was provided the financial security of a new husband without the church having to pay extra support. Secondly, the personal music collection of the deceased director remained at the church for continued use.

With so few sacred works available in print, a *regens chori* had to maintain his own library of musical copies. Where he went, his music library (including orchestral parts) went also; the music was usually his personal property.[28] Although Johann Georg Zechner (1716–78) worked several years at St. Veit's in Krems before moving to Stein an der Donau, only one of this productive composer's works is found in Krems today exactly because of this practice.[29] When Gregor Werner (1693–1766) came to Eisenstadt as Prince Esterházy's Kapellmeister in 1728, he brought with him much badly needed music that rejuvenated the chapel's repertoire.[30] Pater Franz Sparry (1715–67), *regens chori* 1747–67 at Kremsmünster, introduced that monastery to much Italian music from his own library, while his successor, Pater Georg Pasterwitz (1730–1803), personally acquired or copied out many new works for this Benedictine cloister.[31] Clerical *regentes chororum* often left such valuable musical legacies to their church or order. It is not surprising that in his 1796 *Jahrbuch* Schönfeld listed several *regentes chororum* of Prague as "Liebhaber" possessing sizeable music collections.[32] The importance of this portability of whole church music collections is often forgotten in references to dissemination. The practice often preserved the integrity of large collections, thus facilitating study today of a particular director's repertoire.

In the eighteenth century every music director was required to provide his church with adequate music, often of his own composition. If a particular Mass was too long or too short, lacked a fugue at the appropriate moment (e.g., "Cum Sancto Spiritu"), or was too taxing for the soprano soloist, the Kapellmeister or *regens chori* was responsible for making the requisite alterations or substitutions.[33] For example, a director at Stein an der Donau was supposed to provide motets, concertos, and sonatas for his church's services.[34]

The "Instruction" cited above for St. Veit's in Krems is an example of how the choir director was often personally responsible for the choirboys—from their attire to their education. In Melk Abbey at the end of the seventeenth century, the *regens chori* and his *Sängerknaben* had to appear before the prelate at mealtime and be prepared to offer a "musicalische Distraction."[35] Joseph Haydn might have had a different career had not the Kapellmeister of St. Stephen's, Georg Reutter, Jr., stopped at Hainburg in his search for new choirboys to train and educate. Thus directors often had to be good teachers. Pasterwitz at Kremsmünster, for example, was also a fine lecturer in philosophy and mathematics as well as a capable music director.[36]

Obviously the professional requirements for a *regens chori* could be quite high, especially when the multifaceted responsibilities just discussed were demanded. For the more prestigious directorships the competition was fierce, with good connections, seniority, previous experience, reputation, and letters of high recommendation all playing a role in the selection process. When Florian Gassmann died in 1774, there were four able candidates for the job of *Hofkapellmeister:*[37]

1. Leopold Hofmann, Kapellmeister at St. Stephen's and St. Peter's, 2nd *Hoforganist,* age 35
2. Giuseppe Bonno, *Hofkomponist,* age 63
3. Tobias Gsur, *k.k. Hofmusicus* (bass), *regens chori* at the *Schottenkirche,* age 49
4. Joseph Starzer, *k.k. Hofmusicus* (violinist) age 48

Each man petitioned Emperor Joseph II for the post; Johann Wenzel Count von Sporck, the *Hof- und Kammermusik-Direktor,* favored Bonno. Then the emperor appointed Bonno for financial, political, and seniority reasons, despite Bonno's advanced age and Hofmann's superior qualifications.[38]

Unfortunately, little is known at present about the selection procedures for other choir directorships in Vienna. We do know that in a monastery either a layman or a cleric served as *regens chori* and that, outside of nunneries, women rarely held such a post.[39] Family ties and personal connections undoubtedly had an influence on the choice. Nepotism was probably the reason why Georg Reutter, Jr. succeeded his father as Kapellmeister at St. Stephen's in 1738. Later, as we have seen, Georg, Jr. was to have a "monopoly" over the city's most prestigious church music positions.

Nepotism may also have played a role in a Karl Gsur (b. 1735) singing bass at the Schottenkirche in 1783 when Tobias Gsur was the *regens chori* there.[40] Several of the letters which Leopold Mozart wrote home to Salzburg in 1767-68 describe the sometimes offensive musical politics and intrigues that threatened the young Wolfgang's advancing reputation in Vienna.[41] These letters illustrate the power which certain musicians possessed and sought to preserve.

In *Der vollkommene Kapellmeister* (Hamburg, 1739) Johann Mattheson's discussion of the many abilities and qualifications needed by the ideal choir director seems as valid for Austria as for northern Germany. In his final chapter Mattheson provides the following advice:[42]

1. Strive for "a certain authority" without being "offensive or scandalous" and attain a "good reputation and esteem" (§6)
2. Strive for affability, yet be serious when admonishing or contradicting someone (§§7-8)
3. Write your scores as legibly and neatly as possible (§§9-12)
4. During a performance use the hands, gestures, and eyes to keep the musicians together with a precise but flexible beat (§§11, 13-14)
5. Be able to sing well, at least with "taste, style, or method" (§15)
6. Be able to play the keyboard well (§16)
7. Select your performers wisely (§§17-20)
8. Tune up carefully (§§17, 21-22)
9. Use rehearsals intelligently, to improve performance and correct the music (§§17, 23-24)
10. During a performance stay calm and attentive, think quickly, and in church forget not your "honest devotion" (§§17, 25-27)
11. Position your musicians prudently, according to their quantity and the hall (§§28-31)
12. Let your ensemble know beforehand how to proceed should a musical mishap occur during the performance (§32)
13. For variety's sake, perform other composers' music as well as your own (§§33-34)

In Part II of the treatise, Mattheson similarly discusses the attributes of a good composer. Since most choir directors at that time were also composers, a summary of these "requirements" would complete a general portrait of the ideal *regens chori*:[43]

1. Be an educated, scholarly man, with a knowledge of music history (§§2-5; also Part I, Chapter 4, §51)
2. Understand Greek or, at least, Latin as well as French and Italian (§§6-7, 12-13)

3. Be a poet or well-acquainted with the poetic art (§§8–11)
4. Understand thorough bass (§§34–35)
5. Be a singer or at least sing well internally (§§38–44)
6. Play the keyboard well, and, if possible, other instruments (§§45–48)
7. Possess a "natural ability or innate instinct and spirit" (§§49–54)
8. Have diligence (§§55–56)
9. Persevere and be enthusiastic (§§57–60)
10. Personally understand and feel different affections, emotions, and passions (§§64–68)

The many musicians of the period (including Haydn) who read *Der vollkommene Kapellmeister* probably took many of these suggestions to heart.

Among the 28 Mass composers studied in the following chapters we find several who, although not necessarily choir directors, had other specialties, including one that was nonmusical.

organists	Albrechtsberger, Arbesser, Hofmann, Monn, Wagenseil
violinists	Dittersdorf, Ziegler
tenors	Karl Friberth, Joseph Krottendorfer
bass	Tobias Gsur
opera composers	Gassmann, Hasse
lute virtuoso	Carl Kohaut
gamba virtuoso	Tuma
singer/dilettante	Marianne Martínez
church musician	Joseph Seuche
"free" composer	Vaňhal
lawyer	Sonnleithner

In Vienna a *regens chori* often held this post until death. Robert Haas's list of musicians found in the *Sterbelisten* of the *Wiener Diarium* includes several directors who were still working as *regentes chororum* at the time of death.[44] The generous pensions which were offered to the imperial court's employees are well documented; little is known, however, about retirement pensions for Viennese musicians outside the court. In 1771 Florian Gassmann founded the *Tonkünstler-Societät* to present concerts during Advent and Lent and in the process raise funds for the widows and orphans of its musician members. Among the members of the *Societät* prior to 1783 we find several local *regentes chororum*:

Johann Georg Albrechtsberger (Karmeliterkirche)
Karl Friberth (Pfarrkirche am Hof and elsewhere)

Florian Gassmann (*Hofkapellmeister* 1772–74)
Tobias Gsur (Schottenkirche)
Franz Haunold (Wiener-Neustadt)
Simon Kölbel (Karlskirche)
Johann Michael Spangler (St. Michael's)
Franz Ullmann (St. Leopold's)[45]

In 1828 Franz Xaver Glöggl (1764–1839) wrote a handbook for church musicians which includes his generation's definition of a good *regens chori:* "The choir director (*Chordirector*) is the *Geist* and soul of the church music, upon him depends everything belonging to a church music that arouses devotion."

"If he himself is not a composer, just the same he must possess a genuine power of judgement with respect to the *character* of the pieces as well as a knowledge of the voice, instruments, and the Latin language."[46] Thus, a *regens chori* in the eighteenth century had to be a person of diversified talents if he hoped to meet all of his various responsibilities. Not only was he a conductor but usually also an organist, cantor, and composer who, in addition, often had to direct the opera, the citizens' chorus, or orchestra of a city or court.[47]

Masses in Performance

Introduction

During the eighteenth century in Vienna, Masses were composed for performance only in the church, i.e., only in conjunction with the appropriate rites and services. Masses performed as concerts were extremely rare until the early nineteenth century. The few reported concert performances were usually linked to an informal gathering rather than any public event like the well-known *concert spirituel* of Paris. As already noted, some church services did approach the outward appearance of a concert because of the quantity of vocal and instrumental music included. Apparently some churches went so far as to advertise their music. In 1781 the anonymous critic of Vienna's "too operatic" church music commented: "... they [the public] read on a printed poster that all men, women, and maiden sisters of an honorable brotherhood or even of a high brotherhood (*Erzbruderschaft*) are most cordially invited in Christ's name to a solemn musical High Mass without the customary communion offering (*unter Ablegung des gewöhnlichen Opfers*)."[48] In 1782 Mozart describes how he (as alto), violinist Joseph Starzer (tenor), and organist Anton Teiber (bass) were meeting each Sunday noon at the home of Baron van Swieten (treble!) to sing through all kinds of church music.[49] Not until 1819 did Vienna have its own *concert spirituel,* founded by Franz

Gebauer (1783/84–1822), the choirmaster at St. Augustine's.[50] Only then did the Viennese begin to publicly perform Masses and other sacred music outside the church service on a regular basis.

The sacred music of several Viennese composers was heard in concerts elsewhere during the late eighteenth century. On 4 April 1778 Mozart informed his father that the Paris *concert spirituel* was to perform his arrangement of Holzbauer's "Miserere."[51] The next year, on 9 December 1779, the Kyrie and Gloria from the then late Florian Gassmann's ample *St. Cecilia Mass in C* were performed under Johann Adam Hiller (1728–1804) as part of the Advent series of his *concerts spirituels* at the Thomashaus am Markt in Leipzig.[52] The Parisian *concerts* also provided the opportunity for four public performances of Joseph Haydn's *Stabat Mater* (Hoboken XX[bis]) in April 1781.[53]

The rare *concert spirituel* aside, Masses in eighteenth-century Vienna were conceived as functional music to be used for heightening the worshipers' devotion during the service. In any study, these works must be seen in their liturgical context. By his bull of 14 July 1570 Pope Pius V made binding the *Missale Romanum,* a product of the Council of Trent (1545–47, 1551–52, 1562–63).[54] This "improved" Roman Missal became the basic norm for the Western Church until the extensive changes begun by the Second Vatican Council's Constitution on the Sacred Liturgy in 1963.[55] The writings of the distinguished scholar and theologian Josef Jungmann (1889–1975) clarify the history and traditions of the Roman Catholic Mass before the Second Vatican Council. In his emphasis on the importance of historical context in reference to the liturgy he points out that: "Undeniably the past two thousand years have left us an overabundance of forms, many of which are no longer understood as expressions of what they were originally meant to convey, so that they obscure the holy rather than reveal it. Such forms are often taken in isolation from their original context (in which they alone have real meaning) and are attributed an independent value."[56] This statement also applies to music: awareness of context helps us understand the origins, structure, and musical style of the Mass.

The Liturgical Context

For the Catholic faithful, Mass is the central institution of religious practice. Over the centuries it has grown up around a text commemorating the Last Supper when Christ used the bread and wine as eternal symbols of the flesh and blood of his body which was about to be crucified.[57] Thus the Mass is essentially a sacrament of sacrifice. With the words of consecration over the elements of bread and wine, Christ and his sacrifice become present again. Behind this central sacrament of the Eucharist, the Mass has always had four basic purposes: adoration, thanksgiving, petition (prayer or supplication), and expiation (atonement).[58]

In Vienna of the mid-eighteenth century, Mass was quite different from what one witnesses today. There was still an enormous distance between the faithful and the priests celebrating Mass before the altar. The worshipers were mere spectators, having little or no active participation in the service. Only the priest (celebrant) and his assistants had an active role. Even greater distance arose because the ceremonies were still conducted in Latin, even then little understood by the people.[59] Thus, the average worshiper was merely a viewer and listener.[60] Emphasis was upon the visual (the majestic sanctuary, the instructive stained-glass windows, paintings and sculpture, the priestly vestments, the Blessed Sacrament, etc.) and the aural (intoned psalms, prayers, special music, etc.). Marcel Brion finds the theatrical magnificence of Baroque churches corresponding to the "Austrian religious feeling which delights to see liturgical ceremonies take place amidst a splendour equal to that of Hofburg receptions."[61] The church sought to inspire devotion by keeping a veil of mystery around the liturgy and exploiting the effects of candles, smells, and bells. Jungmann forcefully reminds us how the eye was satisfied during a Mass of the Baroque period:

> The new age sought not the sight of the holy, but the sight of the beautiful in art and universe. And so the church became a great hall, its walls shimmering with marble and gold. The paintings on the ceilings, which grew right out of the plaster of the entablature, made the room appear to fade away into heavenly glory. The *presbyterium* is hardly any longer distinct from the nave, and along with the latter it mounts upwards, by force of the cupola or dome, into a higher unity. At its base the glance falls on the mighty structure of the high altar in which the design of the Gothic altarpiece has been reconstructed architecturally. The prominent thing in this structure is the altar-piece itself, perhaps also the exposition throne for the Blessed Sacrament, and finally the tabernacle which has become part and parcel of the plan.... The interior of the church has become a great hall filled with sensuous life. Even the galleries and boxes are there. And the liturgy itself is conceived of as a play, to be looked at and listened to. But it is no longer—as it was in the Middle Ages—the Mass itself with its succession of ceremonies which bears this dramatic character. Only the adoration of our Lord at the consecration retains its position as the dominating climax.[62]

The liturgical calendar determined many details of the Mass ceremony—from the degree of solemnity to the chants which were to be included or omitted. Mass was said every day, but High Masses, with special music such as the concerted Masses under study, were reserved for Sundays and holy days. The normal or ferial Mass was used on weekdays which did not coincide with a special feast. The Gloria and Credo were omitted during Advent and Lent, while the Agnus was dropped only at the Easter Vigil Mass.[63]

In appendix A are lists of fixed and movable feasts (with German and Latin names) which were especially significant for the liturgical year in

eighteenth-century Vienna. The fixed feasts of local interest, some of which
are represented by the Masses under study, included:

12 February	Wedding anniversary of Maria Theresa and Francis I (1736)
13 March	Birthday of Emperor Joseph II (1741)
19 March	St. Joseph, patron saint of Austria; nameday of Joseph II
1 May	Sts. Philip and James; St. Bridget's Day
13 May	Birthday of Empress Maria Theresa (1717)
26 July	St. Anne, Mother of the B.V.M.[64]
18 August	Death of Francis I, husband of Empress Maria Theresa (1765)
28 August	St. Augustine; birthday of Empress Elisabeth Christine, widow of Charles VI
2 September	St. Stephen of Hungary, guardian angel of Vienna and its cathedral
12 September	Procession celebrating repulsion of the Turks (1683)
1 October	Birthday of Emperor Charles VI (1685)
15 October	St. Theresa; nameday of Maria Theresa
20 October	Death of Emperor Charles VI (1740)
4 November	St. Charles Borromeo; nameday of Charles VI
15 November	St. Leopold, *Landespatron*
19 November	St. Elisabeth; nameday of Empress Elisabeth Christine
22 November	St. Cecilia, patron of musicians' brotherhood
28 November	Death of Empress Maria Theresa (1780)
30 November	St. Andrew Apostle, patron of Order of Golden Fleece
6 December	St. Nicholas, patron of *Nicolasbruderschaft* of musicians
8 December	Immaculate Conception of B.V.M.; birthday of Francis I (1708)

As the above list suggests, the namedays of statesmen, churches, monastic
orders, and brotherhoods as well as anniversaries of all kinds—births,
marriages, deaths, military campaigns, victories, and even eradication of a
pestilence—also occasioned special Masses in Vienna during this period. For
example, the Hofkapelle parts for Wagenseil's *Missa solenne Immaculatae*

Conceptionis (M. 70) indicate that it was performed 15 October 1743, the nameday of Empress Maria Theresa. Visits by high officials and dignitaries also occasioned special festivities. When Pope Pius VI celebrated Easter Mass on 31 March 1782 at St. Stephen's Cathedral in Vienna, the late *Dom-* and *Hofkapellmeister* Reutter was honored (posthumously) by having his Kyrie and Gloria performed for the occasion.[65]

Lastly, the influence of local liturgical practice upon Mass settings must be considered. In his excellent account of church music at the court of Emperor Charles VI, Friedrich Wilhelm Riedel discusses how the *Hof* had three grades of ceremony (*Toison-, Pontifikal-,* and *gewöhnliche-Gottesdienste*) and how the length and form of ceremony were affected by these grades.[66] Riedel relies on a number of documents describing *Hof* practices in detail—Kilian Reinhardt's *Rubriche Generali* of 1727 being especially helpful.[67] Walter Senn informs us that Salzburg's cathedral had *Chorordnungen* that were very explicit about which days had a *Missa solemnis* and which had a *Missa brevis.*[68] In Mannheim Mozart remarked how the Masses there were very short and organ playing replaced the Benedictus.[69] And in Salzburg, in 1772 the new Archbishop, Hieronymus Colloredo, demanded that Masses last no longer than three quarters of an hour.[70] Unfortunately, apart from a few hints in contemporary newspapers, diaries, and books, we presently lack detailed descriptions of local liturgical practice for most of Vienna's churches during the second half of the eighteenth century.

The Role of Church Music: Contemporary Views

With so strong an emphasis upon the visual and aural, music naturally had a vital function. Numerous musical treatises discuss the "true" role of church music and often complain about its abuses. In his *Gradus ad Parnassum* (1725) the Viennese *Hofkapellmeister* Fux warns his students never to forget the purpose of church music: "to arouse prayerful devotion (*Andacht*) during a service."[71] In a *Critischer Musikus* article dated 15 October 1737, J. A. Scheibe has the same view: "The chief purpose of church music is principally to edify the listeners, to encourage their prayer (*zur Andacht aufmuntern*) so as to thereby awaken in them a quiet and holy reverence before God's presence."[72] Scheibe adds that it would be appropriate to the understanding and dignity of the music if composers would strive to observe this purpose more exactly than they had been doing.

In *Der vollkommene Kapellmeister* (1739) Mattheson holds the typical view that church music was for praising God and instilling devotion in the faithful: "For example in churches, where the main consideration is devotion, one will seldom succeed where devotion is not stimulated through means which can set astir all types of temperaments at the proper time and in their measure."[73] When describing the *Stylo Ecclesiastico* in his 1745 *Tractatus musicus*, the Benedictine composer-theorist Meinrad Spiess says the main goal of the church style is the same as that for all music: "the encouragement and inducement to praise and honor God."[74] On 19 February 1749 Pope Benedict XIV issued the famous "Annus qui" which attempted to regulate certain aspects of sacred music that had become too theatrical. According to this papal encyclical, figural sacred music should "be of such a nature as to arouse among the faithful, sentiments of piety and devotion and to uplift the soul toward God."[75] ("Cantus iste ille est, qui fidelium animos ad devotionem et pietatem excitat.")[76] In 1778 Joseph Martin Kraus, a German musician who later became a Kapellmeister in Stockholm, criticized contemporary sacred music and demanded that it arouse "inspiration and total devotion."[77]

The anonymous author of the 1781 Josephine polemic against secularism in Vienna's churches bluntly sets forth two purposes of church music which are not unlike those already described: "First, to glorify the praise and honor of God. Secondly, to touch the hearts of the people and incite them to pray."[78] Nine years later, in his *Gründliche Anweisung zur Composition*, Albrechtsberger remarks how "each of us Christians knows that the aim of church music is not amusement, but prayer and the honor of God (*Andacht und Ehre Gottes*)."[79] In the article "Kirchenmusik" for his 1802 *Lexikon*, Heinrich Koch shows how secularized and cosmopolitan the church style had become in the post-Josephine period: "Church music may appear in whatever form it wants so long as it maintains the character of solemnity and devotion."[80] And finally, in 1828 the Linz *Domkapellmeister* Franz Xaver Glöggl reminds choir directors that church music, especially that for voices, assists the priest and at times acts as his voice during a service.[81]

Two currents run through most of the above testimony. First, the function of sacred music was to inspire piety and prayerful devotion (*Andacht*); a secular tone was to be avoided. Second, the distance between worshipers and celebrants was implied by the absence of any mention of congregational participation. It was not until the enlightened reign of Joseph II that congregational singing in German was enthusiastically promoted.[82]

The Mass Ordinary

A Roman Catholic Mass consists of two principal parts: (1) Mass of the Catechumens (Fore-Mass; *Vormesse*); and (2) Mass of the Faithful (Eucharist). With its entrance rituals and the liturgy of the word, the Mass of the Catechumens is an instructional service preparing the faithful for the Holy Eucharist to come. It reawakens them to their concepts of faith.[83] In the eighteenth century this was the part of the Mass that, with all its additional music, could resemble a concert. With the Offertory (following the Credo), the Mass of the Faithful begins. Here is the focal point of the Mass, i.e., the actual "sacrifice" where supposedly only the baptized are allowed to be present and partake of communion and where the action is focused primarily upon the altar. In each of these principal parts some sections were sung and some spoken, with some texts being chosen according to the season or feast (Proper) and others remaining constant and invariable (Ordinary). Observing these distinctions, the chart of figure 2-2 outlines the various items of a Sunday Mass in eighteenth-century Austria.[84]

Continuing a tradition that goes back to the fourteenth century, the concerted Mass cycles of eighteenth-century Austria usually set the five main chanted sections of the Ordinary, i.e., Kyrie, Gloria, Credo, Sanctus, and Agnus Dei.[85] In the early history of the Church these sections were sung by the congregation rather than the clergy or choir.[86] Figure 2-2 shows how these five sections were distributed throughout the Mass and, with the exception of the Kyrie-Gloria pair, separated by various chants, prayers, blessings, readings, and ceremonies.[87] This distribution should not be forgotten when we attempt to view these settings as unified or integrated cycles.

Indeed, the Mass Ordinary should be seen only within the context of the entire Mass liturgy. The Kyrie is a response to the priest's opening penitential prayers, and the Gloria prepares the opening prayer (Collect) of the celebrant. The Credo concludes the readings and lessons with a personal creed. Then the Sanctus continues the prayer of thanksgiving begun by the Preface and accompanies the start of the Canon; the Benedictus announces Christ's "arrival" at consecration. Finally, the Agnus Dei accompanies the distribution of Communion with calls to the sacrificial lamb and pleas for mercy and peace.

Other Considerations

Besides liturgical requirements, Mass composition was sometimes affected by church and state regulation of sacred music. The "Annus qui," promulgated by Pope Benedict XIV in 1749, attempted to regulate church music. As we have already seen, it forbade the use of theater style and theater instruments and demanded complete, audible liturgical texts.[88] This was one of the recurring attempts by the Catholic Church to prevent secular elements from infiltrating the sanctuary.[89]

On 24 December 1753, partly under the influence of the "Annus qui," the arch-episcopal *Konsistorium* of Vienna issued a decree that has been interpreted as expressly forbidding the use of trumpets and timpani in church services and processions.[90] An imperial *Hofreskript* of 26 January 1754 has been seen as supporting this same ban for the entire Hapsburg Empire.[91]

Figure 2-2. The Mass in the Eighteenth Century

Liturgical Section	SUNG Ordinary	SUNG Proper	SPOKEN/RECITED Ordinary	SPOKEN/RECITED Proper	Comment/Actions
I. MASS OF THE CATECHUMENS					
A. Opening (Entrance) Rite					
	1. Asperges me[a]				Preparation for Mass; cleansing of soul with holy water.
		2. INTROIT (Introitus)	---Penitential Prayers at the foot of the altar (Stufengebet)[b]		Clergy enter and begin private prayers; greeting, kissing, and incensing of altar; change of vestments.
	3. KYRIE				Celebrant moves before center of altar.
	4. GLORIA				Celebrant gives Gloria intonation.
				5. Collect (Oration)	First audible recitations by celebrant; this opening prayer is the climax of the opening rites.
B. Liturgy of the Word (Service of Readings)					
				6. Epistle	
		7. GRADUAL			Introduced by procession with candles and incense; people stand.
		8. ALLELUIA or TRACT[c]			
				9. Gospel (Evangelium)	
				10. Homily (Predigt)	This optional sermon interprets the Biblical texts of the day.
	11. CREDO				
II. MASS OF THE FAITHFUL					
A. Offertory Rite					
		12. OFFERTORY (Offertorium)	---Prayers over the gifts (Oratio super oblata; Opferungsgebete)		Monetary gifts collected; incensing of gifts, clergy, and people; washing of hands; prayers in low voice.
				13. Secret (Secreta)	Recited softly.
				14. Preface (Prefatio; Great Prayer of Thanksgiving)	Recited aloud.
	15. SANCTUS-BENEDICTUS				
B. Eucharistic Prayer (Canon actionis)					
			16. Canon[d]		Inaudible recitations; bell warns of elevation of Host after consecration when silence reigns; more incensing.
(continued on next page)					

a"Vidi aquam" during the Paschal season. i.e. Easter until Whitsunday.

bThese consist of: "Trinitarian blessing," antiphon "Introibo ad altare Dei," Psalm 42 ("Judica me Deus"), "Confiteor," "Misereatur," "Indulgentiam," "Deus tu conversus," and "Aufer a nobis."

cA sequence (prosa) follows the Alleluia for the Octaves of Easter, Whitsunday, and Corpus Christi. The sequence "Dies irae" follows the Tract of the Requiem Mass. The Stabat Mater is sung for the Feast of the Seven Dolours of the B.V.M. (September 15).

dThe Canon consists of: "Te igitur," intercessory prayers ("Memento" and "Communicantes"), "Hanc igitur," "Quam oblationem" (epiclesis or consecration), "Qui pridie," "Unde et memores" (anamnesis or recollection), petitions seeking acceptance of the sacrifice ("Supra quae" and "Supplices"), "Memento" of the dead, "Nobis quoque," and concluding doxologies. The "Benedictus qui venit" usually began only after the consecration and elevation.

Figure 2-2 (concluded)

Liturgical Section	SUNG		SPOKEN/RECITED		Comment/Actions
	Ordinary	Proper	Ordinary	Proper	
C. Communion Cycle			17. Lord's Prayer (Pater noster)		
			18. Fraction, Commingling, "Pax Domini," Kiss of Peace		
	19. AGNUS DEI				
		20. COMMUNION (Communio)--Various prayers			Faithful approach in hierarchical order to receive consecrated Host.
				21. Post-Communion	
D. Concluding Rite	22. Ite, missa est[e] (Dismissal)				Sung facing the people.
			23. "Placeat" Prayer		Farewell kiss of the altar; deeply bowed; spoken with a quiet voice.
			24. Closing Blessing ("Benedicat vos")		Priest raises eyes and hands toward heaven.
			25. Last Gospel[f] (Schluss-Evangelium)		Spoken quietly by rote; bishop may start leaving the altar.
			26. Final Blessings		
			27. Recession[g]		The faithful depart.

[e] A general blessing called Prayer over the People (*Oratio super populum*) precedes the Dismissal only during Lent.

[f] John 1: 1-14 ("In principio erat verbum").

[g] Canticle "Benedicite omnia opera Domini" (*Canticum trium Puerorum*, Daniel), Psalm 150 ("Laudate Dominum in sanctis"), et al.

Recently, Friedrich Riedel has presented a new interpretation of the *Hofreskript,* one that accounts for why trumpets and timpani continued to be used in some services:

> [What the *Hofreskript*] meant were *intradas* by trumpet choirs (sometimes even doubled) which played on high feasts at the beginning and end of High Mass as well as after the Gospel; also in a Te Deum they played before its beginning, before the verse "Te ergo quaesumus" (at genuflection), and at the end, and also between verses of the processional litany. The use of obbligato trumpet parts for concerted church music was not affected, as proven by contemporary performance remarks and directories.[92]

The *Hofreskript* of 1754 was thus probably a ban on just martial trumpet fanfares.

Although the *Hofkapelle* held to this prohibition until 1767, various accounts and the performance materials themselves indicate that this ban was not strictly obeyed elsewhere.[93] However, it was occasionally enforced; during the summer of 1757 St. Veit's in Krems received a reprimand from the Lower Austrian *Kreisamt* for having used two choirs of trumpets and timpani during a Mass celebrating a victory.[94] The ban was apparently lifted unofficially in 1767 after the Archbishop of Vienna, Cardinal Migazzi, sought a relaxation of the order upon the occasion of a thanksgiving service for the recovery of Maria Theresa from an illness.[95] From then on, Emperor Joseph II restricted the use of trumpets and timpani to only certain occasions, and he wished to be personally informed of each such use.[96]

In the 1780s, under the influence of the Enlightenment, Joseph II enacted various *Verordnungen* (decrees) that indirectly restricted the use of instruments for church music and also fostered congregational singing in the vernacular.[97] The imperial *Hofdekret* of 23 February 1783 engendered changes—mostly economically, politically, and socially motivated—whose end result was to simplify the liturgy and allow the people more participation in and understanding of their religious services.[98] In their correspondence from 1782 on, Mozart and his father frequently lament the changed state of church music resulting from the repercussions of the new policies.[99] That neither Haydn nor Mozart composed a Mass during the remainder of Joseph II's reign is often cited as one effect of the *Verordnungen* beginning in 1783.

The preceding discussions have considered the meaning of the Eucharist, the assigned role of music in the Mass, and the various influences of the church year, local practice, and decrees—all part of the background for sacred music in Vienna during this period. The analyses of later chapters will show how the structure and style of concerted Masses responded to this background. Because "church style" was still considered an isolated style by many of the composers and theorists defining the function of church music above, a review of what constituted this style is necessary for a true perspective on these Masses.

Church Style

Since Marco Scacchi's treatise of 1649, church music had been considered one part of a "trinity" of musical styles, the other two being chamber and theater music.[100] During the eighteenth century, theorists, scholars, and lexicographers continued to support the same functional divisions. Walther (1732) writes that the "Kirchen-Styl" is very different from the "theatralischer oder Cammer-Style"; while Mattheson (1739) says Scacchi's division "is not only absolutely correct, but also necessarily thus, and could and must not be done in any other way...."[101] Style, then, remained closely dependent upon the use to which the music was put.

Even at the end of the eighteenth century, composers still regarded church music as necessarily distinct. In a letter of 1778 from Mannheim, Mozart reminds his father that he can adequately adopt and imitate all manners and styles of composition.[102] When Mozart applies to the Municipal Council of Vienna for the position of *Kapellmeisteradjunkt* at the cathedral in May 1791, he justifies his service "on account of my thorough knowledge of both the secular and ecclesiastical styles of music."[103] In his *Gründliche Anweisung zur Composition,* the Viennese composer Albrechtsberger has a chapter entitled "Von dem Kirchen- Kammer- und Theater-Styl und von der Kirchen-Musik mit begleitenden Instrumenten."[104] He admits (and regrets) that by that late date (1790) these three styles were heard mixed together in many places. Nonetheless he claims it necessary—"for the understanding of old music books"—to inform his readers how each style used to be treated.

By 1802, however, the definitions in Koch's *Musikalisches Lexikon* clearly reflect a new view of style. In his article "Style," Koch classifies music in two overlapping ways:[105]

I. Two *Hauptarten* based on musical treatment, i.e.,
   A. Strict style (*strenger/gebundener Stil*)
   B. Free style
II. Three *Hauptarten* based on the feelings (*Empfindungen*) being expressed, i.e.,
   A. Church style
   B. Chamber style
   C. Theater style

Because church music was now described as bearing elements of both the free (galant) and strict styles, the old definitions based only upon use and affect were obsolete.[106] In his article on the Mass, Koch speaks highly of the musical treasures then beginning to collect dust in church archives: "Many Catholic churches possess very precious collections of such pieces [i.e., Mass settings] by composers old and new, pieces in which the reverence and solemnity of the church style is retained, still unmixed with the chamber and theater styles."[107]

Practically speaking, the division of music into three styles was no longer valid, except perhaps on a purely theoretical level. "Church style" became the synonym for strict or learned style, while other (i.e., secular) styles infiltrated the music actually heard in sanctuaries.[108] As Friedrich Riedel writes: "After the death of Charles VI, the purposeful connections between the gradation of ritual and musical style seem to have gradually faded from consciousness so that it came more and more to an equalization."[109]

Figure 2-3 summarizes the adjectives and other generalizations used by several composers, theorists, and critics to describe "church style" from 1725 to 1802. As can be seen, most definitions require church music to (1) promote solemnity, seriousness, and prayerful devotion (the German word *Andacht* is often used); and (2) reflect the meaning and spirit of the text. Later chapters will show how nearly every Mass examined for this study possesses these basic attributes of the church style. Interestingly is how most of these authors (particularly Fux, Spiess, Quantz, and Sulzer) place the church style above all other styles in terms of relative importance, compositional demands, and craftsmanship.[110] As usual, theory was lagging behind the actual practice. Opera, chamber, and symphonic music, where most significant new developments were then being achieved, were thus paradoxically ranked below church music until the end of the century.

For Fux the various genres of the church style are products of the different texts. Thus Masses, motets, psalms, songs of praise (*Lobgesänge*), etc. all have their individual styles which Fux groups under two chief types: (1) a cappella style; and (2) mixed style (*vermischter Styl, stile misto,* or *stilus mixtus*). The latter style describes works mixing concerted sections for voices and instruments with polyphonic a cappella sections. He asks composers not to dilute (*vermengen*) the church style by also using theater elements or dance tunes "as unfortunately many do."[111]

In *Der vollkommene Kapellmeister* (1739) Mattheson reminds composers that church style is determined more by the worship service itself than by the building in which it occurs; sacred music is not limited to a particular edifice and may be performed in a theater or concert hall.[112] Mattheson is one of the first writers to concede that the theater and chamber styles share some traits with the church style. Within "church music" Mattheson distinguishes some six secondary styles:[113]

*1. Ligature style (monophonic chant)
*2. Motet style (colorful counterpoints upon a few words)
3. Madrigal style (ingenious setting of a short poem; with words as "masters" of the music and with basso continuo)
4. Instrumental style (*stylus symphoniacus;* oratory in sound—for imitation and accompaniment of singing)

5. Canonic style (best used with instruments only so that no textual meaning is lost)
6. Melismatic style (chorale style; strophic songs)

* Used only in the church (§ 51)

Aside from printing short musical examples of each of these styles, Mattheson hesitates to describe the styles in any elaborate detail. He is following his own advice that "several cited qualities never constitute one single principal style."[114] Incidentally, Mattheson also does not ban cheer from church music:

> Yet one should not... indiscriminately abandon all vivacity in the sacred service, especially since the style of writing under discussion [instrumental style] often naturally requires more joyousness and cheerfulness than any other, namely according to the subject and circumstance giving occasion for it. . . . Only the appropriate discretion and moderation with the joyful sounds of the clarino trumpets, trombones, violins, flutes, etc., must never be lost sight of, nor be to the slightest detriment to the familiar commandment, which says: *Be joyous, yet in fear of God.*[115]

Similar to Fux, Meinrad Spiess (1745) groups church music into two manners (*Arten*), the first of which has two subdivisions:

I. A cappella
   A. *Stylus ligatus* (based upon preexistent chant)
   B. *Stylus solutus* (based upon a free but appropriate subject)
II. *Modo mixto (stylus mixtus, die vermischte Art)*

For the mixed style, where concertante instruments perform together with one or more voices in a mixture of homophony (*ariose*) and polyphony, Spiess begs composers not to "overshoot the limits of church gravity and modesty."[116]

Quantz (1752) compares church style with that of opera. He admits that church music can use both serious and light styles, letting prayerful devotion set their limits. His comments on the high value of church composition are worth mentioning: "A composer who cannot make an impression in church, where he is more restricted, will surely have even less success in the theater, where he has more freedom. But from him who already knows how to make an impression despite various restraints, from him can be expected great things when he has complete freedom."[117]

Finally, in his *Jahrbuch* for 1796, Schönfeld presents what seems to be a much more accurate account of existent musical styles than those already cited. In the opening sentence of a chapter entitled "Basis of Musical Composition in Vienna" (*Grundfuss der in Wien bestehenden Musikverfassung*), Schönfeld divides all music into no fewer than five categories: (1)

Figure 2-3. Eighteenth-Century Descriptions of "Church Style"

Writer	Adjectives
J. J. Fux (1725)[a]	arousing only prayerful devotion; following meaning of text; timeless; eternal; easy to sing; pleasing in melody; as perfect as possible; exactly according to the rules of composition
J. Walther (1732)[b]	arousing devotion; majestic; serious; respectable; elevating the spirit toward God
J. A. Scheibe (1737)[c]	following the meaning, emphasis, and declamation of the text; majestic; very serious; according to the rules of composition; penetrating, magnificent, and sublime in character
J. Mattheson (1739)[d]	arousing devotion and contemplation; majestic; serious; noble; splendid; rapturous; magnificent; instilling fear of God; promoting repentance and supplication; honoring, exalting, and praising God; edifying; elevated in style
M. Spiess (1745)[e]	majestic; serious; pious; modest; displaying much care, diligence, and workmanship
J. J. Quantz (1752)[f]	arousing prayerful devotion or sorrow; serious; more pompous and grave than opera; moderate and restrained in tempo and execution; pious; praising God
C. Burney (1772)[g]	grave; "scientific" (i.e., with good harmony, learned modulation, and fugues); without frivolity

J. G. Albrechtsberger (1790)[h]	following meaning of text; serious; pious; noble; magnificent; cheerful (when required)
J. G. Sulzer (1793)[i]	arousing prayerful devotion; following meaning and declamation of text; solemn; omitting all artificiality, excessive ornament, and showiness
H. C. Koch (1802)[j]	arousing prayerful devotion; solemn; dignified; expressive of worthy, lofty, and pious feeling; omitting excessive ornament and virtuosic showiness; able to move the heart

---

[a]Fux, *Gradus ad Parnassum,* Mizler trans., pp. 181–82, 192–93.

[b]Walther, "Stylus," *Musicalisches Lexicon,* p. 584.

[c]Scheibe, *Critischer Musikus* (29 Oct. 1737), p. 168, (7 Jan. 1738) p. 219.

[d]Mattheson, *Der vollkommene Kapellmeister,* pt. I, ch. 10, sec. 10, Harriss trans., p. 191; sec. 12 and 38, Harriss trans., pp. 192 and 198.

[e]Spiess, *Tractatus musicus,* p. 161; cf. Ratner, *Classic Music,* p. 7.

[f]Johann Joachim Quantz, *Versuch einer Anweisung die Flöte traversiere zu spielen* (Berlin: J. F. Voss, 1752) XVII, vii, sec. 12, 21–22, 53, pp. 245, 289–90, 266.

[g]Burney, *Musical Tours,* ed. Scholes, II, pp. 113–14.

[h]Albrechtsberger, *Gründliche Anweisung zur Composition,* p. 378.

[i]Sulzer, "Kirchenmusik," *Allgemeine Theorie,* 4th ed. (1793) III, 20–22. This article was probably written jointly by Sulzer and J. P. Kirnberger; cf. Howard Serwer, "Sulzer," *New Grove Dictionary of Music and Musicians,* XVIII, p. 365.

[j]Koch, "Styl, Schreibart," *Musikalisches Lexikon,* col. 1453–54.

church, (2) concert, (3) military, (4) theater, and (5) dance.[118] Theoretical writing was at last beginning to catch up with musical practice. He names two branches of church music: chant (*Choralmusik*) and instrumental music. The first type is customary where only a chorus sings, as in the *Metropolitankirche* (St. Stephen's) and the monks' churches. The second type probably refers to instrumentally accompanied church music. "Instrumental music may be considered half extinct. One hears it in parish churches only on Sundays and in the other churches only on holy days."[119] Six years earlier, after the death of the Emperor Joseph II in 1790, the restrictions upon orchestrally accompanied services had been lifted so as to allow again the use of instruments at institutions that could afford it.[120]

Clearly the term "church style" had a different, more complicated meaning by the end of the eighteenth century. Ever an elusive concept, style now had to be more specifically qualified because it could refer to the use, the manner, or the effect of music. The old triumvirate of church, theater, and chamber styles no longer sufficed; the cross influences among all three had become too numerous. The gradual secularization of the church style created a divergence of attitudes among composers, critics, and church fathers.

The papal "Annus qui" of 1749 was but one manifestation of the church's reaction to the change. This encyclical demanded that ecclesiastical music be composed in a style different from that of the theater; solos, duets, trios, etc., as well as theatrical instruments were expressly forbidden.[121] Josephinism of the 1780s merely exacerbated the tensions, which were tentatively resolved by the conservative tide of Cecilianism in the nineteenth century.

As responsibility for the music fell more and more into laymen's hands, composers often forgot that the music was supposed to support the liturgical action. "Music spread its gorgeous mantle over the whole Mass, so that the other details of the rite scarcely had any significance. Encouraged by the moderate attitude of the Council of Trent, it had developed into mighty proportions."[122] As we have seen, some Masses became almost "church concerts with liturgical accompaniment."[123] The singers had been moved from the cathedral's choir to galleries (balconies), chants were omitted, and other music was substituted for the day's Proper or played during liturgically required silences.[124]

Many critics attacked this musical secularization in the church. In his account of a visit to Vienna in 1772, Charles Burney displays a very conservative attitude toward church style. In his opinion, composers such as the *Hofkapellmeister* Gassmann would do better to follow the example of many earlier composers and specialize in only one style so as not to mix attributes of the different styles.

But, in general, those succeed best in writing for the church, stage, or chamber, who accustom themselves to that particular species of composition only.

I do not call every modern oratorio, mass or motet, *church music;* as the same compositions to different words would do equally well, indeed often better, for the stage. [125]

Thus, for Burney, church music should remain a serious and solemn genre. In 1777, after lauding the merits of plainsong, Joseph Martin Kraus was blunt in his attack of contemporary Catholic figured music: "Allein, ihre Figuralmusik ist für Kirchen Unsinn—wahrer Unsinn." [126] He goes on to criticize inappropriate instrumentation, volume, and counterpoint:

In a not too medium-sized town I heard one such [Mass] performed and remain eternally astonished to this day. Before the first Kyrie there was a noisy overture with trumpets and timpani, followed by the chorus rejoicing with all its force; and so that nothing was spared in glorifying the affair, the organist pulled out all the stops and used all ten fingers for each chord played. Schmidt, Holzbauer, Brixi, [and] Schmidt of Mainz have produced such Masses that, with other words set to them, you could make miniature operas (*Operettchen*) out of them. Take the more solidly (as one calls it) crafted works of Wassmut, Pögel, Richter, the great Fux, [and] Gassmann—for what purpose must a mere *Amen* be repeated several hundred times? Is not the music in the churches supposed to be mostly for the heart? Do fugues serve that end? [127]

This indictment of counterpoint obviously conflicts with most views about the suitability of the strict style for the church.

Among the often vicious reprobations in the anonymous *Ueber die Kirchenmusik in Wien* (1781) we find:

It is especially in a [certain] monastic church of our city where things go a bit too far with respect to the music, and every Christian who does not have a wooden insensibility must be disturbed in prayer. The clerical choir director himself, in whose musical round dance (*Runde*) everything sings and whistles, composes mostly his own pieces or whatever they are called. There is hardly any opera—*buffa* as well as *seria*—which he does not know how to plunder line by line (as the experts told me) and use most cleverly. On the day of a production the top male and female singers of our stages appear in the middle of the church to be heard. . . .

Really! If we were to be led blindfolded into this church on a feast day, e.g., in the octave of St. John, we would have to believe that we had entered a playhouse, were not a "Pax vobis" or a purely annoying offertory bag to make us aware of the holy place.

Who, then, can really maintain that one would be able to pray fervently in the theater while listening to a Venetian marketplace, a Röschen and Kollas, [or] a love story of the working class? Why? Because the enticing song, the pleasing tones conquer our senses.

I myself was present in this church when they performed such arias that had been removed from operas and metamorphosed into a *Salve Regina* or a *Regina coeli*. . . . Moreover, an undertone of *Bravo, Schön,* and *che viva* was heard from most of the listeners. [128]

Similar attacks elsewhere in this pamphlet make it clear why the author preferred to remain anonymous.

In his account of Vienna's church music in 1781, Friedrich Nicolai likewise condemns the influence of opera:

> With respect to composition, Catholic Church music up until several years ago still had much of its own special character. But nowadays operatic music also forces its way into churches everywhere, and, what is worse, [it is] the insipid Italian opera music of the new style. In Vienna, too, I found it all too conspicuous. During many a Credo or Benedictus I knew not whether perhaps I was hearing music from an Italian *opera buffa.*[129]

As will be seen in the analytical chapters to follow, all of these criticisms can be justified to a certain extent when we consider the various operatic techniques (e.g., solo arias, ensembles, quasi recitatives, etc.) used in some Masses. In addition to the opera contrafacta already known, others undoubtedly lurk within Masses and other sacred compositions—borrowings which only time and careful study will uncover.[130]

When the position of the church in Vienna's musical life and the diverse talents of that city's musicians are considered, it is no surprise that all styles— sacred and secular—were blending inevitably into the cosmopolitan style we associate with the mature Classic era. In his study of the Masses of Hasse, David Wilson has properly viewed the new church style at the end of the century as the result of a reconciliation between the *stile antico* and *stile moderno,* i.e., between strict counterpoint and a style that blends polyphony, homophony, chorus, instruments, and solo voices.[131] Henry Raynor has noted that composers of church music could hardly avoid expressing themselves with the newly developing musical resources (i.e., opera, symphony, etc.).

> The musical value of these works [i.e., Viennese Masses of Haydn, Mozart, and Beethoven], even to non-Catholic or irreligious minds, is oddly involved with the fact of their unsuitability for church use, but the musical principles involved show that the composers of these doubtful [i.e., criticized] Masses were writing music that came naturally to them. Their style was anything but restricted; those we have mentioned had an enormous emotional range; they could not, however, worship God in a foreign language.[132]

And what were composers' views of what specifically constituted church style? Fux asks that melodies follow the meaning and declamation of the text and be easy to sing: "... this happens if the composer sets no words under the smallest note values, unless a vowel is part of a melisma, in which case the short notes occur according to the skill of the singer."[133] In 1737 Scheibe offers a series of recommendations for composers of Masses. These suggestions may be summarized as follows:[134]

1. Masses consist of choruses as well as movements for one, two, and three voices
2. Choruses are best set as fugues, with double counterpoints, canons, etc. and with a straightforward, singable subject (*Hauptsatz; Thema*) that is not too elaborate
3. Chromatic melodies are best used for appropriate words and as fugal subjects with short, simple countermelodies
4. Most apt for choral fugues is a short theme which has little or no chromaticism and scarcely exceeds the octave in range
5. Melody must agree with the meaning, emphasis, and declamation of the text
6. Be careful with word repetitions; do not repeat words of little importance or affect
7. Use of instruments for such choruses must be clever and splendid (*sinnreich und prächtig*), support the words or voices, clarify the intent of the text, strengthen the harmony, and provide "filler" when necessary
8. The higher instruments should not be lacking in melody; if they do not double voices, they should have "a new and flowing or running song" (*einen neuen und fliessenden, oder laufenden Gesang*) or else present a counterpoint which does not obscure the words
9. No trumpets or timpani should be used in Masses for the dead
10. In solo voiced movements the instruments provide a quiet, gentle, and pleasant accompaniment, and the harmony should remain concise and penetrating
11. In slow movements the soloist's melody should be of the most natural and singable kind
12. Use care if the solo voice is allowed to compete with a solo instrument; other instruments must play softly, and the two main participants must carry on in an agreeable manner
13. In solo movements: "There can be no lengthy or facile jokes, games, rufflings (*Kräuseln*), or coloraturas (*Coloriren*), but seriousness and splendor must always dominate"
14. Vocal duets and trios may also be used effectively, with or without instrumental accompaniment; the voices must interact and keep up a continuous, interesting competition between themselves, without superfluous ornamentation
15. Seek variety and change (*Wechsel*) from movement to movement

Albrechtsberger (1790) offers specific suggestions about key (e.g., a major key is best for a solemn Mass), tempo (allegro should be avoided in the Kyrie, "Qui tollis," "Crucifixus," and "Dona nobis"), and instrumentation.[135] In 1793 Sulzer has many recommendations for figural church music, including:

1. The music had best have a simple melody, using one of the old modes (*die alten Tonarten*) which is best suited for the *Affekt* of the piece
2. The correct declamation of the text must be preserved
3. Chromaticism and enharmonics are useful for a livelier or even a more violent (*heftiger*) *Affekt*
4. Fast notes in the lower voices as well as arias with runs and cadenzas are to be avoided.[136]

Several of Mozart's letters show his concern for well-crafted sacred music.[137] In 1763, while in Bologna with Gluck, the 24-year-old Dittersdorf was somewhat appalled by secular elements in a Vesper by the local *maestro di cappella* named Mazzoni: "With choruses and instruments, the music made use of more than one hundred persons. The composition was beautiful and magnificent, though it seemed to me a little too cheerful and profane for the church; for, excepting the exemplary fugues, it resembled *opera seria* more than church music."[138] In his late years, Haydn told his biographer Griesinger that he had required three months to compose a Mass as opposed to one month for each of the "London" symphonies.[139] And as for the cheer which many criticized in his Masses, Haydn said he thought more about the "qui tollis" (salvation) than about the "peccata" (sin) in the text.[140] Usually, however, a composer's attitude toward sacred music was rarely expressed in words. We obtain a better idea of their "views" by studying and listening to the scores. Only then can we adequately judge to what degree each composer met the liturgical requirements and followed the norms of "church style."

3

The Composers

This chapter introduces (in alphabetical order) the 28 composers under study, with special emphasis upon biographical details relating to their sacred music. To the extent possible, the composers' church music activities in Vienna, their Mass output, and contemporary reports about their music for the church are discussed. Pertinent biographical data for composers who have been amply treated elsewhere (e.g., *New Grove*) will be given summarily.[1]

Johann Georg Albrechtsberger
b. 3 February 1736, Klosterneuburg
d. 7 March 1809, Vienna

As a highly praised teacher and theorist, Albrechtsberger needs little introduction. However, it is perhaps not always realized how esteemed he was as an organist and how active he was as a composer of church and keyboard music.[2]

After studies in Vienna in the late 1740s and early 1750s (possibly including organ lessons with Monn), Albrechtsberger held a succession of organist positions in Hungary and Lower Austria (including Melk). In the late 1760s he returned to Vienna, settling there with his wife whom he married in 1768. Soon thereafter, we know he held the following Viennese appointments:

1772–93	*Regens chori*	Karmeliter-Kirche in the Leopoldstadt[3]
1772–91	2nd *Hoforganist*	Imperial Court
1791–93	1st *Hoforganist*	Imperial Court (succeeding Arbesser)
1791–93	*Kapellmeister Adjunkt*	St. Stephen's (succeeding Mozart)
1793–1809	*Kapellmeister*	St. Stephen's (succeeding Hofmann)

As we have seen, in 1783 Albrechtsberger was one of the best paid choir directors in Vienna.

Albrechtsberger composed over 30 Masses.[4] In 1769 the *Wiener Diarium* reported that a *Cäcilienmesse* by Albrechtsberger was performed on St. Cecilia's Day.[5] Otherwise we have few contemporary accounts of performances of his Masses. Recent reactions to his church music, especially to the later works, criticize its sectional formality and obvious functionalism.[6] In his treatise of 1790 Albrechtsberger seems to regret the then current practice of mixing three musical styles (church, chamber, and theater) in compositions destined for church use.[7]

In the present study Albrechtsberger is represented by four *missae breves* (M. 1, 2, 3, 5) and one *missa longa* (M. 4) dating from 1755 to 1781.[8] Contrary to what we might expect, he used a variety of textures, energetic syllabic choruses (ex. 7-4), movements which juxtapose chorus and soloists in *concertato* fashion (ex. 7-7) as well as masterful fugues at the expected places. In some of his solo numbers he can be harmonically expressive and adventurous (see the "Et incarnatus" of ex. 8-13). Few movement subdivisions, limited key choice from movement to movement, melodic reprises (ex. 7-4), and "segue" markings in his holograph scores all show a commitment to concise and well-integrated settings. His Masses maintain a pace that would not unduly delay the service. It may have been Albrechtsberger's concern for overall unity that led him to reuse Kyrie music for each of the "Dona" settings in the present sample. Over a third of Albrechtsberger's Masses are accompanied only by two violins and organ continuo; Masses using oboes and flutes are dated 1781 (M. 4) and later, with relatively few winds employed during the period of retrenchment under Joseph II.

[Franz Paul] Ferdinand Arbesser
b. ca. 1719 (place unknown)
d. 12 December 1794, Vienna

Little is known about Ferdinand Arbesser except that he served as first *Hoforganist* from 6 May 1772 until his pensioning on 1 December 1791 when Albrechtsberger succeeded him in the post.[9] According to Anton Mörath, Arbesser had served as a *Kapellmeister* in Krumau (Český Krumlov) from 1747 to 1751.[10] Although no known records confirm it, Arbesser may have served earlier than 1772 as *Hoforganist*, perhaps as early as 1763 when Gottlieb Muffat (d. 1770) retired.[11] We know Arbesser was already in Vienna by 1771 because in June of that year he was taken with imperial subvention into the newly founded *Tonkünstler-Societät*.[12] Arbesser must have been a fairly gifted organist, considering that he would have played continuo under Gassmann's direction and that Albrechtsberger, regarded as Vienna's best organist, succeeded him as *Hoforganist*.

Research thus far reveals that Arbesser wrote no more than the four Masses listed by Reichert.[13] Both of the masses selected for this study (M. 6 and 7) are typical examples of a mid-eighteenth-century *missa brevis*, the kind Joseph Haydn would have heard and sung in his youth.[14] His style is generally conservative and horizontally oriented. The violin parts to the Kyrie of the *Missa Nubes pluant justum* (M. 6) show that Reutter was not the only one guilty of "rushing strings" in his church music. The pastoral "Dona nobis pacem" is perhaps the best movement of this somewhat pedestrian Mass. The other Mass (M. 7) is notable for the flexible alternation between soloists and chorus in nearly every movement (see ex. 6-9). Based on initial stylistic comparison, Arbesser is the most likely composer of the *Missa brevis "Rorate coeli desuper"* also attributed to Reutter and Joseph Haydn (Hob. XXII: 3).[15]

Giuseppe Bonno
b. 29 January 1711, Vienna
d. 15 April 1788, Vienna

Son of an imperial footman, Giuseppe Bonno worked at court most of his life. Emperor Charles VI sent him as a teenager to Naples for 10 years of musical training, supposedly under Durante and Leo. Back in Vienna, Bonno became a *Hofscholar* in composition on 9 May 1737 and studied with court organist and composer Johann Georg Reinhardt (1676/77–1742).[16] A negative light is shed on either the training Bonno received in Italy or on his abilities when Fux, in his appraisal of the then 26-year-old "student," attests that Bonno "was not yet instructed enough in the fundamental rules of counterpoint."[17] Nevertheless, two years later (1739) Bonno was named a *Hofkomponist*, a position he retained for the next 35 years. (He did, however, lose out to Predieri in a bid to become *Vize-Hofkapellmeister* that same year.) Not earning an adequate income as *Hofkomponist*, Bonno was also active as a composition and singing teacher (Dittersdorf, Friberth, and Martínez were among his pupils) and as the *Hauskapellmeister* to Field Marshal Joseph Friedrich, Prince von Sachsen-Hildburghausen (from 1749 to 1761).[18]

Finally in 1744, at the then advanced age of 63, Bonno landed a distinguished position: he became *Hofkapellmeister* upon the death of Florian Gassman, a man 18 years his junior. Apparently Bonno's many years of experience at court and Count von Sporck's wish not to let Hofmann receive the post led to this appointment.[19] Bonno also succeeded Gassmann as director of the concerts presented by the *Tonkünstler-Societät* (1774–81/82)[20] and was secretary of Vienna's *Cäcilien-Kongregation* in 1783.[21] In sum, Bonno was a very late bloomer whose position and prestige seems to have been based more upon seniority and court connections than upon musical talent.[22]

Bonno composed some 30 complete Mass settings.[23] According to Angermüller in *New Grove*, most of Bonno's church music dates from after 1763, the year he stopped composing music for the stage.[24] Even up to 1774 the bulk of his output remained compositions for the chamber and theater.[25] The three Masses in the present sample (M. 8, 9, 10) are all *missae breves* from this late period when he was *Hofkapellmeister*.[26] These settings show that, despite some lack of imagination in melody, rhythm, and harmony, the aged Bonno was attuned to contemporary trends in the texture, size, and instrumentation of concerted settings. He wrote no long number Masses with separate movements for soloists. Indeed movements are few, and vocal solos are always integrated into the choral numbers.[27] Even the Benedictus is usually choral in his Masses.

Wellesz's praise of the instrumentation in Bonno's operas applies equally to his Masses.[28] Often movements begin with an extended orchestral introduction (see ex. 6-7). Pairs of oboes and violas are usually part of the full orchestra, and Bonno retained the four-trumpet brass section (2 clarini, 2 [low] trombe) typical of earlier Masses by *Hofkapelle* composers.[29] Obbligato writing for woodwinds and violoncello is another progressive trait (see ex. 6-7) as is the use of sonatalike form in two of the Kyries (M. 8 and 9). Pasteovers and other alterations made by Bonno to scores from the *Hofkapelle* collection show a concern for his overly repetitive style with its all too regular cadences.

Johann Nepomuk Boog
b. ca. 1724 (place unknown)
d. 21 April 1764, Vienna

Although little is known at present about the life of Boog (Pock, Bockh, Pogg), his church compositions are preserved at several cloisters and libraries in Vienna, Lower Austria, and Moravia. He preceded Leopold Hofmann as *regens chori* at St. Peter's in Vienna, the music collection of which (now in the Austrian National Library) contains several of Boog's church compositions.[30] The title page of an a cappella Mass dated 1745 and preserved at the Gesellschaft der Musikfreunde indicates that Boog studied with Tuma.[31] Later Boog taught thoroughbass to Franz Joseph Aumann (1728–98) at Vienna's Jesuit Seminar.[32]

Research thus far shows Boog to have written about 16 Masses. The three concerted Masses inspected for this study include two *missae breves* (M. 11, 12), and a *missa longa* (M. 13). Boog is an impressive craftsman who does not shy away from composing choral fugues or from carefully indicating dynamic contrasts. His style is nonetheless conservative: movements are often unified by a single accompaniment figure throughout, sequences are frequent, and hemiolas show Boog to be not yet a blind observer of the barline. One of his Masses preserved at Göttweig is written for a double chorus of eight voices, a

Plate 4.　St. Peter's as Viewed from the Graben

Boog and Hofmann were choir directors here. Engraving by Salomon Kleiner (*Wahrhafte und genaue Abbildung aller Kirchen und Klöster* [Vienna, 1724–37], pt. IV, pl. 1. Historisches Museum der Stadt Wien) scoring that was becoming more and more rare in Masses of this period. Boog's Masses are true number Masses, with each movement being a separate entity unto itself. Boog rarely departs from the central key of each Mass. Trombone parts show that Boog still used this instrument at St. Peter's for choral doubling and occasional obbligatos. Nevertheless, as the number of musical examples by Boog in the later chapters shows, his Masses are quite representative of the stylistic mainstream in Vienna at mid-century.[33]

Anton Carl
b. ca. 1717 (place unknown)
d. 1 July 1784, Vienna

Although as many as 22 Masses are attribtued to him, we know very little about Anton Carl (Karl). According to the 1783 index of Vienna's church music personnel, Carl was the pensioned *regens chori* at St. Augustine's (a church physically attached to the *Hof*) as well as the active *regens chori* at the nearby Kirche zum heiligen Geist im Bürgerspital where he apparently lived.[34] As we saw earlier, he was one of Vienna's best paid choir directors. The city death records indicate that Carl was also "k. k. Totenmusikdirektor"; that is, he was in charge of music for the *Totenbruderschaft*, an imperially endowed brotherhood at St. Augustine's.[35] He may have been identical with one of—or related to—the two Anton Karls serving as bass and tenor at St. Augustine's in 1783.[36] Ambros Carl (ca. 1677–1754), an earlier *regens chori* at the Kirche zum heiligen Geist im Bürgerspital, could also have been a relative.[37]

Carl's *Missa solennis in C* (M. 14) is an elaborate *missa longa* in a fairly conservative style.[38] It is a number Mass with two to four subdivisions for each part. In most of the choral movements there are vocal solos alternating with the chorus. The bass and alto soloists each have an aria ("Quoniam" and "Benedictus," respectively), while the soprano soloist has what approaches accompanied recitative for the moving "Et incarnatus" (ex. 8-16). In the "Benedictus" the first violinist switches to a viola. Both the Kyrie and Gloria end with a fugue. Despite the number quality of this multi-movement Mass, Carl achieves a certain degree of continuity by not always having movements end in the same key with which they began.

Karl Ditters von Dittersdorf
b. 2 November 1739, Vienna
d. 24 October 1799, Schloss Rothlotta, Neuhof (Bezirk Pilgram), Bohemia, Czechoslovakia

Dittersdorf was a virtuoso violinist as well as composer of operas, oratorios, symphonies, concertos, and a quantity of church and chamber music. Thanks to his autobiography (1801) we know many details about his career.[39] In his youth he studied music at the Jesuit Seminar where Joseph Ziegler was one of his teachers.[40] It was Ziegler who suggested that Dittersdorf play violin at the Schottenkirche to improve his sightreading.[41] As the following résumé indicates, Dittersdorf remained in Vienna as a performer until his 1763 concert tour of Italy.

1751–61	*Kammerknabe* to Prince von Sachsen-Hildburghausen (Vienna) for whom Bonno (Dittersdorf's composition teacher), Friberth, and Gluck also worked
1761–63	Violinist in the *Hof* opera orchestra, Vienna
1765–69	*Kapellmeister* to the Bishop of Grosswardein (Oradea, Rumania)
ca. 1769–96	*Kapellmeister* to Prince-Bishop of Breslau, Count Schaffgotsch, in Johannisberg (near Jauernig)
1796–99	Guest, during his retirement, of Baron Ignaz von Stillfried, Schloss Rothlotta

Although from 1765 on he was employed elsewhere as a music director, Dittersdorf occasionally visited Vienna (1773, 1786); musical scores and catalogues indicate that his new compositions continued to be performed there. After Gassmann died in 1774, Joseph II invited Dittersdorf to be the new *Hofkapellmeister*. Dittersdorf declined the position. In Vienna he also came into contact with Haydn, Mozart, Paisiello, and Vanhal.

Dittersdorf composed at least a dozen Masses in his lifetime.[42] For the present sample the three Masses catalogued by Krebs in 1900 have been analyzed (M. 15–17).[43] All three are extended *missae longae* totaling more than 1,100 measures each.[44] Despite some conservative tendencies (e.g., long fugues, hemiola, "number" settings with three to six movements for the Gloria and Credo, and displays of solo coloratura), Dittersdorf is one of the most progressive composers under study. For him, musical form usually takes precedence over the text; the traditional rhetorical devices of the Mass are seldom used. Thus, for example, we frequently find movements resembling sonata form (ex. 6-11). His orchestrations (always using oboes and sometimes violas) stand out for their inspired employment of obbligatos (ex. 9-12).[45] There is a greater than usual variety in the choice of meters (especially 2/4). In addition, Dittersdorf is not averse to reusing melodic material in varied form for a later part of a Mass to strengthen the work's unity (ex. 10-9).

Dittersdorf's church music was well received by his contemporaries in Vienna. One of the more glittering reviews appeared in the *Anhang* to number 84 of the *Wiener Diarium* in 1766. It singles out his Masses for special praise.

Herr Carl Ditters, his passages are mostly fiery, violent, daring, but they always have a dominating melody that pleasantly and attractively connects them. Whenever he appears, he is new; and one notices that there is a genius in him that seeks to rise up and to reach the highest degree of perfection. Even there when he does not wish to, he pleases, because he understands how the national taste can be linked pleasantly with the art. Up to now a Ditters has understood best how to honor the nation, in that he is a good composer as well as a great violinist. His last works, especially the Masses, contain fugues which will stand up to the most severe criticism. In his concertos a brilliant melody usually predominates, which appears to be placed with such order and choice that the work reaches all the perfection of which this instrument is capable. Should not, or can not, time give us a Bach in him?[46]

Earlier, when Dittersdorf was only 26, the *Wiener Diarium* had praised his Mass for the feast of the Styrian *Landes-patron:* "The music [was] by the famous Herr Carl Dieters who joined the charming with the artistic (*das anmuthige mit dem künstlichen*) according to church style and won the approval deserved from all experts."[47] In another issue of 1766 the *Diarium* even mentions a specific compositional technique of the Mass: "The Mass was a totally new experience in which the so-called cantus firmus was so ingeniously combined (*künstlich verbunden*) with the instrumental music (after the Roman church style) that it not only served to edify the devout congregation but also was generally approved by the cognoscenti."[48]

As the old catalogues and collections tell us, Dittersdorf's church music was widely disseminated. We already saw how his C Major Mass was part of the extensive music performed for a service in Furth in 1773.[49] As late as 1820, in Alt-Lerchfeld, Ferdinand Schubert (Franz's brother) performed Dittersdorf's so-called "Franziskaner-Messe," a unison Mass with organ accompaniment.[50] Further study of Dittersdorf's Masses may well show that, contrary to what the article in *New Grove* has suggested, his church works do not necessarily have less historical importance than his theater works.

[Franz] Karl Friberth
b. 7 June 1736, Wullersdorf (Lower Austria)
d. 6 August 1816, Vienna

Karl Friberth (Friebert) is best known for his activities as a tenor in Vienna and Eisenstadt. However, as was noted in the first chapter, he was also a composer as well as one of Vienna's busiest choir directors. During the 1750s he sang at St. Stephen's and at the concerts run by his singing teacher Bonno for Prince von Sachsen-Hildburghausen.[51] Friberth studied composition with

Gassmann and possibly Joseph Haydn.[52] In 1776, after 17 years as a tenor for his close friend Haydn and his Esterházy patrons in Eisenstadt, Friberth returned to Vienna where he sang and directed the music in both "Jesuit" churches (Kirche am Hof and Universitäts-Kirche) and, up to 1783, at several smaller churches.[53] In his *Jahrbuch* of 1796 Schönfeld still lists Friberth as Kapellmeister at the two "Jesuit" churches and the "Wällsche Kapelle" in the Minoriten-Kirche.[54] At the latter church Friberth was occasionally allowed to use singers from the Italian opera.[55] Friberth's high rank among Vienna's musicians is demonstrated by his various activities in the *Tonkünstler-Societät* from its founding in 1771 and by the fact that he (along with Bonno and Hofmann) was one of the few choir directors with the title Kapellmeister instead of *regens chori.*[56]

Friberth composed mostly church music, including nine Masses.[57] His *Missa in D* (M. 18, dated 1774) is a moderately sized *missa longa.*[58] Not surprisingly, the work shows Friberth's strength to be the movements for solo voice rather than the choruses. Operatic influences include virtuosic coloratura covering a wide range (e.g., alto up to f#[2] in the "Quoniam"), finalelike themes (e.g., the "Dona" marked Prestissimo), dramatic fermatas, etc. Except for the "Gratias" (B minor), "Et incarnatus" (D minor), and "Benedictus" (A major), the Mass is entirely in D major. Phrases of regular length and rondolike themes are just two of the characteristics which place Friberth stylistically in the younger generation along with Dittersdorf, Vařhal, and Haydn.

Although this particular Mass rarely rises above mediocrity, Friberth was respected and honored during his lifetime. Nicolai, for instance, praised the "beautiful music" for a Mass heard 17 June 1781 at one of the Jesuit churches where Friberth directed.[59] "On account of his service to music,"[60] Friberth went to Rome in 1796 to receive the Order of the Golden Spur from Pope Pius VI. That same year Schönfeld includes Friberth along with Albrechtsberger, Beethoven, Haydn, Martínez, Sonnleithner, Vařhal, et al. in his *Jahrbuch*'s list of composers who have written music "worthy of attention."[61]

His compositions, which consist mostly of church music and several arias, distinguish themselves mainly in the fact that they are distinctly, [and] most correctly, very pleasant to the ear and heart, and in vocal textures (*Stimmensätze*) they are brilliant without being overburdened. At the same time he observes a deeply felt aesthetic. His singing is flexible and fluent; never is it empty or too obscured by the instruments.[62]

Plate 5. Kirche am Hof (obere Jesuiten-Kirche until 1773) Where Karl Friberth Served
Several Years as Kapellmeister
Engraving by Salomon Kleiner
(*Wahrhafte und genaue Abbildung aller Kirchen und Klöster* [Vienna, 1724–37],
pt. I, pl. 9. Historisches Museum der Stadt Wien)

Plate 6. Following a Procession from the Service in St. Stephen's,
Pope Pius VI Blesses More Than 30,000 Viennese from
the Balcony of the Kirche am Hof on Easter Sunday
in 1782
Engraving by Karl Schütz
(Vienna: Artaria, 1783; Albertina, Vienna)

Florian Leopold Gassmann
b. 3 May 1729, Brüx (Most), Bohemia
d. 20 January 1774, Vienna

Gassmann was first and foremost a composer of operas, symphonies, and chamber music. Most of his church music was written after he succeeded Reutter as *Hofkapellmeister* in 1772, just two years before his own untimely death.[63] After several years of work and study in Italy, Gassmann had come to Vienna in 1763 as a composer of ballets for the theater.[64] He rapidly won favor at court and in 1764 became "Kammer-Musikus" to Joseph II who was especially fond of his music.[65] In 1771 Gassmann was one of the founders of Vienna's distinguished *Tonkünstler-Societät*.[66] By 1772 Gassmann's standing among his colleagues had grown to such an extent that his appointment to the *Hofkapellmeister* post probably came as no surprise.

Gassmann composed five Mass settings, which represent only about one-tenth of all his church music.[67]

Kosch No.[68]	Earliest Known Year	Title (with principal sources)	
1	1772	*Missa* [brevis] *in B-flat*	(A-Wn: H.K. 24)
2	1775	*Missa* [solemnis] *in F*	(A-Wn: H.K. 28)
3	1775	*Missa solemnis in C*	(A-Wn: H.K. 29; score published in *DTÖ*, vol. 83, p. 1–54)
4	1771	*Missa solemnis in C*	(A-Wn: H.K. 30; D-brd-B: mus. ms. 7120 as *St. Cecilia Mass*; M. 19)
5	?	*Missa in D* (for men's voices [TTB]; lacks Sanctus-Agnus)	(autograph score at A-Wgm: I-7506)

Only the last two (Kosch Nos. 4 and 5) are number Masses that divide the Gloria and Credo each into four or more solo and choral movements. Kosch believes that the first three (Kosch Nos. 1–3), which have fewer movements and are for orchestra and chorus only (i.e., without solos) were composed while Gassmann was *Hofkapellmeister* (1772–74).[69]

The *St. Cecilia Mass* (Kosch No. 4 = M. 19) was probably from Gassmann's first years in Vienna (i.e., between 1763 and 1771).[70] This *missa longa* exists in two versions; in a Berlin score there are a Credo (longer) and Sanctus (shorter) different from those in the *Hofkapelle* parts at the Austrian

National Library in Vienna.[71] The work is representative of the mixing of older and newer styles common at that time. Grand choral fugues still close each part of the Mass, and the Gloria consists of six separate movements, including duets, trios, and quartets as well as choruses.[72] Progressive features include metric and harmonic variety (2/4 is used), regular, balanced phrases, lack of excessive coloratura, cello and woodwind obbligatos (e.g., "Laudamus"), and greater use of the solo quartet (e.g., "Christe," "Qui tollis," and "Agnus"). Despite the overall serious tone of the work, Gassmann's prowess as an opera composer is (like Bonno's) omnipresent (e.g., in the vocal lines, key plans, and instrumentation). George Hill's remark (1980) about Gassmann's considerable lyric gifts[73] and the following observations by Burney (1772) about Gassmann's opera *I Rovinati* would apply equally to the present Mass: "There was a contrast, an opposition and dissimilitude of movements and passages, by which one contributed to the advantage and effect of another, that was charming; and the instrumental parts were judiciously and ingeniously worked."[74]

Gassmann acquired a good reputation; and even after his premature death in 1772, his works continued to be performed.[75] In 1777 Joseph Martin Kraus names Gassmann among composers "of more solidly crafted things."[76] Four years later Nicolai notes that Gassmann was a "man of exemplary talent" who died "in his best years."[77] A 1795 biographical sketch of the composer remarks how no one heard Gassmann's Requiem performed "without it leaving a great impression upon the heart."[78] The following year Schönfeld's *Jahrbuch* describes then *Hofkapellmeister* Salieri as "a pupil of the great Gassmann, former *k.k. Kapellmeister* and ardent admirer of the immortal Gluck, whose style he chose as a model."[79]

[Laurenz and Adam] Grassl

In the archives of Austria, Moravia, and southern Germany, some 14 Masses from the late eighteenth century are attributed to Grassl (Graßl, Grasl, Gras[s]el). There appear to have been two composers with the name Grassl at this time: Laurenz (Lorenz, Laurentius) and Adam (Adamo). However, these first names are seldom provided in the musical sources or catalogues; further study is needed to distinguish between the two men.

The collection of manuscript biographies assembled for the Gesellschaft der Musikfreunde in 1826 gives us the following information about Laurenz Grassl: "Laurenz Grassl was a native Austrian. He was employed as a tenor and sub-cantor at St. Stephen's Cathedral in Vienna and died 16 June 1805. He wrote many small Masses and other church pieces, which were formerly disseminated throughout Austria and to other provinces and which are still found in several choirs of the countryside."[80] A "Laurentius Grassl" was active ca. 1769 as organist at the pilgrimage church in Mariazell.[81] In 1783 Laurenz was singing tenor at the Karmeliter-Kirche in the Leopoldstadt (under Albrechtsberger) and at St. Peter's (under Hofmann and Preindl).[82] Like Friberth, he was a tenor who also composed sacred music. In his catalogue of Prague's Loreta Kapelle collection, Pulkert reports that Laurenz Grasl is identified as "Maest. di Capp. Vien."[83] Laurenz may have been a pupil of Haydn since the parts of a *Missa solemnis in C* at the Benedictine Abbey in Ottobeuren list the composer as "Gras[Grasl?]/Scolare di Gius: Haydn."[84]

No biographical information is available on Adam Grassl. Two Masses were found to bear this first name in a few sources: *Missa Pastoralis Ex C* (M. 20, before 1774) and *Missa in D Pastoralis* (at Göttweig and Melk).[85] Herzogenburg's *Catalogus Selectiorum Musicalium*, which was begun in 1751, lists three Masses by "Adamo Grassel." However, pending further investigation, these Masses cannot be positively attributed to Adam; they could also be by Laurenz.

Despite its *missa longa* proportions and full orchestra (including obbligatos for clarini and trombones), the *Missa Pastoralis Ex C* is a mediocre work lacking in variety. Every movement except the "Laudamus" (F-C major) and "Et incarnatus" (F major) has C as its tonic. All solos are incorporated into choral movements except for the "Et incarnatus," an alto binary aria.

Tobias Gsur
b. ca. 1725 (place unknown)
d. 20 May 1794, Vienna

Tobias Gsur was *regens chori* at the Schottenkirche for well over 30 years. In his autobiography Dittersdorf relates that the violin teacher Ziegler sent him to Gsur at this church where "the best Masses, motets, Vespers and litanies were performed" by a good-sized (*wohlbesetztes*) orchestra.[86] From Dittersdorf, Eitner estimates that Gsur became choir director there around 1750.[87] Court documents inform us that Gsur had been hired in 1749 as a bass at the Hofmusikkapelle,[88] a post which he apparently held simultaneously with that at the Schottenkirche. In 1771 he joined Vienna's newly founded *Tonkünstler-Societät*.[89]

Along with Bonno, Hofmann, and Starzer, Gsur was one of the four candidates for *Hofkapellmeister* upon the death of Gassmann in 1774. According to the above mentioned documents, Gsur had been substituting for Gassmann during the latter's final illness and was even considered for the job of *Vize-Hofkapellmeister*. However, Count von Sporck convinced Joseph II only to appoint the aged Bonno as *Hofkapellmeister*; Gsur was to assist

Plate 7. The Benedictine Schotten-Kirche auf der Freyung Where Tobias Gsur Served as
Regens Chori for over 30 Years

This church was also where Ziegler told young Dittersdorf to go for violin
sightreading practice and "the best Masses." In the center background from left to
right are seen the tops of Kirche am Hof, St. Stephen's, and St. Peter's. Engraving
by Salomon Kleiner

(*Wahrhafte und genaue Abbildung aller Kirchen und Klöster* [Vienna, 1724–37],
pt. I, pl. 4. Historisches Museum der Stadt Wien)

Bonno (without title) for the yearly sum of 200 fl. Sporck did not want Hofmann appointed because he feared Gsur would then become Kapellmeister at St. Stephen's.

At his death in 1794 at the age of 69, Gsur was still employed as a bass at court. Because the Vienna death roll lists him only as a "k. k. Hof- und Kammermusikus," it might be assumed that by this date Gsur had already given up the directorship at the Schottenkirche.[90]

Gsur composed a small amount of church music; only seven Masses have been traced thus far. Kellner indicates that Gsur's music was well liked at Kremsmünster.[91] The two *missae breves* in the present sample (M. 21, 22) probably date from the late 1760s and show Gsur to be a most competent and consistent composer.[92] He usually gives each voice part at least one solo, often requiring extended coloratura on single syllables. Occasionally Gsur also exploits the dynamic contrast between *f* and *p*. Limited counterpoint and no fugues are found in these works. In ex. 10-1A Gsur shows his concern for musical unity by motivically tying together the "Agnus Dei" and "Dona nobis" of the Mass.

Johann Adolf Hasse
b. 23/24 March 1699, Bergedorf (near Hamburg)
d. 16 December 1783, Venice

Hasse was a renowned senior statesman of opera composers during this period. Trained in Naples and working chiefly out of Dresden until 1764, the peripatetic "Saxon" visited Vienna at least three times during his long career: 1733–34, 1760–62, and 1764–73.[93] As yet, there is little record of performances of his church music in Vienna.[94] However, as Walther Müller has pointed out, the quantity of contemporary performance materials found in the Austrian National Library (including the former *k.k. Hofbibliothek* collection), the Gesellschaft der Musikfreunde, and various Austrian monasteries (e.g., Göttweig, Herzogenburg, Klosterneuburg, Kremsmünster, Lambach, and Melk) strongly suggests that the Viennese knew Hasse's Masses as well as they did his operas.[95] In Vienna Hasse held no fixed position, although he did write several operas, became a favorite at the court of Empress Maria Theresa, was a friend of Metastasio, and made the acquaintance of Charles Burney.[96]

Hasse composed some 15 Masses. The three included in the present sample (M. 23–25; in G, d, and D) are all *missae longae* for which parts exist in Viennese archives.[97] Despite an old-fashioned multi-movement approach, which even includes the traditional closing fugues, the works stand apart from other Viennese Masses for several reasons: (1) because of an orchestration that emphasizes variety and always includes two oboes, one viola, and sometimes two horns (rarely trombones); (2) because of the skillful, often virtuosic, *bel canto* vocal writing; and (3) because of the absence of many of the traditional musico-rhetorical figures for expressing the text. These differences were probably observed by Vienna's younger composers, who then began applying some of these traits to their own Masses during the 1770s and 1780s. Hasse mainly wrote number Masses, with each of the several movements usually restricted to a single tempo, meter, and key. Seldom does a movement end in a different key than that with which it began. Every Mass also has two to four solo movements (see ex. 7-23).[98]

The *Missa in G* (M. 23, which actually ends in D major) is dated 1753 according to the autograph in Milan.[99] Its "Quoniam" resembles a bass buffa aria (ex. 7-23). The *Missa in D Minor* (M. 24, which ends in D major) was first performed 29 June 1751 at the consecration of the Catholic Hofkirche in Dresden.[100] This Mass has a pastoral "Qui tollis" (6/4 in G major, for tenor soloist and chorus), a Credo whose beginning is based upon a plainchant intonation, and an expressive solo trio for the "Et incarnatus" (ex. 8-11). The *Missa in D* (M. 25; undated) is unusual because of the three *trombe* in addition to the two clarini (ex. 6-1). The text telescoping in the Credo is unusual for a Mass this size.

As Wilson remarks, never was a composer so quickly forgotten as Hasse.[101] Yet, while he lived, Hasse was most respected and honored by those who knew his music, undoubtedly including many of the other composers in this study as well as Burney, who wrote:

> I have never yet conversed with a single professor on the subject, who has not allowed him [Hasse] to be the most natural, elegant, and judicious composer of vocal music, as well as the most voluminous now alive; equally a friend to poetry and the voice, he discovers as much judgement as genius, in expressing words, as well as in accompanying those sweet and tender melodies, which he gives to the singer. Always regarding the voice, as the first object of attention in a theatre, he never suffocates it, by the learned jargon of a multiplicity of instruments and subjects; but is as careful of preserving its importance as a painter, of throwing the strongest light upon the capital figure of his piece.[102]

Leopold Hofmann
b. 14 August 1738, Vienna
d. 17 March 1793, Vienna

Son of a chamber servant at the imperial *Hof*, Leopold Hofmann's earliest known job was as a "Musikus" at St. Michael's in the late 1750s where he probably played violin.[103] In about 1764 he became *regens chori* at St. Peter's (probably as a successor to Johann Nepomuk Boog).[104] In 1769 Hofmann succeeded Wagenseil as *Hofklaviermeister* in charge of teaching keyboard to Maria Theresa's daughters. After the death of *Hof- und Domkapellmeister* Georg Reutter in 1772, Hofmann became Kapellmeister at St. Stephen's, a

Plate 8.   St. Michael's Where Johann Michael Spangler Was Choir Director in the 1770s and 1780s

Hofmann was probably a violinist here in the late 1750s under then director Ferdinand Zangl. Martinez, Metastasio, and Haydn were among the numerous celebrities who at one time dwelled in the "Michaelerhaus" seen at the left. One of Martinez's Masses was performed at St. Michael's in 1763. During the 1750s Holzbauer directed music at the Burg-Theater across the street to the right (out of view). Engraving by Salomon Kleiner (*Wahrhafte und genaue Abbildung aller Kirchen und Klöster* [Vienna, 1724–37], pt. I, pl. 10. Historisches Museum der Stadt Wien)

position which, together with the choir directorship at St. Peter's, he held until his retirement 20 years later.[105] When Gassmann died in 1774, Hofmann applied for the *Hofkapellmeister* position but lost out to Bonno who, despite less talent, had more seniority and political pull.[106] In 1791 Mozart was to have become Hofmann's assistant at the Cathedral, a job later given to Albrechtsberger.

Hofmann composed approximately 33 Masses.[107] They are mostly orchestral Masses that quickly reveal the gifts of this experienced composer-violinist who also wrote several symphonies, concertos, keyboard pieces, and much chamber music. Two long and two short Masses by Hofmann have been included in the present sample (M. 26, 29, and M. 27, 28).[108] The *Missa Sancti Erasmi in D* (M. 26) is Hofmann's longest Mass (1,123 measures). It is also his only Mass having several other solo movements besides the "Et incarnatus" and "Benedictus." In the other three Masses the solos are usually interspersed within choral movements, in what Prohászka calls the South German-Austrian-Venetian manner (see ex. 7-10 and 10-2).[109] Most instrumental parts (especially violins) exhibit an unusual number of markings denoting dynamics and phrasing (ex. 8-1, m. 17f.). Hofmann rarely fails to include a few captivating instrumental obbligatos in these works (ex. 7-20 for 2 violoncellos). The *Missa in D* (M. 29) has a virtuosic flute solo in nearly every movement (ex. 9-10). Yet, despite all their interesting orchestral features and harmonic variety, Hofmann's Masses often seem somewhat stiff and old-fashioned because of fussy rococo rhythms in the accompaniment and a Baroque-like unity of *Affekt*.

Hofmann was considered one of Vienna's best composers. The 1766 *Wiener Diarium* article "Von dem Wienerischen Geschmack in der Musik" discusses him immediately after Reutter:

> *Herr Leopold Hoffman,* his path soars ever upwards. The *serious* with the *pleasant, melody* with correctness, characterize his pieces above all others. He is the only one to approach the church style of *Hrn. von Reuttern.* His Masses are full of majestic and grand thoughts, which elevate and inflame the praise of God and the prayer in the temple.... But serious though this style is, as pleasant and attractive he in his symphonies, concertos, quartets and trios; one may say that Hoffmann, after *Stamitz,* is the only one to give to the transverse flute the proper lightness and melody.[110]

In 1773 Hofmann wrote a Mass (possibly M. 26) in honor of Joseph Hörl, Vienna's newly selected *Bürgermeister,* and thereby won a gold medal from the city magistrate.[111] When Hofmann applied to be *Hofkapellmeister* the next year, the following appraisal of his abilities was prepared for the court:

> With respect to composition, particularly of church music, Leopold Hofmann has, with general approval, produced the most and best proofs of his abilities [in comparison with the other applicants, i.e., Bonno, Gsur, and Starzer]; at the same time he understands the rite of

Ad. R. M.
PIO SEXTO PON. ROM.
PASCHA CELEBRANTE
VIENNÆ. IN TEMPLO
S. STEPHANI.
A. MDCCLXXXII.

Feyerliche Begehung des Oster Festes in der St Stephans Dom Kirche
zu Wien von PIVS dem VI Röm. Papst. Im Jahr 1782

Cum Priv. S.C.M.   in Wien bey Artaria Compß.

Plate 9.   Pope Pius VI Celebrates Mass according to Roman
           Ritual in St. Stephen's Cathedral on Easter Sunday
           in 1782
           Domkapellmeister Hofmann undoubtedly prepared the
           musicians seen singing in the opening between the curtains
           to the right. Engraving by Karl Schütz
           (Vienna: Artaria, 1783; Albertina, Vienna)

the Church and has directorial experience as *regens chori* in various churches for several years before becoming Kapellmeister at St. Stephen's, a position to which he has so far brought much honor.[112]

The last phrase conflicts with the rather negative report of Burney who, although he enjoyed Hofmann's symphonies, found little to praise about the music heard at St. Stephen's in 1772.[113] It is perhaps also surprising that Hofmann was never a member of Vienna's *Tonkünstler-Societät*. In 1781 Nicolai observed that, after Haydn, Hofmann and Vaňhal were doing the most to improve musical taste in Austria; Nicolai also praised what Hofmann had done to improve the lyrical quality of violin music.[114]

Ignaz Holzbauer
b. 17 September 1711, Vienna
d. 7 April 1783, Mannheim

Ignaz Holzbauer studied law at the University of Vienna and would have joined the Jesuits had not his commitment to music changed his mind. Musically he was an autodidact who secretly took lessons with members of the choir at St. Stephen's and read Fux's *Gradus ad Parnassum*—all without his father's knowledge.[115] Fux supposedly evaluated Holzbauer, declared him a born genius, and urged him to travel to Italy to clear his head of "superfluous ideas." By the end of the 1730s Holzbauer had returned from studies in Venice. In 1737 (at the latest) he was Kapellmeister for Count Franz von Rottal at Holešov (Holleschau) in Moravia. (This job explains the existence of several of his early Masses in Moravian archives.)[116] Then, from 1741 to 1751 (with two years out [1744–46] for a second Italian trip during which he met Sammartini), Holzbauer was music director at the Imperial Burgtheater across the street from St. Michael's. Here he began his successful career as an opera composer. In November 1751 (if not earlier) the Württemberg *Hof* in Stuttgart appointed Holzbauer as its Kapellmeister. Two years later he became Kapellmeister and composer for the Palatinate Elector (*Kurpfalz*) Karl Theodor in Mannheim, where he joined J. Stamitz and F. X. Richter in "founding" that town's well-known symphonic style.

Holzbauer composed about three dozen Masses.[117] The present study has examined four Masses (M. 30–33) that date from before his move to Stuttgart.[118] (Masses from the later, Mannheim period are very different because of the splendid orchestra—with more winds—at the composer's disposal.) The *Missa in A minor* (M. 31, before 1747) and *Missa St. Andreae in E minor* (M. 32, before 1744) are both *missae breves* with text telescoping in some sections. With their use of the minor mode and Kyries that open with *stile antico* counterpoint, both seem based upon Fuxian models. The a cappella writing during the "Et incarnatus" (M. 32) or the "Crucifixus" (M.

31) is particularly effective and dramatic. The other two Masses, the *Missa in C* (M. 30, before 1739) and *Missa in F* (M. 33, before 1745), are both *missae longae*. The *Missa in C,* which is the earliest dated Mass for Holzbauer, is an expansive multi-movement number Mass. The Gloria alone has eight separate movements using a total of 10 tempos. A second soprano soloist is required for four movements of the Mass, including the quintet "Crucifixus" and the fanfarelike opening of the "Et resurrexit" (ex. 8-5). A copy at the Schottenkirche indicates that this Mass was performed in Vienna (beginning in 1760, at the latest). The *Missa in F* is quite different from the other three Masses. Its string parts have intricate, difficult, and fussy rhythms as well as numerous expressive marks not found in the other Masses; a much more experienced string ensemble would be needed for performance. Since a score based only upon Mannheim parts (now in Munich's Bavarian State Library) and not upon the earlier dated Brno parts (now missing) was consulted, perhaps the difference in instrumental writing is a result of Holzbauer's recasting this work for the Mannheim ensemble. Schmitt, Bush, and Altmann have observed that Holzbauer did rewrite other Masses. In any case, thematic catalogues show that the early, original version did begin in the Italian manner, i.e., with a tiny sinfonia (ex. 6-4) which is related to the music of the Kyrie that follows. The *Missa in F* also includes a soprano rage aria ("Quoniam"), two duets ("Christe" and "Laudamus"), and a trio ("Benedictus").

Holzbauer's operatic interests surface in each of these Masses. Whether he is dovetailing a series of sections with different tempos or using choral recitative accompanied by unsettling modulations (ex. 7-26), he exhibits enormous invention in exploring the (albeit limited) dramatic potential of the Mass. Often he also tries to melodically unify his Masses (ex. 6-4; 8-6). Although a bit of an iconoclast vis-à-vis most traditions of Mass composition (e.g., he seldom uses the traditional musicorhetorical figures at the expected places), Holzbauer sometimes did write acceptable fugues (even double fugues) to close the Gloria, Credo, and Sanctus (see ex. 9-9).

In 1777 Kraus complained about Holzbauer's excessively operatic Masses.[119] In November of that same year, however, Mozart wrote his father about hearing a 26-year-old "very fine" Mass by Holzbauer. Mozart adds: "He writes very well—a good church style, good writing [*Satz*] for the voices and instruments, and good fugues."[120]

Carl von Kohaut
bapt. 26 August 1726, Vienna
d. 6 August 1784, Vienna

Little is known about the lute virtuoso Carl von Kohaut. He may have studied music with his father Jakob Carl, a musician at the *Hof*.[121] Besides writing several brilliant pieces (including concertos) for lute, Kohaut composed about eight Masses which are today preserved in a few archives of Lower Austria and Czechoslovakia. In 1758 Kohaut entered state service and became a *Hof* secretary, accompanying Emperor Joseph II and State Chancellor Count Kaunitz on foreign travels. The lutenist was also a member of Baron van Swieten's domestic music circle.[122] When Burney was visiting Vienna in 1772, a Monsieur L'Augier told him to add Kohaut ("a great lutentist") to the list of the city's fine musicians.[123] On 17 March 1777 the *Tonkünstler-Societät* performed a "Grosse Sinfonie" and a "Grosses [Violin] Concertino" by Kohaut.[124]

Kohaut's *Missa Sancti Willibaldi* (M. 34, before 1763) is a solemn *missa longa* of moderate size. Stylistically the work presents nothing to set it very much apart from the common practices of the day. Except for the "Et incarnatus" (solo quartet accompanied only by continuo) and the "Benedictus" (alto aria, ex. 9-16E), all vocal solos are parts of choral movements. The Gloria, Credo, Sanctus, and Agnus Dei all conclude with the traditional fugue (ex. 7-11; 8-19). "Osanna II," however, presents an interesting double fugue reworking (in ₵ instead of C meter) of the "Osanna I" fugue.

[Johann Baptist] Joseph Krottendorfer
b. 26 April 1741, Purgstall (Lower Austria)
d. 10 April 1798, Vienna

Joseph Krottendorfer (Grottendorfer) grew up in a musical family. His father was a teacher and *regens chori* in Purgstall. Two younger brothers, Andreas (b. 1744) and Johann Michael (b. 1746, later choir director under the name Ubaldus at Herzogenburg), also had musical careers.[125] At some point in the early 1760s Joseph served temporarily as organist in Herzogenburg before becoming a chamber musician at the Imperial *Hof* in Vienna in 1766. Five years later, in 1771, he was among the group of 32 *Hof* musicians whose membership in the *Tonkünstler-Societät* was underwritten by Empress Maria Theresa; Krottendorfer frequently performed in the Society's semiannual concerts.[126] In 1772 when Gassmann reorganized the *Hofkapelle* after the death of Reutter, Krottendorfer was appointed as a tenor. He held this post for 26 years, working under *Hofkapellmeister* Gassmann, Bonno, and Salieri.[127]

Krottendorfer composed over one hundred works, most of which were for the church.[128] Research thus far has uncovered about 10 Masses by the composer. Their extensive dissemination in collections of sacred music in Czechoslovakia and Lower Austria shows that these Masses remained popular well into the first half of the nineteenth century.[129] Krottendorfer's Masses that are dated later than ca. 1770 often include parts for two oboes and a viola in addition to the usual strings, clarini, and timpani. The *Missa in C*

(M. 35, before 1764) is a *missa brevis*.[130] Most vocal solos occur within choral movements. The "Et incarnatus" is a tenor solo, and the "Benedictus" a solo quartet. During the "Agnus Dei" a single trombone accompanies the alto soloist. Stylistically the work is mediocre, unimaginative, and somewhat old-fashioned, adhering as it does to traditional forms, tempos, and rhetorical figures. There is scarcely any variety in tonality (C major) or meter (C); only the "Benedictus" has a tonic other than C, and only the "Quoniam" and "Et resurrexit" are in 3/4. Nonetheless, in the opinion of the 1793 *Wiener Schriftsteller- und Künstlerlexikon* (p. 48) Krottendorfer's compositions "evidence much study of composition as well as a refined [*geläuterten*] taste."[131]

Marianne von Martínez
b. 4 May 1744, Vienna
d. 13 December 1812, Vienna

Although her music was little disseminated and soon forgotten, Marianne von Martínez (Martines) was one of the first women in Vienna to show that a woman could compose as well as sing and play the pianoforte.[132] Indeed she was a woman of many musical talents, having had the benefit of lessons with Porpora, Bonno, Haydn, and Metastasio.[133] After his visit to Vienna in 1772, Burney devoted several paragraphs to praising this young lady. For example:

> Metastasio desired her to shew me some of her best studies; and she produced a psalm for four voices, with instruments. It was a most agreeable *Mescolanza* [mixture], as Metastasio called it, of *antico e moderno*; a mixture of the harmony, and contrivance of old times, with the melody and taste of the present. It was an admirable composition, and she played and sung it in a very masterly manner, contriving so well to fill up the parts, that though it was a full piece, nothing seemed wanting.[134]

The next year (1773) Miss Martínez was honored with membership in the Accademia Filarmonica of Bologna.[135] In a story about this achievement, the *Wiener Diarium* of 4 August 1773 (No. 62) reports:

> ... The authentic diploma, written with the most honorable expressions, has already been sent to her here. Certainly, through this spontaneous (*freiwillige*) acceptance, the Academy does justice to the special and unusual merits of Mademoiselle Martines. The full membership [of the Academy] could not admire enough the fusion of grace (*Zierlichkeit*), genius, nobility of expression, and astonishing precision in the compositions of the new candidate. Such a unanimous judgement could cause one to reproach the Academy for not having earlier taken advantage of the honor of accepting so worthy a member into their most illustrious society. How very happy a patriot must be to observe daily more and more how the German nation endeavors to advance (*hervorzuthun*) so well in all the arts! What an excellent and special honor it is for the fair sex to again be able to produce a member of whom so many a city has cause to be jealous. Thanks be to the glorious government of our respected Empress, under whom all kindred arts have been rising so high and leading one soon to expect a certain degree of perfection.

In the fourth book of his *De cantu et musica sacra* published the next year, Martin Gerbert mentions Martínez in a footnote to a paragraph on current Spanish [*sic*] composers. He says that some years before he had personally received from Martínez a copy of one of her *missae solemnes* that was well suited for the church style. [136]

Undoubtedly because of her sex, Martínez could not make a living as a professional musician. Instead she taught singing and became a popular dilettante, using her connections with the *Hof* and aristocracy, together with her musical talents, to hold musical soirées at least once a week starting in the early 1780s. Haydn and Mozart were among the more famous musicians who attended. In 1782 her oratorio *Isacco* (text by Metastasio) was twice performed during the Lenten concerts of the *Tonkünstler-Societät*. [137] In Schönfeld's *Jahrbuch* for 1796 Martínez is listed under "illustrious persons" in the first chapter, which is entitled "Special Friends, Patrons, and Connoisseurs in Vienna." In second chapter ("Virtuosos and Dilettantes of Vienna") Schönfeld calls her "one of the best connoisseurs among our numerous dilettantes" and praises her musicianship. [138] He adds: "She has written Masses and very many arias that at times approach the style of Jommelli, and in every regard she is a great pillar (*Stütze*) of the musical art." [139] As the ultimate honor, Schönfeld lists Martínez in the list of composers who have written something "which can be worthy of some attention," a list that also includes Albrechtsberger, Beethoven, Friberth, Haydn, Kozeluch, Salieri, Sonnleithner, Steｐan, Vaňhal, et al. [140]

Martínez composed four Masses, the autographs of which are in the Gesellschaft der Musikfreunde. Her third and fourth Masses were selected because they have existed not only in score but also in parts; the Masses were actually performed during the eighteenth century. They show a strong Italian influence in their multi-movement number format, vocal writing, use of oboes, and extended orchestral introductions. [141] In fact, her *Terza Messa* (M. 36) has almost the same distribution of text and movements as a *Grande Messe* (in D) published by her teacher Porpora. [142]

Both Masses in the present sample are *missae longae*. In the *Terza Messa* (M. 36, in D; 1761) two flutes play only once—during the "Laudamus" duet for soprano and alto; the only solo for the trombones accompanies the tenor soloist at "Benedictus." This was probably the Mass that prompted the *Wiener Diarium* for Wednesday, 30 September 1761 (No. 78) to report: "Yesterday in the *k.k. Hof-Pfarrkirche der P.P. Michaelern* the titular feast of the Holy Archangel Michael was celebrated with a High Mass, for which the music was composed here by Mademoiselle Martínez (a virtuosa of only 16 years in age) and which, on account of its excellence, was admired by all connoisseurs." Martínez often uses a fluid alternation between the chorus and soloists, as in the "Dona nobis pacem" of her *Missa in C* (M. 37; see ex. 10-11 for this *concertato* effect). The expected places in both Masses exhibit a command of the fugal art which must have impressed Martini and the members of the *Accademia* in Bologna (ex. 6-19; 7-11; 8-19). However, certain oversights in her autograph scores reveal some lack of practical experience in matters of orchestration. Overall, Metastasio is correct in calling her music an "agreeable mixture" of old and new stylistic elements. Pfannhauser believes that the "Christe" of her first Mass (also in C) may even have been one of the models for the young Mozart when he was working on the *Waisenhaus Mass* (K. 139) in 1768. [143]

Mathias Georg Monn
b. 9 April 1717, Vienna
d. 3 October 1750, Vienna

Little is known about Mathias Georg Monn, who died at the relatively young age of 33. Nonetheless, his symphonic, chamber, and church music have received widespread attention and comment over the years. Kirkendale calls him "perhaps the most accomplished fugue-writer of the older Viennese school"; and Joseph II was particularly fond of Monn's music. [144] His Masses must have been highly esteemed in the eighteenth century, for we find monasteries like Göttweig, Kremsmünster, and Seitenstetten acquiring and performing them one and two decades after his death.

Documents at the Augustinian monastery of Klosterneuburg indicate that Monn was a choir boy there in the early 1730s. [145] By the end of the decade (1738 at the earliest) he had become the organist at St. Charles Borromeo in Vienna, a post apparently held until his death in 1750. [146] Albrechtsberger allegedly studied thoroughbass and composition with Monn. [147]

Monn composed about six Masses. [148] All three in the present sample (M. 38, 39, 40) are of the multi-movement *missa longa* type. [149] The style is basically late Baroque, with unifying instrumental ritornellos, spun-out melodies, hemiola, maintenance of one affect per movement, and ternary arias. Monn exhibits his mastery of fugue (perhaps learned from Fux?) at all the usual places (see ex. 6-19, 7-11, 8-19) and, occasionally, elsewhere in the Mass (e.g., "Crucifixus" in M. 39). Despite a conservative surface, these Masses exude energy and imagination (see ex. 6-2). They often show concern for harmonic continuity and variety (e.g., dovetailing movements or ending movements in a new key). Vocal solos are frequently integrated into the choral movements (ex. 6-8). The *Missa in C* (M. 38, 1741) is a monumental work of 1,321 measures. Its intricate string and vocal solo writing (see ex. 7-21) would be a mighty challenge for most ensembles today. The slow introduction to its Kyrie is especially dramatic in its melodic leaps, pauses, and harmonic unrest (ex. 6-2). The quasi-canonic "Quoniam" is a tour-de-force rage aria requiring a bass with a solid tessitura of two octaves ($F-f^1$). In Monn's *Missa in D* (M.

40) the "Benedictus" for soprano and solo violin has a restless quality which (abetted by the minor key) is unusual for this text. One almost wishes that Monn had written some operas.

[Franz] Silverius Müller

b. 27 February 1754, Oberhöflein
(near Geras, Lower Austria)
d. 21 August, 1812, Vienna

Silverius Müller received his musical training from the Piarist order, of which he was an ordained priest. From 1770 to 1783 he worked primarily as a *regens chori* and instructor at three Piarist colleges, beginning with the church of Maria Treu in Vienna (1770–71).[150] As a result of the reforms initiated under Joseph II, Müller held no more musical posts after 1783, the year he returned to Maria Treu as its *Valetudinarius*. In 1793 the *Wiener Schriftsteller- und Künstler-Lexikon* called Silverius Müller "a capable composer and creditable man of music, although he is not well-known. His style is original and deserves more recognition."[151]

In addition to a large quantity of chamber music, Müller composed at least two Masses (in C and D). Parts for the *Missa in D* (M. 41, n.d.) are preserved in the music collection of Maria Treu in Vienna.[152] This delightful *missa longa* of moderate size has a modern cast. There are no more than three movements in each part of the Mass, and all vocal solos are incorporated into the choral movements. Müller unifies the Credo by using the same bass line at "Credo," "Et resurrexit," and "Et in Spiritum."

Luca Antonio Predieri

b. 13 September 1688, Bologna
d. (exact date unknown) 1767, Bologna

Predieri is the only native Italian and the oldest composer in the present sampling; and he marked the end of an era of direct Italian influence in Vienna (e.g., A. Pancotti, M. A. Ziani, A. Caldara, A. Vivaldi, F. Conti, N. Porpora, and M. Palotta). Predieri studied composition with musician relatives and with Giacomo Antonio Perti in Bologna, where Predieri played violin and viola and served as *maestro di cappella* at various churches.[153] Before the end of 1737 he came to Vienna and eventually (1739) succeeded Caldara as *Vize-Hofkapellmeister*. After the death of Fux in 1741, Predieri, with Reutter's assistance, was in charge of the *Hofmusikkapelle*. Not until September 1746 was Predieri officially appointed *1st Hofkapellmeister*. He retired in 1751 but kept the title, although Reutter was in charge; in 1765 Predieri returned to Bologna where he died two years later.

Predieri composed at least 14 Masses, all of which could be termed *missae breves*.[154] Both Masses in the present sample (M. 42, 43) are from the mid-1740s and are marked by a paucity of separate movements, an absence of fugue, text telescoping in the Credo, alternation of chorus and soloists in the same movement (see ex. 7-8), and the use of brief instrumental introductions. Frequent awkwardness in the part-writing and harmony may perhaps explain why this music was so little disseminated outside of Vienna.

[Johann] Georg von Reutter, Jr.
bapt. 6 April 1708, Vienna
d. 11 March 1772, Vienna

Reutter is a central figure in Viennese church music of this period. His father, Georg Sr. (1656–1738), was an organist at the *Hof* and Kapellmeister at St. Stephen's. Undoubtedly because of his father's influence, Georg Jr. played the organ at St. Stephen's, in the *Hof*, and elsewhere in Vienna during the 1720s.[155] He studied composition only with Caldara, the *Vize-Hofkapellmeister*, and in 1728 or 1729 the *Hof* sent Reutter to study in Venice and Rome. Early in 1731 he was appointed *Hofkomponist*, during which time he composed several operas and oratorios. After the death of his father in 1738, Reutter officially became 1st (or *Essential-*) Kapellmeister at St. Stephen's. It was in this post that Reutter "discovered" Joseph Haydn's talents in Hainburg. As the following résumé shows, Reutter's "monopoly" of the top choir directorships in Vienna was beginning to form.

1738-72	1st Kapellmeister at St. Stephen's
1741-47	Assistant to Predieri at *Hofmusikkapelle*
1747-51	2nd *Hofkapellmeister*
1751-69	Acting *Hofkapellmeister* (for pensioned Predieri)
1756-72	2nd Kapellmeister (*Gnadenbild-Kapelle*) at St Stephen's
1769-72	*Hofkapellmeister* (officially)

Thus, by 1756 he was essentially in charge of all sacred music at court and in the cathedral. Reutter also provided music for St. Augustine's and the Jesuit Churches.[156] When he replaced Predieri at the *Hof* in 1751, severe budgetary restrictions and a new system of administration led to a decline in the Hofmusikkapelle, a decline which has usually, and perhaps unfairly, been blamed on Reutter.[157]

No other composer in the present study was more prolific in Mass composition than Reutter. About 72 Masses have been attributed to him.[158] The six in the present sample include four *missae breves* (M. 44, 46, 47, 48) and two *missae longae* (M. 45, 49), the latter two coincidentally being the earliest of those chosen.[159] The four *missae breves* stand apart from the longer Masses because of their lack of isolated solo movements and because vocal solos usually appear as interludes within a choral movement (ex. 7-3). The two *missae longae* are both multi-movement number Masses with Glorias of more than three movements.

Although one sometimes receives the impression that Reutter composed these works in a hurry, certain musical elements make them more than just mediocre, functional Masses. For example, in the *Missa Sancti Placidi* (M. 44, before 1756) a violin figuration found in several movements helps to unify the entire Mass.[160] The *Missa Sancti Mariani* (M. 47, 1759) has a Kyrie with a double reprise structure and thematic dualism that may have been inspired by sonatas of the day (ex. 6-10). These Masses also include impressive, sometimes virtuosic obbligatos for the violin, clarino trumpet (ex. 7-15, 7-24), trombone, bassoon (ex. 6-6), organ (ex. 9-11), or even timpani (ex. 10-17). In two of the Masses (M. 44 and 47) Reutter's long, close ties with church music (and perhaps his acquaintance with the species counterpoint examples of Fux) are manifested in his use of *cantus firmus* technique to base a movement upon part of a plainsong (ex. 5-2). Reutter is also fond of placing brief orchestral introductions at the head of choral movements.

Reutter's Masses were abundantly disseminated throughout Austrian lands during his lifetime. He was certainly not a stellar composer, and, like that of Hasse, his music was soon forgotten. Burney arrived in Vienna six months after Reutter's death and visited St. Stephen's where they were playing some loud music by "Reüter, an old German composer, without taste or invention."[161] The famous *Wiener Diarium* article describing the local musical scene in 1766 was kinder and extraordinarily perceptive:

> The first [composer that comes to mind] is Herr Georg von Reutter, *k.k. Kapellmeister*, who is unquestionably the strongest composer to sing the praise of God, and is the model for all the men working in this sphere. For who knows better than he how to express the magnificent, the joyous, the triumphant, when the text requires it, without falling into the profane or theatrical? Who is more pathetic, more rich in harmonies than he, when the text demands sadness, a prayer, or pain? His Masses always gather a crowd of people about them, and every man leaves them edified, convinced, and wiser than before.[162]

Ferdinand Schmidt
b. 1693/94 (place unknown)
d. 11 August 1756, Vienna

We know almost nothing about the life and works of this composer whom the young choirboy Joseph Haydn must have encountered at St. Stephen's in the early 1740s. Ferdinand Schmidt served as *regens chori* at the Dorothea-Kirche and at the Maria Loreto Chapel in St. Augustine's.[163] In 1743 he became Kapellmeister of the *Gnadenbild-Kapelle* in St. Stephen's, a post which *Dom-Kapellmeister* Reutter also wanted but did not receive until Schmidt's death thirteen years later. Apparently Schmidt died in abject poverty, without even enough money to cover the expense of his burial.[164]

Schmidt composed about 14 Masses, several of which were widely disseminated throughout Lower Austria and Czechoslovakia from the 1720s to the 1750s. When Gregor Werner (1693–1766) came to Eisenstadt in 1728, he brought along a *Missa Sancti Nicolai* by Schmidt.[165] Between 1739 and 1747 the Benedictine Abbey in Kremsmünster acquired at least five of his Masses, including a *Missa Sancti Bernardi Abbatu* which Kremsmünster's *regens chori* Franz Sparry called a "praeclarum opus" (remarkable work).[166] Pfannhauser reports that the Schottenkirche in Vienna performed Schmidt's *Missa Sancti Ferdinandi* in 1747 and 1749.[167]

The two Masses in the present sample, *Missa Sanctae Caeciliae in C* (M. 50) and *Missa Primitiarum in C* (M. 51), were acquired by the Benedictine Abbey Göttweig in 1746 and 1747 respectively.[168] Both are monumental, Baroque-like multi-movement number Masses (6+ movements in the Gloria, 5+ in the Credo). Conservative as they may be, the works are impressive for their instrumental introductions (ex. 6-3, 6-20), clarini solos, harmonic, metric, and textural variety (ex. 7-9; 8-14), and vocal coloratura (ex. 9-2, 9-14). Sometimes Schmidt's string parts have the rushing scale accompaniment also found in Arbesser, Monn, and Reutter (ex. 8-2). Nonetheless, the expressivity and inventiveness of many passages in these Masses should draw more attention to the music of this relatively unknown composer.

Joseph [Franz] Seuche
b. 1701/02, German Bohemia
d. 3 February 1790, Vienna

Some 19 Masses are attributed to Joseph Seuche (Seiche, Seüche) in various archives and old catalogues of Lower Austria and Czechoslovakia. Vienna's *Todtenprotokoll* of 1790 describes him simply as a "Kirchenmusikus."[169] In the inventory of church music personnel for 1783 he is listed as a violinist at St. Michael's, a post which he had probably held since about 1750.[170]

The two Masses in the present selection, the *Missa Sancti Joachimi in A minor* (M. 52) and the *Missa Ex D* (M. 53), are both *missae breves*. Most vocal solos are incorporated into the choral movements, and in the Credo the text is telescoped. They are conservative and functional pieces in the truest sense of both terms.[171] Occasionally the melodies and declamation seem awkward for the voice.

Christoph Sonnleithner
b. 28 May 1734, Szegedin, Hungary
d. 25 December 1786, Vienna

Although he was one of Vienna's best lawyers, Christoph Sonnleithner seems too good a composer to be labeled a dilettante. He wrote several symphonies, 36 string quartets, trios, and much sacred music before ill health forced him to cease composing.[172] His first musical studies (violin and voice) were with his uncle Leopold Sonnleithner, *regens chori* at the Karmeliter-Kirche (St. Joseph's) in the Leopoldstadt. Christoph later studied composition with *Hoforganist* Wenzel Raimund Birck (1717/18–1763).

Some 14 Masses are attributed to Sonnleithner. The five in the present sample (M. 54–58) are all *missae longae* of the newer multi-movement type, in which each part of the Mass consists of no more than four independent movements.[173] Sonnleithner's Masses are a blend of the conservative (e.g., fugues, *colla parte* trombones, no woodwinds, repeated accompaniment figures) and the progressive (e.g., fewer movements, use of 2/4 and 3/8 meter, thematic differentiation and functionalism, sonatalike double reprise, most solos incorporated into the chorus). It seems that Sonnleithner frequently borrowed melodies from himself. For example, the "Et vitam" fugue subjects of M. 56 and M. 57 closely resemble each other (ex. 8-19; see "Agnus Dei" of M. 54 and 55, M. 57 and 58).

Sonnleithner's music was highly praised both before and soon after his death. His Masses were widely disseminated from the late 1750s through the 1780s. Vienna's *Allgemeine Musikalische Zeitung* reported in 1817 that Sonnleithner had been a "favorite composer" of Emperor Joseph II.[174] According to an anecdote, Joseph Haydn even outbid the son Joseph Sonnleithner in order to acquire some of Christoph's manuscript scores at the auction of *Hofrat* Bernhard Ritter von Kees's large music library.[175] In 1794 the *Wiener Theater Almanac* reported posthumously:

> Herr Christoph Sonnleithner, a lawyer, possessed a very solid style [*gründlichen Satz*] and from his early youth on, until a few years before his death, composed many High Masses, Requiems, and smaller church pieces which were esteemed by all connoisseurs and are still played in many churches. He has the honor of having been one of the first of those who knew how to join taste and solidity [*Gründlichkeit*] in this type of composition.[176]

Two years later Schönfeld lists Sonnleithner among the Viennese composers (including Beethoven, Haydn, et al.) who have written music worthy of attention.[177] The 1817 biography in the *Allgemeine Musikalische Zeitung* of Vienna praises his style at greater length:

He had a pure style [*reinen Satz*] and was one of the first who knew how to unite taste with art and rigorousness in sacred music. His compositions were written in a simple, gentle style and had an individual stamp.

Only with difficulty will one discover errors of musical grammar in his works, since he seldom composed anything without also seeking to satisfy the higher demands of art—for which reason his church works are more or less adorned with rich fugues and excellent contrapuntal passages. Even when he sometimes (like almost all contemporaries) did not adhere to the churchly character as much as one would like, an intimate, warm feeling and expressive ideas, whose wealth appears everywhere, act as compensation. Intelligibility and order (which attest to thinking, knowledgeable, and sure composers), warmth of the heart, good treatment of the voice, a natural instrumental style, knowledge of musical effects— these traits form the outline of his musical character.[178]

Sonnleithner's balanced style may have had an effect upon contemporary composers. Pfannhauser believes that the "Benedictus" of Sonnleithner's *Missa in C* (M. 55, before 1765; see ex. 9-16B) may have inspired that same movement in Mozart's *Waisenhaus Mass*, K. 139, of 1768.[179]

Georg Strasser
b. unknown
d. unknown

The second half of the eighteenth century found several musicians with the name Strasser in Vienna. Some seventeen Masses from the period bear this name in various archives of Lower Austria. Because the manuscripts rarely give first names, we cannot always be positive which Strasser is meant. More research is needed to clearly identify and distinguish each Strasser.

At least eight Masses are attributed to a Georg Strasser who may be identical with the choir directors listed for the following five churches in Vienna in 1783:

Georgius Strasser	Paulaner-Kirche
Johann Georg Strasser	Karmeliter-Kirche auf der Laimgrube
Johann Georg Strasser	Maria-Hilf
Georgius Strasser	Stiftskirche zum Heiligen Kreuz
Georg Strasser	St. Anne's (former church of Jesuit novitiates; music personnel released in 1783)[180]

Kellner reports that Kremsmünster acquired six Masses by Georg Strasser, "Kapellmeister des Collegio Nobile Emmanuele" in Vienna, during Sparry's tenure there as choir director (1747–67).[181] The *Missa in E* (M. 59) of the present sample may be by Georg Strasser. The copy at hand is one of three Masses (in E-flat, E, and F) attributed to an "N. Strasser" in the Sammlung

Gilg acquired by the Austrian National Library in 1908. (In Lambach and Seitenstetten the E major Mass bears only the name "Strasser.") The first initial "N" is possibly erroneous because the F major Mass is attributed to Georg Strasser in copies at Göttweig and Lambach; while the E-flat major is attributed to Novotny (see Hob. XXII: Es12) in these and other locations.[182]

In any case, the *Missa in E* (M. 59) is definitely by one member of the Strasser musical family in Vienna. Composed sometime before 1784, the Mass is a *missa brevis* of few movements.[183] Except for the Sanctus, each part of the Mass consists of a single continuous movement. The declamatory, syllabic Gloria has one tempo throughout. The standard fast-slow-fast sections of the Credo are joined by rhythmic elisions, probably to keep the Mass brief. Undemanding vocal solos are heard at "Qui tollis" (alternating with the chorus) and "Benedictus" (solo quartet). Every movement has 3/4 meter, a highly unusual occurrence for this period. Otherwise the work is fairly typical of the concise and efficient Austrian *missa brevis* in the early 1780s.

Franz Tuma
b. 2 October 1704, Kostelec nad Orlicí, Bohemia
d. 30 January 1774, Vienna

After initial training with his organist father in Kostelec, gamba virtuoso Franz Tuma continued his musical studies in Prague (possibly with Bohuslav Černohorský).[184] Some time in the early 1720s he moved to Vienna where he studied with Fux and worked as a Vice-Kapellmeister at an unnamed institution.[185] By 1729 he was playing and composing music for Count Franz Ferdinand Kinsky, High Chancellor of Bohemia, who soon (ca. 1731) made Tuma his Kapellmeister. After the count's death in 1741, Tuma became Kapellmeister for the private chapel of the dowager Empress Elisabeth Christina, widow of Charles VI. Tuma held this post until her death in 1750, at which time he was pensioned by the *Hof*. He remained active as a performer and composer in Vienna until about 1768 when he retired to the Premonstratensian monastery at Geras in Lower Austria. When Burney visited Vienna in 1772, he encountered neither the music nor the name of Tuma.

In addition to chamber and symphonic music, Tuma wrote a large quantity of sacred music. His approximately 65 Mass settings (dating mostly from the 1730s through the 1750s) make him the second most prolific composer (after Reutter) in the present study.[186] The four concerted Masses of the present sample include two *missae longae* (M. 60–61) and two *missae breves* (M. 62–63).[187] That Tuma is of the older generation is clear from the well-crafted, often complex counterpoint repeatedly found in these Masses (ex. 6-15A). Even the *missae breves* have fugues or fugatos. His essentially

Baroque style is further underscored by a multi-sectional approach (e.g., 12 tempo changes in the Gloria of M. 61, see fig. 7-2), the occasional absence of specific tempo markings, the influence of church modality upon harmony and melody (the minor mode is often heard), and the use of traditional musico-rhetorical figures expressive of the text. Like other composers of his generation (e.g., Monn, Reutter, and Wagenseil) Tuma often uses two low trumpets (specified *trombe*) in addition to the clarini. Trombones are usually given obbligatos (ex. 7-19; 10-5). The *Missa Sancti Stephani* (M. 63; before 1747) is significant for its being a relatively early example of a *missa brevis* (333 m.) incorporating the traits of a longer, number Mass. To help create the illusion of fewer movements desired in such a short Mass, Tuma uses rhythmic elisions to join together several adjacent sections that are distinguished by new keys, meters, and tempos in both the Gloria and Credo. In the Agnus Dei of the *Missa Tibi soli di Psalm 50* (M. 60) Tuma boldly employs a style resembling accompanied recitative (ex. 10-5). This is but one example of how Tuma frequently juxtaposed the older and newer styles of his day.

Jan Křtitel [Johann Baptist] Vaňhal
b. 12 May 1739, Nové Nechanice, Bohemia
d. 20 August 1813, Vienna

After studying and playing organ in his native Bohemia during the 1750s, Jan Vaňhal (Wanhall) arrived in Vienna about 1761, apparently at the invitation of Countess Schaffgotsch, sister-in-law of Breslau's Prince Bishop, who admired his compositions and violin playing.[188] In Vienna Vaňhal studied with Dittersdorf and became essentially a free-lance composer and teacher. After a three-year trip to Italy (1769-71), mental illness forced Vaňhal to convalesce in Croatia. In 1780 he returned to Vienna and to his life of composing and teaching. These were never quite the same; and his productivity decreased after 1790 because of ill health. As Landon writes: "It was one of the great tragedies of Viennese musical life at that time."[189]

Vaňhal composed about 60 Masses, a sizeable number that perhaps indicates an ecclesiastical connection for Vaňhal of which we are not aware.[190] The three Vaňhal Masses in the present sample (M. 64–66) are all *missae longae*.[191] They show Vaňhal to be among the more progressive composers (along with Dittersdorf, Gassmann, Haydn, and Sonnleithner) forging the new language of the emerging Classic style. For example, in just the Kyrie of his *Missa Pastorell in G* (M. 65, before 1782; ex. 6-12) we hear symmetrical phrases (too often repeated *piano*), an essentially homophonic texture, an instrumental introduction (not shown in ex. 6-12), the thematic dualism and double reprise associated with sonata form, a second theme using a Haydnesque device of sustaining a drone beneath a folk-dance-like melody

(m. 36f.), and inclusion of oboes and violas in the church orchestra. In addition, Vaňhal's Masses are firmly rooted in their chosen keys (harmonic variety occurs more within rather than between movements), triple meters and simple meters such as 2/4 and 3/8 are commonly used, vocal solos are nearly always part of the choral movements, and each part of the Mass consists of no more than four movements.

Georg Wagenseil
b. 29 January 1715, Vienna
d. 1 March 1777, Vienna

As a member of the elder generation of this period, Wagenseil had studied with Adam Weger (organist at St. Michael's), J.J. Fux (*Hofkapellmeister*), and Matteo Palotta (*Hof-Komponist*)—a fact reflected by the contrapuntal emphasis in his own Masses.[192] Having been a *Hof-Scholar* for four years, Wagenseil was appointed *Hof-Komponist* in 1739, a post which he retained until his death nearly four decades later. From 1741 until 1750 this celebrated keyboard virtuoso also served as organist in the private chapel of the dowager Empress Elisabeth Christina (where Tuma was Kapellmeister). Beginning in 1749 Wagenseil was also *Hofklaviermeister,* teaching keyboard to the children of Maria Theresa. Among his several famous students was Leopold Hofmann. In 1772 Burney met a "thin and infirm" Wagenseil who by then was an invalid enjoying an annual court pension of 1,500 fl. but who was still teaching and composing.[193]

In addition to several operas, symphonies, concertos, and much chamber and keyboard music, Wagenseil composed at least 17 Masses, most of which date from the 1730s and 1740s.[194] The present sample includes four *missae breves* (M. 67–70).[195] Throughout each of them Wagenseil exhibits a skillful, fluid counterpoint by which each new line of text usually generates a new head motive for imitative treatment (see ex. 6-16). Often Wagenseil creates only the illusion of imitative counterpoint by means of staggered entrances. Chordal homophony is reserved for textual emphasis at "Qui tollis" or "Et incarnatus" and for the more dogmatic clauses of the Credo. Separate formal fugues at the expected places (e.g., "Cum Sancto" and "Et vitam") are rare, since these sections are usually fugatos that are part of a larger contrapuntal movement.[196] Nonetheless, the "shadow" of Fux seems present nearly everywhere in Wagenseil's Masses (e.g., the "Gratias" fugue of the *Missa Transfige cor meum*, M. 69).

Because of the emphasis upon counterpoint, the common Baroque musico-rhetorical figures expressive of the text are used only sporadically. Like other composers at the *Hof*, Wagenseil sometimes uses both high and low trumpets (M. 70) as well as *colla parte* doubling by the cornetto, alto trombone, tenor trombone, and bassoon. The occasional demanding trombone solos (see M. 67 and M. 70) are not surprising coming from the composer of the earliest known concertos for that instrument.[197] Vocal solos which appear frequently within choral movements as well as in separate movements, are always part of a trio texture.[198] The *Missa Transfige cor meum* (m. 69, before 1742), which has the unusual accompaniment of only two *colla parte* violas (or trombones) and continuo, is longest of the four *missae breves* under study (555 m.) and resembles a longer, number Mass because of the multi-sectionalism created by numerous changes of tempo (e.g., nine tempos for the Gloria).

Joseph Paul Ziegler
b. 14 September 1722, Vienna
d. 18 October 1767, Vienna

Dittersdorf called Joseph Ziegler, his second violin teacher (ca. 1753), "a very fine violinist as well as a capable and deserving chamber music composer."[199] It was Ziegler who urged Dittersdorf to play violin at the Schottenkirche in order to acquire sightreading practice. Ziegler taught violin in the Jesuit Seminar of Saints Ignatius and Pankratius "am Stuben-Thor."[200] Until his death he was also a musician at St. Stephen's where he would have played violin under Ferdinand Schmidt and Georg von Reutter, Jr. Ziegler also played at the *Hofkapelle*, his "chamber and sacred compositions were highly esteemed in Vienna," and his playing was praised by Albrechtsberger and both Haydn brothers.[201]

Ziegler composed at least six Masses; they date from the 1750s and 1760s and are preserved in several archives of Lower Austria and Czechoslovakia.[202] Both Masses of the present study (M. 71–72) are multi-movement *missae longae*.[203] They are fascinating works with much variety in meter (including 2/4 and 3/8), tempo (the Gloria of M. 71 has six different tempo markings), and key (the Gloria of M. 71 has seven different keys for its 10 subdivisions). In the *Missa in C* (M. 71, before 1762) movements often end in a new key, fostering a heightened continuity and harmonic bond with the section that follows as well as sometimes entailing a new key signature in the middle of a movement. For this same Mass, Ziegler writes demanding (and almost raging) coloratura for the soprano soloist (ex. 6-18, 7-13). Naturally the violin parts of both Masses dominate the accompaniment in a way expected of a violinist-composer: e.g., concertolike hammerstroke chords, frequent double stops, many articulation marks, undulating ♪♫ tremolos (*ondulé* or *ondeggiando*; see "Crucifixus" of M. 71), and numerous dynamic indications. The *Missa in D* (M. 72, before 1770) reflects current trends in Mass orchestration by including oboe parts that are occasionally obbligato.

Part II

Style of the Concerted Masses

4

Instrumentation and Scoring

The instrumentation of these Masses was flexible; it was a function of local conditions such as available instruments, performers' abilities, choir size, parish rules and traditions, degree of solemnity, etc.[1] Rarely do all extant manuscript sources for a single Mass share identical scoring because of this functional and adaptable nature of the music. Thus, without autograph scores or authentic parts (a common situation with this repertoire), we cannot always establish with certainty the "original" instrumentation.[2] One can, however, extrapolate the probable scoring from the confluence of instrumentations in the various sources or from what appears to have been the instrumentations typical for a composer and his place of work.[3] The present chapter will focus upon the common practices and general trends of scoring observed in Masses by the composers under study.

Common Instrumentations

Study of extant Masses by all the composers in the sample reveals the seven common instrumentations that are summarized in figure 4-1. About three-fifths of the sample (43 of 72) uses one of these seven types of full orchestration; the remaining two-fifths has scorings that are essentially derived from these seven.[4] The types are arranged approximately according to frequency of occurrence in the sample, with type "A" being found most often. However, the quantity of examples is much less significant than how the types are associated with certain composers, institutions, compositional practices, and stylistic trends.

   The first four orchestral types (i.e., "A"–"D" in fig. 4-1) were in use throughout the period of study. Types "B," "C," and "D" are reduced versions of orchestral type "A." Type "B" lacks the trombones while "D" lacks the clarini and timpani; "C" is the so-called Viennese church trio.[5] Orchestration "E" tends to be found in Masses by the older generation of composers, particularly those associated with the *Hofmusikkapelle* where both high and low trumpets (i.e., 2 clarini and 2 trombe) were used. Types "F" and "G" are

Figure 4-1. Common Instrumentation Types with Representative
            Examples and Composers*

Type A	Type B	Type C
2 Clni.	2 Clni.	2 V.
2 Tbn.	Timp.	SATB
Timp.	2 V.	Org./Vlone.
2 V.	SATB	
SATB	Org./Vlone.	
Org./Vlone.		
M. 11, 14, 18, 20,	M. 1, 3, 13, 21,	M. 2, 6, 7, 22,
30, 35, 40, 49,	54, 71	32, 52, 53
50, 55, 56, 57		
Ex. 5-2; 6-3, 8, 13,	Ex. 6-14, 18;	Ex. 6-9; 7-7;
20; 7-6, 26;	7-4, 16	8-13; 9-1,
8-2, 5; 10-7,	17; 8-17;	7, 9
8, 12, 15	9-3	
Boog	Albrechtsberger	Albrechtsberger
Friberth	Boog	Arbesser
Grassl	Friberth	Grassl
Gsur	Grassl	Gsur
Hofmann	Gsur	J. Haydn
Holzbauer	Hofmann	Holzbauer
Kohaut	Kohaut	Mozart (+Va)
Krottendorfer	Mozart (+Va)	Predieri (+Va)
Monn	Sonnleithner	Seuche
Reutter	Strasser	Sonnleithner
F. Schmidt	Wagenseil	Strasser
Seuche	Ziegler	
Sonnleithner		
Strasser		

associated mostly with the younger generation for whom the oboe and viola
were becoming regular components of church music. The continuo, which
was sometimes augmented by the bassoon or violoncello, will be discussed
below.

As figure 4-1 also shows, the four-part chorus and the accompaniment of
two violins and basso continuo (organ and violone) formed the nucleus of
every scoring. "Viennese church trio" is certainly a misnomer for this basic
accompaniment because two violins and continuo had accompanied church
music in several locations throughout Europe since the Baroque era.[6] As past
literature has noted, *missae breves* were often scored with only this
accompaniment (i.e., type "C").[7] However, such short Masses were by no
means limited to this small orchestra; research reveals *missae breves* using
each of the other instrumentations, particularly types "A," "D," and "E."
Local conditions and degree of ceremony undoubtedly had more influence
than a Mass's length upon the instrumentation.

Figure 4-1 (concluded)

Type D	Type E	Type F	Type G
2 Tbn.	2 Clni.	2 Ob.	2 Ob.
2 V.	2 Trombe	2 Clni.	2 Clni.
SATB	2 Tbn.	Timp.	Timp.
Org./Vlone.	Timp.	2 V.	2 V.
	2 V.	SATB	Va.
	SATB	Org./Vlone.	SATB
	Org./Vlone.		Org./Vlone.
M. 31, 58,	M. 12, 46, 47,	M. 5, 15, 17,	M. 4, 64, 65,
61, 63	51, 60	37, 41	72
Ex. 6-15	Ex. 6-10;	Ex. 6-11;	Ex. 6-1, 12;
	7-3, 8,	7-1;	10-13, 16
	9, 15;	10-3, 10,	
	8-8,	11	
	18; 9-2,		
	13; 10-17		
Boog	Bonno	Albrechtsberger	Albrechtsberger
Gsur	(+2Ob, 2Va)	Dittersdorf	Dittersdorf
Hofmann	Boog	Hofmann	Gassmann (+2Va)
Holzbauer	Gassmann	Martínez	Grassl
Monn (+Va)	(+2Ob, 2Va)	Müller	Hasse
Predieri	Monn (+Va)	Strasser	(+2Fl, 2Hn, 2 Tbn)
Reutter	Mozart (+2Ob,		J. Haydn (+Fl, 2EH,
Seuche	2Hn, B.Tbn,		2Cl, 2Bsn, 2Hn)
Sonnleithner	1-2Va)		Hofmann
Tuma	Predieri		Holzbauer (+2Hn)
Wagenseil	Reutter (+2Ob)		Krottendorfer
	F. Schmidt		Vaňhal (2Cl, 2Hn)
	Tuma		Ziegler
	Wagenseil		

*Abbreviations for the instruments are explained in the table at the front of this book. "M" numbers refer to Masses in the sample under study and are found in the thematic catalogue of appendix C. Musical examples (ex.) from these Masses are located in later chapters (6-10).

The listing of composers is based upon information for *all* their known Masses. Instruments in parentheses (e.g., "+2Ob") show how a given scoring type was often augmented by some composers; not all instruments so indicated were always added.

Viennese church orchestras were normally smaller than those heard in theaters and concert halls. In today's terminology most Masses were essentially "chamber" works. Extant performing materials for the Masses usually have only one part per instrument or voice, although materials from the wealthier institutions (e.g., the Hofmusikkapelle) often have duplicate or *"Concertato/Ripieno"* parts. Otto Biba's close analysis of a 1783 inventory of Vienna's church music personnel reveals that generally there were one or two players for each violin part and occasionally a trumpet choir of four; otherwise there was one person per part, even when a choir of boys sang soprano.[8] When a special feast required a larger chorus or more instrumental forces, extra musicians were hired as needed.

As shall be observed in detail in later chapters, instrumentation varies from movement to movement and section to section within each Mass. Not unexpectedly, the full orchestra usually accompanies the sections for chorus. Reduced instrumentation (often just the violins with or without continuo) accompanies most solo sections.[9] Impressive obbligatos for woodwinds, brass, or strings are frequently heard during solo movements such as the "Christe," "Laudamus," "Gratias," "Quoniam," "Et incarnatus," "Benedictus," and "Agnus Dei."

Instrument Functions

In the course of a Mass each instrument has one or more of the following functions: (1) obbligato or *concertato; (2) ripieno* (tutti); (3) doubling of the choral parts (*colla parte*); (4) basso continuo. By no means are these functions mutually exclusive since the instruments generally maintain a flexible relationship with the voice parts they are accompanying.

Obbligatos were usually reserved for the ritornellos (less often for the vocal sections) of movements for solo voice. In eighteenth-century Vienna these parts were commonly entitled "obbligato" or "concertato." As may be seen in the following list, other instruments beside the violin played obbligatos in these Masses:

Flute (see ex. 9-10)
Oboe (see ex. 6-7)
Bassoon (see ex. 6-6, 7; 9-12; also "Laudamus" of Gassmann's *St. Cecilia Mass*)
Clarino (see ex. 6-20; 7-4, 8, 15, 24; 8-5, 17)
Trombone (see ex. 7-9, 19)
Violin (see most examples; especially ex. 7-14; 9-12; also "Et incarnatus" of Gassmann's Mass)
Viola (see ex. 7-20 [ad libitum in place of Vcllo.])
Violoncello (see ex. 7-20; also in Gassmann's Mass)
Organ (see ex. 9-11)

At mid-century most instrumental solos in a Mass were played by the violins, trombones, or, on especially high feasts, clarini.[10] However, by the end of the 1760s the quantity of obbligatos seems to increase, and the woodwinds and lower strings are used almost equally often (e.g., in Masses by Bonno, Gassmann, and Hofmann).

In 1781 the Berlin critic Friedrich Nicolai, who did not like everything he heard in Vienna's churches, was especially impressed by the obbligatos during a Mass:

I seldom heard anything moving *(herzrührendes)* or elevated *(erhabenes)*. What should have been magnificent was mostly just thundering *(rauschend)*. There were a few exceptions. For example, on June 17th in the Kriegskirche or former Jesuit Church, I heard beautiful music for a Mass. Indeed it was in the modern taste but full of noble and new ideas. The Sanctus was accomplished merely by an obbligato solo violin which was even played quite well. The Agnus Dei was accompanied by a thoroughly obbligato trombone which was played distinctly *(rein)* and intelligently.[11]

In a chapel at St. Augustine's where Anton Carl was *regens chori,* Nicolai happened to hear music for one of the *Todtenmessen* held there every Monday. The poorly played accompaniment consisted of two violins (one player on each), violoncello, violone, two trombones, and a positive organ. Although the choir was also "very weak," he found the composition—possibly by Fux or Caldara, he thought—to be quite noteworthy.

[There were] short, always contrapuntal movements *(Sätze)* along with a very simple, noble singing full of expression. Particularly moving for me was a beautiful, moderately slow aria sung by a choirboy who had a pure, gentle, [and] flexible alto voice, which seemed yet unrefined in consideration of the execution and placement of the tones *(portamento di voce).* The accompaniment was merely a concertante tenor trombone; there were no other instruments. Nonetheless, in this strange but simple combination there was so much to arouse a mysterious, solemn, and sublime feeling! These long drawn-out, gentle, always connected tones incited a silent amazement *(ein stilles Staunen).* Especially a few passages where the trombone gradually descended into the depths and held while the alto voice, which had had a pause of a few measures, again sang a soft, gradually intensifying long tone—these passages went right to the heart. I have heard nothing more appropriate *(zweckmässigeres)* for a long time.[12]

The *ripieno* parts usually provide the tutti ritornellos, accompaniment figures, and harmonic "filler" for the choral movements. Strings and continuo commonly fulfill these *ripieno* functions. *Ripieno* melody often adheres to one unifying figuration or motive per section (ex. 6-7, 6-10; 7-1, 7-3, 7-4, 7-16, et al.). At other times the *ripieno* parts combine choral doubling with short, independent interludes during the vocal pauses (ex. 6-12, 7-9). (N.B.: Sometimes the parts labeled *ripieno* do *only* choral doubling.)

Two kinds of vocal doubling are found in these Masses: literal (i.e., *colla parte*) and timbral. In the latter type *ripieno* instruments freely double the vocal parts, often in a different octave or in an elaborated version (see ex. 6-12; 7-15, 7-26, et al.; also the "Christe" of Gassmann's *St. Cecilia Mass*). Another kind of timbral doubling is the so-called Viennese unison *(Wiener unisono)* or octave coupling between instruments; it occurs mostly between the violins and oboes in these Masses (see ex. 6-12).[13]

Literal orchestral doubling of the chorus (i.e., *colla parte*) is frequently overlooked in this repertoire. The instruments used for such doublings varied from place to place, even for the same Mass; undoubtedly they depended upon both the size and ability of the chorus as well as the instrumentalists available.[14] Figure 4-2 lists some of the literal doublings encountered in the present Masses. Not only in fugues (where every instrument doubled a voice) but usually everywhere else in the Mass the choral parts were intensified by this kind of doubling. Frequently the doublings are not specifically indicated in the titles, scores, or even parts for the Masses. In the latter case the doubling parts may have been later discarded as superfluous or, more likely, the instrumentalists read from the vocal parts.[15]

One of the older doublings uses the cornetto, two trombones, and bassoon to support the chorus (type "A" in fig. 4-2); this doubling had been commonly used in the *Hof* since the reign of Charles VI and can be found in Masses by Monn, Predieri, Tuma, and Wagenseil.[16] Use of trombones for vocal doubling begins to die out in Vienna during the 1770s, although the list of church music personnel for 1783 indicates their continued presence in the 1780s.[17] In his 1790 discussion of church music with instrumental accompaniment, Albrechtsberger still informs students that "the first trombone [goes] with the alto, the second with the tenor, [and] the third (which is seldom still used) with the bass voice."[18] Interestingly, none of the Masses in the present study are known to require a bass trombone, which was probably deemed unnecessary because the continuo (organ, violone) usually doubled the bass voice. However, that early tradition appears to have been maintained in Salzburg (e.g., Mozart, K. 139, 317).[19] By 1790 Albrechtsberger considers the cornetto "an unusual *(seltsames)* instrument" for doubling the soprano.[20] At that time violins or oboes commonly played an elaborated doubling of the soprano part. Instrumental doubling of the vocal passages marked "solo" is relatively rare (see ex. 7-13, 7-18).

Of course, other doublings were used; for example, around mid-century the viola (often called violetta) sometimes doubled the sopranos or altos if it was not being used to double the continuo an octave higher (e.g., in M. 69 by Wagenseil). Instrumental doublings of the chorus must have saved rehearsal time with the singers; in addition, the *colla parte* instruments provided a necessary support for the (often single-voice) choral parts pitted against the accompanying instrumental forces in Vienna's all too resonant churches.

The omnipresent basso continuo is perhaps the most conservative feature in all these Masses. Most performing materials from the period include both an organ and violone part for the continuo. (In the several instances where only an organ part exists, the violone player would have stood behind the organ bench.) "Violoncello" parts for continuo were rare during most of this period; they begin to supplement (or replace) the violone during the 1770s. The 1783 inventory of church music personnel shows cellists employed regularly at only about half of Vienna's churches.[21]

Exact instrumentation of the continuo depended upon local

Figure 4-2. Vocal Doublings (i.e., *colla parte*) in the Masses

Voice Being Doubled:	SOPRANO	ALTO	TENOR	BASS	Examples
Type A	Cornetto (Zink)	Trombone I	Trombone II	Bassoon	Ex. 6-2, 6
Type B	Violins (unisono)	Trombone I	Trombone II	b.c.	M. 63
Type C	- -	Trombone I	Trombone II	b.c.	Ex. 6-8; 7-9
Type D	Violin I	Violin II/ Trombone I	Trombone II	b.c.	Ex. 6-15A; 7-9
Type E	Violin I	Violin II	Viola	b.c.	Hob.XXII: 5

circumstances and was not always explicitly stated in the title pages, covers, catalogues, parts, etc. Continuo parts from the Hofmusikkapelle for Masses by Bonno, Gassmann, Monn, Predieri, Reutter, Tuma, and Wagenseil are usually also supplied for the bassoon, violoncello, and "M.D.C." *(maestro di cappella).*[22] At St. Peter's the continuo for Hofmann's Masses also included the violoncello (see ex. 7-5). Researchers must always be on the lookout for continuo parts that were originally marked "violone" but later changed to "violoncello" by the addition of four letters.

The continuo keyboard is always the organ, although there are reports that a harpsichord was sometimes used out of necessity.[23] The organist's realization provides harmonic filler which is particularly necessary for solo movements where a trio texture often predominates (ex. 7-12, 7-14, et al.). As Biba remarks: "The organist was actually the musical center for these small and transparent instrumentations; he was decisive for the musical performance."[24] The organ rarely stops playing during a concerted Mass. During a fugal exposition it acts as a *basso seguente,* thus doubling each entrance when the voices enter in descending order. Occasionally, for dramatic effect (e.g., during the "Et incarnatus" of M. 8, 9, 10, 15 [ex. 8-4, m. 16ff.], and 32) the organ will pause for a few measures. Frequently, too, the organ will stop playing to let only the two violins accompany a solo voice during a multi-sectional movement for chorus and soloists (see ex. 6-10; 7-3AB, 7-8 et al.).

The interpretation of the terms "solo" and "tutti" in the continuo parts remains in dispute. When "solo" does appear, it can have any one or more of the following meanings:

1. The voices have a true solo (i.e., single voices are exposed)
2. The continuo should play softer so as not to cover the solo; the organist might change registrations
3. Fewer instruments (only one?) should play continuo during this passage

The first meaning appears to hold for all the present Masses, although Biba and others question how much of a distinction truly existed between the solo and tutti passages when there was usually only one person per vocal part.[25] *Piano* dynamics in the upper instruments often parallel such "solo" indications in the continuo and thus support the second interpretation (see ex. 7-12, 17). In truth there seems to have been no consistent use of these terms. Performers today had best continue using common sense and judgement informed by the individual context and instrumentation when interpreting "solo" and "tutti" in continuo parts.

Voices

All the present Masses are scored for a four-part SATB chorus. Double choruses, such as those found in Baroque Masses by Schmeltzer, Ziani, and Fux or in more contemporary settings by Pergolesi, Martini, and other Italians, are rare. Church records for 1783 make it seem likely that only one person sang from each part (see n. 8 above). Indeed, duplicate vocal parts are a rarity among the performing materials for these Masses and exist for only the most elaborate settings. However, considering the large size (often a 10-staved, vertical format) of contemporary vocal parts and the available iconographical evidence, we should not rule out the possibility that two or more singers could share a vocal part. In addition, the existence of "solo" and "tutti" passages distinguished by more and less elaborate vocal writing suggests that there were two or more voices on a part, with the ablest voice of each part singing the solos. In some Masses an additional voice part (often a soprano or bass) is required for certain ensembles of equal voices, e.g., SS duets, SSA trios, etc. (see ex. 8-5, 9-16E).[26]

Instrument Deployment: Miscellaneous Trends

Woodwinds provide chiefly harmonic filler and timbral doubling (e.g., *Wiener unisonos*) in these Masses. The flute, clarinet, and English horn were not part of the regular church orchestra at this time. The flute, however, is occasionally obbligato for isolated movements (e.g., 2 flutes for the "Christe," "Et incarnatus," and "Benedictus" in M. 4 by Albrechtsberger).[27] Hofmann's *Missa in D* (M. 29) which has a flute obbligato for every movement is a rarity (see ex. 7-10, 9-10). Probably influenced by theater orchestras, some Viennese composers began using oboes in Masses during the 1760s. Gassmann's *St. Cecilia Mass* (M. 19, before 1771) treats the oboe flexibly by giving it the following duties:

1. Obbligato melodies (e.g., "Christe" and "Benedictus")
2. Choral doubling (e.g., "Kyrie II," "Quoniam," "Cum Sancto," and "Agnus Dei")
3. Harmonic filler (e.g., "Kyrie I" and "Gloria")
4. Fixed timbral doubling—usually with the violins (e.g., "Christe," "Laudamus," and "Qui tollis")
5. Varying timbral doublings, i.e., doubling changes in the course of a movement (e.g., "Domine Deus, Rex," and "Benedictus")

Oboes are often used during ritornellos; they are seldom heard when a soloist is singing or the dynamic level is *piano*. Not until the 1790s do clarinets come into regular use. Bassoons were used mostly for an occasional expressive obbligato or "Viennese unison" (see ex. 6-6, 6-7; 9-12; "Laudamus" of Gassmann's *St. Cecilia Mass;* "Benedictus" of Haydn's *St. Cecilia Mass,* Hob. XXII; 5). At court the bassoon continued to augment the thoroughbass during tuttis.

Brass instruments had very specific duties in most Masses of this period. High or clarini trumpets (invariably with accompanying timpani) continued to symbolize solemnity as they had during the high Baroque.[28] Clarini parts were often marked "ad libitum," thus allowing their omission from ordinary Masses and their inclusion in solemn High Masses where they were also used for intradas. Clarini are commonly heard in the opening and closing choral movements of each part of the Mass (ex. 6-3, 7-1, 10-14, et al.), less often in solo movements (ex. 7-24). Performance materials indicate that works with clarini and timpani were still performed outside of the *Hof* after the ban of 1753 (see chapter 2, nn. 93–94). Pairs of low trumpets (called "trombe" and often written in the alto C-clef) are occasionally present to accentuate the rhythms and augment the harmonies of the higher, more melodic clarini (ex. 7-2, 7-3, 7-9, 7-15, et al.).[29]

Horns are rarely used in these Masses.[30] Horn parts were sometimes added later as the tastes and orchestral personnel of an institution changed. In Gassmann's *St. Cecilia Mass,* for example, attempts to replace the clarini with horns in certain movements of some manuscripts have perhaps permanently obscured the original use of horns in that Mass.[31] Having both clarini and horns in a Mass at this time may be suspect since both instruments were frequently played by the same persons.[32] Not until the 1790s (e.g., in M. 66 by Vaňhal) do we find composers regularly scoring separate parts for horns.

The use and importance of the trombone in these Masses has often been undervalued or even overlooked. A pair of trombones is commonly found in performing materials from the period. Besides doubling the alto and tenor parts of the choir, trombones often have short, expressive obbligatos, especially at "Gratias," "Qui tollis," "Et incarnatus," and "Agnus Dei" (see ex. 7-9, 7-19; 8-1; 10-7). As Robert Wigness has shown, the trombone did indeed still flourish.[33] The trombone's long-standing use in sacred music undoubtedly led to its frequent association with the divine and supernatural in operas by Gluck, Mozart, and others.[34] Some trombone solos are challenging, often demanding lip trills and lengthy sixteenth-note runs. When doubling voices, the trombone (like most doubling instruments) usually plays simplified rhythms so as to avoid rapid or unnecessary repeated notes (see ex. 7-6).

As already indicated, timpani were used only in conjunction with the trumpets (whose rhythms they usually shared). The absence of timpani parts from scores or performing materials when clarini are present does not preclude their use; timpanists could easily have improvised their parts from those of the clarini.[35] No matter what the key, all timpani parts are written in the key of C, using only tonic and dominant pitches. Example 10-17B (Reutter's *Schimmelmesse*) shows one of the rare instances when the timpani are played somewhat independently.

Not unexpectedly, the violins are principal carriers of melody, second only to the voices. Movements without violins are exceedingly rare; only occasionally might they be briefly silent for effect (e.g., at "Crucifixus" in M. 40, 53, and 54). Since we seldom find more than one copy of each string part, it can probably be safely assumed that, except for special feasts, there were usually no more than two players on each violin part.[36] The busy, seemingly endless rush of sixteenth notes in the violin accompaniments to the choral movements of these Masses was part of the accepted style and should not be associated only with Reutter (see ex. 7-3A, 6).[37] Sometimes the violin figurations are so elaborate and fussy that one must wonder how clearly they would be heard in a spacious, resonant sanctuary. Do such violins help or hinder the voices? In his composition treatise, Albrechtsberger makes a special point of discussing this type of string accompaniment:

> Lastly, one ought to know that if one desires to set obbligato violins with running or skipping notes against a chorus, sixteenth and thirty-second notes make the best effect; however, to give the last named [note values] to the violone and other bass instruments would create an unpleasant rumble *(Poltern)*. To achieve variety one can alternate the violins' rapid notes in each measure or half measure. It is also good if the bass instruments and thoroughbass make the alternation with violins that are playing in unison.[38]

As example 7-4 later shows, Albrechtsberger himself liked to use the alternation accompaniment just described.

Strings play arco most of the time, although pizzicato or muting is occasionally required for special effect in some sections such as the "Qui tollis," "Et incarnatus," "Benedictus," and "Agnus Dei" (ex. 10-4F). The frequent and often virtuosic obbligatos for solo violin as well as the violin's doubling of the chorus have already been discussed. Dittersdorf and Hofmann, both expert violinists themselves, have challenging and carefully written violin parts in their Masses.

Starting in the 1770s the viola (also called violetta) plays an increasingly independent role in these Masses. Prior to that decade it appears only sporadically, mostly to double either the basso continuo *(all'ottava)* or an inner voice. The few users of obbligato viola before 1750 include Holzbauer (M. 33), Monn (M. 38, 39), and Hasse (M. 23–25).[39] They may have influenced its later independent use in Masses by Albrechtsberger (M. 4), Bonno (M. 8, 9), Dittersdorf (M. 16), Gassmann (M. 19), Hofmann, Sonnleithner (M. 57), and Vaňhal (M. 64, 65). Gassmann's *St. Cecilia Mass* (M. 19, with 2 violas) and Vaňhal's *Missa Pastorell in G* (M. 65, see ex. 6-12) exhibit this greater freedom with viola parts that frequently switch functions during the course of a single movement. In isolated movements requiring viola solos, a violinist commonly played the viola. This practice is demonstrated by the existence of such viola solos only in first violin parts (e.g., "Gratias" in M. 57 by Sonnleithner; "Benedictus" in M. 14 by Anton Carl).[40]

Except at court where it was usually part of the basso continuo, the violoncello was used occasionally (sometimes in pairs) for elegant obbligatos (ex. 7-20). The inspiration for such solos may have come from Naples where Masses since the start of the century had often included elaborate solos for cello.[41] Symptomatic of the cello's growth as an independent member of the orchestra by the 1770s is its solo treatment in the first Kyrie and "Qui tollis" of Gassmann's *St. Cecilia Mass* (M. 19). Its use as continuo in the remainder of this Mass reflects the instrument's acceptance as a regular member of the orchestra.

The violone is almost always a part of the basso continuo in these Masses; it never has a solo. Exactly what instrument played these violone parts remains an issue of debate; smaller than today's string bass, the instrument probably varied in size from place to place since there was not yet a uniform contrabass.[42]

As already indicated, the organist had one of the most important roles in the church orchestra. Along with other duties during the service (e.g., preludes, postludes, improvisations, epistle sonatas, versets, chant accompaniments), for *every* movement of the concerted Mass the organist played continuo, provided an often necessary harmonic filler, and even gave vocal cues.[43] It is thus not surprising that a badly tuned organ ruined many a Mass for Burney while he was in Vienna.[44] Occasionally the organ would pause momentarily for expressive purposes during the "Qui tollis," "Et incarnatus," or "Crucifixus" (see ex. 7-25). Austrian organs at this time rarely had pedals, and only the bigger churches had more than one manual and a few stops. (The violone and other continuo instruments could make up for the lack of pedals.) The range of organs rarely exceeded $C-c^3$, with most instruments lacking the chromatic tones below F.[45] Both Bonno and Wagenseil used the designations "aperto" (open) and "serrato" (closed) in place of dynamic markings for the organ.[46]

Three of the Masses in our sample (M. 17, 45, 64) are usually termed "organ solo Masses" (a better description would be "organ *concertato* Masses") because one or more movements have an independent part written out for the organist's right hand. According to Landon, these organ solo Masses have "always been regarded as something of an Austrian specialty."[47] Such solos are most commonly found in the "Benedictus" where an organ introduction provides a kind of elevation music (see ex. 9-11). Usually no exceptional technical prowess is required for these short solos.

Summary

In studying these Masses, one should never lose sight of the potential flexibility in their scoring. Orchestration (including specific doublings) was more a function of the local performing conditions and ceremonial requirements than of a composer's volition. Thus, discrepancies in the instrumentation of a given Mass can be widespread. Examination of only Haydn's and Mozart's Masses does not give one a true picture of the variety of orchestrations in use. Nonetheless, seven common instrumentations—all built around the "Viennese church trio"—are found in the majority of Masses (fig. 4-1); other scorings tend to be derivatives of these basic seven. In general, the trend in Mass instrumentation is away from the *colla parte* trombones and low trumpets (trombe) of Monn, Predieri, Reutter, Tuma, and Wagenseil. By the 1770s, perhaps through the influence of the symphony and opera (and Hasse?), the oboe and viola are becoming standard in the Masses of younger composers like Albrechtsberger, Dittersdorf, Gassmann, Hofmann, and Vaňhal.

The orchestra fulfills obbligato, *ripieno, colla parte,* and continuo duties; the latter (increasingly anachronistic) was usually assumed by at least the organ and violone. Expressive instrumental obbligatos (heard chiefly in the ritornellos of movements for solo voice) are found throughout this period, with woodwind solos increasing in frequency and variety. The marking "solo" in the vocal and instrumental parts has various and sometimes ambiguous meanings; consideration of the context usually leads to a correct interpretation of the term. The existence of vocal "solo/tutti" markings, paralleled by changes in melodic style, texture, and accompaniment, speaks strongly for more than one voice on a part. However, the presence of *colla parte* instruments and single copies of each voice part may support the hypothesis that only solo voices sang throughout. More research on the performing materials and more practical experiments must be conducted before this riddle is satisfactorily answered. Masses are believed to have been performed ordinarily with one instrumentalist to a part, except for the violins which normally had two per part. The standard chorus of these Masses is four-part SATB, with an extra soprano or bass part occasionally added for duets in isolated movements. With its basso continuo, harmonic filler, and occasional vocal cues, the organ has a central role in all of these Masses. Austrian composers also frequently enriched their settings with one or two solo interludes for the instrument.

5

General Form and Style of the Masses

This chapter is designed as an introduction to the five analytical chapters that follow. Discussion focuses on the Mass as a whole and on common elements of style and form. The aim is to give the reader a bird's eye view of the 72 Masses under study.[1] What was "normal" in these Masses? What were their commonalities? By no means can (or should) these observations apply to all settings; after all, composers did vary their Masses—albeit inconsistently—according to the degree of ceremony, the place, and the performing conditions. To complicate matters, musical style was also undergoing fundamental changes which some analysts relate to an evolutionary movement from high Baroque to galant, rococo, and pre-Classic styles. For specific uses of the forms discussed, for textual-musical relationships, and for most of the musical examples mentioned, the remaining chapters should be consulted.

The Mass as a Cycle

It is a matter of debate whether and to what extent we can view a Mass setting as a unified cycle. As we saw in chapter 2 (fig. 2-2), various liturgical acts and even other musical selections originally separated every part of the Mass Ordinary except the Kyrie and Gloria. This situation may have been what deterred most composers from attempting to integrate their settings by any means other than key and scoring. Moreover, there appears to have been a certain flexibility and interchangeability in how Mass settings and their individual sections functioned.

Composers were undoubtedly aware that the integrity of their Masses was not sacred and that, as in opera, practicalities might at any time make the reworking or substitution of a movement necessary. For example, a choir director might substitute the fugue from another composer's Mass in order to make the work fit the solemnity of the occasion.[2] Some composers wrote "insertion" movements for such a purpose; many of Mozart's isolated Mass movements can be explained by this practice.[3] Michael Haydn's later expansion of the Gloria of his brother's *Kleine Orgelsolomesse* (Hob. XXII:7) is one of the better known examples.[4] In his autobiography, Dittersdorf reports how Padre Martini in Bologna did not hesitate to substitute an eight-voiced "Amen" from one of his Vespers for the "Amen" at the end of a Credo.[5] Study of the Hofmusikkapelle's repertoire and its *Kalendarium* in the appendix of Reinhardt's "Rubriche Generali" (1727) shows that frequently not all parts of a Mass Ordinary were by the same composer—especially during an extended Pontifical Mass.[6] For example, on 21 June 1739 (Feast of St. Aloysius) at the Schlosskapelle, a Credo by Fux was inserted in a Mass by Ziani.[7] Indeed, the physical make-up of performing materials for many long Masses must have encouraged such pasticcio Masses; often there are three separate folders for the parts to the Kyrie-Gloria, Credo, and Sanctus-Agnus Dei.[8]

The eighteenth-century composer's relatively flexible attitude toward the integrity of his Masses not only tempers to what extent we should consider each setting a unified entity but also leads to problems in performance and authenticity. For example, there are two different settings of both Credo and Sanctus for Gassmann's *St. Cecilia Mass* (M. 19). Did Gassmann write both settings or did someone later insert substitutions by another composer? Hasse's *Missa in G* (M. 23) has two versions of the "Dona nobis pacem"; in Berlin (Mus. ms. 9484) the "Dona" reuses the music of Gloria's "Amen," while in Vienna (Mus. Hs. 17320) it has its own fugue.[9] Which version is Hasse's? Are they both by him? These are just a few of the countless examples of conflicting or alternate versions to be found in the Masses of this period.[10]

Often the practice of substituting movements in a Mass with music from other settings hampered legitimate dissemination of a work and led to conflicting attributions. For example, Boog's *Missa in C* (M. 12) which is found under his name in six locations (including St. Peter's, Vienna, where he was choir director) was somehow attributed to Monn in an expanded version preserved at Kremsmünster.[11] Many such problems of substitution and attribution exist; attempts at their solution are now only beginning as by-products of authenticity studies of the major composers.[12]

Keeping in mind the possibility of such substitute movements and alternate versions, but knowing that most of the time a composer's Mass (except for the Credo on certain occasions) was performed in its entirety, we now examine the Masses as a whole.

During the period under study, the overall dimensions of Mass settings remained basically constant. Of course, Mass lengths did vary according to whether a composer was writing a *missa longa* or a *missa brevis*.[13] Figure 5-1 presents a list of Mass lengths (arranged in order of diminishing size) for comparing all the settings in the sample. Using Mozart's and Haydn's settings entitled "Missa brevis" as points of reference, we might consider most Masses that last approximately 570 measures or more as *missae longae*.[14] Masses shorter than 570 measures usually have some of the typical trademarks of a *missa brevis* (i.e., polytextuality, no fugues, few solos, simple straightforward style and scoring, Kyrie and Gloria as single movements). Figure 5-1 also includes the lengths of well-known Masses as well as choral and instrumental works by Bach, Beethoven, Handel, Haydn, Mozart and Scarlatti for comparison purposes. (Obviously these totals do not reflect differences in meter or tempo.)

The larger *missae longae* can last from 75 minutes (Haydn's *St. Cecilia Mass*; 1,744 measures) to 113 minutes (Bach's *B-minor Mass*; 2,492 measures). These lengths are roughly equivalent to Part I or II of Handel's *Messiah*. A moderate sized *missa longa* lasts about half an hour (e.g., Haydn's *Missa Cellensis*, Hob. XXII: 8; 927 measures), the length of many classical symphonies.[15] *Missae breves* are from about 10 to 25 minutes in duration. Certainly composers must have had these durations in mind before writing a Mass. Was the Mass to be a quarter, half, or whole hour or even longer? In the autograph scores of several composers, e.g., Albrechtsberger and Haydn, we see a measure total carefully placed at the end of each movement; perhaps they were counting minutes as well as measures.[16] In any case, composers were concerned about the temporal dimensions of their settings. It is well known that Mozart had to fit his Masses into a service lasting no longer than three quarters of an hour from 1772 on.[17]

Proportions among the five parts of a Mass varied. They were primarily a function of both the text and the temporal demands of the liturgy, as well as the composer's aesthetic sense. The Kyrie-Gloria pairing was often more extended and more elaborate than the remainder of the Mass. As figure 5-2 indicates, over two-thirds of the settings (46 of 67) have a Kyrie and Gloria which account for more than two-fifths of the Mass; in the majority of these the Kyrie and Gloria actually take up more than half of the Mass. Obviously the prolixity of the Gloria's text is a factor in this imbalance.[18] These opening two parts were often so long and intricate (e.g., 757 measures, 57 percent of the Mass, and seven movements in M. 38 by Monn) that they provided a kind of concert—with choruses, arias, duets, etc.—to precede the lessons and Holy Eucharist. Undoubtedly the Credo, Sanctus, and Agnus Dei were proportionally smaller so as not to impede the momentum of that part of the service.[19]

As the details in the following chapters will show, composers exercised a certain amount of freedom in how they divided each of the five parts of the Mass into various movements and sections, providing them with different tempos, meters, keys, themes, and scorings. In formal discussion below, the

Figure 5-1. Comparative Table of Mass Lengths*

Missae longae		Measure Total
J. S. Bach	B-minor Mass, B. W. V. 232 (1733-39)	2,492
Beethoven	Missa solemnis, Op. 123 (1818-22)	1,932
J. Haydn	"St. Cecilia" Mass, Hob. XXII: 5 (1766)	1,744
Gassmann	St. Cecilia Mass, M. 19 (before 1771) [Vienna version]	1,441
Monn	Missa in C, M. 38 (1741)	1,321
Holzbauer	Missa in C, M. 30 (before 1739)	1,298
Martínez	Messe No. IV, M. 37 (1765)	1,266
Beethoven	Mass in C, Op. 86 (1807)	1,254
Dittersdorf	Missa ex D, M. 17 (before 1777)	1,242
J. Haydn	The Six Late Masses, Hob. XXII: 9-14 (1796-1802)	990-1,159
Mozart	Mass in C Minor, K. 427 (1782-83) [incomplete]	1,127+
Hofmann	Missa Sancti Erasmi in D, M. 26 (before 1779)	1,123
Vaňhal	Missa Pastorell in G, M. 65 (before 1782)	1,120

*All Masses in the sample of 72 are listed (in descending order of lengths) except M. 16, 41, 44, 46, 48, and 55, for which all information was not available. However, M. 46 and 48 are probably also *missae breves*.

Figure 5-1 (cont'd.)

		Measure
Missae longae (cont'd.)		Total
Dittersdorf	Missa in C, M. 15 (before 1773)	1,118
Mozart	Mass in C Minor ("Waisenhausmesse"), K. 139 (1768)	1,112
Mozart	"Dominicus" Mass in C, K. 66 (1769)	1,069
Vañhal	Missa in C, M. 64 (before 1778)	1,047
F. Schmidt	St. Cecilia Mass in C, M. 50 (before 1746)	1,042
Albrechtsberger	Missa Dei Patris in C, M. 4 (1781)	1,002
Monn	Missa solemnis in B-flat, M. 39 (before 1750)	997
J. Haydn	Grosse Orgelmesse in E-flat, Hob. XXII: 4 (before 1774)	965
A. Scarlatti	St. Cecilia Mass in A (1720)	950
Vañhal	Missa solemnis in F, M. 66 (before 1797)	944
Reutter	Missa Sancti Caroli, M. 49 (1734) [in DTÖ 88]	933
Sonnleithner	Missa solennis in C, M. 56 (before 1763)	931
J. Haydn	Missa Cellensis in C, Hob. XXII: 8 (1782)	927
Hasse	Missa in G, M. 23 (1753)	921
Martínez	Terza Messa, M. 36 (1761)	906
Hasse	Mass in D Minor, M. 24 (before 1751)	903

Figure 5-1   (cont'd.)

	Missae longae (cont'd.)	Measure Total
Sonnleithner	Missa in F, M. 58 (before 1769)	893
Tuma	Missa in Chordis et organo, M. 61 (before 1743)	882
Monn	Missa in D, M. 40 (before 1750)	868
Mozart	Trinitatis Mass in C, K. 167 (1773)	863
Ziegler	Missa in C, M. 71 (before 1762)	862
Mozart	Missa (longa) in C, K. 262 (1776)	824
Sonnleithner	Missa ex C, M. 54 (before 1771)	820
Friberth	Missa in D, M. 18 (1774)	ca. 818
F. Schmidt	Missa Primitiarum in C, M. 51 (before 1747)	806
Holzbauer	Missa in F, M. 33 (before 1745)	766
Grassl	Missa Pastoralis ex C, M. 20 (before 1774)	766
Sonnleithner	Missa sollemnis in C, M. 57 (before 1758)	759
Tuma	Missa Tibi soli di Psalm 50, M. 60 (before 1750?)	720
Ziegler	Missa in D, M. 72 (before 1770)	690
A. Carl	Missa solemnis in C, M. 14 (before 1751)	673

Figure 5-1 (cont'd.)

		Measure Total
Missae longae (cont'd.)		
Hofmann	Missa in D, M. 29 (before 1772)	672
Mozart	"Credo" Mass in C, K. 257 (1776)	666
Boog	Missa in C, M. 13 (before 1763)	638
Mozart	Coronation Mass in C, K. 317 (1779)	628
Reutter	Missa Lauretana in C, M. 45 (before 1742)	596
Hasse	Missa in D, M. 25 (before 1783)	594
Kohaut	Missa Sancti Willibaldi in C, M. 34 (before 1763)	583

Missae breves (in title)

Mozart	K. 49, 65, 192, 194, 220, 258, 259, 275	356-569
J. Haydn	Hob. XXII: 1, 3, 7	91-312

Probable Missae breves (although not so titled)

Wagenseil, M. 69	555	Albrechtsberger, M.2	525
Holzbauer, M. 31	551	Hofmann, M. 28	505
Bonno, M. 9	537	Hofmann, M. 27	503
Mozart, K. 337	530	Boog, M. 12	480
Bonno, M. 8	529	Reutter, M. 47	477
J. Haydn, Hob. XXII: 6	527	Holzbauer, M. 32	474
Albrechtsberger, M. 3	526	Wagenseil, M. 70	454
Albrechtsberger, M. 5	526	Bonno, M. 10	433

Figure 5-1 (concluded)

Probable <u>Missae breves</u> (cont'd.)

Strasser, M. 59	429	Predieri, M. 43	368
Arbesser, M. 7	428	Tuma, M. 62	333
Boog, M. 11	413	Tuma, M. 63	333
Gsur, M. 22	407	Wagenseil, M. 68	299
Gsur, M. 21	391	Seuche, M. 52	298
Krottendorfer, M. 35	391	Albrechtsberger, M.1	277
Wagenseil, M. 67	390	Seuche, M. 53	202
Predieri, M. 42	381	Arbesser, M. 6	199

<u>Other Works - For Comparison of Dimensions</u>

Handel	<u>Messiah</u> (1742)		
	Part I		1,275
	Part II		1,132
	Part III		838
		TOTAL	3,245
Beethoven	Symphony No. 9, Op. 125 (1823-24)		2,203
Beethoven	Symphony No. 5, Op. 67 (1805-7)		1,566
Mozart	Symphony No. 41, K. 551 (1788) "Jupiter"		924
J. Haydn	Symphony No. 7 (1761) "Le Midi"		416
J. Haydn	Piano Sonata No. 62 in E-flat, Hob. XVI: 52 (1794)		272

Figure 5-2. Percentage of Mass Occupied by Kyrie-Gloria

Kyrie-Gloria % of Mass*	Quantity of Examples	Mass Nos.
70% or more	1	M. 26
60-69%	6	M. 19, 24, 36, 49, 60, 61; also Haydn, Hob. XXII:5
50-59%	20	M. 4, 5, 8, 18, 21, 23, 29, 30, 33, 37-40, 50, 54, 62, 63, 66, 71, 72
41-49%	19	M. 9, 10, 15-17, 20, 22, 25, 32, 35, 42, 45, 51, 52, 56, 58, 64, 65, 70; also Haydn, Hob. XXII:8, 10-14
40% or less	21	M. 1-3, 6, 7, 11-13, 27, 28, 31, 34, 43, 47, 53, 57, 59, 67-69; also Haydn, Hob. XXII: 1, 3, 4, 6, 7, 9
TOTAL	67	

*These percentages are based upon measure counts only; differences caused by changes in meter or tempo are not reflected. Complete measure counts were not available for Mass Nos. 41, 44, 46, 48, and 55.

word "part" is reserved for the major divisions of the Mass; i.e., the Mass Ordinary consists of five "parts": Kyrie, Gloria, Credo, Sanctus, and Agnus Dei. Within a part, the term "movement" will be used for a continuous, complete, and independent division defined by a full cadence at its conclusion. "Section" and "subsection" refer only to the smaller components that make up a movement's form.[20] A movement is not necessarily restricted to a single tempo, meter, scoring, and key, although these elements may contribute to its independence. Slow subsections (introductions, interludes, and conclusions) are thus considered parts of the fast section to which they are joined by means of a half-cadence, overlapping cadences, dovetailing, or the like.[21]

Each part of the Mass consisted of one to 10 separate movements, with the long texts of the Gloria and Credo usually engendering the most movements. *Missae breves* naturally had fewer movements than *missae longae*. After the middle of the century, composers in general seemed to compose longer movements and limit each part of the Mass to no more than four movements. Some idea of the greater continuity arising from a Mass with fewer movements may be drawn from figure 5-3 which compares the movements (vis-à-vis text) of an early and late Mass from the period. Monn's Gloria of six separate movements made up of 10 different tempos is typical of the earlier "number Masses" with their series of independent solos and choruses. Vaňhal's Mass is representative of the greater conciseness associated with the Masses of the Classic era.

As will be seen, composers usually tried to vary the meter and tempo from movement to movement. The most common meters were C, 3/4, and ¢, with composers often using the latter in *stile antico* fugues. Perhaps influenced by secular forms such as dance, chamber music, and opera buffa, Masses after mid-century use a greater variety of meters than before, including 3/8, 6/8, and 2/4; 3/2 and 6/4, along with the hemiola, seem to be used less and less frequently from that point on. Composers were also becoming more precise about tempo indications during this period. Before about 1750 it was not unusual to find no tempo marking for some movements, especially fugues, e.g., the "Et vitam" of Monn's *Missa in C* (see fig. 5-3). Adler has pointed out that in Fuxian and earlier Masses only tempo deviations from a basic norm tended to be indicated.[22] Of course, when the composer was directing the performance, tempo markings were not absolutely necessary. But the ever-increasing dissemination of this church music prompted composers at this time to pay more attention to tempo and other expression marks.

The only factors which unify most Masses into a coherent cycle are key and scoring. In almost every Mass all five parts begin and end in the same central tonality.[23] The number of keys used as the main key of a Mass is limited. Major keys (especially C major and keys of one to three sharps or flats) are preferred. The tonalities E, B, and A-flat are relatively rare, while Masses based on C-sharp (D-flat), F-sharp (G-flat), and C-flat major are virtually non-existent during this period.[24] As Landon correctly points out, C major was the predominant key for Masses from 1750 to 1800; it was *the* key for *missae solemnes* using natural trumpets and timpani.[25] Minor keys, despite their potential appropriateness for the penitent mood of the opening Kyrie, are infrequently used as the central tonality, with such Masses often concluding in the parallel major.[26]

Within each part of the Mass composers usually seek variety in key, as will be seen later. Mode aside, key choice seems not to be based upon the various key characteristics so carefully delineated by Mattheson, Schubart and other theorists.[27] Rather, key selection is a practical matter chiefly affected by the following considerations:

1. The key's relationship to the central tonality of the Mass (e.g., use of the submediant for the "Christe" or the subdominant for the "Benedictus")

Figure 5-3. Movement Layouts of Monn's *Missa in C* (M. 38) and Vaňhal's *Missa Pastorell* in G (M. 65)

Monn's Missa in C (M. 38, 1741)					Text	Vaňhal's Missa Pastorell in G (M. 65, before 1782)				
I. Adagio	C 3/4	in C	22 m.	chorus	Kyrie (slow)	—				
Allegro	"	"	163 m.	chorus & soloists	Kyrie (fast)	I. Allegro moderato	3/4	in G	164 m.	chorus & soloists
II. Allegro	C	in C	35 m.	chorus	Gloria	II. Allegro moderato	¢	in G	65 m.	chorus
III. Andante	3/4	in G	122 m.	SA duet	Laudamus					
IV. Un poco allegro ma non molto	C	in e	58 m.	chorus	Gratias					
					Domine Deus, Rex	III. Andante molto	3/8	in C	131 m.	SA duet & chorus
V. Adagio-Andante-Presto-Adagio	C-3/2-C	in C-F	62 m.	chorus	Qui tollis					
VI. Allegro ma non troppo	¢	in d	205 m.	B solo	Quoniam	Allegro	3/4	in G	100 m.	chorus
VII. Adagio-Allegro	C	in C	90 m.	chorus	Cum Sancto					
VIII. Allegro	C	in C	42 m.	chorus	Credo	IV. Allegro moderato	3/4	in G	93 m.	chorus
IX. Adagio	C	in c-g	34 m.	SATB solos	Et incarnatus	V. Adagio	2/4	in D-b	33 m.	SATB solos & chorus
X. Allegro	3/4	in C	52 m.	chorus & S solo	Et resurrexit	VI. Allegro moderato	3/4	in G	150 m.	chorus
Andante un poco	C	in C-G	55 m.	"	Et in Spiritum					
XI. Allegro-Adagio	3/4	in C	18 m.		Et expecto					
--(Allabreve)--	¢	"	155 m.	chorus	Et vitam					
XII. Andante	C	in C	9 m.	T solo	Sanctus	VII. Adagio	3/4	in G-D	22 m.	chorus
Allegro	"	"	26 m.	chorus	Pleni sunt coeli	VIII. Allegro	2/4	in G	19 m.	chorus
					Osanna I	IX. Allegro	3/8	in G	38 m.	chorus
XIII. Allegro	C	in a	70 m.	chorus	Benedictus	X. Andante	2/4	in G	104 m.	chorus
					Osanna II	XI. Allegro	3/8	in G	38 m.	chorus
XIV. Adagio	C	in c	15 m.	AS solos & chorus	Agnus Dei	XII. Adagio	3/4	in g	47 m.	chorus
Allegro	C	in c	88 m.	chorus	Dona nobis	Allegro moderato	2/4	in G	116 m.	SATB solos & chorus

2. The key's relationship to the keys of adjacent movements (e.g., third relationships common at "Quoniam" and "Et resurrexit," contrasts of mode at "Christe," "Qui tollis," and "Et incarnatus," etc.)

3. The key's suitability for the instruments and voices used

In discussing the Masses of Fux, Riedel makes an observation that relates to the last factor named above:

> The tonal structure of the Masses was critically determined by the trumpets since all sections with trumpets had to be in C major. Excursions into other keys were thus only possible in the "trumpet-free" sections. Narrow limits were placed on the modulatory scheme above all in the closing movements because composers often preferred to have the trumpet choir flourish climactically only for the final cadences.[28]

Use of English horns may have been the practical reason why Haydn wrote his *Grosse Orgelsolomesse* (Hob. XXII: 4, before 1774) in the rather unusual key of E-flat.[29]

There are just over 100 movements for solo voice in the sample under study, with soprano arias being most common (over two-fifths of the examples). Perhaps because of their usual position as inner movements, such solos generally make use of a greater variety of keys than do the overall Masses themselves. For instance, about a third of the solos are in minor keys. Voice range must also have played a role in the selection of keys for arias. Almost one-third (14 of 46) of all soprano solo numbers are in G major; A minor and B minor are also commonly found keys for this voice.[30] A more equal distribution of keys is found for the other voice parts, although alto arias are most frequently in F major (seven of 20 examples); the most common keys for tenor arias are F and A (both four of 19), for bass arias, G and C (six and five, respectively, of 21).

Before leaving harmonic considerations, a few additional comments about tonal movement within the Masses are in order. Modulation is often closely allied with the text at this time. As will be seen, "Qui tollis peccata mundi," "Et incarnatus," and "Agnus Dei" are commonly marked by chromaticism and harmonic instability. Imperfect cadences are frequently used at the ends of inner movements so as to avoid the sound of complete closure and to thereby generate greater continuity over an entire part of the Mass.[31] Looking at the period as a whole, we find a trend away from tonal variety within movements. This change parallels the move toward multiplicity of themes and motivic development—traits which arose as composers abandoned the practice of maintaining only one "Affekt" per movement.

Scoring also helps make a unified cycle of the Mass. By choosing from the same group of soloists and instruments throughout a Mass, the composer lends greater continuity from one part to the next. For example, one or two instruments are sometimes given obbligato solos in each part of the Mass.[32] Certainly the triumphant clarini heard at the end of Ferdinand Schmidt's *Missa Sanctae Caeciliae in C* (ex. 10-15) recall those which open the Mass (ex. 6-3) and strengthen the work's unity. Most composers also allow each vocal soloist to be heard at least once in every part of the Mass.[33] Beginning and ending each part of the Mass with the full chorus is another integrating element.

Neither melodic reiteration nor variation technique plays a major role in unifying these Masses. Except for the frequent settings of the "Dona nobis" which reuse music from the Kyrie (see fig. 10-7) or the occasional fugue that ends both the Gloria and Credo (see fig. 7-16), each part of the Mass is melodically independent. Common melodic recurrences within each part include repeating "Kyrie I" for "Kyrie II" (after the "Christe") and using the same "Osanna in excelsis" before and after the "Benedictus." The more interesting melodic repetitions are those which are actually variations or derivatives of the original versions (see ex. 7-5; 10-1). Linking together separate movements of the whole Mass with a returning accompaniment figure, as in Reutter's *Missa Sancti Placidi in C* (M. 44, Hofer No. 33), is relatively rare at this time.[34]

In sum, key and scoring are the primary means of unifying these Masses. Melodic connections between movements are rarely found except in the few places where, by tradition, music was sometimes repeated. In this repertoire composers constantly sought contrast from movement to movement.[35] Usually each part of the Mass was a separate entity in and of itself, often equaling in dimensions and variety a contemporary symphony. As the remaining chapters will show, unity was still strongest at the movement level. The more comprehensive and audible cyclic unity associated with the Romantic era was only foreshadowed at this time.

Musical Style and Text Treatment

> Thus, whether he begins in a major or minor key, a good composer who understands Latin can design his movement according to the words *(nach den Wörten)*, sometimes with a different tonality, sometimes with another tempo, sometimes with unexpected turns of phrase or chords, sometimes with high or low notes, sometimes with *piano* or *forte* etc.[36]

This advice from Albrechtsberger to novice composers of church music in 1790 accurately reflects the aesthetic behind most of the Masses under discussion. Ultimately the unalterable liturgical text was the principal determinant of form in all these works, and the best composers chose their styles "according to the words." Accordingly, much attention will be devoted to musico-textual relationships in the analytic discussions of the remaining chapters.

As James Dack has suggested, composers tended to approach the Mass text in one of two ways:[37] either they created a multi-sectional setting arising from a line-by-line treatment of the text, or they adopted an independent musical design. The first approach is commonly found in settings of the longer texts, e.g., the Gloria and Credo, where the number and character of the verses foster an efficient form. In the second approach a musical structure such as ternary form, binary aria, sonata, rondo, or fugue supports a relatively short text (e.g., the "Kyrie," "Benedictus," and "Dona"). Obviously this latter approach allows the composer much more freedom because he can do things like choose melodies, repeat words and phrases, or modulate to new keys according to a design that was not imposed upon him by the text.

By no means are these two approaches mutually exclusive; combinations are found. Time and evolving traditions can eventually transmute a musical structure that closely follows the text into a conventional form. For example, composers often used similar tripartite designs for the "Kyrie" (in a single movement), the "Qui tollis," and the "Agnus Dei." Which approach do they represent, the line-by-line or the independent approach? It is difficult to say, since the texts themselves are tripartite. In many settings the three "Agnus Dei" invocations use the same melody, and the harmony modulates at "miserere nobis." Are these similarities the results of composers individually using the line-by-line approach, or have these similarities already become part of the musical vernacular of the Mass? Admittedly, these distinctions are not always sharp; and the insights they reveal about stylistic development will remain negligible until there is a more solid chronology for the church music of this period.

The form and style of a Mass also depended upon factors other than the text and the composer's volition. The degree of solemnity, the time allotted for performance, the available performers and soloists, and other local conditions must have influenced many compositional decisions. Unfortunately information about such details remains scarce and often cannot be directly related to specific Masses and their designs.

Because multi-sectional parts such as the "Gloria in excelsis Deo" and "Credo in unum Deum" are so closely tied to their texts, generalizations about them are best left for the detailed analyses in the remaining chapters. It should be said, however, that in these movements the musical rhetoric of the Baroque era remains alive, especially where the quantity of words offers a bounty of opportunities for hypotyposis (word painting), exclamatio, parrhesia, pathopoeia, noema, suspiratio, and other musical figures.[38] The remainder of this chapter will concentrate upon movements which have been more or less freed from the text and built upon existing musical forms.

In the Masses there are five basic vocal textures:

Choral
1. Polyphonic choruses (with or without solos) (ex. 6-4B, 6-15A, 6-19; 7-2, 7-11, et al.)
2. Homophonic, declamatory choruses (with or without solos) (ex. 6-1, 6-3, 6-12, 6-13; 7-1, et al.)
3. Choruses in the mixed style combining 1 and 2 (ex. 6-6, 6-8, 6-9, 6-10, 6-17, 6-20, et al.)

Solo
4. Homophonic arias for solo voice (ex. 7-12, 7-13, 7-19, 7-20, 7-24, et al.)
5. Solo ensembles of two or more voices (homophonic/polyphonic) (ex. 7-6, m. 25ff.; 7-10, et al.)

Movements that open or close a part of the Mass usually have the choral textures 1, 2, or 3. Textures 4 and 5, however, are usually reserved for inner movements such as the "Christe," "Gratias," "Et incarnatus," and "Benedictus." Texture 1 is manifest in the fugues and fugatos often used to end each part of the Mass; it is the descendant of the a cappella *stile antico*, the style about which Christian Friedrich Michaelis wrote in 1814: "Religious concepts carry the stamp of eternity, and music cannot express this better than by the marvelous art of counterpoint, of canonic, and fugal writing, which has been brought into contempt only through injustice, irresponsibility, and ignorance."[39] In all fugues of concerted Masses at this time, instruments (at least strings and continuo) played *colla parte,* i.e., they doubled the choral voices. Texture 2 undoubtedly derives from the Venetian polychoral style of the preceding century, while texture 3 is the newer *stile misto* discussed by Fux, Spiess, and others.[40] Textures 4 and 5 are descendants of Italian secular monody and opera (especially Neapolitan) of the previous century. In demonstrating the eclectic nature of these Masses, one might name the first four of these textures the Roman, Venetian, Viennese, and Neapolitan styles. Such labels, however, only tend to solidify false stereotypes associated with these cities. More significantly, these textural types parallel some of the various styles cited by eighteenth-century theorists in their discussions of church style. For example, the "motet" and "madrigal" styles in Mattheson's *Der vollkommene Kapellmeister* are equivalent to textures 1 and 4; his "instrumental style" is present in the orchestral accompaniments to the Masses.[41]

During the period under study the degree to which these textures were employed was changing. By the 1770s the fugal and solo textures (nos. 1 and 4) were serving less and less for isolated movements. At this later time fugues seldom matched the intricacy, craftsmanship, and scope of those found in earlier Masses (e.g., Holzbauer, Monn, Tuma, and others). Rather, fugue had come to be employed more as a section of a movement rather than a movement by itself. Independent arias, such as those found at several points in Masses by Dittersdorf, Hasse, Hofmann, Holzbauer, Krottendorfer, Martínez, Monn, Reutter, F. Schmidt, and Tuma, were also beginning to appear less frequently. Instead, solos were integrated more and more into movements for chorus (texture 3) or solo ensemble (texture 5). The "Benedictus" remained the only section commonly set for soloists. The aged *Hofkapellmeister* Bonno especially liked the alternation of chorus and soloists in the several Masses he wrote in the late 1770s and early 1780s; in fact, there are no separate solo movements in any of his Masses.[42] This trend away from arias toward mixed ensembles of chorus and soloists possibly reflects contemporary developments in genres such as the concerto, symphony, and operatic finale. The change may also have been part of the reaction to demands for fewer operatic traits in the church music. In any case, the skill of the younger composers in this study (e.g., Gassmann, Dittersdorf, Sonnleithner, and Vaňhal) can often be measured by how deftly they use and combine the various textures described above.

Although their mandate was to set every word, composers occasionally would repeat, rearrange, or even omit some words of the Mass.[43] Interesting are the changes in text caused not by oversight but by the demands of the music. Obviously in movements set to short texts (e.g., solo arias) word repetitions cannot be avoided (see ex. 7-12, 7-13, 7-20, and 7-24). In choral movements word repetitions often add an effective stress to significant words like "pax" at "Et in terra pax" and "non" at "non erit finis" (see ex. 7-6, 7-15, 7-17, 8-18). Occasionally there are repetitions because one movement ends with the same words that begin the next movement or section (e.g., "Dona nobis pacem" in M. 65). In the eighth chapter we shall see how the so-called Credo Masses augment musical unity by periodically repeating the word (and melody to) "Credo." Yet, when the liturgy requires that certain words (e.g., "Kyrie eleison," "Qui tollis," "Sanctus," and "Agnus Dei") be repeated once or twice, composers do not always comply; often for musical reasons there are too many or too few repetitions of the words.[44]

The most ubiquitous (and infamous) rearrangement of the Mass text is found in the telescoping or polytextuality of the more dogmatic verses in the Gloria and Credo of a *missa brevis*. To dispose of lengthy texts in a few measures and thereby keep the movements brief, composers had the different voice parts sing different segments of the Mass text simultaneously. For example, the Gloria of Haydn's *Missa brevis in F* (Hob. XXII: 1) or his *Kleine Orgelmesse* (XXII: 7) produces babel not unlike that of a medieval polytextual motet.[45]

Sonnleithner often takes liberties with the text. In two of his Glorias (M. 56 and 58) we find "et conglorificamus te" instead of "glorificamus te"; in the Agnus Dei of three Masses (M. 56–58) he presents the words "miserere nobis" a third time, i.e., after the third "Agnus Dei" which is supposed to be followed directly by the "Dona." (The latter instances allow Sonnleithner a greater musical symmetry in the tripartite form derived from the "Agnus Dei" text.) Some other kinds of textual rearrangements and repetitions caused by the musical structure may be seen in the "Gloria" (m. 36ff.) and "Quoniam" (m. 41ff.) of Gassmann's *St. Cecilia Mass*. In four Masses (Hob. XXII: 9–12) Joseph Haydn omits "Qui ex Patre Filioque procedit." No one really knows why. Thus we should realize that, despite all the papal bulls and imperial decrees outlawing such textual corruptions, composers did exert some creative influence over the treatment of the text, especially during the final quarter of the century.

Along with the changing textures and rhetorical figures, several vocal styles contribute to the heterogeneous style that characterizes most of these Masses. One finds coloratura arias, buffa arias, "rage" arias, recitative, and even dance-like numbers. The florid coloratura of some arias testifies to the extraordinary abilities of the singers for whom composers were writing these solos. Significant words in the text are frequently underscored by extensive runs, e.g., "eleison" (ex. 6-18, m. 16ff.), "glorificamus" (ex. 7-6, m. 15f.; ex. 7-7, m. 15f.), "gloriam" (ex. 7-6, m. 21f.), "Laudamus" (ex. 7-12), "Jesu" (ex. 7-21, m. 34f.; ex. 7-24, m. 19f.), etc.[46] Often such melismas are preceded by a calm passage of longer notes which may allow the singer an expressive *messa di voce* (ex. 7-13, m. 33f.). Vienna's bass soloists must have had particularly agile techniques, considering the sizeable leaps (often a tenth or more) frequently demanded of them during florid passages (see the elevenths in ex. 7-21). The influence of *opera buffa* seems strong when voices sing phrases consisting of short repeated motives covering a wide range at a fast pace (ex. 7-23; ex. 10-16). *Sturm und Drang* elements such as the minor mode, syncopated motives, dynamic accents, etc. occur in some tempestuous numbers that could be called rage arias.[47] A few solos even include a fermata that provides an opportunity for a cadenza (see ex. 10-15, m. 62). Sometimes the influence of dance music is observable in movements using triple meter at a moderately fast tempo; often we are reminded of the melodic style and phrasing of the minuet (ex. 5-1 and ex. 6-12).

Masses show the influence of the theater style perhaps most obviously in movements which resemble accompanied recitative. Although secco recitatives are never found in these works, the inherently more "dramatic" texts (e.g., "Qui tollis peccata mundi," "Crucifixus," and "Agnus Dei") occasionally inspire composers like Carl, Dittersdorf, Holzbauer, Monn, Schmidt, and Tuma to use the musical inflection, disjunct vocal line, rhythmic

Example 5-1.   Marianne von Martinez, *Terza Messa*, M. 36 (1761),
Sanctus (Andante), measures 1–8.

irregularity, and sustained instrumental chords of accompanied recitative (ex. 7-9, m. 14f.; 7-26; 8-16; 10-4E; 10-5). Whether for soloists or chorus, such recitatives do much to enliven the Mass when they occur.[48]

Most of the time, any vocal passage marked "solo" in the score or parts is distinguished in several ways from the sections marked "tutti." Generally such a vocal solo:

1. has a more florid melody, often including long runs and large leaps
2. is part of a more transparent and contrapuntal texture
3. has a much lighter orchestral accompaniment (usually only the violins and continuo)
4. has "solo" also indicated in the organ continuo part (usually)

In other words, these "solo" passages are more soloistic in style than the tutti (i.e., choral) sections. (For examples of these two styles juxtaposed see ex. 6-8, 6-9, 6-10, 6-12, 6-18; 7-1, 7-3, 7-6, 7-7, 7-8, 7-9, 7-10, et al.) Although in some instances the "solo" marking might simply be a warning to the singers (as in modern orchestral parts) that the passage so marked is sung apart from the rest of the chorus (i.e., it is exposed), the more florid style of these "solos" supports the belief that only one singer (probably the most able member of that section of the chorus) sang them. More research is needed before we can be sure just how many singers generally performed these Masses in church.[49]

Forms

The most commonly used form for the closed solo numbers in these Masses is the binary aria. This scheme is the basis for most vocal duets, trios, and quartets, as well as for solos. Its format is actually that of the first part of a *da capo* aria, that is, the first stanza (the *A* section) which is repeated *"da capo"* at the end. Complete *da capo* arias *(ABA)* are virtually never found in these Masses because the form is incompatible with the ongoing liturgical text.[50] Often given to comprimario characters in opera, the binary aria consists of two vocal strains: one modulating to a related key (V or vi in major, III or v in minor keys), the other strain returning to the tonic. Each strain is articulated by a full cadence at its end. As can be seen in figure 5-4, instrumental ritornellos precede and follow both strains so as to provide an introduction, interlude, and closing that successively confirm each of the three main key areas.

Usually the ritornello of a binary aria shares its melody with the vocal section (ex. 7-12, 7-19), although the older generation of composers tends to give the ritornello a separate melodic and rhythmic character (ex. 7-20, 7-24, and 9-5). Sometimes the instrumental ritornello is an elaborated version of the

Figure 5-4. Outline of the Typical Binary Aria

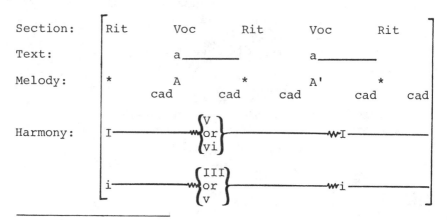

Rit = Ritornello (instruments only)
Voc = Vocal sections
cad = cadence
*Ritornello melodies may or may not be related to those of the voice.

melody to be presented by the voice (ex. 9-10). The complete text is generally repeated for the second vocal section (*A'* in fig. 5-4) which normally opens with the same melody as the first vocal section (ex. 7-12, 7-24).[51]

Ternary (three-part) arias occur less frequently in the Masses and date mostly from before 1750.[52] This form is similar to that for most of the arias and duets in Bach's *B-minor Mass* ("Laudamus," "Qui sedes," "Quoniam," and "Et in unum Dominum"). It follows the same pattern as the binary aria except that another vocal strain and ritornello are sandwiched between the two vocal strains of the binary form so that an additional related key (usually vi or IV in major, v in minor keys) may be heard (see fig. 5-5). Again the complete text is usually heard in each strain. Ternary arias exhibit a greater variety in melodic form than binary arias. The third vocal strain may begin like the previous two strains (e.g., "Christe," m. 100 of Gassmann's *St. Cecilia Mass,* or m. 138 of Reutter's *Missa Sancti Caroli* [M. 49, *DTÖ* 88, p. 7]). In other instances, since we have already heard melody *A* twice, the final strain presents a new melody (e.g., "Christe," m. 43 of Monn's *Missa in D* [M. 40], or m. 58 of Bach's *B-minor Mass,* and "Laudamus," m. 33 of Holzbauer's *Missa in C* [M. 30]). In some instances each strain begins with a new vocal melody (e.g., "Laudamus" in both Reutter's *Missa Sancti Caroli* [M. 49; *DTÖ* 88, pp. 17ff.] and Bach's *B-minor Mass*).

Thus by no means were these aria forms strictly adhered to in every case. A variety of modifications could occur. The ritornello might be omitted at the beginning or end to allow a more direct vocal connection with an adjacent

Figure 5-5.   Outline of the Typical Ternary Aria

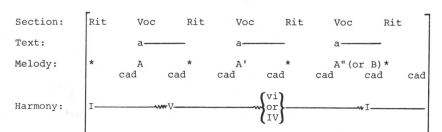

(For abbreviations see fig. 5-4)

movement (e.g., "Gratias" of M. 57, "Benedictus" of M. 52 and 53). A vocal strain might modulate to an unexpected key (e.g., "Crucifixus" of M. 51 goes to ii instead of V or vi). Rather than confirm a key, a ritornello might modulate to a new key *before* the voice reenters (e.g., "Benedictus" of Monn's *Missa in D* [M. 40, ex.9-5, m. 53–68] or Hasse's *Mass in D Minor* [M. 24, m. 29–35]).[53] In the "Benedictus" of Sonnleithner's *Missa in C* (M. 55; before 1765) the penultimate ritornello modulates back to the tonic so that a sonata-like "double reprise" (thematic and harmonic) occurs at the start of the final vocal strain.[54] After about 1760, such "double reprises" during the final vocal strain increase in frequency in these Masses. The relationship of these reprises to the developing sonata form remains to be examined in depth.

Another modification of the binary and ternary arias creates what is known as the "motto aria" (Ger. *Devisenarie*). Here the opening phrase of the vocal soloist is sung (with or without a preceding ritornello) and then immediately repeated with its continuation after an intervening ritornello (see ex. 7-12, 7-19, 7-20; 9-5). As Reichert notes, motto arias were common in Masses during the first half of the eighteenth century;[55] during the present period they were becoming less and less fashionable. Just the same, Boog, Hofmann, Monn, and Ferdinand Schmidt continued to include effective motto arias in some of their Masses.[56]

Occasionally we encounter a "one-part" solo number consisting of a single vocal strain with or without enclosing ritornellos (ex. 9-8).[57] That so many of these examples are short "Benedictus" settings perhaps indicates that composers were reacting to the exigencies of the ongoing liturgy at this high point of the Mass.

The lengths of solo numbers vary extensively according to the overall size and solemnity of a particular Mass, as well as according to the form and meter in use. Binary solos range from 13 measures ("Benedictus" in M. 53, a *missa brevis*) to 134 measures ("Benedictus" in M. 17, a *missa longa*). For ternary solos the range extends from 35 measures ("Benedictus" in M. 39, a *missa longa*) to 205 measures ("Quoniam" in M. 38, a *missa longa*).

Solo quartets occur with increasing frequency throughout the period under study. Just over half of the Masses in the sample have at least one section requiring a quartet of vocal soloists. "Crucifixus," "Agnus Dei," "Laudamus te," and "Benedictus" (in that decreasing order) are the texts where such quartets commonly occur (see ex. 6-8, 6-12; 7-6, 7-10; 8-1, 8-4; 9-8, 9-16A, B, D; 10-2, 10-6A, 10-12, 10-13, 10-16). The trend in such numbers was away from the contrapuntal quartet of soloists singing successively alone or in pairs (ex. 7-6, 7-10; 8-1; 9-8; 10-2, 10-12, 10-13, 10-16) toward the more homophonic quartets such as we hear in Gassmann's *St. Cecilia Mass* ("Christe," "Qui tollis," and "Agnus Dei") or Vaňhal's *Missa Pastorell* (ex. 6-12).

As we stated earlier, most choral movements which are not fugues have multi-sectional forms that closely parallel the changing text. These will be discussed separately in each of the remaining chapters. In some movements that follow the aria forms discussed above, the chorus either (1) alternates with the soloists, usually entering at the end of each solo strain (e.g., "Quoniam" of M. 39, "Christe" of M. 24), or (2) enters only after the final solo strain (e.g., "Gratias" of M. 50, "Quoniam" of M. 55).

After about 1760, elements of sonata form (e.g., double reprise, thematic functionalism and development) begin to appear in the choruses of these Masses, often mixed with characteristics of the concerto and rondo. Composers of such "progressive" choral movements include Albrechtsberger, Bonno, Dittersdorf, Gassmann, J. Haydn, Martínez, Mozart, Reutter, Sonnleithner, and Vaňhal (see ex. 6-10–12; 7-4; 9-7; 10-11, 10-12). A deterrent to the use of these forms containing a reprise was the ongoing liturgical text. Thus they are used mostly for texts which are short (e.g., "Benedictus"), tripartite (e.g., Kyrie), or which syllabically allow the same music to be used for two different sections of the text (e.g., "Gloria"="Quoniam").

During this period, choral fugues continued to be used often as grand conclusions for each new part of the Mass, especially in the more solemn *missae longae* (e.g., Gassmann's *St. Cecilia Mass*). As we saw in the discussion of church style at the end of chapter 2, fugue was often considered the highest style; for eighteenth-century composers its learned counterpoint best reflected the power, perfection, and perpetuity of the God and church being renewed by the Mass.[58] Unlike chamber music—where fugue had experienced a decline and then a rebirth in Vienna during the 1770s—the Mass and its traditions continued to encourage fugal writing after the death of Fux. Few composers totally avoided fugue in their Masses, although *missae breves* usually lacked extensive fugal writing. Fortunately most composers varied their textures during a Mass and seemed to heed Mattheson's advice: "Fugues are pleasing and nice; but an entire work of nothing but fugues is without vigor and is unpleasant...."[59] Because fugue was essentially an unchanging stylistic artifact in these Masses (i.e., following the usual procedure of two or three expositions separated by episodes, with stretto, inversion, diminution, etc. during the later expositions) the following chapters will not discuss fugal movements in any great detail. Closer study would undoubtedly show trends similar to those discussed by Kirkendale in *Fugue and Fugato in Rococo and Classical Chamber Music* (e.g., influence of galant style upon the subject, increasing use of dynamic and tempo markings, long homophonic episodes, absence of certain contrapuntal artifices, and influence of binary form).

Separate instrumental movements are rarely included in these Masses. The two occurrences in the present sample are early and very short, single-movement sinfonie preceding the Kyrie (see ex. 6-3 and 6-4).[60] Otherwise instruments play alone only in the ritornellos of solo numbers (ex. 7-12 et al.) or in the often lengthy introductions to choral movements (ex. 6-2, 6-5–7; 7-1; 9-13 et al.). The length of such instrumental introductions seems to have been mostly a function of the degree of solemnity desired for a Mass, although the developing genre of the symphony may have influenced their growth during the second half of the century. Composers exposed to the Italian Mass tradition (e.g., Bonno, Gassmann, Hasse, Holzbauer, Martínez, et al.) were especially fond of extended orchestral introductions to their choruses.

Contrafacta and Cantus Firmus Technique

As anyone acquainted with the music of Handel and Bach realizes, the age-old techniques of contrafacta and cantus firmus remained in use during the eighteenth century.[61] Haydn occasionally based a movement upon preexistent material (e.g., Symphonies No. 26 "Lamentatione," 30 "Alleluja," and 45 "Farewell," the Sanctus of the *Heiligmesse*, and the late *Te Deum* for the Empress).[62] Similarly, here and there (especially in the Masses of Reutter and Hasse) one encounters what may or may not be an old chant buried in the counterpoint (see ex. 5-2). These tunes usually occur at the start of the Gloria, Credo, or Sanctus, or in the "Benedictus."[63] Finding such melodies depends on one's recognizing a large repertoire of tunes known to eighteenth-century composers. Future research will undoubtedly uncover more examples of this practice as well as identify many of the cantus firmi. In any case, the incorporation of known liturgical melodies shows the concern of some composers for better integration of their concerted settings into the entire Mass with all its additional ceremony and chant.

Example 5-2.   Georg von Reutter, Jr., *Missa Sancti Placidi in C,*
              M. 44 (before 1756), "Gloria" (Andante), measures
              1–5.

Summary

Form and style in these Masses are primarily functions of the text and of a
longstanding tradition of musico-rhetorical figures associated with specific
words. For most analyses, the text must be the point of departure because of
its extensive control over the musical design. Although each Mass was
conceived as a cycle unified by one principal key and one basic scoring, we

Example 5-2   (concluded)

cannot view these settings as cyclic works in the nineteenth-century sense, especially when we take into account 1) the liturgical ceremony and additional music that would interrupt the flow of a concerted Mass, and 2) the performance flexibility (e.g., substitution movements) that existed. In addition, aside from some traditional musical repetitions (e.g., Kyrie=Dona nobis pacem), most composers were not trying to achieve cyclic unity by means of thematic relationships between different parts of the Mass. Thus, it is appropriate that the analyses in the remaining chapters will discuss separately each of the five principal parts of the Mass.

Nonetheless, composers did show concern for the relative lengths of their Masses. Whether a work was intended to be a *missa brevis* or a *missa longa* seems to have had a decisive effect upon the style of a Mass. Using the lengths of Haydn's and Mozart's Masses as arbitrary guides, one finds that settings with *missa longa* characteristics have a total of at least 570 measures (see fig. 5-1). Within a Mass, the Kyrie-Gloria complex frequently accounts for a disproportionately large and elaborate segment of the entire Mass, as composers often seem to have lavished more attention upon this "concert" which precedes the "business" of the Holy Eucharist. During the period under study, some aspects of the *missa brevis* began to influence the typical design of a *missa longa*. For example, after mid-century each part of a multi-movement *missa longa* usually consisted of no more than four movements each. In other words, there was a trend toward Masses with fewer (although often longer) movements.

Composers' concern for contrast from movement to movement was generally manifest in the changing succession of meters, tempos, keys, vocal textures, vocal styles, and scorings within each part of the Mass. There was a tendency toward greater variety in meter choice during the latter part of the present period as 2/4, 6/8, and 3/8 began to appear nearly as often as C, ¢, and 3/4. Most composers also became more explicit and accurate in their markings for tempo, articulation, and other elements of expression. Some five basic vocal textures, ranging from polyphonic choruses to solo arias and ensembles, were variously employed according to practices established by tradition for certain texts of the Mass. By the 1770s vocal solos tended to be integrated into the choral movements instead of occurring as isolated arias, duets, etc.

Harmonically each part of the Mass usually began and ended in the principal tonality. Because of an association with clarino trumpets, C major was the predominant key in these Masses, although tonalities of one to three sharps or flats were also employed. Keys used for inner movements seem dependent upon both context within the Mass part and the range of the solo voice(s) required. In addition, younger composers were beginning to explore harmonic contrast more within movements rather than between movements as Baroque composers had done.

The forms of these Masses result from either a multi-sectional line-by-line treatment of the text (e.g., most choruses) or the imposition of an existing musical form upon the text (e.g., binary and ternary arias). Designs combining both approaches are also found. Rudimentary traces of sonata form begin appearing in both solo and choral movements after about 1760. Most vocal solos are binary arias or derivatives thereof; *da capo* arias are virtually nonexistent. Throughout this period, fugues continued to serve as magnificent conclusions for many parts of the Mass, especially the Gloria and

Credo. Instrumental interludes are confined primarily to the ritornellos of solos and choruses; isolated sinfonie are a rarity. Occasionally the clarity or integrity of the text is compromised by polytextuality (especially in *missae breves*) or by the addition/subtraction of certain words. To a greater extent than is generally realized, preexistent melodies (often plainchants) occasionally formed the basis for certain movements of these Masses. This "cantus firmus technique" is only one of the many timeless traditions in which the generally conservative style of these Masses is steeped. We shall now investigate each part of the Mass separately and observe more closely the interplay of such traditions with the individual styles of the 28 composers under study.

6

Kyrie

A comparison of the Kyrie settings reveals several traits representative of the stylistic change in the Mass as a whole during this period. In the Kyrie there was a trend toward fewer but longer self-contained movements, greater variety of meters, stronger thematic and harmonic unity, fewer independent solo movements with further integration of vocal solos into choral movements, and some abandonment of fugal writing for the second "Kyrie." By the 1780s composers were viewing the Kyrie on a more integrated level than previously—i.e., as a single continuous movement rather than as three "eleison" invocations demanding to be treated separately.

Because of its short text the Kyrie affords enormous flexibility in musical structure. In his *Gradus* (1725) Fux suggested that brief texts such as the "Kyrie" and "Amen" should be lengthened by varying melody or adding new phrases *(novis subjectis)* to reduce tedium. [1] Accordingly, in many Viennese Kyries loud and stately introductions, ingratiating melodies at fast tempos, resounding choruses, and ornate vocal solos often greeted the recently arrived worshipers (though the music hardly suggested the penitence underlying this part of the service). Nonetheless, all composers recognized the Kyrie's important musical role of establishing the appropriate mood for the Mass as a whole: this opening section had to communicate the degree of solemnity of the occasion. Was it an ordinary Sunday Mass or a special one celebrating an important feast or event? With these concerns in mind, composers showed considerable freedom in their settings of the Kyrie's three simple lines.

Overall Structure

Perhaps taking their cue from plainchant, composers set the Kyrie's three invocations ("Kyrie I," "Christe," and "Kyrie II") in either a through-composed *(ABC)* or ternary (*ABA* or *ABA'*) form. [2] Viennese composers rarely adhered strictly to the threefold repetition of each "eleison" call. Word repetition was more a function of the musical form. In one to three movements the Kyrie's music reflected only the larger three-part structure of the text. The text controlled the music insofar as the Christe (usually the *B* section) was musically set off from the Kyries surrounding it, as figure 6-1 illustrates. The Kyrie is one of the few places in the Mass where a return in the text ("Kyrie eleison") allows a *da capo* repetition in the music.[3]

The present study has revealed that from about the mid-1750s Kyrie settings of one movement began to far outnumber multi-movement Kyries. Of some 27 Kyries dated between 1734 and 1754, only 11 (or 40%) consist of a single movement.[4] In the 37 Masses dated 1755-84, however, we find 31 (or 83%) with single-movement Kyries. This change reflects the gradual decrease in the use of multi-movement designs for the Mass as a whole during this period; it is one of several changes that may be traced to the *missa brevis* whose Kyrie rarely exceeded one movement. With one exception each, all of Haydn's and Mozart's Kyries agree with this trend by having single movements, with and without slow introductions.[5]

Figure 6-1.   Common Forms and Text Divisions of the Kyrie

Text:	Kyrie I	Christe	Kyrie II	
Common Musical Forms	A	B	C	
	A	B	A	
	A	B	A'	
Common Movement Distributions				(single)

The Opening

Most Masses begin with the full available orchestra, including trumpets and timpani if required. In 1737 Scheibe devoted a long paragraph to the inappropriateness of loud brass in this part of the Mass:

> The so-called Kyrie, however, is subjected to great and almost unnatural force. Very often it is set with trumpets and timpani without realizing that neither the opening words nor several later passages of this text can bear such a reveling din *(schwärmendes Getöne).* Nevertheless, certain circumstances compel many a sensible composer to accompany these imploring and supplicating words with such a clamor. The splendor of the courts, the mirth of the feasts, the joyful events that one wishes to celebrate, or even the esteem and glorious memory of the saint or lofty personage being worshiped—[all these conditions] force composers to express even mercy joyfully, magnificently, and martially. And so the pomp, the customs, and arrogant human vanity (which really should be absent when worshiping God) prevail even in the music.[6]

Scheibe was not alone in his complaints as the discussion above of eighteenth-century restrictions upon brass use has shown (see chapter 2). The fact remains that nearly every Kyrie immediately displays its full instrumentation, at least at the first tutti if not in the opening measures. The beginning of Hasse's *Missa in D* is typical (ex. 6-1).

Quite often the Kyrie opens with such a slow introduction for chorus and orchestra. In this case there are two "Kyrie I's," i.e., a slow one joined to a faster one. Such introductions are found in both single- and multi-movement Kyries and are characterized by brevity (2–8 measures in length), a slow tempo (almost always adagio followed by allegro), and an inconclusive cadence (usually half) at the end. The best known example is the opening of Bach's *B-Minor Mass* (B.W.V. 232). In some multi-movement Kyries both "Kyrie I" and "Kyrie II" are preceded by such an introduction.[7] The model for slow introductions seems to come from instrumental music, especially opera overtures and church sonatas. Introductions were already very common in Italian Masses from the end of the seventeenth century; in the first half of the eighteenth century we find them in Masses by Perti, Caldara, Fux, and Pergolesi.

These slow introductions set a solemn, dignified tone by the use of dotted rhythms, the full tutti sonority (no solos), and a basically homorhythmic texture. Leading from the tonic to an open, half-cadence upon the dominant, the section acts as a preparation (or "upbeat") to the Kyrie proper. A sense of expectancy can be aroused that seems appropriate for the clergy's entrance into the sanctuary. Hasse's *Missa in D* (ex. 6-1) has the shortest introduction encountered in this study; it demonstrates the usual tonal movement most succinctly. Haydn places introductions before six of his 13 extant Masses, four of these being in his six late Masses of 1796–1802.[8] Often, as in the Hasse example or in Haydn's *St. Cecilia Mass*, these introductions use the familiar rhythmic topos (♩. ♪ ♩) that is so common for the word "Kyrie" during the eighteenth century.[9] Most introductions are only 5 to 12 measures in length. However, two of Haydn's late Masses (Hob. XXII: 12 and 13) have introductions as long as 28 measures—much longer than those of most earlier Masses. Albrechtsberger, Dittersdorf, Martínez, Monn, and Vaňhal also wrote introductions longer than 12 measures.[10] The opening 22 bars of Monn's *Missa in C* (1741) provide one of the more dramatic examples of such extended slow introductions; unison orchestral writing, large downward leaps, abrupt pauses, and sudden mode shifts all contribute to this expression of the pathos inherent in the text (ex. 6-2). Short masses *(missae breves)* normally lack such introductions; composers probably felt that only longer, more festive Masses deserved to be so weightily framed.

Sometimes, as an alternative to the slow choral introduction, the orchestra plays either a ritornello or a separate sinfonia before the voices

Example 6-1.   Johann Adolf Hasse, *Missa in D,* M. 25 (before
1783), Kyrie (Adagio-Andante), measures 1–7.

Example 6-2. Mathias Georg Monn, *Missa in C,* M. 38 (1741), "Kyrie I" (Adagio), measures 1–22.

Example 6-2   (cont'd.)

Example 6-2   (cont'd.)

Example 6-2 (cont'd.)

Example 6-2   (concluded)

enter. In his musical yearbook for 1777 Kraus complained about such "noisy overtures" before the first choral Kyrie.[11] Short instrumental sinfonias before the first vocal movement were part of the Italian Mass tradition before the end of the seventeenth century. Several Bolognese Masses by G.P. Colonna, M. Cazzati, and G.A. Perti open with a two-movement sinfonia (slow-fast), which in some cases is musically related to the Kyrie that follows.[12] Such sinfonias were rare in Viennese Masses of the mid-eighteenth century; most Masses begin immediately with the chorus and instruments together.[13] In the 1740s, however, we still find examples of these separate "preludes." In Ferdinand Schmidt's *Missa Sanctae Caeciliae* a six-measure Allegro for clarino trumpets, violins, and continuo precedes the short Adagio introduction for chorus (ex. 6-3). Five measures later the Allegro fanfare returns as an 18-bar ritornello leading directly into the chorus. At the first entrance of the chorus (m. 7) a sudden shift to C minor, diminished seventh chords, and chromatic voice leading suggest that Schmidt may have been attempting to express the text's penitence which most composers overlooked.

Several of Ignaz Holzbauer's Masses include a short opening sinfonia of eight to twenty measures. Eduard Schmitt associates this practice with Venice where the composer had studied in the early 1730s.[14] Like the earlier Bolognese composers just mentioned, Holzbauer usually ties this sinfonia motivically to the fast Kyrie that follows. In his *Missa solemnis in F* (ex. 6-4) the theme of the sinfonia (A) does not return until after the "Christe" duet—transformed into the fugue subject for "Kyrie II" (B).

When Viennese composers use an instrumental introduction, it is usually a nonmodulating ritornello which is integrated into the choral Kyrie. These opening ritornellos are more often found in longer Masses and are one to twenty-eight measures in length. As in the case of slow introductions, these are usually absent in *missae breves*. Ritornellos have two important functions: 1) they establish and maintain the movement's principal affect; and for practical purposes, 2) they supply the chorus with its opening pitch. In most cases the ritornello figurations are used again later in the orchestral accompaniment for the entrance of the chorus.[15]

Quite often the melodic material of the ritornello is the same or an embroidered version of that sung by the chorus. This holds true for most of Joseph Haydn's Masses with ritornello openings (e.g., the *Great Organ Mass* [before 1744] or the *St. Nicholas Mass* [1772]). As example 6-5 shows, Marianne von Martínez's *Terza Messa* (M. 36; 1761) begins in this way—the orchestra plays the two contrasting themes of the Kyrie (marked x and y) before the chorus enters. (The rather dramatic use of the fermata over the rest in measure 8 reminds us of a device commonly used by Haydn.)

Obbligato instruments are often prominently displayed in the ritornello. In Reutter's *Missa Sancti Venantii* the ritornellos are played by the solo

Example 6-3. Ferdinand Schmidt, *Missa Sanctae Caeciliae,* M. 50
(before 1746), "Kyrie I" (Allegro-Adagio-Allegro),
measures 1–13, 30–36, and 85–107.

Example 6-3 (cont'd.)

Example 6-3   (concluded)

Example 6-4. Ignaz Holzbauer, *Missa in F,* M. 33 (before 1745),
"Kyrie I" Sinfonia (Allegro spiritoso), measures 1–4;
and "Kyrie II" (Allegro spiritoso), measures 1–16 of
the choral parts.

Example 6-5. Marianne von Martínez, *Terza Messa,* M. 36 (1761),
"Kyrie I" (Allegro), measures 1–15.

bassoon with string accompaniment; in the fifth measure the chorus and remainder of the orchestra enter with a contrapuntal treatment of the same theme, after which the bassoon returns for further solo interludes (ex. 6-6). The 21-bar introduction of Bonno's *Missa in C* (ex. 6-7) soon makes it quite obvious that this Mass is scored for obbligato oboes and bassoon. The *ripieno-concertino* effect borrowed from the old concerto grosso is unmistakable. By contrast, Haydn never so used his obbligato instruments for solo purposes at the outset of a Mass.

Another aspect reminding us of the concerto grosso is the alternation of tutti and solo voices during the Kyrie and later parts of the Mass. One-sixth of the Masses sampled here make use of such alternation during the Kyrie. (Solos were standard practice for the Christe and are discussed below.) The "Kyrie I" Allegro (following an adagio introduction) from Mathias Georg Monn's *Missa in D* shows a typical treatment (ex. 6-8). After the full chorus and orchestra state the main theme (m. 9ff.), the vocal *"concertino"* presents a contrasting melody (m. 23ff.) which is contrapuntally treated in a lighter texture supported only by the continuo. The Kyrie of Gassmann's *St. Cecilia Mass* uses soloists in the same way. Occasionally the solo voices themselves would open the Kyrie, saving the choral tutti until a few measures later—as we see in Ferdinand Arbesser's *Missa Sanctae Susannae* of the early 1750s (ex. 6-9). Such a solo soprano beginning is reminiscent of that heard in Haydn's *Missa Cellensis* (Hob. XXII: 8) of 1782 or Mozart's *Coronation Mass* (K. 317) of 1779. Study of many similar tutti-solo settings shows that pairs of solo voices are usually preferred; even if three or four vocal solists are required for the Kyrie, we hear them almost exclusively in pairs or by themselves, rarely all together. Probably the solo trio or quartet of voices created too dense a texture for the concertino effect still being sought.[16] The ideal sound appears to have remained the trio texture of two solo voices above the basso continuo. This sonority is frequently heard in the solo portions of several Kyries by Haydn and Mozart.[17]

Single-Movement Kyries

A majority of the Kyries in a single movement (26 of the 43 single movements examined) have a fast tempo (usually Allegro) and quadruple meter (C). At quick tempos these movements extend anywhere from 22 to 92 measures (58 average) for quadruple meter and often exceed 100 measures when the meter is triple. For slower tempos there are only about 40 measures on the average.

Single-movement Kyries generally fall into one of three formal types: 1) through-composed, 2) ternary with a literal reprise, and 3) ternary with a varied reprise. As figure 6-2 shows, most composers (or 31 of the 47 single-movement Kyries studied) including Haydn and Mozart prefer a rounded

Example 6-6. Georg von Reutter, Jr., *Missa Sancti Venantii,* M. 48
(before 1761), Kyrie (Andante), measures 1–8.

Example 6-6 (concluded)

Example 6-7. Giuseppe Bonno, *Missa in C*, M. 8 (before 1778),
Kyrie (Allegro e con spirito), measures 1-15.

Example 6-7　(cont'd.)

Example 6-7 (cont'd.)

Example 6-7 (concluded)

Example 6-8. Mathias Georg Monn, *Missa in D,* M. 40 (before 1750), "Kyrie I" (Allegro), measures 9–10 and 22–46.

Example 6-8 (cont'd.)

Example 6-8   (concluded)

Example 6-9. Ferdinand Arbesser, *Missa Sanctae Susannae*, M. 7
(before 1752), Kyrie (Allegro), measures 6–19 (Vln. II
part is missing).

Figure 6-2. Forms of Single-Movement Kyries*

	Kyrie I	Christe	Kyrie II	QUANTITY of Exx.	% of single mvts.
Through-composed	a	b	c	4	8.5%
Ternary	a	b	a	12	25.5%
Ternary (varied reprise)	a	b	a'	31	66.0%

*Lowercase letters are used because all components belong to a single movement.

aba' design with varied reprise. Modulation to a related key at the end of "Kyrie I" helps isolate the "Christe" middle section; and a melodic and harmonic return usually underscores the textual reprise of "Kyrie II." The three above forms were found to be fairly equally distributed over the entire period of this study. However, we must keep in mind that most of these single-movement Kyries are post-1754.

We can perceive the incipient sonata form in only eight of the 31 single-movement Kyries with *ABA'* form.[18] Most such examples are from the 1770s and later. The allegro Kyrie from Reutter's *Missa Sancti Mariani* (before 1759) is an early instance of this sonata treatment (ex. 6-10). Its form appears in figure 6-3.[19] Here we observe thematic differentiation (P and S themes), a full but varied reprise (m. 38), a short modulatory middle section ("Christe," m. 27-37), and a concluding coda (m. 54-73). Of course, in this relatively simple form there are no independent themes functioning for transitional and closing sections, there is little development, and (because the liturgical text must keep moving ahead) there are no repeat signs. Like a ritornello, the tutti P theme returns at several points (including the coda) and thereby reinforces the concerto grosso quality of this movement. (There are, however, no "true" ritornellos for orchestra alone; the chorus and orchestra together make up the *ripieno*). Thus, in its mixture of concerto and sonata form elements, Reutter's Kyrie is both conservative and progressive for its day. The following lists sort out these old and new elements:

Conservative Elements

1. Fugal opening
2. Unity of affect from
   the constantly repeated
   rhythm of the accompaniment
3. Concerto grosso aspects
   a) Ritornello-like use
      of P-theme
   b) Tutti-solo contrasts
4. Trio texture for solos
5. Melodic sequence (Sx)
6. Lack of dynamic indications
7. Hemiola
8. Figured bass

Progressive Elements

1. "Primitive sonata"
   (ternary) form
   a) Melodic function-
      alism, contrast
   b) Limited "development"
      of P theme
   c) Full, varied reprise
2. Kyrie in one movement
3. Triple meter

Reutter's fugal exposition of the main theme, which later returns in a homophonic texture (m. 38-42), is typical of this older generation's continued attempts to keep aspects of the Fuxian *stile antico* alive while assimilating the newer style. The movement is heard again later as the "Dona nobis pacem" at the end of the Mass.

Example 6-10. Georg von Reutter, Jr., *Missa Sancti Mariani*, M. 47 (1759), Kyrie (Adagio-Allegro), vocal score.

Example 6-10 (cont'd.)

Example 6-10 (cont'd.)

Example 6-10   (cont'd.)

Example 6-10 (concluded)

Figure 6-3. Structural Outline of the Kyrie (Allegro) to Reutter's *Missa Sancti Mariani*, M. 47 (before 1759)*

Text:	KYRIE I	KYRIE I			CHRISTE			KYRIE II						
		a			*b*			*a'*						
Forces:	Tutti	Tutti	Solo		Tutti			Tutti	Solo		Tutti			
Melody:	O	P	Sx	Y	P^1	P^2		P^3	Sx^1	y^1	P^4	$\dfrac{Sx^2(x^1)}{P^5(m)}$	P^6	P^7K
Measure:	1	5	17	23	27	31	34	38	42	48	54	58	65	68 (73)
Harmony:	I	I [=G] —V			—vi—			—I						
Section:	[Slow intro.]	[Exposition]			[Development]			[Reprise]				[Coda]		

Sx has some T character
Sy has K character

---

*On the symbols used see n. 19.

A similar synthesis of concerto and sonata elements is found in later Kyries by Haydn, Mozart, and their contemporaries.[20] There the "Christe" is likewise reserved for the middle *b* section that modulates from the dominant back to the tonic—usually via the submediant which conveniently supplies the minor mode that is normally used for the "Christe."

By the end of the 1770s the sonata characteristics have become much more conspicuous in many Kyries. Example 6-11 shows the principal themes for the Kyrie of Dittersdorf's *Missa in C.* The theme for the second key area (S) contrasts with the primary theme (P) by means of static repetitions of "Kyrie" on the same pitch and alternation between the sopranos and the rest of the chorus. For the "Christe" at measure 58 the soprano soloist enters with a new theme (N) that soon blossoms out into an impressive vocal display. In this "development" area we are taken to the submediant (A minor) and then past other keys (e.g., E minor) before returning to the tonic for Kyrie II. Vaňhal's *Missa Pastorell in G* offers yet another example of the sonata-like treatment of the Kyrie. Here the themes of the principal and secondary key areas—like those of many sonatas of the mid-eighteenth-century—are remarkably similar (see m. 20 and 32 in example 6-12). The regular four-bar phrasing speaks for its later date of composition. The frequent parallel thirds and the unusual drone accompaniment during the second key area (m. 36ff.) are some of the more obvious pastoral qualities explaining the title of the Mass. Again the "Christe"—this time for all four vocal soloists—is the modulatory section with the expected arrival upon the submediant (m. 99) before the return of the tonic (m. 109).

As for the other 23 single-movement Kyries in *aba'* form, their structures do not resemble that of the sonata because (1) they lack consistent thematic differentiation, (2) they often do not modulate to the dominant (or mediant) before the "Christe," (3) they have little trace of thematic development, or (4) they lack a simultaneous return of tonic and opening theme. Contrasting melody and harmonies are saved for the "Christe" passage, which is usually a solo. The opening *a* theme indeed returns for "Kyrie II," but it is soon varied in some way. As a result, this section usually parallels "Kyrie I" only at the start of the reprise.[21] This was also a common design for Haydn's and Mozart's single-movement Kyries.[22]

Often the *aba'* design is the result of a fugal treatment of the Kyrie.[23] In such instances the imitative counterpoint for the Kyrie subject is usually reworked in the reprise so that the tonic may be maintained to the end. In the *aba'* Kyrie of *Missa brevis in A* (M. 68) Wagenseil deftly compresses 20 measures of the "Kyrie I" into 13 measures for "Kyrie II" (m. 30-42) by omitting most of the opening contrapuntal duet of "Kyrie I" (m. 2-8).

Three of Christoph Sonnleithner's single-movement Kyries are striking because the principal theme returns in the submediant instead of the tonic key

Example 6-11. Karl Ditters von Dittersdorf, *Missa in C*, M. 15
(before 1773), Kyrie (Allegro), measures 15–22,
39–46, and 58–74.

Example 6-12.   Jan Vaňhal, *Missa Pastorell in G,* M. 65 (before
1782), Kyrie (Allegro moderato), measures 20–123.

(follows 19mm. orchestral intro.)

Example 6-12 (cont'd.)

Example 6-12 (cont'd.)

Example 6-12   (cont'd.)

Example 6-12   (cont'd.)

Example 6-12 (cont'd.)

Example 6-12   (cont'd.)

Example 6-12 (cont'd.)

Example 6-12 (cont'd.)

Example 6-12 (cont'd.)

Example 6-12   (cont'd.)

Example 6-12   (cont'd.)

Example 6-12 (concluded)

for "Kyrie II."[24] Thus the return of the tonic is delayed and is not coordinated with the start of "Kyrie II." For example, in Sonnleithner's *Missa sollemnis in C* (ex. 6-13) the Kyrie theme (m. 5ff.) does return after the "Christe," but it is in A minor and the contours have been slightly changed (m. 64ff.) Not until 11 measures from the end (m. 78) do we hear this theme firmly back in the tonic C major—again somewhat varied from its original shape.

The second most frequently encountered structure for single-movement Kyries (with and without slow introductions) is the *aba* type where "Kyrie II" is a literal repeat of "Kyrie I." Usually such scores are marked *Da Capo, Fine al segno* ⌒ , but sometimes the entire repetition of "Kyrie I" has been written out, as in Arbesser's *Missa Nubes pluant justum* (M. 6). Although this design for a Kyrie suggests little compositional imagination, it can be a satisfactory way of rounding out the whole movement. The *da capo* structure is found in Masses of all dimensions throughout the period under study.[25] Such movements tend to lack harmonic momentum, since the tonic is usually reaffirmed just before the Christe section. Haydn and Mozart, however, never resorted to this rather simplistic structure.

Occasionally, composers using this *aba* arrangement will vary only the final measures of "Kyrie II" (e.g., M. 28) or simply add a coda (ex. 6-14). These changes usually occur because "Kyrie I" does not end in the tonic. Boog's coda (ex. 6-14B, m. 61f.) presents an effective conclusion in the emphatic repetitions of "eleison" laid over modulating harmonies.

One inspired use of this *aba* design is found in Tuma's *Missa Sancti Stephani* where the "pathotype"[26] fugal subject of "Kyrie I" (ex. 6-15A) also generates the melody used for the ritornello and vocal duet of the "Christe" middle section (ex. 6-15B). *Kyrie da Capo sino al Segno* ⅜ *poi segue* is the instruction at the end of the "Christe." A pleasingly integrated *aba* structure results from the more homophonic "Christe" middle section being motivically related to the solid fugal expositions of the surrounding Kyries.

Only four of the 47 single-movement Kyries at hand have a through-composed tripartite structure.[27] This is probably an older, pre-1760 construction since it is frequently associated with fugal movements. In Wagenseil's *Missa Sancti Antonii in D* each of the three lines of text has a different subject which is treated imitatively (ex. 6-16A–C). As the example shows, "Kyrie II" employs double counterpoint. In his *Missa solenne Immaculatae Conceptionis* Wagenseil also uses a new melody for each part of the text (ex. 6-17A–C). Here, however, each section is also texturally varied as

Example 6-13. Christoph Sonnleithner, *Missa sollemnis in C,* M.
57 (before 1758), Kyrie (Adagio-Allegro), measures
1–18 and 59–81.

Example 6-13 (concluded)

Example 6-14. Johann Nepomuk Boog, *Missa in C*, M. 13 (before 1763), Kyrie (Allegro), measures 13–16 and 59–73.

Example 6-14 (concluded)

Example 6-15. Franz Tuma, *Missa Sancti Stephani,* M. 63 (before
1747), Kyrie (Allegro), measures 1–9 and 20–34.

Example 6-15 (concluded)

Example 6-16. Georg Christoph Wagenseil, *Missa Sancti Antonii in D,* M. 67 (before 1741), Kyrie (Allegro), measures 1–3, 21–23, and 32–33 of the soprano part, 32–33 of the alto part.

Example 6-17. Georg Christoph Wagenseil, *Missa solenne*
Immaculatae Conceptionis, M. 70 (1743), Kyrie
(Allegro), measures 1–3, 13–16, and 30–33.

Wagenseil attempts to maintain in a single movement the traits of older and longer cantatalike Masses:

Section	m.	Text	Vocal Forces	Texture
A	1–9	Kyrie I	Tutti	chordal homophony
B	10–30	Christe	Solo Soprano	arialike
C	31–65	Kyrie II	Tutti	fugue

Each section is directly joined with one another; there is no change in meter or tempo. The integrity of the whole is supported chiefly—like so many Kyries of the period—by the violin accompaniment with its recurring triplet figures that help unify the *Affekt*.

"Christe"

Following a centuries-old tradition, Viennese composers normally distinguished the "Christe" from the remainder of the Kyrie. A musical change at this point seems logical because "Christe eleison" is the first invocation of the God-man's name during Mass. To contrast this section with the preceding Kyrie, one or all of the following means were used:

1. New thematic material
2. Vocal solo(s), often highly ornate
3. Contrasting key (usually the submediant)
4. Starting a new movement (i.e., new tempo, meter, etc.)

Haydn and his Viennese contemporaries followed this practice, but Mozart quite often integrated the "Christe" text into the Kyrie.[28] Some of the above characteristics may be seen in the "Christe" excerpts of musical examples already cited (see ex. 6-9, 6-11, 6-12, 6-14–17).

Often the first entrance of the vocal soloist(s) is saved for the "Christe," the opening Kyrie supplications being sung by the impersonal chorus. The individuality of a solo voice at "Christe" adds a human warmth that is most appropriate for this text. In at least 60 of the 72 Masses examined (roughly 83%) the "Christe" involves solo singing—either as a separate movement or as the middle section of a larger single-movement Kyrie.[29] In fact, when solo singers are part of a Mass, the "Christe" is very rarely sung by the chorus alone. Viennese composers prefer using one or two high voices (i.e., soprano alone or soprano with alto) when the "Christe" forms the midsection of a larger single-movement Kyrie. Figure 6-4 shows the distribution of solo voices in "Christes" of the present sample.

Figure 6-4. "Christe" Soloist Use within Single-Movement Kyries

Solo Voice(s)				Quantity of Examples
S	A			11
S				10
S	A	T	B	5
		T	B	4
S			B	3
			B	2
S	A	T		1
S	S			1
S		T		1
	A	T		1
		T		1

Joseph Ziegler's *Missa in C* provides an example of the coloratura often demanded for such a "Christe" solo interlude.[30] In typical fashion the soprano soloist has a few sustained tones before releasing the outpouring of runs, triplets, trills, and *alla zoppa* rhythms. In addition, the e^2 sustained for six beats (m. 19–20) offers the soloist a chance to display the *messa di voce* and prepares the florid climax that follows (ex. 6-18).

A tradition from the previous generation of Fux and Caldara, the "Christe" as a separate movement is found mostly in long Masses that exceed 500 measures in total length. In the 20 independent "Christe" movements examined, there is again a preference for solos by the upper two voices.[31] New tempo, key, meter, instrumentation, as well as an increased lyricism, all help set such a "Christe" apart as the "middle movement" of the entire Kyrie. Figure 6-5 provides a survey of these "Christe" movements. Nearly every composer changes mode for this movement, and more than half of the examples are in the relative minor or major. Less frequently used keys are the subdominant and dominant. Andante is the typical tempo, and most "Christes" are closed movements (i.e., they conclude with a full cadence). Among the Masses of Albrechtsberger, Holzbauer, Monn, Predieri, and Wagenseil there are a few "Christes" which are linked to the following movement ("Kyrie II") by means of either a half-cadence or rhythmic dovetailing (enjambement).[32]

Lengths of these independent "Christes" range from 17 measures in a *missa brevis* by Seuche (M. 52) to 149 measures in Gassmann's expansive *St. Cecilia Mass* (M. 19). As figure 6-5 shows, Haydn's *St. Cecilia Mass*, Hob. XXII: 5, has a "Christe" of 103 measures; the "Christe" of Bach's *B-Minor Mass* has only 85 measures. Usually the "Christe's" length is anywhere from 20 to 63 per cent of the entire Kyrie with all its movements. "Christes" with two or more soloists are generally longer than those for a single vocal soloist.

These independent "Christes" also tend to be longer and more standard in form than the preceding "Kyrie I" movements. With very few exceptions,

Example 6-18. Joseph Ziegler, *Missa in C,* M. 71 (before 1762), Kyrie (Allegro), measures 12–30.

Figure 6-5. "Christe" as a Separate Movement (in Order of Lengths)

M. No.	Composer	Key of Mass	Key of Christe	Soloist(s)	Meter	Tempo	Length mm.	Form
52	Seuche	a	C =III	ATB	C	Allegro	17	3 pt. (NOR)
31	Holzbauer	a	C =III*	SAT	3/4	-	18	t/c (NOR)
60	Tuma	C	a =vi	S	C	Andante	27	2 pt.
50	Schmidt	C	a =vi	SB	C	Andante	37	2 pt.
25	Hasse	D	A =V	SA	C	Andante	38	2 pt.
36	Martínez	C	a =vi	SAB	C	Andante	39	3 pt. (NOR)
51	Schmidt	C	a =vi	S	C	Andante	40	2 pt.
45	Reutter	F	C =I	SA	3/4	Andante	54	2 pt.
33	Holzbauer	C	C =V	SA	3/4	Andante	58	2 pt.
23	Hasse	G	e =vi	SAT/Tutti	2/4	Allegretto	59	2 pt. (NOR)
5	Albrechtsberger	C	c =i*	SATB	3/4	Andante	59	2 pt.
30	Holzbauer	C	F =IV	ST	C	Andante	61	2 pt.
40	Monn	D	b =vi	S	C	Allo modto	63	3 pt. (motto)
61	Tuma	G	e =vi	SB	3/4	Vivace	63	2 pt.
37	Martínez	D	g =iv	SAB	3/4	Andante	67	2 pt. (NOR)
24	Hasse	d	F =III	SA/Tutti	3/8	Andantino	88	2 pt.
26	Hofmann	D	A =V	T	2/4	Andantino	113	3 pt. (sonata?)
4	Albrechtsberger	d	G =IV	SATB	3/4	Andante	120	3 pt.
49	Reutter	C	F =IV	SB	3/8	Poco Ande	145	3 pt. (extended)
19	Gassmann	C	F =IV	SATB	2/4	Ande molto	149	3 pt. (extended)
	J. Haydn, H.XXII:5	C	a =vi	T/Tutti	3/4	Allegretto	103	2 pt.
	W.A. Mozart, K.139	c	F =IV	SATB	2/4	-	36	2 pt. (NOR)
	J.S. Bach, BWV 232	b(D)	D =III	SS	C	-	85	3 pt.

Further information about the sources for these Masses arranged according to "M" number is in the thematic catalogue of appendix C.

2 pt. = two-part aria
3 pt. = three-part aria
t/c   = through-composed
NOR   = no opening ritornello precedes first entry of voice(s)
*   = Christe concludes with a half cadence to the dominant of the Mass' tonic

only two- and three-part aria forms are used—for duets and quartets as well as for solos. Older, more conservative composers seem to prefer ritornello themes which are independent of the vocal melodies. "Christes" for three or more solo voices usually omit the opening ritornello (see the "NOR's" in fig. 6-5). In two of Hasse's "Christes" (M. 24 and 23, dated 1751 and 1776 respectively) the full chorus alternates with the soloists and helps frame the end of each of the two sections in the movement. Haydn uses the chorus in a similar manner during the "Christe" of his 1766 *St. Cecilia Mass* (Hob. XXII: 5).

Multi-Movement Kyries

In the eighteenth century multi-movement Kyries were nothing new; they were commonly found in concerted Masses of the late seventeenth century.[33] As already stated, by the middle of the eighteenth century the trend was toward single-movement Kyries, with or without slow introductions. Nonetheless, the two- and three-movement designs shown in figure 6-6 were encountered in the Masses under study. Such multi-movement structures were used in *missae longae* by the older generation (e.g., Carl, Hasse, Holzbauer, Monn, Predieri, Reutter, Schmidt, Seuche, Tuma, and Wagenseil) and by some of the younger composers (e.g., Albrechtsberger, Boog, Gassmann, Hofmann, Martínez, and Sonnleithner). We can only surmise whether or not the Viennese tradition influenced the young Mozart to set the Kyrie in three movements for his so-called *Waisenhaus Mass, K.* 139. This Mass was composed in Vienna in 1768 and was the only one written by Mozart in which the "Christe" was a separate movement.

As figure 6-6 shows, the "Kyrie II" is usually a choral fugue in these multi-movement Kyries. Such independent fugal settings, like those for the ends of the Gloria and Credo, are part of an old tradition which begins to disappear at this time. They are still found in Masses by Bach, Caldara, Fux, Jommelli, and many others during the eighteenth century. Usually they return us to the tonic key of the Mass (Bach's is an exception—it does not). The fugues are often over 100 measures in length; the instruments usually play *colla parte*. The fugue which concludes the Kyrie of Haydn's *St. Cecilia Mass* (Hob. XXII: 5) is one of the more glorious examples. Because such fugal movements were a stylistic artifact by this time, they shall not be discussed in detail. However, a sampling of several "Kyrie II" fugue subjects reveals the *alla cappella* heritage behind most of them (ex. 6-19). Most of the subjects have the three distinct sections (head motive, expansion, and cadence) which Kirkendale associates with late Baroque and rococo fugues.[34]

Figure 6-6 also shows us that in six instances (or 30% of the Kyries with three movements) composers resorted to the easiest solution for Kyrie II: they

Example 6-19. Selected "Kyrie II" Fugue Subjects (in chronological order)

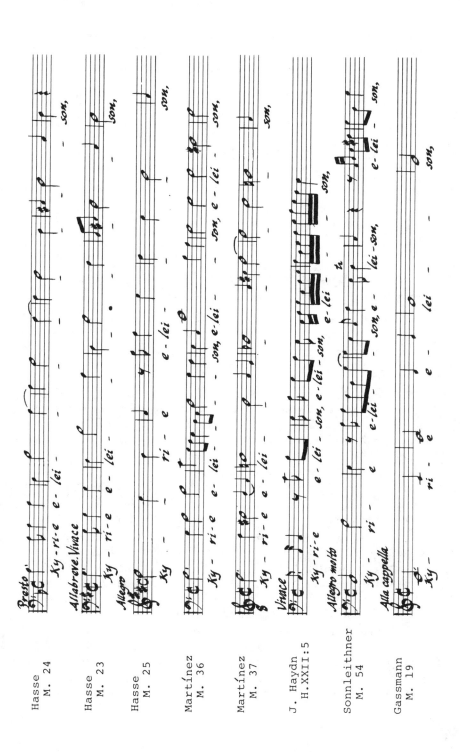

Hasse
M. 24

Hasse
M. 23

Hasse
M. 25

Martínez
M. 36

Martínez
M. 37

J. Haydn
H.XXII:5

Sonnleithner
M. 54

Gassmann
M. 19

Figure 6-6. Multi-Movement Kyrie Designs

TWO MOVEMENTS			Quantity Of Exx.
Kyrie I — Christe ⌐fast ¬		Kyrie II ⌐fugue¬	3
Kyrie I - Christe - Kyrie II ⌐slow ¬		Kyrie II ⌐fugue¬	1

THREE MOVEMENTS			Quantity	% of sample of 3 mvts.
Kyrie I	Christe	Kyrie II		
⌐fast ¬	⌐solo ¬	⌐fugue ¬	8	40%
⌐slow ¬	⌐solo ¬	⌐fugue ¬	4	20%
⌐A ¬	⌐B (solo)¬	⌐A ¬	6	30%
⌐A ¬	⌐B ¬	⌐A' ¬	2*	10%

*both pre-1750

simply repeated Kyrie I to produce a rounded *ABA* structure for the entire Kyrie.[35] If Kyrie I began with a slow introduction, however, this was normally omitted from the *da capo* repetition. Mozart uses this arch scheme in his *Waisenhaus Mass*. When the same thing is done in a *Messa solenne* attributed to Pergolesi, Wienandt accuses the composer of resorting to the "operatic convention" of the *da capo* return.[36] Perhaps limitations of time or performing ensemble forced all these composers to forego the standard fugue for Kyrie II.

Of more interest are the few instances where Kyrie II is a variant of the Kyrie I movement—thus producing the overall *ABA'*. In Ferdinand Schmidt's *Missa Sanctae Caeciliae* the Kyrie II subject is derived from the rising fanfare motive that served for both the clarino trumpet ritornellos and the bass line of "Kyrie I" (compare ex. 6-20 with ex. 6-3 above). What unifies Schmidt's entire Kyrie even more, however, are the nearly identical endings of "Kyrie I" (m. 90—107 in ex. 6-3) and "Kyrie II" (m. 26–38, after the fugal exposition in ex. 6-20). We have already seen how the subject of the "Kyrie II" fugue in Holzbauer's *Missa in F* is based upon the sinfonia heard at the beginning of the Kyrie (ex. 6-4 above). Seeking to unify the beginning and end of his sizeable three-movement Kyrie of 229 measures, Reutter (in his *Missa Sancti Caroli* [M. 49, 1734]), reuses the opening bars of "Kyrie I" as a coda

Example 6-20. Ferdinand Schmidt, *Missa Sanctae Caeciliae,* M. 50
(before 1746), "Kyrie II" (Allegro), complete vocal
score [see ex. 6-3 for "Kyrie I"].

Example 6-20 (concluded)

concluding the "Kyrie II" fugue (see *DTÖ* 88, m. 1–2, 224–25, pp. 1, 13). It is significant that already in the 1740s composers like Schmidt, Holzbauer, and Reutter were seeking to unify the Kyrie as a whole, despite its expansiveness when set as three disparate movements. Ultimately composers found a satisfactory unity in setting the Kyrie-Christe-Kyrie as one single movement.

Summary

The Kyrie was predominantly a joyful section whose fast tempo, major tonality, and full instrumentation rarely suggested the petitions of its text. In longer Masses, a slow introduction was often used to provide the necessary solemnity. Although Kyries were set in one to three movements, the trend during this period moved increasingly toward single movements. Kyrie length was determined by the scale of the mass as a whole. In nearly every case the music attempted to parallel the *ABA* structure of the text, with the "Christe" usually serving as a solo *B* section. By the 1770s the influence of sonata design began to supplant that of the concerto grosso in shaping the Kyrie, even though tutti-solo alternation was retained. Also, by that time homophonic thinking with regularly phrased melodies and slower harmonic rhythm had mostly replaced strict contrapuntal writing, as comparison of Kyries by Wagenseil and Tuma with those by Dittersdorf and Vaňhal makes clear (compare ex. 6-16 and 6-15 with ex. 6-11 and 6-12). Throughout the period under study one finds a few composers concerned with integrating the entire Kyrie, even when it comprises two or three movements. Rondo, strophic, and binary forms such as those encountered in some of Mozart's Kyries (e.g., K. 275, 257, and 258) are not found among the Viennese examples under study. Dittersdorf, Holzbauer, Monn, Vaňhal, and Schmidt seem to have composed the most integrated and imaginative settings of the Kyrie.

7

Gloria

With the Gloria the text changes to one of action. The contrition of the Kyrie
is past, and the congregation begins to glorify, praise, and thank God the
Father, Son, and Holy Ghost. The opening exclamations ("Glory be to God in
the highest," etc.) which echo the words of the angels at the Nativity inspired
the Viennese composers—as well as most of their predecessors—to begin the
Gloria loudly and triumphantly (see ex. 7-1). Once these initial flourishes are
over, however, the ways in which these composers set the Gloria's 18 sentences
diverge markedly. Indeed Reichert's observation that it is difficult to find
consistency of treatment in Viennese Glorias from the first half of the
eighteenth century also holds true to a certain extent for the second half of the
century.[1] The present section will explore this diversity in an attempt to
uncover the commonalities of musical form, rhetoric, and contrast found in
the Glorias under study.

Division of the Text

Viennese composers set the Gloria in one to 10 separate movements. *Missae
breves* usually have the Gloria's 18 sentences compressed into a single
movement, a situation which often leads to problematic polytextuality or text
telescoping. Figure 7-1 shows the pattern of text distribution for all the
Glorias under study, as well as those by Bach, Haydn, and Mozart. Other
Masses might, of course, reveal other distributions, but this chart outlines the
more common patterns. As can be seen, some 13 (approximately 18%) of the
72 Glorias consist of a single movement. Ten of these 13 are from *missae
breves*; longer Masses having single-movement Glorias date from 1760 and
later.[2]

Multi-movement Glorias were nothing new to the eighteenth century.
They were the trademark of so-called cantata Masses which had become
common in Italy and then Vienna during the latter part of the seventeenth
century. Schnoebelen reports that Glorias of eight to 13 movements were
common in Bolognese Masses at that time.[3] Schmeltzer, Biber, Ziani, Fux,
Caldara, and others introduced the multi-movement Gloria to Vienna.[4] Most

Example 7-1.   Marianne von Martínez, *Messe No. 4*, M. 37 (1765),
              Gloria [Allegro], measures 1–32.

Gloria

Example 7-1   (cont'd.)

Example 7-1 (cont'd.)

Example 7-1 (cont'd.)

Example 7-1 (cont'd.)

Example 7-1 (concluded)

Figure 7-1. Gloria Text Divisions

Sentence No.	Text Incipit
1	Gloria in excelsis/
2	Et in terra pax
3-6	Laudamus
7	Gratias
8	Domine Deus Rex
9	Domine Fili
10	Domine Deus Agnus
11	Qui tollis (miserere)
12	Qui tollis (suscipe)
13	Qui sedes
14-16	Quoniam
17	Cum Sancto Spiritu
18	Amen

Column groups (across top): I | II a b c | III a b c d e | IV a b c d e | V a b c d e f | VI a b c d | VII a b | VIII a b | X

Qty. of Ex. in sample of 72: 13 1 1 10 1 1 1 13 1 1 2 2 1 6 1 1 1 1 1 1 1 0 2 2 1 0 1 1 1 1 1

Qty. of Ex. changing tempo within a movement: 1 1 1 5 1 0 1 4 1 1 2 2 0 2 0 0 0 0 0 0 0 1 1 2 1 0 1 0 1 1

Qty. of Mozart Ex. (out of 16): 13 0 0 0 0 0 0 1 0 0 0 0 0 0 0 0 0 0 0 0 0 0 0 0 0 0 1 1 0 0 0

Qty. of Haydn Ex. (out of 13): 4 1 1 2 0 1 4 4 0 0 0 1 0 2 0 0 0 0 0 0 0 0 1 2 1 0 1 1 0 0 0

Type	Mass Nos.
I	M. 1, 3, 6, 9, 10, 27, 32, 42, 43, 46, 53, 59, 68
II a	M. 65
II b	M. 63
II c	M. 7, 8, 12, 35, 41, 48, 52, 54, 55, 57
III a	M. 18
III b	M. 21
III c	M. 66

Type	Mass Nos.
III d	M. 2, 11, 22, 28, 29, 31, 34, 39, 44, 47, 62, 67, 70
III e	M. 16, 58
IV a	M. 4, 72
IV b	M. 20
IV c	M. 24
IV d	M. 5, 13, 14, 45, 56, 64
IV e	M. 37
V	J. S. Bach

Type	Mass Nos.
V a	M. 40
V b	M. 25
V c	M. 17
V d	M. 33
V e	M. 23
V f	M. 15
VI a	Mozart, K. 139
VI b	M. 38, 50
	M. 19, 71

Type	Mass Nos.
VI c	M. 49, 61
VI d	M. 69
VII a	Mozart, K. 427
VII a	M. 60; also Mozart, K. 66 and Pergolesi
VII b	M. 51
VIII a	M. 30
VIII b	M. 26
X	M. 36

of Caldara's Masses divide the Gloria into nine movements.[5] Both of Pergolesi's authentic Masses have Glorias of seven movements, while in Vivaldi's well-known Gloria in D Major (RV589) there are some 11 separate movements.[6] Fifty-nine of the Masses under study here divide the Gloria into two to 10 movements (columns II–X in fig. 7-1). The bulk of these multi-movement Glorias (50 examples or 85%) are from long Masses.[7]

Just how the Gloria's 18 sentences are distributed over several movements varies extensively, as figure 7-1 illustrates. Sometimes individual movements consist of two or more sections, each separated by a different tempo or meter yet joined by rhythmic elision (dovetailing) or resolution of a half-cadence. For example—to take the most extreme case found—in Tuma's *Missa in chordis et organo in G* (M. 61, before 1743) we encounter a dozen changes of tempo or meter during its six-movement Gloria (see fig. 7-2). Similarly, Bach's *B-minor Mass* has some eight changes of meter, scoring, or tempo distributed over the five movements of its Gloria (see column V in fig. 7-1). At one time or another in the Glorias under study such changes demarcate the start of almost every one of the text's 18 sentences.[8] Such diverseness in text and tempo distribution was part and parcel of the Italo-Austrian Mass tradition passed on to these Viennese composers by the generation of Fux and Caldara.

Why were there so many sections for this part of the Mass? Adler's answer that composers were trying not to bore their pious audiences is, at most, partially correct.[9] Scheibe (1737) did ask for "variety and change" from movement to movement.[10] Indeed the Gloria is part of the first half of Mass (Mass of the Catechumens) where, as we have already seen, music often played so extensive a role that a person might believe he were attending a concert rather than a religious rite. Thus, by tradition composers often made the Kyrie and Gloria more elaborate and perhaps even more "secular" than later parts of the Mass. By the start of the eighteenth century, oratorio, opera, and cantata had become genres with which many Mass composers were equally familiar. Faced with the multi-faceted text of the Gloria, composers could hardly avoid the temptation of enlivening and modernizing it with elements from such genres.

Despite the diversity in the distribution of the Gloria text, there are common structural threads running through all the Glorias. First, a three-part textual division ("Gloria"–"Qui tollis"–"Quoniam") is the basis for most Gloria designs. As can be seen in figure 7-1, some 39 of the 59 multi-movement Glorias (66%) begin a new movement with "Qui tollis peccata mundi," and 53 of the same 59 (90%) also start a new movement at "Quoniam tu solus sanctus." This three-part division is undoubtedly based upon a musical tradition that had long reacted to and expressed the surface meaning of the text at these two points (the allusion to evil and pleas for mercy at "Qui tollis" and the resumption of praise at "Quoniam") rather than follow the divisions

Figure 7-2. Movement Plan of the Gloria in Tuma's *Missa in chordis et organo* (M. 61)

Mvt.	Text Incipit	Tempo	Meter	Key*	Vocalists
I.	Gloria (verses 1-4)	⎡1. Allegro	C	G	Chorus/SATB solos
	Adoramus te (v. 5)	⎢2. Adagio			
	Glorificamus te (v. 6)	⎣3. Allegro			
II.	Gratias (v. 7)	[4. Andante	3/4	e	A solo
III.	Domine Deus, Rex(v. 8-10)	[5. Vivace	C	a	TSB solos
IV.	Qui tollis (v. 11A)	⎡6. Adagio	C	e	Chorus/ATB solos
	Miserere (v. 11B)	⎢7. Andante	3/2		
	Qui tollis (v. 12A)	⎢8. Adagio	C		
	Suscipe (v. 12B-13A)	⎢9. Andante	[C]		
	Miserere (v. 13B)	⎣10. Andante	3/2		
V.	Quoniam (v. 14-16)	[11. Spiritoso	3/4	G	S solo
VI.	Cum Sancto (v. 17A)	⎡12. Adagio	C	G	Chorus
	In gloria Dei (v. 17B-18)	⎣13. Alla breve	¢		

*Lowercase letters or Roman numerals refer to minor keys in this and later charts.

implied by the theological meaning.[11] Many Masses, particularly those consisting of four or more movements, also have a structural break before "Cum Sancto Spiritu."

The four most common textual divisions of the Gloria are shown in figure 7-3. These are also shown as the thicker brackets in figure 7-1 (columns I, IIc, IIId, and IVd). Together the four arrangements account for well over half of the Masses studied (42 of the 72; 58%). As figure 7-1 also shows, the greatest diversity is found in the distribution of text up to "Qui tollis" in Glorias of five or more movements.[12]

Figure 7-3. Common Gloria Text Distributions

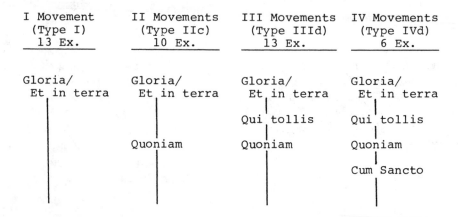

I Movement (Type I) 13 Ex.	II Movements (Type IIc) 10 Ex.	III Movements (Type IIId) 13 Ex.	IV Movements (Type IVd) 6 Ex.
Gloria/ Et in terra	Gloria/ Et in terra	Gloria/ Et in terra	Gloria/ Et in terra
		Qui tollis	Qui tollis
	Quoniam	Quoniam	Quoniam
			Cum Sancto

A second common structural trait is that composers nearly always group certain sentences of the Gloria together as separate movements usually unified by tempo, meter, and key. Each of the following five sentence groupings generally maintains its integrity by being set within the same section of music; the sentences rarely appear in separate movements:

Group	Sentence Number	Text
A	1.	Gloria in excelsis Deo.
	2.	Et in terra pax hominibus bonae voluntatis.
B	8.	Domine Deus, Rex coelestis, Deus Pater omnipotens.
	9.	Domine Fili unigenite, Jesu Christe.
	10.	Domine Deus, Agnus Dei, Filius Patris.
C	11.	Qui tollis peccata mundi, miserere nobis.
	12.	Qui tollis peccata mundi, suscipe deprecationem nostram.
	13.	Qui sedes ad dexteram Patris, miserere nobis.
D	14.	Quoniam tu solus sanctus.
	15.	Tu solus Dominus.
	16.	Tu solus Altissimus, Jesu Christe.
E	17.	Cum Sancto Spiritu in gloria Dei Patris.
	18.	Amen.

Meaning and syntax naturally tie these sentences together. The many ways in which each group may link up with adjacent groups generate the enormous variety in the text distribution of multi-movement Glorias.

One chronological change is noticeable in the text division of these Glorias: after about 1750 composers usually limit their Glorias to one to four movements and Glorias of five or more movements become increasingly rare. Of the 21 Masses dated between 1734 and 1750, 10 (47%) have five movements or more in the Gloria. On the other hand, in the 51 examples dated post-1750, there are only eight Glorias (15%) with five or more movements.[13] By this later period composers were probably finding extended multi-movement Glorias too cumbersome for the greater musical coherence and unity they sought. Official displeasure with operatic style in the church may also have played a role.

Without having closely analyzed each composer's entire output of Masses, it is difficult to assess adequately individual preferences with regard to Gloria structure. However, based upon existing literature and research for the present study, figure 7-4 summarizes the number of movements within all the known Glorias of several representative composers. From the list we can see that the older generation frequently composed Glorias of five or more movements. The younger generation, i.e., Haydn and his contemporaries,

Figure 7-4.   Numbers of Movements in the Gloria

Elder Generation	I	II	III	IV	V	VI	VII	VIII	IX	X	XI	XII
Bonno	I	II										
*Hasse [a]				IV	V							
Holzbauer	I		III		V			(VIII)				
Monn			III		V	VI						
*Reutter [b]	I	II	III	IV	V	VI	VII	VIII				(XII)
Tuma [c]	I	II	III	IV	V	VI	VII	VIII			(XI)	
*Wagenseil [d]	I		III		V	VI						(XII)

Haydn's Generation	I	II	III	IV	V	VI	VII	VIII	IX	X	XI	XII
*Albrechtsberger [e]	I		III	IV								
*Dittersdorf			III		V							
*Gassmann [f]			III			(VI)	(VII)					
*J. Haydn	I	II	III				(VII)					
*Hofmann [g]	I	II	III	IV				(VIII)				
*Mozart	I					(VI)	VII					
Sonnleithner		II	III	IV								
Vanhal		II	III	IV			(VII)					

*Data for these composers are complete.
Parentheses indicate that only one example exists with this many movements.

[a] Müller, "Hasse als Kirchenkomponist," p. 54.

[b] Hofer, "Reutter," pp. 76-78. Glorias of six or more movements were for "die grössten Feierlichkeiten"; six of Reutter's over seventy Masses have Glorias of such extent. The twelve-movement Gloria is found in Reutter's *Missa Sanctae Caeciliae in C* (Hofer No. 79; 1743).

[c] Peschek, "Tuma," pp. 47-48, 143-280 passim. The only eleven-movement Gloria is in Tuma's *Missa Sancti Andreae in D* (Reichert No. 32, Peschek No. C27; n.d.).

[d] Philipp, "Messenkomposition," tables on pp. 83-113. Twelve movements make up the Gloria of Wagenseil's *Missa a 5 in C* (Reichert No. 2; 1738).

[e] Weissenbäck, "Albrechtsberger als Kirchenkomponist," p. 150, states that the composer wrote Glorias chiefly of one or three movements.

[f] Kosch, "Gassmann," p. 224.

[g] Prohászka, "Hofmann," p. 86. She says only one-quarter of Hofmann's Glorias consist of a single movement. Hofmann's only eight-movement Gloria occurs in his *Missa Sancti Erasmi* (M. 26, before 1779), p. 89.

kept mostly to four movements or less, with longer Glorias reserved only for the more festive Masses. The Glorias of Reutter and Tuma display the greatest diversity in structure—from one to 12 movements. Although he was of the elder generation, *Hofkapellmeister* Giuseppe Bonno follows the trend of the 1760s and 1770s (the late period of his life from which most of his sacred music comes) and restricts his Glorias to only one or two movements.

The total length of a Gloria depends largely upon the number of movements over which its text has been distributed. The shortest Gloria encountered in the present study—only nine measures—is from a *missa brevis*, Arbesser's *Missa Nubes pluant justum in B-flat* (M. 6, before 1753). Polytextuality is unavoidable in such a compressed movement. [14] Hofmann's *Missa Sancti Erasmi in D* (M. 26, before 1779) had the longest Gloria: 640 measures for its eight movements. This Mass was undoubtedly composed for a special occasion since Hofmann's Glorias usually consist of no more than four movements. [15] Certainly even longer Glorias were written at this time, as anyone who knows Bach's *B-minor Mass* (769 m. in five movements), Haydn's *St. Cecilia Mass* (821 m. in seven movements), or Mozart's *C-minor Mass* (737 m. in seven movements) could testify.

Tempo

In accordance with the joyful and laudatory text, allegro is the usual beginning tempo for the Gloria. In single-movement Glorias this fast pace often establishes one cheerful affect for the entire movement—even for the somber "Qui tollis." When the Gloria has only two movements, both are generally fast, with perhaps a slow section at "Qui tollis" before the fast "Quoniam." [16] The most common tempo arrangement occurs in the Gloria of three movements: [17]

I.	"Gloria/Et in terra"	Allegro
II.	"Qui tollis"	Adagio
III.	"Quoniam"	Allegro

The tempo schemes of most multi-movement Glorias seem derived from this basic fast-slow-fast design. Even the following common four-movement design is based upon it: [18]

I.	"Gloria/Et in terra"	Fast
II.	"Qui tollis"	Slow
III.	"Quoniam"	Fast
IV.	"Cum Sancto"	Fast, Faster, or Slow Intro./Fast

As already mentioned, one movement may consist of several connected sections, each having a different tempo, meter, or scoring. However, only the final section concludes with a full cadence. Such fluctuations are usually associated with the texts "Domine Deus, Rex," "Qui tollis," and "Cum Sancto Spiritu." Some composers felt that each sentence of these sections deserved a change. Figures 7-5, 7-6, and 7-7 show three of the more typical plans for this intramovement subsectioning. Despite changes in singer, meter, and key, Schmidt tonally unifies his "Qui tollis" by returning to the key of C at the end of that movement's "Qui sedes" (fig. 7-5; see also ex. 7-9). The multi-tempo "Qui tollis" was common in the 1740s and earlier; after that decade composers preferred to restrict the "Qui tollis" to a single tempo. [19]

Throughout the period under study many composers continued the old practice of dividing the final movement into the following two parts: [20]

Figure 7-5. Layout (Excerpt) for the Gloria of Ferdinand Schmidt's *Missa Primitiarum in C* (M. 51, before 1747)

Mvt. No.	Text	Tempo	Meter	Key(s)	Scoring	mm.
III.	Gratias	Adagio	C	in C	A, S solos & chorus	1-26
	Domine Deus, Rex	Andante	"	" "	A solo	27-43
IV.	Domine Fili	Andante	2/4	in F	B solo	1-62
V.	Qui tollis	Adagio	6/8	in c -V/c	Chorus	1-13
	Suscipe	"	C	in E-flat	S solo	14-19
	Qui sedes	Adagio	"	-- C	Chorus	20-26

Figure 7-6. Layout (Excerpt) for the Gloria of Holzbauer's *Missa in C* (M. 30, before 1739)

Mvt. No.	Text	Tempo	Meter	Key(s)	Scoring	mm.
IV.	Domine Deus, Rex	Largo	3/4	in F	A solo	1–79
V.	Domine Fili	Largo	C	in B-flat	T solo	1–34
	Domine Deus, Agnus	Andante	C	in g	TB duet	35–55
VI.	Qui tollis (cf. Ex. VII–33 below)	Grave	C	--V/a	Chorus & S, A solos	1–15
	Suscipe	Largo	3/2	in C	SAT solos & chorus	16–47

Figure 7-7. Layout (Excerpt) for the Gloria of Tuma's *Missa in chordis et organo* (M. 61, before 1743)

Mvt. No.	Text	Tempo	Meter	Key(s)	Scoring	mm.
IV.	⎡Qui tollis	Adagio	C	in e--V/e	Chorus	1-3
	miserere	Andante	3/2	in e	Chorus (fugue)	4-29
	Qui tollis	Adagio	C	in F--V/a	Chorus	30-33
	suscipe	Andante	"	in a--V/e	ATB trio	34-41
	⎣miserere	Andante	3/2	in e (= 1st. miserere)		42-67

"Cum Sancto Spiritu"	slow, choral, homophonic "introduction"
"In gloria Dei" (or Amen)	faster, choral fugue or fugato

Undoubtedly composers felt that an adagio "Cum Sancto Spiritu" provided the desired tempo contrast (and respite) between the fast "Quoniam" and concluding "In gloria Dei." Albrechtsberger, Anton Carl, Dittersdorf, Hasse, J. Haydn, Holzbauer, Monn, Reutter, Tuma, and Vaňhal all followed this tradition in several of their Masses. Of the 27 Glorias which set apart the "Cum Sancto" as a final movement, 12 (44%) begin with such a slow introduction.[21] Of these 12, three Glorias save the change to a fast tempo until "Amen."[22] In example 7-2 by Monn the "Cum Sancto" introduction provides not only a contrast of tempo, meter, and scoring but also a quick, convenient way of modulating from the D minor of the "Quoniam" bass solo to the C major of the "In gloria Dei" choral fugue.

Overall Structure of the Gloria

The chief means of unifying every Gloria is harmonic. Whether there is one movement or 10 movements, this paean to God always provides us with a carefully arranged and balanced tonal journey away from and eventually back to the tonic key of the Mass. Except in a few single-movement Glorias, melodic or rhythmic recurrence is rarely used to produce the overall cohesiveness and unity heard in large-scale cycles of the next century.

Single-Movement Glorias

Most single-movement Glorias are through-composed. Each subdivision of the text is usually set to a new melody and concluded with an authentic cadence. A Gloria by Bonno (fig. 7-8) shows this typical periodic structure. The Gloria is broken up into 14 subsections by a succession of cadences to related keys on both the sharp and flat sides of the circle of fifths. In all such movements the tonic of the Mass traditionally returns just before or at "Quoniam" (m. 118 in fig. 7-8). This is true unless the text has been obscured by polytextuality, in which case no uniform practice exists.

Much of the time a new accompaniment pattern distinguishes each of the Gloria's three main musical divisions ("Gloria," "Qui tollis," and "Quoniam") as in Reutter's *Missa Conceptionis in C* (ex. 7-3). Only three Glorias were found in which the accompaniment remained the same throughout.[23] Distribution of the vocal solos and choruses also follows a traditional alignment with the text and will be discussed in a separate section below.

Example 7-2. Mathias Georg Monn, *Missa in C,* M. 38 (1741), end
of "Quoniam" (Allegro ma non troppo), measures
196–205; "Cum Sancto" (Adagio-Allegro), measures
1–5.

Figure 7-8. Layout for the Gloria of Bonno's *Missa in C* (M. 9, before 1776)

Verse	Voices Used	Text Beginning Each Section	Cadence Tones at Ends of Sections	Cadence Measure(s)
1	Chorus	Gloria	--C	11
2	"	Et in terra pax	--a	19, 21*
3-5	SATB solos	Laudamus te	--D (as V/g)	25
6	Chorus	Glorificamus te	--G	35, 37*
7	TB solos/Chorus	Gratias	--C	45, 47*
8	AT solos	Domine Deus, Rex	--C	49
8-9	Chorus/SB solos	Deus Pater omnipotens	--G	51, 53*
9-10	Chorus/AT solos	Unigenite, Jesu	--D	55, 57*
10	Chorus	Filius Patris	--A, a	60, 63*
11	"	Qui tollis	--F (f)	78, 81*
12	"	Qui tollis	--A-flat	95, 98*
13	"	Qui sedes	--c, C (A-flat decept. in m. 112)	115, 118*
14-16	"	Quoniam	--G	125
17-18	"	Cum Sancto	--C	148 (end)

*Where two measure numbers are cited, the orchestra follows the voices with its own cadence in the same key.

Example 7-3. Georg von Reutter, Jr., *Missa Conceptionis in C*, M. 46 (before 1756), Gloria (Andante), measures 1–9, 46–55, and 73–82.

Example 7-3   (cont'd.)

Example 7-3 (cont'd.)

Example 7-3 (cont'd.)

Example 7-3   (cont'd.)

Example 7-3 (concluded)

Most of Mozart's Glorias consist of a single movement ranging from 49 to 198 measures in length.[24] Structurally they are quite like the Viennese Glorias just described. However, Mozart saves the return of the tonic until either the "Quoniam" or, more often, the "Cum Sancto." Usually he rounds out the Gloria by coordinating this tonic return with a reprise of the Gloria's opening theme or a variation thereof. ("Quoniam" is a compositionally attractive place for reprise because the tri-syllable is accentuated exactly like "Gloria.") In Glorias from two of Mozart's late Masses (K. 317 and 337) the use of this reprise structure with two contrasting thematic groups resembles that in sonata form. Among the 13 single-movement Viennese Glorias examined, only one—that in Albrechtsberger's *Missa Annuntiationis*—has such a thematic return at "Quoniam" (ex. 7-4). As already stated, most Viennese composers seemed to prefer a through-composed form when confining the Gloria to only one movement.[25]

Multi-Movement Glorias

Although the entire Gloria usually constitutes a satisfactorily complete harmonic unit (i.e., it begins and ends in the central tonality of the Mass), many of its inner movements do not.[26] Probably out of concern for large-scale harmonic continuity and growth, many of the Viennese composers often begin and end inner movements in different keys. Sometimes a smooth and graduated modulatory plan for the whole Gloria results. Coupled with a carefully chosen succession of meters, tempos, and instrumentation, such harmonic planning often produces a Gloria with momentum and drive not unlike that experienced during the chain of dovetailed numbers and ensembles in a finale from an eighteenth-century opera.[27]

Although virtually every sequence of keys is unique, all Glorias follow certain general principles in their harmonic plans.[28] The specific harmonic layout is a function of how many movements make up the Gloria: usually the more movements there are, the greater the variety of keys. Most harmonic designs take into consideration two crucial points in the Gloria text: "Qui tollis" and "Quoniam." Basically, composers were continuing an established tradition of associating a minor key with the sin and penitence of "Qui tollis" and changing to a major key when the praising of Christ resumes at "Quoniam." Most harmonic plans—including those for single movement Glorias—were conceived upon these principles.

Of the 39 Glorias which begin a new movement at "Qui tollis," 32 (82%) begin this section in the minor mode. In 26 of these 39 the new mode is emphasized because the preceding movement ends in a major key. The tonic minor, submediant, mediant, and minor dominant of the Mass are the minor keys most often encountered here, as figure 7-9 shows. The great variety of tonalities used at "Qui tollis" stems from the fact that a composer's selection of

Example 7-4. Johann Georg Albrechtsberger, *Missa Annuntiationis,* M. 3 (1763), Gloria (Allegro moderato), measures 1–7 and 32–37.

Example 7-4   (cont'd.)

etc.

Example 7-4 (cont'd.)

Example 7-4 (concluded)

etc.

key depends largely upon how many movements make up the Gloria and what keys have already been used. Nevertheless, most Masses—single-movement Glorias included (see ex. 7-3)—turn to the minor mode for "Qui tollis." Even most of the seven "Qui tollis" movements that begin in the major modulate to the minor before their conclusions.[29]

Figure 7-9. Starting Tonalities for "Qui tollis" Movements

Key	Qty. of Ex.	% of Sample	M. Nos.
i	12	31	20, 28, 31, 34, 44, 50, 51, 56, 62, 63, 64, 71, and Haydn, Hob. XXII: 5
vi	10	26	5, 11, 22, 29, 39, 40, 45, 60, 61, 69, and J. S. Bach
iii	4	10	14, 17, 36, 47
v	3	7.5	19, 26, 49, and Mozart, K. 66, 427
iv	1	2.5	13 and Mozart, K. 139
ii	1	2.5	2
♭vii	1	2.5	23
IV	5	13	15, 24, 37, 67, 70
I	2	5	21, 38
VI	-	-	Haydn, Hob. XXII: 9, 11

Another ingredient of the change at "Qui tollis" is the third relationship usually preferred between the key of this movement and the preceding one. With a minor third down being most frequent, such a third relationship is found in 19 (49%) of the 39 Glorias that have a separate "Qui tollis" movement (see fig. 7-10). For example, following the "Domine Deus" trio in B-flat major in Gassmann's *St. Cecilia Mass*, the "Qui tollis" chorus begins a minor third lower, in G minor. Fifth relationships (up and down) are found in about one-third of the cases (in 12 of the 39). In seven instances only the mode is changed, and in one there is no change.[30] The harmonic instability that results from often adventuresome modulations during the ensuing "Qui tollis" will be discussed separately below.

In 53 (90%) of the 59 multi-movement Glorias the "Quoniam" begins a new movement. Composers sharply contrast this movement with the preceding "Qui tollis" in ways not unlike those heard in the Credo at the

Figure 7-10.   Third Relationships at "Qui tollis"

	Key of Preceding Movement	Key of Qui tollis	Qty. of Ex.	M. Nos.
Down a Third	I	vi	7	5, 11, 22, 29, 39, 60, 69
	V	iii	2	14, 36
	vi	IV	2	24, 67
	♭vii	v	2	19, 49
	III	i	1	31 (Mass in minor key)
	IV	ii	1	2
	V/ii	IV	1	16
	I	VI	–	J. Haydn, Hob. XXII: 9, 11
Up a Third	vi	I	1	21
	ii	IV	1	15
	IV	vi	1	45 and J.S. Bach

change from "Crucifixus" to "Et resurrexit." The "Quoniam" is almost always in a major key. Over half the time this means a switch from the minor to the major mode, a change which aptly expresses the resumption of jubilation and praise found in the text.

Viennese composers again prefer the tonal relationship of a third between the end of the "Qui tollis" and the start of the "Quoniam." Figure 7-11 shows how 23 (43%) of the 53 "Quoniam" movements are in a key a third higher or lower. Composers seem to have enjoyed exploiting the sense of wonderment and awe that such third relationships between movements can induce. Again, fifth relationships are also found (in 16 of the 53). In five Masses there is no change of key for the "Quoniam" movement, usually because the preceding movement modulated to the key of the "Quoniam."[31] This latter type shows a concern for smooth intermovement connections on the part of the composers involved. Even in Masses that do not begin a new movement at "Quoniam" there are third and fifth relationships as well as the mode change at this point (e.g., M. 17, 63, and Mozart K. 139; see ex. 7-3 above). These Masses sometimes use a half-cadence to link the "Qui tollis" with the "Quoniam."[32]

Figure 7-11. Third Relationships at "Quoniam"

	Key of Preceding Movement	Key of Quoniam	Qty. of Ex.	M. Nos.
Up a Third	vi	I	10	5, 11, 12, 22, 29, 44, 61, 62, 67, 70; J. Haydn Hob. XXII: 4, 9, 10, 14; J.S. Bach
	i	III	2	31, 52 (both Masses in minor key)
	III (iii)	V	1	36*
	VI (vi)	I	1	18*
Down a Third	vi	IV	3	15, 49, 69
	I	vi	3	30, 33*, 39
	iii	I	2	4*, 41; Haydn Hob. XXII: 6
	IV	ii	1	38
	V (v)	♮iii	–	Mozart K. 427
	ii	IV	–	Mozart K. 66

*indicates where the preceding movement ends with Picardy third

The tonic is the tonality most often used for the "Quoniam" (in 28 of the 53; see fig. 7-12). This harmonic return to the tonic usually occurs when the "Quoniam" is the Gloria's closing movement. Yet, even among the 25 cases where the "Quoniam" is not the final movement, there are seven instances where it is in the tonic key. The potential problem here of two tonic movements in a row at the close is occasionally obviated by ending the "Quoniam" in a different key; e.g., the "Quoniam" in Ferdinand Schmidt's *Missa Sanctae Caeciliae* (M. 50) begins in the tonic and ends in the subdominant. As the "P" superscripts in figure 7-12 indicate, the dominant and subdominant are the preferred keys when the "Quoniam" is the penultimate movement of the Gloria. In such instances the "Quoniam" acts as a tonal "upbeat" to the final movement of the Gloria. Gassmann's *St. Cecilia Mass* exemplifies this practice which Mozart—but not Haydn—also followed. When the "Quoniam" is the final movement and does not begin in the tonic, there is naturally a modulation to the tonic at some later point, often just before "Cum Sancto" or "Amen" (see ex. 7-2).

Figure 7-12. Starting Tonalities for "Quoniam" Movements

Key	Qty. of Ex.	% of Sample	M. Nos.
I	28	53	4, 5^P, 7, 11, 12, 13^P, 18, 20, 22, 24, 28, 29, 34, 35, 41, 44, 45^P, 47, 38, 50^P, 57, 60^P, 61^P, 62, 64^P, 67, 70, 72; J.S. Bach, J. Haydn Hob. XXII: 4, 5^P, 6, 8-10, 13, 14
V	10	19	2, 8, 14^P, 16^P, 19^P, 26^P, 36^P, 37^P, 51^P, 55
IV	9	17	15^P, 23^P, 25^P, 49^P, 54, 56^P, 58^P, 69^P, 71^P, and Mozart K. 66^P
III	2	3.5	31, 52 (both Masses in minor key)
vi	3	5.5	30^P, 33^P, 39
ii	1	2	38^P
iii	-	-	Mozart K. 427

Superscript "P" indicates penultimate movement of Gloria.

The preceding discussion of the "Qui tollis" and "Quoniam" as critical points in the harmonic plan of the Gloria helps to explain why some movements do not end in their opening keys, although they conclude with a full cadence. Being more concerned about harmonic continuity and the expressive effect of these two sections, composers did not always worry about harmonic unity within the sections. In sum, a section of the Gloria will end in a different key than it began in because (1) the key of the next movement (especially "Qui tollis" and "Quoniam") is being prepared, commonly by setting up a third, unison, or fifth relationship; (2) contrast in mode or tonic with the following movement is desired for expressive reasons; or (3) it is the final movement of the Gloria, and the tonic key must return for the conclusion.

The six-movement Gloria of Ferdinand Schmidt's *Missa Sanctae Caeciliae* demonstrates some of these principles (see fig. 7-13). Both the "Laudamus" and "Quoniam" end in a different key to disguise the fact that the following movement begins in the same key. The "Gratias" concludes in C major (I) to set up the major-minor contrast traditionally heard at "Qui tollis." For "Quoniam" we have the usual return of the major mode as well as the tonic of the Mass. As a rule, movements for the vocal soloists are closed ones, i.e., they begin and end in the same key; choral movements (with or without solo passages) often end in a new key.

Figure 7-13.   Gloria Tonal Plan of F. Schmidt's *Missa Sanctae*
Caeciliae in C (M. 50, before 1746)

Key(s)	Text	Voices	Lengths
I	Et in terra	BB solos	41 mm.
vi-I	Laudamus	Chorus	26
vi-I	Gratias	AT solos, chorus	50
i-♭III-♭VII-i	Qui tollis	Chorus, SA solos	61
I-IV	Quoniam	TBB solos	99
I	Cum Sancto	Chorus	117

Gloria total 394 mm.

Several composers—Boog, Friberth, Gassmann, Gsur, Hasse, Hofmann, Krottendorfer, Martínez, Sonnleithner, and Vaňhal—are content with "number" Glorias. They tend to keep each movement of the Gloria a separate harmonic unit, almost like the parts of a number opera.[33] All movements begin and end in the same key (although not always with a perfect authentic cadence). Here the overall harmonic plan is founded upon the order and variety of the keys used. Often each movement is centered upon a different degree of the scale. Several of Joseph Haydn's Masses (Hob. XXII: 4, 5, 8, and 9) have Glorias of this type. The six-movement number Gloria of Gassmann's *Missa Sanctae Caeciliae in C* has one of the more logical harmonic plans (fig. 7-14). The second and third movements take us two steps around the flat side of the circle of fifths (F and B-flat). Then we hear the "Qui tollis" in the submediant to B-flat (G minor, the traditional mode here) before the "Quoniam" returns us to the major mode (G major), the key parallel to that of the "Qui tollis." This key (G) provides the expected and welcome move in the other (sharp) direction along the circle of fifths. Finally, the return to the tonic C major for the "Cum Sancto" fugue creates a satisfying sense of tonal closure for the entire Gloria. Analysis shows that Gassmann and his contemporaries paid careful attention to the degree of finality at the ends of the Gloria's inner movements, as plagal and imperfect cadences often lead one movement to the next and reduce the discreteness of the individual numbers.

Figure 7-14.   Gloria Tonal Plan of Gassmann's *Missa Sanctae*
Caeciliae in C (M. 19)

Key	Degree	Text	Voices	Lengths
C	(=I)	Gloria	Chorus, SATB solos	71 mm.
F	(=IV)	Laudamus	SATB solos	192
B♭	(=♭VII)	Domine Deus, Rex	SAT solos	130
g	(=v)	Qui tollis	Chorus, SATB solos	38
G	(=V)	Quoniam	Chorus	60
C	(=I)	Cum Sancto	Chorus	75

Gloria total 566 mm.

A few generalizations may be made about the keys chosen for the early movements of a multi-movement Gloria. As figure 7-15 shows, the subdominant and dominant are favorite keys for starting second movements. We also see that the submediant (seven instances) and supertonic (two instances) were occasionally used for second movements of the Gloria. The tonic is frequently reused as the key for the "Gratias" or "Domine Deus, Rex" when these are third or later internal movements. In addition, the later a movement occurs, the greater the selection of key possibilities. Thus we find the lowered leading tone (♭VII) for two settings of the "Domine Deus, Rex" (M. 19 and 49) as well as frequently in the "Qui tollis" that follows.[34]

As stated at the outset, melodic or rhythmic recurrence is an intramovement matter in the Gloria and is rarely used to relate one movement to another. If there is a later reference to an earlier movement, it is usually found at "Quoniam" where the mood, tempo, and tonality of the Gloria's opening often return. Of the 59 multi-movement Glorias examined, only two examples were found. In Albrechtsberger's *Missa Dei Patris in D minor* (M. 4, 1781) the first 25 measures of the "Quoniam" repeat the opening music of the Gloria. This return corresponds with Albrechtsberger's practice in some of his single-movement Glorias (see ex. 7-4). Similarly, in Hofmann's *Missa in C* (M. 28, before 1762) the cycle is unified by borrowing violin figurations from the "Gloria" for use in the "Quoniam" (see ex. 7-5A and 7-5B).[35] In his quest for unity Haydn, too, later writes "Gloria" and "Quoniam" movements that resemble each other (Hob. XXII: 8 [1782] and 10 [1796]). In his *Missa in tempore belli* (Hob. XXII: 9 [1796]) accompaniment motives are reused; and in the *Nelson Mass* (Hob. XXII: 11 [1798]) whole sections are replayed literally for the "Quoniam."

On the other hand, external connections between the Gloria and later parts of the Mass are found in seven of the seventy-two Masses studied. Such ties are mostly the result of literal repetitions (with new words) of certain movements from the Gloria, as the list in figure 7-16 shows. The most common connections are between the "Cum Sancto," the "In gloria Dei," or the "Amen" of the Gloria and the end of the Credo or Agnus Dei. The relationship occurs about 25 percent of the times when these three Gloria sections appear as separate movements (7 out of 28 such examples). We can never be certain if these composers intended to create a higher cyclical unity for the Mass or whether it was simply a matter of time-saving expediency. Nonetheless such literal restatements of the music do help to integrate the entire Mass and often to underscore the similarities in the texts.

Use of Soloists and Chorus

Despite an overall diversity in the deployment of voices (see fig. 7-2 and 7-8), certain verses of the Gloria are usually reserved for soloists, others for the chorus. No matter whether the Gloria consists of one or several movements,

Figure 7-15. Starting Tonalities for "Laudamus," "Gratias," and "Domine Deus, Rex" Movements

| | | Examples (according to M. Nos.) | | |
Text	Key	Second Movements	Third Movements	Fourth Movements
Laudamus (15 Ex.)	in IV	19, 17, 20, 33, 40, 71; Mozart K. 66 & 427	36	
	in V	4, 25, 30, 38, 51, 72; Mozart K. 139; Haydn Hob. XXII: 5; Bach		
	in vi	50, 60		
Gratias (14 Ex.)	in IV	23, 69; Haydn Hob. XXII: 8 & 14	60	
	in vi	18, 26, 61; Haydn Hob. XXII: 4 & 10	50	
	in ii	49	Mozart K. 427	
	in I	-	25, 30, 40, 51; Bach; Mozart K. 66 & 139	
	in iii	38; Haydn Hob. XXII: 5		
	in II	-	-	36
Domine Deus, Rex (18 Ex.)	in IV	65	-	30; Bach; Mozart K. 139
	in vi	21, 24	17	-
	in ii	15	33, 61, 69; Mozart K. 427	-
	in ♭III	66	-	-
	in I	-	26, 72	60; Haydn Hob. XXII: 5
	in iii	-	4	-
	in ♭VII	-	19, 49	-
	in V	-	71	36; Mozart K. 66

Example 7-5. Leopold Hofmann, *Missa in C*, M. 28 (before 1762),
A: "Et in terra pax" (Allegro), measures 1–2; B:
"Quoniam" (Allegro) measures 1–2.

Figure 7-16. External Connections between the Gloria and Later Movements

Mass No.	Composer	Gloria Section	Section Where Later Reused
4	Albrechtsberger	Gloria in excelsis	Et vitam (Credo)
57	Sonnleithner	Cum Sancto (fugue)	Et vitam (Credo)
26	Hofmann	Cum Sancto (fugue)	Dona nobis (Agnus Dei)
45	Reutter	In gloria	Et vitam (Credo reworking)
38	Monn	In gloria (fugue)	Dona nobis (Agnus Dei)
69	Wagenseil	Amen (fugue)	Amen (Credo)
23	Hasse	Amen (fugue)	Dona nobis (Agnus Dei)
34	Kohaut	Amen (fugue)	Dona nobis (Agnus Dei)
Hob. 1	J. Haydn	Amen	Amen (Credo)
Hob. 7	J. Haydn	Amen	Amen (Credo)

soloists generally sing at "Laudamus," "Gratias," "Domine Deus, Rex," and "Quoniam." Depending upon the scope and dimensions of a Mass, such solos take the form of either an interlude within a larger choral number (ex. 7-6, m. 11ff.) or an independent number such as an aria, duet, etc. (ex. 7-12). Characteristic of nearly all such solos within choral movements are melodies that begin on an upbeat or weak beat tied over into the next strong beat (see ex. 7-6 and 7-10). Sometimes these same lines of text are sung alternately—polychoral fashion—by the soloist and choir, as in the Gloria from Albrechtsberger's *Missa in E* (ex. 7-7).

Frequently soloists are used at the very beginning of the Gloria and later at "suscipe" during the "Qui tollis." Solo settings of the opening words "Gloria in excelsis Deo" probably derive from the old practice of having the celebrant chant this intonation text (see ex. 7-8).[36] Occasionally the soloists delay their entrance until after a brief initial statement by the chorus (see ex. 7-1). Usually

Example 7-6. Johann Nepomuk Boog, *Missa in C*, M. 11 (before 1752), "Gloria" (Allegro).

Example 7-6 (cont'd.)

Example 7-6 (cont'd.)

*Timp: Notes 1-4 G instead of C in Ms.

Example 7-6 (cont'd.)

Example 7-6 (cont'd.)

Example 7-6   (cont'd.)

Example 7-6 (cont'd.)

Example 7-6 (cont'd.)

Example 7-6 (concluded)

Example 7-7. Johann Georg Albrechtsberger, *Missa in E,* M. 2
(1756), "Gloria" (Allegro moderato) measures 1–20.

Example 7-7 (cont'd.)

Example 7-7   (cont'd.)

Example 7-7 (concluded)

Example 7-8.   Luca Antonio Predieri, *Missa Nativitatis in C*, M. 42
(before 1747), "Gloria" (Allegro), measures 1–8.

sung by a soprano, these opening Gloria solos also recall the angels' voices announcing a similar message at the Nativity. Arbesser, Bonno, Krottendorfer, Reutter, Schmidt, Tuma, Wagenseil, and Ziegler also begin some of their Glorias with such solos.[37] This practice is also found in Masses by Caldara and other Italians.[38] The powerful and dramatic soprano solos which begin the Glorias of Haydn's *Nelson Mass* and *Harmoniemesse* (Hob. XXII: 11 [1798] and 14 [1802]) undoubtedly come out of this tradition.

In 30 of the 68 Glorias which use vocal soloists there are solos at "suscipe deprecationem nostram" (see fig. 7-17). Here composers use the "humanity" and intimacy of a single voice to mirror the redemption and comfort inherent in the text's plea ("receive our prayer") and thereby provide a welcome contrast for the sins ("peccata") just bewailed by the impersonal chorus at "Qui tollis." The switch to the major mode at "suscipe" in example 7-9 (m. 14ff.) was common for this text.

Figure 7-17 illustrates the changing distribution by text of solos in the 68 Glorias that require vocal soloists. The usual deployment of soloists and chorus can be summed up as follows:

Chorus	Soloist(s)
Gloria in excelsis Deo	
	Laudamus te
	Gratias agimus tibi
	Domine Deus, Rex coelestis
Qui tollis peccata mundi	
	Quoniam tu solus sanctus
Cum Sancto Spiritu	

Of course, this distribution represents only the common practice; there were no hard and fast rules in this matter, as the percentages in figure 7-17 indicate. Frequently the chorus is juxtaposed with soloists in the same movement so that certain phrases such as "Glorificamus te," "propter magnam gloriam tuam," and "Domine Deus, Agnus," or "miserere nobis" may be emphasized (see ex. 7-6 and 7-10).

The "Qui tollis" and "Cum Sancto" are nearly always reserved for the chorus; in nine Glorias there are no further solos from "Qui tollis" until the end.[39] The use of soloists during the "Cum Sancto," "In gloria Dei," or "Amen"—something quite frequent in Haydn's late Masses—is rare among these composers.[40] These latter texts were normally set together as a fugue during this period. Some 45 of the 72 Masses under study (62.5%, or nearly two-thirds of the sample) have a fugue or fugato for these concluding texts of the Gloria. Example 7-11 offers a selection of some of the typical subjects encountered in these contrapuntal movements.[41]

Figure 7-17. Use of Soloists and Chorus in the Glorias (by Text
           Subdivision)*

Text Incipits	Quantity Using Soloists	% of Sample Using Soloists	Overall Change In Solo Use***	Quantity Using Chorus Only
Gloria in excelsis**	12	26.7		33
Et in terra pax	13	19.1	- 7.6%	55
Laudamus te	50	73.5	+54.4	18
Benedicimus te	47	69.1	- 4.4	21
Adoramus te	46	67.6	- 1.5	22
Glorificamus te	39	57.4	-10.2	29
Gratias agimus tibi	48	70.6	+13.2	20
propter magnam gloriam	40	58.8	-11.8	28
Domine Deus, Rex	57	83.8	+25.0	11
Domine Fili unigenite	59	86.8	+ 3.0	9
Domine Deus, Agnus	45	66.2	-20.6	23
Filius Patris	43	63.2	- 3.0	25
Qui tollis peccata	15	22.1	-41.1	53
Suscipe deprecationem	30	44.1	+22.0	38
Qui sedes	21	30.9	-13.2	47
Miserere nobis	5	7.4	-23.5	63
Quoniam	49	72.1	+64.7	19
Cum Sancto Spiritu	3	4.4	-67.7	65
In gloria Dei Patris	2	2.9	- 1.5	66
Amen	3	4.4	+ 1.5	65

*68 of the 72 Glorias involve soloists as well as chorus.

**In 23 Masses the Gloria intonation was not set; therefore the sample for this text consisted of only 45 Masses; cf. n. 36.

***These figures represent the percentage change in the second column.

Example 7-9. Ferdinand Schmidt, *Missa Primitiarum in C*, M. 51
(before 1747), "Qui tollis" (Adagio).

Example 7-9   (cont'd.)

Example 7-9 (cont'd.)

Example 7-9 (cont'd.)

Example 7-9 (cont'd.)

no - stram, sus - ci - pe, sus - ci - pe, sus - ci - pe.

Example 7-9 (cont'd.)

Example 7-9 (concluded)

Example 7-10. Leopold Hofmann, *Missa in D*, M. 29 (before 1772), "Gloria" (Allegro), measures 12–17.

Example 7-11. Selected "Cum Sancto," "In gloria," and "Amen"
Fugue Subjects.

"Cum Sancto"

Bonno
M. 8

Dittersdorf
M. 16

Hasse
M. 25

Hofmann
M. 26

Hofmann
M. 29

Martínez
M. 37

Schmidt
M. 50

Sonnleithner
M. 56

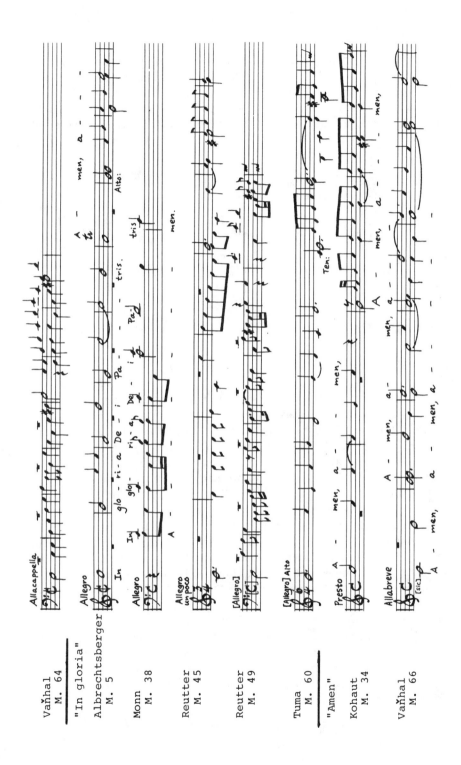

A breakdown of Gloria solos according to voice type generally reveals an even distribution. Unless special circumstances demanded otherwise, most composers give approximately equal exposure to each solo voice, as in the Gloria from Vaňhal's *Missa in C* (see fig. 7-18). Sopranos and basses are selected for solo duties somewhat more often than other voice parts (especially at "Quoniam"); alto solos are least frequent. For duets the soprano-alto pair is most favored by these composers.

Figure 7-18.   Voice Deployment in the Gloria of Vaňhal's *Missa in C* (M. 64, before 1778)

	Tempo	Meter	Key	Text	Voice(s)
I.	Allegro moderato	C	in C	Gloria	Chorus
				Laudamus	S, A solos
				Gratias	Chorus
				Domine Deus, Rex	T solo
				Domine Deus, Agnus	B solo
				Filius Patris	Chorus
II.	Adagio	3/4	in c	[Qui tollis	Chorus
III.	Allegro	3/4	in C	[Quoniam	Chorus
IV.	Alla cappella	¢	in C	[Cum Sancto	Chorus

Independent solo movements of the Gloria usually have the two- or three-part aria forms discussed in chapter five. The "Laudamus" from Schmidt's *Missa Primitiarum* is in the form of a miniature two-part motto aria for tenor (ex. 7-12). Most solo settings of the "Laudamus" are much longer than this example; about 75 measures is the average length. In Ziegler's *Missa in C* the "Quoniam" is an impressive two-part coloratura aria for soprano (ex. 7-13). "Quoniam" solos run from 32 to 205 measures in length, with about 80 measures being average.

Because of their three-part structure, the sections beginning with "Domine Deus, Rex" and "Qui tollis" inherently lend themselves to some kind of tripartite musical treatment—most often the varied repetition scheme A A^1 A^2. The opening movement from the Gloria of Reutter's *Missa Sancti Placidi* displays this typical design at "Domine Deus, Rex" (ex. 7-14). The dizzying flights for solo violin between the vocal entries are typical of the demands which Reutter often put on his solo instrumentalists.

Choruses tend to be through-composed, closely following the order of the text, although some choral movements are unified internally by short orchestral interludes that recur several times in ritornello fashion. For example, in the Gloria of Bonno's *Missa in C* (M. 8, before 1778) the melodies of measures 16–25 of the orchestral introduction return four times as interludes preceding the "Et in terra," "Laudamus," "Gratias," and "Domine Deus, Rex" of this otherwise through-composed movement.

Example 7-12. Ferdinand Schmidt, *Missa Primitiarum in C*, M. 51 (before 1747), "Laudamus" (Andante).

Example 7-12 (concluded)

Example 7-13. Joseph Ziegler, *Missa in C,* M. 71 (before 1762), "Quoniam" (Allegretto).

Example 7-14. Georg von Reutter, Jr., *Missa Sti. Placidi*, M. 44
(before 1756), "Gloria" (Andante), measures 21–52.

Example 7-14   (cont'd.)

Example 7-14 (cont'd.)

Example 7-14 (concluded)

Musical Rhetoric of the Gloria

For all composers the Gloria text is fertile soil for cultivating a myriad of rhetorical figures, many of which derive from the Renaissance and Baroque periods. Fostering a through-composed form in many choral movements, these figures usually enliven the music and, somewhat like a musical gloss, serve one or more of three basic purposes: (1) to convey the spirit or mood of the text; (2) to illustrate the meaning of specific words (word painting or *hypotyposis);* and (3) to lend emphasis to particular words. The figures appear in all kinds of Gloria movements except fugues where monothematicism and imitative counterpoint deter their use. Because of their compactness and frequent polytextuality, single-movement Glorias also tend to lack such rhetorical figures. In the following line-by-line discussion of the Gloria text, the more common musical figures will be enumerated and, in some cases, illustrated.

Gloria in excelsis Deo.

As stated at the outset of this chapter, nearly every Gloria begins with an evocation of joy (see ex. 7-1, 7-3–8). In addition to the fast tempo and major mode, ascending melodic figures, chordal declamation by the full chorus, melismas on the word "gloria" and proclamatory opening solos all contribute to this vivacious mood. The following and succeeding outlines show where illustrations of these and other characteristics may be found in the Masses and, specifically, in the musical examples of this chapter.[42]

I.   Elements of Joy (according to M. Nos.)

A.   Ascending melodies *(anabasis)*

1.   Voices   M. 2 (ex. 7-7), 18, 22, 24, 37, 45 (ex. 7-15), 61, 72.

2.   Orchestra   M. 2 (ex. 7-7), 3 (ex. 7-4), 9, 10; 11 (ex. 7-6), 14, 16, 17, 19, 23, 24, 25, 28 (ex. 7-5), 29, 30, 33, 34, 35, 36, 37 (ex. 7-1), 38, 39, 41, 45 (ex. 7-15), 48, 64, 68.

B.   Syllabic, chordal declamation by chorus *(noema)*   M. 4, 9, 19, 35, 36, 37 (ex. 7-1), 41, 45 (ex. 7-15), 49.

C.   "*Glo*-ri-a" melismas   M. 42 (ex. 7-8), 51.

D.   Solo voice at start   M. 7, 8, 9, 35, 37 (ex. 7-1, m. 30–32), 42 (ex. 7-8), 45 (ex. 7-15), 51, 70, 71 (ex. 7-16).

Example 7-16 by Ziegler demonstrates the word painting still commonly found at the words "in excelsis"; such a specialized ascending figure often permeated this entire opening section. For Kirkendale the rising melodies aptly parallel the celebrant's raising his arms for joy at this part of the service.[43]

Gernot Gruber has pointed to the martial elements often heard at the start of a Gloria as representative of God's omnipotence in the form of Christ and his heavenly legions.[44] In examples 7-15 and 7-16 we observe the "military" instruments (usually clarini and timpani) commonly reserved for this section (see ex. 7-1, 7-3, 7-4, et al.). Other martial aspects include fanfare-like vocal melodies (ex. 7-15), dotted and dactylic rhythmic topoi (♩♪ ♩, ♫ ♫, etc.), and agitated accompaniments which sometimes mimic the clashing, sword swinging, and general pandemonium of battle.

II. Martial Elements

    A. Brass and timpani in use — M. 9, 10, 19, 33, 35, 36, 37 (ex. 7-1), 41, 42 (ex. 7-8), 45 (ex. 7-15), 49, 54 (ex. 7-17), 71 (ex. 7-16).

    B. Vocal fanfare allusions — M. 20, 21, 33, 45 (ex. 7-15), 54 (ex. 7-17).

    C. "Gloria" rhythmic topoi

        1. Dotted patterns

        "Glo-ri-a"

        ♪ ♪ ♩ — M. 19, 20, 21, 22, 35, 49.
        ♪ ♪ ♪ — M. 10, 33.
        ♩ ♪ ♪ — M. 18.
        ♩. ♪ ♪ — M. 8, 42.

        2. Dactylic pattern

        ♪♪♪ — M. 9, 10, 37 (ex. 7-1), 41, 45 (ex. 7-15).

    D. Agitated orchestral accompaniments

        1. "Stile concitato" (with tremoli) — M. 4, 18, 19, 20, 25, 46.

        2. Rushing scales — M. 16, 46 (ex. 7-3), 19.

        3. Dynamic contrasts — M. 19, 37 (ex. 7-1).

        4. Restless syncopations — M. 8, 16.

Even when a Gloria lacks the opening intonation (as in ex. 7-17), the joyful and martial elements are usually heard.

Example 7-15. Georg von Reutter, Jr., *Missa Lauretana in C*, M. 45 (1742), "Gloria" (Andante), measures 1–8.

Example 7-15   (concluded)

Example 7-16. Joseph Ziegler, *Missa in C,* M. 71 (before 1762), "Gloria" (Allegro), measures 1–7.

Example 7-16 (concluded)

sis De - o. Et in ter - ra pax ho - mi - ni - bus, pax,

in ex-cel-sis, in ex-cel-sis De-o. Et in ter - ra pax ho - mi - ni - bus, pax,

in ex-cel-sis, in ex-cel-sis De-o. Et in ter - ra pax ho - mi - ni - bus, pax,

in ex-cel-sis, in ex-cel-sis De-o. Et in ter - ra pax ho - mi - ni - bus, pax,

etc.

Example 7-17.   Christoph Sonnleithner, *Missa ex C*, M. 54 (before 1771), "Et in terra" (Allegro), measures 1–20.

Example 7-17 (cont'd.)

Example 7-17 (concluded)

Et in terra pax hominibus bonae voluntatis.

Here most composers, including Haydn and Mozart, favor a more pictorial approach. "Peace" is commonly depicted by a combination of longer note values, softer dynamic level (usually *piano*), and lower pitches. Sometimes the softening in dynamics is a result of a lightening in the overall texture (i.e., fewer instruments play or only the soloists sing here). In truly Baroque spirit, descending melodies frequently correspond to the words "et in terra" (see ex. 7-15). Many Glorias emphasize the "pax" by means of numerous repetitions. This stress on peace perhaps reflects some composers' inner yearnings during an era plagued by many wars.[45]

I. Word painting *(hypotyposis)*

    A. Descending "et in terra" melodies *(catabasis)* — M. 2 (ex. 7-7), 4, 9, 13, 19, 22, 34, 35, 43, 47, 48, 50, 54 (ex. 7-17), 58, 62.

    B. Softer dynamic level or lighter texture — M. 12, 14, 15, 16, 17, 19, 20, 21, 22, 23, 25, 26, 28, 29, 33, 37, 38, 41, 58, 63, 65, 66, 70.

    C. Longer, "calmer" note values — M. 4, 10, 14, 16, 17, 21, 22, 23, 27, 29, 33, 36, 37, 38, 41, 49, 61, 71 (ex. 7-16).

    D. Markedly lower pitches — M. 18, 22, 23, 33, 37.

II. Word emphasis

    A. Repetitions of "pax" *(repetitio; anaphora)* — M. 11, 12, 13, 19, 20, 33, 34, 35, 36, 42, 43, 45 (ex. 7-15), 48, 49, 54 (ex. 7-17), 61, 62, 63, 70, 71 (ex. 7-16).

    B. Unison singing — M. 33, 63, 66.

    C. Loud again at "bonae voluntatis" — M. 12, 16, 21, 28, 41, 70.

Laudamus te. Benedicimus te.

For the Gloria's series of "we" clauses ("we praise, bless, adore," etc.) there is usually a return to the joyful elements heard at the beginning. In addition to fanfarelike motives, choral exclamations *(noema)*, loud dynamics, and exuberant "Lau-*da*-mus" melismas (ex. 7-3, 7-4, 7-6, 7-12, and 7-17), this section often uses solo-tutti alternations to create *coro spezzato* effects that resemble the echoing voices of a large throng (see ex. 7-3 and 7-7).

Adoramus te.

Some composers add a somewhat sensuous connotation to this text by means of chromaticism (ex. 7-17), melismas on "A-do-*ra*-mus" (ex. 7-6), strikingly longer note values (ex. 7-17 and 7-18), lower pitches (ex. 7-18), or a softer dynamic level (ex. 7-17). Kirkendale likens the latter two features to the celebrant's bowing his head at this point.[46] Using a technique found earlier in Caldara, Tuma sometimes underscores this personal declaration of love for the Godhead with a few measures at a slower tempo (M. 60 and 61).[47]

Glorificamus te.

Generally these words return us to an atmosphere of praise and joy (as represented by loud dynamics, ascending melodies, etc.). Many composers place a brilliant melisma on the word "glo-ri-fi-*ca*-mus" (ex. 7-6 and 7-7). As figure 7-17 above indicates, this text often coincides appropriately with a new entrance by the full chorus (ex. 7-10).

Gratias agimus tibi propter magnam gloriam tuam.

The "Gratias" is most often sung by a soloist, the full choir frequently entering at "propter magnam" (see fig. 7-17). Expressive melismas on "*ma*-gnam" or "*glo*-riam" (see ex. 7-6) are also common for this section. Such coloratura doubtlessly attests to the technical prowess of the vocalists for whom these Masses were originally written. Several composers set this section apart by an unusual orchestration that reflects the godly "magnam gloriam" being acknowledged. A local practice also found in Caldara's Masses is the use of one or two obbligato trombones for the "Gratias." Reutter, Schmidt, Sonnleithner, Tuma, and Wagenseil—all (except for Sonnleithner) members of the elder generation—continue this custom (see ex. 7-19).[48] An unusual accompaniment by two obbligato violoncellos is found in the lovely two-part motto aria that is the "Gratias" of Hofmann's grandiose *Missa Sancti Erasmi in D* (ex. 7-20).[49] The violoncellos' rhapsodic arpeggiation and the dense string texture during the vocal pauses have a stunning effect.

Domine Deus, Rex coelestis, Deus Pater omnipotens.
Domine Fili unigenite, Jesu Christe.
Domine Deus, Agnus Dei, Filius Patris.

These three "inactive" verses (they are just a series of names) are generally assigned to soloists, and relatively few rhetorical figures are encountered. Quite common, however, are melismas for emphasis on the words "Pater,"

Example 7-18.   Johann Adolf Hasse, *Missa in D,* M. 25 (before
1783), "Laudamus" (Andante), measures 16–22.

Example 7-19. Franz Tuma, *Missa in chordis et organo in G,* M. 61 (before 1743), "Gratias" (Andante), measures 1–20.

Example 7-20. Leopold Hofmann, *Missa Sancti Erasmi in D*, M. 26 (before 1779), "Gratias" (Andante), measures 1–20.

Example 7-20 (concluded)

"unigenite," "Jesu," and "Patris" (see ex. 7-6, 7-14, and 7-21). As in example 7-21 by Monn, virtuosic solo leaps and dotted rhythms are occasionally used here to suggest the power and regality of the Godhead (see also M. 26, 55, 64, 70, and 71). In some Glorias the words "Jesu Christe" are marked by longer note values than those of adjacent passages (ex. 7-14, m. 36f.; also M. 44). Word painting of "coelestis" (i.e., melodies ascending toward "heaven") is surprisingly infrequent (e.g., M. 14 and 61). As figure 7-17 indicated, several composers emphasize the third verse ("Domine Deus, Agnus Dei") by a return to the chorus; in other instances soloists are heard together for the first time at this text (see ex. 7-6, m. 34 and Gassmann's *St. Cecilia Mass*). In addition to providing a musical climax, both means of coming together suggest the theological oneness of the Father and Son proclaimed in the text.

Qui tollis peccata mundi, miserere nobis.
Qui tollis peccata mundi

Normally the "Qui tollis" stands apart from the rest of the Gloria because of its slower tempo, minor mode *(mutatio)*, choral setting, and harmonic instability. For most composers it is the emotional heart of the Gloria; for theologians it states a fundamental tenet of Christianity: the forgiveness of sins. The words "peccata" (sins) and "miserere" (have mercy) receive special attention from the composers who use various means to illustrate the suffering which, for an eighteenth-century person, was the expected consequence of all the world's evil: diminished and augmented intervals, chromatic melodies, rhythmic agitation, melodic sighs, accented dissonances, dynamic contrasts, woefully descending melodies, and dramatic pauses or gaps (see fig. 7-19). Several composers, young and old alike, employ white notation (i.e., 3/2 and ₵ meters) which Elaine Walter has also found at the same point in Caldara's Masses. In such instances the composer seems "more intent on spinning out his expressive style and thus is more concerned with melody and harmony than rhythm" (see ex. 7-22).[50]

The dissonances often associated with "miserere" (see ex. 7-22) perhaps indicate that miserableness rather than pity was understood as the underlying affect here. Word repetition and extended melismas were also frequently used to emphasize the words "qui tollis," "peccata," and "miserere" (see ex. 7-3B, 7-9, 7-22, 7-25, 7-26, 7-27 and Gassmann's *St. Cecilia Mass*).

Suscipe deprecationem nostram.

As already indicated, composers occasionally distinguish this text with solo singing (see fig. 7-17 and ex. 7-9, 7-26, 7-27). In addition, the tempo often accelerates slightly (usually to Andante), the meter changes (often to triple), and the mode switches to major.[51] The music of the "Suscipe" thus attempts to

Example 7-21. Mathias Georg Monn, *Missa in C*, M. 38 (1741), "Gratias" (Un poco allegro ma non molto), measures 23-41 of the bass and tenor parts.

Figure 7-19. "Qui tollis" Elements Suggesting Suffering and
Torment (according to Mass Numbers)

1. Diminished or augmented
   intervals (passus
   duriusculus)

   M. 4, 9, 16, 23, 36, 37, 47,
   55, 56 (Ex. 7-22), 62, 67

2. Melodic chromaticism
   (pathopoeia)

   M. 3, 4, 12, 13 (Ex. 7-27),
   16, 17, 19, 30 (Ex. 7-26),
   33, 34, 36, 38, 41, 43, 46
   (Ex. 7-3B), 49, 50, 51 (Ex.
   7-9), 59, 60, 63, 67, 70

3. Sighing figures (♪♩ , ♪♪ , etc.)

   a. Voices

   M. 13 (Ex. 7-27), 16, 19,
   23, 25, 46 (Ex. 7-3B), 49,
   50, 51 (Ex. 7-9), 56 (Ex.
   7-22), 57, 64

   b. Orchestra

   M. 9, 11, 13 (Ex. 7-27),
   19, 39, 54, 55, 63, 64

4. Expressive leaps
   (exclamatio)

   M. 22, 30 (Ex. 7-26), 41,
   56 (Ex. 7-22), 62

5. Dissonant harmonies (parrhesia)

   a. Diminished seventh
      chords

   M. 1, 3, 19, 26, 30 (Ex.
   7-26), 41, 45 (Ex. 7-25),
   46 (Ex. 7-3B), 49, 50, 55,
   56 (Ex. 7-22), 67, 68

   b. Poignant suspensions
      (syncope) [especially
      for "miserere"]

   M. 9, 16, 30, 39, 55, 56 (Ex.
   7-22, m. 13f.), 63

6. Rhythmic agitation

   a. Tremolo accompaniment

   M. 23, 35, 47

   b. Stormy accompaniment
      figures, arpeggios, etc.

   M. 29, 30 (Ex. 7-26), 34,
   45, 65

   c. Pulsating, "running"
      accompaniment

   M. 23, 26, 34, 41, 44, 45,
   46 (Ex. 7-3B), 47, 48,
   49, 55, 58, 64

   d. Syncopated accompaniment
      figures (♪ ♩ ♪ etc.)

   M. 17, 19, 41, 43

   e. Gapped accompaniment
      patterns (e.g., ♪ ♪♪♪)

   M. 2, 14, 39, 50, 57, 71

7. Melody broken up by rests
   (suspiratio)

   M. 13 (Ex. 7-27), 15, 19
   23, 33, 34, 56 (Ex. 7-22),
   61, 62, 63, 64, 68

8. Dynamic shading and
   contrast

   M. 8, 9, 10, 12, 13 (Ex.
   7-27), 15, 16, 17, 19,
   23, 30, 41, 46 (Ex. 7-3B),
   47, 48, 51 (Ex. 7-9), 55,
   56 (Ex. 7-22), 57, 59, 64,
   70, 72

9. Syllabic declamation by
   the chorus (noema)
   [often at "miserere"]

   M. 9, 13 (Ex. 7-27), 15,
   19, 29, 32, 45 (Ex. 7-25),
   46 (Ex. 7-3B), 59, 68, 71

Example 7-22. Christoph Sonnleithner, *Missa solennis in C,* M. 56
(before 1763), "Qui tollis" (Adagio), measures 1–24.

Example 7-22   (cont'd.)

Example 7-22   (cont'd.)

Example 7-22 (cont'd.)

Example 7-22 (cont'd.)

Example 7-22 (concluded)

convey a sense of hope and comfort to the faithful seeking to have their prayers ("deprecationem") heard and answered. The transparent sound of a solo soprano accompanied by only a single trombone and two violins in the "Suscipe" of Schmidt's *Missa Primitiarum* (ex. 7-9, m. 14ff.) is typical of the orchestral effects sometimes used to heighten the solace of this section.

Qui sedes ad dexteram Patris, miserere nobis.

Often this text is set to the same music—somewhat varied—as one or both of the preceding "Qui tollis" sentences. Otherwise composers prefer allusions to God's authority and power of judgment in the form of a broader, more majestic style, one that often includes the addition of brass and timpani (see ex. 7-9 and M.30). Word painting in the form of a longer note for "sedes" (sits) is also common (see ex. 7-9 and Gassmann's *St. Cecilia Mass*).

Quoniam tu solus sanctus.
Tu solus Dominus.
Tu solus Altissimus.

Here the Gloria almost invariably makes a triumphant return to the elements of joy and praise (fast tempo, major mode, fanfare figures, rising melodies, melismas, brass and timpani, etc.). "Solus" and "Altissimus" are repeatedly targets of word painting. Over two-thirds of the Masses use vocal soloists at "Quoniam"—perhaps because of the "solus" idea dominating the text. Ascending melodies or high pitches are often heard at "Altissimus" (see ex. 7-13, m. 32; also Gassmann's *St. Cecilia Mass*). Hasse in his *Missa in G* obviously makes a conscious effort at "reverse word painting" when "Altissimus" comically sends the bass soloist to the lower part of his register (see ex. 7-23). Octave leaps (a kind of *exclamatio*) sometimes lend the appropriate pomposity and stateliness to the word "Sanctus" (see ex. 7-3C and Gassmann's *St. Cecilia Mass*), while lengthy melismas commonly underscore "Jesu" (ex. 7-13, 7-24, and Gassmann's *St. Cecilia Mass*). Effectively annunciatory, a bold, virtuosic, and very Baroque clarino trumpet shares center stage with the soprano soloist in the "Quoniam" from Reutter's *Missa Lauretana* of 1742 (ex. 7-24).[52]

Cum Sancto Spiritu, in gloria Dei Patris.
Amen.

Viennese composers of the third quarter of the eighteenth century continued to prefer a choral fugue for this peroration of the Gloria (see ex. 7-11). Fugue was their best way of expressing a timeless religious concept such as the eternal

Example 7-23. Johann Adolf Hasse, *Missa in G,* M. 23 (1753),
"Quoniam" (Allegro con spirito), measures 19–27.

Example 7-24. Georg von Reutter, Jr., *Missa Lauretana in C,* M.
45 (1742), "Quoniam" (Un poco allegro).

Example 7-24   (concluded)

glory of God. As mentioned earlier, a slow introduction appropriate for "Sancto" is occasionally used for the opening three words, the fugue then being delayed until "in gloria" or "Amen" (see ex. 7-2). Fugal writing here seems to inhibit composers' use of rhetorical figures, although some joyful elements continue to be heard. For example, melismas on "*glo*-ria" and "*A*-men" are common and, on occasion, serve to expand this relatively brief text to over one hundred measures of climactic counterpoint (e.g., Gassmann's *St. Cecilia Mass*).

"Qui tollis" as a Modulatory Movement

Whether it is a separate movement or part of a longer one, the "Qui tollis" is usually the most tonally unstable area of the Gloria. In response to the more active text and to the larger, intermovement tonal plan, most composers increase the number of chord changes per bar and juxtapose striking modulations, thereby generating a strong sense of harmonic uncertainty for this section.[53] Only about half the time does the "Qui tollis" end in the same key in which it started, usually because the key of the succeeding "Quoniam" is being prepared. The vocal parts from Reutter's *Missa Lauretana* show how contorted the harmonies of the "Qui tollis" can become (ex. 7-25). This section can expose the weaknesses of composers unversed in sophisticated voice leading and modulation. The "Quoniam" is generally heard as a welcome antidote to such harmonic uneasiness (see ex. 7-24 for the "Quoniam" that follows Reutter's "Qui tollis"). Multi-sectional settings of the "Qui tollis" were common up to the 1750s (see above, at n. 19). Example 7-9 shows how changes of vocalists, tempo, and meter add to the instability created by chromatic vocal lines and constant modulation.

Beneath the harmonic turmoil reserved for the "Qui tollis," a basic scheme was commonly used. Closely allied with the three-part text, this formula hitches a string of modulations to three harmonic areas marked by full and half-cadences (see fig. 7-20). In simple terms, each of the three sentences is associated with a harmonic movement toward a new key, with half-cadences usually occurring at the commas ("mundi" and "Patris") and full cadences at the periods ("nobis" and "nostram"). Most "Qui tollis" sections, including several by Haydn and Mozart, are derived from such a scheme. The moments of greatest modulation and harmonic tension conveniently coincide with the pleas of "miserere" and "suscipe" where diminished seventh chords and sinuous chromatic lines invariably lead to new harmonic regions. The design is also a natural one for any composer sensitive to the litanylike repetitions of the text ("Qui tollis...Qui tollis...Qui sedes..."). Occasionally tutti-solo alternations reinforce the text's responsorial nature (see M. 11, 13 [ex. 7-27], 14, 28, and 29; also Haydn's Masses, Hob. XXII: 9 and 11).

Example 7-25. Georg von Reutter, Jr., *Missa Lauretana in C*, M. 45 (1742), "Qui tollis" (Adagio assai), vocal parts and continuo only.

Example 7-25 (concluded)

Example 7-26. Ignaz Holzbauer, *Missa in C,* M. 30 (before 1739),
"Qui tollis" (Grave-Largo), measures 1–7.

Example 7-26   (concluded)

Figure 7-20. A Typical Harmonic Scheme for the "Qui tollis"

Text	Harmonic Event
Qui tollis	Initial minor key
peccata mundi,	Half cadence (usually V/i)
miserere	Modulation (often with dim. 7th chords)
nobis.	Full cadence in new key (usually III, v, or i)
Qui tollis	New Key (often major)
peccata mundi,	Half cadence (in the new key)
suscipe deprecationem	Modulation
nostram.	Full cadence in second new key (often iv, III, VI, i or ♮VII)
Qui sedes	Second New Key
ad dexteram Patris,	Half cadence (in second new key)
miserere	Modulation
nobis.	Full cadence (usually to i or III)

As mentioned earlier, a tripartite form of varied repetition (AA^1A^2) is common for the "Qui tollis."[54]

A	Qui tollis ... nobis.
A^1	Qui tollis ... nostram.
A^2	Qui sedes ... nobis.

Variants in each presentation of A are usually products of the changing text (e.g., "suscipe" in A^1 instead of the "miserere" of A) and the modulations to new keys. One also finds ternary forms (ABA^1), bar forms $(AAB$ or $AA^1B)$, and through-composed forms (ABC) in use.[55] The "Qui tollis" from Boog's *Missa in C* (ex. 7-27) may serve as a concise prototype of the AA^1A^2 form and the standard harmonic scheme outlined above. The more original composers will often expand upon the basic scheme in various ways (see ex. 7-9 and 7-26).

Example 7-27. Johann Nepomuk Boog, *Missa in C*, M. 13 (before 1763), "Qui tollis" (Largo).

*Largo in Org. & Ten.

Example 7-27 (cont'd.)

Example 7-27   (cont'd.)

Example 7-27 (concluded)

Summary

We have observed the diversity of ways in which Viennese composers continued to set the Gloria during this period. Consisting of from one to 10 independent movements, Glorias selected for this study are from nine to 640 measures in length. They exhibit elaborate combinations of soloists, chorus, and instrumentalists that served as miniature "concerts" elevating the spirits of worshipers in preparation for the liturgical events to follow. During this period the tendency was toward Glorias of fewer movements and with greater tonal control; most Glorias have one to four movements. Comparison of figures 7-2 and 7-18 exemplifies this change supporting heightened concinnity.

Despite the variety in settings there are some common patterns and techniques that were part of the local tradition:

1. Text is the overriding determinant of structure, except in purely solo numbers.
2. The movement layout of most Glorias derives from the basic three-part, fast-slow-fast, major-minor-major division of the text ("Gloria," "Qui tollis," and "Quoniam").
3. Certain sentences are nearly always set together (often in groups of three).
4. The practice of subdividing certain movements (e.g., "Qui tollis") with changes of tempo, meter, key, or performer lasted up to the 1750s.
5. Certain verses, especially "Laudamus," "Gratias," "Domine Deus, Rex," and "Quoniam," are usually sung by soloists.
6. Instrumental obbligatos are common with certain solos.
7. Most Glorias exhibit tonal planning marked by harmonic continuity between movements, third relationships between certain sections, the "Qui tollis" as an unstable harmonic area, and the "Quoniam" as a place for tonal reprise.

The Glorias are unified chiefly by tonal means. Melodic and rhythmic recurrences throughout multi-movement Glorias are rare, although certain music (e.g., "Cum Sancto" or "In gloria Dei") frequently is reused in a later part of the Mass (e.g., "Et vitam" of the Credo or "Dona nobis pacem" of the Agnus Dei).

Most composers were also still employing a variety of rhetorical figures to illustrate the text, evoke a certain affect (joy and suffering being common here), and emphasize specific words. Although a few composers seemed to avoid using these traditional figures (e.g., Arbesser, Holzbauer, Seuche, Strasser, and Wagenseil), it is significant that some of the figures remained in use and were incorporated into the more progressive style found in the Glorias of Bonno, Dittersdorf, Friberth, Gassmann, Haydn, Mozart, and Vaňhal.

8

Credo

Viennese composers approached the Credo with much less imagination than they did other parts of the Mass. With the exception of the "Et incarnatus," which always received special treatment, they tended to set the Credo's 18 verses in a straightforward, businesslike manner for a number of possible reasons:

1. The Credo has the longest text of the Ordinary.
2. The text consists mostly of a series of dogmatic affirmations.
3. Concluding the Liturgy of the Word, which sometimes includes a lengthy homily, the Credo prepares the Mass of the Faithful (Eucharist) that is about to begin, i.e., the Credo is a formal recitation on the border between two sections of the Mass and thus does not demand an elaborate setting.
4. Gregorian chant Credos are mostly syllabic and unornamented.

From most Credos one has the impression that composers lavished little time upon them. The Credos in Haydn's shorter Masses (Hob. XXII: 1, 3, 6, 7) are examples of the polytextuality which was frowned upon by the church and was endemic to most *missae breves.*[1] The declamatory, parlando choral writing and the almost mechanical alternation of chorus and soloists—both characteristic of the Credo's outer movements in longer concerted Masses— may be seen in Reutter's *Missa Sancti Caroli* (*DTÖ* vol. 88, p. 36ff.). Usually the Credo text exerts full control over the setting; relatively few words are repeated, and most vocal rhythms are direct derivatives of the syllabically declaimed text. This chapter will elucidate the compositional traditions which tend to make the Credo one of the least inspired parts of the Mass, but one which at the same time offered an attractive challenge to the more innovative composers.

Overall Structure

With only a few exceptions all Credos—including those in both long and short Masses—are designed around a tripartite division of the text: (1) "Credo/Patrem," (2) "Et incarnatus est," (3) "Et resurrexit."[2] As can be seen in figure 8-1 (under III[b]), some 43 of the 71 Credos under study (60.6%) consist of exactly these three movements. Another 12 Credos—usually from the earlier Masses—further subdivide the text with movements starting at "Qui propter nos homines," "Crucifixus," "Et in Spiritum Sanctum," "Confiteor," "Et expecto," or "Et vitam" (e.g., fig. 8-8). Of the 16 Credos whose movements overlap the basic tripartite structure (columns I–III[a] in figure 8-1) 11 have a new section beginning at "Et incarnatus" or "Et resurrexit."

The Credo's three basic movements are most commonly differentiated by tempo, meter, mode, and scoring as follows:

	Tempo	Meter	Mode	Scoring
"Credo/Patrem"	fast (92%)	duple (71%)	major (94%)	full orch.
"Et incarnatus"	slow (90%)	duple (68%)	minor (68%)	reduced orch. (without brass)
"Et resurrexit"	fast (97%)	triple (46%) or duple (54%)	major (97%)	full orch.

(Percentages are of the sample of 69 multi-movement Credos.) A kind of "arch" structure results, the center being the "Et incarnatus"—the spiritual core of the Credo where one of Christianity's greatest mysteries is described.

The usual opening tempo for the Credo is allegro or a form thereof (e.g., allegro molto, allegro di molto, allegro spiritoso, allegro con spirito, spiritoso, and allegro moderato). In most multi-movement Credos the first change in tempo occurs at "Et incarnatus" where adagio is the norm.[3] In 14 Credos there is a new, often slightly faster tempo for the "Crucifixus."[4] To reflect the triumphant turn in the text ("He is risen!") the Credo's opening tempo almost invariably returns at "Et resurrexit." Changes of tempo are relatively rare after this point, with the exception of those Credos where the "Et vitam" is a separate fugal movement or follows a brief "mortuorum" adagio.[5] In general, then, most composers use a fast-slow-fast tempo scheme for their Credos, a design which is also common in much Baroque instrumental music as well as in the Kyrie and Gloria of the Mass.

Most composers vary the meter from movement to movement, although in 16 Credos one meter is maintained despite changes in tempo, key, scoring,

Figure 8-1. Credo Text Divisions

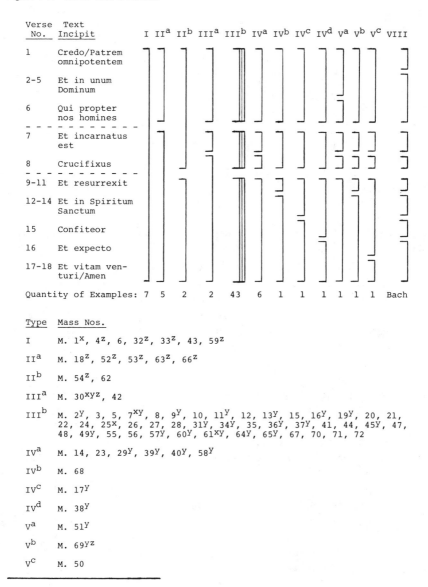

Verse No.	Text Incipit	I	II^a	II^b	III^a	III^b	IV^a	IV^b	IV^c	IV^d	V^a	V^b	V^c	VIII
1	Credo/Patrem omnipotentem													
2-5	Et in unum Dominum													
6	Qui propter nos homines													
7	Et incarnatus est													
8	Crucifixus													
9-11	Et resurrexit													
12-14	Et in Spiritum Sanctum													
15	Confiteor													
16	Et expecto													
17-18	Et vitam venturi/Amen													
Quantity of Examples:		7	5	2	2	43	6	1	1	1	1	1	1	Bach

Type	Mass Nos.
I	M. 1^x, 4^z, 6, 32^z, 33^z, 43, 59^z
II^a	M. 18^z, 52^z, 53^z, 63^z, 66^z
II^b	M. 54^z, 62
III^a	M. 30^{xyz}, 42
III^b	M. 2^y, 3, 5, 7^{xy}, 8, 9^y, 10, 11^y, 12, 13^y, 15, 16^y, 19^y, 20, 21, 22, 24, 25^x, 26, 27, 28, 31^y, 34^y, 35, 36^y, 37^y, 41, 44, 45^y, 47, 48, 49^y, 55, 56, 57^y, 60^y, 61^{xy}, 64^y, 65^y, 67, 70, 71, 72
IV^a	M. 14, 23, 29^y, 39^y, 40^y, 58^y
IV^b	M. 68
IV^c	M. 17^y
IV^d	M. 38^y
V^a	M. 51^y
V^b	M. 69^{yz}
V^c	M. 50

x = Crucifixus is a separate subsection within a movement.

y = Et vitam is a separate subsection within a movement.

z = Multi-sectional (i.e., one or more movements may be divided into separate subsections other than "x" and "y" above).

etc.[6] As already indicated, duple-duple-triple is the most frequently encountered pattern of meters for the Credo. However, as can be seen in figure 8-2, the arrangements duple-duple-duple and duple-triple-duple are almost equally common. Meter selection is restricted mostly to C and 3/4, with the "expressive" 3/2 often reserved for the "Et incarnatus" and the Allabreve ₵ for the final "Et vitam" fugue (see ex. 8-13 and 8-19). Dancelike triple meters in the outer movements often serve to enliven the dogmatic text (see ex. 8-9 below). In only two instances (M. 55 and 69) is there a change of meter for the closing "Amen" section.

The Credo shows less harmonic adventuresomeness than the Gloria. The tonic of the Mass opens the Credo and almost always returns for the "Et resurrexit."[7] Like the "Qui tollis" of the Gloria, the "Et incarnatus" is usually a tonally unstable movement, beginning in a minor key (about 68% of the time), modulating through several keys (with "Crucifixus" in a new key), and ending in a key different from that in which it began (over 50% of the time). As can be seen in figure 8-3, the relative minor (vi), tonic minor (i), and subdominant (IV) were the keys most often used (over 80% of the time) for beginning the "Et incarnatus." Interesting is how nearly one-third of the settings begin the "Et incarnatus" in a major key (see the upper case Roman numerals in fig. 8-3). The major "Et incarnatus" settings by Hasse, Holzbauer, Monn, Predieri, Tuma, and Wagenseil date from the 1740s and 1750s and serve as conceivable antecedents for a practice which Haydn took up only in his Masses of the late 1770s.[8] However, in most of the major "Et incarnatus" settings (16 of the 22) the minor mode eventually appears, albeit belatedly at "Crucifixus."[9]

Usually the entire "Et incarnatus"—"Crucifixus" section modulates so that it concludes in a key which is a third or fifth above or below the key of the "Et resurrexit" to follow (see fig. 8-4). As at "Quoniam" in the Gloria, composers enjoy exploiting the marvelous effect of this harmonic contrast coupled with a change in tempo, meter, mode, and scoring; Bach's *B-minor Mass* offers the best-known example of this kind of striking contrast between "Crucifixus" and "Et resurrexit." In about one-fifth of the examples there is no change of tonic pitch at this point, the "Et incarnatus" having already modulated to the key of the "Et resurrexit."

The full orchestra (including brass and timpani) is normally used for the start of the Credo and at "Et resurrexit." A greatly reduced ensemble—frequently only strings and continuo—accompanies the somber "Et incarnatus est." As figure 8-5 indicates, obbligatos were often part of the "Et incarnatus" accompaniment in Masses by Albrechtsberger, Bonno, Dittersdorf, Gassmann, Hofmann, Reutter, Sonnleithner, Tuma, and Wagenseil. Since nearly one-quarter of the Masses under study have obbligatos at this point, it should be no surprise that Mozart makes exquisite concertante use of a solo flute, oboe, and bassoon in the "Et incarnatus" of his

Figure 8-2. Meter Use in the Credo (Credo/Patrem–Et
             incarnatus–Et resurrexit)

Duple-Duple-Triple
(C-C-3/4 unless otherwise
  indicated)

    17 Ex.   M. 2, 11, 14, 15, 30, 34, 35,
                              36, 38, 39, 40, 49, 51 (2/4-C-
                              3/4), 54, 56, 57, 71 (C-2/4-3/4)

Duple-Triple-Duple
(C-3/4-C)

    14 Ex.   M. 3 (C-3/2-C), 7, 13, 16 (¢-3/4-¢),
                              22 (C-3/2-C), 24, 31 (C-3/2-C),
                              32 (C-3/2-C), 42, 44 (C-3/2-C), 47,
                              52 (C-3/2-C), 53, 68 (C-3/2-C)

Duple-Duple-Duple
(C-C-C)

    16 Ex.   M. 1, 8, 10, 19 (Vienna version),
                              21, 25, 26, 29, 33, 45 (C-C-2/4),
                              50, 60, 61, 62, 63, 72

Triple-Duple-Triple
(3/4-C-3/4)

    8 Ex.   M. 4 (3/8-C-3/4), 12, 20 (3/4-
                              2/4-3/4), 27, 28, 41, 65 (3/4-
                              2/4-3/4), 70 (3/4-C-3/2)

Triple-Duple-Duple
(3/4-C-C)

    6 Ex.   M. 9, 18 (3/4-C-2/4), 23, 37,
                              67 (3/2-C-¢), 69 (3/2-C-C)

Duple-Triple-Triple
(C-3/4-3/4)

    3 Ex.   M. 19 (Berlin version), 48,
                              55 (C-3/2-3/4)

Triple-Triple-Triple
(3/4-3/4-3/4)

    5 Ex.   M. 17, 58 (3/4-3/2-3/4), 59,
                              64 (3/4-3/2-3/4), 66

Triple-Triple-Duple

    1 Ex.   M. 5 (3/8-3/4-C)

Meter Changes also at "Crucifixus"
¢   M. 39, 61, 69
C   M. 32, 42, 58
3/4   M. 23, 51
3/2   M. 29

Meter Changes also at "Et vitam"
¢   M. 7, 34, 36, 37, 38, 69
C   M. 2, 39, 40, 49, 51
3/4   M. 45, 50
3/8   M. 17
6/4   M. 9

One Meter AND Tempo Throughout Credo
           M. 6, 43

Figure 8-3. Starting Tonalities for the "Et incarnatus"

Starting Key	Qty. of Examples	M. Nos.
vi	23	M. 2, 7, 10, 14, 16, 21, 22, 24, 25, 26, 28, 34, 45, 47, 48, 53, 56, 57, 58, 59, 60, 62, 72
i	19	M. 1, 3, 11, 13, 18, 27, 33, 35, 38, 39, 44, 49, 50, 51, 52, 54, 55, 70, 71
IV	14	M. 4, 5, 8, 9, 15, 17, 19, 20, 29, 30, 41, 42, 64, 69
V	4	M. 23, 65, 66, 68
VI	2	M. 31, 63 (both Masses in minor key)
v	2	M. 36, 61 (both follow a "Credo" ending in ♭VII)
iv	1	M. 12
iii	1	M. 67
♭iii	1	M. 37
III	1	M. 32 (Mass in minor key)
I	1	M. 40

69 Masses with multi-movement Credos

Figure 8-4. Key Relationships between the End of the "Crucifixus"
and "Et resurrexit"

Key Relationships	Quantity of Examples	Keys Employed
Up a third	21	vi-I (15 Ex.), VI-I (2), iv-VI (1), ii-IV (2), i-III (1)
Down a third	11	iii-I (7), ♭III-I (2), III-I (1), vi-IV (1)
Up a fifth	11	IV-I (8), iv-I (3)
Down a fifth	9	v-I (4), V-I (2), ♭VII-IV (2), i-IV (1)
No change of tonic	14	(the mode changes minor-major in 8 of these)
Half cadence elision	3	V/i-i (1), V/i-I (1), V/vi-I (1)

C-minor Mass, K. 427, of 1782–83. Example 8-1 shows a similar concertante use of trombones and violins during the "Et incarnatus" of Hofmann's *Missa in honorem Sanctae Theresiae*. Such obbligatos are often found when the "Et incarnatus" has recurring orchestral ritornellos.

Figure 8-5. "Et incarnatus" Obbligatos

Instruments (pairs)	*Masses Where Used*
Trombones	M. 27 (ex. 8-1), 45, 56, 60, 61, 67, 70
Oboes	M. 8 (solo), 10, 16 (solo), 17
Flutes	M. 4 (mostly in unison with violins), 29 (solo)
Bassoons	M. 48
Violoncellos	M. 9
Violin	M. 19 (Vienna version)

Vocal soloists mostly alternate with the chorus during the Credo and sing fewer independent numbers than they do in the Gloria. The full chorus nearly always opens the Credo, even in the 36 instances where the intonation's text ("Credo in unum Deum") has been set. A syllabic, almost parlando style is typical of the choral writing here.[10] Soloists usually begin singing successively (and more melismatically) at "Et in unum Dominum" so that a concertante style results (see ex. 8-2). In shorter Masses offensive telescoping of the texts (polytextuality) often occurs here and later, during the "Et resurrexit." By the end of the Credo's first movement, generally at "Qui propter nos homines," if not at "Genitum," the chorus has resumed its declamatory singing.

Example 8-1. Leopold Hofmann, *Missa in honorem Sanctae Theresiae in C,* M. 27 (before 1760), "Et incarnatus" (Adagio).

Example 8-1   (cont'd.)

Example 8-1 (cont'd.)

Example 8-1   (cont'd.)

Example 8-1 (cont'd.)

Example 8-1   (concluded)

pul - tus est.

Example 8-2. Ferdinand Schmidt, *Missa Sanctae Caeciliae*, M. 50
(before 1746), "Credo" (Andante).

Example 8-2 (cont'd.)

Example 8-2 (cont'd.)

Example 8-2 (cont'd.)

Example 8-2 (cont'd.)

Example 8-2 (cont'd.)

Example 8-2 (cont'd.)

Example 8-2 (cont'd.)

Example 8-2 (cont'd.)

Example 8-2 (cont'd.)

Example 8-2 (cont'd.)

Example 8-2   (cont'd.)

Example 8-2   (cont'd.)

Example 8-2   (concluded)

Although some three-fifths of the "Et incarnatus" settings are for solo voices (see fig. 8-6), the remainder are for chorus—putting in doubt the generalizations by analysts who claim that by the second half of the eighteenth century composers preferred soloists for the "Et incarnatus."[11] Whether for chorus or solo voices, the "Et incarnatus" always has a clearly audible text, one rarely distorted by polytextuality.[12] A solo soprano or solo quartet is common for the beginning of the "Et incarnatus," with a new soloist (most often a bass) taking over at "Crucifixus" (see fig. 8-7 and examples 8-1, 8-3, and 8-4). In the "Et incarnatus" of Vaňhal's *Missa solennis in F* we observe the intricate coloratura sometimes demanded of soloists in this section (Example 8-3, m. 65ff.). In addition, the asterisks in figure 8-7 show that over half of the 25 "Et incarnatus" settings which start with chorus alone switch to vocal soloists for the "Crucifixus."

The "Et resurrexit" nearly always returns us to the vocal treatment heard at the outset of the Credo: syllabic choral declamation, tutti-solo concertante style, and occasional polytextuality.[13] Again the chorus usually begins this movement alone.[13] However, an opening with vocal soloists can heighten the sense of triumph in the text, as the "Et resurrexit" from Holzbauer's *Missa in C* demonstrates (ex. 8-5). The "Et resurrexit" of Mozart's *"Waisenhaus" Mass*, K. 139 (Vienna, 1768), similarly begins with a soprano solo. As figure 8-6 shows, soloists usually do not begin singing in this movement until "Et iterum venturus est" or "Et in Spiritum Sanctum." Generally each solo voice is then heard successively at least once. Choral outbursts are common at "judicare" and "simul adoratur" for reasons to be discussed below. By "Et expecto" or, at the latest, "Et vitam venturi" the chorus has usually resumed singing, often (about 40% of the time) concluding the Credo with a learned fugue or fugato.

Total lengths of the Credos range from 16 measures in Arbesser's *Missa nubes pluant justum* (M. 6) to 356 measures in Monn's *Missa in C* (M. 38). The average length is about 164 measures, with the "Et incarnatus" having roughly one-half to three-quarters as many measures as either of the Credo's outer movements. By comparison, Haydn's Credos range from 24 measures (Hob. XXII: 3) to 386 measures (Hob. XXII: 5).

Forty-two percent of the time (in 28 of 67 examples) the halfway point in the Mass's total length is reached before the Credo (in other words, the Credo, Sanctus, and Agnus Dei often account for much less than three-fifths of the Mass's length).[14] This situation corroborates the general impression that for most composers the bulk of musical interest and "weight" lies in the Kyrie and Gloria.

Figure 8-6. Use of Soloists and Chorus in the Credo* (by Text Subdivision)

Text	Quantity Using Soloists	% of Sample Using Soloists	% Change in Solo Use	Quantity Using Chorus Only
Credo in unum Deum**	0	--	--	30
Patrem omnipotentem	11	17.2%	+17.2%	53
Et in unum Dominum	29	45.3	+28.1	35
Qui propter nos homines	13	20.3	-25.0	51
Et incarnatus est	39	60.9	+40.6	25
Crucifixus	43	67.2	+ 6.3	21
Et resurrexit	7	10.9	-56.3	57
Et iterum venturus est	21	32.8	+21.9	43
Et in Spiritum Sanctum	39	60.9	+28.1	25
Et expecto	8	12.5	-48.4	56
Et vitam venturi	2	3.1	- 9.4	62
Amen	1	1.6	- 1.5	63

*Only 64 of the 71 Credos under study involved soloists as well as chorus; the percentages refer to this sample of 64. M. 1, 5, 9, 17, 59, 64, and 72 are for chorus alone throughout.

**In the sample of 64 Credos, only 30 set the opening intonation; the Berlin version of M. 19 also does so but was not counted here. Thus, 34 Credos (including the Vienna version of M. 19 and in addition to M. 1 and 59) begin with the text "Patrem omnipotentem."

Figure 8-7.   Vocal Soloists Used at "Et incarnatus" and
"Crucifixus"

Text	Voice(s)	Quantity of Examples	M. Nos.
Et incarnatus	S	12	M. 3 (Ex. 8-13), 19 (Vienna version), 27 (Ex. 8-1), 29, 36, 38 (Ex. 8-12A), 44, 48, 49, 66 (Ex. 8-3), 71
	SATB	5	M. 14, 15 (Ex. 8-4), 26, 34, 65
	AT	5	M. 7, 22, 60, 61, 67
	SA	4	M. 4, 41, 47, 70
	T	3	M. 16, 28, 35
	A	2	M. 20, 45
	B	2	M. 50, 53
	ATB	2	M. 21, 24 (Ex. 8-11)
	ST	1	M. 62
	TB	1	M. 55
	SAT	1	M. 69
	S/Chorus	1	M. 43
Crucifixus (new soloists)	B	8	M. 7, 25*, 27 (Ex. 8-1), 29 (Ex. 8-15), 45, 67, 70, 71
	SATB	7	M. 3, 13, 18*, 28, 40*, 52*, 55
	ATB	6	M. 12*, 38, 44, 48, 49, 62
	T	3	M. 42*, 50 (Ex. 8-14), 58*
	SA	2	M. 23*, 32*
	SAT	2	M. 53, 57*
	S	2	M. 14 (Ex. 8-16), 51*
	TB	1	M. 47
	SSTB	1	M. 16
	SSATB	1	M. 30*
	B/Chorus	1	M. 33*
	SAT/Chorus	1	M. 43
	Same soloists as "Et incarnatus"	8	M. 20, 21, 22, 26, 34, 35, 66, 69
	Chorus alone enters	9	M. 15, 19 (Vienna version), 24, 36, 41, 60, 61, 65, 69

*Indicates that the "Et incarnatus" began with the full chorus alone.

Example 8-3. Jan Vaňhal, *Missa solennis in F*, M. 66 (before 1797), "Credo" (Andante) measures 48–80 [= "Et incarnatus"; for preceding section see ex. 8-10].

Example 8-3 (cont'd.)

Example 8-3 (cont'd.)

Example 8-3 (concluded)

Example 8-4. Karl Ditters von Dittersdorf, *Missa in C*, M. 15
(before 1773), "Et incarnatus" (Adagio).

Example 8-4 (cont'd.)

Example 8-4   (cont'd.)

Example 8-4   (cont'd.)

Example 8-4 (cont'd.)

Example 8-4 (concluded)

Example 8-5. Ignaz Holzbauer, *Missa in C,* M. 30 (before 1739), "Et resurrexit" (Allegro), measures 1-9.

Example 8-5 (concluded)

Most of the time the three movements of the Credo form three disparate sections. However, several composers use some of the following techniques for unifying the Credo as a whole:

1. "Credo" refrain throughout opening movement

   M. 4 (Albrechtsberger, 1781),
   M. 30 (Holzbauer, before 1739),
   M. 55 (Sonnleithner, before 1765),
   M. 56 (Sonnleithner, before 1763)

2. "Credo" refrain at ends of opening and closing movements

   M. 8 (Bonno, before 1778)

3. Musical reprise at "Et resurrexit"
   a) Return of only the accompaniment figures that opened the Credo

   M. 16 (Dittersdorf, n.d.),
   M. 19 (Gassmann, Vienna version, before 1771),
   M. 26 (Hofmann, before 1779),
   M. 27 (Hofmann, before 1760),
   M. 28 (Hofmann, before 1762),
   M. 47 (Reutter, before 1759; ex. 8-8)

   b) Varied return of the Credo's opening bars

   M. 64 (Vaňhal, before 1778),
   M. 65 (Vaňhal, before 1782; ex. 8-9),
   M. 66 (Vaňhal, before 1797)

   c) Literal reprise of entire first movement

   M. 17 (Dittersdorf, before 1777)

4. "Et vitam" as a varied reprise of "Et resurrexit"

   M. 18 (Friberth, 1774),
   M. 19 (Gassmann, Berlin version, before 1771),
   M. 64 (Vaňhal, before 1778),
   M. 65 (Vaňhal, before 1782),
   M. 72 (Ziegler, before 1770)

Interspersing the opening word "Credo" and its theme between various verses of the Credo's extensive text makes both syntactical and musical sense: the listener is reminded that a series of beliefs is being enumerated, and greater musical unity is achieved for the entire Credo. In his investigation of this subject, Georg Reichert found that such "Credo Masses" were frequent during the eighteenth century, especially in the works of Predieri, Jommelli, Wagenseil, as well as Joseph Haydn (Hob. XXII: 5) and Mozart (K. 192 and 257).[15] However, the examples by Albrechtsberger, Holzbauer, and Sonnleithner (listed under type "1" above) limit the "Credo" refrain to the first movement and do not have it return during the "Et resurrexit." For example, in the Credo of Holzbauer's *Missa in C* the opening melody and text shown in example 8-6 return four times during the first movement (after "invisibilium," "unigenitum," "Deo vero," and "facta sunt"). Mozart, who spoke highly of Holzbauer's Masses, used a similar but more famous theme to unify the entire Credo of his *Missa brevis in F* (ex. 8-7).

Much more common among the composers under study was the limiting of the Credo's musical reprise to only the accompaniment figures or opening measures of "Et resurrexit" (listed under type "3" above). In Reutter's *Missa Sancti Mariani,* the same violin figurations open the "Credo" and "Et resurrexit" movements (ex. 8-8). As in several of the Masses of Mozart and Haydn, Vaṅhal's Masses often use a slightly recast version of the Credo's beginning—melody as well as accompaniment—for the start of the "Et resurrexit."[16] In the *Missa pastorell in G* Vaṅhal seems to be mixing this practice with the refrain form of the older so-called Credo Masses. The opening Credo "refrain" returns four times—each time to a different text: "Qui propter nos homines," "Et resurrexit," "Et unam sanctam catholicam," and "Et vitam" (ex. 8-9).[17] Dittersdorf's expedient for unifying the Credo by using the same 65 measures of music for both the "Credo" and "Et resurrexit" movements is unique but unimaginative (M. 17).

Occasionally a Credo has musical ties with other parts of the Mass Ordinary. As was seen in figure 7-16 of the previous chapter, in three cases the Credo's "Et vitam" or "Amen" is a repetition or derivative of music already heard in the Gloria. In one instance (Boog's *Missa in C,* M. 13) the "Et vitam" is heard later, in slightly reworked form as the "Dona nobis pacem" at the end of the Mass.

Figures 8-8 and 8-9 summarize the range of the Credo's overall structure during this period. In figure 8-8 (Monn) we see the older multi-movement Credo with several connected subdivisions in different keys and tempos; Holzbauer, Schmidt, and Wagenseil also wrote such settings. Figure 8-9 (Albrechtsberger) depicts the three-movement scheme which was becoming the standard for most Credos during the second half of the eighteenth century.

Musical Rhetoric of the Credo

Undoubtedly because of the nature of the text—a series of dogmatic affirmations—Viennese composers use rhetorical figures less intensively in the Credo than in the Gloria. Generally the outer movements ("Credo" and

Example 8-6. Ignaz Holzbauer, *Missa in C,* M. 30 (before 1739),
          "Credo" (Allegro), measures 1–2 of the soprano part.

Example 8-7. Wolfgang Amadeus Mozart, *Missa brevis in F,* K.
          192 (1774), "Credo" (Allegro), measures 1–2 of the
          soprano part.

Example 8-8. Georg von Reutter, Jr., *Missa Sancti Mariani in G,*
M. 47 (1759), "Credo" (Allegro), measures 1–5, and
"Et resurrexit" (Allegro), measures 1–6.

Example 8-8　(cont'd.)

Example 8-8   (cont'd.)

Example 8-8 (concluded)

Example 8-9. Jan Vaňhal, *Missa Pastorell in G*, M. 65 (before
1782), A–B: "Credo" (Allegro moderato), measures
1–8, 70–77, C–D: "Et resurrexit" (Allegro moderato),
measures 1–8, 81–88, E: "Et vitam" (Allegro),
measures 109–16 [choral parts only].

Figure 8-8. Movement Plan of the Credo in Monn's *Missa in C*
(M. 38, 1741)

Mvt.	Text Incipit	Tempo	Meter	Key	m.	Voices
I.	Credo in unum Deum	1. Allegro	C	C	42	Chorus
II.	Et incarnatus est	2. Adagio	C	c-g	34	SATB solos
III.	Et resurrexit	3. Allegro-	3/4	C-G	52	S/Chorus
	Et in Spiritum	4. Andante un poco	C		55	S solo
IV.	Et expecto	5. Allegro-	3/4	C	8	Chorus
	Mortuorum	6. Adagio-	"		7	Chorus
		7. Allegro-	"		3	Orch.
	Et vitam venturi	8. Alla breve	¢		155	Chorus (fugue)

Figure 8-9. Movement Plan of the Credo in Albrechtsberger's
Missa S. Mathiae in E (M. 2, 1756)

Mvt.	Text Incipit	Tempo	Meter	Key	m.	Voices
I.	Patrem omnipotentem	1. Allegro	C	E	33	Chorus/ SATB solos
II.	Et incarnatus est	2. Adagio	C	c#	18	Chorus
III.	Et resurrexit	3. Allegro-	3/4	A-E	74	Chorus/ AT solos
		4. Allegro moderato	C		30	Chorus (fugue)

"Et resurrexit") have accompaniment figures which evoke the sense of resolution and triumph behind these texts. The 10 verses from "Et in unum Dominum Jesum Christum" through "cujus regni non erit finis" narrate the birth, life, death, and resurrection of Christ, and it is here that word painting is most plentiful. The central "Et incarnatus" uses several specific figures of melody, harmony, dynamics, etc. to reflect the mystery and suffering of Christ's incarnation and crucifixion. Henry Raynor pithily describes most Austrian composers' approach to the Credo thus: "...its purely dogmatic clauses are usually declamatory, and the narrative section [is] treated as a composer's purple patch."[18]

Credo in unum Deum ... invisibilium

"But what was a composer to do with the doctrinal parts?" H. C. Robbins Landon justly asks that question in his discussion of Haydn's *Heiligmesse*.[19] As we have seen in the preceding section, a few composers rely upon recurring musical events (e.g., "Credo" refrains and ritornellos) to help integrate this section. Others use cantus firmus technique by incorporating chant into their settings.[20] Mostly, however, Charles Rosen's description of the Credo in Haydn's *Theresa* Mass (Hob. XXII: 12) as "turgid and unimaginative" applies to the syllabic and homophonic settings encountered here.[21] Some composers (especially Predieri, Seuche, Tuma, and Wagenseil) create a pseudo-polyphony out of staggered vocal entries, often telescoping the text in the process.[22] The only musical figures frequently used are fanfares and ascending melodies (*anabasis*) which may allude to the omnipotent Godhead overseeing "heaven and earth" (see ex. 8-2).

Et in unum Dominum Jesum Christum ... descendit de coelis

As figure 8-6 showed, "Et in unum Dominum" is where the soloists often begin singing (in 19 of 64 cases or about 30%). This change to solo voices perhaps parallels that heard earlier at "Christe eleison" and "Domine Fili unigenite" when Christ was also the subject of the text; a single voice may have been considered the best means of representing Christ's humanity (see ex. 8-2, m. 10f.).[23] Almost as frequently the chorus appropriately reenters a few measures later at "Qui propter nos homines" where the first person plural ("nos") refers to all of "us" whom Christ has saved (ex. 8-2, m. 31f.).[24]

Perhaps the most ubiquitous case of word painting in the Mass occurs with "descendit de coelis" where falling vocal melismas (*catabasis*) appear at least 70 percent of the time. This and a few other examples of word painting were a fixture of the Viennese tradition in the eighteenth century. On occasion some composers take a more innovative path. For example, Ferdinand

Schmidt hides the descending motives in the accompaniment at this point (ex. 8-2, m. 35), and Vaňhal exaggerates the "descent" in a rather *buffo* manner (ex. 8-10).

Et incarnatus est ... Et homo factus est

As it has been for centuries, the "Et incarnatus" is the true heart of the Credo—its 24 words describing the mystery, life, death, and suffering of Christ. For Viennese composers this text almost always engenders a plaintive, dramatic, or intense style. Because of the text's narrative quality, most settings of the "Et incarnatus" are relatively short and through-composed (see ex. 8-11). "Et incarnatus" and "Crucifixus" together average only about 33 measures in length. Full-blown numbers such as arias with recurring themes and ritornellos are rare, even though soloists are commonly used (see ex. 8-3 above).[25] As already indicated, the "Et incarnatus" usually stands apart because of its slower tempo, minor mode, harmonic instability, reduced orchestration (no brass or timpani), and occasional instrumental obbligatos (see ex. 8-1, 8-4, 8-11, and Gassmann's *St. Cecilia Mass*).

Comparison of "Et incarnatus" settings reveals that several of the opening vocal themes resemble each other in their pathos. There appear to have been a few families of "Et incarnatus" melodies or topoi (see ex. 8-12A–C). One type (A) has the voice begin on the tonic, leap up to the fifth degree, and then descend (mostly stepwise) to the tonic which is usually weakened by an affective appoggiatura or accented neighboring tone on "-natus est." Another melody type (B) opens with the skip of a perfect fourth and follows the basic outline of 5–1–7–1 in scale degrees. Still another type (C) rises the minor sixth from the dominant to the mediant and then falls the diminished fourth to the leading tone before returning to the tonic, as though this *passus duriusculus* suggests the "incarnation" of the text. These topoi were by no means codified melodic formulas consciously employed by the composers, but the types conveniently summarize the kinds of melodic style used in the "Et incarnatus." Not all "Et incarnatus" themes are so imbued with pathos as these types indicate; some composers use the major mode and more cheerful themes which perhaps reflect the "Maria Virgine" rather than the mysterious "incarnatus" of the text (see ex. 8-3 and 8-4 above as well as some of Haydn's late Masses).

The next few musical examples serve to illustrate the more common musical figures of the "Et incarnatus" and "Crucifixus." The "Et incarnatus" from Albrechtsberger's *Missa Annuntiationis* is typical of the many settings using expressive white notation which emphasizes harmony and melody over rhythm.[26] The proper air of mystery is set up by the solo soprano voice winding its way through a diminished fourth (*passus duriusculus*) and

Example 8-10. Jan Vaňhal, *Missa solennis in F,* M. 66 (before
1797), "Credo" (Allegro), measures 31–47 [for
succeeding section see ex. 8-3].

Example 8-10   (cont'd.)

Example 8-10 (cont'd.)

Example 8-10 (concluded)

scen - - dit, de - - scen - - dit.

pro - pter nos,   pro - pter nos.

pro - pter nos,   pro - pter nos.

Example 8-11. Johann Adolf Hasse, *Missa in D Minor*, M. 24
(1751), "Et incarnatus" (Non troppo lento).

Example 8-11 (cont'd.)

Example 8-11 (cont'd.)

Example 8-11 (cont'd.)

Example 8-11 (cont'd.)

Example 8-11 (concluded)

Example 8-12. "Et incarnatus" Solo Melodic Types (in chronological order according to type).

crescendoing through two chromatic half-steps (*pathopoeia*) while violins and continuo maintain a quiet ("sanft"), measured accompaniment of repeated tones (ex. 8-13). Some Masses create an even more subdued accompaniment by muting the strings, leaving the strings out entirely, or having the continuo not play during the instrumental interludes.[27] Albrechtsberger's rather abrupt modulation to the relative major for the soprano's second phrase (ex. 8-13, m. 7) suggests the transformation inherent in Christ's incarnation. Many composers make this allusion by modulating to a related key for the words "Et homo factus est" (see ex. 8-1, m. 7; ex. 8-13, m. 21). Dissonant, diminished seventh chords (*parrhesia*) are frequently employed to intensify the harmonic uncertainty (ex. 8-13, m. 15). In addition, sudden contrasts in dynamics are occasionally called for in the accompaniment to heighten the dramatic tension (ex. 8-13, m. 6–7, 21, 30, 35, 41, 53, 55).

Crucifixus etiam pro nobis...et sepultus est

For most composers the "Crucifixus" is the dramatic climax of the entire Credo, the moment when the intensity of expression reaches its peak. Often *forte* dynamics are called for, and the mode returns or shifts to minor (*mutatio*) (see ex. 8-4, m. 9f.; ex. 8-13, m. 32; ex. 8-15). In some cases the excitement and turmoil of the crucifixion is mirrored by a more agitated accompaniment (ex. 8-4, staccato octaves; ex. 8-14, repeated staccato sixteenth notes). In the "Crucifixus" of Ferdinand Schmidt's *Missa Sanctae Caeciliae* the rhythmic agitation seems to be interrupting a pompous march (to Calvary?) of dotted notes (ex. 8-14). Sizable leaps in the vocal melody (*exclamatio, hyperbole,* and *passus duriusculus*) often add to the drama (ex. 8-1, octaves, perfect twelfths, thirteenths, and diminished sevenths; ex. 8-13, sixths and octaves; ex. 8-14, sixths; ex. 8-15, sixths, diminished sevenths, octaves).

Example 8-15 (Hofmann) emphasizes what so many "Crucifixus" settings use to express the suffering and sorrow of the crucifixion scene: descending chromatic melody (*pathopoeia*). Bach, Haydn, Mozart, and most of the Viennese composers under study allow chromaticism to wring blood and torment from the music at "Crucifixus," "sub Pontio Pilato," or especially "passus" (ex. 8-11, m. 23–27; ex. 8-13, m. 35–39; ex. 8-15, m. 1–9). The chromatic descent often covers a perfect fourth (ex. 8-11, 8-15).

Other means of heightening the impact of this section include emphatic repetition of key words (e.g., "passus" in ex. 8-1, 8-11, 8-14), "wailing" melismas on "passus," and poignant suspensions reflecting the pain of "Crucifixus" (ex. 8-11) or "passus" (ex. 8-14 and 8-16). In the "Crucifixus" of his *Missa solennis in C* Anton Carl resorts to a style resembling opera's accompanied recitative in order to further intensify this dramatic scene (ex. 8-16).

Example 8-13. Johann Georg Albrechtsberger, *Missa Annuntiationis,* M. 3 (1763), "Et incarnatus" (Adagio molto).

Example 8-13   (cont'd.)

Example 8-13   (cont'd.)

Example 8-13 (cont'd.)

Example 8-13   (cont'd.)

Example 8-13 (cont'd.)

Example 8-13   (concluded)

Example 8-14. Ferdinand Schmidt, *Missa Sanctae Caeciliae,* M. 50
(before 1746), "Crucifixus" (Adagio).

Example 8-14 (concluded)

Example 8-15. Leopold Hofmann, *Missa in D,* M. 29 (before
1772), "Crucifixus" (Larghetto).

Example 8-15   (concluded)

Example 8-16. Anton Carl, *Missa solennis in C,* M. 14 (before
1751), "Crucifixus" (Adagio).

There is usually a sense of anticlimax for "et sepultus est." A soft dynamic is commonly specified here, and voices descend in long notes to the lower part of their ranges (ex. 8-3, 8-4, and 8-13).[28] The softness is occasionally exaggerated by having the chorus sing these words a cappella (ex. 8-4 and 8-13).

Et resurrexit tertia die...cujus regni non erit finis

In most settings the "Et resurrexit" provides the necessary catharsis for the tension accumulated during the preceding section. The heavens seem to open up, and the God-man stands triumphantly before us. Musically the full orchestra (brass and timpani included), the chorus, the major mode (usually the tonic key), and the fast tempo of the Credo's beginning all return to celebrate this victory, this fundamental tenet of Christianity. Sometimes this section begins with a soprano solo or, as in example 8-17, a short instrumental introduction.[29]

As example 8-17 shows, ascending melodies, triadic vocal lines (see bass, m. 3), repeated-note accompaniments, and even fanfares for clarini may combine to generate the appropriate level of exhilaration.[30] Many (if not all) musical elements heard at the start of the Credo return, especially the syllabic, declamatory writing for chorus.[31] This section closes the narration of Christ's life and is the composer's final "purple patch" suitable for word painting, as the following list of rhetorical traditions shows:

"ascendit in coelum" —ascending motives (*anabasis*)	M. 1, 4, 8, 9, 11–15, 18, 19 (Vienna version), 21, 23, 27–29, 30, 33, 35–38, 40, 49, 50, 51, 57, 58, 60, 61, 63, 67, 68, 70, 71
"sedet" (sits) —longer notes	M. 1, 4, 8, 9, 16, 19 (Berlin version), 23, 28, 37, 49, 68
"judicare" —long, sustained notes (God's implacable judgment)	M. 16, 19 (Berlin version), 26, 27, 30, 34, 38, 39, 49, 56, 60, 61, 63
—brass tatoos (power)	M. 4, 9, 12, 15, 20, 28, 30, 35, 39, 48, 51, 57
—entrance of chorus (*noema;* voices of judgment)	M. 11, 12, 27, 28, 30, 31, 56, et al.

Example 8-17. Johann Georg Albrechtsberger, *Missa Annuntiationis,* M. 3 (1763), "Et resurrexit" (Allegro), measures 1–4.

"mortuos"
—subito *piano,* often with
longer, lower pitches and
brief reference to minor
mode (*mutatio*); *forte*
again at "cujus regni"

M. 2, 8, 11-14, 18, 26-28,
30, 34, 38, 39, 45, 48, 49,
57, 63, 64, 65, 69, 70, 71

"non erit finis"
—several repetitions of
these words "without end"

M. 2, 4, 12, 13, 15, 17, 18,
19 (Berlin version), 26-28,
30-32, 34, 36-39, 45, 48-51,
57, 60, 68, 70, 71, 72

Composers' continual reliance on these old, established devices is symptomatic of the perfunctory treatment usually observed in this final part of the Credo.

Et in Spiritum Sanctum . . . resurrectionem mortuorum

Many short Masses begin (if not continue) telescoping the text in this section which dryly enumerates the fruits of salvation. In many concerted Masses there begins a series of vocal solos not unlike that heard at "Et in unum Dominum" during the first part of the Credo (see ex. 8-18).[32] Despite the abstract language, a few words are commonly given special treatment:

"simul adoratur"
—full chorus enters
(simultaneously; *noema*)

M. 8, 12 (ex. 8-18), 14,
19 (Berlin version), 20, 30,
31, 34, 39, 52, 56-58, 69,
70, 71

"et in unam sanctam
catholicam"
—two or more voices in
unison

M. 1, 15, 18, 20

—several repetitions
of one tone

M. 4, 5, 8-10, 15, 16, 18,
20, 23, 26, 32, 49, 61

"resurrectionem"
—ascending melody
(*anabasis*)

M. 3, 21, 33, 36, 38, 60, 70

A strong Viennese tradition appears to have been the slow, soft performance of the word "mortuorum" at the end of this section (see ex. 8-18, mm. 79-82). The sustained tones here result from either a temporarily slower tempo

Example 8-18.   Johann Nepomuk Boog, *Missa in C*, M. 12 (before
1764), "Et resurrexit" (Allegro), measures 31–90.

Example 8-18 (cont'd.)

Example 8-18   (cont'd.)

Example 8-18 (cont'd.)

o - que   pro- ce - - - - - dit.

Example 8-18   (cont'd.)

Example 8-18 (cont'd.)

Example 8-18 (cont'd.)

Example 8-18 (cont'd.)

Et u - nam san - ctam, san - ctam ca - tho-li-cam

Solo

Example 8-18   (cont'd.)

Example 8-18 (cont'd.)

Example 8-18 (cont'd.)

Example 8-18 (cont'd.)

Example 8-18 (cont'd.)

Example 8-18 (cont'd.)

Example 8-18   (concluded)

(usually adagio for two to twelve measures) or longer note values. The use of the minor mode (*mutatio*), diminished seventh chords, dramatic rests (*abruptio*) and fermatas, or a drastically reduced scoring often intensifies this gruesome apocalyptic view of the dead.

Et vitam venturi saeculi. Amen.

"Et vitam" usually returns us to a fast tempo or more agitated rhythms, a loud dynamic level, and the major mode. Often this section has a stretto quality making it a kind of coda for the entire Credo. Over one-third of the multi-movement Credos (27 of 69) have a fugue at this point. As in the "Cum Sancto" of the Gloria, fugue is the "timeless" compositional style, one best suited for the world's eternal life avowed in the text. Example 8-19 shows a selection of "Et vitam" subjects which last anywhere from one measure (M. 2, 60, and 61) to nine measures (M. 34). Other multi-movement Credos maintain a homophonic texture for this final section (see ex. 8-18) or, at most, create a pseudopolyphony (M. 3, 6, 8, 15, 32, and 44) or fugato (M. 10, 67, and 69). If present, polytextuality usually stops before or at the start of this section. Only a few Masses thematically tie the "Et vitam" to an earlier part of the Credo (see above, at nn. 15-17).

Summary

Because of its long doctrinal text, the Credo usually inspires the least imaginative setting of the Mass. Nearly all composers tend to follow the same basic mold. Most Credos consist of three movements: "Credo" (or, if the intonation is not set, "Patrem omnipotentem"), "Et incarnatus est," and "Et resurrexit." The three movements are distinguished by tempos (usually fast-slow-fast), meters (often duple-duple-triple), keys (usually I-vi-I), modes (usually major-minor-major), and scorings. Frequently the "Et vitam" is set apart as a fugal finale. The earlier settings subdivide the Credo into even more sections (see fig. 8-8). Total lengths of Credos range from 16 to 356 measures, averaging about 164. A few composers unify their settings with thematic refrains or reprises; many only reuse earlier accompaniment patterns at "Et resurrexit." The outer movements ("Credo" and "Et resurrexit") are usually declamatory, syllabic choruses accompanied by the full orchestra. *Missae breves* often resort to polytextuality for both these sections. Soloists generally alternate with the chorus at standard points in the text (e.g., solos at "Et in unum Dominum Jesum Christum" and "Et in Spiritum Sanctum"). The sense of triumph at the "Et resurrexit" is sometimes enhanced by a third relationship between its key and that of the preceding "Crucifixus," or by having a solo voice opening the movement.

Example 8-19.   Selected "Et vitam" Fugue Subjects

Example 8-19   (concluded)

Framed by the faster outer movements, the "Et incarnatus" is the musical and spiritual heart of a Credo setting. Its reduced scoring (usually without brass and timpani), its short through-composed form, its tonal instability and modulatory nature, the instrumental obbligatos occasionally complimenting the solo voice(s), the minor mode, and the intensely expressive style all reflect the mystery of the incarnation of God. "Et incarnatus" settings in the major mode are also found throughout the period (in about one-third of the sample). In these cases, the minor mode usually makes a later appearance—at "Crucifixus," which is often the climax of the "Et incarnatus." The similar contours of several "Et incarnatus" themes reveal a few of the melodic types (topoi) which were commonly employed for this section.

In general, there is a less intensive use of rhetorical figures in the Credo than in the Gloria. Most examples of such figures occur during the Credo's narration of the life of Jesus Christ (i.e., from "Et in unum Dominum Jesum Christum" through "cujus regni non erit finis"), with the "Et incarnatus" and the "Crucifixus" being the most expressive sections.

9

Sanctus

Liturgical demands are most strongly apparent in the settings of the Sanctus. Faced with the necessity of fitting some of the music into the relatively brief period that precedes the silence at consecration, composers have little time or incentive here for unusual and expansive forms. Therefore (except for the "Benedictus") most Sanctus settings are brief, consisting of only two or three movements, requiring few solos, closely adhering to the text, and allowing practically no repetition of words. The structure is usually through-composed. Despite these limitations, most composers do succeed in creating functional settings that evoke affects appropriate to this holiest part of the service.

In eighteenth-century concerted settings the first division of the Sanctus (i.e., up through the "Osanna in excelsis" preceding the "Benedictus") had to be short for a practical reason: silence had to reign during the consecration *(die Wandlung)* and elevation of holy elements.[1] Only after the consecration had been signaled by the elevation of the Host and by the ringing of bells might the choir begin the "Benedictus." This delay of the "Benedictus" had been authorized in the post-Reformation *Caeremonial episcoporum* of 1600.[2] The rubric explains why the "Benedictus" is usually a separate movement in these concerted Masses.

Glöggl (1826) asked that the Sanctus be performed "majestically." It was not to be too long "because during the consecration strict silence must prevail over the organ as well as choir so that nobody is disturbed in the worship of the moment." He also suggested that after consecration the "Benedictus" should be sung "in a lofty manner" *(in einem erhabenen Charakter).*[3]

Overall Structure

The movement structure of nearly every Sanctus is thus based upon the premise that the "Benedictus" follows elevation and should begin a new musical movement.[4] Figure 9-1 shows the various distributions of text for all

Figure 9-1. Sanctus Text Divisions

Text Incipit	I	IIa	IIb	IIIa	IIIb	IVa	IVb	V
Sanctus								
Dominus Deus Sabaoth								
Pleni sunt coeli								
Osanna I								
---------- (Elevation) --								
Benedictus								
Osanna II								

Quantity of Examples: 1 1   18 2   40   4   4   1

Type	Mass Nos.*
I	32
IIa	70
IIb	1, 3, 5, 9, 18, 19 (Berlin version), 20, 23, 24, 27, 29, 35, 38, 43, 46, 47, 52, 54, 68
IIIa	42, 71
IIIb	2, 4, 6, 7, 8, 10, 11, 12, 15, 16, 17, 21, 22, 25, 26, 28, 30, 33, 34, 36, 37, 39, 40, 41, 44, 45, 49, 51, 53, 55, 56, 57, 58, 59, 61, 63, 64, 66, 67, 72
IVa	14, 50, 62, 69
IVb	13, 19 (Vienna version), 31, 60
V	65

*M. 48 lacks a Sanctus

settings under study. The most common plan divides the Sanctus into the following three movements:

I. "Sanctus, Sanctus, Sanctus Dominus Deus Sabaoth. Pleni sunt coeli et terra gloria tua. Osanna in excelsis."
II. "Benedictus qui venit in nomine Domini."
III. "Osanna in excelsis."

Forty of the 71 settings (56% of the sample) have this format (Type III[b] in fig. 9-1). Eighteen others (25%) connect the "Benedictus" with the second "Osanna" and thus have only two movements (Type II[b]). In 61 settings (86%) the first part of the Sanctus is divided into the following slow and fast sections:[5]

SLOW   "Sanctus, Sanctus, Sanctus Dominus Deus Sabaoth."

FAST   "Pleni sunt coeli et terra gloria tua. Osanna in excelsis."

Sanctus settings consisting of four or five movements often treat the first "Osanna" as a movement separate from the "Pleni sunt coeli" (see Types IV[b] and V in fig. 9-1).

The most common tempo scheme in the Sanctus is as follows:[6]

"Sanctus"		Adagio
"Dominus Deus Sabaoth"		
"Pleni sunt coeli"		Allegro
"Osanna I"		
"Benedictus"		Andante
"Osanna II"		Allegro

Usually composers vary the meter from movement to movement, as the examples in figure 9-2 illustrate. The most common meters are C and 3/4; the duple 2/4 occurs only in Masses dated 1770 and later.[7] The majority of Sanctus settings (49 examples, or 69%) begin with quadruple meter (C), with changes of meter occurring at "Pleni," "Benedictus" (most often), and "Osanna." Some 17 settings (24%) maintain the same meter throughout the Sanctus despite changes in tempo, key, and scoring. The alla breve (₵) found in 13 "Osanna II" settings is usually associated with a fugal style reminiscent of the *stile antico*.

Sanctus settings run from 38 to 221 measures in length, with an average of approximately 102 measures. The brevity of the Sanctus is more apparent when we consider that the Kyrie, with far fewer words, is often about the same length as, or much longer than, the Sanctus.[8]

Figure 9-2. Sanctus Meters: Some Common Arrangements*

Sanctus	Pleni	Benedictus	Osanna II**	Mass Numbers
C	3/4	C	3/4	M. 10, 11, 27, 28
C	3/4	C	C	M. 14, 41, 61, 70
C	C	3/4	C	M. 12, 15, 18, 21
C	---	3/4	C	M. 5, 23, 56
C	---	3/8	C	M. 40, 52
C	C	C	¢	M. 2, 34, 49, 57, 67, 69
3/4	C	3/4	C	M. 7, 24, 37

*This chart shows only the meter arrangements that occur in more than one Mass of the sample. Twenty-eight of the Sanctus settings have unique metric plans. C meter throughout the Sanctus occurs in M. 3, 8, 22, 25, 26, 29, 35, 38, 39, 43, 44, 46, 58, 71; 3/4 meter throughout in M. 42, 47, and 59.

**Although less than half the sample reuses Osanna I for Osanna II, every Osanna II is in the same meter as Osanna I with the exception of M. 2, 9 (ex. 9-6), 14, 30, 32, 34, 41, 49, 51, 55, 57, 61, 67, 69, and 70.

With the exception of the "Benedictus," the Sanctus is sung mostly by the chorus.[9] Figure 9-3 shows solo distribution among the 66 settings that require vocal soloists. Employment of soloists during the "Sanctus" and "Pleni" sections appears to have been part of an earlier tradition that lasted up to the early 1760s; most later Masses require only the chorus here.[10] If soloists begin the Sanctus, the full chorus enters later, usually at "Dominus Deus Sabaoth" or, more often, "Pleni sunt coeli" where the word "pleni" may thus be aptly depicted (see ex. 9-1).[11] Another practice occasionally encountered throughout the period under study is the use of soloists to start "Osanna." The delayed tutti entrance by the chorus in such "Osannas" often produces a suitably splendid effect (see ex. 9-2 at m. 16).[12]

As can be seen in figure 9-3, the "Benedictus" is usually reserved for the vocal soloist, with soprano or tenor solos, duets, and quartets being most common. Here the influence of opera, oratorio, and cantata is most obvious in the forms, coloratura, and instruments employed (see ex. 9-5, 9-7). Figure 9-3 also reveals that about one-fifth of the sample uses only the chorus (i.e., no soloists) during the "Benedictus"; such choral settings are found throughout the period under study in Masses by Holzbauer, Reutter, Tuma, Dittersdorf, and Vaňhal.[13] Use of the chorus here could possibly be the influence of Fux and his generation, most of whose "Benedictus" settings require the chorus.

Harmonically the Sanctus usually follows a standard plan: it begins and ends in the tonic key of the Mass, with the first "Osanna" also ending in that key. Most of the time the slow opening "Sanctus" section connects directly with the faster "Pleni sunt coeli" by means of either a half-cadence (54% of the sample) or a rhythmic elision over a cadence (24%), as seen in figure 9-4.

Figure 9-3. Use of Soloists and Chorus in the Sanctus* (by Text Subdivision)

Text	Quantity Using Soloists	% of Sample Using Soloists	Quantity Using Chorus Alone	Mass Nos. Using Soloists
Sanctus	11	17%	55	M. 6, 32, 36, 37-39, 43, 44, 51, 63, 68
Pleni sunt coeli	9	14%	57	M. 13, 42, 43, 50, 51, 66, 67, 69, 70
gloria tua	11	17%	55	M. 8, 13, 30, 39, 42, 50, 51, 67, 69, 70
Osanna I	9	14%	57	M. 13, 21, 22, 27, 35, 37, 53, 57, 58
Benedictus	55	83%	11	S: M. 7, 13, 17, 18, 22, 26, 28, 29, 40, 42, 45, 50, 54 (w/chor.), 58, 60, 62
			A:	M. 14, 16, 34, 39, 57, 61
			T:	M. 6, 23, 36, 37, 52, 53, 56, 66, 72
			B:	M. 21, 25, 49, 51, 71
			Duets:	M. 3, 19 (Vienna version) 24, 27, 46, 64, 67-70
			Trios:	M. 33, 38?, 43
			Quartets:	M. 4, 19 (Berlin version), 30, 31, 35, 55, 59
Osanna II	9	14%	57	M. 13, 21, 22, 27, 37, 51, 52, 53?, 58

*This information is based upon the 66 Masses in the sample which have a Sanctus requiring both soloists and chorus.

Example 9-1. Ignaz Holzbauer, *Missa S. Andreae Apost.*, M. 32
(before 1744), Sanctus (Largo-Allegro), measures
1–19 (for continuation see ex. 9-9).

Example 9-1   (cont'd.)

Example 9-1 (concluded)

Example 9-2.   Ferdinand Schmidt, *Missa Primitiarum in C,* M. 51
(before 1747), Osanna II (Andante).

Example 9-2 (cont'd.)

Example 9-2 (cont'd.)

Example 9-2 (cont'd.)

Example 9-2 (concluded)

Figure 9-4.   Harmonic Articulation between "Sanctus" and "Pleni"

Type of Articulation	Keys at End of "Sanctus"-Start of "Pleni"	Qty. of Ex.	% of Sample
Half cadence	$V/I^{(i)} - I^{(i)}$	29	
	V/vi - I	5	
	V/vi - vi	2	54%
	V/V - V	2	
Rhythmic elision over a cadence, usually with a change in tempo or meter		17	24%
Full cadence	V ‖ I	2	
	vi ‖ I	2	
	I ‖ I	2	12%
	iii ‖ I	1	
	III ‖ I	1	
No stop or change		8	10%
		71	100%

Example 9-3 (m. 7) shows the typical kind of half-cadence connection at this point, while example 9-1 (m. 9) demonstrates how a rhythmic elision sometimes joins the two sections. Occasionally such half-cadences and elisions also connect the "Pleni" section to the first "Osanna," although usually the "Pleni" leads directly into the first "Osanna" without any change of tempo, meter, or scoring.[14]

In the Sanctus there is a greater emphasis upon the subdominant than in any other part of the Mass. Of the 60 Sanctus settings that open with an essentially homophonic texture, some 13 (22%) commence with a slow, majestic I–IV chordal progression which reflects the character of the text (see ex. 9-4). In 28 cases the first "Osanna" concludes with a plagal (IV–I) cadence, a cadence which otherwise seldom occurs in these Masses but which does produce the degree of articulation needed for the brief liturgical "interruption" (i.e., elevation) that precedes the "Benedictus" (see ex. 9-2).[15] In addition, the "Benedictus" is frequently (31% of the time; see fig. 9-5) in the subdominant key of the Mass. Thus, in retrospect, the earlier references to the subdominant could be interpreted as a kind of "foreshadowing" of this "Benedictus" tonality.

Figure 9-5 summarizes the keys for the "Benedictus" movements in the sample. As just indicated, the subdominant tonality is the usual choice. Many settings, however, are in the submediant, tonic, or dominant key, though most

Example 9-3. Johann Nepomuk Boog, *Missa in C,* M. 13 (before 1763), Sanctus (Adagio-Allegro), measures 1-15.

Example 9-3   (cont'd.)

Example 9-3   (concluded)

Example 9-4. Four Sanctus Beginnings.

     A.   Mathias Georg Monn, *Missa in C,* M. 38
           (1741), vocal score of measures 1–3.

     B.   Georg von Reutter, Jr., *Missa Lauretana in C,*
           M. 45 (1742), vocal score of measures 1–3.

Example 9-4. Four Sanctus Beginnings (concluded)
- C. Tobias Gsur, *Missa in C,* M. 21 (before 1770), vocal score of measures 1–3.

- D. Karl Ditters von Dittersdorf, *Missa in C,* M. 16 (n.d.), vocal score of measures 1–6.

Figure 9-5. Benedictus Keys

Key in Terms of Tonality of Mass	Quantity of Examples	Percent of Sample
IV	22	31%
vi	16	23
I	15	21
V	13	18
i*	2	3
iii	1	1.7
III*	1	1.7
VI*	1	1.7

*With the exception of one "Benedictus" in i (M. 45, in C Major), the settings in i, III, and VI are from Masses in minor keys (i.e., M. 32, 31, and 63).

of them share the contrast of key which sets the "Benedictus" apart as a middle section of the Sanctus. The God-man "who comes in the name of the Lord" has entered the picture, and a departure (a sojourn) away from the home key makes for an effective musical analogy.

The fact that so many of the "Benedictus" settings (27%) are in minor keys seems surprising considering the nature of the text (an enthusiastic blessing and acclamation). The majority of such minor settings—by Arbesser, Boog, Hasse, Holzbauer, Monn, Predieri, Reutter, Schmidt, Tuma, and Wagenseil—occur in the 1740s and earlier, tapering off noticeably during the 1750s and 1760s.[16] Perhaps these composers were reacting to the text with a Baroque Pietism, i.e., more to the torment and sacrifice of Christ than to the good news of His salvation. Example 9-5 is the "Benedictus" from Monn's *Missa in D* (probably of the 1740s) and is typical of an extended two-part motto aria in a minor key and with a theme that evokes pathos.

As stated at the outset, the Sanctus is usually through-composed, partly because of the time limitations imposed by its liturgical place and function. However, following a tradition that extends back to ninth-century plainsong, most composers link the "Osanna" settings that precede and follow elevation. They make "Osanna II" either a repetition (42% of the sample) or a variation of "Osanna I."[17] Only a few composers (e.g., Arbesser, Monn, Schmidt, Sonnleithner, Tuma, and Wagenseil) prefer to conclude the Sanctus with a

Example 9-5. Mathias Georg Monn, *Missa in D,* M. 40 (before 1750), "Benedictus" (without tempo).

Example 9-5 (cont'd.)

*m.46-48 in A·G̊ source: (sic)

Example 9-5 (cont'd.)

Example 9-5   (cont'd.)

Example 9-5 (cont'd.)

Example 9-5 (concluded)

new "Osanna" (usually a short fugue). When "Osanna II" is a variation of "Osanna I," the differences are normally the result of adding music to the beginning so as to make a better transition from the "Benedictus" (e.g., M. 59). Example 9-6, however, shows Bonno's clever recasting of "Osanna I" in a new meter for "Osanna II." Kohaut in one of his Masses (M. 34) expands the four measures of the "Osanna I" theme into the countersubject of an impressive 52 measure "Osanna II" double fugue.

"Benedictus"

As a separate movement the "Benedictus" generally follows the form of a binary aria. The first vocal section (which may be preceded by an instrumental ritornello) modulates to a related key (most often V, vi, v, or III), which a short ritornello then reaffirms. In the new key, the second vocal section often begins with a restatement (transposed) of the opening theme and then returns to the tonic key before the ritornello closes the movement. Figure 9-6 demonstrates how duets, trios, quartets, and choruses also use this form and its derivatives for the "Benedictus." If the "Benedictus" connects directly with the following "Osanna II," the final ritornello of the "Benedictus" may not be retained.

"Benedictus" settings from the 1760s and later begin to anticipate elements of sonata form.[18] In these instances the opening vocal theme reappears in the tonic as well as the related key during the course of the two- and three-part aria forms (see those listed in fig. 9-6 as "with Reprise in I"). The earliest dated example of double reprise encountered in this study is the "Benedictus" from Boog's *Missa in C* (M. 11, before 1752). During the next two decades younger composers like Albrechtsberger, Dittersdorf, Hofmann, Krottendorfer, Vaňhal, and (especially) Sonnleithner often borrowed this reprise form for their "Benedictus" settings, even stating two themes in some instances.[19] In the binary aria the double reprise of tonic and opening melody usually occurs one to ten measures into the second vocal section (e.g., in M. 11, 12, 17, 20, 22, 35, 58, and 66). In the three-part aria forms, the tonic reprise commences with the third vocal section (e.g., M. 4, 15, 26, and 54), the retransition having occurred during the penultimate ritornello. Example 9-7 by Sonnleithner shows this latter type of double reprise and also demonstrates the thematic functionalism that was well in place by the early 1770s. Figure 9-7 is an outline of the movement's form. The alternation of chorus ("Tu") and soloists ("S") reminds us of some "Benedictus" settings by Haydn (Hob. XXII: 4, 8, 11, 12, 13, 14) and Mozart (K. 139, 258, 262).

Example 9-6. Giuseppe Bonno, *Missa in C,* M. 9 (before 1776).
A. "Sanctus" (Allegro), measures 22–26 ["Osanna I"]

Example 9-6 (concluded)

B. "Benedictus" (Adagio-Andante), measures 10–13
    ["Osanna II"]

Figure 9-6. Benedictus Designs

Two-Part Forms	Qty. of Ex.	% of Sample*	Mass Nos.
Aria	21	30%	M. 6, 7, 14, 16, (Ex. 9-12), 21, 28, 29, 34, 40 (motto, Ex. 9-5), 42, 45, 49, 50, 52, 53, 56, 60-62, 71, 72
Duet	8	11	M. 3, 19 (Vienna version),24, 27, 46, 64 (w/2 themes), 67, 68
Trio	1	1.5	M. 33
Quartet	3	4	M. 19 (Berlin version), 30, 59
Chorus	4	5.5	M. 1, 2, 5, 41?
Two-Part with Reprise in I			
Aria	4	5.5	M. 17, 22, 58 (w/2 themes), 66
Quartet	2	3	M. 35, 55 (both w/2 themes)
Chorus	3	4	M. 11, 12, 20
TOTAL TWO-PART	46	64.5%	
Three-Part Forms			
Aria	5	7	M. 13, 25, 39, 51, 57 (also Monn version of M. 12)
Chorus	1	1.5	M. 38 (trio?)
Three-Part with Reprise in I			
Aria	1	1.4	M. 26
Chorus	2	2.8	M. 15, 65 (2 themes)
Quartet	2	2.8	M. 4, 54 (w/chorus, both sonata-like; Ex. 9-7)
TOTAL THREE-PART	11	15.5%	
One-Part Forms			
Aria	4	5.5	M. 18, 23, 36, 37
Duet	2	3	M. 69, 70
Trio	1	1.5	M. 43
Quartet	1	1.5	M. 31
Chorus	4	5.5	M. 8-10, 63
Fugue/Fugato	2	3	M. 32, 47
TOTAL ONE-PART	14	20%	
	71		

*This chart tabulates the forms for 71 "Benedictus" settings, including both versions of M. 19. M. 44 and 48 are not included.

Example 9-7.   Christoph Sonnleithner, *Missa ex C,* M. 54 (before
                1771), "Benedictus" (Andante), measures 1–109.

Example 9-7 (cont'd.)

Example 9-7 (cont'd.)

Example 9-7 (cont'd.)

Example 9-7   (cont'd.)

Example 9-7   (cont'd.)

Example 9-7 (cont'd.)

Example 9-7   (cont'd.)

Example 9-7 (cont'd.)

Example 9-7 (cont'd.)

Example 9-7 (cont'd.)

Example 9-7 (concluded)

Figure 9-7. Layout of "Benedictus" from Christoph Sonnleithner's *Missa ex C* (M. 54, before 1771)*

Section:	A				B			A		
	Rit	Voc Tu · S · Tu	Rit Tu		Voc S · Tu · S · Tu	Rit Tu		Voc Tu · S · Tu	Rit Tu	
Motive:	a x b y	a c/x d e b	b y		f c/x d b y	b y		a/x d' b	b y	
Measure:	1	13 24	46 53		56 71 78			81 99 106	108	
Harmony:	I		V			vi——————I				

"Exposition" "Development" "Reprise"

S - Soprano solo
Tu - Tutti Chorus
x and y are orchestral motives
Rit - Ritornello
Voc - Vocal Part
x and f derive from "a"

*See also ex. 9-7

The one-part "Benedictus" is usually a simple, cursory setting of only 20 to 30 bars on the average. It occurs in both long and short Masses throughout the period under study (see fig. 9-6). Example 9-8 by Holzbauer is typical of this short kind of "Benedictus" that has little (or no) room for modulations and orchestral interludes. In this case and others (e.g., M. 36, 37, and 39) an overly long "Osanna II" (75 measures) is perhaps the reason for abbreviating the "Benedictus" that precedes.

Fugal settings of the "Benedictus" are rare—the compassionate nature of the text warrants ingratiating cantilena more than learned counterpoint. However, the two contrapuntal settings in the sample deserve mention because their approaches are unique to this study. In his E-minor Mass (M. 32, before 1744) Holzbauer combines the second "Osanna" with the "Benedictus" by writing a double fugue in which the principal subject of half and whole notes has the "Benedictus" text while the countersubject continually reiterates "Osanna in excelsis" in quarter notes (ex. 9-9). In the *Missa Sancti Mariani in G* (M. 47, before 1759) Reutter has the voices enter successively with a subject probably based upon a plainchant "Benedictus." This sort of cantus firmus treatment is occasionally encountered in other "Benedictus" settings of the period.[20]

In 55 "Benedictus" settings an instrumental introduction or ritornello precedes the first entry of the voice(s). Ranging from two to 36 measures in length, these introductions average about 11 measures; most of the longer ones date from the 1760s and later.[21] However, these ritornellos are never long enough to indicate that they were played during that part of the Canon which precedes elevation, as some analysts have suggested.[22] About 30 percent of these opening ritornellos have thematic material independent of that introduced by the voice (see ex. 9-5 by Monn). The remaining 70 percent follow the trend of the period by having the instrumental introduction and voice share the same theme or a variant thereof. In example 9-10 by Hofmann a flute solo begins the "Benedictus"; its opening two measures are a highly ornamented and contracted version of the soprano's first three bars (see m. 9-12).

This last example (Hofmann) also shows how throughout this period the "Benedictus" was frequently a movement for instrumental as well as vocal solos. When present, obbligato instruments always hold forth during the opening and closing ritornellos. For example, in so-called organ Masses the organ's most extensive solos are usually found in the "Benedictus" (see ex. 9-11).[23] Figure 9-8 lists instruments employed for "Benedictus" obbligatos in the Masses under consideration. In his undated *Missa in C* (M. 16), Dittersdorf has an obbligato bassoon and violin weave a most expressive and elaborate

Example 9-8. Ignaz Holzbauer, *Missa in A Minor*, M. 31 (before
1747), "Benedictus" (without tempo marking).

Example 9-9. Ignaz Holzbauer, *Missa S. Andreae Apost.*, M. 32
(before 1744), "Benedictus" (Allabreve), measures
20–41 [for preceding section see ex. 9–1].

Example 9-9 (concluded)

Example 9-10. Leopold Hofmann, *Missa in D,* M. 29 (before
1772), "Benedictus" (Allegretto), measures 1–11.

Example 9-11. Georg von Reutter, Jr., *Missa Lauretana in C, M.
45 (1742), "Benedictus" (Andante un poco),
measures 1–8.

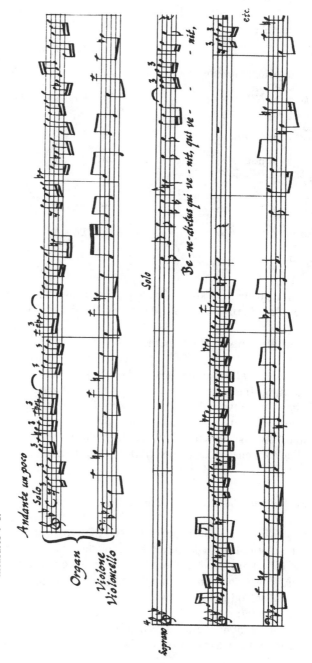

Figure 9-8. "Benedictus" Obbligatos

Instrument(s)	Mass Nos.
Flute	M. 4, 29 (Ex. 9-10), 24
2 Flutes, 2 Horns	M. 66
2 Oboes	M. 10, 19 (Vienna version), 33
Oboe, Bassoon	M. 8
2 Trombones	M. 36
Violin	M. 57
Violin, Bassoon	M. 16 (Ex. 9-12)
Viola	M. 14
Organ	M. 17, 45 (Ex. 9-11)

introduction to the alto's aria (ex. 9-12). Instrumental obbligatos similarly open the "Benedictus" of many Masses by Haydn and Mozart.

Rhetorical Elements of the Sanctus

Because of the small amount of text and the lack of "action words" begging for word painting, the music of the Sanctus tends to reflect the overall mood rather than the individual words of the text. For the opening "Sanctus" most composers seek to evoke the majesty and power of God. Usually at "Pleni sunt coeli" and "Osanna in excelsis" the choir celebrates the omnipresent glory of God, while at "Benedictus" soloists lyrically express the warm compassion felt by God's people toward Jesus.

Sanctus, Sanctus, Sanctus Dominus Deus Sabaoth

In approximately two-thirds of the Masses the proper stateliness and dignity for this holy of holies are achieved by loud, sustained, widely spaced chords from the full chorus and orchestra (*noema*; see ex. 9-4, 9-13). The adagio tempo and slowly changing harmonies add to the pomp. Occasionally a short instrumental introduction prepares the opening choral statement as in the Sanctus of Reutter's *Missa Conceptionis in C* (ex. 9-13).[24] Often octave leaps in the bass accompany the word "Sanctus" in a kind of musical representation (*exclamatio*) of the magnitude of God's holiness (see ex. 9-4B). Bach uses this

Example 9-12. Karl Ditters von Dittersdorf, *Missa in C,* M. 16
 (n.d.), "Benedictus" (without tempo marking),
 measures 1–12.

Example 9-12   (concluded)

Be - - ne-di-ctus qui ve-nit, qui ve-nit   in   etc.

Example 9-13. Georg von Reutter, Jr., *Missa Conceptionis in C,*
M. 46 (1756), Sanctus (Andante-Adagio), measures
1–9.

Example 9-13   (concluded)

same device in the Sanctus of his *B-minor Mass.* Some composers fill the pause between each choral exclamation of "Sanctus" with rapidly ascending and descending runs (*anabasis, catabasis*) that perhaps depict the battles waged by the Sabaoth or armies of God (see ex. 9-4C by Gsur).[25] About one-third of the Sanctus settings begin with a staggered homophony, a pseudopolyphony, or actual imitative polyphony (ex. 9-1 and 9-3)—each echoing the reiterated "Sanctus" acclamations of a congregation. As we have seen in the preceding chapters, a "learned" contrapuntal texture was often used with texts referring to the eternally present God.

Pleni sunt coeli et terra gloria tua. Osanna in excelsis.

At "Pleni sunt coeli" the tempo is accelerated and the heavens seem to open up in a manner recalling the similar change between "Crucifixus" and "Et resurrexit" in the Credo. The quickening pace parallels the growing joy of the congregation preparing to "see" Christ anew—liturgically as the Host of Holy Communion and musically as the "Benedictus" movement. In Gassmann's *St. Cecilia Mass* (Vienna version, m. 9–11) a short fanfare by two clarini brilliantly introduces this new section.

Often we observe the only true word painting of the Sanctus during this section. Some composers allude to "Pleni" (full) with a simultaneous reentry by the full chorus and orchestra (see ex. 9-1). There are also ascending melodies for "coeli" and "excelsis" (see ex. 9-1, 9-3, and 9-6). Falling lines or leaps frequently depict "terra" in contrast to the heights of "coeli" (ex. 9-1 and 9-3). As was commonly the case in the eighteenth century, melismas often emphasize the word "gloria" (see ex. 9-1), which sometimes appears as a brief coloratura tour de force (see ex. 9-14). About two-thirds of the "Osanna" settings are short fugues or fugatos whose polyphony (or pseudopolyphony) resembles the echoing shouts of the crowds greeting Jesus (see ex. 9-6).[26]

Benedictus qui venit in nomine Domini

With its short text, the "Benedictus" is more conducive to the use of conventional musical forms than to word painting. Occasionally a close approximation of word painting involves either a rising sequence of "qui venit" repetitions or a wandering melisma on "venit" or "nomine" (ex. 9-15). A reduced orchestra (often only the strings and continuo with, as we saw earlier, one or two possible obbligatos) usually accompanies the soloists. The brass and timpani are normally silent for this movement.[27]

Viennese "Benedictus" settings often resemble each other because they

Example 9-14. Ferdinand Schmidt, *Missa Primitiarum in C,* M. 51
(before 1747), "Pleni sunt coeli" (Allegro), measures
26–33 of the soprano part.

Example 9-15. A. Johann Georg Albrechtsberger, *Missa
Annuntiationis,* M. 3 (1763), "Benedictus"
(Andante), measures 10–13 of the soprano and
alto parts;
B. Franz Tuma, *Missa in G,* M. 62 (1746),
"Benedictus" (Andante), measures 7–9 of the
soprano part.

share pastoral qualities, and like the "Et incarnatus," can be related to a few melodic types or topoi. Pastoral aspects include simplicity and tenderness of expression, lilting rhythms, homophonic textures, folk-like melodies often in parallel thirds, major keys, and woodwinds—all reminiscent of the first Christmas when shepherds greeted the infant Jesus.[28] Gernot Gruber has noticed how many of the melodies rely mostly upon stepwise motion and set "Benedictus" and "qui venit" to expressive appoggiaturas.[29] Example 9-16 attempts to classify several "Benedictus" themes according to their shared melodic traits. Hearing each of these melodies, one after the other, makes their familial ties most clear. A few of the melodies in triple meter even approach the minuet in their dancelike quality (see M. 15, 18, 42, and 55 in ex. 9-16). As we have seen, melodies of "Benedictus" settings in a minor key evoke quite different affects (see ex. 9-5).

Summary

The Sanctus usually consists of three movements: "Sanctus," "Benedictus," and "Osanna II." Because of both practical requirements and paucity of words, this part of the Mass is relatively brief, averaging just over 100 measures in length. The generally syllabic outer movements are sung by the chorus, while the more lyrical and central "Benedictus" is normally reserved for vocal soloists and, occasionally, instrumental obbligatos. With the opening "Sanctus" often having both slow and fast sections, the common tempo configuration for the three movements is adagio-allegro, andante, and allegro. The meters C and 3/4 usually alternate from movement to movement; 2/4 begins to appear in Sanctus settings from the 1770s on. Harmonically the Sanctus gives much weight to the subdominant, which often appears in slow chord progressions, in plagal cadences concluding the "Osanna," and as the key of the "Benedictus."

The "Benedictus" normally has the form of a two- or three-part aria. Elements associated with sonata form (e.g., double reprise and thematic functionalism) begin appearing in the 1760s. The ritornellos and solo voices were tending more often to share the same theme in the "Benedictus." During the 1750s and 1760s minor keyed "Benedictus" settings became more and more rare.

Overall, rhetorical figures are sparsely employed in the Sanctus. The settings tend to depict the general moods of the text (power and majesty, contrite compassion, and joyful praise) rather than paint individual words. Throughout the period most composers continue the old practice of reusing "Osanna I" for "Osanna II."

Example 9-16. Thematic Types of the "Benedictus"

A. Appoggiatura from above and anticipatory note for "di-ctus"

Albrechtsberger
M. 4

Bonno
M. 8

Bonno
M. 10

Dittersdorf
M. 17

Martínez
M. 37

Schmidt
M. 50

Ziegler
M. 72

B. Mordent (lower neighbor) for "di-ctus"

Carl
M. 14

Monn
M. 39

Sonnleithner
M. 55

Sonnleithner
M. 58

Strasser
M. 59

Tuma
M. 61

Example 9-16 (concluded)

C. Successive Appoggiaturas for "di-ctus"

Sonnleithner
M. 56

Vaňhal
M. 66

D. Appoggiatura for "di-ctus"

Krottendorfer
M. 35

Ziegler
M. 71

E. Successive Appoggiaturas for "ve-nit"

Albrechtsberger
M. 2

Hofmann
M. 27

Kohaut
M. 34

Reutter
M. 46

Sonnleithner
M. 57

F. Appoggiatura for "ve-nit"

Boog
M. 11

Dittersdorf
M. 15

Friberth
M. 18

Holzbauer
M. 33

10

Agnus Dei

The Agnus Dei usually concludes the musical portion of the Mass.[1] Most composers approach this part of the Mass with an efficiency manifested in relatively short movements, reliance upon formal stereotypes, lack of rhetorical figures, and the reuse of music heard earlier. Continuing a tradition that goes back to the a cappella and concerted Masses of the seventeenth century, composers set the Agnus in two connected sections: "Agnus Dei" and "Dona nobis pacem."[2] Solemnly invoking the Lamb of God, the first section ("Agnus Dei") usually follows the tripartite form of the text closely. The "Dona nobis pacem," a short plea for peace, exhibits greater freedom in treatment since composers rely upon a variety of conventional musical forms (e.g., fugues, *concertato* procedures, ritornellos, etc.). The "Dona" generally concludes the Mass in a joyous, festive, and lively manner not unlike that of an operatic finale.

Overall Structure

The Agnus is essentially a single movement of two sections, a slow "Agnus Dei" joined by a half-cadence with the faster "Dona nobis pacem." Only eight of the 70 Agnus settings examined have two separate movements (see columns II, II^a, and II^b in fig. 10-1).

The Agnus is usually the shortest part of the Mass, with lengths ranging from 23 to 193 measures. The average length is about 87 measures; longer Agnus settings are usually the result of having a fugue for the "Dona nobis pacem" or balancing the larger proportions of a solemn Mass. The "Dona nobis pacem" is generally about twice as long as the "Agnus Dei."

Vocal soloists are used primarily only during the first section of the Agnus, i.e., the "Agnus Dei." As will be seen shortly, the solo-tutti alternations during this section usually follow the three-part structure of the text. Figure 10-2 shows how the majority of settings change from soloists to chorus for "Agnus Dei III." The "Dona nobis pacem" is generally for chorus; only one-third of the 70 settings examined also require vocal soloists here.[3] Ten Agnus settings (14%) are entirely for chorus.[4]

Figure 10-1. Agnus Text Divisions

	I	II	II^a	II^b
Agnus Dei I				
Agnus Dei II				
Agnus Dei III				
Dona nobis pacem				"Dona II"

Quantity of Examples: 62   1   6   1

Type   Mass Numbers*

I   Sixty-two Masses (all except those listed
       below); M. 24, 60, and 66 lack a half cadence
       before "Dona"

II_a M. 25
II_b M. 40, 43, 47, 55, 56, 67
II^b M. 3 (two "Dona" movements)

*Seventy Agnus settings are accounted for; Mass Nos. 16 and 48 lacked a complete Agnus.

Figure 10-2. Use of Soloists and Chorus in the Agnus Dei (by Text
              Subdivision)

Text	Quantity Using Soloists	% of Sample Using Soloists	Quantity Using Chorus Only
Agnus Dei I	47	78%	13
Agnus Dei II	51	85%	9
Agnus Dei III	13	22%	47
Dona nobis pacem	23	38%	37

*Based upon the 60 Masses having an Agnus that requires both soloists and chorus. See n. 4.

The usual tempo relationship between the "Agnus Dei" and the "Dona nobis pacem" is slow-fast. The common "Agnus" tempos (in order of decreasing frequency) are adagio, andante, largo, and grave; the "Dona" tempos are allegro, andante, allegro moderato, and alla breve.

The majority of Agnus settings have a change of meter for the "Dona nobis pacem." As may be seen in figure 10-3, the meter of the "Dona" is often triple. Triple, dancelike "Dona nobis pacem" settings apparently were already in use during the first quarter of the eighteenth century.[5] There is no observable change in meter use during the period of study except perhaps for the introduction of 2/4 meter during the 1770s.[6]

The "Agnus Dei" and "Dona nobis pacem" are almost always melodically independent of each other. Motivic connections such as those encountered in one Mass each by Gsur and Hasse are relatively rare (see ex. 10-1). However, relationships between the "Dona" and earlier parts of the Mass (e.g., "Kyrie II" or "Cum Sancto Spiritu") are fairly common and will be discussed below. Perhaps not surprisingly, no Mass makes a melodic link between the words "Agnus Dei" and "Qui tollis peccata mundi" in the Gloria and those same words in the Agnus.

Tonally the Agnus begins in the tonic major, the tonic minor, or, less frequently, the relative minor of the Mass. The tonic major appears to be used less frequently in "Agnus Dei" settings after about 1760.[7] A half-cadence usually closes the "Agnus Dei" (in 61 of 70 examples) and leads us directly into the "Dona nobis pacem" which is always in the tonic key of the Mass. Figure 10-4 summarizes the more common overall harmonic plans. The tripartite harmonic design of the opening "Agnus Dei" section will be discussed shortly.

"Agnus Dei" as a Tripartite Introduction

Most of the time several musical elements (i.e., melody, harmony, and texture) articulate and emphasize the three-part nature of the "Agnus Dei" text. Three melodic schemes are commonly used throughout the period under study: strophic variation (AA^1A^2), through-composed (ABC), and bar (AA^1B) forms.[8]

Agnus Dei, qui tollis peccata mundi, miserere nobis.	Agnus Dei, qui tollis peccata mundi, miserere nobis.	Agnus Dei qui tollis peccata mundi	Quantity of Examples
A	A^1	A^2	28
A	B	C	21
A	A^1	B	17
A	A	B	1
A	B	B^1	1

Figure 10-3. Meter Use in the Agnus ("Agnus Dei"–"Dona nobis
pacem")

Meters	Quantity of Examples	Mass Nos.
C - 3/4	14	M. 3, 6, 7, 20, 28, 30, 32, 36, 37, 41, 47, 55, 68, 70,
3/4 - C	6	22, 23, 33, 44, 45, 67
C - ¢	4	M. 9, 39, 40, 69
3/4 - ¢	2	M. 10, 19
3/2 - C	2	M. 5, 71
3/2 - 3/4	2	M. 31, 72
C - 3/8	2	M. 43, 58
C - 2/4	2	M. 15, 17
3/4 - 2/4	2	M. 64, 65
C - 6/8	1	M. 46
C -12/8	1	M. 29
3/2 - 6/4	1	M. 52

39 change meter

No Change of Meter

C - C	27	M. 1, 4, 8, 11-14, 18, 21, 24, 26, 27, 34, 35, 38, 42, 49, 50, 51, 53, 54, 56, 57, 60, 61-63
3/4 - 3/4	4	2, 25, 59, 66

31 do not change meter

Example 10-1. Related "Agnus Dei" and "Dona" Settings

A. Tobias Gsur, *Missa in D,* M. 22 (before 1769),
"Agnus Dei" (Adagio), measures 1–2 of the
alto; "Dona nobis" (Allegro), measures 52–53
of the soprano.

B. Johann Adolf Hasse, *Missa in D Minor,* M. 24
(1751), "Agnus Dei" (Andante), measures 11–16
of the alto solo; "Dona nobis" (no tempo),
measures 37–40 of the chorus.

Figure 10-4.   Agnus Harmonic Plans (Beginning and Ending
               Tonalities)

Quantity of Examples	% of Sample*	Agnus Dei	Dona nobis pacem	Mass Nos.
19	27.5%	i - - - or (V/I ↘ / V/i ↗)	I - - - - - -	M. 2, 4, 8, 9, 10, 11, 12, 13, 17, 26, 36, 37, 46, 53, 64, 65, 70, 71, 72
19	27.5%	I - - - - or (V/I ↘ / V/i ↗)	I - - - - - -	M. 1, 14, 18 21, 22, 23, 30, 33, 35, 39, 41, 44, 57, 58, 59, 61, 62, 68, 69
9	13%	vi - - - or (V/I ↘ / V/i ↗)	I - - - - -	M. 15, 20, 27, 28, 29, 34, 42, 45, 51,
3	4%	I - - -V/vi ⌒ I	- - - - - -M. 6, 19, 49
3**	4%	i - - -V/i ⌒ i	- - - - - -M. 31, 32, 52
3	4%	I - - - - - - - - -	- - - -M. 24, 60, 66
3	4%	I - - - -‖ I	- - - - - -M. 40, 47, 67
2	3%	vi - - -V/vi ⌒ I	- - - - - -M. 50, 54
2	3%	IV - - - or (V/I ↘ / V/i ↗)	I - - - - - -M. 5, 7
7	10%	(various unica, e.g. i-V/vi I, III-V/i i, V-I‖I, vi-vi‖I, i-i‖I, et al.)	M. 3, 25, 38, 43, 55, 56, 63

*This information covers 70 Masses; Mass Nos. 16 and 48 lack a complete Agnus. I = the tonic of the Mass.
**All three Masses are in a minor key.

Short instrumental interludes often separate the three sections. Surprisingly, the round *ABA* form so frequent in plainsong settings of the Agnus is not encountered. Mass Nos. 6 and 19 by Arbesser and Gassmann, respectively, as well as many of Haydn's Masses (Hob. XXII: 4, 7, 8, 10, 12-14), are examples of the first type (AA^1A^2). Example 10-5 shows a through-composed "Agnus Dei" by Tuma (M. 60). In example 10-2 by Hofmann the "Agnus Dei" has a modified bar form (AA^1B), which Haydn also uses (see Hob. XXII: 5, 6, 9). "Agnus I" and "Agnus II" are begun with bass (m. 3) and soprano (m. 9) soloists, respectively, singing the same melody; more soloists enter for each "miserere nobis." New melodic material is heard with the choral entrance at "Agnus III" (m. 12).

The harmonic layout of the "Agnus Dei" also confirms a tripartite form. Each of the three "Agnus" invocations usually leads to and confirms a new key. Often the text "miserere" takes us abruptly to this new key. As already stated, the third "Agnus" generally ends upon a half cadence (V/I, V/i, or V/vi) that leads directly into the faster "Dona nobis pacem." Figure 10-5 shows the 14 most common modulation schemes for the "Agnus Dei"; Roman numerals represent the keys in terms of the beginning tonality of the Agnus (which is not always the key of the Mass, see fig. 10-4). As can be seen, "Agnus Dei" settings that start in a minor key usually cadence onto the mediant or dominant minor just before "Agnus II" and onto a different key (often i, III, iv, v, vi, or ♭VII) just before "Agnus III." In a similar way, settings in a major key cadence onto the supertonic, mediant, dominant, or submediant before "Agnus II" and onto another key (vi, I, ii, iii, or V) before "Agnus III." These harmonic plans represent over half of the sample. Other unique key plans are found, but they all reflect a similar three-part structure. Dittersdorf, for example, in the "Agnus Dei" of his *Missa in C* (before 1773) modulates only a half step higher for each of the "Agnus" invocations; thus we hear i–♭II–♮ii (i.e., A minor–B-flat major–B minor)—certainly an unusual and affective harmonic path (see ex. 10-3). Some of the plans outlined in figure 10-5 also occur in the Masses of Joseph Haydn: plan "A" in Hob. XXII: 5 and 6, "D" in XXII: 12, and "F" in XXII: 8. In Mozart's Masses we find plans "F" (K. 139, 192) and "J" (K. 167, 257, 258, 262, 317, 337).

Disposition of the soloists and chorus also supports the three-part form of the "Agnus Dei." Usually a change to another soloist or the entry of the chorus marks the beginning of each "Agnus" invocation. As we have seen in figure 10-2, "Agnus III" is generally reserved for the chorus (in 78% of the sample). Figure 10-6 summarizes the solo-chorus distribution in the "Agnus Dei" of 70 Masses. We have already seen the most common arrangement (solo-solo-chorus; type A) in example 10-2. In several instances (types C, D, G, H, I, and J) there is also a change of singers at "miserere" so that a five-part "Agnus Dei" often results.[9] Even when only one soloist or only the choir sings

Example 10-2. Leopold Hofmann, *Missa in C,* M. 28 (before
1762), "Agnus Dei" (Adagio).

Example 10-2 (cont'd.)

Example 10-2 (cont'd.)

Example 10-2 (concluded)

Figure 10-5. Common Harmonic Plans of the "Agnus Dei" (up to
"Dona nobis pacem")

	Agnus I	Agnus II	Agnus III	Quantity of Examples	Mass Nos.
A.	i - - -	III - - -	v - - -	7	M. 9, 36, 46, 53, 56, 65, 70
B.	i - - -	III - - -	VI - - -	4	M. 17, 54, 55, 72
C.	i - - -	v - - -	i - - -	4	M. 1, 12, 13, 42
D.	i - - -	v - - -	III - - -	2	M. 2, 64
E.	i - - -	v - - -	♭VII - - -	2	M. 38, 45
F.	i - - -	III - - -	i - - -	2	M. 27, 29
G.	i - - -	III - - -	iv - - -	2	M. 28 (Ex. X-2), 52
H.	I - - -	V - - -	vi - - -	6	M. 21, 22, 33, 35, 57, 59
I.	I - - -	ii - - -	vi - - -	5	M. 6, 39, 60 (Ex. X-5), 62, 68
J.	I - - -	V - - -	I - - -	3	M. 58, 63, 66
K.	I - - -	ii - - -	iii - - -	2	M. 24, 61
L.	I - - -	vi - - -	iii - - -	2	M. 44, 49
M.	I - - -	vi - - -	V - - -	2	M. 14, 40
N.	I - - -	iii - - -	ii - - -	2	M. 19, 47

$$\overline{45}^{*}$$

---

*Mass Nos. 3, 4, 5, 7, 8, 10, 11, 15 (ex. 10-3), 20, 23, 26, 30, 31, 34, 37, 41, 43, 50, 51, 67, 69, and 71 have unique three-part harmonic plans for the "Agnus Dei." Nos. 18, 25, and 32 follow other plans. Nos. 16 and 48 lack a complete Agnus.

Example 10-3. Karl Ditters von Dittersdorf, *Missa in C*, M. 15 (before 1773), "Agnus Dei" (Grave).

* *Andante in Soprano; Adagio in Alto.*

Example 10-3 (cont'd.)

Example 10-3   (cont'd.)

Example 10-3 (cont'd.)

Example 10-3   (cont'd.)

Example 10-3 (cont'd.)

Example 10-3 (cont'd.)

Example 10-3 (concluded)

Figure 10-6. Chorus and Soloist Distribution in the "Agnus Dei"
(up to "Dona nobis pacem")

	Agnus I . . miserere		Agnus II . . miserere		Agnus III	Examples
A.	1st Solo - - - - - -		2nd Solo - - - - - -		Chorus	23
B.	Solo -				Chorus	6
C.	1st Solo	Chorus	2nd Solo	Chorus	Chorus	5
D.	1st Solo	Chorus	2nd Solo	Chorus	Solo/Chorus	3
E.	Chorus - - - - - - -		Solo- - - - - - - - -		Chorus	3
F.	1st Solo - - - - - -		2nd Solo - - - - - -		3rd Solo	2
G.	1st Solo	Chorus	2nd Solo - - Chorus		3rd Solo ·	1
H.	Chorus	1st Solo	2nd Solo	3rd Solo	Chorus	1
I.	Chorus - - - - - - -		1st Solo	Chorus	2nd Solo	1
J.	Chorus/Solo Chorus		2nd Solo - - - - - -		Chorus	1
K.	Solo	Chorus -				1
L.	Solo -					5
M.	Chorus -					18
						70

Type Mass Nos.

A. 2, 7, 12, 13, 27, 28 (Ex. 10-2), 33, 34, 38, 45, 49, 50, 53, 55, 58, 60 (Ex. 10-5), 61, 62, 63, 68, 69, 70, 71
B. 17, 20, 25, 29, 44, 52; also Mozart, K. 139, 337
C. 11, 43, 46, 54, 57; also Mozart, K. 66, 259
D. 6, 19, 56
E. 30, 39, 40
F. 51, 67; also J. Haydn, Hob. XXII: 11
G. 66; also Mozart, K. 192, 194
H. 31
I. 37
J. 42
K. 36
L. 22, 23, 24, 32, 35; also J. Haydn, Hob. XXII: 5, 14, and Mozart, K. 317
M. 1, 3, 4, 5, 8, 9, 10, 14, 15 (Ex. 10-3), 18, 21, 26, 41, 47, 59, 64, 65, 72; also J. Haydn, Hob. XXII: 1, 3, 4, 6-10, 12, 13, and Mozart, K. 49, 65, 167, 275

the "Agnus Dei" (as in types B, K, L, M of fig. 10-6), instrumental interludes, melodic repetition, and harmonic movement together articulate a tripartite form. Most composers strictly adhere to the three-part text and avoid additional repetitions of the words "Agnus Dei."[10]

Single vocal soloists are generally preferred in the "Agnus Dei" section. However, duets, trios, and quartets are found in settings by Arbesser, Boog, Dittersdorf, Gassmann, Gsur, Hofmann (ex. 10-2), Holzbauer, Kohaut, Monn, Predieri, Reutter, Seuche, Sonnleithner, Vañhal, Wagenseil, and Ziegler.[11] Gassmann's *St. Cecilia Mass* presents a balanced alternation of solo quartet and chorus, the latter entering at each plea for mercy ("miserere nobis").

Expressive Devices of the "Agnus Dei"

Composers generally evoke a solemn, pious mood for the "Agnus Dei" (and for the simultaneous distribution of the Eucharistic Sacrifice) by means of a calculated combination of melodic types, timbres, dynamics, and harmonic unrest.

Comparison of all "Agnus Dei" melodies reveals certain similarities which again allow one to group themes according to type. Several of the melodies have almost the declamatory character of recitative—often beginning with an accented upward leap of a perfect fourth, interrupting phrases irregularly with rests or leaps, and having a certain amount of rhythmic freedom and an accompaniment of sustained chords (ex. 10-4). The "Agnus Dei" from Tuma's *Missa Tibi soli* might even be classified as accompanied recitative were another text substituted (ex. 10-5). Often an "Agnus Dei" in a minor key has a pathos not unlike that heard earlier during the "Qui tollis" of the Gloria or the "Et incarnatus" of the Credo (ex. 10-7). "Agnus Dei" settings in a major key usually have a more comforting tone which often resembles that of the "Benedictus," especially when the word "Dei" is set to appoggiaturas (ex. 10-6; see also ex. 10-4C and ex. 9-16).

The "Agnus Dei" is another part of the Mass where Viennese composers liked to use one or two obbligato trombones. Reutter, Tuma, and Wagenseil, as well as younger composers like Boog, Grassl, Krottendorfer, and Sonnleithner, use the trombone's dark, rather melancholic sonority to add solemnity to the movement (ex. 10-5 and 10-7).[12] Most Masses (about 72% of the sample) begin the "Agnus Dei" directly with the voices; obbligato instruments either provide a counterpoint to the voice part(s) (ex. 10-5) or play a short ritornello between each "Agnus" statement (ex. 10-7, m. 12ff.). A few composers (especially Hasse, Hofmann, Mozart, and Sonnleithner) have a short ritornello (one to fifteen measures) preceding the first vocal entry and setting the appropriate mood for the "Agnus Dei" (ex. 10-2 and 10-7). In

Example 10-4.   Selected "Agnus Dei" Openings (vocal scores)

A.   Mathias Georg Monn, *Missa in C,* M. 38
(1741), "Agnus Dei" (Adagio), measures 1–5.

B.   Franz Tuma, *Missa in G,* M. 62 (before 1746),
"Agnus Dei" (Adagio), measures 1–3.

C.   Franz Tuma, *Missa Sancti Stephani,* M. 63
(before 1747), "Agnus Dei" (Andante),
measures 1–4.

Example 10-4. (cont'd.)

D. Joseph Franz Seuche, *Missa in D,* M. 53
(before 1773), "Agnus Dei" (Andante),
measures 1–3.

E. Karl Ditters von Dittersdorf, *Missa ex D,* M.
17 (before 1777), "Agnus Dei" (Adagio),
measures 1–7.

Example 10-4 (concluded)

F. Leopold Hofmann, *Missa Sancti Erasmi in D,*
   M. 26 (before 1779), "Agnus Dei" (Adagio),
   measures 1–5.

G. Joseph Haydn, *Missa Cellensis,* Hob. XXII: 5
   (1766), "Agnus Dei" (Largo), measures 1–4.

Example 10-5. Franz Tuma, *Missa Tibi soli di Psalm 50*, M. 60
(probably before 1750), "Agnus Dei" (Largo)

Example 10-5 (cont'd.)

Example 10-5   (cont'd.)

Example 10-5 (concluded)

Example 10-6. Joseph Krottendorfer, *Missa in C,* M. 35 (before
                    1764), "Agnus Dei" (Adagio), measures 1–9.

Example 10-7. Christoph Sonnleithner, *Missa solennis in C,* M. 56
(before 1763), "Agnus Dei" (Adagio), measures
1–17.

Example 10-7 (cont'd.)

Example 10-7 (cont'd.)

Example 10-7   (cont'd.)

Example 10-7 (cont'd.)

Example 10-7 (concluded)

Masses by Bonno, Haydn, Hofmann, Reutter, Sonnleithner, and Vaňhal, muted strings are another timbral means of creating the usually subdued tone of this section.[13] In general, except for the trombone obbligatos and a flute solo in one of Hofmann's Masses (M. 29), obbligatos for wind instruments (such as the beautiful trio for oboe, bassoon, and organ in Mozart's 1780 Mass in C major, K. 337) are relatively rare in this section.

The "Agnus Dei" is one of the composers' favorite sections for dynamic effects and contrasts, as an examination of the previous examples demonstrates. Dynamic markings usually appear only in the instrumental accompaniment and not in the vocal parts. Often the pleas of "miserere" are set apart by a sudden *forte* (ex. 10-7) or *piano* (ex. 10-3). Regular dynamic accents in the accompaniment (such as the recurring *fp*'s in the violins at "miserere" in ex. 10-7) are also common.[14] In some cases the orchestra is required to play loudly only during its more agitated ritornellos and softly when accompanying the voices (ex. 10-2).

The words "qui tollis peccata mundi" or "miserere nobis" are often coupled with harmonic instability. It is debatable whether such tonal restlessness stems more from the text, with its "sins of the world" and yearning for God's mercy, or from an established practice (discussed above) of having each "Agnus" invocation modulate. Nonetheless, we frequently encounter sudden diminished seventh chords and chromatic voice leading on the words "peccata" (ex. 10-3, m. 21) and "miserere" (ex. 10-2, 10-7, and 10-8). With "miserere" the chromaticism aptly expresses the pleading in the text.

"Dona" as a Finale to the Mass

With "Dona nobis pacem," the tonic major key of the Mass usually returns and the tempo quickens to bring the Mass to a resounding conclusion. The change at this section may recall the spirit of the change heard earlier at "Quoniam" and "Et resurrexit." Grandiose fugues, reuse of earlier material, and *concertato* procedures commonly make the "Dona" (with its brief text of only three words) into a cogent, almost operalike finale for the Mass.

By the mid-eighteenth century the reuse of earlier music for the "Dona nobis pacem" was a common practice.[15] As figure 10-7 shows, in over one-third of the Masses (25 of 70 instances) the "Dona" is an exact or varied repetition (with new words) of the Kyrie, the end of the Gloria, or the end of the Credo. Most common is reuse of the Kyrie, either in part (usually the faster "Kyrie" section or the "Kyrie II" fugue) or in its entirety. Gassmann's *St. Cecilia Mass* (M. 19) is typical in its reuse of the "Kyrie II" fugue. In manuscript scores and parts the designation "Kyrie ut supra" often indicates this musical repetition, and underlay of the new words ("Dona nobis pacem") is thus left up to the copyists or singers.[16] Since both "Kyrie eleison" and

Example 10-8. Ferdinand Schmidt, *Missa S. Caeciliae* in C, M. 50
(before 1746), "Agnus Dei" (Andante), measures
1-9.

Figure 10-7. External Connections between the "Dona" and Earlier
              Movements

Earlier Section Being Reused	Mass Nos.
Kyrie (in its entirety)	M. 59
Kyrie (fast section only)	M. 1, 11, 47
Kyrie I	M. 2, 3*, 4, 5
Kyrie II**	M. 12, 19, 39, 40, 45, 67
Kyrie (derivatives)	M. 16 (Ex. 10-9), 28, 44, 49 (DTÖ 88)
"Cum Sancto" of Gloria	M. 26, 72
"In gloria" of Gloria	M. 38
"Amen" of Gloria	M. 23 (Berlin version) 34
"Et vitam" of Credo**	M. 13, 51

*In Albrechtsberger's *Missa Annuntiationis B.M.V.* (M. 3) there are three "Dona" sections. The first and third replay the music of Kyrie I, while the second is a new fugue.
**The Kyrie II and "Et vitam" settings reused are usually fugal movements.

"Dona nobis pacem" consist of six syllables, use of the same music for these two sections is accomplished relatively easily, although not without some problems of accentuation (see n. 16). The practice makes sense because the "Dona," like the Kyrie, is also an entreaty to God. One might go so far as to understand this return to music heard at the start of Mass as a parallel to the worshipers' leaving the "holy of holies" and returning to the world from which they came. This large-scale musical return also satisfactorily unifies and rounds out the Mass as a whole.

The five instances where the "Dona" is only a derivative of the Kyrie are interesting for the transformations involved and for the change in proportions. In the *Missa in C* (M. 28) Hofmann reduces the 85 measures of the fast Kyrie down to 45 measures for the "Dona" which begins (m. 1–20) and ends (m. 29–34, 39–45) with the same music as the "Kyrie." The "Kyrie" has a slow introduction of only six measures, while the slow "Agnus Dei" (different music) lasts 15 measures. Perhaps the longer "Agnus Dei" introduction led Hofmann to shorten the music being reused for the "Dona." In the *Missa Sancti Caroli* (M. 49; score in *DTÖ* 88) Reutter shortens the "Dona" (actually a repetition of the "Kyrie II" fugue) by omitting a five-measure coda which had served only to relate "Kyrie II" musically to the beginning of "Kyrie I." In M. 16 Dittersdorf is most imaginative in his reworking of the opening adagio Kyrie for the allegro "Dona nobis"; the disjunct bass line of the earlier adagio becomes the subject of the allegro fugue (see ex. 10-9). Monn uses the opening and closing of "Kyrie I" for the "Agnus Dei" of his *Missa Solemnis in B-flat* (M. 39); he then reuses the "Kyrie II" fugue for the "Dona."

For many composers the fugue remained the tried and true way to close the Mass. About half of the Masses in the sample (36 of 70) have a fugal "Dona nobis pacem." About two-thirds of these fugues are from Masses written before 1760 by composers such as Albrechtsberger, Arbesser, Boog, Hasse, Holzbauer, Monn, Predieri, Reutter, Schmidt, Tuma, and Wagenseil. "Dona" fugues continue to appear after this date, albeit less frequently, in Masses by some of these composers as well as in the Masses of Bonno, Gassmann, Gsur, Hofmann, Kohaut, and Sonnleithner. Almost half of these fugues are repeats of movements heard earlier in the Mass. Most impressive and effective as a "Dona" finale are the double fugues found in Masses by Holzbauer, Monn, and Tuma—all members of the older generation.[17] Returning to fugue at the conclusion of the Mass again, as in earlier movements at "Cum Sancto Spiritu," "Et vitam," and "Osanna," evokes the idea of eternity associated with both God's church and the old art of imitative counterpoint.

The more imaginative settings of the "Dona" are those employing both soloists and chorus. Over one-third of the Masses under study have some kind of *concertato* treatment in this section.[18] Often the alternation of solo and

Example 10-9. Karl Ditters von Dittersdorf, *Missa in C*, M. 16
(n.d.)
A. "Kyrie" (Adagio), measures 12–21

Example 10-9 A (cont'd.)

Example 10-9 B.   "Dona nobis pacem" (Allegro), measures 1–20

Example 10-9B (cont'd.)

Example 10-9B (cont'd.)

Example 10-9B (concluded)

choral forces generates a momentum and excitement comparable to that experienced during an operatic finale. Occasionally soloists are brought in for only the final measures to intensify the climax of the work (e.g., M. 66; see J. Haydn, Hob. XXII: 14 and Mozart, K. 317). In other settings the soloists are part of a choral fugue where they present 1) the first exposition of the subject in all voices (M. 7, 8, 30, 68), 2) one or more internal episodes (M. 31, 50 [ex. 10-15], 63), or 3) a coda for the movement (M. 9).

In "Dona" settings by Carl, Dittersdorf, Haydn, Holzbauer, Martínez, Mozart, Seuche, Sonnleithner, and Ziegler, the juxtaposition of chorus and soloists often resembles that of *ripieno* and *concertino* in concertos from the period. Here the chorus normally unifies the movement with a recurring refrain (ritornello) that reaffirms each new key to which the soloists move during their more melismatic flights. There is considerable variety and freedom in overall design, but generally the soloists have two to four passages interspersed between choral sections. The "Dona nobis pacem" of Dittersdorf's *Missa ex D* (M. 17, before 1777) is typical of this kind of treatment (ex. 10-10).[19]

The most progressive approach to *concertato* treatment is found in "Dona" settings that rely upon sonata- and rondolike forms. We have already discussed the mixture of sonata and concerto elements in the Kyrie of Reutter's *Missa Sancti Mariani* (M. 47, 1759), which reuses the music of the Kyrie for the "Dona nobis pacem" (see fig. 6-3 and ex. 6-10). In example 10-11 we see how Marianne von Martínez similarly blends aspects of the concerto (tutti-solo alternation, ritornellos) and sonata form (thematic functionalism, double reprise, etc.) in her *Messe Nr. 4* (M. 37, 1765). As in the Reutter Mass just cited, the second theme of the movement is set apart as a vocal solo (ex. 10-11, m. 7). Figure 10-8 illustrates the structure of the entire movement.[20] Dittersdorf's *Missa in C* (M. 15, before 1773) also mixes sonata and concerto attributes in a lively 2/4 "Dona" finale that has regular four-bar phrases and frequent alternation between the soprano soloist and chorus.

By the 1770s sonata and rondo designs begin to dominate settings of the "Dona." In the sample under study, Grassl (M. 20, before 1774), Müller (M. 41, n.d.), and Sonnleithner (M. 55, before 1765) follow more or less a sonata design for the "Dona." Figure 10-9 shows the plan of Sonnleithner's "Dona." The alternation between soloists and chorus shows how the concerto influence remained strong (ex. 10-12, mm. 19–24). A new use of vocal forces during the reprise (i.e., chorus instead of soloists at m. 62, four soloists instead of one at m. 68) resists the thematic compartmentalization typical of a concerto grosso and instead provides a refreshing change at this climax of the finale. Thematic functionalism is evident in the consistent use of a transitional theme (T: mm. 25 and 68); the "development" area is based mostly upon melodies already heard (mm. 37–61).

Example 10-10. Karl Ditters von Dittersdorf, *Missa ex D,* M. 17
(before 1777), "Dona nobis pacem" (Allegro),
measures 1–45.

Example 10-10 (cont'd.)

Example 10-10   (cont'd.)

Example 10-10   (cont'd.)

Example 10-10 (cont'd.)

Example 10-10 (cont'd.)

Example 10-10   (concluded)

Example 10-11. Marianne von Martínez, *Messe No. 4*, M. 37 (1765), "Dona nobis pacem" (Allegro), measures 1–20.

Example 10-11 (cont'd.)

Example 10-11 (cont'd.)

Example 10-11 (concluded)

Figure 10-8. Structural Outline of the "Dona nobis pacem" (Allegro) to Martinez's *Messe Nr. 4* (M. 37, 1765)*

Forces:	Chorus	Solo Chorus								Orch.	Chorus	Chorus	Solo Chorus	Solo Chorus			Solo Chorus			
Melody:	Pa	b	S	(Pa)	Pa^1	b^1	c	d	K	1N	2N (Pa)	3N	4N (Pc)	K^1	K^2(S)	(Pa)	Pa b^2	S	K^3	
Measure:	1	5	7		17	20	24	26	35	38	48	55	62	65	75	85	96	99	103	105	110	125 (end)
Harmony:	I------V------										(V/V Ped.)				V------V		
Section:	"Exposition"										"Development" [New ideas, some derived from Pa, Pc, K and S]						"Reprise"			
	"Ritornello"			"Ritornello"													"Ritornello"			

*See ex. 10-11

Figure 10-9. Structural Outline of the "Dona nobis pacem" (Allegro) to Sonnleithner's *Missa in C* (M. 55, before 1765)*

Forces:	S solo/Chorus	S Solo	Chorus	A/S solos		Chorus	Chorus	SATB Solos	Chorus	
Melody:	P	T	S	P^1	P^2	S^1 ext.	P^3	T	S	K(S)
Measure:	19*	25	28	37	43	47 51	62	68	75 83	91 (end)
Harmony:	I----------------V---------------vi-----------------I-----------------V----------------I									
Section:	"Exposition"			"Development"			"Reprise"			

*Measures 1-18 constitute the "Agnus Dei," a slow introductory section.

ext. = extension

*See ex. 10-12

Example 10-12. Christoph Sonnleithner, *Missa in C,* M. 55 (before
1765), "Dona nobis pacem" (Allegro), measures
19–62.

Example 10-12 (cont'd.)

Example 10-12 (cont'd.)

Example 10-12 (cont'd.)

Example 10-12 (cont'd.)

Example 10-12   (cont'd.)

Example 10-12 (cont'd.)

Example 10-12 (cont'd.)

Example 10-12 (cont'd.)

Example 10-12 (cont'd.)

Example 10-12 (concluded)

Although less frequently used, rondo form (coupled with tutti-solo alternation) fosters an energetic finale for the Mass, as it does so often in instrumental music of the period.[21] In Vaňhal's *Missa pastorell in G* (M. 65, before 1782) the basic form is $ABA^1B^1A^2$. The lively opening tune (A) is sung primarily by pairs of soloists and has the unmistakable character of a 2/4 rondo finale theme (ex. 10-13).

Purely choral settings which are neither fugues nor the forms just discussed account for only about 15 percent of the "Dona" settings in the sample. Despite their lack of solo-tutti contrast or thematic functionalism and development, these choral movements can still be effective finales by virtue of their interesting juxtaposition of chordal and contrapuntal passages (M. 56 and 70), recurring choral refrains (M. 64 and 71), and rounded ABA' forms (M. 35, 42, and 44). Through-composed "Dona" settings are rare; there are only two examples in the sample (M. 18 and 53).

Expressive Devices of the "Dona"

With so short a text and a form inspired by instrumental music, it should come as no surprise that the "Dona nobis pacem" usually lacks the wealth of rhetorical figures found in some other parts of the Mass. However, a few devices which appear sporadically should be mentioned. "Pacem" provides the only opportunity for word painting, and several composers (including Dittersdorf, Gsur, Haydn, Mozart, Seuche, Sonnleithner, Tuma, Vaňhal, and Wagenseil) occasionally set this word *piano* or in a low register (ex. 10-14). In some Masses the idea of peace takes the form of a generally pastoral style, often characterized by triple meters, melodies in thirds, folklike melodies, and dronelike sustained or repeated tones (see ex. 10-13; also J. Haydn, Hob. XXII: 6).

Some composers exploit many of the characteristics of an operatic finale: agitated repeated-note accompaniments (ex. 10-17), alternation of chorus and soloists (discussed above), a sudden, tension-filled fermata upon a dominant seventh chord near the end (M. 50 [ex. 10-15], 64, and J. Haydn, Hob. XXII: 9, 10, 12), and a rip-roaring triumphal conclusion accompanied by brass and timpani (ex. 10-15). Indeed, the images of battle and victory conjured up by certain settings are sometimes strong enough to make one believe the composer may have been alluding to wars being waged at the time or he may have felt the need to express musically the wars (internal, external, or personal) from which believers were seeking relief. Thus Runestad's justification for the happy endings in most of Haydn's Masses also applies to many of the present Masses:

> The function of the music which concludes the Mass is precisely the same as that which closes the symphony. In both, the emotional level is lightened to provide relief from tension and dramatic impact of earlier movements, particularly in development sections of sonata forms and in the heavy, penitential parts of the Gloria and Credo.[22]

Example 10-13. Jan Vaňhal, *Missa Pastorell in G*, M. 65 (before 1782), "Dona nobis pacem" (Allegro moderato), measures 1–17 [see also ex. 10-16].

Example 10-13   (cont'd.)

Example 10-13 (concluded)

Example 10-14. Georg Christoph Wagenseil, *Missa solenne Immaculatae Conceptionis,* M. 70 (1743), "Dona nobis pacem" (Allegro), measures 17–20.

Example 10-15. Ferdinand Schmidt, *Missa Sanctae Caeciliae in C,*
M. 50 (before 1746), "Dona nobis pacem"
(Allegro), measures 52–68.

Example 10-15   (cont'd.)

Example 10-15 (cont'd.)

Example 10-15 (concluded)

In one Mass (M. 65) Vaňhal seems to have confused the style of the "Dona" with that of an *opera buffa*; the repetitive runs of its closing theme are more spritely than serious (ex. 10-16).

A cheerful conclusion to the Mass was nothing new to Austria. Earlier composers (e.g., Ziani, Pachschmidt, Fux, and Caldara) had used triple meter and happy, folklike melodies to end their Masses.[23] However, a few composers during the present period chose to conclude their Masses quietly (e.g., M. 6 by Arbesser). Such soft endings may be more in keeping with the "peace" hoped for in the text. Brand writes that a quiet conclusion—like the one at the end of Haydn's *Kleine Orgelmesse* (Hob. XXII: 7)—suggests the beseeching of the people.[24] In some Masses a plagal cadence or a brief adagio coda may lend additional serenity.

This chapter would not be complete without recounting the old Viennese anecdote pertaining to the "Dona nobis pacem." Georg von Reutter composed a Mass that came to be nicknamed "Die Schimmelmesse." This Mass is thought to be Reutter's *Missa Conceptionis B. M. V.* (M. 46, Hofer No, 68; before 1756).[25] The story has it that when Reutter composed the "Dona" of this Mass, the aging Kapellmeister was contemplating a verse of Virgil that describes the sounds of horses' hoofbeats. The unusual 6/8 movement moved Empress Maria Theresa to question Reutter about the piece. He answered that he had hoped to hint that, at his advanced age and with his busy schedule, he should not have to walk everywhere. Immediately the Empress granted his wish and presented him with his very own equipage drawn by white horses or *Schimmel*. Example 10-17 shows the opening and closing measures of this "Dona." The lumbering bass accompaniment, the steady "hoofbeat" sixteenth-notes in the violins, the fugal entries of the voices chasing each other, and especially the "galloping" timpani notes of the final bars—all seem to fit the story. Actually, however, such settings in compound meter were not all that rare (see the "Dona's" listed for 12/8 and 6/4 in fig. 10-3). Interestingly, the fugue which closes Haydn's *Grosse Orgelmesse* (Hob. XXII: 4), a work written over a decade later, is also in 6/8 and very much resembles this "Dona" by his teacher—even in its equestrian aspects. Whether or not the *Schimmelmesse* story is true, it is pleasing to know that some of these Masses were multi-functional and that they did affect the minds of their listeners, even though not always in the most pious of ways.

Summary

The Agnus has three invocations to the Lamb of God joined with pleas for mercy and spiritual peace. It is usually the shortest part of the Mass, averaging about 87 measures in length and consisting of two distinct sections: a slow

Example 10-16. Jan Vaňhal, *Missa Pastorell in G*, M. 65 (before
1782), "Dona nobis pacem" (Allegro moderato),
measures 32–37 [see also ex. 10-13].

Example 10-17.   Georg von Reutter, Jr., *Missa Conceptionis in C*;
M. 46 (1756), "Dona nobis pacem" (Allegro
molto).
A.   measures 1–11

Example 10-17 (cont'd.)
 B. measures 51–58

Example 10-17 (concluded)

introductory "Agnus Dei" connected by a half-cadence to a faster "Dona nobis pacem" which is also marked by changes in meter, melody, and scoring. The "Agnus Dei" almost always begins in the Mass's tonic major, tonic minor, or relative minor, while the "Dona" always begins and ends in the tonic key. Nearly always the "Agnus Dei" follows a tripartite design that is reflected in the melody (AA^1A^2, ABC, or AA^1B), the harmony (three successive tonalities), and the disposition of the soloists and chorus (often solo-solo-chorus). Certain melodic types, e.g., melodies with pathos or recitativelike declamation, appear frequently in the "Agnus Dei." A tradition of using trombone obbligatos during the "Agnus Dei" was maintained by some of the composers. In a few of the "Agnus Dei" settings the strings are muted or dynamic contrasts are used to stir the affections of listeners. Harmonic instability and chromaticism are common at the words "peccata" and "miserere."

Compared with the "Agnus Dei," the "Dona nobis pacem" settings exhibit greater variety. In about a third of the Masses the music of the "Dona" recapitulates an earlier movement (usually all or part of the Kyrie); these are chiefly choral fugues and rounded ternary forms. Almost another third of the Masses present a new fugue at this point. About a quarter of the settings imaginatively use both chorus and soloists in forms that often resemble the concerto grosso or, by the 1770s, the sonata, rondo, and their hybrids. Despite the general lack of rhetorical figures in this section, some composers do set the word "pacem" to softer notes or conclude the movement quietly. In general, however, composers treat the "Dona nobis pacem" almost as an operatic finale and use the full ensemble (brass and timpani included) to reflect the triumph and majesty of God whose eternal presence is being celebrated by the communicants partaking of the Eucharistic meal.

Conclusions

In September 1777 the Benedictine Abbey at Kremsmünster (some 130 miles east of Vienna) held an eight-day festival celebrating the one-thousandth anniversary of its founding. Viennese church music was much in evidence. Eleven of the 16 Masses during the festival were by composers associated with Vienna. There were three settings by Reutter, three by Hofmann (two of which were called "prächtig" at the time), two by Franz Novotny, and one each by Sonnleithner, Haydn (no first name given), and Holzbauer.[1] Such an isolated event, together with the wide-ranging manuscript dissemination of Viennese sacred music throughout Lower Austria, Czechoslovakia, and Hungary, testifies to the significant influence of the imperial city's music throughout the Austro-Hungarian Empire.

The foregoing chapters have shown how much the church contributed to Vienna's musical life in the second half of the eighteenth century, be it providing numerous musicians with employment (not always at the best wages) or encouraging the study, practice, and composition of music. The composers of sacred music formed a diverse lot: they included singers, instrumentalists, dilettantes, freelancers, and lawyers, as well as organists and choir directors. As we have seen, their Mass settings were equally diverse— running from routine, functional, and uninspired to distinctive, imaginative, and stirring. Previous reports on a decline in Viennese sacred music during this period are somewhat exaggerated. Although nearly every Mass followed the liturgical dictates for performance during an actual service, most composers seemed to express themselves freely in their own stylistic vein despite papal and imperial decrees that attempted to ban theatrical elements from church music.

One looks in vain for a clear evolution in the style of these Masses. Continuous stylistic change is not easily discernible because church music with its unchanging Latin texts was, by nature, conservative and tended to maintain the traits and traditions of an already established "church style" (e.g., fugal conclusions, rhetorical figures, organ basso continuo, *colla parte* trombones, etc.). Such stylistic traditions affected compositional freedom to varying degrees, depending upon the composer and the situation. In addition, at least two different generations of composers with widely differentiated backgrounds were contributing to the large repertoire of concerted Masses. Undoubtedly the varying local circumstances also influenced the size, scoring, and degree of difficulty of a Mass.

We thus receive the general impression that these Masses retained many Baroque traits until well into the 1770s, only then gradually borrowing new stylistic elements from other, more innovative genres such as the sonata, symphony, opera, and chamber music. In most Masses, particularly in the choral movements, music and text remained closely allied, with musical form and rhetorical figures heavily dependent upon the order and meaning of the words. Solo movements continued to use existing binary and ternary aria designs which had been borrowed from opera during the Baroque era. By the 1770s only a few composers (e.g., Dittersdorf, Haydn, Mozart, Reutter, Sonnleithner, and Vañhal) were incorporating elements of the sonata and symphony into their Masses.

Traits that seemed to remain relatively constant during the four decades 1741–83 include the organ figured bass, the Viennese *Kirchentrio* as the orchestral core, the frequent and often challenging instrumental obbligatos during ritornellos, the use of fugue (or fugato) for concluding movements, the reduction to a trio texture whenever the soloists are singing, and the *concertato* alternation of tutti and solo voices during choral movements. In addition, certain instrumental obbligatos (e.g., the trombone at "Gratias" and "Agnus Dei") continued to be associated with specific texts.

Nonetheless, despite the generally conservative nature of the genre, we do observe at least six stylistic trends that by the 1770s were paving the way for grander, more symphonic Masses of Haydn, Beethoven, Schubert, and others after 1790:

1. *Fewer but longer movements.* The era of the Baroque multi-movement "number" Mass was coming to a close. After about 1770, Glorias and Credos rarely consisted of more than four movements each. In making longer, tonally more unified movements that fit into the larger plan of the entire Mass, composers like Albrechtsberger, Bonno, Dittersdorf, Haydn, Sonnleithner, Vañhal, and others were espousing an aesthetic that seems rooted in the *missa brevis* tradition and was concurrently reflected in the instrumental music of the developing Viennese Classic style. As Kirkendale has written: "...the musical sensibility of the baroque and rococo was focused more upon details than on the whole, more upon contiguity and continuation than upon the overall formal plan."[2] Reviewing the present Masses, we observe the younger composers beginning to reject this Baroque concern for the immediate moment and the minute detail and thinking more in terms of a larger and often bolder conception.

2. *Greater unity of key.* Hand in hand with a more comprehensive view of the Mass went an increased concern for tonal unity. Individual movements (for that matter, entire Masses) tended to begin and end in the same key, rather than change tonality because of a desire to foster harmonic continuity at the immediate, local level. Tonal unity and clarity were further promoted by a growing predisposition for homophony and by the resultant broad harmonic strokes, i.e., slower harmonic rhythms, which composers used increasingly (see ex. 6-12 by Vaňhal). As each new chord came to be sustained for a half or a full measure rather than just a single beat, composers were becoming more "measure oriented" or barline conscious. This change lent greater harmonic focus and thrust to the Mass but also reduced rhythmic flexibility and freedom somewhat, as phrases assumed more or less regular and symmetrical lengths, hemiola became less common, and the emphasis changed from horizontal to vertical thinking.

3. *Greater variety in meter.* Composers were starting to employ other meters, including 2/4, 3/8, and 6/8 in addition to the ubiquitous C, ¢, and 3/4. The increasing use of the "new" meters that were already common in instrumental music may be considered further evidence of the secularization that continued to take place in church music. Metric variety also helps offset the potentially dull effect of music that is particularly conscious of the barline.

4. *Vocal solos within choral movements instead of as independent arias.* Perhaps in response to critics' complaints about too many operatic characteristics in church music, composers began giving vocal soloists fewer separate numbers and, instead, assigning them selected texts to sing (often alone or in duo) within movements that were essentially choral. The *missa brevis* tradition, with its succinct forms and paucity of independent solos, was likely influential in this change.

5. *More independent oboe, viola, and 'cello parts; decrease in solos for the trombone.* Despite a generally conservative approach to instrumentation based upon the so-called *Wiener Kirchentrio* nucleus (two violins and basso continuo), by the end of the 1760s composers were freeing the oboe, viola, and 'cello from their former *colla parte* subjugation. Undoubtedly orchestral practices in opera and especially in the newly evolving symphony led composers like Dittersdorf, Hasse, Haydn, Sonnleithner, and Vaňhal to enrich church music orchestration by the independent use of these instruments. The trombone continued to be an important part of the church orchestra throughout most of this period—even more so than is generally realized from the Masses of Haydn and Mozart. However, by the 1780s trombones were beginning to play fewer obbligatos, as composers preferred to highlight some of the church orchestra's new constituents. Other developments in orchestration included more idiomatic writing for each instrument and greater precision in the notation of tempo, dynamics, articulation, and other expressive devices.

6.   *Forms reflect the influence of sonata and concerto designs.* By the end of the 1760s choral movements and solo arias had both begun exhibiting sonata characteristics (i.e., thematic groups, thematic functionalism, double reprise, etc.), particularly in Masses by Reutter, Sonnleithner, and Vaňhal. Concerto elements (e.g., tutti-soli alternations, unifying ritornellos) occur in Masses throughout the period of study, sometimes in conjunction with sonatalike schemes. These influences are all part of the increasingly cosmopolitan nature of church music, a cosmopolitanism that was certainly reflected in Koch's elaborate definition of "church style" in 1802. Opera continued to have an effect upon the Mass in the stylistic borrowings from bel canto aria, recitative, coloratura, *stilo buffo,* cadenzas, etc.

Individual studies of a single composer's Mass output would undoubtedly reveal a few other stylistic tendencies not mentioned here (where the purpose has been to present the overall picture). When examining these Masses it is crucial to keep their functionalism in perspective and realize that most composers probably did not consider this genre the ideal outlet for their creative impulses.

The present study has surveyed several composers' handling of the same, unchanging text for the Mass Ordinary over a 42 year period in one of Europe's most influential musical centers. The analyses have revealed how deeply entrenched in tradition many of the Masses were. Nevertheless, several Masses stand apart because they exhibit the relatively progressive influence of other genres such as opera, concerto, sonata, and symphony.[3] In some cases these latter genres may have inspired the larger, more comprehensive thinking that we witness at the end of the period under discussion, as composers seemed to aim for greater coherence among the various movements of a Mass. True, these genres were not restricted to functioning within an established liturgical framework. On the other hand, although the concerted Mass was only an accompaniment to the ceremonies leading up to and including a reenactment of the Lord's Last Supper and sacrifice, we know from contemporary accounts that the music played a vital role in arousing piety in the hearts and minds of the faithful, many of whom could not actively partake of communion. Several of the composers discussed in this study (e.g., Arbesser and Reutter) took this practical role for their Masses very seriously. As a result, their music may fail when heard outside of the liturgical context. But such failure would seldom occur with most of the Masses examined here; rather, Fellerer's observation about the effect of Enlightenment philosophy upon church music rings true: "In the anthropocentric interpretation of the Enlightenment, the music itself became the carrier of expression and was no longer defined by the liturgy. In many ways the liturgy became the plot for the ruling musical design which sought to grip and inspire the people, just as in opera and concerts."[4]

The present project has also sought to reveal the problems of sacred music research in the pre-Classic era and worthwhile directions for future research in this still relatively unexplored territory. We need to know more about the performance practices of the various institutions which performed these Masses. How many performers were actually involved? We need more repertoire studies of individual churches and more information about the genesis and performance of sacred music. A thorough examination of church music reports in the *Wiener Diarium* would be most valuable. Surely many more documents such as those discovered and published by Otto Biba and others need to be recovered from Vienna's archives and churches and reviewed for the additional perspectives they provide for the church music of this period. Were any of these Masses transported to and performed in Italy where the Hapsburgs still had some authority? After enactment of Joseph II's restrictions of 1783, where and why did concerted Masses continue to be performed with trumpets and timpani? Countless composer attributions await further authenticity verification before an accurate history of the present repertoire may be completed. Several of Vienna's church archives with significant eighteenth-century music collections remain uncatalogued or inaccessible to all musicologists; one hopes this situation will change before it is too late to retrieve the music.

Was this music successful in its day? From most reports the answer is decidedly yes, if we mean a Mass was successful in fulfilling its function within the liturgy. As the thematic catalogue shows, some Masses continued to be performed for decades after their composition; some performance dates extend even into the middle of the nineteenth century. Whether the Masses would be successful today must hinge upon how they could work in the concert hall, a setting for which they were definitely not intended. Our century, often entranced by the sheer beauty of Masses from the nineteenth century, needs to be reminded of the equally expressive repertoire from Vienna during the second half of the eighteenth century, a repertoire for which Dittersdorf, Gassmann, Haydn, Mozart, Reutter, Sonnleithner, and Vaňhal (among others) created some of their most distinguished compositions.

The preceding chapters will have served a useful purpose if they enhance our appreciation of the little known but important repertoire of the concerted Mass in Vienna and thereby help us understand the sources of the great sacred works of Haydn and Mozart. Better yet, one hopes that in the near future some of the more deserving settings might be enjoyed on programs along with the better known examples by the two giants of the period. [5]

Appendix A

The Liturgical Year in Vienna

<u>Significant Fixed Feasts</u>

January
1   Circumcision of Our Lord (In Circumcisione Domini;
        Beschneidung Christi; Beschneidung des Herrn)
        [Octave day of Christmas]
6   Epiphany (Adoration of the Magi; In Epiphania Domi-
        ni; Dreikönigtag; Tag der heiligen drei Könige)
20 St. Fabian & St. Sebastian
22 St. Vincent
-- Marriage of the B.V.M.
25 Conversion of St. Paul (Pauli Bekehrung)

February
2   Purification of the B.V.M. (Candlemas; Lichtmess)
6   St. Dorothy (Dorothea)
8   St. John of Matha (Johann von Matta)
9   St. Apollonia
12 Wedding anniversary of Maria Theresa and Francis I
24 St. Matthias the Apostle (Matthäus)

March
7   St. Thomas Aquinas (Thomas von Aquin)
13 Birthday of Emperor Joseph II (1741)
19 St. Joseph, patron saint of Austria; nameday of
        Joseph II
21 St. Benedict (Benedikt)
24 St. Gabriel the Archangel (Gabriel Erzengel)
25 Annunciation of the B.V.M.

April
2   St. Francis of Paula (Paola; Franz von Paula)
23 St. George (Georg)
25 St. Mark Evangelist

May
1   Sts. Philip & James Apostles (Philipp und Jakob);
        St. Bridget's Day
8   Apparition of St. Michael Archangel (Erscheinung
        des Erzengels Michael)
13   Birthday of Empress Maria Theresa (1717)

June
13   St. Anthony of Padua (Anton von Padua)
24   St. John the Baptist (Johannes der Täufer;
        Johann des Täufers)
29   Sts. Peter & Paul Apostles

July
2   Visitation of the B.V.M. (Maria Heimsuchung)
--   Separation of the Apostles (Scheidung der Aposteln)
16   Our Blessed Lady of Mt. Carmel (Aufenthalt Maria
        vom Berge Carmel)
22   St. Mary Magdalen (Maria Magdalena)
23   St. James Apostle
26   St. Anne, Mother of the B.V.M. (Anna)
31   St. Ignatius [Loyola of the Jesuits]

August
1   St. Peter's Chains (Petri Kettenfeier)
3   The Finding of the Body of St. Stephen (Erfindung
        des heiligen Stephan)
4   St. Dominic (Dominicus)
6   Transfiguration of Our Lord Jesus Christ (Ver-
        klärung Jesu)
7   St. Cajetan
10   St. Lawrence (Lorenz)
15   Assumption of the B.V.M. (Mariä Himmelfahrt)
16   St. Joachim; also St. Roch (Rochus)
18   Death of Francis I, husband of Empress
        Maria Theresa (1765)
23   St. Philip Benizi (Philipp Benitius)
24   St. Bartholomew Apostle (Bartholomäus)
28   St. Augustine (Augustin); birthday of Empress
        Elisabeth Christine, widow of Charles VI
29   Beheading of St. John the Baptist (Johannes Ent-
        hauptung)

September
2   St. Stephen, King of Hungary (Stephan); guardian of Vienna
4   St. Rosalia of Palermo
8   Nativity of the B.V.M. (Maria Geburt)
12   The Most Holy Name of Mary (Maria Namensfest);
        Procession celebrating repulsion of the
        Turks (1683)(Entsatz von der türkischen
        Belagerung)

14   Exaltation of the Holy Cross (Kreuzerhöhung und
        -Erfindung)
15   The Seven Dolours of the B.V.M.
21   St. Matthew Apostle & Evangelist (Evangelist Matthäus)
24   Our Lady of Ransom (Maria de Mercede)
28   St. Wenceslaus of Bohemia (Wenzel)
29   St. Michael the Archangel (Michael Erzengel)

October
1   Birthday of Emperor Charles VI (1685)
4   St. Francis of Assisi (Franz der Bekenner)
7   Our Lady of the Most Holy Rosary (Maria Rosen-
        kranzfest)
15   St. Theresa (Teresa; Theresia); nameday of Maria
        Theresa
18   St. Luke Evangelist
19   St. Peter of Alcántara (Peter von Alkantara)
20   Death of Emperor Charles VI (1740)
21   St. Ursula
28   Sts. Simon the Canaanean & Jude [=Lebbaeus,
        Thaddeus] Apostles (Simon und Juda)

November
1   All Saints Day (Allerheiligen)
2   All Souls' Day (Allerseelentag).
4   St. Charles Borromeo (Karl Borromäus; Caroli)
11   St. Martin of Tours
15   St. Leopold, Landespatron
19   St. Elizabeth (Elisabeth); nameday of Empress
        Elisabeth Christine
21   Presentation of the B.V.M.
22   St. Cecilia (Caecilia; Cäcilie); patron of
        musicians' brotherhood
25   St. Catherine (Katharina)
28   Death of Empress Maria Theresa (1780)
30   St. Andrew Apostle (Andreas); patron of Order of
        Golden Fleece (Toisonisten)

December
3   St. Francis Xavier (Franz Xaver)
6   St. Nicholas (Nikolaus); patron of Nicolasbruder-
        schaft of musicians
8   Immaculate Conception of the B.V.M. (die unbefleckte
        Empfängnis Mariens; Mariä Empfängnis);
        birthday of Francis I (1708)
21   St. Thomas Apostle
24   Vigil of Christmas (In Vigilia Nativitatis Domini;
        Vigil der Christnacht; Heiligenabend)
25   Christmas Day, Nativity of Our Lord Jesus Christ
        (Christ-Tag; Weihnacht; 1. Weihnachtstag)

26   St. Stephen (Stephanstag; 2. Weihnachtstag)
27   St. John Apostle & Evangelist (3. Tag der
         Geburtsfeier des Herrn)
28   Holy Innocents (Tag der unschuldigen Kinder)
29   St. Thomas of Canterbury
31   St. Silvester

Significant Movable Feasts

No. of
weeks
before/
after
Easter

-9   Septuagesima Sunday

-8   Sexagesima Sunday

-7   Quinquagesima Sunday

      Ash Wednesday (Aschermittwoch; Cinerum); Lent begins

-6   1st Sunday of Lent (Fastenzeit; Dominica I. in
         Quadragesima)
      Ember Week (Wed., Fri., Sat.)

-5   2nd Sunday of Lent (Dominica II. in Quadragesima)

-4   3rd Sunday of Lent (Dominica III. in Quadragesima)

-3   4th Sunday of Lent (Dominica IV. in Quadragesima;
         Sonntag Laetare)
-2   Passion Sunday (Dominica de Passione; Passion des Herrn)

-1   Palm Sunday (Palmsonntag; 2nd Sunday of the Passion)

      Holy Week (Karwoche)
         Maundy Thursday (Gründonnerstag)
         Good Friday (Karfreitag)
         Holy Saturday (Karsamstag)

      EASTER SUNDAY (Ostersonntag; Ostern; Dominica Resur-
         rectionis; Pascha)

+1   Low Sunday (Quasimodo; Dominica in Albis)

+2   2nd Sunday after Easter (Dominica II. post Pascha)

+3   3rd Sunday after Easter (Dominica III. post Pascha)

+4   4th Sunday after Easter (Dominica IV. post Pascha)

+5   5th Sunday after Easter (Dominica V. post Pascha)

Rogation Days, Litanies (Bittage)(Mon.-Wed.)

Ascension (In Ascensione Domini; Christi Himmelfahrt) (Thurs.)

+6   Sunday within the Octave of Ascension (Dominica infra Octavam Ascensionis; Sonntag Exaudi)

+7   Pentecost, Whit Sunday (Dominica Pentecostes; Pfingsten)

Ember Week, Whitsun Week

+8   Sunday of the Blessed Trinity (In Festo Sanctiss. Trinitatis; Dominica I. post Pentecosten; Dreifaltigkeitsfest)

Corpus Christi (In Festo Corporis Christi; Fronleichnam)(Thurs.)

+9   Sunday within the Octave of Corpus Christi, 2nd Sunday after Pentecost (Dominica infra Octavam Corporis Christi)

The Most Sacred Heart of Jesus (Sacratissimi Cordis Jesus)(Fri.)

+10   Sunday within the Octave of the Sacred Heart, 3rd Sunday after Pentecost (Dominica infra Octavam Sacratissimi Cordis Jesu)

+11   4th Sunday after Pentecost (Dominica IV. post Pentecosten)

etc.

The above calendar of fixed and movable feasts has been culled from various sources, including:

Willi Apel, *Gregorian Chant* (Bloomington, IN: Indiana University Press, 1958), pp. 9–12.

L. W. Cowie and John S. Gummer, *The Christian Calendar* (Springfield, MA: G. & C. Merriam, 1974), passim.

Ludwig Ritter von Köchel, *Die kaiserliche Hofmusikkapelle in Wien von 1543 bis 1867* (Vienna: Beck and Hölder, 1869; reprint ed., Hildesheim: G. Olms, 1976), pp. 135–44 [material from Kilian Reinhardt's *Rubriche Generali*].

Liber Usualis, ed. the Benedictines of Solemnes (Tournai: Desclee, 1956), pp. xli–xlix.

Appendix B

Choirmasters of Vienna during the Eighteenth Century

The following enumeration of the choirmasters (and some organists) in some of Vienna's better known churches during the period 1741-1783 is included as a reference for future studies of sacred music. It is a <u>working</u> list and is by no means comprehensive. Future research will undoubtedly fill in its gaps and correct its errors.

Churches are listed by the names used in the preceding chapters. Alternative names appear in parentheses. The churches are arranged according to the Roman numerals used in the 1783 "Index of All [Church] Music Personnel" transcribed in Otto Biba's valuable study "Die Wiener Kirchenmusik um 1783." The general location of many of these churches may be seen in the map of fig. 2-1 at the start of chapter 2.

I. St. Stephen's Cathedral (Stephansdom; Metropolitan-kirche; Pfarrkirche zu St. Stephan; Dompfarrkirche)

Essential-Kapellmeister
1738-1772 Georg von Reutter, Jr.
1772-1793 Leopold Hofmann
1793-1809 Johann Georg Albrechtsberger
Gnadenbild-Kapellmeister (ended after 1783)
1727-1742 Johann Georg Reinhardt
1743-1756 Ferdinand Schmidt
1756-1772 Georg von Reutter, Jr.
1772-1783 Leopold Hofmann
Organists
1738-1759? Anton Weckh (Neck?)
1761-1803? Matthäus Mittmayr (Mathias Mittelmayr)

II. Schotten-Kirche (Benediktinerchor auf der Freyung; Pfarrkirche der Benediktiner unsere liebe Frau zu den Schotten)

Regens chori
1749/50-1794 Tobias Gsur
1794-1824   Joseph Eybler

III. St. Peter's (Pfarr[kirche] zu St. Peter; Peterskirche)

Regens chori
? -1764 Johann Nepomuk Boog (Pock)
1764?-1793 Leopold Hofmann (Kapellmeister)
1793-   Joseph Preindl

IV. Kirche am Hof (Pfarrkirche am Hof; S. Maria am Hof;
     Obere Jesuitenkirche; Zu den neun Chören der Engel)

Kapellmeister
before 1783-1816 Karl Friberth

V. Dominikaner-Kirche (Pfarr-Kirche bei den Dominikanern;
    Klosterkirche Maria Rotunda)

VI. St. Augustine's (Augustinerkirche; Pfarrkirche bei
     den PP. Augustiner Barfüsser; Hofkirche St. Augustin;
     includes the Loreto-Kapelle and Totenbruderschaft)

Regens chori
? -1784 Anton Carl

VII. St. Michael's (Michaelerkirche; Pfarrkirche zu St.
      Michael; Klosterkirche St. Michael des Barnabiten-
      konventes)

Regens chori
? -1775   Ferdinand Zangl
before 1783-1794 Johann Michael Spangler

VIII. Franziskaner-Kirche (Pfarrkirche bey den Franzis-
       kanern; Klosterkirche St. Hieronymus; PP. Francis-
       cani Minores Observantes)

IX. St. Leopold's (Pfarrkirche in der Leopoldstadt)

Regens chori
1737?-1745   Ferdinand Bindl
? -1780   Franz Ullmann (Uhlmann)
before 1783-1817? Franz (Wenzel?) Groschopf

X. Karmeliter-Kirche (Pfarrkirche St. Joseph; Kirche der
    Carmeliter Barfüssern [die discalceaten Carmeliter]
    in der Leopoldstadt; Kirche der hl. Theresiae;
    Carmelite Church)

Regens chori
? - ?   Leopold Sonnleithner (uncle of Christoph)
1772-1792   Johann Georg Albrechtsberger
1792-1794   Joseph Eybler

XIV. Waisenhaus-Kirche (Waiserhaus unserer lieben Frau
am Rennwege; Pfarrkirche Maria Geburt)

XV. St. Charles Borromeo (Karlskirche; St. Caroli Borro-
maei; Ordenskirche St. Karl der Kreuzherren)

Regens chori
? -1781 Leopold Himmelbauer
1781-1806? Simon Thadäus Kölbel

Organist
ca. 1738-1750 Mathias Georg Monn

XVI. Paulaner-Kirche (Klosterkirche zu den heiligen
Schutzengeln, zu den heiligen Engeln [SS. Angelorum];
Pfarrkirche bei den Paulanern)

Regens chori
? - 1783 Georg Strasser

XX. Karmeliter-Kirche auf der Laimgrube (Klosterkirche
St. Joseph auf der Laimgrube)

Regenschori
in 1783: Johann Georg Strasser

XXI. Maria Hilf (Wallfahrts- und Klosterkirche Maria Hilf
der Barnabiten [auf der Laimgrube])

Regenschori
in 1783: Johann Georg Strasser

Organist
in 1783: Ignaz Strasser

XXIV. Maria Treu (Piaristen-Kirche in der Josephstadt;
Pfarrkirche bei den Piaristen; Wallfahrtskirche
Maria Treu)

Regens chori
1770-1771 Silverius Müller
See also the list in Otto Biba, "Piaristenorden," 150-
57.

XXV. Trinitarier-Kirche (Weis-Spanier Kirche; Klosterkirche zur heiligen Dreifaltigkeit der Trinitarier;
Pfarr bey den Trinitariern)

XXVII. Serviten-Kirche (Pfarr bei den Serviten in der
Rossau; Kirche Mariae Verkündigung)

XXVIII. Wällsche National Kapelle (Kapelle St. Katharina; Maria Schnee; sanctuary of the Italian congregation from 1773 until 1784, when destroyed)

Kapellmeister
1776-1784   Karl Friberth

XXIX.   Stiftskirche zum heiligen Kreuz (Kirche der Kriegschule auf dem Laimgrube)

Regens chori
in 1783:   Georg Strasser

XXXI.   Trattnerische Kapelle (St. Georgs-Kapelle im Trattner hof)

Kapellmeister
in 1783:   Karl Friberth

XXXII. St. Ivo (Kirche in der Juristen-Schule; Kirche der juridischen Fakultäts; run by the Piarists)

Kapellmeister
in 1783:   Karl Friberth

XXXIII. Kapelle Sts. Philipp und Jakob (Kirche im Köllner Hofe; Kirche der Hieronymitanern)

Kapellmeister
in 1783:   Karl Friberth

XXXIV. St. Johannis Nepomucensis Spital (Kapelle St. Johann von Nepomuck [auf der Landstrasse])

Kapellmeister
in 1783:   Karl Friberth

XXXV.   Universitäts-Kirche (Untere Jesuiten-Kirche; Kirche der Societät Jesu [today's Jesuiten-Kirche]; Akademische Kirche; Kirche Sts. Ignaz und Franz Xaver)

Choralist
in 1783:   Karl Friberth

XXXVI. Minoriten-Kirche (Klosterkirche zum heiligen Kreuz [S. Cruci, St. Croix]; Wällsche [Italian] National Church [after 1784])

Regens chori
  ? -1766 P. Alexander Giessel, OFMConv. (organist?)
in 1783:   P. Mauriz Hofman (d. 1823)

XXXVII. Dorothea-Kirche (Klosterkirche St. Dorothea der
Augustiner-Chorherren)

Regens chori
? -1742 Mathias Timmer (d. 1742)
? -1756 Ferdinand Schmidt (d. 1756)
1776- ? Chorherr Joseph Leopold Hodinar

XXXVIII. Kirche zum heiligen Geist im Bürgerspital (Kirche
im Bürgerspital; Pfarrkirche St. Clara; Königin-
kloster; Bürgerspital-Kirche; located next to the
Kärntnertor-Theater)

Regens chori
? - 1754 Ambros Carl (d. 1754)
in 1783: Anton Carl (d. 1784)

XL. St. Anne's (Kirche St. Anna; Klosterkirche der
Jesuiten [novitiates' church])

Regens chori
in 1783: Georg Strasser

XLIV. Kirche Maria de Mercede (Kirche zu unser lieben
Frauen de Mercede; Spannische Spital-Kirche;
Spitals-Kirche)

XLV. St. Ruprecht's (Ruperti Kapellen)

LII. Barmherzige Brüder in der Leopoldstadt (Klosterkirche St. Johannes der Täufer; Fratres misericor-
diae; Konvent der barmherzigen Brüder)

Regens chori
1754- ? Abund Mikysch (d. 1782, Graz)

Joseph Haydn worked here in his youth.

--. Maria Stiegen-Kirche (Passauische Pfarrkirche zu
unser lieben Frauen-Stiegen)

Regens chori
? - 1753 Franz Erhard

--. Schwarzspanier-Kirche (Kirche St. Mariae von Berg
Serrato; Kirche zu unser lieben Frau de Monte Serrato)

--.   Hof-Musikkapelle (Hofburg-Kapelle)

Kapellmeister (Hofkapellmeister)
1715-1741 Johann Joseph Fux
1741-1751 Luca Antonio Predieri (officially named 1746)
1751-1772 Georg von Reutter, Jr. (officially named in
           1769)
1772-1774 Florian Leopold Gassmann
1774-1788 Giuseppe Bonno
1788-1824 Antonio Salieri

Vice-Kapellmeister
1716-1736 Antonio Caldara
1739-1741 Luca Antonio Predieri (officially until 1747)
1741-1751 Georg von Reutter, Jr. (officially named in
           1746)
1751-   no one listed officially (Tobias Gsur may
           have carried out these duties unofficially;
           Gsur eventually substituted for the ailing
           Hofkapellmeister Gassmann)

Appendix C

Thematic Catalogue of the Seventy-Two Selected Masses (M. 1-72)

Introduction to the Catalogue

This thematic catalogue of the seventy-two selected Masses discussed in the foregoing pages is a "working" catalogue. It remains in progress, and, as will be seen, the kinds and amounts of information for each manuscript vary according to the sources available. The Masses, with their numbers M. 1-72, have been arranged in alphabetical order according to composer. For each Mass one will find the following data:

Title(s)

A standard title has usually been derived from the title found in the chief source consulted, i.e., the source marked by an asterisk (*) before its library siglum. (Microfilm copies of all Masses so marked are in the author's possession.) Alternative titles appear in parentheses.

Date

Usually the earliest known date is supplied.

Scoring

Instrumentation is generally based upon the conflation of the sources. Parentheses indicate parts which are undoubtedly ad libitum additions.

Thematic Incipit for Kyrie I

Because slow introductions are sometimes absent from certain sources, incipits for fast Kyries succeeding a slow
Kyrie are also supplied. For the sake of compactness,
clefs and key signatures appear only at the start of
the incipits, unless there is a change for the fast
Kyrie.

Autograph Score and Manuscript Copies

Locations of the manuscript sources are indicated mostly
by the library sigla of RISM (found at the front of each
volume of The New Grove Dictionary of Music and Musicians).
Other sigla are explained in the list that follows. Unless
otherwise indicated, most sources agree with the scoring
shown atop the page of the entry. However, the special
use of the following words should be noted:

> "including" - indicates instrumental or vocal parts
>> existing in addition to those listed at the
>> start of the entry.

> "lacking" - indicates parts which are listed in the
>> general scoring at the head of the entry but
>> which apparently were never part of the
>> source being cited.

> "missing" - indicates parts which, according to cover
>> titles, old catalogues, etc., were supposed to
>> be present in the source but which are now
>> lost.

In addition, unless noted otherwise, all sources agree
with the composer attribution given atop the entry, and
all copies are manuscript parts, not scores.

<u>Printed Edition</u> (when known)

<u>References</u>

Various old and modern catalogues which refer to the Mass
are cited here for support of authorship and dating.
Items which do not appear in the general bibliography at
the end of this volume will be found in the following
lists of thematic catalogues and literature.

<u>Remarks</u>

These are normally comments upon the size (including a
Mass's total length in measures) and other special attributes of the Mass. At the end, locations of musical
examples from the Mass are listed.

Sigla for the Thematic Catalogues Cited

A-GÖ	Göttweig, 1830. Brook no. 471. See Riedel ed.
A-H	Herzogenburg, 1751. Brook no. 582-83.
A-KN	Klosterneuburg, 1790. Brook no. 668.
A-LA	Lambach, 1768. Brook no. 708.
A-M	Melk, 1821. "Catalog aller auf dem Stifts-Chore von Melk vorhandenen Musikalien" (cf. Freeman, p. xvi).
A-SEI	Seitenstetten, 1807. Brook no. 1203.
A-Ws	Schotten (Vienna), 1857. Brook no. 1417.
A-WIL	Wilhering, 1860. Index quorumcumque musicorum operum quae . . . collecta et conscripta sunt ab Adolpho Festl Organista Hilariae, monast: s. Ord. Cist. 1860."
A-Wn	Austrian National Library, Vienna, Sm. 2454 (ca. 1785). Brook no. 1409. (Hof-Kapelle) Sm. 2457. Brook no. 1411. Sm. 2464 (1825). Brook no. 1412.
CS-RAJ	Rajhrad, 1771. Brook no. 1019.

CS-VC   Valtice (Feldsberg), Inventarium der Barmherzigen
         Brüder
CS-P   Prague, Barmherzige Brüder, 1829.
D-FS   Freising, 1796. Brook no. 399.
D-HR   Harburg, 1976 (see Haberkamp ed.).
D-SI   Sigmaringen, 1768. "Catalogus über zer-
         schiedene musicalische Wercke . . . con-
         signirt von mir Georgio Wernhamer." Brook
         no. 1217.

RISM Library Sigla

(See the front of any volume of The New Grove Dictionary)

A-KS   Krems, Stadtpfarre St. Veit
A-MT   Maria Taferl, Pfarre der Wallfahrtskirche
A-RB   Reichersberg, Augustiner-Chorherrenstift
CS-LIT   Litoměřice, Státní Archiv (Pulkert catalogued
         Mss. from the Prague Loreta collection here;
         these Mss. are now at CS-ZI)
CS-ZI   Žitenice, Státní Archív v Litoměřicích--pobočka
         Poděbrady
D-B   Berlin (West), Staatsbibliothek Preussischer
         Kulturbesitz
D-Bds   Berlin (East), Deutsche Staatsbibliothek
D-FW   Frauenwörth, Benediktinerinnenabtei Frauen-
         wörth im Chiemsee

Special Literature

Bárdos, Kornél. Pécs zenéje a 18. században. Budapest:
    Akademiai Kiado, 1976.

Brook, Barry S. Thematic Catalogues in Music: An Anno-
    tated Bibliography. Hillsdale, NY: Pendragon, 1972.

Freeman, Robert N. Franz Schneider (1737-1812): A The-
    matic Catalogue of His Works. New York, NY: Pen-
    dragon, 1979.

Prohászka, Hermine. "Leopold Hofmann und seine Messen,"
    Studien zur Musikwissenschaft XXVI (1964) 106-39.

Reichert, Georg. "Zur Geschichte der Wiener Messenkompo-
    sition in der ersten hälfte des 18. Jahrhunderts."
    Unpublished Ph.D. dissertation, Vienna, 1935.

Riedel, Friedrich Wilhelm, ed. Der Göttweiger thematische
    Katalog von 1830 [by Wondratsch], 2 vol. Munich
    and Salzburg: Emil Katzbichler, 1979.

Schnürl, Karl. Das alte Musikarchiv der Pfarrkirche
     St. Stephan in Tulln (A-TU). Tabulae Musicae
     Austriacae, vol. 1. Vienna: Österreichische
     Akademie der Wissenschaften, 1964.

Weissenbäck, Andreas. "Thematisches Verzeichnis
     der Kirchenkompositionen von Johann Georg
     Albrechtsberger," Jahrbuch des Stiftes Kloster-
     neuburg VI (1914) 1-160.

Johann Georg ALBRECHTSBERGER   M. 1

Missa in C
(Missa Conceptionis B.M.V.)

1755, rev. [?] 1779

SATB 2 Clni Timp 2 V Org

AUTOGRAPH SCORE:
  *H-Bn: Ms. mus. 2.450, <u>Missa in C</u>, "Composui Jourini [?]
    Anno 1755/Ren: 1779. <u>Vienna</u>," 30 p.

COPIES:
  A-GÖ: "comparavit . . . 1760."
  A-M: I.346.

REFERENCE:
  A-GÖ cat.
  Weissenbäck no. 3.

REMARKS:
  Missa brevis, 277 m. in total.

  Copy (now destroyed) in the archive of St. Stephen's
    Cathedral, Vienna, was entitled "Missa Conceptionis
    B.M.V."(Weissenbäck, p. 3).

Johann Georg ALBRECHTSBERGER

Missa S. Mathiae

1756

SATB   2 V   Org

AUTOGRAPH SCORE:
  *H-Bn: Ms. mus. 2.600, <u>Missa in E-dur S: Mathiae</u>,
      "Auth: G. A. 756," 41 p.

COPIES:
  A-KN   [?]
  A-KR
  A-SEI

REFERENCES:
  A-KN cat.
  Weissenbäck no. 5.

REMARKS:
  525 m. in total.
  Weissenbäck, p. 5, gives a different "Dona nobis pacem"
    (C meter) than the autograph (reprise of Kyrie music;
    3/4 meter). Cf. Andreas Weissenbäck, "Johann Georg
    Albrechtsberger," <u>Studien zur Musikwissenschaft</u>
    XIV (1927) 152.
  See Ex. 7-7, 8-19, 9-16E, and Fig. 8-9.

Johann Georg ALBRECHTSBERGER

Missa Annuntiationis B.M.V.

1763

SATB   2 Clni   Timp   2 V   Org

AUTOGRAPH SCORE:
  *H-Bn: Ms. mus. 2.587, <u>Missa Annuntionis [sic] B:M:V:</u>,
    "Finem composui 763. 22, Xbris [Decembris?]," 70 p.

COPIES:
  A-KN
  A-M
  A-SEI
  A-TU: 11 parts, performed 12 times 1800-1819.
  H-VEs: M.2.cl.40, 11 parts, including Vlone.

REFERENCES:
  A-KN cat. [?]
  Schnürl no. 2.
  Hob. C8 [?] and C44 lists work as by "Haydn" at
    CS-Bm (Minoriten) and A-KS respectively.
  Weissenbäck no. 32.

REMARKS:
  526 m. in total.
  See Ex. 7-4, 8-12C, 8-13, 8-17, and
    9-15A.

Johann Georg ALBRECHTSBERGER   M. 4

Missa Dei Patris

1781

SATB   2 Fl   2 Ob   2 Clni   Timp   2 V   Va   Org

AUTOGRAPH SCORE:
  *H-Bn: Ms. mus. 2.454, <u>Missa Dei Patris</u>, "781," 136 p.

COPIES:
  A-KN
  A-Wn: [?; not located in 1979]

REFERENCES:
  A-KN cat. [?].
  Weissenbäck no. 52.

REMARKS:
  Missa longa, 1,002 m.
  Although the Mass begins in D minor, Kyrie II, Gloria,
    Credo, Sanctus, and Agnus Dei are in D major.
  2 Fl appear only in "Christe," "Et incarnatus," and
    "Benedictus."
  See Ex. 9-16A.

Johann Georg ALBRECHTSBERGER   M. 5

Missa Sancti Leopoldi

(before 1801)

SATB   2 Ob   2 Clni   Timp   2 V   Org

AUTOGRAPH SCORE:
  *H-Bn: Ms. mus. 2.484, Missa Scti. Leopoldi, "Auth:
  G: Albrechtsberg:" n. d., 47 p.

COPIES:
  A-KN
  A-TU: 9 (11?) parts, performed 11 times 1801-1818.

REFERENCES:
  A-KN cat. [?].
  Schnürl no. 1.
  Weissenbäck no. 157.

REMARKS:
  Weissenbäck, p. 104, indicates the existence of a
    Vlone part.
  526 m. in total.

Ferdinand ARBESSER   M. 6

Missa Nubes pluant justum

(before 1753)

SATB   2 V   Org

COPIES:
 *A-GÖ: "comparavit 1753."
  A-LA: M380 (olim 277), attributed to "Reutter" (see
     Hofer no. 16).

REFERENCES:
  A-LA cat., p. 61 as "Arbesser," p. 62 as "Reutter."
  A-RAJ cat., p. 20 as "Reutter."
  Reichert, Arbesser no. 4.
  Lang, under "Reutter."
  A-GÖ cat.
REMARKS:
  Missa brevis, 199 m. in total.

  A similar conflicting attribution exists for Haydn's
  Missa "Rorate coeli desuper" (Hob. XXII: 3).

Ferdinand ARBESSER   M. 7

Missa Sanctae Susannae

(before 1752)

SATB 2 V Org

COPY:
 *A-GÖ: lacks V II part; "comparavit 1752"; performed
    some 29 times between 1761 and 1785.

REFERENCE:
 A-GÖ cat.
 Reichert, Arbesser no. 3.

REMARKS:
 428 m. in total.
 See Ex. 6-9 and 8-19.

Giuseppe BONNO

M. 8

Missa [in C]

(before 1778)

SATB   2 Ob   (2) Bsn   2 Clni   2 Trombe   Timp
       2 V   (2) Va   Vlone   Org

COPIES:
 *A-Wn: Mus. Hs. 15858, score with autograph alterations.
 " "   H.K. 106, 33 parts dated 1778, "No: 10."

REFERENCES:
 A-Wn cat. S.m. 2454, p. 96, "No: 10."
 Schienerl no. 10.

REMARKS:
 529 m. in total.
 Oboe and bassoon obbligatos.
 See Ex. 6-7, 7-11, and 9-16A.

Giuseppe BONNO   M. 9

Missa [in C]

(before 1774)

SATB   2 Ob   2 Bsn   2 Clni   2 Trombe   Timp
       2 V   2 Va   2 Vc   Vlone   Org

COPIES:
  *A-Wn: Mus. Hs. 15859, score with autograph [?] alterations.
  " "   H.K. 45, parts dated 1774, performance dates 1776-98,
  "No: IV."

REFERENCES:
  A-Wn cat. S.m. 2454, p. 94, "No: 4."
  Schienerl no. 4.

REMARKS:
  537 m. in total.
  Oboe, bassoon, viola, and cello obbligatos.
  See Ex. 8-19, 9-6, and Fig. 7-8.

Giuseppe BONNO   M. 10

Missa con 2 oboe obligati

(before 1781)

SATB   2 Ob   2 Clni   2 Trombe   Timp
2 V   Vlone   Org

COPIES:
  *A-Wn: Mus. Hs. 15872, score with autograph alterations.
  " "   H.K. 94, 31 parts dated 1781, "No: XI."

REFERENCES:
  A-Wn cat. S.m. 2454, p. 96, "No: 11."
  Schienerl no. 11.

REMARKS:
  433 m. in total.

Johann Nepomuk BOOG   M. 11

Missa in C

(before 1752)

SATB   2 Clni   Timp   2 Tbn   2 V   Vlone   Org

COPIES:
  A-Ee: 87, Kasten I, Fach 2, "Missa S. Floriani" by
     "Boock," performed 1754-1762.
  A-Ek: A22, "Missa Solennis QUasi Cedrus exaltata Sum
     in libano" by "Nepomuceno Boog," lacks 2 Tbn, 11 parts.
  A-KR: C19,733, "Missa solemnis in C."
  *A-Wn: Fond Nr. 24 (St. Peter's Collection), A 41,
     "2. Missa in C . . . Del Auth: Boog Pro Choro
     St. Petri," 21 parts, including concertato and ripieno
     SATB, extra set of V. I and V. II, Violoncello, and
     MDC.

REFERENCES:
  A-GÖ cat. "descripta . . . 1752," without Vlone.
  A-H cat. "Missa Sancti Floriani," no. 109.
  CS-VC cat., no. 7, p. 1.

REMARKS:
  413 m. in total.
  See Ex. 7-6, 8-12C, 8-19, and 9-16F.

Johann Nepomuk BOOG (d. 1764)   M. 12

Missa in C

(before 1764)

SATB   2 Clni   Timp   2 Tbn   2 V   Vlone   Org

COPIES:
  A-Ek: A21, "Missa . . . Del Sigre. Giovanne Nepomu-
    ceno Boog," 13 parts.
  A-KR: C10,673.
  A-KR: C14,708, "Missa ex C . . . Del Sigre. Monn,"
    according to score made from this source (see A-Wn),
    12 parts, lacks Timp.
  *A-Wn: Fond Nr. 24 (St. Peter's Collection), A 42,
    "1. Missa in C . . . Del Sigre. Boog. Pro Choro
    St. Petri," 23 parts, including concertato and ripieno
    SATB, extra set of V. I and V. II, Vc, and MDC.
  *A-Wn: Mus. Hs. 5532, "Missa ex C" by Monn, score
    prepared in 1935 by Frl. Haager from Georg Reichert's
    score extracted from A-KR parts, lacks Timp.
  CS-Bm: A.18.466, "Missa S. Josephi," 9 parts,
    lacks Timp, 2 Tbn, and Vlone.

REFERENCES:
  A-SEI cat.
  A-KN cat. p. 43, without specific attribution but on
    page headed by "Boog/Paumonn."
  Reichert, "Monn" no. 1.

REMARKS:
  480 m. in total.
  See Ex. 8-18.

Johann Nepomuk BOOG   M. 13

Missa in C

(before 1763)

SATB   2 Clni   Timp   2 V   Vlone   Org

COPIES:
  A-KR: C10,675, "Missa S. Michaelis."
  A-H: 59, "Missa in C . . . Del Sign: Boog. Pro Choro
     Ducumbg. 1767," 11 parts.
 *A-Wn: Mus. Hs. 23.029, "Missa in C . . . Del Sigre:
     Joseph Hayden" [!], 10 parts, Vlone lacking.
  CS-BRnm: Trenčin HS 3P 55, dated 1765.
  CS-Bm: Nikolsburg Sammlung, "Missa in C . . . Jos:
     Haydn."
  CS-LIT: Loretánský hudební archív, 543, lacks Timp and
     Vlone.

REFERENCES:
  A-GÖ cat. "Missa Auxilium Christiano . . . comparavit 1763."
  A-H cat. "Missa ex C," no. 162.
  A-KN cat., p. 22, no. 131.
  A-SEI cat.
  Hoboken XXII: C24.

REMARKS:
  Missa longa, 638 m.
  See Ex. 6-14, 7-27, 8-19, and 9-3.

Anton CARL

Missa solennis in C

(before 1751?)

SATB   2 Clni   Timp   2 Tbn   2 V   Org

COPIES:
- A-H: I,116, "Missa Ascensionis Domini," with Va obbligato, 2 Trombe, Vlone, lacking 2 Tbn.
- A-KN: As no. 25 by Reutter, with Va and Vlone, 17 parts.
- A-M: I,31.
- CS-Bm: A12.164, "Missa in C," earliest date 1773, from Rajhrad collection.
- *D-SWl: Ms. 5276/1, "Missa solennis . . . Del Sig: Stephan [!]," 9 parts, lacking 2 Tbn, Timp.

REFERENCES:
- A-H: Listed in 1751 catalogue, with Va, Vlone.
- A-GÖ: "pro choro Gottw. 1754," Riedel no. 91, with Vc.
- A-LA: Listed in 1768 catalogue, with Vlone.
- CS-Raj: 1771 cat., p. 30, "Missa Nr. 190, procuravit RP Maurus Haberhauer."
- Kade, no. 1 under "Giuseppe Antonio Stephan," II, 256.
- Hofer, Reutter no. 48, p. 25-26.
- Reichert, Anton Carl no. 4.

REMARKS:
Missa longa, 673 m. in total.
Viola solo (in place of V. I) during the "Benedictus."
See Ex. 6-19, 8-16, and 9-16B.

Karl Ditters von DITTERSDORF   M. 15

Missa solemnis in C

(before 1773)

SATB   2 Ob   2 Clni   Timp   2 V   Vlone   Org

COPIES:
A-GÖ: 17 parts, including 2 horns, earliest per-
   formance 22 Nov. 1774.
A-LA: M297, 11 parts, without 2 Ob.
A-TU: 13 parts.
*A-Wn: H.K. 500, "No. 4 Missa," 16 parts, including
   Canto Ripieno and extra V. I and II.
CH-E: Ms. 3666, "Missa pro Feriis Rogationum," 13 parts,
   including 2 Hn, Va, without 2 Clni, Timp.
CS-Bm: A.3203 (Vischkov), without Timp, Vlone; per-
   formed 1784-85.
CS-Bm: A.12.205 (Rajhrad), without Vlone, dated 1773.
"   "   A.21.641 (Brno, Petrov), lacking S, V I, Org.
CS-Pnm: XXXVIII.A.34 (Broumov), without Timp, Vlone;
   Sherman diss., p. 222, indicates 2 sets of parts here.
D-Dlb: Includes Va.
D-HR: III 1/2 2O 121, includes V solo part, without
   Vlone, dated April 1781.
D-Mbs: Kyrie & Gloria only, dated Feb. 1793, without
   2 Ob, according to Istel, p. 182.
A-MB: V.6, attributed to Michael Haydn, according
   to Sherman diss., p. 222.
D-Tl: A105, B215, G64, and A30.
I-Fc: As "Giuseppe Haydn," dated 1787, cf. Hob. XXII: C35.
REFERENCES:
D-SI cat., includes Fl solo, omits Timp, Vlone.
CS-Raj cat., no. 135, p. 23.
A-GÖ cat., "comp[aravit] . . . 1774," Riedel no. 102.
A-KN cat., no. 96, p. 16.

M. 15 (cont'd.)

Mannheim <u>Inventarium</u> of 1792, as described by Schmitt
   diss., <u>p. 94-95.</u>
D-FS cat., no. 67.
Mannheim <u>Catalogus</u> of 1803, as described by Schmitt
   diss., <u>p. 94-95.</u>
A-Ws cat., fol. 9.
Krebs, <u>Dittersdorfiana</u>, no. 326, p. 142.
Hoboken, <u>XXII: C35</u>
Sherman diss., doubtful M. Haydn no. 15, p. 222.
Schnürl no. 72.
REMARKS:
Missa longa, 1118 m. in total.
Virtuosic violin solo in Gloria; coloratura soprano
   and alto solos.
See Ex. 6-11, 8-4, 9-16F, 10-3.

Karl Ditters von DITTERSDORF   M. 16

[Missa in C]

(before 1799)

SATB   2 Ob   Bsn   2 Clni   [Timp?]
       2 V   2 Va   [Vlone   Org]

AUTOGRAPH SCORE:
*A-Wn: Mus. Hs. 19197, lacks title page and title,
   "Ditters" appears atop first page; final sheet
   is missing (score thus lacks the end of Osanna II,
   the start of the Agnus Dei, and the end of the
   "Dona nobis pacem"; vertical format, 22 x 36.5 cm.,
   24-28 staves per page.

REFERENCE:
   Krebs, Dittersdorfiana, no. 327, p. 142. Krebs
   entitles the work "Missa 4 vocum cum instru-
   mentis" and cites only the above score at A-Wn.

REMARKS:
   Missa longa, 1112+ m. in total.
   According to Dr. Günter Brosche at A-Wn, the above
   score has been determined to be an autograph. No
   additional confirmation of this fact has been
   found.
   Only "Fondamento" is indicated for the bass, except
   in the "Benedictus" where the Bsn plays obbligato.
   See Ex. 7-11, 8-12A, 8-19, 9-4D, 9-12,
      and 10-9.

Karl Ditters von DITTERSDORF   M. 17

(Missa in D)

(before 1777)

SATB 2 Ob 2 Clni Timp 2 V Vlone Org

COPIES:
  A-GÖ: 14 parts, earliest performance date 6 Sept. 1777,
    lacking Vlone as well as the 2 Hn indicated in the
    A-GÖ cat.
  *A-Wn: F.5 (Mödling) 859, "Missa ex D . . . Del Sigre.
    Car. Ditters. Ex rebus Joann. Mich. Gabmayr,"
    13 parts.
  A-Wn: Mus. Hs. 22246, "Missa ex D" from the Archiv
    Schminder in St. Pölten, Clni parts differ from those
    in the Mödling source above, 13 parts.
  CS-Bm: A.7581, "Missa in D," lacks Timp; omits Adagio
    and begins with the Allegro.
  CS-Pnm: XXXVIII.A.31 (Broumov), "Missa solemnis ex D,"
    lacks Vlone; omits Adagio and begins with the Allegro.
  D-B: Mus. ms. 5000, 11 parts.
  D-Bds: Mus. ms. 30170, Kyrie-Gloria only.
  D-BGD: 116, begins with the Allegro, 13 parts.

REFERENCES:
  A-KN cat., no. 95, p. 16.
  A-GÖ cat., Riedel no. 103, lists "2 Corni" and lacks
    Vlone. Riedel indicates that the 2 Hn [now missing]
    were substitute parts for the 2 Clni.
  Krebs, Dittersdorfiana, no. 328, p. 142. Krebs noted that
    the Dombibliothek in Breslau possessed parts.

REMARKS:
  Missa longa, 1242 m. in total. Organ solo in "Benedictus."
  See Ex. 8-19, 10-4E, and 10-10.

Karl FRIBERTH   M. 18

Missa [in D]

1774

SATB   2 Trombe   2 Tbn   Timp   2 V   Vlone   Org

AUTOGRAPH SCORE:
  *S-Smf: "Missa di Carlo Friberth 1774," 109 p. of music,
    55 fol., vertical format, 22 x 36 cm.

REFERENCES:
  Georg Kinsky, Musikhistorisches Museum von Wilhelm Heyer
    in Köln: Katalog, 4 vols. (Leipzig: Breitkopf and
    Haertel, 1910-16) IV, 109, autograph no. 165.
  Georg Kinsky, [Verzeichnis der] Versteigerung von Musiker-
    Autographen aus dem Nachlass des Herrn Kommerzienrates
    Wilhelm Heyer, 4 parts (Karl Ernst Henrici and Leo
    Liepmannssohn-Antiquariat, 1926-28) pt. 4, p. 19,
    item no. 117.

REMARKS:
  Missa longa, ca. 818 m. in total.
  The Stockholm autograph has numerous corrections and
    crossings out by the composer.
  See Ex. 9-16F.

Florian Leopold GASSMANN   M. 19

Missa in C
(Missa Sanctae Caeciliae)

(before 1771)

SATB 2 Ob 2 Bsn 2 Hn? 4 Clni Timp
      2 V 2 Va Vc Vlone Org

COPIES:
  A-GÖ: Only 1 Bsn extant; lacks 2 Tbn, Vc, and
    Vlone listed in GÖ cat.; "comp[aravit] . . . 1771";
    also lacks 2 Hn and has only 2 Clni.
  A-KN: Score and parts.
  A-LA: M460, 16 parts, has only 2 Clni, lacks 2 Hn, Timp,
    and Vlone.
  A-TU: 15 parts, has only 1 Bsn and 2 Tpt, lacks 2 Hn
    and 2 V; performed six times 1791-1811.
 *A-Wn: H.K. 30, "Missa in C," 22 parts, includes two
    different sets of 2 Hn parts (one for the entire Mass
    and one for only Sanctus-Osanna), lacks Vlone part
    (Vc part appears to have originally read "Violone");
    Clni I and II have been altered in "Gloria" to in-
    clude pitches of the Clni III and IV added for that
    movement; 2 Bsn are in a single part.
  A-W, Staatsakademie, Musikarchiv, Abteilung für Kirchen-
    und Schulmusik, according to Kosch diss. (1924).
 *D-B: Mus. ms. 7120, "Missa St. Caeciliae [later entry],
    Missa C dur von F. L. Gassmann, kaiserl. Kapellmeister
    zu Wien, +1774, in Partitur von Leopold Kozeluchs
    Hand," 72 pages of score, has only 2 Clni, different
    2 Hn parts; Org and Vlone designated as "Fondamento";
    handwriting is similar to that of Dittersdorf "auto-
    graph" for M. 16 above; "Ex Bibliotheca Poelchaviana."
  D-B: Mus. ms. $\frac{7120}{1}$, 8 vocal parts (solo & ripieno),
  with performance dates in 1789 and 1791.

M. 19 (cont'd.)

   D-B: Mus. ms. 7126, Agnus Dei, including a "Dona nobis
                  ̄5̄
      pacem" (in A) by F. X. Richter, score, 9 fol.

   USSR-KAu: Re b 11, fol. I-II (former Königsberg Uni-
      versitätsbibliothek, according to Kosch diss.) score/parts.

REFERENCES:
   A-GÖ cat., Riedel no. 167, includes 2 Tbn, has only 2 Clni,
      and lacks 2 Hn.
   A-LA cat., p. 18, lacks 2 Hn, Timp, and Vc; has only
      2 Clni.
   A-KN cat., p. 18.
   A-Wn cat., S.m. 2464, Messe "No. 4," 22 parts.
   Kosch diss., no. 4, p. 40, "Missa solemnis in C."
   Schnürl no. 118.
   Landon, Haydn: Chronicle and Works, II, 229, indicates
      that (according to Kosch?) the Mass was "composed about
      1765" and may have inspired Haydn's own "St. Cecilia
      Mass," Hob. XXII: 5.

REMARKS:
   Missa longa, 1,441 m. in total (A-Wn "Vienna" version);
      1,429 m. in the D-B "Berlin" version which has a dif-
      ferent Credo, Sanctus, and Benedictus. This latter
      "Berlin" version is also found at A-GÖ and A-LA;
      because of its longer Credo, which reuses earlier
      motives of the Mass, and its use of the solo quartet,
      this version could be Gassmann's original.

   Kosch diss., p. 42, indicates this Mass was probably
      performed 9 Dec. 1779 at the concert spirituel in
      the Thomashaus, Leipzig, under J. A. Hiller.

GRASSL

(Missa Pastoralis in C)

(before 1774)

SATB 2 Clni 2 Tbn Timp 2 V Vlone Org

COPY:
  *A-Wn: Mus. Hs. 22251, "Missa Pastoralis Ex C . . .
  Del Sigre. Adamo Grasl, Ex Partibus Josephi Daninger."
  On back of cover: "in festo Epiphan: Dni 1776"; at
  end of canto: "1774." 14 parts, including one part
  that contains both S and V II; the Vlone also appears
  to be a later addition.

REFERENCE:
  CS-VC cat.   "Nro: 4," "Missa Pastorales . . . Grasl."

REMARKS:
  Missa longa, 766 m. in total.

Tobias GSUR   M. 21

Missa in C

(before 1770)

SATB   2 Clni   Timp   2 V   Org

COPY:
  *A-GÖ: "Missa," 10 parts, produced 27 times from
    23 July 1770 to 1811.

REFERENCE:
  A-GÖ cat., Riedel no. 194, "comp[aravit] . . . 1770."

REMARKS:
  Missa brevis, 391 m. in total.
  See Ex. 9-4C.

Tobias GSUR

Missa in D

(before 1769)

SATB 2 V Org

COPIES:
*A-GÖ: "Missa ex D," 7 parts, produced 24 times from
24 February 1769 until 1811.
CS-Bm: A.12,363, "Missa in D," adds 2 Clni, 2 Tbn,
Timp and Vc, 13 parts, from the Rajhrad collection,
dated 1849.

REFERENCES:
A-GÖ cat., Riedel no. 193, "comp[aravit] . . . 1769."
CS-RAJ cat., "Nro. 185 Missa in D . . . Tobia Xur . . .
procuravit P. M. Haberhauer," adds 2 Clni, Timp.

REMARKS:
Missa brevis, 407 m. in total.
See Ex. 10-1A.

Johann Adolf HASSE   M. 23

Missa in G

1753

SATB 2 Ob 2 Clni 2 Tbn Timp
2 V Va Vlone Org

AUTOGRAPH SCORE:
  I-Mc: dated 1753, according to <u>New Grove</u>, VIII, 290.

COPIES:
  A-Gd: Ms. 29, "Missa in G," score?, 79 fol., from
    the Ebiswald Pfarre, lacks 2 Tbn.
  ?A-LA: not listed in Lang's diss., although <u>New Grove</u>
    VIII, 290, cites this source.
  A-KR: A38,97, includes 2 Fl, 2 Hn.
  A-Wn: Mus. Hs. 17320, 27 parts, including 2 Fl, 2 Hn,
    2 Bsn; Ob I and Clno I missing; lacks 2 Tbn.
  *D-B: Mus. ms. 9484, "Missa in G," score, oblong for-
    mat, "Ex Bibliotheca Poelchaviana."
  D-Dlb: Ms. 2477/D/43, score, includes 2 Fl and 2 Hn;
    has a different Sanctus and Agnus; lacks 2 Tbn.
  A-Gö: lacks 2 Tbn, includes 2 Fl and 2 Hn.

REFERENCES:
  A-Gö cat., Riedel no. 218, "comp[aravit] . . . 1776,"
    lcaks 2 Tbn, includes 2 Fl and 2 Hn.
  A-LA cat., p. 54.
  A-Wn cat., Sm. 2464, 2465, 2466, Mass "No: 2."
  Müller, <u>Hasse als Kirchenkomponist</u>, no. 9, p. 156.
  Wilson, "<u>Selected Masses of Hasse</u>," p. 44-45.

M. 23 (cont'd.)

EDITIONS:
"Crucifixus" arranged for soprano and alto with keyboard
accompaniment in: Johann Adolf Hasse, Ausgewählte
geistliche Gesänge für Alt und Sopran mit Orgel-
oder Klavierbegleitung, ed. Otto Schmid, Musik am
sächsischen Hofe, vol. 8 (Leipzig and Dresden: Breitkopf & Haertel, 1905) p. 20-22.
"Benedictus" arranged for tenor and keyboard accompaniment
appears in vol. 7 of Musik am sächsischen Hof, ed. Otto
Schmid (according to Müller, p. 156).

REMARKS:
Missa longa, 921 m. in total.
Müller, Hasse als Kirchenkomponist, gives a few
excerpts, p. 58, 71-74.
There are challenging coloratura lines for the vocal
soloists.
See Ex. 6-19 and 7-23.

Johann Adolf HASSE   M. 24

Missa in d

1751

SSATB   2 Fl   2 Ob   2 Hn   2 Clni   Timp
2 V   Va   Vlone   Org

AUTOGRAPH SCORE:
  I-Mc: autograph of a later version, according to
  New Grove, VIII, 290.

COPIES:
  A-GÖ: includes Vc; 2 V parts are missing.
  A-Wn: Mus. Hs. 17321, "No. 1 Missa in D: mj:,"
  31 parts, including Vc and misc. duplicate parts.
  A-Wn: H.K. 291, "Missa in D [minore]," 40 parts,
  including Bsn and Vc; performing dates begin 1821.
  CH-E: Ms. 3926, "No: 4, Missa Solemnis ex D . . .
  Del Sig: H'," 12 parts and score, copied by Sigis-
  mund Keller in 1872, lacking 2 Ob, 2 Clni, Timp,
  and Vlone.
  *D-B: Mus. ms. 9485, "Missa in D con Stromenti," score,
  44 fol., Vlone not specified.
  D-B: Mus. ms. 9485, score, "Missa Dedicationis Templi,"
                        ‾1‾
  "Fin in Carolath, die 17. Aprilis, 1789."
  D-Bds: 9485, parts.
          ‾1.3.‾
  D-Dlb: Ms. 2477/D/502, score.
  "   "   Ms. 2477/D/44, parts, including 2 Bsn, lack-
  ing 2 Clni and Timp.
  DK-Kk: Mu.6501.1433, Kyrie only, score, lacking 2 Fl,
  2 Hn, 2 Clni, and Timp.

M. 24 (cont'd.)

GB-L-m: Additional 32393, score (from Otto Jahn
library), late 18th C., fol. 15-67.
I-Nc: Ms. 36.2.16, "Missa detta riformata," score,
includes 2 Bsn, lacks 2 Fl and 2 Hn, dated 1875.
US-Bp: M.250.19, No. 3, "Missa dedicationis templi," score, lacks 2 Fl and Timp?

REFERENCES:
A-GÖ cat., Riedel no. 216, "comp[aravit] . . . 1771,"
including Vc.
A-Wn cat., Sm. 2464, Mass "No: 1," 41 parts.
A-KN cat.
Müller, Hasse als Kirchenkomponist, no. 5, p. 153.
Wilson, "Selected Masses of Hasse," p. 38-40.

EDITIONS:
*Complete score (based chiefly upon the score at D-Dlb)
is found in Wilson, "Selected Masses of Hasse," 145-
256.
"Domine Deus" arranged for keyboard [!] in: Johann
Adolf Hasse, Ausgewählte Werke von J. A. Hasse,
für Klavier bearbeitet, ed. Otto Schmid, Musik am
sächsischen Hofe, vol. 2 (Leipzig and Dresden:
Breitkopf & Haertel, 1900) p. 28-30.
"Agnus Dei" arranged for alto and keyboard in: Johann
Adolf Hasse, Ausgewählte geistliche Gesänge für Alt
und Sopran mit Orgel- oder Klavierbegleitung, ed. Otto
Schmid, Musik am sächsischen Hofe, vol. 8 (Leipzig and
Dresden: Breitkopf & Haertel, 1905) p. 14-16.

REMARKS:
Missa longa, 903 m.
Müller, p. 153, indicates that this Mass was first performed at the consecration of the Catholic Hofkirche
in Dresden in 1751. Müller also provides a few
excerpts from the Mass, p. 75-77.
New Grove, VIII, 290, indicates the first performance (?)
occurred 29 June 1751 in Dresden.
The second soprano part differs from the first soprano
only during the "Laudamus" of the Gloria.
See Ex. 8-11 and 10-1B.

Johann Adolf HASSE   M. 25

Missa in D

(before 1783)

2 Ob   2 Clni   3 Trombe   Timp
2 V   Va   Vlone   Org

COPIES:
  A-KR: A38,98, in the key of C, lacking 2 Ob and
    3 Trombe.
  A-LA: M18, "Missa," 15 parts, 2 Clni and Clno prin-
    cipale instead of 2 Clni and 3 Trombe.
  *A-Wn: Mus. Hs. 17319, "Missa in D," 31 parts,
    including several extra older and newer parts.
  CS-LIT: Sign. 549.

REFERENCES:
  A-LA cat., p. 16.
  A-Wn cat., Sm. 2464, 2465, 2466, in C [!] major.
  Joseph Mantuani, ed., Tabulae codicum manu scriptorum
    praeter Graecas et orientales in Bibliotheca Pala-
    tina Vindobonensi asservatorum, vol. 9: Codicorum
    Musicorum (Vienna: Gerold, 1897) Cod. 17319.
  Müller, Hasse als Kirchenkomponist, no. 2, p. 150.
  Wilson, "Selected Masses of Hasse," p. 36-37.

REMARKS:
  Missa longa, 594 m. in total.
  The Mass seems to require three trumpets (2 Clni and a
    Trombe principale); in the A-Wn source Clni I, II
    = Trombe I, II respectively.
  Müller, p. 55, believes A-KR has the "original"
    scoring, i.e. SATB 2 Clni Timp 2 V Va Vlone Org.
  See Ex. 6-1, 6-19, 7-11, and 7-18.

Leopold HOFMANN

Missa Sancti Erasmi in D

(before 1779)

SATB 2 Clni Timp 2 V Org

COPIES:

A-GÖ: "Missa," includes Vlone.
A-KN: includes 2 Tbn.
A-KR
A-SEI: includes 2 solo Vc for "Gratias."
A-TU: includes Vlone, performed 32 times 1789-1819.
A-Wn: H.K. 466, Missa "No: III," 41 parts.
" "   F. 24 (St. Peter) A152, 14 parts.
*D-B: Mus. ms. 10722, "Missa di Leopoldo Hofmann in
  Vienna," score, 61 fol., including 2 Fl ("Christe"),
  2 Ob, 2 Va, and 2 Vc.
D-B: Mus. ms. $\underline{10722}_{1}$, 35 parts, including 2 Fl ("Chri-
  ste"), 2 Ob, Bsn, 2 Va, 2 Vc, Vlone; from Opernhaus-
  Bibliothek.
D-HR: Ms. 153, 11 parts, including Vlone.

REFERENCES:

A-GÖ cat., Riedel no. 276, "comp[aravit] . . . 1779."
CS-Raj cat., p. 35.
Prohászka, "Hofmann," no. 18 and 18a, p. 123-24.
Schnürl no. 198.

REMARKS:

Missa longa, 1,123 m. in total.
Prohászka distinguishes between the Missa S. Erasmi (no.
  18) and a Missa in D (no. 18a). These are different
  versions of the same Mass. Prohászka no. 18a begins

M. 26 (cont'd.)

    with a four-measure Adagio (see incipit below)
that is found in the sources at A-GÖ, A-KN, A-KR,
A-Wn, D-HR as well as the CS-Raj catalogue.
This version of the Mass also has a different
arrangement of the "Benedictus"; cf. Prohászka,
p. 124.

Alternative
  Opening

(Prohászka
 no. 18a)

See Ex. 7-11, 7-20, and 10-4F.

Leopold HOFMANN

M. 27

Missa in honorem Sanctae Theresiae in C

(before 1760)

SSATB 2 Ob 2 Clni 2 Tbn Timp
2 V Org

COPIES:
A-GÖ: "Missa Stae. Theresiae," lacks S II and 2 Ob.
A-H: lacks 2 Ob.
A-HE: IX e 3, "Missa in C . . . Haydn."
A-KN: lacks 2 Tbn.
A-KR
A-LA: M39, "Missa in C . . . Post Centenar Repetitionem productem ultimo ad nauseam, 2da febr: 1780," 11 parts.
A-SEI
*A-Wn: F.24 (St. Peter) A143, "No. 1 Missa in C in Honorem Stae. Theresiae . . . Ad chorum St: Petri, Del Sigre: Leopoldo Hoffmann," 26 parts, including Vc, Vlone, and MDC.
CS-LIT: Sign. 519.
D-DS: Mus. ms. 554, only Kyrie-Gloria, 21 parts.
F-S, Cathedral archive possessed in 1909 F. X. Richter's arrangement of this Mass, including Bsn, 2 Hn, 2 Trombe, Va, Vc, and Vlone. Cf. Franz X. Mathias, "Thematischer Katalog der im Strassburger Münsterarchiv aufbewahrten Kirchenmusikalischen Werke Fr. X. Richters (1769-1789)," in Riemann Festschrift (Leipzig: M. Hesse, 1909) no. 102, p. 422.
I-Fc

REFERENCES:
A-H cat.
A-GÖ cat., Riedel no. 265, "comp[aravit] . . . 1760," does not mention S II or 2 Ob.
A-LA cat.

M. 27 (cont'd.)

CS-Raj cat., p. 30.
Joseph Haydn-Institut, Cologne, Stammkartei XXIII: C10.
Prohászka, "Hofmann," no. 2, p. 107.

REMARKS:
Missa brevis, 503 m. in total.
S II sings independently in Sanctus, Benedictus, and
    Agnus Dei.
See Ex. 8-1 and 9-16E.

Leopold HOFMANN   M. 28

Missa in C

(before 1762)

SATB 2 Clni 2 Tbn Timp 2 V Org

COPIES:
  A-GÖ: "Missa Stae. Barbarae," lacks 2 Tbn.
  A-H
  A-Krems a. d. Donau, Stadtpfarramt, "Missa Solemn
    in C . . . Del Sig: Mozart," parts, includes 2 Ob,
    Bsn, Vlone but lacks 2 Tbn.
  A-KN
  A-KR
  A-LA: M25, "Missa in C," 10 parts, lacks 2 Tbn.
  A-SF: "zu Ehren des Hlg. Franz X."
  A-TU: includes Vlone; S missing.
 *A-Wn: F.24 (St. Peter) A145, "No. 3 Missa in C . . .
    Ad Chorum St: Petri, Del Sigre: Leopoldo Hoffmann,"
    19 parts, includes Vc and MDC parts, Timp and
    Vlone [mentioned on cover] are lacking.
  CS-KRm: A.1127/Br. C-218.
  CS-LIT
  CS-Pnm: XXXVIII.A.41, "Missa II. Cl[asse] ex C."
   "   "   XLVI.D.220 (Strahov).
  D-OB: MO 525, dated 1774.

REFERENCES:
  A-GÖ cat., Riedel no. 266, "comp[aravit] . . .
    15 8bris 1762," without 2 Tbn.
  A-LA cat., p. 18, no. 3.
  A-H cat., no. 141, including Vlone, lacking 2 Tbn.
  Schnürl no. 196.
  Köchel, <u>Mozart Verzeichnis</u>, 6th ed., no. C 1.34.
  Prohászka, "Hofmann," no. 19, 124-25.

M. 28 (cont'd.)

REMARKS:
  Missa brevis?, 505 m. in total.
  The Adagio introduction to the Kyrie is absent in
    the copies at A-LA, A-Krems, and CS-Pnm (XXXVIII.
    A.41).
  See Ex. 7-5 and 10-2.

Leopold HOFMANN   M. 29

Missa in D

(before 1772)

SATB   Fl   2 Ob   2 Clni   Timp   2 V   Org

COPIES:
  A-GÖ: "Missa," Ob II missing.
  A-KN
  A-Wn: F.24 (St. Peter) A148, "No. 5 Missa in D
    Immaculatae Conceptionis B:M.V: . . . Ad chorum
    St: Petri, Del Sigre. Leopoldo Hoffmann,"
    inside cover: "1772 / 26.Nov. S:St: /
    15.[19?] Nov. S:St: hora ii," 33 parts, including
    2 Tbn, Vc, Vlone, MDC; 2 Ob (added later) = SA.

REFERENCES:
  A-GÖ cat., Riedel no. 275, "comp[aravit] . . . 1778."
  A-H cat.
  A-LA cat., p. 62, Fl and Timp not listed.
  A-KN cat.
  Prohászka, "Hofmann," no. 17, p. 122-23.

REMARKS:
  Missa longa, 672 m. in total.
  The solo flute has impressive passage-work in every
    movement.
  See Ex. 7-10, 7-11, 8-15, 8-19, and 9-10.

Ignaz HOLZBAUER   M. 30

Missa in C

(before 1739)

SSATB   2 Clni   2 Tbn   Timp   2 V   Vlone   Org

COPIES:
  A-Ws: Holzbauer no. 1, "Missa Sti. Bernardi," two
    fascicles of parts, including Bsn conc. and Vc
    conc., lacking 2 Clni, Timp; 2 Tbn are ripieni;
    earliest performance date 1760.
 *CS-Bm: A.2163 (St. Jakob, Brno), "Missa cum Clarinis
    obligatis et Trombonibus obligatis.Del Sig: Holtz-
    bauer," 2 Tbn are missing; Vlone lacking.
  CS-Bm: A.20.809 (Augustinerkloster Altbrünn), "Missa
    . . . Holtzbaur," including Bsn "or" Vc conc.,
    lacking Timp, Vlone; copyist's date at end of
    soprano part is "1739"; 1748 appears on several
    parts.

REFERENCES:
  Reichert, "Geschichte," Holzbauer no. 2.
  E. Schmitt, "Kurpfälzische Kirchenmusik," this Mass
    was not included, but Klaus Altmann (Bonn) has in-
    formed me that Schmitt gives this work the number
    "1" in his revised, unpublished thematic catalogue
    of Holzbauer's Masses.

REMARKS:
  Missa longa, 1,298 m. in total.
  S II sings in Gloria, Credo, Crucifixus, Et resurrexit,
    and Benedictus.
  "Credo" type Mass.
  See Ex. 6-19, 7-26, 8-5, 8-6, 8-19, and
    Fig. 7-6.

Ignaz HOLZBAUER   M. 31

Missa in a

(before 1747)

SATB 2 V Org

COPIES:
  *CS-Bm: A.19.144 (Augustinerkloster Altbrünn), "Missa
    . . . Authore Virtuoso Domino Holtzbauer, Pro Choro S:
    Montano," at end of B: "Descripsit Antonius Fran-
    ciscus Xaverius Waltus Pro Choro Sacro montano pro
    tunc brevi forsitan Secundus Bassista in Honorem
    B:V:M: Czastorhoviensi, ex S: Pauli Primi Eremitae
    A[nno] 1747, d[en]: 29 Apr[il]."
  D-Mbs: Mus. ms. 2297, "Missa," 15 parts, including
    2 Ob, Bsn, 2 Va, and Vc; Org and SA conc. are missing;
    lacks Benedictus.

REFERENCES:
  CS-Raj cat., p. 16, Missa "Nro. 96, Missa in A mr:
    Auth: Holtzbauer."
  D-Mbs, Hofkapelle cat., fol. 227^V, "Holzbauer, Nro. 1,
    brevis," including 2 Ob, Bsn, 2 Hn, and Va. Cf.
    Gertruat Haberkamp and Robert Münster, ed., Thematischer
    Katalog der ehemaligen Musikhandschriftensammlungen der
    königlichen Hofkapelle und der Kurfürstin Maria Anna
    in München, Kataloge Bayrischer Musiksammlungen, vol. 9.
  Reichert, "Geschichte," Holzbauer no. 20.
  Schmitt, "Kurpfälzische Kirchenmusik," Holzbauer no. 7,
    p. 309; no. 8 in Schmitt's revised, unpublished cat.

REMARKS:
  Missa brevis, 551 m. in total. See Ex. VIII-19 and IX-8.
  Version at D-Mbs begins in ₵ meter with doubled rhythmic
    values.

Ignaz HOLZBAUER   M. 32

Missa Sancti Andreae Apostoli

(before 1744)

SATB 2 V Vlone Org

COPIES:
- A-HE: IX,C,2, "Missa . . . Ignaz Holzbauer," includ-
  ing 2 Tbn, performance date 25 Jan. 1749.
- A-M: I,22, "Missa in Em."
- A-Wn: Mus. Hs. 5530, score of only Gloria and Credo,
  prepared from A-HE parts by Fräulein Haager for
  Georg Reichert in 1936.
- *CS-Bm: A.20.673 (Augustinerkloster Altbrünn), "Missa
  S: Andreae Apos: . . . Pro Choro Sacro Montano,"
  two later hands have added "Ignoto" and "Sig: Holz-
  bauer," lacks Vlone, at end of T: "Descripsit pro
  Choro Sacro-Montano Samuel Cassarus Salomon p: t:
  Tubicem: 1744 Die 17 July."

REFERENCES:
  Reichert, "Geschichte," Holzbauer no. 21.
  Schmitt, "Kurpfälzische Kirchenmusik," no. 15, p. 313;
  no. 18 in Schmitt's revised, unpublished catalogue.

REMARKS:
  Missa brevis, 474 m. in total.
  See Ex. 9-1 and 9-9.

Ignaz HOLZBAUER   M. 33

Missa in F

(before 1745)

SATB 2 Ob 2 Hn 2 Trombe Timp
      2 V Vlone Org

COPIES:
  CS-Bm: A.19.102 (Augustinerkloster Altbrünn), "Missa
    solemnis in F . . . Del Sigre: Ignazio Holtzbaur,"
    dated 1745; these parts were missing in 1980;
    supposed to also include Vc.
 *D-Mbs: Mus. ms. 2301, "Missa Del Sig: Holzbauer, Cat:
    No: 13, fol. 264.," 21 parts, including 2 Va;
    Vlone and Vc play from the same part.

REFERENCES:
  Reichert, "Geschichte," Holzbauer no. 12.
  Schmitt, "Kurpfälzische Kirchenmusik," Holzbauer no. 9,
    p. 310; no. 10 in Schmitt's revised, unpublished cat.

REMARKS:
  Missa longa, 766 m. in total.
  Klaus Altmann (University of Bonn) has prepared a score
    based upon the parts at D-Mbs.
  See Ex. 6-4 and 9-16F.

Carl von KOHAUT   M. 34

Missa Sancti Willibaldi in C

(before 1763)

SATB   2 Clni   Timp   2 V   Vlone   Org

COPIES:
  *A-GÖ: "Missa Scti. Willibaldi . . . Carolo Kohaut,"
    9 parts, lacking Timp and Vlone, "comparavit . . .
    1763."
  A-M: I,13, 12 parts, lacking Timp, including 2 Tbn.
  A-SEI: "Missa solemnis in C . . . Kohaut, Sub R. P. M.
    Ober 1771," 12 parts, including Timp "al piacere."
  CS-KU: Klášter voršilek, Hr 431, "Missa in C, Author
    huius preciosi Sacri, et connexi Operis est virtuosus
    Dominus Kohaut," including 2 Clni "ad libitum,"
    lacking Timp and Vlone, A is missing.

REFERENCES:
  A-GÖ cat., Riedel no. 342, without mention of Timp
    and Vlone.

REMARKS:
  Missa longa?, 583 m. in total.
  See Ex. 7-11, 8-19, and 9-16E.

Joseph KROTTENDORFER

M. 35

Missa in C

(before 1764)

SATB 2 Clni 2 Tbn Timp 2 V Vlone Org

COPIES:

A-Ek: A96, "Missa in C, dedicato Scto. Gabrieli Arch-
angelo . . . Del Sigre: Grottendorffer," 11 parts,
lacking 2 Tbn.

*A-Wn: Mus. Hs. F 5 (Mödling) 593, "Nro. 9 Missa in
C . . . Del Sig: Krottendorfer," including "Sparti-
tura" (partial score), 16 parts.

CS-Bm: A.35.906 (Augustinerkloster, Altbrünn), only
V I and Org remain extant.

CS-Bm: A.13.003, as a work by "Schneider."

CS-LIT: Sign. 282 (Loretanský), "Missa in C . . .
Del Sig: Leopoldo Hofmann, Ex Mus. Jos. Strobach,"
lacks Vlone; 2 Tbn missing.

H-P: Bárdos no. 181, "Missa in C No: 7," 11 parts,
lacking 2 Tbn (although Tbn solo of "Agnus" is
indicated), performed 1776-98, remark: "ista Missa
valde bona."

A-GÖ: "Missa Sti. Bernardi," lacking 2 Tbn (although
there exists a Tbn part for the Agnus Dei solo),
Timp missing.

REFERENCES:

CS-Raj cat., p. 15, "Nro. 90, Missa in C, Aut:
Schneider," lacking 2 Tbn and Timp.

A-GÖ cat., Riedel no. 349, "comp[aravit] 1764."

A-KN cat., Missa no. 138, p. 23, [anonymous].

A-SEI cat., "Krottendorfer," lacking 2 Tbn, Org.

M. 35 (cont'd.)

Anton Maria Klafsky, "Thematischer Katalog der Kirchen-
musikwerke von Michael Haydn," DTÖ vol. 62 (Vienna,
1925) no. 33.
Hoboken, Haydn Werkverzeichnis, XXII: C17.
Pulkert, Domus Lauretana Pragensis, no. 393, vol. I,
p. 199, as a work by Leopold Hofmann.
Kornél Bárdos, Pécs zenéje a 18. században (Budapest:
Akademiae Kiado, 1976) no. 181.
Robert N. Freeman, Franz Schneider, doubtful no. 62.

REMARKS:
Missa brevis, 391 m. in total.
V I at A-Wn includes Tbn I "Agnus Dei" solo in its
part, probably as an ad lib. alternative.
See Ex. 9-16D and 10-6.

Marianne von MARTÍNEZ   M. 36

(Missa in C)

1761

SATB   2 Fl   2 Ob   2 Clni   2 Tbn   Timp
        2 V   (Vlone   Org)

AUTOGRAPH SCORE:
  *A-Wgm: I.1639, "Terza Messa Della Sigra Marianna
    Martines, a di 10. Agosto del 1761," 156 p.,
    Vlone and Org are not denoted.

REFERENCE:
  D-Mbs, Hofkapelle cat., fol. 231ʳ, "Missae Delle
    Sigra Marianna Martines, Nro. 1," score indicated,
    including 2 Va, Vc, and Org; lacking 2 Tbn.
    Cf. Gertraut Haberkamp and Robert Münster, ed.,
    Thematischer Katalog der ehemaligen Musikhandschriften-
    sammlungen der königlichen Hofkapelle und der Kur-
    fürstin Maria Anna in München, Kataloge Bayrischer
    Musiksammlungen, vol. 9.

REMARKS:
  Missa longa, 906 m. in total.
  2 Fl play in "Laudamus," 2 Tbn in "Benedictus."
  See Ex. 5-1, 6-5, 6-19, and 8-19.

Marianne von MARTÍNEZ   M. 37

(Missa in D)

1765

SATB   2 Ob   2 Clni   Timp   2 V   (Vlone   Org)

AUTOGRAPH SCORE:
* A-Wgm: I.1640, "Messe No. IV," "Originale Della
  Quarta Messa di Marianna Martines, Luglio 1765,
  174 p.; Vlone and Org are not denoted in the
  bass part.

REFERENCE:
   A-Ws cat., fol. 25, "Mariane Martinez, Missa Solem.
   vell de Domin. in D^d," 31 parts indicated, including Vc, Vlone, Org, and Bsn "unis[ono]."

REMARKS:
   Missa longa, 1,266 m. in total.
   See Ex. 6-19, 7-1, 7-11, 8-19, 9-16A,
     10-11, and Fig. 10-8.

Mathias Georg MONN   M. 38

Missa in C

1741

SATB   2 Clni   2 Trombe   2 Tbn   Timp
       2 V   Va   Vlone   Org

COPIES:
  A-H: "Missa Beatus vir . . . Monn," lacking 2 Trombe
    and 2 Tbn.
  A-M: I,60, lacking 2 Trombe and 2 Tbn.
 *A-Wn: Mus. Hs. 17314, "Missa in C: mj: . . . Monn,"
    77 parts in two fascicles (Kyrie-Gloria and Credo-
    Agnus Dei) with many duplicate parts; includes
    Ob unisono, Bsn, Vc, and MDC; "Messa composta l'anno
    1741, dal maestro di capp: Giov. Mat. Monn."
    S. Vernon Sanders (University of Regina, Saskatche-
    wan) has prepared a manuscript score from these parts
    which once belonged to the Hofmusikkapelle.

REFERENCES:
  A-H cat., no. 125, "Missa Beatus vir," without 2 Trombe
    and 2 Tbn.
  Reichert, "Geschichte," Monn no. 2.

REMARKS:
  Missa longa, 1,321 m. in total.
  Difficult vocal and instrumental writing.
  See Ex. 6-2, 7-2, 7-11, 7-21, 8-12A,
    8-19, 9-4A, 10-4A, Fig. 5-3, and Fig. 8-8.

Mathias Georg MONN (d. 1750)   M. 39

Missa solemnis in B-flat

(before 1750)

SATB 2 V Va Vlone Org

COPIES:
  A-GÖ: "Missa Sti. Fridolini," 8 parts, lacking Vlone,
    with ten performance dates from 16 Dec. 1761 until
    15 Mar. 1801.
  A-LA: M310, "Missa Ex B," 9 parts.
  A-M: I,59, 11 parts, including 2 Tbn.
 *A-Wgm: Q 214 (I.8161), "Missa solemnis . . . Auth.
    Dnõ. Monn," score, 92 fol., Vlone not specified.
  A-Wn: Mus. Hs. 17315, "No. 3, Missa in H:b:, Monn,"
    15 parts in two fascicles (both identified with
    "No. 25").
  A-WIL: Ms. 644, no. 2 (according to Philipp).
  A-WIL: Ms. 645a, "Missa Sti. Fridolini . . . Ex Rebus
    Raymundi Abbatis Hilariensis Authore Del Sigr: Monn,"
    8 parts, lacking Vlone (according to RISM).

REFERENCES:
  A-H cat., no. 115, "Missa Sti. Aldobici," 9 parts.
  A-LA cat., p. 26, 9 parts.
  A-KN cat., p. 16, Missa no. 93, "M. Monn."
  A-GÖ cat., Riedel no. 358, 8 parts, "1761," without Vlone.
  A-WIL cat., under "Missae sine tubis."
  Reichert, "Geschichte."
  R. Philipp, "Messenkomposition der Wiener Vorklassiker."

REMARKS:
  Missa longa, 997 m. in total.
  See Ex. 6-19, 8-19, and 9-16B.

Mathias Georg MONN (d. 1750)   M. 40

Missa in D

(before 1750)

SATB   2 Tbn   2 V   Vlone   Org

COPIES:
  *A-GÖ: "Missa . . . Authore Monn," 11 parts, including
    2 Clni ("ad lib."), lacking Vlone, performance dates
    from 27 May 1753 until 17 Mar. 1776. No Timp.
  A-LA: "Missa Ex D . . . Monn," 10 parts.
  A-SEI: D,XVIII,4b, "Missa in D dur . . . Del Signore
    Mann [sic] 1787," 5 parts, lacking 2 Tbn, 2 V, Vlone,
    performance dates 1827-71.

REFERENCES:
  A-SEI cat., "Mann."   A-LA cat., p. 26, "Monn."
  A-GÖ cat., "Missa . . . des[cri]pta 1753," including
    2 Clni [no Timp], lacking Vlone.
  Reichert, "Geschichte."
  Philipp, "Messenkomposition der Wiener Vorklassiker."

REMARKS:
  Missa longa, 868 m. in total.
  See Ex. 6-8, 6-19, 8-19, and 9-5.

P. Silverius MÜLLER (d. 1812)   M. 41

Missa in D

(before 1812)

SATB   2 Ob   2 Clni   Timp   2 V   Vlone   Org

COPY:
  A-Wp: "Missa," 13 parts.

REMARKS:
  Missa longa?
  Müller was Sub-Regenschori at A-Wp 1770-71.
 *Otto Biba (Vienna) prepared a score from the parts
   at A-Wp. Portions of this score were consulted
   for the present study.

Luca Antonio PREDIERI   M. 42

Missa Nativitatis

1747

SATB (Bsn) 2 Clni 2 Trombe (Cornetto) 2 Tbn Timp
             2 V Vlone Org

COPIES:
 A-LA: M196, 17 parts, including 3 Tbn (instead of only
    2 Tbn) and Va; lacking Bsn and Cornetto.
 A-LA: M211, 7 parts, lacking Bsn, 2 Clni, 2 Trombe,
    Cornetto, 2 Tbn, Timp, and Vlone.
 *A-Wn: H.K. 406, "31. May 1747, Missa Nativitatis . . .
    Del Sig: Predieri, Vice Maestro di Capella di S: M:
    Anno 1747," 23 parts in two fascicles, including
    Vc, MDC, and ripieno voice parts.

REFERENCES:
 A-LA cat., p. 31 (2 times).
 Heinrich Freunschlag, "Luca Antonio Predieri als Kirchen-
    komponist" (unpublished Ph.D. dissertation, University
    of Vienna, 1927) cat. no. 7.

REMARKS:
 Missa brevis, 381 m. in total.
 At A-Wn the Cornetto, 2 Tbn, and Bsn are ripieno
    parts (i.e. = SATB); Org does not always equal Vc, Vlone.
 No examples.

Luca Antonio PREDIERI   M. 43

(Missa in C)

1746

SATB   2 Bsn   2 Clni   2 Trombe   (Cornetto)   (2 Tbn)   Timp
2 V   Vc   Vlone   Org

COPY:
*A-Wn: H.K. 410, "29. May 1746, Kyrie et Gloria . . .
Del Sig: Predieri, Vice Maestro di Capella della
S: C: e Real Mta. 1746," 24 parts, including MDC
and ripieno vocal parts, in two fascicles.

REFERENCE:
Heinrich Freunschlag, "Luca Antonio Predieri als Kirchenkomponist" (unpublished Ph.D. dissertation, University
of Vienna, 1927) cat. no. 11.

REMARKS:
Missa brevis, 368 m.
At A-Wn the Cornetto, 2 Tbn, and Bsn are ripieno
parts (i.e. = SATB);   the 2 Bsn play obbligati
in the Gloria.
No example.

Georg von REUTTER, Jr.   M. 44

Missa Sancti Placidi
(Missa Sancti Georgii)

(before 1748)

SATB   (Bsn)   2 Clni   2 Trombe (Cornetto) 2 Tbn Timp
2 V   Vlone   Org

COPIES:
A-H: parts, lacking Bsn, 2 Trombe, Cornetto, and 2 Tbn;
performed 1804.
A-KN: No. 20, parts, lacking Bsn, 2 Trombe, Cornetto,
and Timp.
A-KN: No. 29, parts.
A-M: parts, lacking Bsn, 2 Clni, 2 Trombe, Cornetto,
and Timp.
A-Wn: H.K. 1023, 1023*, "Missa Sti. Georgii," "in pieno
no. 19," "in concto no. 11," parts, including Vc,
dated 1748.
A-Wn: (St. Peter Sammlung) "No. 3," lacking Bsn, 2 Trombe,
Cornetto, and Timp.
A-Wm: parts (according to Hofer).
A-Wp: parts, lacking Bsn, 2 Trombe, Cornetto.
A-W, St. Michael's: parts, lacking Bsn, 2 Clni, 2 Trombe,
Cornetto, and Timp.
A-GÖ: "Missa Sti. Georgii," 11 parts, lacking Bsn,
2 Trombe, Cornetto, Timp, and Vlone.

REFERENCES:
A-H cat.
A-GÖ cat., Riedel no. 465, "comp[aravit] . . . 1756."
CS-Raj cat., p. 12, no. 70.
A-Wn cat. Sm. 2454, "Messe in Concto No: 11 in C,"
without 2 Clni, 2 Trombe, Cornetto, Timp.

M. 44 (cont'd.)

A-Wn cat. Sm. 2454, p. 33, "Messe in Pieno No: 19 in C,"
    without Cornetto; "S: Georgi."
A-Wn cat. Sm. 2457, fol. 20ᵛ.
A-Ws cat., no. 250, Reutter no. 16.
Vorau ms. catalogue.
Hofer, "Thematisches Verzeichnis der Werke Georg
    Reutters d.J.," cat. no. 33.
Landon, Haydn: Chronicle and Works, I, 92-94.

REMARKS:
 Missa brevis?
 *Otto Biba (Vienna) prepared a score from the parts
    at A-Wp. Portions of this score were studied for
    the present project.
 2 Tbn are obbligati in Agnus Dei; otherwise the
    Cornetto, 2 Tbn, and Bsn are probably ripieno
    parts (i.e. = SATB).
 See Ex. 5-2 and 7-14.

Georg von REUTTER, Jr.   M. 45

Missa Lauretana

1742

SATB (Bsn)   2 Clni 2 Trombe (Cornetto) 2 Tbn Timp
                        2 V Vlone Org

COPIES:

  A-Ek: 139/47, parts, Ob instead of Cornetto;
     lacking 2 Clni, 2 Trombe, and Timp.

  A-GÖ: "Missa Sti. Magnoaldi," 14 parts, only 1
     Tromba (instead of 2 which the old cat. of 1830
     originally indicated but then changed to 1), also
     lacking Bsn and Cornetto; Vlone added later.

  A-KR: B,35,532, includes only SATB, Cl, T Tbn, 2 V,
     Vlone, and Org.

  A-LA: M369, "Missa nova . . . Reitter," lacking
     Bsn, 2 Trombe, and Cornetto.

  A-SEI: parts, lacking Bsn, 2 Trombe, and Cornetto.

A-Wn: H.K. 754, "Missa Lauretana . . . Del Sig:
     Reutter Comp: di S:M:R:e Maestro di Capla di Sto
     Steffano, 1742," "No. 5," parts in 3 fascicles,
     including Vc, MDC, and duplicate parts for 2 V and
     ripieno SATB; earliest performance 17 June 1742.

  A-Wn: H.K. 754, "Missa Lauretana," "No. 10," later
     parts, performed 1798-1842.

  A-Wn: (St. Peter Sammlung) "No. 7," lacking Cornetto
     and Bsn; different arrangement.

  A-Ws: Ms. 18,330?

  A-W, St. Michael's: parts, lacking Bsn, 2 Trombe and
     Cornetto.

  A-WIL: Ms. 841, lacking Bsn and Cornetto.

  D-B: Mus. ms. 18390, "Missa . . . Del Sige: Giorgio
               1
    de Reüttern, Maestro Capla di Sac: Caes: M: e: Rle:

M. 45 (cont'd.)

M: D: C: di Sto. Steffano," 14 parts, lacking Bsn
and Cornetto, only 1 Tromba (instead of 2).
Provenance: Opernhaus Bibliothek, 18th C.

REFERENCES:
A-GÖ cat., Riedel no. 459, "descripta 1751," does
not mention Bsn, Cornetto, and Vlone. "1 Tromba"
originally read "2." Cf. Riedel no. 485.
A-LA cat., p. 33.
A-Wn cat., Sm. 2454, p. 2, "Messe in Concto No: 5 in C,"
does not mention Bsn, 2 Trombe, Cornetto, and Timp.
A-Wn cat., Sm. 2454, p. 31, "Messe in Pieno No: 10 in C,"
does not mention Bsn, 2 Clni, 2 Trombe, Cornetto, Timp.
A-Wn cat., Sm. 2457, fol. 21.
A-Wn cat., Sm. 2464, p. 121, no. 1, "tutti" type;
"Benedictus organo solo ist auch für die Violinen
gesetzt."
Hofer, "Reutter Verzeichnis," cat. no. 45.
REMARKS:
Missa longa, 596 m. in total.
In A-Wn, H.K. 754* there are two "Benedictus" settings:
one in C minor for organ solo and another in A minor
for 2 V and continuo with S solo. Copies at A-GÖ,
A-LA, A-SEI, and A-Ws apparently have the latter
version.
See Ex. 6-19, 7-11, 7-15, 7-24, 7-25,
8-12, 8-19, 9-4, and 9-11.
Cornetto, 2 Tbn, and Bsn are chiefly ripieno parts
(i.e. = SATB).

Georg von REUTTER, Jr.   M. 46

Missa Conceptionis

(before 1749)

SSATB (Bsn)   2 Clni   2 Trombe (Cornetto) 2 Tbn   Timp
                2 V   Vlone   Org

COPIES:
   A-Ek: Ms. 6/93, parts, lacking Bsn, 2 Trombe, Cor-
      netto, and Timp.
   A-GÖ: "Missa Conceptionis B:M:V:," everything missing
      except for S and V I (Riedel no. 457).
   A-GÖ: "Missa," 12 parts, lacking S II, Bsn, 2 Trombe,
      Cornetto, and Vlone (Riedel no. 498).
   A-H: lacking S II, Bsn, 2 Trombe, Cornetto, 2 Tbn,
      and Org; Timp missing; performed 1771-.
   A-HE: 16 parts.
   A-KN: 19 parts.
   A-KR: B,34, 526.
   A-LA: Sign. 372, "Missa ex C," 13 parts, lacking
      Bsn, 2 Trombe, Cornetto, and S II.
   A-M: "Missa Conceptionis."
   A-SEI
   A-Wm: "Missa S. Francisci de Paula."
  *A-Wn: H.K. 780, "No: 10, Missa Conceptionis B:V:M:
      . . . Del Sig: Giorgio de Reütter MDC: di Sac: Ces:
      Maj," 21 parts in 2 fascicles, including Vc and MDC
      as well as 2 ripieno Tbn; Org missing; performed
      eight times between 21 Dec 1771 (S. St[ephan] hora 11)
      and 1 Sept. 1774. No Credo is present.
   A-Wn: H.K. 780*, "Conceptionis Missa, No: 18," origi-
      nal title ["Sancti Franc: de Paula"] was crossed out;
      20 parts, including Ob, Va, Vc, and MDC (2), and extra
      Org; lacking S II, 2 Trombe, and Cornetto. Credo present.

M. 46 (cont'd.)

A-W, St. Michael's.
A-Z: No. 195.
CS-KRE: 185 (Františkánska Knižnica), "Missa S: The-
resiae in C," 13 parts, including 2 Ob, lacking S II,
Bsn, 2 Trombe, Cornetto, 2 Tbn.
CS-LIT: Sign. 478, "Missa . . . Reuther," 11 parts,
lacking S II, Bsn, 2 Trombe, Cornetto, and Vlone.
D-AL: No. 152.
D-OB: MO 716, "Die Schimmel-Messe . . . Giorgio de
Reuttern, Maestro di Capla di Sac: Caes: M: e Rle,
M:D:C: di Sto. Steffano," 13 parts, lacking Bsn,
2 Trombe, Cornetto, and Vlone; earliest performance
date: 24 June 1756.

REFERENCES:
A-GÖ cat., Riedel no. 457, "Missa Conceptionis B:M:V:,"
without Bsn, 2 Trombe, Cornetto, and Vlone, "1749."
A-GÖ cat., Riedel no. 498, "Missa," without S II, Bsn,
2 Trombe, Cornetto, and Vlone; = revision of pre-
ceding entry; "comp[aravit]. . . 1783."
A-H cat., no. 104.
A-LA cat., p. 33.
CS-Raj cat., p. 13.
A-Wn cat., Sm. 2454, p. 3, "Messe in Concto No: 10 in C,"
does not mention S II, Bsn, 2 Trombe, Cornetto, Timp.
A-Wn cat., Sm. 2454, p. 33, "Messe in Pieno No: 18 in C,"
does not mention S II, Bsn, and Cornetto.
Vorau ms. catalogue.
A-Wn cat., Sm. 2457, fol. 18.
Hofer, "Thematisches Verzeichnis der Werke Georg Reut-
ters D.J.," cat. no. 68.
Klafsky, "Thematischer Katalog der Kirchenmusikwerke
von Michael Haydn," DTÖ vol. 62 (Vienna, 1925) no. 28.
Sherman, "The Masses of Johann Michael Haydn," p. 221,
doubtful no. 11.
Pulkert, Domus Lauretana Pragensis, no. 547.

REMARKS:
Missa brevis.
The Credo was lacking in the A-Wn source used.
S II has a part independent from S I in the "Benedictus."
Hofer believes this Mass to be the so-called "Schimmel-
Messe"; cf. chapter 10, n. 25, and Ex. 10-17.
See Ex. 7-3, 9-13, 9-16E, and 10-17.
Cornetto, 2 Tbn, and Bsn are chiefly ripieno parts
(i.e. = SATB).

Georg von REUTTER, Jr.   M. 47

Missa Sancti Mariani

1759

SATB (Bsn) 2 Clni 2 Trombe (Cornetto) 2 Tbn Timp
2 V Vlone Org

COPIES:
  A-Ek: 91/9.
  A-Gö: "Missa Sti. Mariani," lacking Bsn, Cornetto,
    and Vlone, including extra V I and II parts.
  A-H: parts acquired 1763, lacking Bsn, 2 Trombe, and
    Cornetto.
  A-HE: "Missa G," 21 parts.
  A-KN: No. 7, 15 parts, lacking Bsn, 2 Trombe, Cornetto,
    and 2 Tbn.
  A-KN: No. 8, lacking Bsn, Cornetto, and Timp.
  A-KR: B,35,529.
  A-L: parts with performance dates 1828-63.
  A-LA: M368 (olim no. 274), lacking Bsn, 2 Trombe, and
    Cornetto.
  A-Wm
 *A-Wn: H.K. 762, "No: 16 Missa Sancti Mariani . . . Del
    Sigre. Giorgio de Reüttern, Maestro di Capla di Sac:
    Ces: M: e M:D:C: di Sto Steffano 1759," 29 parts in
    each of three fascicles, including Vc, MDC, and extra
    copies of SATB (2 each) and 2 V (1 each); performance
    dates beginning 23 Oct. 1765.
  A-Wn: H.K. 762*, "Missa Sancti Mariani," 40 parts,
    library cat. calls this "eine Bearbeitung," probably
    equals "No. 24" in the A-Wn cat. cited below.
  A-Wn: (St. Peter Sammlung) "No. 6."
  A-Ws: No. 3, 19 parts, lacking Bsn, 2 Trombe, Cornetto.
  A-W, St. Michael's, parts, lacking Bsn and Cornetto

M. 47 (cont'd.)

A-Z: No. 134.
CS-Pnm: XXXVIII.A.69 (Broumov), "Missa solemnis . . .
    Giorgio de Reüttern, M:D:C: dell Imp. e Real Corte,"
    15 parts, including 2 Ob; lacking Bsn, 2 Trombe, Cor-
    netto.
Raudnitz, Count Lobkowitz, X A b 15 (according to
    P. Norbert Hofer's 1947 Reutter catalogue).

REFERENCES:
A-H cat., Mass no. 153.
A-GÖ cat., Riedel no. 471, "Missa Sancti Mariani,"
    lacking Bsn, 2 Trombe, and Cornetto, "comp[aravit
    . . . 1762."
A-LA cat., p. 35.
A-Wn cat., Sm. 2454, p. 4, "Messe in Conc̲t̲o No. 16 in G,"
    does not mention Bsn, Cornetto.
A-Wn cat., Sm. 2454, p. 34, "Messe in Pieno No. 24 in G,"
    does not mention Bsn and Cornetto; includes 2 Va.
A-Wn cat., Sm. 2457, fol. 20.
A-Ws cat., vol. 1, fol. 30^v, no. 237.
Hofer, "Thematisches Verzeichnis der Werke Georg Reut-
    ters d.J.," cat. no. 39.

REMARKS:
Missa brevis, 477 m. in total.
Cornetto, 2 Tbn, and Bsn are chiefly ripieno parts
    (i.e. = SATB); 2 Tbn obbligati in Gloria.
See Ex. 6-10, 8-8, and Fig. 6-3.

Georg von REUTTER, Jr.   M. 48

Missa Sancti Venantii

(before 1761)

SATB   2 Bsn   2 Clni   2 Trombe (Cornetto) 2 Tbn   Timp
                2 V   Vlone   Org

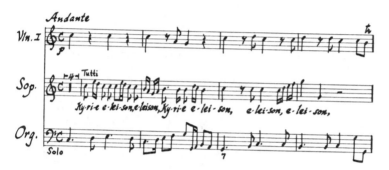

COPIES:
  A-Ek: 5/33, lacking Bsn, 2 Trombe, Cornetto, and 2 Tbn.
  A-H: lacking Bsn, 2 Trombe, COrnetto, and 2 Tbn; "com-
    paravit . . . 1802."
  A-KN: "No. 6," 13 parts, lacking 2 Clni, 2 Trombe, and
    Timp.
 *A-Wn: H.K. 789, "No. 9, Missa Sancti Venantii . . .
    Del Sigre. Giorgio de Reüttern, Maestro di Capla di
    Sac: Ces: M: e M.D.C. di Sto. Steffano," 20 parts
    in 2 fascicles, including Vc and MDC, earliest per-
    formance dates: 18 Nov. 1765 (Kyrie-Gloria) and
    13 April 1761 (Credo).   Sanctus and Agnus are absent.
  A-Wn: H.K. 789*, "Missa Sancti Venantii," 39 parts,
    library cat. calls this "eine Bearbeitung," probably
    equals "No. 16" in the A-Wn cat. cited below;
    includes Sanctus and Agnus Dei; dated 1762.
  A-Gö: "Missa," lacking 2 Trombe, Cornetto;
    Bsn is missing; extra copies of V. I and Vlone.

REFERENCES:
  A-Gö cat., Riedel no. 500, "Missa," does not mention
    2 Trombe, Cornetto, and Vlone, "comp[aravit] . . .
    1785."
  A-Wn cat., Sm. 2454, p. 3, "Messe in Concto No. 9 in C,"
    without mention of rip. Bsn, Cornetto, 2 Tbn.

M. 48 (cont'd.)

> A-Wn cat., Sm. 2454, p. 32, "Messe in Pieno No. 16 in C,"
> without mention of rip. Bsn, Cornetto, 2 Tbn (although
> they may be implied by the designation "Rip:").
> A-Wn cat., Sm. 2457, fol. 19.
> Hofer, "Thematisches Verzeichnis der Werke Georg Reut-
> ters d.J.," cat. nos. 56 and 57.

REMARKS:
> Missa brevis.
> There are several Bsn and Org solos.
> The Sanctus and Agnus Dei were lacking from the A-Wn
> source consulted.
> Cornetto, 2 Tbn, and Bsn II are chiefly ripieno parts
> (i.e. = SATB).
> See Ex. 6-6 and 8-12A.

Georg von REUTTER, Jr.

M. 49

Missa Sancti Caroli

1734

SATB Bsn 2 Clni 2 Tbn Timp
2 V Vc Vlone Org

AUTOGRAPH SCORE:
  A-HE: Sammelband IIc, "Missa S. Caroli . . . D: G:
    Reütter," 55 fol., at end of score: "Finis. 1734."

COPIES:
  A-Ee: 106/11, "Missa S. Caroli," Kyrie and Gloria
    only.
  A-KN: "No. 27," Kyrie and Gloria only, including
    2 Trombe.

REFERENCE:
  A-KN cat.
  Hofer, "Reutter Verzeichnis," cat. no. 60.
EDITION:
  *Georg Reutter, d.J., "Missa Sancti Caroli," in Kirchen-
    werke, ed. P. Norbert Hofer and Leopold Nowak,
    Denkmäler der Tonkunst in Österreich, vol. 88
    (Vienna: Österreichischer Bundesverlag, 1952)
    p. 1-57, 102. (Edition based upon A-HE)

REMARKS:
  Missa longa, 933 m. in total.
  See Ex. 6-19, 7-11, and 8-19.

Ferdinand SCHMIDT   M. 50

Missa Sanctae Caeciliae

(before 1746)

SSATBB   2 Clni   2 Tbn   Timp   2 V   Vlone   Org

COPIES:
  *A-GÖ: "Missa," 13 parts in each of 2 fascicles
    (Kyrie-Gloria and Credo-Agnus), lacking Vlone.
  A-H: I,32, "Missa SS. Magorum," 16 parts, including
    Bsn and Tromba I.
  A-KN: "Nr. 2 Missa in C," including Tromba I;
    there is a second Credo for SATB Bsn Cornet[to]
    2 Tbn 2 V Vc Org.
  CS-Bm: A.2264, "Missa Stae. Barbarae," 17 parts,
    including 2 Trombe and extra V I and II.

REFERENCES:
  A-GÖ cat., Riedel no. 528, "Missa," without mention
    of B II and Vlone, Kyrie-Gloria "descrips[it] . . .
    7 Dec. 1746," Credo-Agnus "die 9 Dec. 1746."
  A-H cat.
  A-KN cat., p. 33, Missa no. 150, "Schmidt."
  Reichert, "Geschichte," p. 116-17, Schmidt no. 7.

REMARKS:
  Missa longa, 1,042 m. in total.
  S II sings independently only in Credo, B II only in
    Gloria. Outstanding obbligati for 2 Clni.
  At A-GÖ the work was performed 5 times from "22 Nov.
    1756 [sic]" until 1772.
  See Ex. 6-3, 6-20, 7-11, 8-2, 8-14, 8-19,
    9-16A, 10-8, and 10-15.

Ferdinand SCHMIDT

M. 51

Missa Primitiarum

(before 1747)

SATB 2 Clni 2 Trombe 2 Tbn Timp
2 V [Vlone] Org

COPY:
  *A-GÖ: "Missa Primitiarum a: Canto, Alto, Tenore,
    Basso, Violinis 2bus, Clarinis 2bus, Trombon 2bus,
    Trombis 2bus, Tympano, con Organo, Auth: Domino
    Schmid, Chori Gottwic: 1747," 14 parts, lacking
    Vlone, with Trombe I and II called Clni III and
    IV (using G-clefs); performed 20 Jan. 1757.

REFERENCE:
  A-GÖ cat., Riedel no. 529, "1747."
  Reichert, "Geschichte," Schmidt no. 8.
REMARKS:
  Missa longa, 806 m. in total.
  Clno I plays several solo obbligati.
  See Ex. 7-9, 7-12, 8-19, 9-2, 9-14, and
    Fig. 7-5.

Joseph SEUCHE   M. 52

Missa Sancti Joachimi

(before 1754)

SATB 2 V [Vlone] Org

COPY:
*A-GÖ: "Missa S. Joáchimi a Canto, Alto, Tenore,
    Basso, Violinis IIbus: & Organo, Auth. Dno:
    Seü[c]he, Pro choro Gottw. 1754," 7 parts,
    lacking Vlone; performed about 24 times from
    5 Dec. 1754 until 1785.

REFERENCE:
    A-GÖ cat., Riedel no. 589, "Missa Sti. Joachimi,"
    without mention of Vlone, "1754."

REMARKS:
    Missa brevis, 298 m. in total.
    Text telescoping in Credo.
    No example.

Joseph SEUCHE

M. 53

Missa in D

(before 1773)

SATB 2 V [Vlone] Org

COPIES:
*A-GÖ: "Missa Ex D: a 4, Canto, Alto, Tenore, Basso,
   Violino Primo, Violino Secundo con Organo, Del Sigre:
   Seuche, Comparavit R:P: Marianus 1773," 7 parts,
   without Vlone; performed approximately 12 times
   from 27 Jan. 1774 until 1785.
   CS-LIT: Sign. 550, "Missa in D," 11 parts, including
   2 Ob and 2 Clni.(Loreto Sammlung).

REFERENCES:
   A-GÖ cat., Riedel no. 593, "Missa," without mention
   of Vlone, "comp[aravit] . . . 1773."
   CS-VC cat., Missa "N: 32, Seüche."
   CS-Raj cat., p. 19, "Nro. 110 Missa in D . . . Haydn."
   Hoboken, Haydn Werkverzeichnis, XXII: D3.
   Pulkert, Domus Lauretana Pragensis, cat. no. 629.

REMARKS:
   Missa brevis, 202 m. in total.
   Text telescoping in Credo. Awkward voice leading.
   See Ex. 10-4D.

Christoph SONNLEITHNER   M. 54

Missa in C

(before 1771)

SATB   2 Clni   Timp   2 V   Vlone   Org

COPIES:
*A-GÖ: "Missa ex C," 10 parts, lacking Vlone, per-
     formed approximately 23 times from 30 Sept. 1771
     to 22 April 1810.
  A-SEI: E,I,3a, "Missa solennis in C . . . 1790,"
     11 parts; performance dates up to 1813.
  CS-Bm: A.13.020 (Rajhrad), "Sonnenleuthner: Missa
     in C," 10 parts, lacking Vlone, earliest performance
     1773.
  CS-LIT: Sign. 511, "Missa in C," 11 parts, including
     2 Ob, lacking Timp and Vlone (Loreto Sammlung).

REFERENCES:
  A-GÖ cat., Riedel no. 603, "comp[aravit] . . . 1771,"
     without mention of Vlone.
  A-H cat., no. 169, "Missa in C . . . Sonleitner."
  CS-Raj cat., p. 30, "Nro. 191: Missa in C, Del Sigre.
     Sonnenleütner, without mention of Vlone and Org.
  CS-VC cat., p. 5, "Missa No: 40," "Sonnleithner."
  A-SEI cat., "Sonleutner," without mention of Org.

REMARKS:
  Missa longa, 820 m. in total.
  See Ex. 6-19, 7-17, 9-7, and Fig. 9-7.

Christoph SONNLEITHNER   M. 55

Missa in C

(before 1765)

SATB 2 Clni (Timp) 2 V Vlone Org

COPIES:

A-GÖ: "Missa B:M:V:," 10 parts, lacking Vlone.

A-M: I,62, 10 parts, lacking Timp.

A-SEI: E,I,3b, "Missa solennis in C, 11 parts, Timp "ad libitum," performance dates 1771-84.

A-Wgm: I.22296, "Missa in C," 10 parts, lacking Timp.

A-Wp: parts.

CS-Bm: A.21.674 (Petrov, Brno), 5 parts, including Tbn; the SATB, Timp, Vlone, and Org parts are missing.

CS-Bm: A.468 (Liprúk), "Sonnenleitner, Missa Scti. Laurentis," 5 parts, lacking Timp and Vlone; 2 V and 2 Clni are missing; dated "1765."

CS-Bm: A.13.022 (Rajhrad), "Sonnenleithner: Missa in C," 11 parts, including 2 Tbn, lacking Timp and Vlone; "1851."

H-P: "Missa in C," 11 parts (Bárdos no. 291).

REFERENCES:

A-GÖ cat., Riedel no. 601, "Missa B:M:V:," lacking mention of Vlone, "comp[aravit] . . . 1765."

A-H cat., Missa no. 161, "Sonnleitner," 12 parts, including 2 Tbn, lacking Timp.

CS-Raj cat., p. 23, "Nro. 133, Missa in C. Auth: Sonnenleüthner, without mention of Timp, Vlone, and Timp.

CS-VC, p. 1, "Missa No. 3, Sonnleithner."

A-KN, p. 21, without attribution.

A-SEI, "Sonleithner."

Kornél Bárdos, <u>Pécs zenéje a 18. században</u> (Budapest: Akadémiae Kiadó, 1976) cat. no. 291.

M. 55 (cont'd.)

REMARKS:
  Missa longa.
  "Credo" type Mass.
 *Otto Biba (Vienna) prepared a score from the parts
    at W-p. Portions of this score were examined for
    the present study.
  "Benedictus" cited by Karl Pfannhauser, "Zu Mozarts
    Kirchenwerken von 1768," <u>Mozart Jahrbuch 1954</u>, p. 162,
    as possible model for Mozart, K. 139 "Quoniam."
  See Ex. 8-12C, 9-16B, 10-12, and Fig. 10-9.

Christoph SONNLEITHNER   M. 56

Missa solennis in C

(before 1763)

SATB 2 Clni 2 Tbn Timp 2 V Vlone Org

COPIES:
  A-GÖ: "Missa de B: V: Mariae," 13 parts (Vlone
    added later), including extra V I and VII as well
    as an extra complete set of parts in Wondratsch's
    hand.
  A-H: 853, "Lit.E.N.145, Missa ex C . . . Del Sig:
    Sonnleithner, Pro choro Duc: 1763," 13 parts,
    with performance dates 1763-79.
  A-M: I,63, 12 parts, lacking Timp.
  A-SEI: E,I,3c, "Missa Solemnis . . . Auth: Sig:
    Sonnleithner, Sub P: M: O: 1770," 13 parts, with
    performance date up to 1790.
  A-SF: II,407, "Messe in C-dur," 8 parts, lacking
    2 Clni, 2 Tbn, and Timp; with performance dates.
 *A-Wgm: Q 431 (I.1628), "Missa solennis . . . Del
    Sigre. Sonnleithner," score (probably 19th C.),
    189 p.
  CS-Bm: A.2249 (St. Jakob, Brno), "Sonnenleitner:
    Missa," Timp omitted from title; only Vlone and
    Org parts present.
  CS-Bm: A.13.021 (Rajhrad), "Sonnenleuthner: Missa
    in C," 13 parts, lacking Vlone, including extra
    Tbn I; earliest performance date 1772.
  CS-Pnm: XLVI.B.348 (Strahov), "Missa Nro: 3: in C
    Majore . . . Sonnleithner," lacking Timp and Vlone,
    including 2 Va as alternatives to 2 Tbn.
  CS-Pnm: XLVI.B.356 (Strahov), "Missa Tono C maj: au-
    thore Sonnleithner, Nro: 3," score of Gerlak Strniště,
    including Va, lacking 2 Clni, 2 Tbn, and Timp.

M. 56 (cont'd.)

REFERENCES:
 A-GÖ cat., Riedel no. 599, without mention of Vlone;
  "comp[aravit] . . . 1765."
 A-H cat., no. 145, "Missa ex C, Sonnleithner."
 CS-RAJ cat., p. 23, "Nro. 134, Missa in C, Auth:
  Sonnenleüthner."
 CS-VC cat., p. 1, Missa "No. 1, Sonnleithner."
 A-KN cat., p. 22, Missa no. 132, "Sonnleithner."
 A-SEI cat., "Sonleutner."
 CS-P, Barmherzige Brüder cat., Missa no. 17, "Sonnen-
  leiter," 12 parts, lacking Vlone.

REMARKS:
 Missa longa, 931 m. in total.
 2 Tbn are obbligati in Agnus Dei.
 See Ex. 7-11, 7-22, 8-19, 9-16C, and 10-7.

Christoph SONNLEITHNER   M. 57

Missa sollemnis in C

(before 1758)

SATB 2 Clni 2 Tbn Timp 2 V Vlone Org

COPIES:

A-GÖ: "Missa Sti. Meinradi," 12 parts, lacking
Vlone, including extra V I and V II.

A-H: 855, "Lit:E. No. 144, Missa . . . Authore
Sonnleithner, Pro Choro Ducumbg," 12 parts,
lacking Timp, with performance dates 1758-80.

A-SEI: E.I.3d, "Missa in C Solemnis . . . Del Sig.
Sonnleithner," 12 parts, lacking Timp, with performance dates 1773-89; 2 Clni are ad lib.

*A-Wgm: I.1624, "Missa Sollemnis in C . . . Del
Signr: Christoph de Sonnleithner, Pr: 13 fl:
30 Xr:," 13 parts.

CS-Bm: A.42.383 (Barmherzige Brüder, Brno), "Sonleithner, Missa," 11 parts, including Va, lacking 2 Tbn
and Timp.

CS-LIT: Sign. 510 (Loreto Sammlung), "Missa in C
S. Mariae Assumptae," 9 parts, lacking 2 Tbn and
Timp; Vlone missing; dated 1766.

CS-Pnm: XXXVIII.A.74 (Broumov), "Missa . . . Sonnen-
leiter," 9 parts, lacking 2 Tbn, Timp, and Vlone.

REFERENCES:

A-GÖ cat., Riedel no. 598, "Missa Sti. Meinradi,"
12 parts, lacking Vlone, "comp[aravit] . . . 1760."

A-H cat., no. 144, lacking Timp.

A-KN cat., p. 28, "Sonleithner."

CS-VC cat., p. 10, "Missa Nro: 88, Sonnleitner."

A-SEI cat., "Sonleutner."

Pulkert, <u>Domus Lauretana Pragensis</u>, cat. no. 638.

M. 57 (cont'd.)

REMARKS:
  Missa longa, 759 m. in total.
  Tbn solos of "Gratias" and "Agnus Dei" also appear
    in 2 V (probably an "ad lib." alternative).
  See Ex. 6-13, 8-19, and 9-16E.

Christoph SONNLEITHNER   M. 58

Missa in F

(before 1769)

SATB   2 Tbn   2 V   Vlone   Org

COPIES:
  A-GÖ: "Missa," 9 parts, lacking Vlone.
  A-LA: M360, "Missa ex F," 10 parts.
  A-M: I,61, 10 parts.
  *A-Wgm: I.22295, "Missa in F . . . Del Sgre. Cristo-
          foro Sonnleithner," 10 parts.
  CS-Bm: A.13.929, ?
  CS-Bm: A.13.023 (Rajhrad), "Sonnenleuthner, Missa in
          F," 9 parts, lacking Vlone, dated 1769.
  CS-LIT: Sign. 512 (Loreto Sammlung), "Missa in F,"
          9 parts, lacking Vlone.
  CS-Pnm: XLVI.B.354 (Strahov), "Missa Nro: 1 in F ma-
          jore . . . Sonnleithner," 11 parts.
  CS-Pnm: XLVI.B.352 (Strahov), "Missa Nro: 1 in F ma-
          jore . . . Sonnleithner," 9 parts, lacking Vlone,
          Ms. (score?) of Gerlak Strniště.

REFERENCES:
  A-GÖ cat., Riedel no. 602, "Missa," lacking Vlone,
     "comp[aravit] . . . 1772."
  A-LA cat., p. 42, lacking 2 Tbn.
  CS-RAJ cat., "Nro: 67, Missa in F, Auth: Sonnenleüthner."
  A-KN cat., p. 22.
  Pulkert, Domus Lauretana Pragensis, cat. no. 639.

REMARKS:
  Missa longa, 893 m. in total.
  2 Tbn are obbligati in Agnus Dei.
  See Ex. 8-19 and 9-16B.

STRASSER

Missa in E

(before 1784)

SATB   2 V   Vlone   Org

COPIES:
    A-LA: M225, "Missa Ex E . . . Strasser," 8 parts,
    dated 1790 (in later hand).
    A-SEI: E,VI,1c, "Missa brevis in E . . . Strasser,"
    8 parts, with performing dates 1784-91.
  *A-Wn: Mus. Hs. 925, "Missa in E . . . Del Sign.
    N. Strasser," 10 parts, including 2 Hn in E (later
    additions), date at end of Org: 18 Sept. 1797.
    Provenance: Sammlung Gilg, 1908. Former owner's
    name: "Fügerl."

REFERENCE:
    A-LA cat., p. 52, "Strasser, No. 1," 8 parts.

REMARKS:
    Missa brevis, 429 m. in total.
    Text telescoping in Credo.
    3/4 meter throughout!
    See Ex. 9-16B.

Franz TUMA (d. 1774)   M. 60

Missa Tibi soli di Psalm 50

(before 1774)

SATB   2 Clni   2 Trombe   2 Tbn   Timp
2 V   Vlone   Org

AUTOGRAPH SCORE[?]:
  A-Wgm: I.1997, "Missa Tibi soli di Psalm 50 . . .
  Authore Francisco Tuma," 16 fol., Vlone and Org
  not specified.

COPY:
  A-Ws: "Nr. 6 Missa Tibi soli," 46 parts, including
  Bsn and Vc.

REFERENCES:
  Reichert, "Geschichte," Tuma no. 11.
  Herbert Vogg, "Franz Tuma (1704-1774) als Instrumentalkomponist" (unpublished Ph.D. dissertation, University of Vienna, 1951), cat. no. 13.
  Alfred Peschek, "Die Messen von Franz Tuma" (unpublished Ph.D. dissertation, University of Vienna,
  1956), cat. no. C12 ("in modernen Stil").

REMARKS:
  Missa longa, 720 m. in total.
  Many tempo markings are absent; probably written
  before 1750.
  See Ex. 6-19, 7-11, 8-12B, 8-19, and 10-5.

Franz TUMA   M. 61

Missa in chordis et organo

(before 1743)

SATB   2 Tbn   2 V   Vlone   Org

COPIES:
*A-GÖ: "Missa In Chordis et Organo . . . L: A: M:
   D: Gl: B: M: V: SS: A: SS: C: Authore D̄no Francisco Tuma, Descripsit R: P: Maurus P: Gött̄w:
   die 25. Sept. 1743," 9 parts, lacking Vlone;
   with 6 performance dates from 1 Nov. 1747 to
   31 Jan. 1790.
A-H: II,112, "Missa Dolorosa."
A-LA: M397, "Missa . . . Franc: Tuma," 10 parts
   each in two fascicles (Kyrie-Gloria and Credo-Agnus),
   including Vc instead of Vlone (Vc for Kyrie-Gloria
   is missing), performance date: 4 Nov. 1753.
A-Ws: "Nr. 2, Missa Sti. Thomae," 17 parts, including
   Bsn, 2 Trombe, and Vc. [Peschek, p. 204, indicates
   this copy is from the 1740's; dates are unreadable.]

REFERENCES:
A-GÖ cat., Riedel no. 619, 9 parts, without mention
   of Vlone, "descrips[it] . . . 25 Sept. 1743."
Reichert, "Geschichte," Tuma no. 27.
Vogg, "Tuma als Instrumentalkomponist," cat. no. 23.
Peschek, "Tuma," cat. no. C10 ("in modernen Stil").

REMARKS:
Missa longa, 882 m. in total.
The present author has prepared a score from the parts
   at A-GÖ.
See Ex. 6-19, 7-19, 8-12B, 8-19, 9-16B,
   Fig. 7-2 and 7-7.

Franz TUMA

Missa in G

1746

SATB (Bsn) (Cornetto) 2 Tbn
2 V   Vlone   Org

COPIES:
  A-H: III,a, "Missa Sti. Antonii," parts, performance
    dates from 8 Dec. 1761 to 19 Oct. 1780 [Peschek, p.
    231; Reichert, "Geschichte" indicates from "1751"].
  *A-Wn: Mus. Hs. 19009, "Missa . . . Del Sg: Francesco
    Tuma, M:D:C: di S: C: Mta: dell' Imple: Elisabetta
    Vedova, 1746," 27 parts, including Vc, MDC, and
    various duplicate parts of V I (2), V II (2), and
    SATB (2 each); unreadable performance dates from
    1746 until 5 April [?] 1750.

REFERENCES:
  A-H cat.
  Reichert, "Geschichte," Tuma no. 29.
  Vogg, "Tuma als Instrumentalkomponist," cat. no. 22.
  Peschek, "Tuma," cat. no. C15 ("in modernen Stil").

REMARKS:
  Missa brevis, 333 m. in total.
  "Credo" Mass type.
  S. Vernon Sanders, Jr. (University of Regina) has pre-
    pared a ms. score of this Mass from A-Wn parts.
  Cornetto, 2 Tbn, and Bsn are chiefly ripieno parts
    (i.e. = SATB).
  See Ex. 9-15B and 10-4B.

Franz TUMA   M. 63

Missa Sancti Stephani

(before 1747)

SATB   2 Tbn   2 V   Vlone   Org

COPIES:
  A-GÖ: "Missa Stae. Mariae Virginis," 8 parts,
    lacking Vlone; Org is missing.
  A-H: II,14, "Missa Experientiae," 10 parts.
  A-Wgm: I.21552, "Missa Scti. Stephani . . . Del
    Sigre. Francesco Tuma," 10 parts, with performance
    dates from 9 Jan. 1763 to 26 Mar. 1770.
  *A-Wn: Mus. Hs. 18992, "Missa Sti. Stephani a
    4 Voces, 2 Violini, 2 Tromboni et Organo," score,
    26 fol., Vlone not specified.
  A-WIL: parts, dated 1757 (according to Peschek, p. 152).

REFERENCES:
  A-GÖ cat., Riedel no. 621, 8 parts, lacking Vlone,
    "descrips[it] die 2 Octob[er] 1747."
  Reichert, "Geschichte," Tuma no. 56.
  Vogg, "Tuma als Instrumentalkomponist," cat. no. 46.
  Peschek, "Tuma," cat. no. C4 ("in modernen Stil").

REMARKS:
  Missa brevis, 333 m. in total.
  See Ex. 6-15 and 10-4C.

Jan VAŇHAL

M. 64

Missa in C

(before 1778)

SATB   2 Ob   2 Clni   Timp   2 V   Va   Vlone   Org

COPIES:

A-Feldkirch, Domarchiv (Vlbg.): II,86.

A-GÖ: "Missa solennis," 13 parts, lacking Va, with a Vc instead of a Vlone part.

A-H: Ms. 897.

A-SB: Ms. 1073.

*A-Wn: Mus. Hs. 22290, "Nro. 88/1, Missa in C . . . Del Signore Vanhall," 16 parts, including extra V I and V II. Provenance: Archiv Schminder, St. Pölten.

CS-Bm: A.392, 7 parts, missing 2 Ob, 2 Clni, Timp, V II, and Vlone.

CS-Bm: A.13.098, "Wannhal: Missa in C . . . 1851," 13 parts, lacking Vlone. Provenance: Rajhrad.

CS-KRm: C569 (Kroměříži, Mořice), "Wanhal: Missa in C Solenn," 14 parts, including 2 Va instead of only one Va, lacking Vlone.

CS-Pnm: XLVI.B.222 (Strahov), "Missa Nro: 1 in C majore . . . Joanne Wanhall," ms. score of Gerlak Strniště, lacking 2 Clni, Timp, and 2 Ob.

CS-Pnm: XLVI.B.223, "Missa Nro: 1," 9 parts, lacking 2 Ob, Timp, Va, and Vlone.

CS-Pnm: XLVI.B.224, "Missa Nro: 1," 12 parts, lacking Timp and Vlone.

D-BNms: Sammlung Klein 202,1, "2 Kyrie von Wanhall," score, 19 p., including two Kyrie's. The first Kyrie is by Vaňhal, including 2 Hn and Org. "transp." [in B-flat instead of C!], lacking 2 Clni and Timp; Vlone not specified. The second Kyrie uses the same

M. 64 (cont'd.)

Adagio opening, followed by a choral "Christe"
(Allegro 3/4 C maj.) and a Kyrie fugue (Allabreve
¢ C maj.). In the first Kyrie the Adagio (as well
as Allegro) returns for Kyrie II after the "Christe."
D-OB: MO 881, "Missa Solennis," 13 parts.

REFERENCES:
  A-GÖ cat., Riedel no. 645, lacking Va, "comp[aravit]
     . . . 1778."
  CS-RAJ cat., no. 356, "Wanhal," without mention of
     Vlone.
  A-KN cat, p. 2, Missa no. 14, "Vanhall."
  "   "   " , p. 18, Missa no. 120, "Wanhal."
  Joseph Haydn-Institut, Cologne, Stammkartei XXIII:
     in 1980 no. C26 in this catalogue indicated parts
     for this Mass under the name "Haydn" at Břevnov,
     I/770 (Miss. 111), "Sacrum solenne in C," now
     at CS-Pnm.
  Alexander Weinmann (Vienna), ms. thematic catalogue
     of Vaňhal (in progress), cat. no. C7. This catalogue
     also cites the following sources for this Mass:
     PL-Wu: Mf 1860 [?] and Guierno (Guesen), Archiv
     der Erzdiözese: AAG Muz.I.49.

REMARKS:
  Missa longa, 1,047 m.
  See Ex. 7-11 and Fig. 7-18.

Jan VAŇHAL   M. 65

Missa Pastorell in G

(before 1782)

SATB   2 Ob   2 Clni   Timp   2 V   Va   Vlone   Org

COPIES:
  *A-Wn: Mus. Hs. 926, "Missa pastorell in G . . . Del
    Sign. Giov. Wanhall," 14 parts, with former owner's
    name: "Flügerl."   Provenance: Sammlung Gilg of 1908.
  CS-Bm: A.3051, "Giov. Vanhal: Missa Pastoralis,"
    13 parts, including Vlone, missing Va obbligata.
    Provenance: Vyškov. Dates on parts: 7 Feb. 1782
    (Org) and 20 Feb. 1782 (Clno II).

REFERENCE:
  Alexander Weinmann, ms. thematic catalogue of Vaňhal
    (in progress 1980), cat. no. G4. This catalogue
    also cites the following sources for this Mass:
    A-W, Pfarrarchiv Rossau (Wien IX) and CS-P, SK,
    CSR-UK 59 R 1275 (including 2 Fl & 2 Hn, lacking
    2 Ob, 2 Clni & Timp) [?].

REMARKS:
  Missa longa, 1,120 m. in total.
  "Credo" type Mass.
  See Ex. 6-12, 8-9, 10-13, 10-16, and Fig. 5-3.

Jan VAŇHAL   M. 66

Missa solennis

(before 1797)

SATB 2 Fl 2 Hn 2 Clni (Timp?)
2 V Va (Vlone) Org

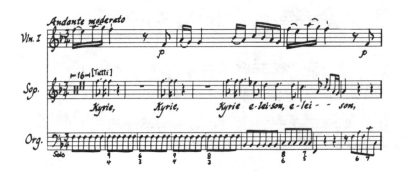

COPIES:
  CS-Bm: A.20.218, parts, with performance dates from
    16 May 1797 to 1812.
  CS-Pnm: XXXVIII.A.85 (Broumov), "Messa per la Solemni-
    tà . . . Auth: Wanhall," 12 parts, lacking 2 Clni,
    Timp, and Vlone.
 *D-B: Mus. ms. 22580, "MISSA SOLENNIS composta di Sign:
    Johann Vanhall in Vien[n]a," score, 56 fol., lacking
    Timp; "Fonda[mento]" not specified as Vlone and Org.
    Provenance: Ex Bibliotheca Poelchaviana, with old
    stamp: "Ex Biblioth. Regia Berolinensi."

REFERENCE:
  Alexander Weinmann, ms. thematic catalogue of Vaňhal
    (in progress 1980), cat. no. F3.

REMARKS:
  Missa longa, 944 m. in total.
  See Ex. 7-11, 8-3, 8-10, and 9-16C.

Georg Christoph WAGENSEIL   M. 67

Missa Sancti Antonii

1741

SATB   (Bsn)   (Cornetto)   2 Tbn   2 V   Vlone   Org

COPIES:
  A-Wn: Mus. Hs. 19041, "11. Giugno 1741 in Possonia,
    No: 1, Missa Sancti Antonii a 4 voci, 2 violini,
    e 2 Tromboni in Conc: Partes 32.   Del Sig: Wagen-
    seill, Comp: di Corte, 1741," 18 parts, including
    Vc and MDC as well as ripieni SATB.
  *D-Bds: Teschner Nachlass Nr. 196, "Messa a 4 con
    stromenti compoșta da Cristoforo Wagenseil, Nach der
    in der Autographen-Sammlung des Aloys Fuchs in Wien
    befindlichen Original-Partitur copirt. G. W. Tesch-
    ner,"   score, fol. 89-106ᵛ in a collection entitled
    "Musica sacra."   This 19th-century score lacks the
    Bsn and Cornetto;   it does not specify Vlone and
    Org for the continuo.

REFERENCE:
  Reichert, "Geschichte," Wagenseil no. 5.

REMARKS:
  Missa brevis, 390 m. in total.
  Cornetto, 2 Tbn, and Bsn are chiefly ripieno parts
    (i.e. = SATB);   the 2 Tbn are obbligati for the
    "Et incarnatus" and "Agnus Dei."
  See Ex. 6-16 and 8-12B.

Georg Christoph WAGENSEIL   M. 68

Missa brevis in A
("Gratias agimus tibi")

1742

SATB (Bsn) (Cornetto) (2 Tbn) 2 V Vlone Org

AUTOGRAPH SCORE:
    D-Bds:Mus. ms. Autogr. Wagenseil 8, "Missa brevis in
    A#, sub Nomine: 'Gratias agimus tibi' a quatuor
    Vocib: 2 Viol. 2 Tromb: et Organo, composita a
    D°: Christoph: Wagenseil, Comp. S. A. M. Imp.
    Austr: Natus 1688 [sic] + 1 Marzio 1777."
    Also on label, in another hand (Fuch's?):
    "Partitura Autographa." Atop first page of music:
    "Messa Nro. 4 Gratias agimus tibi, di Cristoffo[ro]
    Wag[enseil]." 21 fol.

COPIES:
    A-HE: VIII,a,6, "Missa Sti. Francisci Salesii,"
    parts, with penciled remark: "Artificiosa sed
    non ad auditum" [!].
    A-Wn: Mus. Hs. 16994, "Missa Gratias agimus tibi . . .
    Del Sigre: Wagenseil, Orgta: di S: M: Elisabetta
    Vedova, A[nn]o 1742," 18 parts, including Vc and
    MDC as well as ripieni SATB.
    A-WIL: No. 1119, "Missa . . . Auth: Sigre. Wagenseil,"
    8 parts, lacking Bsn, Cornetto, and 2 Tbn.

EDITION:
    Georg Christoph Wagenseil, Missa in A "Gratias agimus
    tibi, ed. Wolfgang Fürlinger, Süddeutsche Kirchenmusik
    des Barock, vol. 3 (Altötting: A. Coppenrath, 1973)
    38 p.

REFERENCES:
    Reichert, "Geschichte," Wagenseil no. 6.
    A-LA cat., p. 46, lacking Bsn, Cornetto.

M. 68 (cont'd.)

REMARKS:
  Missa brevis, 299 m. in total.
  S. Vernon Sanders, Jr. (University of Regina) has pre-
    pared a manuscript score from A-Wn parts.
  See above edition.

Georg Christoph WAGENSEIL   M. 69

Missa Transfige cor meum

(before 1742)

SATB   2 Va   Org

COPY:
  *A-GÖ: "Missa Transfige cor meum, a Canto, Alto,
    Tenore, Basso, Violetta, Trombon. 2bis con Organo,
    L: A: M: D: Gl: B: M: V: SS: A: SS: O: Authore
    Dno. Wagensaill, Comp: D: S: C: M: Imp: Elisabetta
    Crist: Vedova. Descripsit R:P: Maurus P: Gottw:
    die 29 Maÿ 1742," 7 parts; 2 Va are entitled "Vio-
    letta" and "Viola I" (= S & A) respectively;
    2 Tbn mentioned on title page are missing.

REFERENCES:
  A-GÖ cat., Riedel no. 647, without mention of 2 Tbn,
    "descr[ipsit] . . . 1742."
  Reichert, "Geschichte," Wagenseil no. 9.

REMARKS:
  Missa brevis, 555 m. in total.
  Unusual absence of 2 V from the accompaniment.
  No example.

Georg Christoph WAGENSEIL   M. 70

Missa solenne Immaculatae Conceptionis

1743

SATB (Bsn) 2 Clni 2 Trombe (Cornetto) 2 Tbn Timp
           2 V Vlone Org

AUTOGRAPH SCORE:
  *D-Bds: Mus. ms. Autogr. Wagenseil 7, "Missa solenne
     Immaculatae Conceptionis di Cristofforo Wagenseill,
     Comp: di S: R: M: la Regina d'Ongheria e Boemia, etc.
     L'Anno 1743, Mese d'ottobre," 39 fol., the Bsn,
     Cornetto, and Vlone are not expressly called for.

COPIES:
  A-GÖ: "Missa Ascensionis Domini," 12 parts, lacking
     Bsn, 2 Trombe, Cornetto, and Vlone, with performance
     dates beginning in 1764.
  A-KR: C,5,635, "Missa."
  A-Wn: Mus. Hs. 19042, "Missa Immaculatae Conceptionis
     a 4 Voci, 2 Clarini, 2 Violini, e 2 Tromboni in Conc:
     . . . Del Sig: Wagenseil Comp: di S: M: 1743,"
     23 parts in each of two fascicles (Kyrie-Gloria and
     Credo-Agnus), including Vc and MDC as well as ripieno
     SATB parts; only performance date: 15 Oct. 1743.

REFERENCES:
  A-GÖ cat., Riedel no. 648, without mention of Bsn,
     2 Trombe, Cornetto, and Vlone; "comp[aravit] R:P:
     Josephus prod: 1764."
  Reichert, "Geschichte," Wagenseil no. 3.

REMARKS:
  Missa brevis, 454 m. in total.
  See Ex. 6-17 and 10-14.

Joseph ZIEGLER

M. 71

Missa in C

(before 1762)

SATB 2 Clni Timp 2 V Vlone Org

COPIES:
  *A-GÖ: "Missa . . . Authore Sigre. Josepho Ziegler,"
    11 parts, "Violone" later changed to read "Violon-
    cello," 19 performances from 19 Jan. 1764 until 1810.
  A-H: Ms. 139.
  A-KN: No. 133 [161].
  A-KR: B,40,586.
  A-LA: M241, 10 parts, lacking Timp.
  A-TU: Schnürl no. 409, [anonymous], 15 parts, includ-
    ing 2 Ob and 2 Tbn.

REFERENCES:
  A-GÖ cat., Riedel no. 740, without mention of Vlone,
    "comp[aravit] . . . 1762."
  A-LA cat., p. 50, without mention of Timp.
  CS-VC cat., p. 8, Missa "No: 68" by "Strasser."
  A-KN cat., p. 22, Missa no. 133.
  Karl Pfannhauser, "Joseph Ziegler," MGG XIV (1968) col.
    1270.
  Schnürl, cat. no. 409.

REMARKS:
  Missa longa, 862 m. in total.
  See Ex. 6-18, 7-13, and 7-16.

Joseph ZIEGLER   M. 72

Missa in D

(before 1770)

SATB   2 Ob   2 Clni   Timp   2 V   Vlone   Org

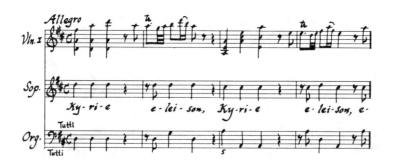

COPIES:
  A-GÖ: "Missa," 12 parts, lacking Vlone, including
    extra S and A parts; with approximately 12 per-
    formance dates from 1 Mar. 1770 until 1806.
  *A-Wp: No. 128, [original cover is missing], 15 parts,
    including extra V I and V II.
  CS-Bm: A.21.687 (Petrov, Brno), "Ziegler," all parts
    except the Org are missing.
  CS-Bm: A.13.164 (Rajhrad), "Ziegler: Missa in D,"
    13 parts.
  A-KR: B,40,583 [?].

REFERENCES:
  A-GÖ cat., Riedel no. 742, without mention of Vlone,
    "comp[aravit] . . . 1770."
  CS-RAJ cat., p. 22, "Nro. 128, Missa in D . . . Ziegler,"
    without mention of Timp, Vlone, and Org.
  Karl Pfannhauser, "Joseph Ziegler," MGG XIV (1968)
    col. 1270.
  Otto Biba (Vienna) is custodian of the music archive
    at A-Wp and kindly allowed photocopies to be made
    of the parts.

REMARKS:
  Missa longa, 690 m. in total.
  See Ex. 9-16A.

Notes

Preface

1. For a description of this seminar see Bruce C. Mac Intyre, "Report from C.U.N.Y.: An Unusual Haydn Seminar," *Current Musicology* 20 (1975): 42–49.

Introduction

1. Guido Adler, "Zur Geschichte der Wiener Messenkomposition in der zweiten Hälfte des XVII. Jahrhunderts," *Studien zur Musikwissenschaft* IV (1916): 9.

2. Alfred Schnerich, *Messe und Requiem seit Haydn und Mozart* (Vienna and Leipzig: C.W. Stern, 1909); Adler, "Geschichte," pp. 5–45.

3. See the bibliography for the contributions by the following authors: Heinrich Freunschlag (1927; on Predieri), P. Norbert Hofer (1915; Reutter), Franz Kosch (1924; Gassmann), Alfred Peschek (1956; Tuma), Roland Philipp (1938; Monn and Wagenseil), Hermine Prohászka (1956; Hofmann), Alfred Schienerl (1925; Bonno), Karl Schnürl (1965; Krottendorfer), Ernst Tittel (1961; Austrian church music), and Herbert Vogg (1951; Tuma).

4. Georg Reichert, "Zur Geschichte der Wiener Messenkomposition in der ersten Hälfte des 18. Jahrhunderts" (Ph.D. diss., Vienna, 1935).

5. For the 72 selected Masses (M. 1–72) see the thematic catalogue in appendix C. On how the composers and Masses were selected, see the latter part of this introduction.

6. However, certain sections were lacking in two of the selected Masses by Reutter: M. 46 (no Credo) and M. 48 (no Sanctus and Agnus Dei); app. C shows other sources which do have these missing sections.

7. This figure is the latest count based upon the author's ongoing research of locating and cataloguing all the Masses by these 28 composers.

8. As the thematic catalogue (app. C) shows, for most of the selected Masses we know only *tempi ante quem* which are usually based upon extant performance dates. Contemporary newspapers, diaries, and other documents are usually not specific enough to help with dating.

   None of the present Masses was published during the lifetime of their composers. The few Masses that were published (e.g., by Lotter in Augsburg) were simple, functional settings (usually without soloists), i.e., ones which could be performed almost anywhere.

It seems that Masses were slowly disseminated in one of four ways: (1) local composers wrote Masses specifically for their own institutions; (2) local copyists prepared performance materials from a Mass borrowed from another institution; (3) choir directors brought new repertoire with them when they moved to a new institution; or (4) an institution would order professionally copied materials from a nearby large city, e.g., Vienna.

On conflicting attributions in Haydn, see my article "Haydn's Doubtful and Spurious Masses: An Attribution Update," *Haydn-Studien* V/1 (1982): 42–54. See also John Spitzer, "Authorship and Attribution in Western Art Music" (Ph.D. diss., Cornell University, 1983), especially chapter 4.

9. Kilian Reinhardt, "Rubriche Generali per le Funzioni Ecclesiastiche Musicali di tutto l'Anno,..." autograph manuscript, Mus. Hs. 2503 in the Austrian National Library; see chapter 2, n. 67. The above description of categories is based upon Friedrich Wilhelm Riedel, *Kirchenmusik am Hofe Karls VI. (1711–1740)* (Munich and Salzburg: E. Katzbichler, 1977), p. 68, see also p. 146f.

10. See Barry S. Brook, *Thematic Catalogues in Music* (Hillsdale, N.Y.: Pendragon, 1972), no. 582, pp. 117–18.

11. Ibid., no. 1409, p. 297. According to Karl Pfannhauser, "Mozart's kirchenmusikalische Studien im Spiegel seiner Zeit und Nachwelt," *Kirchenmusikalisches Jahrbuch* 43 (1959): 168, n. 62, this catalogue was used by Salieri (because of his autograph remark "All' Archivio" on the front cover).

12. "Inventarium der Instrumenten und Musicalien des Kirchenmusikchors der barmherzigen Brüder zu den heiligen Aposteln Simonen et Judam in Prag an[nno]: 1829," now located at CS-Bm (film copy at the Joseph Haydn-Institut, Cologne). "Inventarium" der barmherzigen Brüder in Feldberg (Valtice), n.d., also at CS-Bm (copy at the Haydn-Institut).

13. Brook, *Thematic Catalogues in Music,* no. 1417, pp. 300–301.

14. Johann Gottfried Walther, *Musicalisches Lexicon oder musicalische Bibliothec* (Leipzig: Wolfgang Deer, 1732), pp. 401–2.

15. Reichert, "Geschichte," pp. 4–5; these types are also listed in Adler, "Geschichte," p. 44. Among the Masses by the composers discussed in later chapters, we find titles such as *Missa Sancti Leopoldi* (M. 5), *Missa Primitiarum* (M. 51), *Missa Lauretana* (M. 45), *Missa Pastoralis* (M. 20), *Missa Nativitatis* (M. 42), *Missa Beatus vir* (M. 38), *Missa Tibi soli* (M. 60, from Psalm 50), *Missa solennis* (M. 14, 66), *Missa solemnis* (M. 39, 57), *Missa solenne Immaculatae Conceptionis* (M. 70), *Missa brevis* (M. 68), and *Missa in Chordis et organo* (M. 61).

16. This list was culled from the various titles for manuscripts appearing in my comprehensive thematic catalogue in progress. The titles appear in no special order, although an attempt was made to show the progression from ordinary Sundays to special feasts.

17. H.C. Robbins Landon, *Haydn: Chronicle and Works,* 5 vols. (Bloomington: Indiana University Press, 1980) I, pp. 90–91.

18. Friedrich Wilhelm Riedel, "Liturgie und Kirchenmusik," in *Joseph Haydn in seiner Zeit,* edited by Gerda Mraz, Gottfried Mraz, and Gerald Schlag (Eisenstadt: Kulturabteilung des Amtes der Burgenländischen Landesregierung, 1982), p. 132, prefers to call such an extended Mass a *Missa longa solemnitatis.* Gassmann's *St. Cecilia Mass* (M. 19) is another example of this type.

19. Walter Senn, "Messe, Von 1600 bis zur Gegenwart," in *MGG* IX (1961) col. 184–85, 201.

20. Wolfgang Amadeus Mozart, *Neue Ausgabe sämtlicher Werke,* Ser. I/1, Abt. 1, vol. 2: *Messen,* ed. Walter Senn (Kassel: Bärenreiter, 1975), vii.

21. Ibid., pp. viii–ix. This type is also described in Walter Senn, "Mozart's Kirchenmusik und die Literatur," *Mozart Jahrbuch 1978/79*: 17. Haydn's *Nicolaimesse* (1772), mentioned above is also a mixture of the *missa brevis* and *missa solemnis.* See description by Cornell Jesse Runestad, "The Masses of Joseph Haydn: A Stylistic Study" (D.M.A. diss., University of Illinois at Urbana-Champaign, 1970), pp. 111, 133. Further study may show the origin of this mixed type to be in the *missae mediocres* often written by J.J. Fux; see Riedel, *Karl VI,* pp. 146, 148.

22. For example: Reichert, "Geschichte," pp. 2–3; Hermann Abert, *W.A. Mozart,* 7th ed. (Leipzig: Breitkopf & Härtel, 1955), p. 251; Elwyn A. Wienandt, *Choral Music of the Church* (New York: Free Press, 1965; Da Capo reprint, 1980), pp. 210–12; Runestad, "The Masses of Joseph Haydn," p. 108; Hubert Unverricht, "Die orchesterbegleitete Kirchenmusik von den Neapolitanern bis Schubert," in *Geschichte der katholischen Kirchenmusik,* 2 vols., ed. Karl Gustav Fellerer (Kassel: Bärenreiter, 1976) II, p. 162; James Frederick Dack, "The Origins and Development of the Esterházy Kapelle in Eisenstadt until 1790" (Ph.D. diss., University of Liverpool, 1976), pp. 97–98.

23. Dack, "Esterházy Kapelle," p. 113.

24. Ibid., p. 150.

25. Senn, "Mozart's Kirchenmusik," p. 15.

26. For example, the liturgical term *Missa solemnis* (High or solemn Mass) where most of the texts are sung is the opposite of the *Missa lecta* (Low Mass) where everything is recited; *missa brevis* plays no role here. See *New Grove,* XI, 769 and XII, 364; also Willi Apel, *Harvard Dictionary of Music,* 2nd ed. (Cambridge: Harvard University Press, 1969), p. 533.

27. For example, Haydn's *St. Cecilia Mass* (Hob. XXII: 5) of 1766 was originally the "Missa Cellensis in honorem Beatissimae Virginis Mariae"; a later copy in the Austrian National Library names the work *Missa in C St. Ceciliä* (Mus. Hs. 15810), while a copy (now destroyed) at Darmstadt called it simply *Missa in C,* and in the Breitkopf & Härtel edition (1807) it is entitled *Messe à 4 voix* (see Brand's edition of the Mass, pp. 365–66, and Landon, *Haydn: Chronicle and Works* I, pp. 228ff).

28. The author's thematic catalogue of all known Masses by these and other composers is a continuing project that may eventually be published separately. Anyone wishing to consult these catalogues or the thematic locator prepared from them is encouraged to contact the author.

29. Because the collection of St. Stephen's Cathedral was destroyed during World War II, and because several of Vienna's important church archives remain uncatalogued or inaccessible (e.g., St. Michael's and the Schottenkirche), many of today's extant sources for these Masses are found only in monasteries and archives outside Vienna.

30. Oliver Strunk in the discussion of H.C. Robbins Landon's paper, "Problems of Authenticity in Eighteenth-Century Music," in *Instrumental Music: A Conference at Isham Memorial Library, Harvard University, May 4, 1957,* ed. David G. Hughes (Cambridge: Harvard University Press, 1959; reprint ed., New York: Da Capo, 1972), pp. 55–56.

Chapter 1

1. Floridus Röhrig, "Das religiöse Leben Wiens zwischen Barock und Aufklärung," in *Joseph Haydn in seiner Zeit,* ed. Gerda Mraz, Gottfried Mraz, and Gerald Schlag (Eisenstadt: Kulturabteilung des Amtes der Burgenländischen Landesregierung, 1982), pp. 114, 116. See Friedrich Wilhelm Riedel, "Liturgie und Kirchenmusik," in this same exhibition catalogue, pp. 121–22. The *Hof,* in fact, participated in a large number of religious services, processions, and pilgrimages. Thus upper and lower classes often worshiped together, and, as Röhrig points out (p. 114): "Solange man wusste dass der Kaiser und die Kaiserin mit dem Herzen dabei waren, waren's die Wiener auch."

2. Röhrig, "Das religiöse Leben Wiens," pp. 114, 122. The busy liturgical calendar for the court as reported by Kilian Reinhardt in 1727 is printed in abridged form in Ludwig Ritter von Köchel, *Die kaiserliche Hof-Musikkapelle in Wien von 1543 bis 1867* (Vienna: Beck and A. Hölder, 1869; reprint ed., Hildesheim: G. Olms, 1976), pp. 135–44.

3. Charles Burney, *Dr. Burney's Musical Tours in Europe,* ed. Scholes, 2 vols. (London: Oxford University Press, 1959), II, p. 78.

4. Friedrich Christoph Nicolai, *Beschreibung einer Reise durch Deutschland und die Schweiz, im Jahre 1781,* 4 vols. (Berlin and Stettin: n.p., 1784) IV, p. 544 (=10. Abschnitt: "Von der Musik in Wien").

5. Otto Biba, "Die Wiener Kirchenmusik um 1783," *Jahrbuch für österreichische Kulturgeschichte* vol. I, pt. 2 (Eisenstadt: Institut für österreichische Kulturgeschichte, 1971), pp. 24–51, reproduces the musical personnel of some 46 Viennese churches as enumerated in a detailed "Verzeichnis" dated 4 December 1783.

6. Hermine Prohászka, "Leopold Hofmann und seine Messen," *Studien zur Musikwissenschaft* XXVI (1964), p. 80.

7. Burney, *Musical Tours,* ed. Scholes, II, pp. 105, 122.

8. Nicolai, *Beschreibung* 1781, IV, p. 548. Friedrich Wilhelm Riedel, *Kirchenmusik am Hofe Karls VI.* (Munich and Salzburg: Emil Katzbichler, 1977), pp. 38–39, notes how Masses connected with processions were often held in the Augustinerkirche during the reign of Charles VI. Röhrig, "Das religiöse Leben Wiens," p. 114, has written: "Processions not only correspond to a primitive instinct (Urtrieb) of mankind—one need only regard how eagerly children make processions!—but also they belong to one of the oldest customs of Christianity. Pilgrimages and processions were felt as the symbol of the worldly pilgrimage and accordingly promoted." Röhrig also remarks how these special events provided the people of that era with time for "vacation" and relaxation from work.

9. Processions of penitence (*Bussprozessionen*) with musicians are found in several Viennese engravings by Salomon Kleiner; see, for example, his "Prospect des Hoch-Gräffl. Traunischen Gebäudes in der Herrengassen...," plate 25 in *Wahrhaffte Abbildung,* Historisches Museum der Stadt Wien, Vienna, Austria; reproduced in catalogue *Wien zur Zeit Joseph Haydns: 78. Sonderausstellung des Historischen Museums der Stadt Wien* (Vienna: Museen der Stadt Wien, 1982), pp. 25–26 (catalogue no. 7).

10. Riedel, "Liturgie and Kirchenmusik," p. 122.

11. See Landon, *Haydn: Chronicle and Works* II, p. 121.

12. Richard Kralik, *Geschichte der Stadt Wien und ihrer Kultur*, 2nd edition (Vienna: A. Holzhausen, 1926), p. 277. After a military victory at Görlitz during the Seven Years War, the Emperor and Empress made a pilgrimage to Mariazell for a "Jubiläifest" (Kralik, p. 289).

13. Röhrig, "Das religiöse Leben Wiens," p. 117.

14. Eduard Hanslick, *Geschichte des Concertwesens in Wien* (Vienna: W. Braumüller, 1869–70), p. 11, n. 1. Central brotherhoods were called *Erzbruderschaften.* Hanslick also quotes Geisau, *Geschichte der Haupt-und-Residenzstadt Wien* (1792–93) vol. 4, p. 511, as reporting some 110 *Bruderschaften* in Vienna.

15. Otto Biba, "Die Wiener Kirchenmusik um 1783," in *Beiträge zur Musikgeschichte des 18. Jahrhunderts,* ed. by Gerda Mraz, *Jahrbuch für österreichische Kulturgeschichte* (Eisenstadt: Institut für österreichische Kulturgeschichte, 1971), I, 2, p. 17 and passim, shows how much *Bruderschaft* support for church music was lost when brotherhoods were abolished in 1783.

16. Eduard Hanslick, *Geschichte des Concertwesens in Wien* (Vienna: W. Braumüller, 1869–70), p. 12.

17. Elaine Raftery Walter, "Selected Masses of Antonio Caldara (1670–1736)" (Ph.D. diss., Catholic University of America, Washington, D.C., 1973), p. 58. She notes that Caldara (as Deacon) and Fux were both members of this brotherhood; see Tittel, *Österreichische Kirchenmusik: Werden, Wachsen, Wirken* (Vienna: Herder, 1961), pp. 147–48.

18. Hanslick, *Geschichte des Concertwesens in Wien,* p. 12.

19. J. Ogesser, *Beschreibung der Metropolitan-Kirche zu St. Stephan in Wien* (Vienna: Von Ghelenschen Erben, 1779), p. 293, as cited by Hanslick, *Geschichte des Concertwesens in Wien,* p. 12, n. 2.

20. Constantin Schneider, "Die Kirchenmusik im St. Stephansdom zu Wien," *Musica Divina* 21 (1933):76; Franz Kosch, "Florian Leopold Gassmann als Kirchenkomponist," *Studien zur Musikwissenschaft* XIV (1927):220.

21. H.C. Robbins Landon, *Haydn: Chronicle and Works* (Bloomington: Indiana University Press, 1976–80), II, pp. 229–30 (Landon's translation). Leopold Mozart was apparently so impressed with the activities for 22 November that he hurriedly wrote his Salzburg landlord, Lorenz Hagenauer, on 24 November 1762: "A description of St. Cecilia's Festival I shall postpone until we meet." (Anderson, ed., *Letters of Mozart* no. 7, I, p. 12).

22. Karl Maria Brand, *Die Messen von Joseph Haydn* (Würzburg-Aumühle: K. Triltsch, 1941), p. 61.

23. Tittel, *Österreichische Kirchenmusik,* p. 147.

24. Vienna had two principal Jesuit churches: *Jesuitenkirche am Hof* and *Universitätskirche,* also known as the "obere und untere Jesuitenkirchen," respectively. Burney, *Musical Tours,* ed. Scholes, II, p. 78, believed that Austria's musicality was in part the result of the Jesuit music school in every Roman Catholic town.

25. These Jesuit connections are described in several of Leopold's letters to his wife. See Anderson, ed., *Letters of Mozart* nos. 64, 67, 68, and 178 (13 September 1768, 12 November 1768, 12 December 1768, and 12 August 1773) I, pp. 92, 94, 236.

26. This list is derived from a description of eighteenth-century Austrian practices in Riedel, "Liturgie und Kirchenmusik," pp. 126–31. See Hermann Beck, "Die Musik des liturgischen Gottesdienstes im 18. Jahrhundert," in *Geschichte der katholischen Kirchenmusik*, ed. Karl Gustav Fellerer (Kassel: Bärenreiter, 1976) II, p. 189.

27. Ibid., p. 129. Riedel notes that since the middle of the eighteenth century the dimensions of Gradual music had grown to such an extent that symphonies by Haydn, Dittersdorf, Wagenseil, and other contemporaries were regularly played at this point in the Mass. At the International Haydn Congress in Vienna (10 September 1982) Otto Biba, in his paper on "Nicht-vokalische Kirchenmusik," reported that only *single* movements of symphonies tended to be used as church music. For more on church symphonies see Neal Zaslaw, "Mozart, Haydn, and the *Sinfonia da chiesa*," *Journal of Musicology* I/1 (1982):95–124.

28. Anderson, ed., *Letters of Mozart* no. 67, I, p. 94.

29. Burney, *Musical Tours*, ed. Scholes, II, p. 111.

30. Otto Ursprung, *Die katholische Kirchenmusik* (Potsdam: Akademische Verlagsgesellschaft Athenaion, 1931), p. 219.

31. Biba, "Kirchenmusik 1783," pp. 25, 38–41. A slightly different example would be Tobias Gsur (ca. 1725–94) who in 1783 was a bass for the Hofmusikkapelle while at the same time acting as *regens chori* at the Schottenkirche. Numerous other examples could be cited; see salary discussions below.

32. Ibid. Offers precise information about the musical hiring practices of some 46 Viennese churches; some 286 different names are listed as paid musicians—that is an average of about six musicians per institution.

33. The Michaelerkirche (St. Michael's) and the Schottenkirche were among Vienna's oldest *Stadtpfarrkirchen* (city parish churches) according to Riedel, *Karl VI*, p. 113. The Augustinerkirche (St. Augustine's) and the Jesuitenkirche am Hof were among the churches that became *Pfarrkirchen* in 1783 (Biba, "Kirchenmusik 1783," pp. 25, 26, 57).

    An excellent portrait of musical life at one of these *Klosterkirchen* is Otto Biba's "Der Piaristenorden in Österreich: Seine Bedeutung für bildende Kunst, Musik und Theater im 17. und 18. Jahrhundert," in *Jahrbuch für österreichische Kulturgeschichte*, V (Eisenstadt: Institut für österreichische Kulturgeschichte, 1975). Biba notes that the Piarists hired lay musicians and lay substitute organists at their churches, including their Vienna church, Maria Treu (pp. 111, 113, 120–21).

    The Hofburg (imperial palace) had several private chapels, the principal one being the famous Hofburgkapelle (a structure whose western walls date back to the thirteenth century), and which is the home of today's Vienna Choir Boys. The Hofmusikkapelle was administered by the *Hofkapellmeister* and his assistants. For large services that included processions, the nearby Augustinerkirche was used (Riedel, *Karl VI*, pp. 38–39).

    Except for the Esterházys, little research has been done on the private chapels of other members of the nobility. We do know from Griesinger, for example, that Joseph Haydn played organ for the chapel of Friedrich Wilhelm, Count Haugwitz, soon after the young composer had been dismissed from St. Stephen's (Landon, *Haydn: Chronicle and Works*, I, p. 62).

34. Karl Ditters von Dittersdorf, *Lebensbeschreibung*, ed. Bruno Loets and Norbert Miller (original ed., Leipzig, 1808; modern ed., Munich: Kösel, 1967), pp. 18–19; English edition: *The Autobiography of Karl von Dittersdorf*, trans. A.D. Coleridge (London: R. Bentley and Sons, 1896; reprint ed., New York: Da Capo, 1970), pp. 3–4.

35. Otto Biba, "Der Sozial-Status des Musikers," in *Joseph Haydn in seiner Zeit,* ed. Gerda Mraz, Gottfried Mraz, and Gerald Schlag (Eisenstadt: Kulturabteilung des Amtes der Burgenländischen Landesregierung, 1982), p. 107.

36. Ibid. Even Mozart had to take on pupils to supplement his income upon arriving in Vienna in 1781. Fortunately there seemed to have been an unlimited supply of pupils seeking teachers at that time. See Mozart's letter to his father in Anderson, ed., *Letters of Mozart* no. 406 (26 May 1781) II, p. 736.

37. Georg August Griesinger, *Biographische Notizen über Joseph Haydn,* ed. Franz Grasberger (Vienna: P. Kaltschmid, 1954), p. 61. Landon, *Haydn: Chronicle and Works,* IV, p. 157, reports that publishers paid composers poorly for their church music.

38. Alfred Einstein, *Mozart: His Character, His Work,* trans. Arthur Mendel and Nathan Broder (New York: Oxford University Press, 1945), p. 58.

39. Alfred Francis Pribram, ed., *Materialen zur Geschichte der Preise und Löhne in Österreich* (Vienna: Carl Ueberreuter, 1938). Its many detailed charts, graphs, and lists of costs and salaries are valuable aids when used appropriately. A useful English summary of late eighteenth-century prices in Vienna is found in: Mary Sue Morrow, "Concert Life in Vienna, 1780–1810" (Ph.D. diss., Indiana University, 1984), pp. 111–19. See also Alice M. Hanson, "Incomes and Outgoings in the Vienna of Beethoven and Schubert," *Music and Letters* 64 (1983):173–82.

40. Roman Sandgruber, "Wirtschaftsentwicklung, Einkommensverteilung und Alltagsleben zur Zeit Haydns," in *Joseph Haydn in seiner Zeit,* ed. Gerda Mraz, Gottfried Mraz, and Gerald Schlag (Eisenstadt: Kulturabteilung des Amtes der Burgenländischen Landesregierung, 1982), p. 82.

41. Ibid., pp. 78–79, 81. Contemporary reports also show that the upper classes naturally had higher income expectations. According to Sandgruber, one needed at least 20,000 fl a year to be respectable: "Whoever did not spend at least 20,000 fl a year did not make an impression in Vienna; that is, he lived comfortably but was not noticed, so wrote Johann Pezzl in his 1803 *Skizze von Wien.*" The incomes of princes (100,000–500,000 fl per year) and counts (20,000–80,000 fl per year) were even more impressive (p. 78).

42. Landon, *Haydn: Chronicle and Works,* I, pp. 235–36.

43. Christoph-Hellmut Mahling, "Orchester, Orchesterpraxis und Orchestermusiker zur Zeit des jungen Haydn (1740-1770)," in *Der junge Haydn,* ed. Vera Schwarz (Graz: Akademische Druck- und Verlagsanstalt, 1972), p. 109.

44. Sandgruber, "Wirtschaftsentwicklung," p. 80.

45. Biba, "Sozial-Status," p. 108. Biba rightly complains about such generalization without regard for what archival material can reveal.

46. Anderson, ed., *Letters of Mozart* no. 398, II, p. 723. In the "decoded" German original published in Ludwig Schiedermair, ed., *Die Briefe Mozarts und seiner Familie,* 5 vols. (Munich: Georg Müller, 1914) no. 68, II, p. 58, the amount reads "lausige 4 hundert gulden."

47. Anderson, ed., *Letters of Mozart* no. 405, II, p. 735.

48. Ibid., no. 409, II, p. 641.

49. Ibid., no. 442 (23 January 1782) II, p. 795. Readers are reminded that 60 kreuzer (kr or X) equaled one gulden (fl).

50. Burney, *Musical Tours*, ed., Scholes, II, p. 124.

51. Landon, *Haydn: Chronicle and Works*, I, pp. 236–37. Landon's information here and below is drawn from advertisements in a 1759 issue of the *Wiener Diarium*. Paper costs are from Pribram, *Materialen zur Geschichte der Preise und Löhne in Österreich*, pp. 335, 505–6, 542.

52. Sandgruber, "Wirtschaftsentwicklung," p. 82.

53. "Index of All Music Personnel, Together with Their Past and Present Paid Salary." Ordered 21 June 1783 and completed 4 December that year, the text of this historically valuable document has been printed in Biba, "Kirchenmusik 1783," pp. 24–51. The salary ranges cited here and below have been extracted from that source; court salaries are from other sources cited below.

54. Köchel, *Die kaiserliche Hof-Musikkapelle* (Vienna: Beck'sche Universitätsbuchhandlung and A. Hölder, 1869; reprint ed., Hildesheim: G. Olms, 1976), p. 72; Egon Wellesz, "Giuseppe Bonno (1710–88): Sein Leben und seine dramatischen Werke," *Sammelbände der internationalen Musikgesellschaft* XI (1909–10), p. 403; Ludwig Stollbrock, "Leben und Wirken des k. k. Hofkapellmeisters und Hofkompositors Johann Georg Reuter jun.," *Vierteljahrschrift für Musikwissenschaft* VIII (1892), p. 180.

55. Landon, *Haydn: Chronicle and Works*, II, p. 201.

56. Köchel, *Die kaiserliche Hof-Musikkapelle*, p. 82; also Stollbrock, "Reuter," p. 184.

57. Ibid. For example, *Hoforganist* Wenzel Birck (1718–63) was receiving an annual salary of 500 fl in 1751. The present writer has not located salary information for St. Stephen's Cathedral, an institution which undoubtedly also paid handsomely.

58. For example, the castrati Domenico Genuesi and Angelo Monticelli were each being paid 2,000 fl annually for singing soprano at the *Hofmusikkapelle* (Köchel, *Hofmusikkapelle*, p. 82).

59. Johann Ferdinand von Schönfeld, *Jahrbuch der Tonkunst von Wien und Prag* (Vienna, Prague: Schönfeld, 1796; reprint ed., ed. Otto Biba, Munich-Salzburg: E. Katzbichler, 1976), p. 97.

60. Burney, *Musical Tours*, ed. Scholes, II, p. 78.

61. Riedel, "Liturgie," pp. 122, 132.

Chapter 2

1. Ludwig Ritter von Köchel, *Die kaiserliche Hof-Musikkapelle in Wien von 1543 bis 1867 nach urkundlichen Forschungen* (Vienna: Beck'sche Universitätsbuchhandlung and A. Hölder, 1869; reprint ed., Hildesheim: G. Olms, 1976), p. 12; Carl Ferdinand Pohl, *Joseph Haydn*, 2 vols. (Leipzig: Breitkopf & Härtel, 1878–82) I, p. 80ff.; Otto Ursprung, *Die katholische Kirchenmusik*, vol. 10 of *Handbuch der Musikwissenschaft*, ed. Ernst Bücken (Wildpark-Potsdam: Akademische Verlagsgesellschaft Athenaion, 1931), p. 241; Tittel, *Österreichische Kirchenmusik: Werden, Wachsen, Wirken* (Vienna: Herder, 1961), p. 173.

2. Charles Burney, *Dr. Burney's Musical Tours in Europe*, ed. Percy A. Scholes (London: Oxford University Press, 1959) II, p. 75; see also pp. 110–11 where Burney describes it as "the hateful sour organ."

3. Ibid., II, p. 114.

4. Emily Anderson, ed. and trans., *Letters of Mozart*, 2nd edition (London: Macmillan; New York: St. Martin's Press, 1966) no. 178, I, p. 236.

5. Burney, *Musical Tours*, ed. Scholes, II, p. 94. Joseph Wöger, Burney's Wegerer, was organist at St. Michael's in 1772 and died in 1778 at the age of 47; Robert Haas, *Wiener Musiker vor und um Beethoven* (Vienna, Prague, and Leipzig: E. Strache, 1927), p. 12.

6. Anderson, ed., *Letters of Mozart* no. 444, II, p. 797.

7. Friedrich Christoph Nicolai, *Beschreibung einer Reise durch Deutschland und die Schweiz im Jahre 1781* (Berlin and Stettin, n.p., 1784), p. 544.

8. Burney, *Musical Tours*, ed. Scholes, II, p. 75.

9. More details about Vienna's churches are found in: Derrjac, *Die Wiener Kirchen des 17. und 18. Jahrhunderts* (n.p., 1906); Alfred Schnerich, *Wiener Kirchen und Kapellen* (Vienna: Almathea, 1921); Friedrich Wilhelm Riedel, *Kirchenmusik am Hofe Karls VI. (1711–1740)* (Munich and Salzburg: Emil Katzbichler, 1977), especially pp. 24–56, 310–11.

10. Nicolai, *Beschreibung 1781*, p. 544.

11. Charles Burney, *A General History of Music*, 2 vols., ed. Frank Mercer (London: G.T. Foulis & Co. Ltd., 1935) II, p. 950.

12. Hermann Beck, "Die Musik des liturgischen Gottesdienstes im 18. Jahrhundert (Messe, Offizium)," in *Geschichte der katholischen Kirchenmusik*, ed. Karl Gustav Fellerer (Kassel: Bärenreiter, 1976) II, p. 181.

13. Otto Biba, "Der Sozial-Status des Musikers," in *Joseph Haydn in seiner Zeit*, ed. Gerda Mraz, Gottfried Mraz, and Gerald Schlag (Eisenstadt: Kulturabteilung des Amtes der Burgenländischen Landesregierung, 1982), p. 109.

14. Ibid., p. 105.

15. Milan Poštalka, "Vaňhal, Johann Baptist," *The New Grove Dictionary of Music and Musicians*, 6th ed., ed. Stanley Sadie (London: Macmillan, 1980) XIX, p. 522.

16. Friedrich Wilhelm Riedel, "Beiträge zur Geschichte der Musikpflege an der Stadtpfarrkirche St. Veit zu Krems," in *Festschrift 950 Jahre Pfarrei Krems* (Krems, 1964), p. 303ff.; Renate Federhofer-Königs, "Zur Musikpflege in der Wallfahrtskirche von Mariazell/Steiermark," *Kirchenmusikalisches Jahrbuch* 41 (1957), pp. 120–21.

17. Further research is needed for verifying such a distinction between *regens chori* and Kapellmeister. We need to know if the designation Meister (master) still implied the training and rank it had under the age-old guild system.

18. Otto Biba, "Die Wiener Kirchenmusik um 1783," in *Beiträge zur Musikgeschichte des 18. Jahrhunderts*, ed. Gerda Mraz (Eisenstadt: Institut für österreichische Kulturgeschichte, 1971), pp. 24–55; cf. chapter 1, n. 53 above. Hans Brunner, *Die Kantorei bei St. Stephan in Wien: Beiträge zur Geschichte der Wiener Dommusik* (Vienna: A. Dürer, 1948), p. 18, notes that the title "Kapellmeister" had been in use at the cathedral since the 1640s. Before then various titles (e.g., *Chormeister, regens chori, Sanchherr*, and *geistlicher Cantor*) are found almost interchangeably in the documents.

19. Johann Gottfried Walther, "Maestro di Capella," in *Musicalisches Lexicon oder musicalische Bibliothec* (Leipzig: W. Deer, 1732; reprint ed., Kassel: Bärenreiter, 1953, 1967), p. 377. Walther says this title originated in Italy when conductors became necessary for choral music sung with more than one voice to a part.

20. Friedrich Wilhelm Riedel, "Liturgie and Kirchenmusik," in *Joseph Haydn in Seiner Zeit,* ed. Gerda Mraz, Gottfried Mraz, and Gerald Schlag (Eisenstadt: Kulturabteilung des Amtes der Burgenländischen Landesregierung, 1982), p. 122.

21. Köchel, *Hof-Musikkapelle,* p. 16.

22. Richard Kralik, *Geschichte der Stadt Wien und ihrer Kultur,* 2nd ed. (Vienna: Adolf Holzhausen, 1926), p. 312. Kurz was the renowned *Stegreifkomödiant* who created the Bernardon character and thereby fostered these farcical plays with improvised dialogue.

23. Karl Ditters von Dittersdorf, *Lebensbeschreibung seinem Sohne in die Feder diktiert* (Leipzig, 1801), ed. Bruno Loets (Munich: Kösel, 1967), pp. 18–19 (Coleridge's English trans., pp. 3–4).

24. Howard Chandler Robbins Landon, *Haydn: Chronicle and Works* (Bloomington: Indiana University Press, 1976–80), I, pp. 350–52.

25. Ludwig Stollbrock, "Leben und Wirken des k.k. Hofkapellmeisters und Hofkompositors Johan Georg Reuter jun.," *Vierteljahrschrift für Musikwissenschaft* VIII (1892), 180–82; the complete contract (in German) is transcribed there.

26. Riedel, "St. Veit zu Krems," pp. 328–29. "Emmer" (*Eimer*) was a liquid measure of about 56 liters; see also Roman Sandgruber, "Wirtschaftsentwicklung, Einkommensverteilung und Alltagsleben zur Zeit Haydns," in *Joseph Haydn in seiner Zeit,* p. 85. *Thurnermeister* were apparently master gymnasts from the town.

27. Ibid., p. 329.

28. Karl Schnürl, "Die Kirchenmusik im westlichen Niederösterreich bis zur Errichtung der Diözese St. Pölten," *Singende Kirche* 13 (1966), p. 180; also Walter Senn, "Mozart's Kirchenmusik und die Literatur," *Mozart Jahrbuch 1978/79,* p. 17.

29. Riedel, "St. Veit zu Krems," pp. 308, 314.

30. James Dack, "The Origins and Development of the Esterházy Kapelle in Eisenstadt until 1790" (Ph.D. diss., University of Liverpool, 1976), p. 101.

31. Altman Kellner, *Musikgeschichte des Stiftes Kremsmünster, nach den Quellen dargestellt* (Kassel: Bärenreiter, 1956), pp. 367–68, 448–50.

32. Johann Ferdinand von Schönfeld, *Jahrbuch der Tonkunst von Wien und Prag* (Vienna and Prague: Schönfeld, 1796), pp. 144–45.

33. See Karl Maria Brand, *Die Messen von Joseph Haydn* (Würzburg-Aumühle: K. Triltsch, 1941), p. 125.

34. Otto Biba, "Zur nicht-vokalen Kirchenmusik der Zeit Joseph Haydns" (unpublished paper delivered 10 September 1982 before the International Haydn Congress, Vienna).

35. Robert N. Freeman, "The Function of Haydn's Instrumental Compositions in the Abbeys," in *Haydn Studies,* ed. Jens Peter Larsen, Howard Serwer, and James Webster (New York: Norton, 1981), p. 200, n. 29.

36. Kellner, *Musikgeschichte Kremsmünster,* pp. 436–47.

37. Egon Wellesz, "Giuseppe Bonno (1710–88): Sein Leben und seine dramatischen Werke," *Sammelbände der internationalen Musikgesellschaft* XI (1909–10), pp. 440–41 (Beilage IV).

38. Documents pertaining to this appointment are collected in: "Allerunterthänigster Vortrag ... Wien den 2ᵗᵉⁿ February 1774," *Hofarchiv 78: Obersthofmeisteramt-Akten* in the Haus-, Hof-, und Staatsarchiv, Vienna; these documents were copied into "Vortrag Nr. 31," *Obersthofmeisteramt-Protokolle 37*, pp. 240–50.

    The documents show great hesitation about having Hofmann give up the cathedral choir directorship because of worries that others (including Gsur) would then apply for this position. There is no record of a competition or *concorso* being held for the position. For further information about von Sporck, see Landon, *Haydn: Chronicle and Works* I, pp. 282, 513.

39. Schnürl, "Kirchenmusik Niederösterreich," p. 182, reports a *regens chori* named Anna Maria Seyserin died in 1781 at Ardagger, just north of Amstetten, Austria.

40. Biba, "Kirchenmusik 1783," p. 24. Other families active in Viennese churches may be found in this inventory of 1783.

41. For example, Anderson, ed., *Letters of Mozart* no. 47 (22 September 1767) I, p. 80, or no. 62 (30 July 1768) I, p. 88.

42. Johann Mattheson, *Der vollkommene Kapellmeister* (Hamburg: C. Herold, 1739; trans. and ed. Ernest C. Harriss, Ann Arbor, Michigan: UMI Research Press, 1981) pt. III, ch. 26, trans. pp. 864–71.

43. Ibid., pt. II, ch. 2, Harriss trans. pp. 249–63, 122.

44. Haas, *Wiener Musiker,* passim, lists the deaths of some 22 Viennese musicians with the title *regens chori* between 1724 and 1797. Since their titles and places of employment are listed beside the dates of death, it has been assumed that they held the named jobs until death.

45. Carl Ferdinand Pohl, *Denkschrift aus Anlass des hundertjährigen Bestehens der Tonkünstler-Societät, im Jahre 1862 reorganisirt als "Haydn" Witwen- und Waisen-Versorgungs-Verein der Tonkünstler in Wien* (Vienna: Carl Gerolds Sohn, 1871), pp. 103–6, 117–27.

46. Franz Xaver Glöggl, *Kirchenmusik-Ordnung: Erklärendes Handbuch des musikalischen Gottesdienstes, für Kapellmeister, Regenschori, Sänger und Tonkünstler* (Vienna: J.B. Wallishauser, 1828), pp. 7–8.

47. Ferdinand Haberl, "Repräsentations- und Gebetsgottesdienst im 18. Jahrhundert," in *Geschichte der katholischen Kirchenmusik,* ed. Karl Gustav Fellerer (Kassel: Bärenreiter, 1976) II, p. 154.

48. *Ueber die Kirchenmusik in Wien* (Vienna: S. Hartl, 1781), pp. 6–7.

49. Anderson, ed., *Letters of Mozart* nos. 446 (10 April 1782), 483 (12 March 1783), and 486 (12 April 1783) II, pp. 800, 842, 845. These men often performed "old" music. The last named letter shows Mozart's displeasure with the current church style: "Hence it is that true church music is to be found *only* in attics and in worm-eaten condition." Teiber (1756–1822) later succeeded Mozart as *Hofkammerkomponist.*

50. Hubert Unverricht, "Die orchesterbegleitete Kirchenmusik von den Neapolitanern bis Schubert," in *Geschichte der katholischen Kirchenmusik,* ed. Karl Gustav Fellerer (Kassel: Bärenreiter, 1976), p. 169; Ernst Tittel, *Österreichische Kirchenmusik: Werden, Wachsen, Wirken* (Vienna: Herder, 1961), p. 254. This concert series ended with the death of Gebauer in 1822 and was revived again 1830–48; see, Eduard Hanslick, *Geschichte des Concertwesens in Wien* (Vienna: W. Braumüller, 1869–70), pp. 307–13.

51. Anderson, ed., *Letters of Mozart* no. 300ᵃ, II, p. 521.

52. Franz Kosch, "Florian Leopold Gassmann als Kirchenkomponist," *Studien zur Musikwissenschaft* XIV (1927), p. 237, n. 57, citing Karl Peiser, *Johann Adam Hiller,* (Leipzig: Gebruder Hug & Co., 1894), p. 28. Also on this same program (9 December 1779) were a Salve Redemptor by Hasse, a concerto for harpsichord, a Magnificat by Seydelmann, a Credo and Sanctus by Michael Haydn, and a sinfonia by Naumann (Peiser, *Hiller*, p. 28).

53. Landon, *Haydn: Chronicle and Works* II, pp. 234, 447.

54. Josef A. Jungmann, *The Mass of the Roman Rite: Its Origins and Development (Missarum Sollemnia)*, 2 vols., trans. Francis A. Brunner (New York: Benziger Brothers, 1951) I, pp. 135–36.

55. Ibid., I, p. 141, and Josef Andreas Jungmann, *The Mass: An Historical, Theological, and Pastoral Survey*, ed. Mary Ellen Evans, trans. Julian Fernandes (Collegeville, Minnesota: Liturgical Press, 1976), pp. 87, 219, 165, 228. In 1969 a new Order of Mass (*Ordo Missae*) was finally published.

56. Jungmann, *Mass*, p. 227.

57. Willi Apel, *Gregorian Chant* (Bloomington, Indiana: Indiana University Press, 1958), pp. 23–24; see the Gospel accounts in Matthew 26:26–28, Mark 14:22–24, and Luke 22:19–20.

58. Jungmann, *Mass*, pp. 90, 143, 149.

59. Jungmann, *The Mass of the Roman Rite*, I, pp. 142–44, 154; see Jungmann, *Mass*, p. 178.

60. Beck, "Die Musik des liturgischen Gottesdienstes," p. 189.

61. Marcel Brion, *Daily Life in the Vienna of Mozart and Schubert*, trans. Jean Stewart (New York: Macmillan, 1962), pp. 26–27.

62. Jungmann, *The Mass of the Roman Rite* I, p. 150. *Presbyterium*, which originally meant *Hochaltarraum*, is another name for *sanctuarium*.

63. Apel, *Gregorian Chant*, p. 31; Jungmann, *The Mass of the Roman Rite* I, p. 461; II, pp. 333, 336–37, and id., *Mass*, p. 207. The Gloria and Credo were also dropped for the Rogation Days and the Requiem Mass. The Credo was used only on Sundays and certain feasts.

64. According to Marcel Brion, *Daily Life in the Vienna of Mozart and Schubert*, pp. 42–43, St. Birgit's (May 1) and St. Anne's (July 26) Days were occasions of "prodigious rejoicing" and special outings every year.

65. This Mass is No. 62 in Hofer's catalogue. Georg Reutter d.J., *Kirchenwerke*, ed. P. Norbert Hofer, in *Denkmäler der Tonkunst in Österreich*, vol. 88 (Vienna, 1952) xiii.

66. Friedrich Wilhelm Riedel, *Kirchenmusik am Hofe Karls VI. (1711–1740): Untersuchungen zum Verhältnis von Zeremoniell und musikalischem Stil im Barockzeitalter* (Munich and Salzburg: Emil Katzbichler, 1977), pp. 62–63. Members of the Order of the Golden Fleece (*Vliess* or *Toison*) attended the highest grade of ceremony, the *Toison-Gottesdienst*. A procession usually accompanied a Pontifical Mass, while the regular Masses (*gewöhnliche Gottesdienste*) were also designated as *Ordinari*. Riedel (p. 26) also lists the occasions for a *Stationsgottesdienst* (Stational Mass) at Court.

67. Ibid., pp. 14–19. Riedel's five principal sources were *Das Ordnungsbuch* of 1715 (list of public events at court), *Die Hofkalendar* (printed list of *Gala- und Toison-Tage*), *Die Zeremonialprotokolle* (reports of special events), the *Wiener Diarium* (local newspaper), and Kilian Reinhardt's *Rubriche Generali* (1727 listing of court feasts, processions, etc.; manuscript S.m. 2503 at the Austrian National Library, Vienna). A summary of the last named source is Köchel, *Hof-Musikkapelle*, pp. 135–44, and Mraz, *Joseph Haydn in seiner Zeit*, pp. 335–36.

68. Walter Senn, "Mozart's Kirchenmusik und die Literatur," p. 15; see also id., "Beiträge zur Mozartforschung," *Acta Musicologica* 48 (1976):220ff.

69. Anderson, ed., *Letters of Mozart*, no. 235 (4 November 1777) I, p. 356. Organ playing for the Benedictus was an old Italian practice dating back to the time of Frescobaldi.

70. Alfred Einstein, *Mozart: His Character, His Work*, trans. Arthur Mendel and Nathan Broder (New York: Oxford University Press, 1945), pp. 34–35, 331.

71. Johann Joseph Fux, *Gradus ad Parnassum, oder Anführung zur regelmässigen musikalischen Composition...*, trans. Lorenz Mizler (Leipzig: Mizlerischer Bücherverlag, 1742), pp. 182, 192. The German text reads "...zur Erweckung der Andacht." For Fux the goal of secular music was "to entertain the spirits of the listeners (*die Gemüter der Zuhörer zu belustigen*) and move them to different passions (*Leidenschaften*)..." (pp. 193–94).

72. Johann Adolph Scheibe, *Critischer Musikus* (Leipzig: B.C. Breitkopf, 1745; reprint ed., Hildesheim: G. Olms and Weisbaden: Breitkopf und Härtel, 1970), p. 161.

73. Mattheson, *Der vollkommene Kapellmeister*, pt. II, ch. 2, §66, Harriss trans. p. 263, see also pp. 55, 198.

74. P. Meinradus Spiess, *Tractatus musicus compositorio-practicus* (Augsburg: Lotter, 1746), p. 161; similarly, in the foreword to his *Der vollkommene Kapellmeister* of 1739 (Harriss trans. p. 55), Mattheson had written: "Now the goal of music is to praise God in the highest, with word and deed, through singing and playing."

75. Cornell Jesse Runestad, "The Masses of Joseph Haydn: A Stylistic Study" (D.M.A. diss., University of Illinois at Urbana-Champaign, 1970), p. 302. So that church music would properly arouse piety, the Pope requested that: (1) the Canonical Hours be chanted only and with devotion; (2) no theatrical elements—neither style nor instruments—may be a part of the Church's music; (3) the sacred texts must be complete and aurally comprehensible; and (4) instrumental accompaniment should not overpower the voices but should instead intensify the expression of the words.

76. Karl Gustav Fellerer, "Die Enzyklika 'Annus qui' des Papstes Benedikt XIV," in *Geschichte der katholischen Kirchenmusik*, 2 vols., ed. K.G. Fellerer (Kassel: Bärenreiter, 1976) II, pp. 149–50; see also Unverricht, "Die orchesterbegleitete Kirchenmusik," II, pp. 157–58.

77. Joseph Martin Kraus, *Etwas von und über Musik fürs Jahr 1777* (Frankfurt, 1778; reprint ed. with commentary by Friedrich W. Riedel, Munich and Salzburg: E. Katzbichler, 1977), p. 95.

78. *Ueber die Kirchenmusik in Wien* (1781), p. 5.

79. Johann Georg Albrechtsberger, *Gründliche Anweisung zur Composition* (Leipzig: J.G.I. Breitkopf, 1790), p. 378.

80. Heinrich Christoph Koch, "Kirchenmusik," in *Musikalisches Lexikon* (Frankfurt am Main: A. Hermann d.J., 1802; reprint ed., Hildesheim: G. Olms, 1964), col. 832.

81. Glöggl, *Kirchenmusik Ordnung*, p. 2.

82. Floridus Röhrig, "Das religiöse Leben Wiens zwischen Barock und Aufklärung," in *Joseph Haydn in seiner Zeit*, ed. Gerda Mraz, Gottfried Mraz, and Gerald Schlag (Eisenstadt: Amt der Burgenländischen Landesregierung, Kulturabteilung, 1982), p. 117; Riedel, "Liturgie und Kirchenmusik," pp. 123–24; Jungmann, *The Mass of the Roman Rite* I, pp. 145–47, 154–55.

83. Jungmann, *The Mass of the Roman Rite* I, p. 474.

84. This diagram is based upon Jungmann, *The Mass of the Roman Rite*, 2 vols., passim; Riedel, "Liturgie and Kirchenmusik," pp. 127–38; Apel, *Gregorian Chant*, pp. 23–26, and id., *Harvard Dictionary of Music*, p. 507; *The Liber Usualis*, ed. Benedictines of Solesmes (Tournai: Desclee, 1956), pp. xv–xvi, 1–10. Items appearing at the same horizontal level on the chart were virtually simultaneous in occurrence.

85. Although part of the sung Ordinary, the opening "Asperges me" and closing "Ite, missa est" remained chanted. Italian concerted Masses (e.g., Pergolesi) were often short Masses that set only the Kyrie and Gloria.

86. Ursprung, *Die katholische Kirchenmusik*, p. 220, as cited by Jungmann, *The Mass of the Roman Rite* I, p. 149, n. 45; see also I, pp. 357, 471; II, pp. 128–29, 130, 132, 335–37; and id., *Mass*, pp. 168–69, 183, 203.

87. The juxtaposition of the Kyrie and Gloria led to the frequent setting of just these two sections alone, a practice very popular in eighteenth-century Italy.

    For an excellent survey of the origins, structure, and liturgical significance of the various parts of the Mass, see: Maurus Pfaff, Richard Crocker, Frederick R. McManus, and Ruth Steiner, "Mass," *The New Grove Dictionary of Music and Musicians*, 20 vols., ed. Stanley Sadie (London: Macmillan, 1980) XI, pp. 770–76; see also the articles on individual parts of the Mass.

88. See n. 75 above.

89. The history of such prohibitions goes back to the Council of Trent and even earlier. See Karl Gustav Fellerer, "Church Music and the Council of Trent," trans. Moses Hadas, *The Musical Quarterly* XXXIX/4 (October 1953):567–94.

90. Otto Biba, "Die Piaristenorden in Österreich: seine Bedeutung für bildende Kunst, Musik und Theater im 17. und 18. Jahrundert," *Jahrbuch für Österreichische Kulturgeschichte*, 1975, p. 113. Riedel, "St. Veit zu Krems," p. 327, n. 97, indicates that this decree is found in *Codex Austriacus* V (24 December 1753), p. 275. Kralik, *Geschichte der Stadt Wien*, p. 280, says the archbishop explained to the Empress that such "noisy (bruyante) music" was not appropriate for the church. Kralik also limits the ban to "Hofmusik."

91. Unverricht, "Die orchesterbegleitete Kirchenmusik," p. 158; Karl Gustav Fellerer, "The Liturgical Basis for Haydn's Masses," in *Haydn Studies*, ed. Jens Peter Larsen, Howard Serwer, and James Webster (New York: Norton, 1981), p. 165. The text of the *Hofreskript* is given in Brand, *Die Messen von Joseph Haydn*, p. 189, cf. pp. 153–54, and Karl Gustav Fellerer, "Liturgische Grundlagen der Kirchenmusik Mozarts," in *Festschrift Walter Senn zum 70. Geburtstag*, ed. Ewald Fässler (Munich and Salzburg: E. Katzbichler, 1975), p. 71, n. 57.

92. Riedel, "Liturgie und Kirchenmusik," p. 123.

93. Biba, "Piaristenorden," p. 113. Fellerer, "Liturgical Basis," p. 165, notes how the imperial decree was ignored "whenever possible," for example, at the annual festal service of the Cecilian Brotherhood.

94. Riedel, "St. Veit zu Krems," p. 327.

95. Fellerer, "Liturgischen Grundlagen Mozarts," p. 71; id., "Liturgical Basis," p. 165; Riedel, "Liturgie und Kirchenmusik," p. 123. Cardinal Migazzi's petition was dated 10 June 1767.

96. Unverricht, "Die orchesterbegleitete Kirchenmusik," p. 160. Probably Joseph II meant that he wished to know of use for *Hof* services only, certainly not for everywhere.

97. Literature about these decrees includes: Fellerer, "Liturgical Basis," pp. 165–66; Biba, "Sozial-Status," p. 110; Brand, *Die Messen von Joseph Haydn*, pp. 187–94; Riedel, "Liturgie und Kirchenmusik," pp. 122–25; Walter Pass, "Josephinism and the Josephinian Reforms Concerning Haydn," in *Haydn Studies*, ed. Jens Peter Larsen, Howard Serwer, and James Webster (New York: Norton, 1981), pp. 168–71; Landon, *Haydn: Chronicle and Works* II, pp. 555–56; Unverricht, "Die orchesterbegleitete Kirchenmusik," p. 160; Reinhard G. Pauly, "The Reforms of Church Music under Joseph II," *The Musical Quarterly* XLIII/3 (July 1957):372–82; Jungmann, *The Mass of the Roman Rite* I, pp. 151–56; *New Oxford History of Music*, 11 vols. (London: Oxford University Press, 1973) VII: *The Age of Enlightenment 1745–1790*, ed. by Egon Wellesz and Frederick Sternfeld, pp. 305–6; Brion, *Daily Life in the Vienna of Mozart and Schubert*, pp. 14, 16–19, 22–23.

98. Fellerer, "Liturgical Basis," p. 167; Biba, "Kirchenmusik 1783," pp. 7–10; Pass, "Josephinism," p. 170.

99. See Anderson, ed., *Letters of Mozart*, nos. 465 and 486 (25 September 1782 and 12 April 1783) II, pp. 822, 845. For an excerpt from the latter, see above n. 49.

100. According to R.J. Pascall, "Style," *New Grove* XVIII, p. 320, these three styles (church, chamber, and theater) were first treated in Marco Scacchi's *Breve discorso sopra la musica moderna* (Warsaw, 1649) where they were termed *stylus ecclesiasticus, stylus cubicularis,* and *stylus scenicus.* Angelo Berardi later continued with this division in his treatises; see Manfred F. Bukofzer, *Music in the Baroque Era* (New York: Norton, 1947), p. 4.

   Eighteenth-century observations on the three styles include: Johann Mattheson, *Das neu-eröffnete Orchester* (Hamburg: B. Schiller, 1713), p. 113; Fux, *Gradus ad Parnassum,* Mizler trans., pp. 193–94; Johann Gottfried Walther, "Stylus," *Musicalisches Lexicon*, p. 584; Mattheson, *Der vollkommene Kapellmeister* I, ch. 10, Harriss trans. pp. 189–226; Meinradus Spiess, *Tractatus musicus*, pp. 161–64; Johann Scheibe, *Critischer Musikus* (20 August 1737, 6 June 1739), pp. 125, 130, 391–94; Johann Georg Sulzer, "Cammermusik," *Allgemeine Theorie der schönen Künste,* 5 vols., 4th ed. (Leipzig: Weidmann, 1792–99; reprint ed., Hildesheim: Olms, 1967, 1970) I, p. 440; Johann Nikolaus Forkel, *Allgemeine Geschichte der Musik,* 2 vols. (Leipzig: Schwickert, 1788, 1801) I, pp. 43–45; Albrechtsberger, *Gründliche Anweisung zur Composition,* (Leipzig: J.G.I. Breitkopf, 1790), ch. 34, pp. 377–79; Koch, "Styl, Schreibart," in *Musikalisches Lexikon,* col. 1451; see also Leonard G. Ratner, *Classic Music: Expression, Form, and Style* (New York: Schirmer, 1980), pp. 7, 23, 161, 172–74.

101. Walther, "Stylus," *Musicalisches Lexicon,* p. 584; Mattheson, *Der vollkommene Kapellmeister,* pt. I, ch. 10, §4, Harriss trans. pp. 189–90.

102. Anderson, ed., *Letters of Mozart* no. 283[a] (7 February 1778) I, p. 468.

103. Ibid., no. 594 (early May 1791) II, p. 950.

104. Albrechtsberger, *Gründliche Anweisung zur Composition,* ch. 34, pp. 377–79.

105. Koch, "Styl, Schreibart," *Musikalisches Lexikon,* col. 1450–51.

106. Ibid., "Kirchenmusik," col. 832–33. Here Koch describes how "die freie Schreibart," which arose from opera, intermixed with church music. He notes that "opinions are still very divided" as to the appropriateness and acceptability of this "free" style and the forms of opera for church music.

107. Ibid., "Missa, Messa, Messe," col. 969; see also Ratner, *Classic Music,* p. 161, where the citation of this quotation does not make clear that Koch was specifically discussing Masses.

108. See Ratner, *Classic Music,* pp. 172–80, 260.

109. Riedel, "Liturgie," p. 132.

110. Fux, *Gradus ad Parmassum,* Mizler trans. pp. 181–82; Spiess, *Tractatus musicus,* p. 161; Johann Joachim Quantz, *Versuch einer Anweisung die Flöte traversiere zu spielen,* trans. Edward R. Reilly (New York: Free Press, 1966), XVIII, § 21–22, pp. 289–90; Sulzer, "Kirchenmusik," *Allgemeine Theorie,* 4th ed. (1793) III, p. 18.

111. Fux, *Gradus ad Parnassum,* Mizler trans., pp. 182, 192. Mary Nicole Schnoebelen, "The Concerted Mass at San Petronio in Bologna ca. 1660–1730: A Documentary and Analytical Study" (Ph.D. diss., University of Illinois, Urbana-Champaign, 1966), pp. 8, 153, describes the *stile misto* as mixing homophonic galant interludes with contrapuntal concerted movements. Such choral settings had the "outward trappings of polyphony," yet the contrapuntal development frequently "dissolved into passages of outright homophony." This mixed style was especially favored by the Neapolitans and usually frowned upon by the music theorists.

      Denis Arnold, "Mass," *New Grove Dictionary of Music and Musicians,* ed. Stanley Sadie (London: Macmillan, 1980) XI, p. 793, notes that this style mixture is drawn from three elements: "choruses in *stile antico* with orchestral doubling of the voices; choruses where the orchestra plays a prominent part in the formal organization; and music for solo voices."

112. Mattheson, *Der vollkommene Kapellmeister,* pt. I, ch. 10, §§ 7–9, Harriss trans., pp. 190–91.

113. Ibid., pt. I, ch. 10, §§ 34–69, 99–101, Harriss trans., pp. 196–210, 220–21. To these styles of church music, theater music adds the dramatic (recitative), hyporchematic (singing and dancing), and fantasy styles (§§ 70–101, trans. pp. 210–21), while chamber music adds the choraic (dancing) style (§§ 102–16, trans. pp. 221–25).

114. Ibid., pt. I, ch. 10, § 12, Harriss trans. p. 192.

115. Ibid., pt. I, ch. 10, §67, Harriss trans., p. 209.

116. Spiess, *Tractatus musicus,* p. 161. For Spiess there was nothing more vulgar than bringing into the church everything frivolous (*alles leichtfertiges*) and amusing (*lustiges*) from the theater, chamber, and table concerts.

117. Johann Joachim Quantz, *Versuch einer Anweisung die Flöte Traversiere zu spielen* XVIII, §§ 21–22, pp. 289–90.

118. Schönfeld, *Jahrbuch der Tonkunst von Wien and Prag* (1796), p. 97.

119. Ibid.

120. Fellerer, "Liturgical Basis," pp. 165–66; id., "Liturgische Grundlagen Mozarts," p. 72ff.

121. Runestad, "The Masses of Joseph Haydn," p. 302. Forbidden instruments included timpani, horns, trumpets, oboes, flutes, *saleri* (?), and mandolins; see n. 75 above.

122. Jungmann, *The Mass of the Roman Rite* I, p. 148.

123. See chapter 1, n. 30.

124. Jungmann, *The Mass of the Roman Rite* I, p. 149, n. 45; Beck, "Musik des liturgischen Gottesdienstes," p. 189; Riedel, "Liturgie und Kirchenmusik," pp. 126-29.

125. Burney, *Musical Tours*, ed. Scholes II, pp. 113-14.

126. Kraus, *Etwas von und über Musik 1777*, pp. 94-95. "Alone, its figured music is nonsense, sheer nonsense for churches."

127. Ibid., pp. 95-96.

128. *Ueber die Kirchenmusik in Wien* (1781), pp. 7-9. On pp. 13-15 there is a most unflattering description of music in a Viennese nunnery where one nun even sang bass! Unverricht, "Die orchesterbegleitete Kirchenmusik," p. 159, believes the author of this polemic was a non-musician trying very hard to promote Josephinian ideas of enlightenment. Biba, "Kirchenmusik 1783," pp. 75-76, n. 15 and 20, reports that a Joseph Richter was the author.

129. Nicolai, *Beschreibung 1781*, pp. 544-45; translation based partially on Runestad, "The Masses of Joseph Haydn," p. 40.

130. There are several contrafacta in Haydn's Masses. The Benedictus of his *Missa Cellensis* of 1782 (Hoboken XXII: 8) is based upon Ernesto's aria, "Qualche volte non fa male," from Act II of his opera *Il mondo della luna* (1777?), and the "Qui tollis" of the *Schöpfungsmesse* of 1801 (Hoboken XXII: 13) is a quote from the *Creation;* see Landon, *Haydn: Chronicle and Works* II, pp. 559-60, and V, p. 201.

131. David James Wilson, "Selected Masses of Johann Adolf Hasse" (D.M.A. diss. in choral music, University of Illinois, Champaign-Urbana, 1973), p. 57.

132. Henry B. Raynor, "Some Reflections upon the Viennese Mass," *The Musical Times* (November 1954):592-95.

133. Fux, *Gradus ad Parnassum*, Mizler trans., p. 182. Here Fux seems to justify an occasional coloratura passage—on the condition that the singer can manage it.

134. Scheibe, *Critischer Musikus* (29 Oct. 1737), pp. 168-74. The numeration of points is mine.

135. Albrechtsberger, *Gründliche Anweisung zur Composition*, ch. 34, pp. 378-79.

136. Sulzer, "Kirchenmusik," *Allgemeine Theorie*, 4th ed. (1793) III, pp. 20-22.

137. For example, Anderson, ed., *Letters of Mozart* no. 358 (13 November 1780, Munich) II, p. 663, shows Wolfgang's displeasure with a facile Mass by Paul Grua (1754-1833): "Things like this one could easily turn out at a rate of half a dozen a day."

138. Dittersdorf, *Lebensbeschreibung*, pp. 115-16 (Coleridge's defective translation, p. 113).

139. Georg August Griesinger, *Biographische Notizen über Joseph Haydn*, new ed. of original of Leipzig, 1810, ed. Franz Grasberger (Vienna: P. Kaltschmid, 1954), pp. 61-62; English translation in: Vernon Gotwals, ed., *Joseph Haydn: Eighteenth-Century Gentleman and Genius* (Madison: University of Wisconsin, 1963), p. 62.

140. Raynor, "Some Reflections," p. 595. See also Landon, *Haydn: Chronicle and Works* IV, p. 124, and V, p. 201; Gotwals, ed., *Joseph Haydn*, pp. 62-63; and Brand, *Die Messen von Joseph Haydn*, pp. 407-8.

Chapter 3

1. Warren Kirkendale, *Fugue and Fugato in Rococo and Classical Chamber Music*, trans. Margaret Bent and Warren Kirkendale (Durham, N.C.: Duke University Press, 1979), pp. 3–14, presents a useful survey of the lives and chamber music activities of many of the same Viennese composers.

2. See Robert N. Freeman, "Albrechtsberger," in *New Grove Dictionary of Music and Musicians,* 6th ed., ed. by Stanley Sadie (London: Macmillan, 1980) I, pp. 224–26; Andreas Weissenbäck, "Johann Georg Albrechtsberger als Kirchenkomponist," *Studien zur Musikwissenschaft* XIV (1927), passim. Dorothea Schröder at the University of Hamburg has just completed a dissertation entitled "Die geistlichen Vokalkompositionen Johann Georg Albrechtsbergers," 1986.

3. Freeman, "Albrechtsberger," *New Grove* I, p. 224. Karl Pfannhauser, in his introduction to an edition of Albrechtsberger's *Messe in Es-dur (Missa Sancti Josephi),* ed. Andreas Weissenbäck, vol. 8 of *Österreichische Kirchenmusik* (Vienna: Doblinger, 1951), indicates that the composer held the Karmeliter-Kirche post from 1771 to 1793.

4. Sources vary. Freeman, "Albrechtsberger," *New Grove* I, p. 225, lists 35 Masses; Weissenbäck, "Thematisches Verzeichnis der Kirchenkompositionen von Johann Georg Albrechtsberger," *Jahrbuch des Stiftes Klosterneuburg* VI (1914) describes only 26; in his introduction to the E-flat major Mass, Pfannhauser (see n. 3 above) mentions 39 Masses. Most of the autograph scores of Albrechtsberger's Masses are now housed in the Széchény National Library, Budapest.

5. Karl Maria Brand, *Die Messen von Joseph Haydn,* Musik und Geistesgeschichte, Berliner Studien zur Musikwissenschaft no. 2 (Würzburg-Aumühle: K. Triltsch, 1941), p. 69.

6. For example, Ferdinand Haberl, "Repräsentations- und Gebetsgottesdienst im 18. Jahrhundert," in *Geschichte der katholischen Kirchenmusik,* ed. Karl Gustav Fellerer (Kassel: Bärenreiter, 1976) II, p. 154, considers most of Albrechtsberger's Masses to be just *Gebrauchsmusik.*

7. See chapter 2 at n. 104.

8. For excerpts from Albrechtsberger's Masses see ex. 6-19; 7-4, 7-7; 8-12C, 8-13; 9-15A, 9-16A, 9-16E; see also fig. 8-9.

9. Ludwig Ritter von Köchel, *Die kaiserlich Hof-Musikkapelle in Wien von 1543 bis 1867 nach urkundlichen Forschungen* (Vienna: Beck'sche Universitätsbuchhandlung and A. Hölder, 1869; reprint ed., Hildesheim: G. Olms, 1976), p. 89; see also Robert Eitner, *Biographisch-bibliographisches Quellen Lexikon der Musiker und Musikgelehrten christlicher Zeitrechnung bis Mitte des neunzehnten Jahrhunderts,* 2nd. rev. ed. (Graz: Akademische Druck- und Verlagsanstalt, 1959–60) I, p. 184, and Carl Ferdinand Pohl, *Denkschrift aus Anlass des hundertjährigen Bestehens der Tonkünstler-Societät, im Jahre 1862 reorganisirt als "Haydn," Witwen- und Waisen-Versorgungs-Verein der Tonkünstler in Wien* (Vienna: Carl Gerolds Sohn, 1871), pp. 102–3.

10. Anton Mörath, *Pflege der Tonkunst durch das Fürsthaus Schwarzenberg im 18. und Beginn des 19. Jahrhunderts* (Krumau, 1901) seperát z Wiener Vaterland, č. 68, z. 10. 3. 1901. This information was kindly supplied by Dr. Theodora Straková from her dissertation "Hudba u Brtnických Collaltů v 17. a 18. století (Musik bei Pirnitzer Collaltů in 17. und 18. Jahrhunderten)," 2 vols., (Ph.D. diss., U.J.E.P. Brno, 1967). In July 1982 at a Haydn conference in Eisenstadt, Otto Biba also reported that Arbesser was working at the Schwarzenberg court in Krumau (see *Jahrbuch für österreichische Kulturgeschichte* of 1983).

11. This mere speculation arises from the fact that Köchel, *Hof-Musikkapelle*, lists no active *Hoforganist* for the years 1763–70. Arbesser may have served in an unofficial capacity during these years when Reutter's budget for the Hofkapelle was severely limited.

12. Pohl, *Tonkünstler-Societät*, pp. 102–3, no. 62.

13. Georg Reichert, "Zur Geschichte der Wiener Messenkomposition in der ersten Hälfte des 18. Jahrhunderts," (Ph.D. diss., University of Vienna, 1935), thematic catalogue for Arbesser.

14. A complete score of the *Missa Nubes pluant justum* appears in appendix F of the author's dissertation at C.U.N.Y.

15. Howard Chandler Robbins Landon, *Haydn: Chronicle and Works*, 5 vols. (Bloomington: Indiana University Press, 1976–80) I, 139, still considers Haydn to be the composer of this rather tiny G-major Mass. See Erich Schenk, "Ist die Göttweiger Rorate-Messe ein Werk Joseph Haydns?" *Studien zur Musikwissenschaft* 24 (1960): 87–105.

16. Rudolf Angermüller, "Bonno," *New Grove* III, p. 27.

17. Egon Wellesz, "Giuseppe Bonno (1710–88): Sein Leben und seine dramatischen Werke," *Sammelbände der Internationalen Musikgesellschaft* XI (1909–10): 438.

18. Angermüller, "Bonno," p. 27; Wellesz, "Bonno," pp. 397–98. Dittersdorf, Friberth, and Gluck also worked for this prince.

19. See the discussion of Tobias Gsur later in this chapter for information about others who applied for this post. Alfred Schienerl, "Giuseppe Bonnos Kirchenkompositionen," *Studien zur Musikwissenschaft* XV (1928): 63–64, believes Bonno came out of retirement to take the post; Salieri and Gsur were his assistants.

20. Angermüller, "Bonno," p. 27. Bonno also served as president of the *Societät* (1774–88).

21. Otto Biba, "Die Wiener Kirchenmusik um 1783," in *Beiträge zur Musikgeschichte des 18. Jahrhunderts*, ed. Gerda Mraz (Eisenstadt: Institut für österreichische Kulturgeschichte, 1971), p. 56.

22. The Mozarts valued Bonno chiefly as an "honest and upright man" and as a useful connection at the *Hof*; see Emily Anderson, ed., *Letters of Mozart* (London: Macmillan; New York: St. Martin's Press, 1966), nos. 398, 460 (11 April 1781, 23 August 1782) II, 724, 816.

23. Schienerl, "Bonnos Kirchenkompositionen," p. 65.

24. Angermüller, "Bonno," p. 27. Wellesz, "Bonno," p. 402, writes that from 1754 on Bonno devoted himself mainly to church music and oratorios. Certainly his production of secular music must have decreased after he left the house of Sachsen-Hildburghausen in 1761.

25. The *Hof-Protokolle* concerning Bonno's appointment as *Hofkapellmeister* in 1774 notes that, although he had written more works for the chamber and theater, he had also composed several church works that had been well received ("mit grossem Beyfall"); see Wellesz, "Bonno," p. 440, for a transcript of this document.

26. Excerpts from Bonno's Masses are found in ex. 6-7, 9-6, and 9-16A; see also fig. 7-8.

27. Schienerl, "Bonnos Kirchenkompositionen," pp. 64, 67, 82. Bonno's Mass scores reflect the solo-tutti alternations in the organ part with the designations "serrato" and "aperto" (closed and open) which create a kind of terraced dynamics. Schienerl (p. 84–85) believes Bonno's solo-tutti movements significantly influenced that type of movement in Masses by other Viennese composers, including Haydn.

28. Wellesz, "Bonno," p. 427.

29. The violas play divisi in the "Qui tollis" of M. 9 (before 1776).

30. Robert Haas, *Wiener Musiker vor und um Beethoven* (Vienna, Prague, and Leipzig: E. Strache, 1927), no. 283, p. 11, indicates that "Johann Pock" was still *regens chori* at his death in 1764. Friedrich Wilhelm Riedel, "Beiträge zur Geschichte der Musikpflege an der Stadtpfarrkirche St. Veit zu Krems," in *Festschrift 950 Jahre Pfarrei Krems* (Krems an der Donau, 1964), p. 334, calls Boog the "Kapellmeister" at St. Peter's. The Portheim Catalogue, a biobibliographical resource in Vienna's Stadtsbibliothek, lists several Boogs whose possible relationship to Johann Nepomuk Boog remains to be clarified. Renate Federhofer-Königs, "Zur Musikpflege in der Wallfahrtskirche von Mariazell/ Steiermark," *Kirchenmusikalisches Jahrbuch* 41 (1957), p. 130, reports that this Styrian church preserves a *Te Deum* by "Giov. Nep. Boog/M.D.C. al S. Pietro a Vienna" along with five other sacred pieces by the composer.

31. Manuscript score I.7420 (=Q344) in the Gesellschaft der Musikfreunde, Vienna; mentioned in Reichert, "Geschichte," p. 102. The Mass's attribution reads: "Sgre. Giovanni Pogg [sic] Scolare del Sgre. Francesco Tuma."

32. Peter Dormann, "Aumann," *MGG* XV, col. 343. Since Albrechtsberger and Michael Haydn also studied there, perhaps Boog was also one of their teachers. Considering certain errors in Boog's counterpoint (see ex. 8-18, m. 47, 56), one assumes he did not teach them composition!

33. Excerpts from Boog's Masses appear as ex. 6-14; 7-6, 7-27; 8-12C, 8-18; 9-3, and 9-16F.

34. Biba, "Kirchenmusik 1783," pp. 26, 45. The 1783 inventory mentions that as part of his pay Carl received free lodging from the Bürgerspital.

35. Haas, *Wiener Musiker,* no. 348, p. 12. On St. Augustine's and its *Loreto-* and *Totenbruderschaft-Kapellen* see Riedel, *Karl VI,* pp. 38–39.

36. Biba, "Kirchenmusik 1783," p. 26.

37. Haas, *Wiener Musiker,* no. 241, p. 10. Pfannhauser, in his introduction to the edition of Albrechtsberger's E-flat major Mass (see n. 3 above), indicates that Albrechtsberger became familiar with the music of Ambros Carl while at Klosterneuburg in the 1740s.

38. Excerpts from Carl's Mass appear as ex. 8-16 and 9-16B. This Mass is attributed to Carl in three manuscripts.

39. Karl Ditters von Dittersdorf, *Lebensbeschreibung seinem Sohne in die Feder diktiert* (Leipzig: Breitkopf & Härtel, 1801); for later editions see the bibliography. A good summary of his life and works is Margaret H. Grave, "Dittersdorf," *New Grove* V, pp. 500–503.

40. Albrechtsberger, Aumann, and Michael Haydn were also studying at the Jesuit School about this time.

41. See the section on Tobias Gsur below and chapter 1 at n. 34. Gsur was then director of music at the Schottenkirche.

42. The quantity of Masses by Dittersdorf remains to be settled. I have located some 12 Masses attributed to the composer. Oldřich Pulkert's catalogue of Dittersdorf's works apparently lists 21 Masses and Requiems (see Barry S. Brook, *Thematic Catalogues in Music: An Annotated Bibliography,* Hillsdale, NY: Pendragon, 1972, no. 306).

43. Carl Krebs, *Dittersdorfiana* (Berlin: Paetel, 1900) nos. 326–28, p. 142. Excerpts from these Masses appear as ex. 6-11; 8-4, 8-12A; 9-4D, 9-12, 9-16A, 9-16F; 10-3, 10-4E, 10-9, 10-10.

44. Since no parts for M. 16 (Krebs no. 326, n.d.) have been found and only the autograph score exists, we remain uncertain as to whether the Mass was ever performed during Dittersdorf's lifetime.

45. Some of the virtuosic violin solos (see ex. 9-12) were perhaps intended for performance by the violinist-composer himself. (The Gloria of M. 15 also has a very difficult violin solo.)

46. Translation from Landon, *Haydn: Chronicle and Works* II, p. 130. Landon says the article appeared in the *Wiener Diarium's* supplement "Gelehrter Nachrichten," 26th number, Saturday, 18 October 1766. We give the citation according to Robert Haas, "Von dem Wienerischen Geschmack in der Musik," in *Festschrift Johannes Biehle zum 60. Geburtstag* (Leipzig: Kistner & Siegel, 1930), p. 64, which reprints the original German text.

47. This quotation is cited by Wilfried Scheib, "Die Entwicklung der Musikberichterstattung im *Wienerischen Diarium* von 1703 bis 1780, mit besonderer Berücksichtigung der Wiener Oper" (Ph.D. diss., University of Vienna, 1950), p. 215. Although Scheib does not give the specific issue for this excerpt, he does indicate (p. 230ff.) that articles mentioning Dittersdorf do appear in *Wiener Diarium* no. 77 of 1765 and no. 103 of 1773.

48. *Wiener Diarium* (1766, no. 73) as cited by Scheib, "Musikberichterstattung," p. 215.

49. See chapter 1 n. 27.

50. This information comes from Schubert's handwritten autobiography; see Ernst Hilmar, "Ferdinand Schuberts Skizze zu einer Autobiographie," in *Schubert-Studien: Festgabe der österreichischen Akademie der Wissenschaften zum Schubert-Jahr 1978* (Vienna: Österreichische Akademie der Wissenschaften, 1978), p. 98, n. 40. Dr. Otto Biba kindly provided this citation and remarked that a unison Mass with such limited accompaniment was typical of the so-called *Franziskaner-Messe* type.

51. Carl Ferdinand Pohl, "Friberth, Karl F." in *Allgemeine Deutsche Biographie* (Leipzig: Duncker und Humblot, 1878) VII, p. 376. Modern biographies of Friberth include: Alfred Orel, "Frieberth," *MGG* IV (1955) col. 944–45; Landon, *Haydn: Chronicle and Works* II, p. 58; anon., "Frieberth," *New Grove*, ed. Stanley Sadie VI, p. 848. In Vienna Dr. Ingrid Fuchs of the Kommission für Musikforschung of the Österreichische Akademie der Wissenschaften is presently completing the Friberth study begun by the late Leopold Voruba.

52. Pohl, "Friberth," p. 376. According to Franz Kosch, "Florian Leopold Gassman als Kirchenkomponist," in *Studien zur Musikwissenschaft* XIV (1927): 222, n. 31, Friberth later (1786) taught voice to one of the late *Hofkapellmeister* Gassmann's daughters; Pohl indicates that Friberth was one of Vienna's respected singing teachers.

53. Since 1773 the Jesuits had no longer controlled these churches. According to Biba, "Kirchenmusik 1783," pp. 25, 38–41, up to 1783 Friberth had also been providing (and directing) music at the following: Wällsche National Kapelle (after 1784, Minoriten-Kirche), Trattnerische Kapelle (ended in 1783), St. Ivo (ended in 1783), Kapelle Sts. Philipp & Jakob (ended in 1783), St. Johannis Nepomucensis Spital (ended in 1783). The regulations enacted under Joseph II ended Friberth's work at the latter four institutions in 1783. It is thus no wonder that Friberth wrote the petition of musicians complaining about the new imperial regulations (Biba, "Kirchenmusik 1783," p. 11). Otto Biba, "Der

Piaristenorden in Österreich: seine Bedeutung für bildende Kunst, Musik und Theater im 17. und 18. Jahrhundert," *Jahrbuch für österreichische Kulturgeschichte* (Eisenstadt: Institut für österreichische Kulturgeschichte, 1975), p. 132, notes how Friberth seems to have used the same ensemble at several of these and other churches. For example, Friberth's musicians provided music for a service 24 September 1780 at St. Thekla.

54. Johann Ferdinand von Schönfeld, *Jahrbuch der Tonkunst von Wien und Prag* (1796), p. 17.

55. Pohl, *Joseph Haydn*, II, (Leipzig: Breitkopf & Härtel, 1882), p. 132, n. 4. On Easter Sunday in 1786 instruments and singers from the Italian opera company were given permission to perform under Friberth in the Minoriten-Kirche (then used by the Italian congregation).

56. Pohl, "Friberth," p. 376, and chapter 2 at n. 18. Otto Biba, "Der Sozial-Status des Musikers," in *Joseph Haydn in seiner Zeit*, ed. Gerda Mraz, Gottfried Mraz, and Gerald Schlag (Eisenstadt: Kulturabteilung des Amtes der Burgenländischen Landesregierung, 1982), p. 111, notes that Friberth freely used the term Kapellmeister; although he oversaw the music for only a few services at the Universitäts-Kirche, Friberth called himself "Universitätskapellmeister."

57. According to his biography in the Sammlung handschriftlicher Biographien (1826) located in the Gesellschaft der Musikfreunde archive, Friberth composed 8 "solo Masses" (1771, 1789, 1792, 1796, 1802, 1807, 1808, 1809) and 1 "tutti Mass" (1812). (All autographs were possessed by his son-in-law Anton Riedl, Expeditions-Direktions Adjunkt bei der vereinigten Hofkanzlei in 1826).

58. For some inexplicable reason, the manuscript biography in the Gesellschaft der Musikfreunde (see preceding note) does not mention specifically a Mass for 1774, the date on the autograph of M. 18.

59. Friedrich Christoph Nicolai, *Beschreibung einer Reise durch Deutschland und die Schweiz im Jahre 1781, nebst Bemerkungen über Gelehrsamkeit, Industrie, Religion und Sitten* (Berlin and Stettin: n.p., 1784), p. 545. He calls the church the "Kriegskirche" or former "Jesuiterkirche." For a translation of Nicolai's description see chapter 4 at n. 11.

60. Pohl, "Friberth," p. 376. One wonders if Pope Pius VI had not perhaps heard Friberth and his musicians during a visit to Vienna's Kirche am Hof in 1782; see the illustration of the Pope's audience held from the balcony of this church in that year (plate 6).

61. Schönfeld, *Jahrbuch der Tonkunst von Wien und Prag* (1796), ch. VII, p. 82.

62. Ibid., p. 17. For a different translation see Landon, *Haydn: Chronicle and Works*, II, p. 58.

63. Franz Kosch, "Gassmann," *Studien zur Musikwissenschaft* XIV (1927): 219, 221. For other biographical surveys see: George R. Hill, "Gassmann," *New Grove* VII, pp. 178–79; Karl Michael Komma, "Gassman," *MGG*, IV (1955) col. 1431–35; Gustav Donath and Robert Haas, "Florian Leopold Gassmann als Opernkomponist," *Studien zur Musikwissenschaft* II (1914):34–211.

64. Kosch, "Gassmann," p. 219. Gassmann was Gluck's successor as a theater composer. Kosch (p. 218f.) considers Gassmann's experiences in Italy (especially Venice and studies with Martini in Bologna) crucial to his eventual development as a church composer.

65. Ibid., pp. 219, 221; see also Pohl, *Joseph Haydn* II, p. 111. During the 1760s Gassmann returned twice to Italy.

66. Pohl, *Tonkünstler-Societät*, p. 103.

67. Kosch, "Gassmann," pp. 222–23.

68. Franz Kosch, "Florian Leopold Gassmann als Kirchenkomponist" (Ph.D. diss., Vienna, 1924), pp. 31–43.

69. Kosch, "Gassmann," pp. 224, 221. By this time Gassmann was apparently "free" of Neapolitan influences. Readers may wish to consult Kosch's edition of Mass No. 3 (*DTÖ*, vol. 83). Kosch (p. 219) feels that the Mass for three men's voices was perhaps a product of Gassmann's years in Venice (probably during the 1750s).

70. Ibid., p. 220. Manuscript parts were acquired at Göttweig in 1771. Landon, *Haydn: Chronicle and Works* II, p. 229, writes that this *St. Cecilia Mass* was composed "about 1765" and cites Kosch, "Gassmann," p. 235f. as his source; Kosch, however, actually provides no such date for the Mass.

71. See M. 19 in the thematic catalogue (app. C) and chapter 5. A future edition will attempt to explain the origin of these two versions. At the moment, the Berlin version seems to be the most widely disseminated version of this Mass.

72. Only the "Berlin version" closes the Credo with an "Et vitam" fugue.

73. Hill, "Gassmann," *New Grove* VII, p. 178; see also Kosch, "Gassmann," pp. 225–26.

74. Charles Burney, *Dr. Burney's Musical Tours in Europe*, ed. Percy A. Scholes (London: Oxford University Press, 1959) II, p. 116; II, pp. 123–24, n. 1. Charles Burney, *A General History of Music, From the Earliest Times to the Present Period*, ed. Frank Mercer (London: G. T. Foulis, 1935) II, pp. 946–51, lists Gassmann among "the great opera composers" of Germany who, along with Gluck, J.C. Bach, and Mislivicek and following the path of Hasse and Graun, have won the public's favor for a new opera style.

75. For example, in 1779 Hiller performed part of the *St. Cecilia Mass* (Kosch No. 4; M. 19) at a *concert spirituel* (see chapter 2, n. 52), and after 1774 Haydn continued to produce Gassmann's operas for the Esterházys.

76. Joseph Martin Kraus, *Etwas von und über Musik fürs Jahr 1777* (Frankfurt, 1778), pp. 95–96. The other composers named are Wassmut, Pögel, Richter, and Fux.

77. Nicolai, *Beschreibung 1781*, p. 527.

78. J. Sonnleithner, "Biographische Skizze über Florian Leopold Gassmann," in *Wiener Theateralmanach für das Jahr 1795*, p. 31, as cited by Kosch, "Gassmann," p. 234. The score of Gassmann's Requiem fragment appears in *DTÖ* vol. 83.

79. Schönfeld, *Jahrbuch der Tonkunst von Wien und Prag (1796)*, p. 52.

80. "Laurenz Grassl," in Sammlung handschriftlicher Biographien, Gesellschaft der Musikfreunde, Vienna. Pohl, *Tonkünstler-Societät*, no. 109, pp. 106, 119, reports that Laurenz joined the society in 1778, died 15 May 1805, and left no known descendants.

81. Federhofer-Königs, "Musikpflege in Mariazell," p. 122, n. 25. This information comes from a lost inventory seen by Dr. E.F. Schmid in 1935; it included two Masses by Laurenz Grassl. Haas, *Wiener Musiker*, does not list either Grassl, although he cites a Lorenz Grass, *Regens chori* in Lichtenthal (probably Pfarr "zu den 14 Nothelfern"), who died 15 March 1728.

82. Biba, "Kirchenmusik 1783," pp. 24, 33. Biba's inventory of 1783 also reports (p. 49) that "Lorenz Grasl" had been singing at St. Ruprecht's before it was closed that year. Perhaps Laurenz is related to the "Ludwig Grassel" who up to 1783 had been a tenor at St. Augustine's (ibid., p. 26).

83. Oldřich Pulkert, *Domus Lauretana Pragensis. Catalogus collectionis operum artis musicae,* Catalogus Artis Musicae in Bohemia et Moravia Cultae Artis Musicae Antiquioris Catalogorum (Prague: Supraphon, 1973), vol. I, under "Grasl."

84. Information about this source (Ottobeuren, MO-440) was obtained from the West German RISM catalogues at the Bavarian State Library in Munich. No reason is given why these catalogues attribute the Mass to Laurenz even though no first name is given in the manuscript.

85. For the sources of *Missa Pastoralis Ex C* see M. 20 in the thematic catalogue of app. C. Robert N. Freeman, *Franz Schneider (1737–1812): A Thematic Catalogue of His Works* (New York: Pendragon, 1979), pp. 80–81, lists the D-major Mass (before 1769) as Schneider doubtful no. 79 and attributes the work to Adam Grassl.

86. Dittersdorf, *Lebensbeschreibung,* pp. 18–19.

87. Eitner, *Quellen-Lexikon* IV, p. 397. Biba, "Kirchenmusik 1783," p. 24, lists Gsur as still being *regens chori* of the Schottenkirche in 1783. Gsur may have been related to Karl Gsur, another bass listed at this church as well as at the Dorothea Kirche and St. Anne's in 1783.

88. Haus-, Hof-, und Staatsarchiv, Vienna: Hofarchiv 78, Obersthofmeisteramt Akten; also Protokolle 37, Vortrag Nr. 31. These documents relate to Gsur's 1774 application for the position of *Hofkapellmeister.* See chapter 2 at n. 37 and 38. See also Köchel, *Hof-Musikkapelle,* pp. 89, 93; A. Kellner, *Musikgeschichte des Stiftes Kremsmünster nach den Quellen dargestellt* (Kassel: Bärenreiter, 1956), p. 379; Wellesz, "Bonno," pp. 440–41.

89. Pohl, *Tonkünstler-Societät,* no. 31, pp. 103, 119. Gsur was among the group of Hofkapelle musicians who became members by imperial subvention.

90. Stadtsbibliothek, Vienna: *Todtenprotokoll 1794,* "G," fol. 31^r. Joseph Eybler apparently succeeded Gsur as *regens chori* at the Schottenkirche in 1794.

91. Kellner, *Musikgeschichte Kremsmünster,* p. 379: "[Gsur] hat eine Reihe beliebter Kirchenkompositionen geschrieben." The cloister at Kremsmünster is, like the Schottenkirche in Vienna, also a Benedictine institution.

92. For excerpts from Gsur's Masses see ex. 9-4C and 10-1A.

93. For further biographical details see: David J. Nichols and Sven Hansell, "Hasse," in *New Grove* VII, pp. 279–93; Anna Amalie Abert, "Hasse," in *MGG* V (1956) col. 1771–87.

94. Carl Mennicke, "Hasse und die Gebrüder Graun als Symphoniker nebst Biographien und thematischen Katalogen" (Ph.D. diss., Leipzig, 1905; Leipzig: Breitkopf & Härtel, 1906), p. 423, reports that in March 1769 Hasse conducted his *Litanie della Beatissima Vergine* at the *Hof* in a performance involving the entire imperial family (cited by David James Wilson, "Selected Masses of Johann Adolf Hasse" [Ph.D. diss., University of Illinois at Urbana-Champaign, 1973], p. 29, and Nichols-Hansell, "Hasse," *New Grove* VIII, p. 284). In addition, in a letter dated 19 November 1768 to G.M. Ortes, Hasse wrote that his "chief passion today" was the church style (Georg Walther Müller, *Johann Adolf Hasse als Kirchenkomponist: ein Beitrag zur Geschichte der neapolitanischen Kirchenmusik, mit thematischen Katalog der liturgischen Kirchenmusik J.A. Hasse's* (Leipzig: Breitkopf & Härtel, 1911, p. 48; Nichols-Hansell, "Hasse," *New Grove* VIII, p. 284, report the year as 1769 instead of 1768).

95. Müller, *Hasse als Kirchenkomponist,* p. 48.

96. Nichols-Hansell, "Hasse," *New Grove* VIII, pp. 280–82. See also Burney, *Musical Tours,* ed. Scholes II, pp. 82, 107, 108.

97. Musical examples from these three Masses (= Müller Nos. 9, 5, and 2) include ex. 6-1, 7-23, 8-11, and 10-1B. Wilson, "Selected Masses of Hasse," 94–110, includes a complete score of the D minor Mass (M. 24).

98. Wilson, "Selected Masses of Hasse," p. 74.

99. Nichols-Hansell, "Hasse," *New Grove* VIII, p. 290.

100. Müller, *Hasse als Kirchenkomponist,* Messe Nr. 5, p. 153; Wilson, "Selected Masses of Hasse," pp. 25–26, 94–95.

101. Wilson, "Selected Masses of Hasse," p. 33.

102. Burney, *Musical Tours,* ed. Scholes II, p. 82.

103. Hermine Prohászka, "Leopold Hofmann und seine Messen," *Studien zur Musikwissenschaft* XXVI (1964): 79. Good surveys of Hofmann's career are found in this source and in: Hermine Nicolussi-Prohászka, "Hofmann, Leopold," in *New Grove* VIII, pp. 634–35. Hofmann's position at St. Michael's is based upon a marriage document of 1758. In his youth he had sung in Tuma's Hofkapelle for the widowed Empress Elisabeth Christina and studied keyboard and composition with Wagenseil.

104. Prohászka, "Hofmann," p. 79, reports that, according to Fétis, Hofmann was choir director there by 1764, but not until 1766 do other documents confirm his being there. According to Biba, "Kirchenmusik 1783," p. 24, Hofmann had the title Kapellmeister at St. Peter's in the church music census of 1783.

105. Hans Brunner, *Die Kantorei bei St. Stephan in Wien: Beiträge zur Geschichte der Wiener Dommusik* (Vienna: A. Dürer, 1948), 19ff., informs us that Hofmann (like Reutter from 1756 on) was Kapellmeister for the cathedral's two music ensembles, i.e. the *Essential-* (or *Haupt-*) *Kapelle* and the *Gnadenbild-Kapelle,* the latter of which was terminated in 1783.

106. See chapter 2 at nn. 37 and 38.

107. For an excellent survey of Hofmann's Masses see Prohászka, "Hofmann," pp. 82–104. Research for the present study shows Hofmann's *Missa in D* (Prohászka catalogue no. 6) to be probably by Joseph Krottendorfer.

108. Musical examples from these four Masses include: 7-5, 7-10, 7-20; 8-1, 8-15; 9-10, 9-16E; 10-2.

109. Prohászka, "Hofmann," pp. 82, 89, 104.

110. *Wiener Diarium* 1766, Anhang of no. 84. Translation from Landon, *Haydn: Chronicle and Works* II, p. 129.

111. Prohászka, "Hofmann," p. 80.

112. Wellesz, "Bonno," Beilage IV, p. 440; see n. 88 above.

113. See chapter 2 at n. 2.

114. Nicolai, *Beschreibung 1781* IV, p. 527. Like Burney, Nicolai was surprised at the rather poor quality of musical performances at St. Stephen's; chapter 2, n. 7.

115. The chief source for most of this information is Eduard Schmitt's "Die Kurpfälzische Kirchenmusik im 18. Jahrhundert" (Ph.D. diss., University of Heidelberg, 1958), p. 287ff. Schmitt had access to Holzbauer's short, published *Selbstbiographie* (ca. 1782). For a general biographical survey of Holzbauer's life and works, see also Floyd K. Grave, "Holzbauer," in *New Grove* VIII, pp. 669–70.

116. Holzbauer may have worked for an Esterházy. According to Pulkert's catalogue of Prague's Loreta Kapelle (CS-LIT), the *Missa in D* (Schmitt no. 22; Reichert no. 8) has an undated title page reading: "Del Sige. Holtzbauer, Maestro di Capella all Principe d'Esterhazi. Ex Mus: Jos: Strobach." Strobach (1731–94) worked in several churches in Prague.

117. Schmitt, "Kurpfälzische Kirchenmusik," p. 308ff., catalogues 25 extant Latin Masses by Holzbauer. Three of these (Schmitt nos. 1, 2, and 24) are actually by other composers (F. Schneider, L. Mozart, and L. Hofmann, respectively). In 1980 Klaus Altmann, who was preparing a dissertation on these Masses at the University of Bonn, kindly showed me Schmitt's revised unpublished catalogue which listed 35 Masses. Three of these Masses may be by other composers: Schmitt's new no. 3 (Bush's A2) may be by Zechner (see Reichert no. 15), new no. 11 (Reichert no. 13; Bush A17) bears a striking resemblance to an F-major Mass by Fux (Köchel 41), and new no. 22 (Bush A20) may be by Brixi. Deanna Day Bush, "The Orchestral Masses of Ignaz Holzbauer (1711–1783): Authenticity, Chronology, and Style with Thematic Catalogue and Selected Transcriptions" (Ph.D. diss., Eastman School of Music, 1982) authenticates 21 Masses; her thematic catalogue lists 35 Latin Masses (27 complete, 4 incomplete, 4 doubtful) including 1 complete Mass not known to Schmitt (A9, attributed to A. Grassl at A-M), 1 new incomplete Mass (I29), and 3 new doubtful Masses (D1, D2, D6), and combining different versions of the same Mass under one number (e.g., A11, A11a, A15, A15a equal Schmitt's nos. 22, 23, 15, 16). Bush does not include Schmitt's new nos. 25, 31, and 33. I have located two additional Masses (1 in C, 1 in d) not listed in these catalogues.

118. Examples from these four Masses by Holzbauer are ex. 6-4; 7-26; 8-5, 8-6; 9-1, 9-8, 9-9, 9-16F; see fig. 7-6.

119. Kraus, *Etwas von und über Musik 1777,* pp. 95–96; see chapter 2 at n. 127.

120. Translation based on Bauer-Deutsch, ed., *Briefe Mozarts,* no. 363 (Mannheim, 4 Nov. 1777) II, p. 102; cf. Anderson, ed., *Letters of Mozart,* no. 235, I, p. 356. This same letter describes the balance problems of the large orchestra and chorus (6 persons per voice part!). In a later letter of 14 Nov. 1777 (Anderson no. 243ª) Mozart expresses amazement at the spirit and fire in this old man's music.

121. Josef Klima, "Kohaut," in *MGG* XVI, col. 1013–14 (Eng. trans. in *New Grove* X, p. 153). Haas, *Wiener Musiker,* no. 268, p. 11, lists "Jakob Carl Kohut" as a "k. Hof-Musikus" who died 17 May 1762.

122. Kirkendale, *Fugue and Fugato,* p. 9. Kirkendale also notes that Kohaut was "highly esteemed" by Joseph II.

123. Burney, *Musical Tours,* ed. Scholes II, pp. 112, 125.

124. Pohl, *Tonkünstler-Societät,* p. 58.

125. Most of the present biographical information is based upon Karl Schnürl, "Josef Krottendorfer: Ein Komponistenschicksal aus der Zeit der Wiener Klassik," *Kulturberichte aus Niederösterreich* (Beilage der amtlichen Nachrichten der niederösterreichischen Landesregierung) 1965, Folge 10, pp. 78–79.

126. Schnürl, "Krottendorfer," p. 78; see also Pohl, *Tonkünstler-Societät,* no. 48, p. 104. Schnürl (p. 79) notes that Krottendorder may also have been a theater violinist at this time because a 1771 *Theateralmanach* lists a "Krottendorfer" in the orchestra of the French theater.

127. Schönfeld, *Jahrbuch der Tonkunst von Wien and Prag* (1796), p. 76, still lists Krottendorfer as a tenor in the *k.k. Hofkapelle.*

128. Schnürl, "Krottendorfer," p. 79. According to Jay Dee Schaefer, "The Use of the Trombone in the 18th Century," *The Instrumentalist* XXII/11 (June 1968): 61, T. Donley Thomas, in an article entitled "Michael Haydn's Trombone Symphony" [*Brass Quarterly* VI/1 (Fall 1968): 6–8], mentions a symphony by Joseph Krottendorfer as an early example requiring two trombones.

129. The parts for two Masses from the *Hof-Musikkapelle* collection (now in the Austrian National Library, Vienna)—a *Missa in D* (H.K. 514) and a *Missa in G* (H.K. 515)—show almost annual performances of these works from 1820 to 1857 (earlier performance dates were probably on older covers that were subsequently discarded).

130. Examples from Krottendorfer's Mass include ex. 9-16D; 10-6.

131. Cited by Otto Biba, "Die Orgelakten des Stiftes Herzogenburg," *Unsere Heimat* (Zeitschrift des Vereins für Landeskunde von Niederösterreich und Wien) 41/1 (1970): 24.

132. There were few other women composers in Vienna at this time. The blind Maria Theresia von Paradis did not become known until the 1780s. Nicolai, *Beschreibung 1781,* p. 554, lists only one other female composer under amateurs (*Liebhaber*): Miss Marianne von Auenbrugger, who was a keyboard player and sister of the master keyboardist Miss Franziska Auenbrugger. (No Masses have been found under the name Auenbrugger in 18th-century catalogues.) Among the few other women composers of the period could be named Maria Cäcilia Barbara Meissner (1728–66), daughter of the Salzburg composer Eberlin.

133. For recent biographies of Martínez see: Helene Wessely, "Martínez," *New Grove* XI, pp. 721–22; idem, "Martinez," *MGG,* VIII (1960), col. 1716–18. According to Schnoebelen, *Padre Martini's Collection of Letters,* no. 3081, p. 371, Martínez also credits her father, *maestro di camera* for the Papal *nuntius* in Vienna, as one of her teachers.

134. Burney, *Musical Tours,* ed. Scholes II, p. 117; see also II, pp. 86, 106–7, 109, 119–20, 122.

135. Mary Nicole Schnoebelen, "The Concerted Mass at San Petronio in Bologna ca. 1660–1730: A Documentary and Analytical Study" (Ph.D. diss., University of Illinois at Urbana-Champaign, 1966), pp. 27–30, presents an excellent description of the Accademia Filarmonica. Schnoebelen (p.30) observes: "Thus, it appears that the actual influence of this organization pertained to standards of performance in church music rather than compositional procedures.... The classical ideals of the *Accademia Filarmonia* were remote from actual practice and made no lasting impression, but its continual demands for excellent performance redounded to the glory of concerted sacred music in Bologna."
   Anne Schnoebelen, *Padre Martini's Collection of Letters in the Civico museo bibliografico musicale in Bologna: An Annotated Index* (New York: Pendragon, 1979), no. 3077, p. 370, relates how Martínez sent (at Metastasio's recommendation) a series of vocal pieces to Padre Martini in 1773. Perhaps these samples of her music paved the way for her being accepted by the Accademia; Martini had helped Mozart obtain membership in 1770 (see Alfred Einstein, *Mozart: His Character, His Work,* trans. Arthur Mendel and Nathan Broder [New York: Oxford University Press, 1945], pp. 146–47).

136. Martin Gerbert, *De cantu et musica sacra, a prima ecclesiae aetate usque ad praesens tempus* (St. Blasien, n.p. 1774), Liber IV: *De cantu et musica sacra posterioris aevi, a saeculo circiter XV. usque ad praesens tempus,* p. 353, footnote "a." The relevant part of

Gerbert's note reads: "...accepique ante aliquot annos *Viennae* ex ipsius manu missam solemnam stylo ecclesiastico accommodatiorem multo, quam pleraeque auctorum virorum nostri temporis melothesiae."

137. Pohl, *Tonkünstler-Societät,* p. 60.

138. Schönfeld, *Jahrbuch der Tonkunst von Wien und Prag (1796),* pp. 2, 41. Schönfeld notes here that Martínez's *Geschmack* is chiefly of the Italian manner.

139. Ibid., p. 42. On p. 71f. Schönfeld describes the dilettante academies held every Saturday at the home of this able musician.

140. Ibid., pp. 81-82.

141. Examples of Masses by Martínez are found below in ex. 5-1; 6-5, 6-19; 7-1, 7-11; 8-19; 9-16A; 10-11; see fig. 10-8.

142. Nicola Porpora, *GRAND MESSE/à Quatre Voix/de/Niccola Porpora...* (Paris: Carli, n.d.) pl. no. 1114RC, 75 p. [= RISM P-5108]. In addition, Martínez (like Porpora and other composers) reuses the music of the first "Qui tollis" for the "Qui sedes" in the Gloria.

143. Karl Pfannhauser, "Zu Mozarts Kirchenwerke von 1768," *Mozart Jahrbuch 1954,* p. 162. In 1768 the Mozarts and the Martínez family dwelt in the same house (the so-called Michaelerhaus) next to St. Michael's.

144. Kirkendale, *Fugue and Fugato,* p. 9.

145. Ingrid Kollpacher, "Monn," *MGG* IX (1961) col. 378-79; see also Judith Leah Schwartz, "Monn," *New Grove* XII, pp. 493-94, and Reichert, "Geschichte," pp. 63-64.

146. Haas, *Wiener Musiker,* no. 222, p. 10.

147. This tale (doubted by many) was related by Johann Fuss, a student of Albrechtsberger; see Robert N. Freeman, "Albrechtsberger," *New Grove* I, pp. 224-26.

148. Reichert, "Geschichte," lists four in his thematic catalogue of Monn's Masses. Evidence now indicates that no. 1 in Reichert's catalogue is actually by Boog instead of Monn (see M. 12 in app. C). Monn appears to have written two Masses in C, two in D, one in G, and one in B-flat.

149. Musical examples from Monn's Masses include 6-2, 6-8; 7-2, 7-11, 7-21; 8-12A, 8-19; 9-4A, 9-5, 9-16B; 10-4A; see also figs. 5-3 and 8-8.

150. For biographical details and further documentation see: Otto Biba, "Müller, Silverius," *New Grove* XII, pp. 771-72; idem, "Müller, Silverius," *MGG* XVI, col. 1303-4; idem, "Piaristenorden," pp. 164-66.

151. *Wiener Schriftsteller- und Künstler-Lexikon* (Vienna, 1793), p. 94, as cited by Biba, "Piaristenorden," p. 166. Müller may have been a good friend of Dittersdorf to whom Müller dedicated his six string quartets published by Torricella of Vienna in 1785 (RISM M-7921; see Biba, ibid., p. 131).

152. Dr. Otto Biba, who has made an inventory of the Maria Treu collection, kindly allowed me to make copies of his score drawn up from the parts to this Mass. Biba, "Piaristenorden," p. 165, cautions that some works by Silverius Müller have, over the years, been misattributed to the celebrated Wenzel Müller.

153. For further biographical details see Anne Schnoebelen, "Luca Antonio Predieri," *New Grove* XV, pp. 207-8; idem, "Concerted Mass in Bologna," p. 126; see also Oscar Mischiati and Luigi Ferdinando Tagliavini, "Predieri," *MGG* (1962) col. 1603, 1605-7.

154. Heinrich Freunschlag, "Luca Antonio Predieri als Kirchenkomponist" (Ph.D. diss., University of Vienna, 1927), p. 4ff. lists 12 Masses plus 11 fragments. I have found two additional Masses attributed to Predieri. Freunschlag's thematic catalogue of Predieri's Masses is now in the *DTÖ* archive at the University of Vienna (Musikwissenschaftliches Institut, call no. Z93).

155. For biographical details see Eva Badura-Skoda, "Reutter," *New Grove* XV, pp. 772–74; see also Norbert Hofer, "Die beiden Reutter als Kirchenkomponisten" (Ph.D. diss., Vienna, 1915); idem, ed., introduction to Reutter's *Kirchenwerke, DTÖ*, vol. 88.

156. Landon, *Haydn: Chronicle and Works* I, p. 89, n. 1.

157. Badura-Skoda, "Reutter," *New Grove* XV, p. 773; see also Köchel, *Hof-Musikkapelle*, p. 31. Köchel (p. 24) calls this the Kapelle's "Jammerperiode" (period of misery).

158. Norbert Hofer, "Thematisches Verzeichnis der Werke Georg Reutters d.J.," Mus. Hs. 28.992 at the Austrian National Library, Vienna, lists some 85 different Masses. However, the following 13 can be attributed to other composers: Hofer nos. 6 (Caldara?), 9 (Seuche), 16 and 37 (Arbesser), 18 (Schneider; see also Freeman, *Schneider*, cat. no. 2), 22 (J. Haydn?, Hob. XXII: 3), 27^b (Ziegler or Strasser?), 41 (Pfeiffer), 48 (Carl), 49 (Hofmann; see also Prohászka, "Hofmann," cat. no. 15), 53^b (Zechner), 65 and 71 (Aumann?). Badura-Skoda, "Reutter," *New Grove* XV, p. 774, reports 81 Masses by the composer. Most of the extant autograph scores of Reutter's Masses are today in Heiligenkreuz.

159. Examples from Reutter's Masses include ex. 5-2, 6-6, 6-10, 6-19; 7-3, 7-11, 7-14, 7-15, 7-24, 7-25; 8-8, 8-12A, 8-19; 9-11, 9-13, 9-16E; 10-17; see also fig. 6-3.

160. See Landon, *Haydn: Chronicle and Works* I, pp. 92–94, for the musical figure mentioned.

161. Burney, *Musical Tours*, ed. Scholes II, p. 122.

162. *Wiener Diarium* (1766) no. 84, Anhang; the translation (slightly amended) is from Landon, *Haydn: Chronicle and Works* II, p. 129.

163. All biographical information is from Karl Pfannhauser, "Schmid(t), Ferdinand," *MGG* XI (1963) col. 1846–47.

164. Landon, *Haydn: Chronicle and Works* I, p. 56. Here Landon also describes the workings of the *Gnadenbild-Kapelle (Gnadenbild Maria Pötsch)* where Schmidt was also called "Maestro di cappella della Madonna."

165. James Frederick Dack, "The Origins and Development of the Esterházy Kapelle in Eisenstadt until 1790" (Ph.D. diss., University of Liverpool, 1976), p. 101.

166. Kellner, *Musikgeschichte Kremsmünster*, p. 354.

167. Pfannhauser, "Schmidt," *MGG* XI, col. 1846.

168. Examples from Schmidt's Masses include ex. 6-3, 6-20; 7-9, 7-11, 7-12; 8-2, 8-14, 8-19; 9-2, 9-14, 9-16A; 10-8, 10-15; see also fig. 7-5.

169. *Todtenprotokoll 1790*, "S," fol. 14^v, in the Stadtbibliothek, Vienna; see *Wiener Zeitung* 1790, p. 365.

170. Biba, "Kirchenmusik 1783," p. 30. In Lambach there are parts for symphonies and sonatas (call nos. 158–59, 153) which read "Del Giuseppe Francesco Seüche/Ad Chorum S: Michaelis Viennae" with performance dates 1750–68.

171. An excerpt from M. 53 by Seuche appears as ex. 10-4D below.

172. Hans Jancik, "Sonnleithner," *MGG* XII (1965) col. 915–16; (no author), "Sonnleithner," *New Grove* XVII, p. 526. Constantin Wurzbach, *Biographisches Lexikon des Kaiserthums Oesterreich, enthaltend die Lebensskizzen der denkwürdigen Personen* . . . (Vienna: k.k. Hof- und Staatsdruckerei, 1856–91) XXXVI, p. 2, indicates that Sonnleithner's doctors forbade him to compose any more church music after its demands had begun to take their toll. Christoph's son, Joseph Sonnleithner (1766–1835), adapted the libretto of *Fidelio* for Beethoven, while his daughter Anna became the mother of the renowned poet, author, and dramatist Franz Grillparzer. Christoph was also the family lawyer for Prince Nikolaus Esterházy (Landon, *Haydn: Chronicle and Works* I, p. 412).

173. For excerpts from Sonnleithner's Masses see ex. 6-13, 6-19; 7-11, 7-17, 7-22; 8-19; 9-7, 9-16B, 9-16C, 9-16E; 10-7, 10-12; see also fig. 9-7, 10-9.

174. "Biographien: Christoph Sonnleithner," *Wiener Allgemeine Musikalische Zeitung* I/33 (August 1817) col. 280.

175. Wurzbach, *Biographisches Lexikon*, XXXVI, p. 2. Cf. Landon, *Haydn: Chronicle and Works* IV, p. 464, who says (mistakenly) that it was the auction of Christoph's library.

176. [Ignaz von Mosel], "Über den Stand der Musik in Wien," *Wiener Theater Almanac auf das Jahr 1794:* 178–79.

177. Schönfeld, *Jahrbuch der Tonkunst von Wien und Prag (1796)*, pp. 81–82. Study of ex. 6-13 below will show, however, that Sonnleithner's music was not free of occasional oversights such as the parallel octaves between outer voices in measure 12.

178. "Christoph Sonnleithner," col. 279–80.

179. Karl Pfannhauser, "Zu Mozarts Kirchenwerke von 1768," p. 155ff.

180. Biba, "Kirchenmusik 1783," pp. 33, 35–36, 39, 46–47. Pohl, *Tonkünstler-Societät*, p. 103, reports that three Strassers joined the newly founded society on 2 May 1771:
    Ignaz (dropped out 1783),
    Georg (dropped out 1783),
    Josef (dropped out 2 June 1772).
    Biba (pp. 35–36) reports that Ignaz played organ at Maria Hilf Kirche where Georg directed. Perhaps these men were sons (?) of Johann Georg Strasser, a "Musikus" who died 2 April 1770 at the age of 70 in Vienna; see Haas, *Wiener Musiker*, no. 306, p. 11.

181. Kellner, *Musikgeschichte Kremsmünster*, p. 381.

182. For the Göttweig attribution to Georg see Friedrich Wilhelm Riedel, ed., *Der Göttweiger thematischer Katalog von 1830* (Munich and Salzburg: E. Katzbichler, 1979) II, p. 96.

183. One musical example from Strasser's Mass is ex. 9-16B.

184. Tuma's biography is amply treated in Milan Poštalka, "Tůma, František Ignác Antonín," *New Grove* XIX, p. 252, and Eva Badura-Skoda, "Tuma," *MGG* XIII (1966) col. 971–75.

185. Friedrich Wilhelm Marpurg, *Historisch-Kritische Beiträge zur Aufnahme der Musik* (Berlin: J.J. Schutzen, 1757); reprint ed., Hildesheim: G. Olms, 1970) III/1, p. 68, lists Tuma as a Vice-Kapellmeister in Vienna in 1722 (cited by Badura-Skoda, ibid., col. 971).

186. The total 65 is from Poštalka, "Tůma," *New Grove* XIX, p. 252; also Theodore Milton Klinka, "The Choral Music of Franz Ignaz Tuma with a Practical Edition of Selected Choral Works" (Ph.D. diss., University of Iowa, 1975), pp. 228–35. Reichert, "Geschichte," gave incipits for 55 Tuma Masses in his thematic catalogue (1935); Peschek, "Tuma," pp. 25, 141–316, listed 66 Masses (including doubtful ones) in his 1956 catalogue.

187. Examples from these Masses by Tuma include: ex. 6-15, 6-19; 7-11, 7-19; 8-12B, 8-19; 9-15B, 9-16B; 10-4B, 10-4C, 10-5; see also figs. 7-2, 7-7.

188. For the few other known details of Vaňhal's biography see: Milan Poštalka, "Vaňhal," *New Grove* XIX, pp. 522–25; idem., "Vaňhal," *MGG* XIII (1966) col. 1255–65.

189. Landon, *Haydn: Chronicle and Works* II, p. 380. Here Landon discusses Vaňhal as one of Joseph Haydn's imitators or *seguaci*.

190. The quantity 60 is from Poštalka, "Vaňhal," *New Grove* XIX, p. 224. In 1979 and 1980 Dr. Alexander Weinmann (Vienna) kindly allowed me to consult his on-going thematic catalogue of Vaňhal which registered only 44 Masses. Landon, *Haydn: Chronicle and Works* II, p. 389, n. 1, mentions his own Vaňhal catalogue (begun in 1951).

191. Examples from Vaňhal's Masses include ex. 6-12; 7-11; 8-3, 8-9, 8-10; 9-16C; 10-13, 10-16; see also figs. 5-3 and 7-18.

192. Further biographical details may be found in John Kucaba, "Wagenseil," *New Grove* XX, pp. 100–103; Helga Scholz-Michelitsch, "Wagenseil," *MGG* XIV (1968) col. 68–74; Kirkendale, *Fugue and Fugato*, pp. 7–8.

193. Burney, *Musical Tours*, ed., Scholes II, p. 112.

194. Kucaba, "Wagenseil," *New Grove* XX, p. 102, lists 18 Mass settings. However, because the *Missa S. Francisci Salesii* (at A-HE) and the *Missa brevis in A* (at D-ddr-Bds) are one and the same Mass, i.e., the *Missa Gratias agimus tibi* (M. 68; Reichert No. 6), the quantity should read 17. Reichert, "Geschichte," lists only 12 Masses for Wagenseil, including a Mass fragment (Kyrie at D-ddr-Bds). Four of Wagenseil's 17 Masses are a capella; the remainder have orchestral accompaniments. Roland Philipp, "Die Messenkomposition der Wiener Vorklassiker G.M. Monn und G. Chr. Wagenseil" (Ph.D. diss., University of Vienna, 1938) passim, discusses chiefly the Masses of Wagenseil and includes useful tables showing their structure (pp. 141–74).

195. Musical examples from Wagenseil's Masses include ex. 6-16, 6-17; 8-12B; 10-14.

196. However, the final 35 measures of the Kyrie in Wagenseil's *Missa solenne Immaculatae Conceptionis* (M. 70, 1743) is a masterful fugal section "Kyrie II" that uses all the traditional technical devices (e.g., augmentation, diminution, inversion); see ex. 6-17C.

197. Wagenseil, *Concerto in E-flat for Trombone and Orchestra* (1742); see C. Robert Wigness, *The Soloistic Use of the Trombone in Eighteenth-Century Vienna* (Nashville: The Brass Press, 1978), p. 19.

198. Philipp, "Messenkomposition," p. 77.

199. Dittersdorf, *Lebensbeschreibung*, p. 18.

200. These few biographical details are from Karl Pfannhauser, "Ziegler," *MGG* XIV (1968) col. 1269–70; see Gernot Gruber, "Ziegler (Zügler)," *New Grove* XX, p. 679.

201. Gruber, "Ziegler," *New Grove*, ibid. Landon, *Haydn: Chronicle and Works* I, p. 102, n. 1, p. 234, reports on a German opera by Ziegler at Vienna's Kärntnertor-Theater.

202. Pfannhauser, "Ziegler," col. 1269–70, cites six Masses (three in C, two in D, one in F) while Gruber, "Ziegler," ibid., cites only five (three in C, one in D, one in A). My own catalogue agrees with Pfannhauser.

203. Musical examples from Ziegler's Masses include ex. 6-18; 7-13, 7-16; 9-16A.

Chapter 4

1. Georg Reichert, "Zur Geschichte der Wiener Messenkomposition in der ersten Hälfte des 18. Jahrhunderts" (Ph.D. diss., University of Vienna, 1935), p. 4, notes the same flexibility of scoring for Masses of the first half of the eighteenth century. For examples of variants in Haydn's scoring of his church music at the end of the century, see Irmgard Becker-Glauch, "Remarks on the Late Church Music," in *Haydn's Studies,* ed. Jens Peter Larsen, Howard Serwer, and James Webster (New York: Norton, 1981), pp. 206–7. An excellent discussion of the specific influences of Viennese church conditions upon orchestration is Otto Biba, "Die Wiener Kirchenmusik um 1783," in *Beiträge zur Musikgeschichte des 18. Jahrhunderts,* ed. Gerda Mraz (Eisenstadt: Institut für österreichische Kulturgeschichte, 1971), pp. 68–79.

2. Study of published and unpublished thematic catalogues of church music (e.g., those for F. Schneider, G. Reutter, et al.) reveals that often composers prepared alternate versions of a Mass. For example, Holzbauer rewrote and rescored some of his earlier Masses for the larger, more capable Mannheim orchestra; see chapter 5, nn. 3 and 10.

3. These principles have been used in determining the instrumentation cited in figure 4-1 and atop each page of the thematic catalogue in appendix C.

4. These variant scorings are generated by the addition (or subtraction) of instruments (e.g., flute, oboes, bassoon[s], horns, clarini, trombones, timpani, viola[s], or violoncello[s]). For example, M. 34 (Kohaut) is type "B" but without timpani; M. 19 (Gassmann; Vienna version) is type "G" but with two bassoons, two horns, two additional clarini (for the Gloria), two violas, and violoncello.

5. Biba, "Kirchenmusik 1783," pp. 75–76, found orchestra types "B" and "D" (fig. 4-1) to be most common according to the 1783 personnel lists.

6. This accompaniment probably evolved from the church trio sonata. According to Friedrich Bayer, "Das Orchester Mozarts im speziellen Dienst der Messkomposition," *Musica Divina* 16 (1928): 23, the term "Viennese church trio" *(Wiener Kirchentrio)* comes from Alfred Schnerich's pathbreaking study *Messe und Requiem seit Haydn und Mozart* (Vienna and Leipzig: C.W. Stern, 1909). The term has often been used by modern writers (e.g., Landon, Prohászka, and Unverricht). Walter Senn, in Mozart, *Neue Ausgabe sämtlicher Werke,* ed. W. Senn, Ser. I, Werkgruppe 1, Abt. 1, vol. 2: *Messen* (Kassel: Bärenreiter, 1975) p. VII, notes how the *Kirchentrio* was not unique to Salzburg. Jon Olaf Carlson, "Selected Masses of Niccolo Jommelli" (Ph.D. diss., University of Illinois, 1974), p. 90, observes that some of Jommelli's early Masses use this trio accompaniment.

7. Hubert Unverricht, "Die orchesterbegleitete Kirchenmusik von den Neapolitanern bis Schubert," in *Geschichte der katholischen Kirchenmusik,* ed. Karl Gustav Fellerer (Kassel: Bärenreiter, 1976) II, p. 162; also Mozart, *Neue Ausgabe,* vol. II: *Messen,* ed. W. Senn, p. VII.

8. Biba, "Kirchenmusik 1783," pp. 68, 71–73, 74; see chapter 1, n. 53 above. According to these findings there was a good numerical balance between voices and violins (i.e., 4:4). Biba observes (p. 69) that Leopold Hofmann at St. Peter's had six violins at his disposal; St. Michael's had 12 (and sometimes even 16) violins for special feasts. Albrechtsberger, however, managed with only two regular violinists at the Karmeliter-Kirche in the Leopoldstadt. Biba has found little proof of castrati singing in Vienna's churches (p. 75).

9. A trio texture continued to be favored for accompanying most vocal solos of the present period. Mary Nicole Schnoebelen, "The Concerted Mass at San Petronio in Bologna ca.

1660–1730: A Documentary and Analytical Study" (Ph.D. diss., University of Illinois at Urbana-Champaign, 1966), p. 173, found this practice already common in Bolognese Masses at the end of the seventeenth century.

10. Reichert, "Geschichte," p. 4, found this situation to be true for most of the first half of the eighteenth century in Vienna. Solos by the bassoon, violoncello, flute, and chalumeau were rare in Masses at that time.

11. Friedrich Christoph Nicolai, *Beschreibung einer Reise durch Deutschland und die Schweiz im Jahre 1781* (Berlin and Stettin: n.p., 1784), p. 545. In a footnote Nicolai (ibid.) adds something about the trombone's use: "In our region [i.e., Northern Germany] the trombone has become almost totally uncommon for full-voiced music. In Austria and Bavaria this instrument is still very much in use and well played, especially in the church. Gluck has used it in his operas and ballets, often with the most successful result."

12. Nicolai, *Beschreibung 1781*, p. 548.

13. According to Hermine Prohászka, "Leopold Hofmann und seine Messen," *Studien zur Musikwissenschaft* XXVI (1964): 83, n. 33, Friedrich Bayer, in "Das Orchester Mozarts im speziellen Dienst der Messkomposition," *Musica Divina* 16 (1928): 60, uses the term *Wiener unisono* in this context.

14. Comparison of thematic catalogues and performing materials often shows how one place would use trombones, another violas, for *colla parte* playing (e.g., in the manuscripts for Tuma's Masses); see Biba, "Kirchenmusik 1783," p. 70. Because there were no regular trombonists in Eisenstadt, Haydn's Masses lack the doublings and obbligatos for this instrument. James Frederick Dack, "The Origins and Development of the Esterházy Kapelle in Eisenstadt until 1790" (Ph.D. diss., University of Liverpool, 1976), p. 111, n. 25, observes that Kapellmeister Werner had rarely employed trombones.

15. See Biba, "Kirchenmusik 1783," p. 70, at n. 4.

16. Friedrich Wilhelm Riedel, *Kirchenmusik am Hofe Karls VI. (1711–1740)* (Munich and Salzburg: Emil Katzbichler, 1977), p. 63; idem, "Beiträge zur Geschichte der Musikpflege an der Stadtpfarrkirche St. Veit zu Krems," in *Festschrift 950 Jahre Pfarrei Krems* (Krems an der Donau, 1964), p. 306; Reichert, "Geschichte," p. 4.

17. Biba, "Kirchenmusik 1783," pp. 70–71.

18. Johann Georg Albrechtsberger, *Gründliche Anweisung zur Composition...* (Leipzig: J.G.I. Breitkopf, 1790), p. 379.

19. Bayer, "Gebrauch der Instrumente," p. 55.

20. Albrechtsberger, *Gründliche Anweisung zur Composition*, p. 379.

21. Biba, "Kirchenmusik 1783," p. 69.

22. See ex. 6-2, 6-6; 7-2, 7-3, 7-8, 7-15, et al., and Gassmann's *St. Cecilia Mass*. A *ripieno* bassoon does not play continuo while a soloist is singing in these Masses (ex. 7-15). According to Riedel, *Karl VI*, p. 64, this expanded continuo for the Hofmusikkapelle goes back to the era of Fux and Caldara, when a theorbo was also used; see Reichert, "Geschichte," p. 4. Biba, "Kirchenmusik 1783," p. 73, finds the bassoon to be no longer a regular part of Vienna's church music in 1783.

23. Riedel, "St. Veit zu Krems," p. 306. Heinrich Stute, "Studien über den Gebrauch der Instrumente in dem italienischen Kirchenorchester des 18. Jahrhunderts" (Ph.D. diss., University of Münster, 1928), p. 25, reports that the Neapolitans sometimes used

harpsichord in their church music. According to David James Wilson, "Selected Masses of Hasse" (D.M.A. diss., University of Illinois at Champaign-Urbana, 1973), p. 82, Hans von Schnoor, in his *Dresden: Vierhundert Jahre deutsche Musikkultur* (Dresden, 1948), p. 97, reports that Hasse's *Mass in D Minor* (M. 24) used a harpsichord for its first performance. Peter Williams, "Continuo," *New Grove Dictionary of Music and Musicians* (1980) IV, p. 690, notes that in some countries organs were not allowed during Lent.

24. Biba, "Kirchenmusik 1783," p. 74.

25. Ibid., pp. 68, 74ff.

26. An additional soprano soloist is required for some sections in M. 24, 27, 30, 46, and 50; an extra bass is needed in M. 50.

27. Other Masses requiring flute(s) include M. 24 (usually doubling the violins), 26 ("Christe"), and 36 ("Laudamus").

28. Riedel, "St. Veit zu Krems," p. 306; idem, *Karl VI,* p. 176; idem, "Liturgie und Kirchenmusik," in *Joseph Haydn in seiner Zeit,* ed. Gerda Mraz, Gottfried Mraz, and Gerald Schlag (Eisenstadt: Kulturabteilung des Amtes der Burgenländischen Landesregierung, 1982), p. 132; Prohászka, "Hofmann," p. 83; Biba, "Kirchenmusik 1783," p. 71. Schnoebelen, "Concerted Mass in Bologna," pp. 110, 296, n. 1, reports that, according to Padre Martini's testimony, Perti's *Mass in D* (1680) was the first concerted Mass to use two trumpets.

29. Hasse's *Missa in D* (M. 25) is remarkable for its use of two high and *three* low trumpets (see ex. 6-1).

30. Horn parts are found in M. 19, 24, 33, 59, and 66. See Biba, "Kirchenmusik 1783," p. 73.

31. In Gassmann's Mass the horns generally serve as harmonic filler, often doubling the pitches or rhythms of the clarini. Prohászka, "Hofmann," p. 83, has similarly found horn parts added later to Hofmann's Masses.

32. Howard Chandler Robbins Landon, *Haydn: Chronicle and Works,* 5 vols. (Bloomington: Indiana University Press, 1976–80) IV, pp. 138, 162.

33. C. Robert Wigness, *The Soloistic Use of the Trombone in Eighteenth-Century Vienna* (Nashville: The Brass Press, 1978), p. 2. See n. 11 above.

34. See Jay Dee Schaefer, "The Use of the Trombone in the 18th Century," *The Instrumentalist* XXII/10 (May 1968): 101–2.

35. For example, in M. 16 (Dittersdorf autograph), 34 (Kohaut), and 37 (Martínez autograph) the timpani are lacking, despite the presence of clarini. Many composers (e.g., Tuma) put trumpet and timpani parts on separate pages perhaps because of a lack of staves; this practice may have led to the absence of these parts in some sources.

36. See Biba, "Kirchenmusik 1783," pp. 68–69, where records for Viennese churches in 1783 tend to confirm this number of players.

37. According to Eva Badura-Skoda, "Reutter," in *The New Grove Dictionary of Music,* 6th ed., 20 vols., ed. Stanley Sadie (London: Macmillan, 1980) XV, p. 773, Pohl used the terms "rauschenden violinen à la Reutter."

38. Albrechtsberger, *Gründliche Anweisung zur Composition* (1790), pp. 377–78.

39. Stute, "Instrumente im italienischen Kirchenorchester," pp. 38–41, demonstrates that the viola was a regular part of the orchestra in Italian Masses of the eighteenth century. Hasse and Holzbauer may have picked up the practice of employing violas during their Italian sojourns.

40. Biba, "Kirchenmusik 1783," p. 69, notes that only once in the 1783 inventory is a violist listed as part of a church's regular music personnel.

41. Stute, "Instrumente im italienischen Kirchenorchester," pp. 14–15. Schnoebelen, "Concerted Mass in Bologna," p. 257, has found violoncello solos in Bolognese Masses by Colonna and Perti at the turn of the seventeenth century.

42. Albrechtsberger, *Gründliche Anweisung zur Composition,* p. 421, gives "contrabass" as another name for "violon." Biba, "Kirchenmusik 1783," pp. 69–70, believes that the old violone by itself would not have provided a rumbling, obtrusive bass tone. In 1783 two Viennese churches still had players of the "bassetl," a member of the gamba family. A *Hof* document cited by Biba (p. 70) shows the violone to be a member of church orchestras in Vienna even as late as 1796.

43. See Hermann Beck, "Die Musik des liturgischen Gottesdienstes im 18. Jahrhundert (Messe, Offizium)," in *Geschichte der katholischen Kirchenmusik,* ed. Karl Gustav Fellerer (Kassel: Bärenreiter, 1976) II, p. 188, On where improvisation occurred in the Mass, see Robert N. Freeman, "The Role of Organ Improvisation in Haydn's Church Music," in *Haydn Studies,* ed. Jens Peter Larsen, Howard Serwer, and James Webster (New York: Norton, 1981), pp. 192–94. Warren Kirkendale, "New Roads to Old Ideas in Beethoven's *Missa Solemnis," The Musical Quarterly* LVI (1970): 689, observes how the organ was the traditional instrument for elevation music. Franz Xaver Glöggl, *Kirchenmusik-Ordnung: Erklärendes Handbuch des musikalischen Gottesdienstes, für Kappellmeister, Regenschori, Sänger und Tonkünstler* (Vienna: J.B. Wallishauser, 1828), p. 9, describes the high qualifications and duties expected of an organist in Austria at the start of the nineteenth century.

44. See chapter 2 at nn. 2–4.

45. Albrechtsberger, *Gründliche Anweisung zur Composition,* p. 416.

46. On Wagenseil's use of these terms see Philipp, "Messenkomposition," p. 186. Rudolf Nützlader, "Salieri als Kirchenmusiker," *Studien zur Musikwissenschaft* XIV (1927): 171, finds these same markings in Salieri's first Mass (in D).

47. Landon, *Haydn: Chronicle and Works,* I, pp. 87–88, discusses Haydn's Masses of this type (Hob. XXII: 4, 7, 11). Excerpts from Reutter's *Missa in B-flat* (Hofer no. 15, before 1746) are also shown. Riedel, "St. Veit zu Krems," p. 314, indicates that Zechner's *Missa Sancti Christophori* (at Göttweig, before 1737) is "one of the earliest examples of an organ solo Mass." Zechner's *Missa in C* (Göttweig no. 72, before 1762) is the rare example of a Mass with such an organ solo in every movement. Prohászka, "Hofmann," p. 82, indicates that five Masses by Leopold Hofmann (Prohászka nos. 7, 8, 9, 10, and 15) use the organ in such a concertato fashion. Two of Mozart's Masses (K. 259 and 337) are also of this type.

Chapter 5

1. A catalogue of the 72 Masses appears in Appendix C.

2. Karl Maria Brand, *Die Messen von Joseph Haydn* (Würzburg-Aumühle: K. Triltsch, 1941), pp. 125–26.

3. For example, Mozart wrote several independent Kyries, e.g., K. 33, 89, 90, 91, 221, 322, 323, and 341. In a letter dated 5 April 1778 (Emily Anderson, ed. and trans., *Letters of Mozart and His Family,* 2 vols., 2nd ed. (London: Macmillan; New York: St. Martin's Press, 1966) II, no. 300ª, p. 521), Mozart himself relates how he had to compose substitution movements for a Holzbauer *Miserere* before it could be performed at the *Concerts spirituels* in Paris. Alfred Schienerl, "Giuseppe Bonnos Kirchenkompositionen," *Studien zur Musikwissenschaft* XV (1928): 69, reports that Bonno composed some 50 Mass inserts (*Messeinlagen*) in addition to 30 Masses and two Requiems. Mary Nicole Schnoebelen, "The Concerted Mass at San Petronio in Bologna ca. 1660–1730: A Documentary and Analytical Study" (Ph.D. diss., University of Illinois at Urbana-Champaign, 1966), pp. 257, 304, discusses how G.A. Perti, *Maestro di cappella* at Bologna's San Petronio from 1696 to 1756, wrote *versetti separati* to replace Mass movements which he had written earlier.

4. See Howard Chandler Robbins Landon, *Haydn: Chronicle and Works,* 5 vols. (Bloomington: Indiana University Press, 1976–80) II, p. 554.

5. Karl Ditters von Dittersdorf, *Lebensbeschreibung seinem Sohne in die Feder diktiert* (Leipzig: Breitkopf & Härtel, 1801), pp. 121–22. In this instance Martini wanted to give Dittersdorf and Gluck the opportunity to hear the "Amen" a second time.

6. Friedrich Wilhelm Riedel, *Kirchenmusik am Hofe Karls VI....* (Munich and Salzburg: Emil Katzbichler, 1977), pp. 64, 226.

7. Ibid., p. 225.

8. Such is often the case for Reutter's Masses preserved in the Hofmusikkapelle (H.K.) collection of the Austrian National Library, e.g., M. 45 and 47. Roland Philipp, "Die Messenkompositionen der Wiener Vorklassiker G.M. Monn und G. Chr. Wagenseil" (Ph.D. diss., University of Vienna, 1938), p. 53, remarks on this same phenomenon when he notes that parts for the Masses by Monn and Wagenseil are usually in two folders: Kyrie-Gloria and Credo-Sanctus-Agnus Dei.

9. Georg Walther Müller, *Johann Adolf Hasse als Kirchenkomponist: ein Beitrag zur Geschichte der neapolitanischen Kirchenmusik, mit thematischem Katalog der liturgischen Kirchenmusik J.A. Hasse's* (Leipzig: Breitkopf & Härtel, 1911), pp. 71, 74.

10. For example, at Klosterneuburg Ferdinand Schmidt's *Missa Sanctae Caeciliae in C* (M. 50; Reichert no. 7) has two versions of the Credo, one long and one short. Klaus Altmann, who is writing a dissertation on the Masses of Holzbauer at the University of Bonn, reports that comparison of early and later sources shows how Holzbauer rewrote and rescored several of his Masses for the Mannheim ensemble. Study of recently published catalogues for church music by other composers of the period shows how often there exists more than one version of a Mass; e.g., see Robert N. Freeman, *Franz Schneider (1737–1812): A Thematic Catalogue of His Works* (New York: Pendragon, 1979), passim; Hermine Prohászka, "Leopold Hofmann und seine Messen," *Studien zur Musikwissenschaft* XXVI (1964): 117–19, 123–24; Deanna Day Bush, "The Orchestral Masses of Ignaz Holzbauer (1711–1783): Authenticity, Chronology, and Style with Thematic Catalog and Selected Transcriptions" (Ph.D. diss., Eastman School of Music, 1982), pp. 345–90.

11. Georg Reichert, "Zur Geschichte der Wiener Messenkomposition in der ersten Hälfte des 18. Jahrhunderts" (Ph.D. diss., University of Vienna, 1935) who did not catalogue Boog's Masses, lists this Mass as No. 1 under those attributed to Monn. Interesting is how Kremsmünster actually has both the "Monn" (Ser. C, Fasc. 14, Nr. 708) and the "Boog" (Ser. C, Fasc. 10, Nr. 673) versions of the Mass.

12. For example, Erich Schenk, "Ist die Göttweiger Rorate-Messe ein Werk Joseph Haydns?" *Studien zur Musikwissenschaft* 24 (1960): 87–105, and Bruce C. Mac Intyre, "Haydn's Doubtful and Spurious Masses: An Attribution Update," *Haydn-Studien* V, 1 (1982): 42–54.

13. In the eighteenth century, Masses were categorized according to occasion (*missa solemnis, mediocris,* etc.), instrumentation (e.g., with or without trumpets, timpani, soloists, etc.), and general style (e.g., a cappella, *stile misto,* etc.) as well as length. The terms *missa longa* and *missa brevis* are used here to avoid the confusion resulting from the disagreement between the liturgical and musical meanings of *missa solemnis, missa mediocris,* etc. For further discussion of these terms, see the Introduction.

14. *Missae breves* by Haydn and Mozart are 91–569 measures in length; see the middle group in fig. 5-1.

15. These timings are based upon the following recordings: J. Haydn, *Caecilienmesse* and *Mariazeller Messe,* performed by the Stuttgart Kammerchor, conducted by Frieder Bernius (Vox FSM-43041/42); J.S. Bach, *h-moll Messe,* performed by the Kölner Kantorei, conducted by Volker Hempfling (EMI-Electrola, Köln, no. 667–391/392/401).
    These durations are even more awesome when we remember that liturgical ceremonies preceded and followed most of the movements at that time.

16. Can it be coincidence that three of Albrechtsberger's Masses total 525 or 526 measures (see fig. 5-1)?

17. See chapter 2, n. 70.

18. In about three-fifths of the Masses (41 of 67) the Gloria is the longest (in measure count) of the five parts of the Mass. In about one-quarter of the settings (18 of 67) the Credo is the longest. The Kyrie is never the longest part of a Mass.

19. This disproportion seems even more intentional when one realizes that the text of the Credo is nearly twice that of the Gloria. In *missae breves* there is less of an imbalance; the movement lengths tend to be more in proportion with text lengths.

20. Typographically, quotation marks are used when referring to a section within a part of the Mass, e.g., "Gloria," "Laudamus"; when no such marks enclose the words, the entire part is meant, e.g., Kyrie, Gloria, Credo.

21. This strict and admittedly narrow definition of "movement" is best suited for a uniform description of how variously composers distributed the text in their settings.

22. Guido Adler, "Zur Geschichte der Wiener Messenkomposition in der zweiten Hälfte des XVII. Jahrhunderts," *Studien zur Musikwissenschaft* IV (1916): 42.

23. For the exceptions where the central tonality of a Mass changes (often at Gloria), see chapter 7, n. 26 and n. 26 below. Unity of key was, of course, nothing new for Masses; see Adler, "Geschichte," p. 35.

24. This information is based upon the author's comprehensive Mass thematic locator in progress. The sharp keys G, D, and A appear to outnumber the flat keys F, B-flat, and E-flat in frequency of use.

25. Landon, *Haydn: Chronicle and Works* IV, pp. 400–401; on the frequent use of C major for Masses before 1750 see Adler, "Geschichte," p. 40. Fifty-four percent of the present sample (39 of 72) are C-major Masses.

26. For example, Albrechtsberger's *Missa Dei Patris* (M. 4), Hasse's *Missa in D Minor* (M. 24), Haydn's *Nelson Mass* (Hob. XXII: 11), and Mozart's *Waisenhaus-Messe* (K. 139) all end in the parallel major; see n. 23 above. The four Masses (in the present sample) that both begin *and* end in a minor key are by Holzbauer (M. 31 and 32 in A minor and E minor, respectively), Seuche (M. 52 in A minor), and Tuma (M. 63 in D minor).

27. Johann Mattheson, *Das neu-eröffnete Orchester* (Hamburg: Benjamin Schiller's Witwe, 1713), pp. 231–53; Christian Friedrich Daniel Schubart, *Vaterländische Chronik* (1787); idem, *Ideen zu einer Aesthetik der Tonkunst*, ed. L. Schubart (Vienna: J.V. Degen, 1806). See Rita K. Steblin, *A History of Key Characteristics in the Eighteenth and Early Nineteenth Centuries* (Ann Arbor, Michigan: UMI Research Press, 1983); and George J. Buelow, "An Evaluation of Johann Mattheson's Opera *Cleopatra*," in *Studies in Eighteenth-Century Music: A Tribute to Karl Geiringer on His Seventieth Birthday*, ed. H.C. Robbins Landon and Roger E. Chapman (New York and London: Oxford University Press, 1970), p. 98. In 1828 Glöggl, *Kirchenmusik-Ordnung: Erklärendes Handbuch des musikalischen Gottesdienstes, für Kapellmeister, Regenschori, Sänger und Tonkünstler* (Vienna: J.B. Wallishauser, 1828), pp. 8–9, discussed key characteristics for church music and borrows many of Schubart's ideas.

28. Riedel, *Karl VI*, p. 176.

29. Landon, *Haydn: Chronicle and Works* II, p. 244.

30. Eight and six examples, respectively, exist for solos in A and B minor. Most minor keys in these Masses use a Dorian key signature (i.e., one less flat than usual); see ex. 7-22.

31. See, for examples, the Gloria of Gassmann's *St. Cecilia Mass* (M. 19) or Albrechtsberger's *Missa Dei Patris* (M. 4). For probably the same reason, plagal cadences were also used frequently at the ends of movements (especially the "Osanna").

32. In Hofmann's *Missa in D* (M. 29, Prohászka no. 17) the flutist has a solo in nearly every movement; see ex. 7-10 and 9-11. In Reutter's *Missa Sancti Venantii* (M. 48, Hofer no. 57) a bassoon solo occurs in each part of the Mass; see ex. 6-6. Further details about scoring practices are in chapter 4.

33. Nevertheless, the Masses overall seem to show a distinct preference for soprano solos.

34. Landon, *Haydn: Chronicle and Works* I, p. 92, shows the unifying violin "Leitmotiv" of this Mass which also goes by the name *Missa Sancti Georgi*.

35. Composers in fact seemed to be following Scheibe's advice that they seek variety and change in their Masses. See chapter 2 at n. 134 (point no. 15).

36. Johann Georg Albrechtsberger, *Gründliche Anweisung zur Composition*...(Leipzig: J.G.I. Breitkopf, 1790), p. 378. See chapter 2, at n. 136 above, for Sulzer's similar suggestion in *Allgemeine Theorie* (1793).

37. James Frederick Dack, "The Origins and Development of the Esterházy Kapelle in Eisenstadt until 1790" (Ph.D. diss., University of Liverpool, 1976), p. 123.

38. For definitions of these and other musical figures, see George J. Buelow, "Rhetoric and Music," in *New Grove* XV, pp. 795–800.

39. C.F. Michaelis, "Ueber das Alte und Veraltete in der Musik," *Allgemeine musikalische Zeitung* 16 (1814): 325–28, as cited and translated by Warren Kirkendale, *Fugue and Fugato in Rococo and Classical Chamber Music*, trans. Margaret Bent and Warren Kirkendale (Durham, N.C.: Duke University Press, 1979), p. 33.

40. See chapter 2, at n. 111 and 116.

41. See chapter 2, at n. 113. Mattheson's "ligature" (chant) and "canonic" styles do not apply to the present Masses.

42. Schienerl, "Bonnos Kirchenkompositionen," p. 82.

43. The papal "Annus qui" of 1749 had specifically demanded complete texts; see chapter 2, n. 75.

44. For example, in M. 18, 20, 41, and 64 as well as Haydn, Hob. XXII: 4 and 8, the second "Qui tollis" of the Gloria is omitted. Ex. 9-14 by Boog is a Sanctus in which the opening word has been repeated more than required.

45. Arbesser's *Missa Nubes pluant justum* (M. 6) is a *missa brevis* with polytextuality in both the Gloria and Credo. Cornell Jesse Runestad, "The Masses of Joseph Haydn: A Stylistic Study" (Ph.D. diss., University of Illinois at Urbana-Champaign, 1970), p. 52, believes this expedient allowed the introduction of eighteenth-century forms such as the sonata, rondo, and ternary designs into the Mass.

46. Coloratura at such places was nothing new for Vienna; it occurred in Masses at the end of the seventeenth century (see Adler, "Geschichte," p. 34).

47. For example, "Quoniam" settings by Holzbauer (M. 33) and Monn (M. 38; end of this example is seen in ex. 7-2) as well as two "Domine Deus" settings by Dittersdorf (M. 15 and 17) have this "rage" quality; see ex. 9-5 by Monn.

48. Sacred motets of the period, including those by Gassmann, often consisted of a recitative, aria, and chorus; see Franz Kosch, "Florian Leopold Gassmann als Kirchenkomponist," *Studien zur Musikwissenschaft* XIV (1927): 230.

49. Generally only one or two parts (*concertato* and *ripieno*) for each voice are found in the performance materials for these Masses; see chapter 4, above. Using a 1783 inventory of music personnel in Vienna's churches, Otto Biba ("Die Wiener Kirchenmusik um 1783," in *Beiträge zur Musikgeschichte des 18. Jahrhunderts,* ed. Gerda Mraz (Eisenstadt: Institut für österreichische Kulturgeschichte, 1971), pp. 68, 74–76) finds that, as a rule, there was just one person per voice part; only in the larger and wealthier churches or on special feasts were the voices doubled. Choirboys usually sang soprano.

50. *Da capo* arias are found, however, in the freer church music genres, e.g., in motets by Gassmann and Hofmann. Riedel, *Karl VI,* p. 178, notes that Caldara has a *da capo* "Christe" aria in his *Missa Assumptionis B.M.V.* (A-Wn: H.K. 204/205). Heinrich Stute, "Studien über den Gebrauch der Instrumente in dem italienischen Kirchenorchester des 18. Jahrhunderts" (Ph.D. diss., University of Münster, 1928), p. 6, also found the binary aria most common among the 243 concerted Italian Masses in the Santini collection.

51. By exception, the "Christe" in Schmidt's M. 51 begins the second vocal strain with a new melody.

52. The 19 examples of ternary aria occur in 14 of the Masses and include settings of the "Christe" (M. 19, 14, 49), "Laudamus" (M. 30, 38, 40, 49), and "Gratias" (M. 60), "Domine Deus, Rex" (M. 30), "Quoniam" (M. 38, 39, 60, 61), and "Benedictus" (M. 4, 12, 13, 25, 51, 57).

53. According to David James Wilson, "Selected Masses of Johann Hasse" (D.M.A. diss., University of Illinois at Champaign-Urbana, 1973) p. 76, Hasse often had the second ritornello (instead of the second vocal strain) modulate back to the tonic.

54. In addition, the contrasting themes (m. 1 and 25 etc.) of this solo quartet in binary aria form exhibit the thematic functionalism associated with the sonata; the opening theme is quoted in Karl Pfannhauser, "Zu Mozarts Kirchenwerken von 1768," *Mozart Jahrbuch 1954*, p. 162. See ex. 9-7 for the same procedure in another "Benedictus" by Sonnleithner (M. 54, for soprano and chorus). In the "Benedictus" of Hofmann's M. 26 (a ternary aria) the tonic return occurs even before the penultimate ritornello and third vocal strain repeat the opening theme in the tonic. The "Gratias" from this same Mass (M. 26, before 1779) has a "double reprise" during the final vocal strain of the two-part motto aria. Monn (M. 39 and 40) occasionally also makes his ritornellos modulate.

55. Reichert, "Geschichte," p. 17.

56. For other motto arias see the "Laudamus" of M. 51, the "Domine Fili" and "Domine Deus, Agnus" of M. 26, and the "Quoniam" of M. 13 and 51.

57. Usually these movements remain in one key. Examples of this one-part form include: "Et in terra" of M. 50, "Crucifixus" of M. 23 and 50, and "Benedictus" of M. 18, 23, 31, 36, 37, 63, 69, and 70. This form might be considered analogous to a cavatina in opera.

58. See n. 39 above and Kirkendale, *Fugue and Fugato*, pp. xxv, 3–5, 33; Henry B. Raynor, "Some Reflections upon the Viennese Mass," *The Musical Times* (Nov. 1954): 594.

59. Mattheson, *Der vollkommene Kapellmeister* (1739), pt. I, ch. 10, §44, Harriss trans. p. 199. Rather surprisingly, canon does not occur anywhere in the present sample of Masses. See chapter 2 at n. 127.

60. A sinfonia commonly preceded certain movements (especially Kyries) of seventeenth- and early eighteenth-century Masses in northern Italy; see Schnoebelen, "Concerted Mass in Bologna," pp. 167–68, 171–72, 175, 180–81, 202, 251, 277–78, 351. Reichert, "Geschichte," p. 13, considers instrumental pieces before the Kyrie (e.g., sonata, sonatina, intrada) as leftovers from the seventeenth century; see Adler, "Geschichte," p. 20. Unverricht, "Die orchesterbegleitete Kirchenmusik," pp. 164–65, calls such instrumental introductions (often found in Jommelli's Masses) an Italian trait which was not always found in Viennese and South German Masses. See chapter 6, n. 12.

61. See, for example, "For unto us a child is born," etc. from Handel's *Messiah* or the Credo from Bach's *B-minor Mass*. In chapter 2 at note 116 we also saw how Meinradus Spiess still identifies the *stilus ligatus* (based on plainsong) as one of the principal church styles.

62. Landon, *Haydn: Chronicle and Works* I, pp. 92–93, 143; II, 273, 291–95, 303; IV, 139, 151–52, 607.

63. For example, Reutter's *Missa Sancti Placidi in C* (M. 44, Hofer no. 33; before 1756) uses preexistent chants in its Gloria (ex. 5-2), Credo, Sanctus, and "Benedictus"; see Landon, *Haydn: Chronicle and Works* I, pp. 92–93, for an excerpt from the latter movement. Reichert, "Credo-Messen," p. 121ff., notes that many composers (e.g., Fux, Ziani, J.G. Reinhardt, Pruneder, Oettl, Pachschmidt, Donberger, F. Conti, and F. Schmidt) used the plainchant intonation as a basis for their concerted settings of the Credo. Apparently Dittersdorf also once used a cantus firmus; see his biography in chapter 3.

    Dorothea Schröder, who recently completed a dissertation on Albrechtsberger's sacred works (University of Hamburg, 1986), has informed me that the "Benedictus" of the latter's *Choralmesse* (ca. 1808; Weissenbäck no. 166; H-Bn: Ms. mus. IV.1.101) is based upon Handel's "See the conqu'ring hero comes." She indicates that Abbé Stadler uses a similar procedure (with an unknown melody) in the "Benedictus" of one of his Masses (A-Wn: S.m. 21.527). Thus, the use of cantus firmus technique and its freer offshoots continued even into the nineteenth century.

Chapter 6

1. Johann Joseph Fux, *Gradus ad Parnassum, Sive Manuductio ad Compositionem Musicae Regularem, Methodo nova...* (Vienna: Van Ghelen, 1725) Exercitii V, Lectio VII, "De Stylo a Capella," p. 244; in Mizler's translation, p. 184. Fux uses the word "nausea" which Mizler translates as "Eckel" and we as "tedium."

2. In the present discussions Kyrie refers to this entire part of the Mass Ordinary (Christe included), while "Kyrie I" and "Kyrie II" refer, respectively, to the texts before and after the "Christe."

3. Other such places in the Mass include the "Qui tollis" of the Gloria and the "Agnus Dei"; all of these texts have a litany quality because of their repetitiveness.

4. On the location and significance of these dates (which are usually only *tempi ante quem*), see the introduction to this study. "Movement" is used here in the sense of a musical division made independent by means of a different tempo, meter, key, or scoring and concluded by a full cadence; short, slow introductions and conclusions have been considered parts of the movements to which they are attached.

5. Only Haydn's *St. Cecilia Mass* (Hob. XXII: 5, 1766) and Mozart's *Waisenhaus Mass* (K. 139, 1768) have Kyries consisting of three separate movements.

6. Johann Adolph Scheibe, *Critischer Musikus* (Leipzig: B.C. Breitkopf, 1745) (29 October 1737) p. 172. Later on this same page Scheibe qualifies this statement by asking that the sound of the martial instruments be dampened and that the other winds restrict themselves to a certain "melancholy."

7. Tuma seemed especially fond of putting a slow introduction before both "Kyrie I" and "Kyrie II"; e.g., in his *Missa Tibi soli di Psalm 50*, M. 60, Reichert No. 11 (n.d.) and *Missa in chordis et organo*, M. 61, Reichert No. 27 (1743). This practice is also found in Masses by Italians such as Bettoni, Caldara, and Paisiello, as well as by Fux.

8. These introductions (with lengths in parentheses) are in Hoboken XXII: 5 (7 mm.), 8 (8 mm.), 9 (10 mm.), 10 (12 mm.), 12 (28 mm.), and 13 (28 mm.). The *Theresienmesse* (XXII: 12) is unique for using solo voices for the introduction and its varied return at the end of the Kyrie. Introductions occur in six of Mozart's 16 complete Mass settings (K. 49, 65, 66, 139, 257, and 317). In the *Coronation Mass* (K. 317; 1779) the slow introduction returns to conclude the Kyrie.

9. Warren Kirkendale, "New Roads to Old Ideas in Beethoven's *Missa Solemnis,"* *The Musical Quarterly* LVI (1970): 666–67, discusses the widespread use of this topos—a fact confirmed by a glance through the thematic catalogue in the appendix of this study.

10. Kyries by Albrechtsberger (M. 4: 13 mm.), Dittersdorf (M. 15: 14 mm. and M. 16: 27 mm.), Martínez (M 37: 13 mm.), Monn (M. 38: 22mm.), and Vaňhal (M. 64: 16 mm.) were among the examples encountered.

11. Joseph Martin Kraus, *Etwas von und über Musik fürs Jahre 1777* (Frankfurt, 1778); reprint ed., ed. Friedrich Wilhelm Riedel as vol. 1 of *Quellenschriften zur Musikästhetik der 18. und 19. Jahrhunderte* (Munich and Salzburg: E. Katzbichler, 1977), pp. 95–96. He may also have been referring to independent instrumental intradas which usually opened Masses on festive occasions such as Easter.

12. Mary Nicole Schnoebelen, "The Concerted Mass at San Petronio in Bologna ca. 1660–1730: A Documentary and Analytical Study" (Ph.D. diss., University of Illinois at

Urbana-Champaign, 1966), p. 202. During the eighteenth century, orchestral introductions were often used in Masses by Italian composers, e.g., the opening 82 measures of Paisiello's *Missa concertata in B-flat* (Santini P-20, as described by Heinrich Stute, "Studien über den Gebrauch der Instrumente in dem italienischen Kirchenorchester des 18. Jahrhunderts" [Ph.D. diss., University of Münster, 1928], p. 9).

13. These orchestral "preludes" had not been totally absent from earlier Viennese Masses. Heinrich Schmeltzer's *Missa nuptialis* (before 1680) begins with a nine-measure independent sonata; see *Messen von Heinrich Biber, Heinrich Schmeltzer, Johann Casper Kerll*, ed. Guido Adler, vol. 49 of *Denkmäler der Tonkunst in Österreich* (Vienna: Österreichischer Bundesverlag, 1918), p. 48.

14. Eduard Schmitt, "Die Kurpfälzische Kirchenmusik im 18. Jahrhundert" (Ph.D. diss., University of Heidelberg, 1958), pp. 309, 290.

15. Among the numerous Kyries which open with an instrumental ritornello before the entry of voices are: Dittersdorf's *Missa in C* (M. 16, see ex. 10-9A) and Hofmann's *Missa in honorem S. Theresiae* (M. 27). Instrumental ritornellos introduce six of Joseph Haydn's Masses (Hob. XXII: 4, 6, 11, 12, 13, 14) and run from three to 14 measures. Ten of Mozart's 16 complete Masses have such instrumental beginnings, lasting from two to 13 measures in length (K. 66, 139, 167, 192, 220, 257, 259, 262, 317, and 427); in K. 66, 139, 257, 262, and 427 the introduction melodies are independent from those of the chorus.

16. For further examples of this use of paired vocal soloists in the Kyrie, see examples 6-8–10 in this chapter. Haydn's charming first Mass, the *Missa brevis in F* (Hob. XXII: 1), similarly makes use of two soprano soloists in the Kyrie as well as in later sections of the Mass.

17. This texture is found in Haydn, Hob. XXII: 1, 6, 8, 9, 11, 12, 13, 14, and Mozart, K. 66, 139, 192, and 317. Some of their Masses stand apart for using all four vocal soloists (SATB) together as a quartet contrasting with the choral tutti; these are Hob. XXII: 6, 9, 12–14, and K. 257–58, 262, and 275—all Masses from 1772 and later.

18. These are Bonno's *Missa in C* (M. 8, before 1778) and *Missa in C* (M. 9, before 1776), Dittersdorf's two Masses in C (M. 15 and 16, before 1773 and n.d.), Friberth's *Missa in D* (M. 18, 1774), Reutter's *Missa Sancti Mariani* (M. 47, before 1759), and Vaňhal's *Missa solemnis in F* (M. 66, probably 1780s) and *Missa pastorell in G* (M. 65, before 1782).

19. The analytic symbols are from Jan LaRue, *Guidelines for Style Analysis* (New York: Norton, 1970), pp. 153–72: O = introductory material, P = primary materials, S = secondary, contrasting functions, T = transitional functions, K = closing, articulative functions, N = new theme with less definite function, m = motive; x and y are subphrases; superscripts denote variants; parentheses denote origin of later, new ideas.

20. This synthesis is best seen in the Kyrie of three Masses by Haydn (Hob. XXII: 4, 8, and 11) and a *missa brevis* by Mozart (K. 192).

21. By exception, the Kyrie of Hofmann's *Missa in honorem S. Theresiae* (M. 27, before 1760) has used only the *final* 19 measures of "Kyrie I" for "Kyrie II."

22. This partial parallelism applies to nine Kyries by Haydn (Hob. XXII: 1, 3, 6, 7, 9, 10, 12–14) and four by Mozart (K. 65, 194, 317, and 427).
    A similar Kyrie form is found in Arbesser's *Missa Sanctae Susanne* (beginning shown in ex. 6-9) where in the reprise the contours of the opening theme are smoothed out, and all four voices (tutti instead of solo) weave a denser counterpoint than before. This treatment is commonly found in such *missae breves*.
    Monn's *Missa in C* of 1741 (M. 38) is an example of a longer Mass having a single-movement Kyrie with this *ABA'* design.

23. Examples of this contrapuntal type include Gsur's *Missa ex D* (M. 22, before 1769), Predieri's *Missa Nativitatis in C* (M. 42, before 1747), and Reutter's *Missa Sancti Venantii* (M. 48, before 1761) and his *Missa Conceptionis B.V.M.* (M. 46, before 1756).

24. These are Sonnleithner's *Missa in C* (M. 55, before 1765), *Missa sollemnis in C* (M. 57, before 1758), and *Missa in F* (M. 58, before 1769). The first and last of these three are basically contrapuntal movements.

25. The twelve cases found in my sample of 72 Masses were in M. 3*, 6*, 13 (with coda), 17, 20, 28 (with slight change at end), 32*, 35, 56, 63, 64, and 69*. The asterisks indicate *missae breves*.

26. Warren Kirkendale, *Fugue and Fugato in Rococo and Classical Chamber Music*, trans. Margaret Bent and Warren Kirkendale (Durham, N.C.: Duke University Press, 1979), p. 91, coined the designation "pathotype" for this common type of Baroque fugue subject in a minor key.

27. Through-composed tripartite Kyries of one movement are found in M. 11, 53, 67, and 70.

28. In eight of Mozart's Masses (K. 49, 66, 139, 257–59, 262, and 275) the "Christe" recurs after *each* singing of "Kyrie eleison," i.e., there is not one isolated "Christe" section surrounded by Kyries. These "Christe" repetitions result mainly from a reprise structure (*ABA*) in which the "Christe" appears in the opening *A* section rather than being saved until the modulatory middle section.

29. Of course, this practice was nothing new in Vienna. In Fux's Masses the Christe was almost always for soloist(s), usually a duet or trio, with violins (Friedrich Wilhelm Riedel, *Kirchenmusik am Hofe Karls VI. (1711–1740): Untersuchungen zum Verhältnis von Zeremoniell und musikalischen Stil im Barockzeitalter* (Munich and Salzburg: Emil Katzbichler, 1977), p. 177). Schnoebelen reports that this practice was common in Bologna of the late seventeenth century (Schnoebelen, "Concerted Mass in Bologna," p. 208). Hasse commonly set the Christe as a duet (Georg Walther Müller, *Johann Adolf Hasse als Kirchenkomponist...* (Leipzig: Breitkopf & Härtel, 1911), p. 57).

30. This Mass (M. 71; before 1762) has florid coloratura for most of its vocal solos. Another example of "Christe" coloratura was already seen in Dittersdorf's *Missa in C* (ex. 6-11).

31. The only choral "Christe" encountered was a fugal one (32 measures in length) in Wagenseil's *Missa Transfige cor meum* (M. 69, before 1742).

32. Albrechtsberger's *Missa Sancti Leopoldi* (M. 5, before 1801; "Christe" ends upon the dominant of the tonic key), Holzbauer's *Missa in A minor* (M. 31, before 1747; "Christe" ends upon the dominant of the tonic key), Monn's *Missa Solemnis in B-flat* (M. 39, before 1750; "Christe" ends upon dominant of the submediant, the key of the "Christe"), Predieri's *Missa in C* (M. 43, before 1746; rhythmic dovetailing), and Wagenseil's *Missa Transfige cor meum* (M. 69, before 1742; rhythmic dovetailing).

33. Schnoebelen, "Concerted Mass in Bologna," pp. 202–3.

34. Warren Kirkendale, *Fugue and Fugato*, p. 89ff.

35. This *ABA* three-movement design was found in M. 4, 5, 26, 31, 51, and 52.

36. Elwyn A. Wienandt, *Choral Music of the Church* (New York: Free Press, 1965; reprint ed., New York: Da Capo, 1980), p. 207. Wienandt was referring to the Mass in vol. XXIII (pp. 1–63) of the Pergolesi *Opera Omnia*, ed. Francesco Caffarelli (Rome, 1939–42), a Mass which is no longer considered authentic; see Marvin Paymer, *Giovanni Battista Pergolesi (1710–1736): A Thematic Catalogue of the Opera Omnia with an Appendix Listing Omitted Compositions* (New York: Pendragon, 1977), pp. 15–16.

Chapter 7

1. Georg Reichert, "Zur Geschichte der Wiener Messenkomposition in der ersten Hälfte des 18. Jahrhunderts" (Ph.D. diss., University of Vienna, 1935), p. 14.

2. The three *long* Masses having single-movement Glorias are: Hofmann's *Missa in honorem Sanctae Theresiae in C* (M. 27, before 1760), and both Bonno's *Missa in C* (M. 9, before 1776) and his *Missa con 2 oboe obligati in C* (M. 10, before 1781). Here is yet another indication that after 1750 composers were setting the Mass in fewer movements than previously.

3. Mary Nicole Schnoebelen, "The Concerted Mass at San Petronio in Bologna ca. 1660–1730: A Documentary and Analytical Study" (Ph.D. diss., University of Illinois at Urbana-Champaign, 1966), p. 205. As Riedel has suggested to me, "number Mass" is probably a better, less confusing term for such extended, multi-movement Masses.

4. See the discussion in Guido Adler, "Zur Geschichte der Wiener Messenkomposition in der zweiten Hälfte des 17. Jahrhunderts," *Studien zu Musikwissenschaft IV* (1916): passim, and in Reichert, "Geschichte," p. 14; see also Hermine Prohászka, "Leopold Hofmann und seine Messen," *Studien zur Musikwissenschaft XXVI* (1964):89.

5. Elaine Raftery Walter, "Selected Masses of Antonio Caldara (1670–1736)," Studies in Music no. 51 (Ph.D. diss., Catholic University of America, 1973), pp. 133–34.

6. Both Pergolesi Masses (Paymer Nos. 46 [in D, 1733] and 47 [in F, 1732]; divide the Gloria into sections like those under VII[a] in figure 7-1, i.e., "Gloria," "Laudamus," "Gratias," "Domine Deus Rex," "Qui tollis," "Quoniam," and "Cum Sancto." Alessandro Scarlatti's *Missa St. Caeciliae* of 1720 divides the Gloria into nine separate movements: "Gloria," "Et in terra," "Laudamus," "Gratias," "Domine Deus Rex," "Domine Deus Agnus," "Qui tollis," "Quoniam," and "Cum Sancto."

7. Multi-movement Glorias occur in the following nine *missae breves:* M. 21, 22, 31, 48, 52, 62, 63, 67, 69.

8. "Benedicimus te" is always part of the "Laudamus te" preceding it, and "Tu solus Dominus" is always connected with "Quoniam tu solus sanctus."

9. Adler, "Geschichte," pp. 41–42.

10. See chapter 2 at n. 134.

11. According to Josef Andreas Jungmann, *The Mass of the Roman Rite: Its Origins and Development (Missarum Sollemnia)* (Vienna: Herder, 1949), 2 vols., trans. Francis A. Brunner (New York: Benziger Brothers, 1951) I, p. 349, the Gloria breaks down theologically into three parts: "Gloria," "Laudamus," and "Domine Fili." Pedantic theologians certainly might object to musically separating the "Qui tollis" from the preceding "Domine Fili" which supplies the antecedent for "who taketh away the sins of the world." Unlike most of his contemporaries, Joseph Haydn usually followed the view of theologians; in six of his nine multi-movement Glorias the "Qui tollis" is *not* the start of a new movement but rather the middle section of a movement begun earlier in the text, usually at "Gratias."

12. When there are five or more movements, the Gloria's final three movements are usually "Qui tollis," "Quoniam," and "Cum Sancto Spiritu."

13. These post-1750 examples are found in extended Masses by Dittersdorf (M. 15, 17), Gassmann (M. 19), Hasse (M. 23, 25), Hofmann (M. 26), Martínez (M. 36), and Ziegler (M. 71). The pre-1750 examples are by Holzbauer, Monn, Reutter, F. Schmidt, and Wagenseil; see figs. 7-1 and 7-4.

14. A famous case of Gloria polytextuality is in Joseph Haydn's *Missa brevis Sancti Joannis de Deo* (Hob. XXII: 7). To meet Salzburg's demands for textual clarity, his brother Michael in 1795 wrote a longer version of this Gloria and eliminated the troublesome telescoping of text (see Howard Chandler Robbins Landon, *Haydn: Chronicle and Works*, 5 vols. (Bloomington: Indiana University Press, 1976–80) II, p. 554).

15. See fig. 7-4, n.g. Perhaps this Mass is the *Festmesse* which Hofmann composed in honor of the newly elected mayor of Vienna in 1773; see Proñaszka, "Hofmann," p. 80.

16. Such a tempo insertion creates a fast-slow-fast arrangement. For example, in Arbesser's *Missa Sanctae Susannae in C* (M. 7, before 1752) we find:

I.	Allegro	C	in B-flat	"Gloria"
	Largo	3/2	in C minor–E-flat	"Qui tollis"
II.	Allegro	C	in B-flat	"Quoniam"

In M. 12, 35, 41, 52, and 55 both Gloria movements are fast; in M. 7, 8, and 57 a slower section interrupts one of the fast movements.

17. This fast-slow-fast arrangement is in 13 Masses: M. 2, 11, 22, 28, 29, 31, 34, 39, 44, 47, 62, 67, and 70; these fall under column III[d] in figure 7-1.

18. This four-movement arrangement occurs in six Masses: M. 5, 13, 14, 45, 56, and 64, with M. 5, 14, and 45 having "Cum Sancto Spiritu" as a slow introduction before "In gloria Dei." See column IV[d] in figure 7-1.

19. The latest example found of a multi-tempo "Qui tollis" was in Kohaut's *Missa Sancti Willibaldi in C* (M. 34, before 1763). Other composers of such a multi-sectional "Qui tollis" were Holzbauer (M. 30), Monn (M. 38 and 39), F. Schmidt (M. 50 and 51), Tuma (M. 60 and 61), Wagenseil (M. 69), and Ziegler (M. 71).

20. During the first half of the eighteenth century such slow choral introductions at "Cum Sancto" are found in Masses by Italians such as Caldara, Pergolesi, and Perti (see Reichert, "Geschichte," pp. 12, 16; Schnoebelen, "Concerted Mass in Bologna," p. 291; Walter, "Selected Masses of Caldara," pp. 188, 190).

21. The 12 Masses treating the "Cum Sancto" as the final movement of the Gloria are M. 5, 14, 15, 17, 23, 33, 38, 45, 49, 60, 61, and 66; see Ex. 7-11 below. Six other Masses which do not treat the "Cum Sancto" as a separate movement nonetheless have a slower tempo here (M. 11, 29, 34, 39, 54, and 63).

22. M. 23, 33, and 66.

23. This rigidity of accompaniment for the Gloria occurred in two Masses by Albrechtsberger (M. 1 and 3) and one by Hofmann (M. 27). Such lack of change is often found in compressed Glorias that are polytextual, e.g., J. Haydn's *Missa brevis Sancti Joannis de Deo* (Hob. XXII: 7).

24. The *Coronation Mass*, K. 317 (1779), has the longest Gloria, *Missa brevis in D minor*, K. 65 (1769), the shortest. Local time limitations imposed by the Salzburg Archbishop upon Mass length (no longer than three-quarters of an hour) restricted 13 of Mozart's 16 Masses to Glorias of one continuous movement (see chapter 2 at n. 70).

25. Joseph Haydn's single-movement Glorias (Hob. XXII: 1, 3, and 7) are essentially through-composed movements; polytextuality in Nos. 3 and 7 allows practically no musical-textual relationships to be used. The Gloria of the *Theresienmesse in B-flat* (Hob. XXII: 11) is also through-composed if its three, harmonically connected sections are considered as one movement, although one might make a case for the similarity between the opening themes of its "Gloria" and "Quoniam."

26. By exception, some eighteenth-century Masses shift their harmonic centers with the start of the Gloria. At this point in his *Missa in G* (M. 23, before 1753) Hasse changes the tonal center to D major, in which key the Mass eventually concludes. (Bach does the same thing in his *B-minor Mass.*) In his *Missa solemnis in F* (M. 66, before 1797) Vaňhal changes here to C major which remains the tonal center of the Mass until the Agnus Dei, when F major returns. More common is a mode change (from minor to major) in the tonic of the Mass at this point (e.g., Albrechtsberger, M. 4 [D major–D minor]; Hasse, M. 24 [D major–D minor]; Mozart, K. 139 [C minor–C major]). In these instances the change is perhaps text-inspired.

27. This continuous, *Kettenfinale* effect is especially evident in "Qui tollis" settings that consist of a series of short sections, each with a different meter, tempo, etc. (see fig. 7-6, 7-7, 7-8), as well as in the connected Gloria sections of M. 2, 16, 42, and 57.

    Landon, *Haydn: Chronicle and Works* IV, p. 399, has termed such harmonic planning in *The Creation* "progressive tonality."

28. Only two pairs of Glorias sharing exactly the same general harmonic plan were found:

    Reutter and Tuma (M. 44 & 62)
    "Gloria"   I—IV
    "Qui tollis"   i—vi
    "Quoniam"   I—I
    Gsur and Hofmann (M. 22 & 29)
    "Gloria"   I
    "Qui tollis   vi
    "Quoniam"   I

    In only one case did a Gloria share an overall harmonic plan with one by Haydn or Mozart:

    S. Müller (M. 41) and J. Haydn (Hob. XXII: 6)
    "Gloria"   I—vi
    "Quoniam"   I—I

29. That Haydn often began his "Qui tollis" in the major mode is one of several reasons why some critics have found his Masses too "cheerful"; see Landon, *Haydn: Chronicle and Works* IV, pp. 124–30, 169–70. Two of Dittersdorf's Masses (M. 15 and 16) similarly begin the "Qui tollis" in a major key.

30. The relationship is up a fifth in M. 17, 40, 44, 51, 61, 62, and 63; down a fifth in M. 13, 23, 26, 37, 70, and Mozart, K. 427. There is a change from the tonic major (I) to the tonic minor (i) in M. 20, 28, 34, 50, 56, 64, 71, and Haydn, Hob. XXII: 5; in M. 47 the mediant key (iii) is retained.

31. No key change is found in Masses by Krottendorfer, Martínez, Reutter, and Tuma (M. 35, 37, 45, 47, and 60).

32. Such linkage by means of a half-cadence before the "Quoniam" occurs in M. 17, 40, 65; J. Haydn, Hob. XXII: 11; Mozart, K. 139.

33. The examples are found in M. 5, 11, 13, 18, 19, 21, 22, 24, 25, 26, 28, 29, 35, 36, 56, 58, 61, 64, and 66. Among these composers, Gassmann and Hasse are the only ones having extensive operatic experience. It is perhaps significant that most of these composers are from the younger generation under study.

34. Flatted seventh keys generally appear in Glorias having five or more movements. See figure 7-13 for an example of the flatted seventh degree at "Qui tollis."

35. Prohászka, "Hofmann," p. 97, finds large-scale cyclical use of themes to be rare in Hofmann's Glorias; she cites his *Missa Sancti Peregrini* (Prohászka No. 32) as the only example.

36. Apparently degree of solemnity determined whether a composer set the Gloria's intonation text ("Gloria in excelsis Deo") or not. Thus most multi-movement *missae longae* include the intonation, while most *missae breves* omit it (see Prohászka, "Hofmann," p. 96). Twenty-six of the 72 Masses under study (36%) lack this intonation text; 16 of these 26 (62%) are *missae breves*. However, no hard and fast rules can be applied because of several exceptions; e.g., the following long Masses lack the intonation: M. 13, 39, 40, 50, 54–58. (Sonnleithner seems never to have set the intonation in his Masses.) M. 21, 22, and 42 are *missae breves* which do include the intonation.

37. Glorias beginning with solos occur in M. 7, 8, 9, 35, 45 (see ex. 7-15 below), 51, 61, 70, and 71 (see ex. 7-16).

38. For example, Caldara's *Mass in G Minor* (1772, autograph score in Dresden; copy also at Austrian National Library, Vienna, Mus. Hs. 16260; Mass "H" in Walter, "Selected Masses of Caldara," p. 112); also found in later Masses by Jommelli: *Mass in F* (Venice, 1745; copy at Conservatorio, Naples, Ms. 22.6.5) and *Mass in D* (Stuttgart, 1766; printed ed. by Porro of Paris, 1766); see Jon Olaf Carlson, "Selected Masses of Niccolo Jommelli" (D.M.A. diss., University of Illinois at Champaign-Urbana, 1974), pp. 17–57.

39. M. 2, 4, 9, 10, 21, 22, 53, 64, 65. These nine represent only about 13% of the sample.

40. Such solos were encountered in the Glorias of the following Masses:

M. 44	(Reutter)—soprano at "Amen" sings opposite chorus [=end of Quoniam movement]
M. 46	(Reutter)—soprano at "Cum Sancto" [=end of single-movement Gloria]
M. 48	(Reutter)—soprano and alto at "Amen" sing opposite chorus [end of Quoniam]
M. 69	(Wagenseil)—tenor and bass at "Cum Sancto" [=end of single-movement Gloria]
M. 72	(Ziegler)—soprano and alto at "Cum Sancto/Amen" [end of Quoniam]

Mozart uses soloists during the Amens of three Glorias: K. 192, 317, and 337.

41. The common order of fugal entries among all the fugues of these Masses was bass, tenor, alto, and soprano. Johann Mattheson, *Der vollkommene Kapellmeister* (Hamburg: C. Herold, 1939), ed. and trans. Ernest C. Harriss, Studies in Musicology no. 21 (Ann Arbor, Michigan: UMI Research Press, 1981), p. 730 belittles this ordering which he terms "the old trodden path"; see Warren Kirkendale, *Fugue and Fugato in Rococo and Classical Chamber Music*, trans. Margaret Bent and Warren Kirkendale (Durham, N.C.: Duke University Press, 1979), pp. 62–63.

42. The outlines indicate where examples of specific figures may be found. Certainly not every example has been cited, but the numbers give us an approximate idea of how often the musical figures occurred.

    Terms in parentheses are from seventeenth- and eighteenth-century treatises concerning musical figures, i.e. *Figurenlehre;* see George J. Buelow, "Rhetoric and Music," in *The New Grove Dictionary of Music and Musicians* ed. Stanley Sadie, 6th ed., 20 vols (London: Macmillan, 1980) XV, pp. 793–803.

43. Warren Kirkendale, "New Roads to Old Ideas in Beethoven's *Missa Solemnis,"* *The Musical Quarterly* LVI (1970): 668.

44. Gernot Gruber, "Musikalische Rhetorik und barocke Bildlichkeit in Kompositionen des jungen Haydn," in *Der junge Haydn,* ed. Vera Schwarz (Graz: Akademische Druck- und Verlagsanstalt, 1972), pp. 180–81.

45. According to Prohászka, "Hofmann," p. 86, Hofer in his 1915 dissertation on Reutter (p. 121) claims a Neapolitan origin for this practice of repeating the word "pax."

46. Kirkendale, "New Roads," p. 668.

47. A slower tempo for "Adoramus" occurs in Caldara's *Missa* [in C], Manuscript score Mus. Res. *MRDI in the New York Public Library; this Mass is apparently not discussed in Walter, "Selected Masses of Caldara."

48. The "Gratias" requires trombone(s) in M. 45, 47, 49, 50, 51, 57, 60, 61 (ex. 7-19), 62, 63, and 70—all Masses dated before 1760. According to Walter, "Selected Masses of Caldara," pp. 61–84, Caldara's *Missa Gratiarum* (autograph score at A-Wgm dated 1727, copy also at A-Wn, Mus. Hs. 15896; Mass "A" in Walter's catalogue) and *Missa Desiderii* (n.d., A-Wn, Mus. Hs. 15901; Mass "F") have a trombone solo at "Gratias." Two trombones are required at this point in Caldara's *Mass in C* at the New York Public Library (see n. 47 above).

49. The violoncello scoring is based on the parts at Seitenstetten; see Prohászka, "Hofmann," p. 123. In the West Berlin score (Mus. ms. 10722) both "Viole obl." and "Violoncelli obl." are indicated; a later hand appears to have changed these designations into "due Viole obl. o due Violoncelli obl."

50. Walter, "Selected Masses of Caldara," p. 156; see also 143–44. Masses using white notation meters for the "Qui tollis" or its subsections include those by Albrechtsberger, Arbesser, Holzbauer, Martínez, Monn, Reutter, Sonnleithner, Tuma, Wagenseil, and Ziegler; i.e., M. 5, 7, 30, 31, 37, 38, 44, 56, 61, 62, 63, 67, and 71.

51. Seven Masses in the sample of 72 change meter or tempo at "Suscipe":

	"Qui tollis"		"Suscipe"		Composer (Date)
No. 30	C	Grave	3/2	Largo	Holzbauer (1739)
No. 34	C	Adagio	3/4	Andante	Kohaut (1763)
No. 38	C	Adagio	3/2	Andante	Monn (1741)
No. 51	6/8	Adagio	C	Adagio	Schmidt (1747)
No. 61	C	Adagio	C	Andante	Tuma (1743)
No. 69	C	Adagio	C	Adagio	Wagenseil (1742)
No. 71	¢	Adagio	3/8	Andante	Ziegler (1762)

This tempo change seems to have become less common after the 1740s.

52. Clarini are also highlighted in "Quoniam" settings by Predieri, Schmidt, and Tuma; see M. 42, 50, and 60.

53. Prohászka, "Hofmann," p. 86, calls the "Qui tollis" the *Durchführungsatz* of the Gloria and compares it to the "Crucifixus" of the Credo.

54. This AA^1A^2 type of "Qui tollis" occurs in M. 1, 9, 10, 12, 13 (ex. 7-27), 15, 17, 26, 28, 29, 42, 48, 54, 55, 56 (ex. 7-22), 57, and 59; see J. Haydn, Hob. XXII: 5 and 9; W. A. Mozart, K. 262 and 427.

55. Examples of these "Qui tollis" forms include the following Masses:
    ABA^1—M. 36, 63
    AAB (AA^1B)—M. 3, 5, 16, 19, 47, 49
    ABC—M. 22, 23, 42, 43, 45 (ex. 7-25).

Chapter 8

1. Polytextuality (text telescoping) occurs in 23 (32%) of the 71 Credos studied; 16 (70%) of these 23 Credos are from *missae breves*. The 23 examples are found in M. 1, 3, 6, 11, 19 (Vienna version), 21, 22, 25, 31, 32, 33, 42, 43, 44, 47, 48, 52, 53, 59, 62, 63, 66, and 69.

2. This division disagrees with the theological division in Josef Andreas Jungmann, *The Mass of the Roman Rite: Its Origins and Development (Missarum Sollemnia)* (Vienna: Herder, 1949), 2 vols, trans. Francis A. Brunner (New York: Benziger Brothers, 1951) I, p. 463: Credo (God the Creator), Et in unum Dominum Jesum Christum (Christ), and Et in Spiritum Sanctum (Gifts of Salvation). Credos in the following Masses totally avoid the tripartite musical division: M. 6, 33, 42, 43, and 62. M. 46 lacks a Credo.

3. Other forms of adagio such as poco adagio (M. 41) and adagio molto (M. 3, ex. 8-13) are also found at "Et incarnatus." In nine instances grave or a form thereof (e.g., largo e maestoso, largo ma non troppo, and larghetto) is used here. Faster tempos employed for "Et incarnatus" are:
    Andante: M. 5, 6, 20, 48, 60, 66 (ex. 8-3)
    Moderato: M. 8
    Non troppo lento: M. 24 (ex. 8-11)

4. The following four Credos change to a faster tempo at "Crucifixus": M. 23 (Lento), 25 (Andante), 39 (Un poco allegro), and 69 (Allabreve). M. 29 (Larghetto; ex. 8-15) and M. 32 (Largo) have a slower tempo, while the following Masses begin a new section yet retain the previous tempo for the "Crucifixus": M. 14 (ex. 8-16), 30, 40?, 42, 50 (ex. 8-14), 51, 58, and 62?. (Question marks indicate that the tempo is not specified but is assumed to be that of the preceding section.)

5. The following Masses have a new tempo at "Et vitam": M. 2, 9, 17, 19 (Berlin version), 51, 60?, 61?, 69. New movements (and tempos) are also found at "Et in Spiritum Sanctum" (M. 68, 69), "Confiteor" (M. 17), "Et expecto" (M. 38), and "Et vitam" (M. 50). Unlike Bach (see column VIII in fig. 8-1) and Mozart (see K. 49, 66, 139, 167, 262), most Viennese composers make the "Et resurrexit" the final movement of the Credo

6. M. 1, 8, 10, 19 (Vienna version), 21, 25, 26, 33, 50, 60, 62, 63, and 72 keep to a quadruple meter (C) while M. 17, 59, and 66 are triple meter (3/4) throughout the Credo.

7. The 10 exceptions to this pattern of harmonic return (with tonality of start of "Et resurrexit" in parentheses) are the following: M. 2 (IV), 7 (ii), 19 (IV; Vienna version), 23 (IV), 24 (IV), 31 (III), 32 (III), 37 (IV), 63 (VI), and 68 (IV).

8. Irmgard Becker-Glauch, "Die Kirchenmusik des jungen Haydn," in *Der junge Haydn,* ed. Vera Schwarz (Graz: Akademische Druck- und Verlagsanstalt, 1972), p. 76, observes that Haydn used major keys for the "Et incarnatus" only from 1775 on. A resultant need for modal contrast may partially explain why five of Haydn's Masses (Hob. XXII: 7, 10, 11, 12, 13) oddly begin the "Et resurrexit" in the minor mode. Only two of the Masses under study (M. 7, 52) use a minor key for the "Et resurrexit."

9. This striking effect of delaying the mode change until "Crucifixus" occurs in M. 5, 8, 9, 15, 17, 19 (Vienna version), 23, 29 (ex. 8-15), 30, 31, 40, 41, 42, 63, 65, 69. In some seven instances (M. 1, 7, 33, 39, 51, 58, 59) a "Crucifixus" in the major mode follows an "Et incarnatus" begun in the minor.

10. The intonation has not been set in 37 of the 71 Credos in the sample: 1–4, 6–8, 10, 12, 19 (Vienna version), 28, 31–35, 37, 40, 42, 43, 45, 47, 48, 52–54, 57–61, 63, 66–70. Since only 17 (46%) of these 37 are from *missae breves,* it would appear that inclusion of the intonation depends more upon the circumstances of the service for which a Mass was originally composed rather than upon its overall length. Only four of the Credos begin with vocal soloists: M. 34 (Kohaut), 52 (Seuche), 61 (Tuma), and 68 (Wagenseil).

   Hasse (M. 24) and Reutter (M. 44) each wrote a Credo which, like that in Bach's *B-minor Mass,* begins with a concerted setting of the oldest Gregorian chant intonation (see *The Liber Usualis with Introduction and Rubrics in English,* ed the Benedictines of Solesmes (Tournai: Desclee, 1956), p. 64). Georg Reichert, "Mozart's 'Credo-Messen' und ihre Vorläufer," *Mozart Jahrbuch 1955*:121ff., cites several earlier examples of this cantus firmus technique in Masses by Fux, Ziani, J. G. Reinhardt, Pruneder, Oettl, Pachschmidt, Donberger, Fr. Conti, and Ferdinand Schmidt.

11. See Guido Adler, "Zur Geschichte der Wiener Messenkomposition in der zweiten Hälfte des XVII. Jahrhunderts," *Studien zur Musikwissenschaft IV* (1916):21, and Alfred Orel, "Die katholische Kirchenmusik von 1600 bis 1750," in *Handbuch der Musikgeschichte,* 2 vols., 2nd ed., ed. Guido Adler (Berlin-Wilmersdorf: H. Keller, 1930), p. 520. Hermine Prohászka, "Leopold Hofmann und seine Messen," *Studien zur Musikwissenschaft XXVI* (1964): 87, should thus not have been so surprised to find Leopold Hofmann preferring the "Et incarnatus" as a choral movement.

12. When telescoping of the text occurs in the Credo, it usually ceases by "descendit de coelis," if not earlier at "Genitum, non factum" or "Qui propter nos homines."

13. The "Et resurrexit" begins with vocal soloists in five Masses of the sample: M. 12 (Boog), 30 (Holzbauer), 38 (Monn), 42 (Predieri), and 68 (Wagenseil).

14. For about two-thirds of the Masses (43 of the 67 for which measure counts were available) the cumulative lengths for the Credo, Sanctus, and Agnus Dei amounted to less than 60 percent of the entire Mass's length.

15. Georg Reichert, "Mozart's 'Credo-Messen' und ihre Vorläufer," *Mozart Jahrbuch 1955:* 121 ff.; see also Reichert, "Zur Geschichte der Wiener Messenkomposition in der ersten Hälfte des 18. Jahrhunderts" (Ph.D. diss., University of Vienna, 1935), pp. 27–57, from which the *Mozart Jahrbuch* article was derived. Jommelli's *Mass in D* (published 1766 in Paris) is a "Credo Mass" in which the "Credo" refrain interestingly recurs at a higher pitch level each time; see Jon Olaf Carlson, "Selected Masses of Niccolò Jommelli" (Ph.D. diss., University of Illinois at Champaign-Urbana, 1974), p. 53.

16. Such a varied reprise at "Et resurrexit" is found in two early Masses by Joseph Haydn (Hob. XXII: 6 and 8) and six Masses by Mozart (K. 220, 257, 258, 259, 317, and 337). Some of their Masses call for a reprise of only the violin figurations at this point (Hob. XXII: 3 and K. 167 and 259).

17. Mozart uses a similar structure in his *Missa brevis in F,* K. 192 (Salzburg, 1774). There a four-note theme (ex. 8-7 above) recurs with the word "Credo" as well as with "Crucifixus," "Confiteor," "Et vitam," and "Amen." Perhaps this means for unifying the Credo derives from the ritornello and reprise forms of the aria, concerto, and sonata.

18. Henry B. Raynor, "Some Reflections upon the Viennese Mass," *The Musical Times* (Nov. 1954): 593.

19. Howard Chandler Robbins Landon, *Haydn: Chronicle and Works,* 5 vols. (Bloomington: Indiana University Press, 1976–80), IV, p. 146.

20. See n. 10 above.

21. Charles Rosen, *The Classical Style: Haydn, Mozart, Beethoven* (New York: Norton, 1971), p. 370.

22. Such "pseudo-polyphonic" Credos are found in M. 1, 4, 6, 19 (Vienna version), 33, 38, 42, 43, 48, 52, 53, 58, 60 (fugal?), 61, 67, and 69. On text telescoping see nn. 1 and 12 above.

23. The following Credos change from chorus to vocal soloists at "Et in unum Dominum": M. 2, 7, 12, 13, 19 (Berlin version), 26–29, 31, 37, 40, 45, 49, 50, 51, 63, 70, and 71.

24. The full chorus enters at "Qui propter nos homines" in M. 12, 13, 19 (Berlin version), 27–29, 33, 49, 50, 63, 70, and 71.

25. The following 10 solo numbers were found:

M. 16	Dittersdorf	SSTB ternary ensemble
19	Gassmann	S binary aria with chorus (Vienna version)
20	Grassl	A binary aria
22	Gsur	AT binary duet
29	Hofmann	S binary aria
35	Krottendorfer	T binary aria
50	Schmidt	B binary aria
51	Schmidt	S binary "Crucifixus" aria
66	Vaňhal	S binary aria (ex. 8-3)
71	Ziegler	S binary aria linked to B binary aria

26. See chapter 7 at n. 50. M. 3 (ex. 8-13), 22, 31 32, 44, 52, 55, 58, 64, and 68 use 3/2 meter for the "Et incarnatus"; M. 29 (ex. 8-15) uses 3/2 and M. 69 uses ¢ for the "Crucifixus" (see fig. 8-2). Gernot Gruber, "Musikalische Rhetorik und barocke Bildlichkeit in Kompositionen des jungen Haydn," in *Der junge Haydn,* ed. Vera Schwarz (Graz: Akademische Druck- und Verlagsanstalt, 1972), p. 187, reports that Hans Heinrich Unger, in his *Die Beziehungen zwischen Musik und Rhetorikum im 16.–18. Jahrhundert* (Würzburg: Triltsch, 1941), p. 121f., traces the use of long notes at "Et incarnatus" back to Josquin.

27. M. 9, 10, and 47 as well as J. Haydn, Hob. XXII: 5 require muted strings for the "Et incarnatus." In M. 64 (Vaňhal) the violins play pizzicato. M. 7, 14, 32, and 34 have no strings at this point, while M. 8, 9, 10, and 32 leave out continuo during the instrumental interludes.

28. Bach does the same thing in the *B-minor Mass* (m. 49), as do both Haydn and Mozart in several of their Masses.

29. A solo voice begins the "Et resurrexit" in M. 12, 30 (ex. 8-5), 38, 42, and 68.

30. Brass fanfares open the "Et resurrexit" in M. 3, 14, 18, 35, 36, 38, 45, 49, 51, 56, and 57. Vocal "fanfares" open this section in M. 3, 5, 14, 20, 26, 28, 31, 37, 41, 48, 50, 54, 58, 60, and 69.

31. On musical reprises at "Et resurrexit" see ex. 8-8 and 8-9.

32. Soloists begin singing at "Et in Spiritum Sanctum" in M. 10, 12, 15, 19 (Berlin version), 20, 27–30, 32, 34, 36–39, 45, 48, 50–52, 57, 60, 61, 63, 69, 70, and 71. Some Masses start the vocal solos earlier in this movement, often at "Et iterum"; see n. 29 above.

Chapter 9

1. Josef Andreas Jungmann, *The Mass of the Roman Rite: Its Origins and Development (Missarum Sollemnia)* (Vienna: Herder, 1949) II, pp. 216–17. Soft organ playing ("ernst und melodiös") was allowed in some churches during this holiest moment; see Karl Gustav Fellerer, "Die Enzyklika 'Annus qui'," II, p. 151 and id., "Kirchenmusik und Aufklärung," in *Geschichte der katholischen Kirchenmusik*, 2 vols., ed. Karl Gustav Fellerer (Kassel: Bärenreiter, 1976) II, p. 199.

2. *Caeremonial episcoporum* (Rome, 1600) II, 8, p. 70f., as cited by Jungmann, *The Mass of the Roman Rite* II, p. 137, n. 44. Apparently extended musical settings are what prompted the move of the "Benedictus" from its original position before the consecration. See figure 2-2.

3. Franz Xaver Glöggl, *Kirchenmusik-Ordnung: Erklärendes Handbuch des musikalischen Gottesdienstes, für Kapellmeister, Regenschori, Sänger und Tonkünstler* (Vienna: J.B. Wallishauser, 1828), pp. 16–17. Jungmann, *The Mass of the Roman Rite* II, p. 137, notes that in some extended settings the Sanctus and "Benedictus" filled the required silence during consecration.

4. In only two cases (M. 32 [ex. 9-1] by Holzbauer and M. 70 by Wagenseil) does the first "Osanna" not end with an authentic or plagal cadence. See Robert Freeman, "The Role of Organ Improvisation in Haydn's Church Music," in *Haydn Studies*, ed. Jens Peter Larsen, Howard Serwer, and James Webster (New York: Norton, 1981), p. 194, on how the organ was frequently played (often improvised) between the "Sanctus" and "Benedictus" of Austrian Masses at this time.

    Subsections of the Sanctus will be designated with quotation marks, i.e., "Sanctus" (first section of the Sanctus), "Pleni sunt coeli," "Benedictus," etc.

5. This slow-fast arrangement applies to all Masses except M. 1, 4, 33, 40, 43, 44, 47, 50, 67, and 69. However, in M. 5 (Albrechtsberger) the allegro begins earlier than "Pleni," at "Dominus Deus Sabaoth," and in M. 50 (Schmidt) there is a four-measure adagio coda on "Dominus Deus Sabaoth" at the end of an Andante "Sanctus." Interestingly, in M. 1 Albrechtsberger reverses the usual tempo relationship by using allegro for the "Sanctus" and andante for the "Pleni." Georg Reichert, "Zur Geschichte der Wiener Messenkomposition in der ersten Hälfte des 18. Jahrhunderts" (Ph.D. diss., University of Vienna, 1935), p. 20, found that during the first half of the eighteenth century only rarely did the "Sanctus"-"Pleni"-"Osanna" complex consist of more than a single movement; only the larger Masses were multi-movement here.

6. At least one-third of the settings in the sample have this common tempo arrangement; see M. 3, 5, 12–15, 17, 21, 22, 25–27, 35, 39, 52–57, 61, 64, 65, and 71.

7. The meter 2/4 occurs in Sanctus settings by Dittersdorf (M. 17), Gassmann (M. 19), Grassl (M. 20), Vanhal (M. 64–66), and Ziegler (M. 72).

8. Such is the case at least 49% of the time. The following 33 Masses have Kyries which are longer (in measure count) than their respective Sanctus settings: M. 3–5, 8, 9, 15, 19, 23–27, 29, 30, 32, 33, 36–40, 43, 45, 49, 50, 52, 58, 60, 61, 63, 64, 66, and 70. The average Kyrie's length is about 105 measures.

9. Only five Sanctus settings in the sample (M. 1, 2, 5, 20, and 47) are entirely for chorus.

10. In the sample under study, Masses by Martínez (M. 36 and 37, dated 1761 and 1765 respectively), Boog (M. 13, before 1763; see ex. 9-3), and Vaňhal (M. 66, before 1797) were the latest examples employing solos for the "Sanctus" or "Pleni." Interestingly, Joseph Haydn "revived" this practice in two of his late Masses: Hob. XXII: 9 (1796) and 12 (1799).

11. M. 32, 36, 38, 43, 44, 51, 63, and 68 open the Sanctus with vocal solos; in M. 6 and 39 the soloists enter only at "Dominus"; in M. 37 the soloist alternates with the chorus. Except for M. 43 and 51, all of these change to full chorus for "Pleni sunt coeli."

12. Such solo-tutti "Osanna" settings go back to the seventeenth century in Vienna; see Guido Adler, "Zur Geschichte der Wiener Messenkomposition in der zweiten Hälfte des XVII. Jahrhunderts," *Studien zur Musikwissenschaft* IV (1916): 21.

13. The choral "Benedictus" settings were in M. 8–12, 15, 32, 41, 44, 63, and 65.

14. Between "Pleni" and the first "Osanna" there is a half-cadence in M. 17, 33, 36, 37, and 53, rhythmic elision in M. 4, 11, 16, 19 (Berlin version), and 43, and full cadence in M. 13, 19 (Vienna version), 31, 60, and 65.

15. A plagal cadence concludes the first "Osanna" in M. 1–5, 13–15, 17, 20–22, 28, 30, 31, 35, 44, 46, 47, 51, 54, 56, 59, 61–63, 71, and 72. Often the second "Osanna" also ends with a plagal cadence. Plagal cadences also occur occasionally at the end of the "Dona nobis pacem."

16. The latest minor-keyed "Benedictus" settings were in M. 13 (Boog, before 1763), 28 (Hofmann, before 1762), and 71 (Ziegler, before 1762). The other, earlier settings are in M. 7, 11, 23, 30, 32, 33, 38, 40, 43, 45, 50, 60, 62, 69, 70, and 71.

    Joseph Haydn wrote four of his 13 extant, "Benedictus" settings in a minor key: Hob. XXII: 5 (1766), 8 (1782), 9 (1796), and 11 (1798). Two of these (nos. 8 and 9) do, however, end in a major key, thus conveying some sense of the Redeemer's comfort.

17. The repetition of "Osanna I" for "Osanna II" is often indicated in the parts by "Osanna ut supra." A glance through *The Liber Usualis, with Introduction and Rubrics in English,* ed. the Benedictines of Solesmes (Tournai: Desclee, 1956), p. 21ff., shows that about half of the Sanctus chants have such a repetition linking the two "Osannas." Polyphonic Masses of the sixteenth century also had this repetition; see Reichert, "Geschichte," pp. 23–24. Exact repetition for "Osanna II" occurs in M. 3–5, 8, 10–13, 15, 17, 19 (both versions), 23, 25, 27, 31, 33, 36–38, 42, 45–47, 53?, 54, 58, 60?, 64–66; variation occurs in M. 1, 9, 16, 20–22, 24, 26, 28, 29, 34, 43, 44, 52, 59, 71, and 72.

18. Because its short text (six words) does not itself offer any internal repetitions to guide musical form, the "Benedictus"—more than any other text of the Mass Ordinary—allows composers maximum freedom in design. Thus, sonata elements appeared here early.

19. Here the earliest dated example of a "Benedictus" with two contrasting thematic areas that both return in the tonic is by Joseph Krottendorfer (M. 35, before 1764). However, a true "development" is lacking, since the tonic reprise occurs only one measure into the second vocal section.

20. In the *Missa Sancti Mariani* the subject is probably derived from the "Benedictus" of Mass VIII in the *Liber Usualis*, p. 39. In the "Benedictus" of his *Missa Sancti Placidi* (M. 44, before 1756) Reutter has the sopranos alone (similarly accompanied by running violin figures) sing a tune derived from another "Benedictus" chant (probably from *Liber Usualis*, p. 63, rather than the Tonus Pellegrinus suggested by Landon, *Haydn: Chronicle and Works*, I, p. 93). Other examples of "Benedictus" settings using a cantus firmus include Tuma's *Missa Sancti Stephani* (M. 63, before 1747; unknown melody) and Albrechtsberger's *Choral-Messa* (Weissenbäck no. 166, ca. 1808; see Dorothea Schröder, "Die geistlichen Vokalkompositionen Johann Georg Albrechtsbergers," Ph.D. diss., University of Hamburg, 1986).

21. Except for M. 40, 42, and 50, all "Benedictus" settings having opening ritornellos of more than 11 measures date from 1763 and later. Most of Joseph Haydn's "Benedictus" introductions are longer than 11 measures (Hob. XXII: 3 and 6 are the exceptions); Mozart's are mostly shorter, the exceptions being K. 167 and 427.

22. For example, Warren Kirkendale, "New Roads to Old Ideas in Beethoven's *Missa Solemnis,*" *The Musical Quarterly* LVI (1970): 689.

23. Such organ Masses include M. 17 and 45 (ex. 9-12) as well as Masses by J. Haydn (Hob. XXII: 4 and 7) and Mozart (K. 259). For an excerpt from the organ solo in Reutter's *Rosalienmesse* (Hofer no. 15; 1746) see Landon, *Haydn: Chronicle and Works* I, p. 88.

24. An orchestral introduction opens the Sanctus of M. 8, 16, 18, 24, 46, 51, and 66. Introduction lengths range from one to eight measures (see M. 18 and 66). Unlike the Reutter example, these introductions are usually in the same tempo as the rest of the "Sanctus."

25. For the scalar motion at the beginning of the Sanctus in Reutter's *Missa Sancti Placidi* (M. 44, Hofer no. 33), see Landon, *Haydn: Chronicle and Works* I, p. 93. In a few Sanctus settings (e.g., M. 25, 27, 39, and 57) fermatas add even more ceremony (and tension) to the movement by lengthening either the word "Sanctus" or the silence between the repetitions of this word.

26. For an example of a homophonic "Osanna" see ex. 9-2, m. 16f.

27. Clarini and timpani do play during the "Benedictus" of M. 1, 5, 9, 20, 36, and 65.

28. These characteristics are based upon those traits listed for pastoral Masses in Ernst Tittel, "Die Wiener Pastoralmesse," *Musica Divina* 23/12 (1935): 192–96, and Alois Augustin Dimpfl, "Die Pastoralmesse" (Ph.D. diss., University of Erlangen, 1945). The traditions of the provincial pastoral Mass will be treated in Mark Germer, "The Austro-Bohemian Pastoral Mass" (Ph.D. diss., in progress, New York University, expected 1986).

29. Gernot Gruber, "Musikalische Rhetorik und barocke Bildlichkeit in Kompositionen des jungen Haydn," in *Der junge Haydn,* ed. Vera Schwarz (Graz: Akademische Druck- und Verlagsanstalt, 1972), p. 183.

Chapter 10

1. According to Andreas Weissenbäck, "Johann Georg Albrechtsberger als Kirchen-komponist," *Studien zur Musikwissenschaft* XIV (1927): 151, the Communion was usually not sung at this time (see fig. 2-2). During the Agnus Dei the priest distributes the Host of the Eucharist to members of the congregation who come forward.

2. Georg Reichert, "Zur Geschichte der Wiener Messenkomposition in der ersten Hälfte des 18. Jahrhunderts" (Ph.D. diss., University of Vienna, 1935), p. 22. For the sake of clarity, quotation marks will indicate references to this opening "Agnus Dei" section; the entire final part of the Mass Ordinary (including the "Dona nobis pacem") will be designated as simply Agnus Dei (i.e., without quotation marks). The three repeated invocations will be further distinguished as "Agnus Dei I," "Agnus Dei II," and "Agnus Dei III."

3. The 23 "Dona nobis pacem" settings requiring both chorus and soloists are in M. 7-9, 14, 15, 17 (ex. 10-10), 30, 31, 33, 36, 37 (ex. 10-11), 41, 47, 50 (ex. 10-15), 52, 55 (ex. 10-12), 57, 58, 63, 65 (ex. 10-13, 10-16), 66, 68, and 72. The "Dona nobis pacem" is never for soloists only. Most "Dona" fugues require only the chorus.

4. The 10 Agnus settings for chorus only are in M. 1, 3-5, 10, 18, 21, 26, 59, and 64. M. 16 and 48 lack a complete Agnus.

5. Reichert, "Geschichte," pp. 22-23.

6. The earliest 2/4 example of the sample is the "Dona" of a Mass by Dittersdorf (M. 15); the others occur in M. 17, 64, and 65.

7. Some 22 of the 33 Masses dated before 1760 (67%) begin the Agnus in a major key, while only 11 of the 33 dated 1760 or later (33.3%) do the same.

8. Examples of AA^1A^2 are found in M. 1, 4, 6, 8, 10, 15 (ex. 10-3), 19, 21-24, 26, 29, 44, 46, 47, 50, 51, 56-58, 63-66, 68, 70, and 72; ABC in M. 3, 7, 13, 14, 30, 31, 32, 34, 36, 37, 39, 40, 42, 49, 52, 53, 60 (ex. 10-5), 62, 67, 69, and 71; AA^1B in M. 2, 5, 11, 12, 17, 25, 27, 28 (ex. 10-2), 33, 35, 38, 43, 45, 54, 55, 59, and 61; ABB in M. 20; AAB^1 in M. 9.

9. Guido Adler, "Zur Geschichte der Wiener Messenkomposition in der zweiten Hälfte des XVII. Jahrhunderts," *Studien zur Musikwissenschaft* IV (1916): 21, found up to six alternations of solo and chorus in the "Agnus Dei" settings of the late seventeenth century. Reichert, "Geschichte," p. 22, found the arrangement solo-solo-chorus for Agnus I-II-III (type "A" in fig. 10-6) to be also very common in Viennese Masses of the first half of the eighteenth century (see ex. 10-2). Friedrich Wilhelm Riedel, *Kirchenmusik am Hofe Karls VI. (1711–1740)*... (Munich and Salzburg: Emil Katzbichler, 1977), p. 151, indicates that this latter arrangement was typical of Fux's *missae mediocres*.

10. This obedience towards the text contrasts with the freedom found in the Kyries of these same Masses; there the words "Kyrie eleison" were often repeated any number of times. However, in six Agnus settings (M. 15 [ex. 10-3], 33, 55-58) Dittersdorf, Holzbauer, and Sonnleithner repeat "miserere nobis" a second time, i.e., after the third "Agnus Dei, qui tollis peccata mundi" and just before the "Dona." Friberth omits "Agnus III" in his setting (M. 18). In M. 32 Holzbauer has "Agnus Dei" sung only once by each of the three soloists singing simultaneously in counterpoint; in M. 33 Holzbauer has the chorus sing a fourth "Agnus Dei" invocation. In M. 65 (before 1782) Vanhal does what Haydn often does: present the "Dona" text "prematurely"—at the end of the "Agnus Dei," i.e., just before the faster "Dona nobis pacem" proper begins; see Hob. XXII: 5, 9, and 11.

11. "Agnus Dei" vocal duets, trios, or quartets are found in M. 7, 11, 17, 19, 22, 27, 28, 30-34, 40, 42-44, 46, 52, 53, 56-58, 66-71.

12. Trombones accompany the "Agnus Dei" of M. 12 (solo), 20, 35 (solo), 44, 46, 49, 56, 57, 58, 60, 61, 67, and 70. Mozart uses a trio of trombones (ATB) in the "Agnus Dei" of his early C-minor Mass, K. 139, which was probably written for Vienna. Fux and Caldara also used trombones at this point; see Fux's *Missa Lachrymantis Virginis* in C minor (the so-called

Klosterneuburger-Mass) in his *Sämmtliche Werke,* Ser. I, Bd. 2 (1971); Caldara's *Missa Gratiarum,* A-Wn: Mus. Hs. 15896 (1727) [=Mass "A" in Walter, "Selected Masses of Caldara," ex. 4, p. 95].

13.   Strings are muted during the "Agnus Dei" of M. 8 (later crossed out?), 26, 47, 54, 64, 65, J. Haydn, Hob. XXII: 4, and Mozart, K. 317 and 337.

14.   Compare the similar use of *fp* in the "Agnus Dei" of Joseph Haydn's *St. Cecilia Mass,* Hob. XXII: 5. Elsewhere, e.g., in his *Nicolaimesse* (XXII: 6), Haydn sets the "miserere" apart with a *forte* marking. Mozart uses dynamic contrast in several of his "Agnus Dei" settings; see K. 49, 66, 167, 192, 257–59, 262, 275.

15.   Hermine Prohászka, "Leopold Hofmann und seine Messen," *Studien zur Musikwissenschaft* XXVI (1964): 88. Reichert, "Geschichte," p. 24, is not sure just how far back in history such musical repetitions for the "Dona" occur but indicates that they are found in seventeenth-century Masses. The practice was also used by Caldara, many of whose Masses were certainly models for those presently under study.

16.   This "Kyrie ut supra" practice is one of the chief causes of text underlay difficulties in the "Dona." For example, not all musicians used the artificially expanded text "da pacem" (instead of only "pacem") to avoid an awkward syncopated "pacem" when there were several repetitions of "eleison" in the Kyrie being reused. In a Kremsmünster source for M. 12 by Boog, the subject of the "Dona" fugue has this added word:

However, in the St. Peter's collection in Vienna, this same subject avoids the use of "da" but has some awkward word accentuation as a result:

Reichert, "Geschichte," p. 25, found "da pacem" used for "eleison" repetitions in Masses by F. Schmidt, Tuma, Monn, Zechner, Gassmann, and J. Haydn. The authenticity of such "da pacem's" should probably remain in doubt unless there is autograph proof for its use.

Albrechtsberger showed concern for underlay here; so that the new text would be properly set by copyists (e.g., M. 2 and 5), Albrechtsberger in his autographs usually wrote out only the vocal parts for such a "Dona" reusing earlier music.

17.   Double fugue "Dona" settings are found in M. 32, 38, 40, and 63; see J. Haydn, Hob. XXII: 4, 5.

18.   See n. 3 above.

19. Concerto style is also found in the "Dona" of M. 14, 17, 30, 36, 52, 57, 58, 72. Joseph Haydn's *Missa brevis in F* (Hob. XXII: 1) also has this treatment, as do some of Mozart's Masses.

20. On the symbols used in fig. 10-8 and 10-9, see chapter 6, n. 19.

21. Mozart's concerted settings that use rondo form for the "Dona" are K. 275 (1777) and 337 (1780). An early Mass by Holzbauer (M. 33, before 1745) has an $ABA^1B^1A^2$ form suggesting a rondo.

22. Cornell Jesse Runestad, "The Masses of Joseph Haydn" (Ph.D. diss., University of Illinois at Urbana-Champaign, 1970), p. 287.

23. Reichert, "Geschichte," p. 22.

24. Karl Maria Brand, *Die Messen von Joseph Haydn* (Würzburg-Aumühle: K. Triltsch, 1941), pp. 142–43. Here Brand also quotes a 1776 letter by *Domkapellmeister* Schmittbauer of Cologne who discusses a quiet ending in one of his own Masses. Other "Dona" settings that end softly occur in Masses by Gsur (M. 21 and 22), Müller (M. 41), and Wagenseil (M. 68).

25. P. Norbert Hofer, "Die beiden Reutter als Kirchenkomponisten," 2 vols. (Ph.D. diss., Vienna, 1915), p. 90. Hofer was influenced by a copy of the Mass at Seitenstetten which has the inscription: "Princeps de Lictenstein Missam hanc tanti fecit, ut auctori in remunerationem dederit 6 equos albos." Another candidate for the *Schimmelmesse* is Hofer's No. 74 which has a "Dona" in 12/8 meter. See Hofer, "Thematisches Verzeichnis der Werke Georg Reutters d.J.," Mus. Hs. 28.992 in the Austrian National Library, Vienna, fol. 37, and idem, *DTÖ*, vol. 88, p. XIII. Ludwig Stollbrock, "Leben und Wirken des k.k. Hofkapellmeisters und Hofkompositors Johann Georg Reuter jun.," *Vierteljahrschrift für Musikwissenschaft* VIII (1892): 193–94, and Carl Ferdinand Pohl, *Joseph Haydn* (Berlin: A Sacco; Leipzig: Breitkopf & Härtel, 1878) I, p. 39, describe the meter of this "Dona" as 12/8.

Conclusions

1. Doberschiz, *Millenarium Cremifanense*, pp. 366, 59, as cited by Altman Kellner, *Musikgeschichte des Stiftes Kremsmünster nach den Quellen dargestellt* (Kassel: Bärenreiter, 1956), p. 468.

2. Warren Kirkendale, *Fugue and Fugato in Rococo and Classical Chamber Music*, trans. Margaret Bent and Warren Kirkendale (Durham, NC: Duke University Press, 1979), p. 71.

3. Progressive traits were found especially in Masses by Albrechtsberger, Dittersdorf, Gassmann, Hasse, Hofmann, Holzbauer, Reutter, Sonnleithner, and Vaňhal.

4. Karl Gustav Fellerer, "Kirchenmusik und Aufklärung," in *Geschichte der katholischen Kirchenmusik*, ed. idem, 2 vols. (Kassel: Bärenreiter, 1976) II, p. 199.

5. The author recommends M. 15 by Dittersdorf, M. 19 by Gassmann, M. 29 by Hofmann, M. 30 by Holzbauer, M. 38 by Monn, M. 44 by Reutter, M. 50 and 51 by Schmidt, M. 56 by Sonnleithner, and M. 65 by Vaňhal.

Bibliography

A. Literature

Adler, Guido. "Zur Geschichte der Wiener Messenkomposition in der zweiten Hälfte des XVII. Jahrhunderts." *Studien zur Musikwissenschaft* IV (1916):5-45.

Albrechtsberger, Johann Georg. *Gründliche Anweisung zur Composition; mit deutlichen und ausführlichen Exempeln, zum Selbstunterrichte, erläutert; und mit einem Anhange: Von der Beschaffenheit und Anwendung aller jetzt üblichen musikalischen Instrumente.* Leipzig: J. G. I. Breitkopf, 1790.

Altmann, Klaus. "Die Messen von Ignaz Holzbauer." Ph.D. diss. in preparation (1980), University of Bonn.

Anderson, Emily, ed. *Letters of Mozart. See* under Mozart, W. A.

Antoniček, Theophil. *Das Musikarchiv der Pfarrkirche St. Karl Borromäus in Wien: Die Drucke.* Tabulae Musicae Austriacae, vol. 4. Vienna: Böhlau, 1968.

_____. *Das Musikarchiv der Pfarrkirche St. Karl Borromäus in Wien: Die Handschriften A-H.* Tabulae Musicae Austriacae, vol. 7. Vienna: Österreichische Akademie der Wissenschaften, 1973.

_____. "Die Stände der Wiener Hofmusik-Kapelle von 1867 bis zum Ende der Monarchie." *Studien zur Musikwissenschaft* 29 (1978):171-95. (A continuation of Köchel's *Die kaiserliche Hof-Musikkapelle . . . 1543-1867*)

Apel, Willi. *Gregorian Chant.* Bloomington, IN: Indiana University Press, 1958.

_____. *Harvard Dictionary of Music.* 2nd ed. Cambridge, MA: Belknap Press of Harvard University Press, 1970.

Bayer, Friedrich. "Das Orchester Mozarts im speziellen Dienst der Messkomposition." *Musica Divina* 16 (1928): 23-27.

_____. "Über den Gebrauch der Instrumente in den Kirchen- und Instrumentalwerken von Wolfgang Amadeus Mozart." *Studien zur Musikwissenschaft* XIV (1927):33-74.

Beck, Hermann. "Die Musik des liturgischen Gottesdienstes im 18. Jahrhundert (Messe, Offizium)." In *Geschichte der katholischen Kirchenmusik,* ed. Karl Gustav Fellerer. Vol. II, 180-89. Kassel: Bärenreiter, 1976.

Becker-Glauch, Irmgard. "Die Kirchenmusik des jungen Haydn." In *Der junge Haydn,* ed. Vera Schwarz, 74-85. Graz: Akademische Druck- und Verlagsanstalt, 1972.

_____. "Remarks on the Late Church Music." In *Haydn Studies,* eds. Jens Peter Larsen, Howard Serwer, and James Webster, 206-7. New York: Norton, 1981.

Biba, Otto. "Beispiele für die Besetzungsverhältnisse bei Aufführungen von Haydns Oratorien in Wien zwischen 1784 und 1808." *Haydn Studien* IV/2 (May 1978):94-104.

_____. "Der Piaristenorden in Österreich: seine Bedeutung für bildende Kunst, Musik und Theater im 17. und 18. Jahrhundert." *Jahrbuch für österreichische Kulturgeschichte,* vol. V. Eisenstadt: Institut für österreichische Kulturgeschichte, 1975.

————. "Der Sozial-Status des Musikers." In *Joseph Haydn in seiner Zeit*, eds. Gerda Mraz, Gottfried Mraz, and Gerald Schlag, 105-13. Eisenstadt: Kulturabteilung des Amtes der Burgenländischen Landesregierung, 1982.

————. "Die Wiener Kirchenmusik um 1783." In *Beiträge zur Musikgeschichte des 18. Jahrhunderts*, ed. Gerda Mraz, 7-79. *Jahrbuch für österreichische Kulturgeschichte*, vol. I, pt. 2. Eisenstadt: Institut für österreichische Kulturgeschichte, 1971.

————. "250 Jahre Musikpflege an der Piaristenkirche Maria Treu in Wien." *Singende Kirche* 17 (1969):62-67.

Blom, Eric, ed. *See* Grove, Sir George, ed.

Blume, Friedrich, ed. *Die Musik in Geschichte und Gegenwart: Allgemeine Enzyklopädie der Musik.* 16 vols. Kassel: Bärenreiter, 1949-79. (Abbreviated in text as *MGG*.)

Brand, Karl Maria. *Die Messen von Joseph Haydn.* Musik und Geistesgeschichte, Berliner Studien zur Musikwissenschaft no. 2. Würzburg-Aumühle: K. Triltsch, 1941.

Brion, Marcel. *Daily Life in the Vienna of Mozart and Schubert.* Trans. Jean Stewart. New York: Macmillan, 1962.

Brook, Barry S. *Thematic Catalogues in Music: An Annotated Bibliography.* Hillsdale, NY: Pendragon, 1972.

Brunner, Hans. *Die Kantorei bei St. Stephan in Wien: Beiträge zur Geschichte der Wiener Dommusik.* Vienna: A. Dürer, 1948.

Bücken, Ernst. *Die Musik des Rokokos und der Klassik.* Vol. 5 of *Handbuch der Musikwissenschaft.* 13 vols. Ed. Ernst Bücken. Wildpark-Potsdam: Athenaion, 1927.

Buelow, George J. "Rhetoric and Music," *New Grove Dictionary of Music and Musicians.* 6th ed., 20 vols. Ed. Stanley Sadie. vol. XV, 793-803. London: Macmillan, 1980.

Bukofzer, Manfred F. *Music in the Baroque Era.* New York: Norton, 1947.

Burney, Charles. *Dr. Burney's Musical Tours in Europe* (London, 1771, 1773). 2 vols. Ed. Percy A. Scholes. London: Oxford University Press, 1959.

————. *A General History of Music, From the Earliest Times to the Present Period* (London, 1776-89). 2 vols. Ed. Frank Mercer. London: G. T. Foulis, 1935.

Bush, Deanna Day. "The Orchestral Masses of Ignaz Holzbauer (1711-1783): Authenticity, Chronology, and Style with Thematic Catalogue and Selected Transcriptions." Ph.D. diss., The University of Rochester, Eastman School of Music, 1982.

Carlson, Jon Olaf. "Selected Masses of Niccolò Jommelli." Ph.D. diss., University of Illinois at Champaign-Urbana, 1974.

Carse, Adam. *The Orchestra in the Eighteenth Century.* Cambridge: W. Heffer, 1940.

Chusid, Martin. "Some Observations on Liturgy, Text and Structure in Haydn's Late Masses." In *Studies in Eighteenth-Century Music: A Tribute to Karl Geiringer on His Seventieth Birthday,* eds. H. C. Robbins Landon in collaboration with Roger E. Chapman, 125-35. New York: Oxford University Press, 1970.

Cowie, L. W. and Gummer, John Selwyn. *The Christian Calendar.* Springfield, MA: G. & C. Merriam Co., 1974.

Dack, James Frederick. "The Origins and Development of the Esterházy Kapelle in Eisenstadt until 1790." Ph.D. diss., University of Liverpool, 1976.

Daninger, Josef G. "Musikästhetische Gedanken zur Instrumentalmesse." *Musica Divina* 2 (1914):19-24.

Deutsch, Otto Erich. "Austrian Currency Values and Their Purchasing Power." *Music and Letters* (July 1934): 236-38.

Dimpfl, Alois Augustin. "Die Pastoralmesse." Ph.D. diss., University of Erlangen, 1945.

Dittersdorf, Karl Ditters von. *The Autobiography of Karl von Dittersdorf* (Leipzig, 1801). Trans. A. D. Coleridge. London: Richard Bentley, 1896. Reprint. New York: Da Capo, 1970.

————. *Lebensbeschreibung seinem Sohne in die Feder diktiert* (Leipzig: Breitkopf & Härtel, 1801). Ed. Bruno Loets with afterword by Norbert Miller. Lebensläufe: Biographien, Erinnerungen, Briefe vol. 12. Munich: Kösel, 1967.

Dlabacz, Gottfried Johann. *Allgemeines historisches Künstler-Lexikon für Böhmen und zum Theil auch für Mähren und Schlesien.* 3 vols. in 1. Prague: Gottlieb Haase, 1815. Reprint. Ed. Paul Bergner (1913). Hildesheim: G. Olm, 1973.

Donath, Gustav and Haas, Robert. "Florian Leopold Gassmann als Opernkomponist." *Studien zur Musikwissenschaft* II (1914):34–211.

Einstein, Alfred. *Mozart: His Character, His Work.* Trans. Arthur Mendel and Nathan Broder. New York: Oxford University Press, 1945.

Eitner, Robert. *Biographisch-bibliographisches Quellen-Lexikon der Musiker und Musikgelehrten christlicher Zeitrechnung bis Mitte des neunzehnten Jahrhunderts.* 2nd rev. ed., 11 vols. Graz: Akademische Druck- und Verlagsanstalt, 1959–60.

Federhofer, Hellmut. "Alte Musikalien-Inventare der Klöster St. Paul (Kärnten) und Göss (Steiermark)." *Kirchenmusikalisches Jahrbuch* 35 (1951):97–112.

———. "Die Musikpflege an der St. Jacobskirche in Leoben (Steiermark)." *Die Musikforschung* 4 (1951): 333–41.

Federhofer-Königs, Renate. "Zur Musikpflege in der Wallfahrtskirche von Mariazell/ Steiermark." *Kirchenmusikalisches Jahrbuch* 41 (1957): 117–35.

Fellerer, Karl Gustav. "Church Music and the Council of Trent." Trans. Moses Hadas. *The Musical Quarterly* XXXIX/4 (October 1953): 567–94.

———. *The History of Catholic Church Music* (Düsseldorf, 1949). Trans. Francis C. Brunner. Baltimore: Helicon Press, 1961.

———. "The Liturgical Basis for Haydn's Masses." In *Haydn Studies,* eds. Jens Peter Larsen, Howard Serwer, and James Webster, 164–68. New York: Norton, 1981.

———. "Liturgische Grundlagen der Kirchenmusik Mozarts." In *Festschrift Walter Senn zum 70. Geburtstag,* ed. Ewald Fässler, 64–74. Munich and Salzburg: Katzbichler, 1975.

———. *Mozarts Kirchenmusik.* Salzburg-Freilassing: Ludwig Schäffler, 1955.

———. *Der Palestrinastil und seine Bedeutung in der vokalen Kirchenmusik in Italien und Deutschland.* Augsburg: B. Filser, 1929.

———. "Text and Music in Mozart's and Haydn's Masses." In *Haydn Studies,* eds. Jens Peter Larsen, Howard Serwer, and James Webster, 416–19. New York: Norton, 1981.

———. "Thematische Verzeichnisse der fürstbischöflichen Freisingischen Hofmusik von 1796." In *Festschrift Otto Erich Deutsch,* pp. 296–303. Kassel: Bärenreiter, 1963.

———. "Verzeichnis der kirchenmusikalischen Werke der Santinischen Sammlung." *Kirchenmusikalisches Jahrbuch* 26 (1931):111–40; 27 (1932):157–71; 28 (1933):143–54; 29 (1934):125–41; 30 (1935):149–68; 31–33 (1936–38) :95–110. (Covers only Abbatini-Purcell)

———. ed. *Geschichte der katholischen Kirchenmusik.* 2 vols. Kassel: Bärenreiter, 1972, 1976. Vol. II: *Von Tridentinum bis zur Gegenwart* includes the following articles by Fellerer: "Die Enzyklika 'Annus qui' des Papstes Benedikt XIV," pp. 149–52; "Kirchenmusik und Aufklärung," pp. 198–201.

Flotzinger, Rudolf and Gruber, Gernot. *Musikgeschichte Österreichs.* 2 vols. Graz. Österreichische Gesellschaft für Musikwissenschaft, 1977–79.

Forkel, Johann Nikolaus. *Allgemeine Geschichte der Musik.* 2 vols. Leipzig: Schwickert, 1788, 1801.

Freeman, Robert N. *Franz Schneider (1737–1812): A Thematic Catalogue of His Works.* Thematic Catalogue Series no. 5. New York: Pendragon, 1979.

———. "The Function of Haydn's Instrumental Compositions in the Abbeys." In *Haydn Studies,* eds. Jens Peter Larsen, Howard Serwer, and James Webster, 199–201. New York: Norton, 1981.

———. "The Practice of Music at Melk Monastery in the Eighteenth Century." Ph.D. diss., University of California, Los Angeles, 1971.

———. "The Role of Organ Improvisation in Haydn's Church Music." In *Haydn Studies,* eds. Jens Peter Larsen, Howard Serwer, and James Webster, 192–94. New York: Norton, 1981.

738   Bibliography

_____. "Zwei Melker Musikkataloge aus der zweiten Hälfte des 18. Jahrhunderts." *Die Musikforschung* XXIII (1970):176–84.

Freunschlag, Heinrich. "Luca Antonio Predieri als Kirchenkomponist." Ph.D. diss., University of Vienna, 1927.

Frost, Bede. *The Meaning of Mass: Dogmatic and Devotional Considerations upon the Divine Liturgy.* London and Oxford: A. R. Mowbray; Milwaukee: Morehouse, 1934.

Fux, Johann Joseph. *Gradus ad Parnassum, oder Anführung zur regelmässigen musikalischen Composition....* Trans. Lorenz Mizler. Leipzig: Mizlerischer Bücherverlag, 1742.

_____. *Gradus ad Parnassum, Sive Manuductio ad Compositionem Musicae Regularem, Methodo nova....* Vienna: Joannis Petri Van Ghelen, 1725.

Georgiades, Thrasybulos. *Music and Language: The Rise of Western Music as Exemplified in Settings of the Mass.* Trans. Marie-Louise Göllner. New York: Cambridge University Press, 1982.

_____. *Musik und Sprache: das Werden der abendländischen Musik dargestellt an der Vertonung der Messe.* Berlin, Göttingen, and Heidelberg: Springer, 1954.

Gerber, Ernst Ludwig. *Historisch-biographisches Lexikon der Tonkünstler (Leipzig, 1790–92) und Neues historisch-biographisches Lexikon der Tonkünstler (Leipzig, 1812–14).* 4 vols. Ed. Othmar Wessely. Graz: Akademische Druck- und Verlagsanstalt, 1966–69.

Gerbert, Martin. *De cantu et musica sacra, a prima ecclesiae aetate usque ad praesens tempus.* St. Blasien: n.p., 1774. Reprint. Ed. Othmar Wessely. Graz: Akademische Druck- und Verlagsanstalt, 1968.

Gesellschaft der Musikfreunde, Vienna. Sammlung handschriftlicher Biographien. Manuscript biographies of numerous Viennese composers; prepared in 1826 and written mostly by the composers or by persons related to or acquainted with them.

Glöggl, Franz Xaver. *Kirchenmusik-Ordnung: Erklärendes Handbuch des musikalischen Gottesdienstes, für Kapellmeister, Regenschori, Sänger und Tonkünstler.* Vienna: J.B. Wallishauser, 1828.

Grasberger, Franz. *Die Musiksammlung der Österreichischen Nationalbibliothek.* Vienna: Bundeskanzleramt, Bundespressedienst, 1970; Vienna: Österreichische Nationalbibliothek, 1978.

Griesinger, Georg August. *Biographische Notizen über Joseph Haydn* (Leipzig, 1810). Ed. Franz Grasberger. Der Musikfreund, vol. 1. Vienna: P. Kaltschmid, 1954.

Groner, Richard. *Wien wie es war: Ein Nachschlagwerk für Freunde des alten und neun Wien.* Revised and expanded by Felix Czeike. Vienna and Munich: Fritz Molden, 1965.

Grove, Sir George, ed. *Grove's Dictionary of Music and Musicians.* 9 vols., 5th ed. Ed. Eric Blom. London: Macmillan; New York: St. Martin's Press, 1954.

Gruber, Gernot. "Musikalische Rhetorik und barocke Bildlichkeit in Kompositionen des jungen Haydn." In *Der junge Haydn,* ed. Vera Schwarz, 168–91. Graz: Akademische Druck- und Verlagsanstalt, 1972.

Gutkas, Karl. "Österreich und Europa zur Zeit Joseph Haydns." *Jahrbuch für Österreichische Kulturgeschichte* II (1972):9–24.

Haas, Robert. "Die Musiksammlung der Nationalbibliothek in Wien: Ein Kapitel aus der Geschichte der musikalischen Denkmalpflege." *Jahrbuch der Musikbibliothek Peters* 37 (1930):48–62.

_____. "Von dem Wienerischen Geschmack in der Musik." In *Festschrift Johannes Biehle zum 60. Geburtstag,* ed. Erich M. Müller, 59–65. Leipzig: Kistner & Siegel, 1930.

_____. *Wiener Musiker vor und um Beethoven.* Vienna, Prague, and Leipzig: E. Strache, 1927.

Haberkamp, Gertraut. *Die Musikhandschriften der Fürst Thurn und Taxis Hofbibliothek Regensburg: Thematischer Katalog mit einer Geschichte des Musikalienbestandes von Hugo Angerer.* Kataloge Bayerischer Musiksammlungen. Vol. 6. Munich: G. Henle, 1981.

————. *Thematischer Katalog der Musikhandschriften der Fürstlich Oettingen-Wallerstein' schen Bibliothek Schloss Harburg, mit einer Geschichte des Musikalienbestandes von Volker von Volckamer.* Kataloge Bayrischer Musiksammlungen. Munich: G. Henle, 1976.

Haberl, Ferdinand. "Repräsentations- und Gebetsgottesdienst im 18. Jahrhundert." In *Geschichte der katholischen Kirchenmusik,* ed. Gustav Fellerer, vol. II, 153–56. Kassel: Bärenreiter, 1976.

Hanslick, Eduard. *Geschichte des Concertwesens in Wien.* 2 pts. Vienna: W. Braumüller, 1869–70.

Hartl, Sebastian. See *Ueber die Kirchenmusik in Wien.*

Hilmar, Ernst. "Ferdinand Schuberts Skizze zu einer Autobiographie." In *Schubert-Studien: Festgabe der österreichischen Akademie der Wissenschaften zum Schubert-Jahr 1978,* eds. Franz Grasberger and Othmar Wessely, 85–117. Heft 19 of Veröffentlichungen der Kommission für Musikforschung, ed. Franz Grasberger. Vol. 341 of Österreichische Akademie der Wissenschaften, Philosophisch-historische Klasse Sitzungsberichte. Vienna: Österreichische Akademie der Wissenschaften, 1978.

Hoboken, Anthony van, ed. *Joseph Haydn: Thematisch-bibliographisches Werkverzeichnis.* 3 vols. Mainz: Schott, 1957, 1971, 1978.

Hofer, P. Norbert. "Die beiden Reutter als Kirchenkomponisten." 2 vols. Ph.D. diss., Vienna, 1915.

————. "Thematisches Verzeichnis der Werke Georg Reutters d. J." Mus. Hs. 28.992 in the Austrian National Library, Vienna.

Hüntemann, Josef Albert. *Die Messen der Santini-Bibliothek zu Münster in Westfalen: Ein Beitrag zur Geschichte der Messe.* Quakenbrück: R. Kleinert, 1928.

Istel, Edgar. "Dittersdorfiana: Einige Beiträge zur Dittersdorf-Bibliographie." *Zeitschrift der Internationalen Musikgesellschaft* IV/4 (1902/03):180–82.

Jungmann, Josef Andreas. *The Mass: An Historical, Theological, and Pastoral Survey.* Trans. Julian Fernandes, ed. Mary Ellen Evans. Collegeville, MN: Liturgical Press, 1976.

————. *The Mass of the Roman Rite: Its Origins and Development (Missarum Sollemnia.* Vienna: Herder, 1949). 2 vols. Trans. Francis A. Brunner. New York: Benziger Brothers, 1951.

Kade, Otto. *Die Musikalien-Sammlung des Grossherzoglich Mecklenburg-Schweriner Fürstenhauses aus den letzten zwei Jahrhunderten.* 2 vols. Schwerin: Sandmeyer, 1893.

[Kandler, Franz Sales.] "Wiens musikalische Kunst-Schätze." *Allgemeine musikalische Zeitung* XXIX (Leipzig, 1827): col. 66–72, 82–87, 125–35, 145–56, 817–24, 881–83.

Karner, Ernest A., ed. *Die Hofmusikkapelle und die Hofburgkapelle in Wien.* Vienna: Hofmusikkapelle Wien, 1977.

Kellner, Altman. *Musikgeschichte des Stiftes Kremsmünster, nach den Quellen dargestellt.* Kassel: Bärenreiter, 1956.

Khevenhüller-Metsch, Rudolf and Schlitter, Hanns, ed. *Aus der Zeit Maria Theresias: Tagebuch des Fürsten Johann Josef Khevenhüller-Metsch, kais. Obersthofmeisters 1742-1776.* 8 vols. [vol. 8 eds. Maria Breunlich-Pawlik and Hans Wagner, 1972], Gesellschaft (Kommission) für neuere Geschichte Österreichs. Vienna: Holzhausen; Leipzig: Engelmann, 1907–25, 1972.

Kirkendale, Warren. *Fuge und Fugato in der Kammermusik des Rokoko und der Klassik.* Tutzing: Schneider, 1966. English edition, revised and expanded: *Fugue and Fugato in Rococo and Classical Chamber Music.* Trans. Margaret Bent and Warren Kirkendale. Durham, NC: Duke University Press, 1979.

————. "New Roads to Old Ideas in Beethoven's *Missa Solemnis.*" *The Musical Quarterly* LVI (1970):665–701.

Kirnberger, Johann P. *Die Kunst des reinen Satzes in der Musik aus sicheren Grundsätzen hergeleitet und mit deutlichen Beispielen erläutert.* 2 vols. Berlin: G. J. Decker & G. L. Hartung, 1771–79.

Klafsky, Anton Maria. "Thematischer Katalog der Kirchenmusikwerke von Michael Haydn." In *Michael Haydn: Kirchenwerke, DTÖ* vol. 62 (Jg. 32/1). Vienna: Universal, 1925.

Kleiner, Salomon. *Wahrhafte und genaue Abbildung aller Kirchen und Klöster, vieler Paläste, Monumente, Spitaler und Bürgerhäuser in Wien und seinen Vorstädten* (Vienna, 1724–37). 4 pts. in 2 vols. Eds. Anton Macku, Alfred May, and Hans Aurenhammer. Graz: Akademische Druck- und Verlagsanstalt, 1971.

Klinka, Theodore Milton. "The Choral Music of Franz Ignaz Tuma with a Practical Edition of Selected Choral Works." Ph.D. diss., University of Iowa, 1975.

Kobald, Karl. *Alt Wiener-Musikstätten.* 2nd rev. and expanded ed. Zürich, Leipzig, and Vienna: Amalthea, 1923.

Koch, Heinrich Christoph. *Musikalisches Lexikon.* Frankfurt am Main: August Hermann, d. J., 1802. Reprint. Hildesheim: G. Olms, 1964.

_____. *Versuch einer Anleitung zur Composition.* 3 vols. Leipzig: Adolf Friedrich Böhme, 1782, 1787, 1793.

Köchel, Ludwig Ritter von. *Chronologisch-thematisches Verzeichnis sämtlicher Tonwerke Wolfgang Amadé Mozarts.* 6th ed. Ed. Franz Giegling, Alexander Weinmann, and Gerd Sievers. Wiesbaden: Breitkopf & Härtel, 1964.

_____. *Johann Josef Fux, Hofcompositor und Hofkapellmeister der Kaiser Leopold I., Josef I. und Karl VI. von 1698 bis 1740 nach urkundlichen Forschungen.* Vienna: Alfred Hölder, 1872.

_____. *Die kaiserliche Hof-Musikkapelle in Wien von 1543 bis 1867 nach urkundlichen Forschungen.* Vienna: Beck'sche Universitätsbuchhandlung and A. Hölder, 1869. Reprint. Hildesheim: G. Olms, 1976.

Komorzynski, Egon. "Die Sankt-Nikolausbruderschaft in Wien (1288 bis 1782)." In *Festschrift Wilhelm Fischer zum 70. Geburtstag,* 71–74. Innsbrucker Beiträge zur Kulturwissenschaft, Sonderheft 3. Innsbruck: Tiroler Graphik, 1956.

Kosch, Franz. "Florian Leopold Gassmann als Kirchenkomponist." *Studien zur Musikwissenschaft* XIV (1927):213–40. (Abbreviated in text as Kosch, "Gassmann")

_____. "Florian Leopold Gassmann als Kirchenkomponist." Ph.D. diss., University of Vienna, 1924.

Kralik, Richard. *Geschichte der Stadt Wien und ihrer Kultur.* 2nd edition. Vienna: Adolf Holzhausen, 1926.

Kraus, Hedwig. "Die Sammlungen der Gesellschaft der Musikfreunde in Wien." *Österreichische Musikzeitschrift* X (1955):68–70.

Kraus, Joseph Martin. *Etwas von und über Musik fürs Jahr 1777.* Frankfurt, 1778. Reprint. Ed. Friedrich Wilhelm Riedel as vol. 1 of *Quellenschriften zur Musikästhetik der 18. und 19. Jahrhunderte.* Munich and Salzburg: E. Katzbichler, 1977.

Krebs, Carl. *Dittersdorfiana.* Berlin: Paetel, 1900.

Krieg, Franz. *Katholische Kirchenmusik, Geist und Praxis, mit geschichtlichen Beiträgen von Ernst Tittel.* Teuffen: Arthur Niggli and Willy Verkauf, 1954.

Landon, Howard Chandler Robbins. *Haydn: Chronicle and Works.* 5 vols. Bloomington, IN: Indiana University Press, 1976–80.

_____. "Problems of Authenticity in Eighteenth-Century Music." In *Instrumental Music: A Conference at Isham Memorial Library, Harvard University, May 4, 1957,* ed. David G. Hughes, 31–56. Cambridge: Harvard University Press, 1959. Reprint. New York: Da Capo, 1972.

Lang, Gerda. "Zur Geschichte und Pflege der Musik in der Benediktiner-Abtei zu Lambach mit einem Katalog zu den Beständen des Musikarchivs." 3 vols. Ph.D. diss., University of Salzburg, 1978.

Larsen, Jens Peter, Howard Serwer, and James Webster, eds. *Haydn Studies: Proceedings of the International Haydn Conference, Washington, D.C., 1975.* New York: Norton, 1981.

————. "Der Stilwandel in der österreichischen Musik zwischen Barock und Wiener Klassik. In *Der junge Haydn,* ed. Vera Schwarz, 18–30. Graz: Akademische Druck- und Verlagsanstalt, 1972.

————. "Über die Möglichkeiten einer musikalischen Echtheitsbestimmung für Werke aus der Zeit Haydns und Mozarts." *Mozart Jahrbuch 1971–72:* 7–18.

Lewis, Anthony and Fortune, Nigel, ed. *Opera and Church Music: 1630–1750.* Vol. 5 of *The New Oxford History of Music,* ed. Jack Westrup et al. London: Oxford University Press, 1975.

The Liber Usualis, with Introduction and Rubrics in English. Ed. the Benedictines of Solesmes. Tournai: Desclee, 1956.

Mac Intyre, Bruce C. "Haydn's Doubtful and Spurious Masses: An Attribution Update." *Haydn-Studien* V, 1 (1982):42–54.

Mahling, Christoph-Hellmut. "Orchester, Orchesterpraxis und Orchestermusiker zur Zeit des jungen Haydn (1740–1770)." In *Der junge Haydn,* ed. Vera Schwarz, 98–113. Graz: Akademische Druck- und Verlagsanstalt, 1972.

Marshall, Robert L. "Bach's Chorus: A Preliminary Reply to Joshua Rifkin." *The Musical Times* 124 (Jan. 1983):19–22.

————. "Bach's 'Choruses' Reconstituted." *High Fidelity* 32 (Oct. 1982):64–66, 94.

Massenkeil, Günther. "Die konzertierende Kirchenmusik." In *Geschichte der katholischen Kirchenmusik,* ed. Karl Gustav Fellerer, vol. II, 92–107. Kassel: Bärenreiter, 1976.

Mattheson, Johann. *Der vollkommene Kapellmeister* (Hamburg: C. Herold, 1739). Ed and trans. Ernest C. Harriss. Studies in Musicology no. 21. Ann Arbor, MI: UMI Research Press, 1981.

Morrow, Mary Sue. "Concert Life in Vienna: 1780–1810." Ph.D. diss., University of Indiana, Bloomington, 1984.

Mozart, Wolfgang Amadeus. *Briefe und Aufzeichnungen: Gesamtausgabe.* 4 vols. Ed. Wilhelm A. Bauer and Otto Erich Deutsch. Kassel and New York: Bärenreiter, 1962–63.

————. *Die Briefe W. A. Mozarts und seiner Familie: Erste kritische Gesamtausgabe.* 5 vols. Ed. Ludwig Schiedermair. Munich: Georg Müller, 1914.

————. *The Letters of Mozart and His Family.* Trans. and ed. Emily Anderson. 2 vols. 2nd edition, ed. A. Hyatt King and Monica Carolan. London: Macmillan; New York: St. Martin's Press, 1966.

Mraz, Gerda, Gottfried Mraz, and Gerald Schlag, eds. *Joseph Haydn in seiner Zeit* (Catalog for exhibition in Eisenstadt, Austria, May 20–October 26, 1982 under the auspices of die Kulturabteilung des Amtes der Burgenländischen Landesregierung). Eisenstadt: Amt der Burgenländischen Landesregierung, 1982.

Müller, Georg Walther. *Johann Adolf Hasse als Kirchenkomponist: ein Beitrag zur Geschichte der neapolitanischen Kirchenmusik, mit thematischem Katalog der liturgischen Kirchenmusik J.A. Hasse's.* Publikationen der Internationalen Musikgesellschaft. 2. Folge, Heft IX. Leipzig: Breitkopf & Härtel, 1911.

New Catholic Encyclopedia. 15 vols. Ed. Catholic University of America. New York: McGraw-Hill, 1967.

New Grove Dictionary of Music and Musicians. See Sadie, Stanley, ed.

Nicolai, Friedrich Christoph. *Beschreibung einer Reise durch Deutschland und die Schweiz im Jahre 1781, nebst Bemerkungen über Gelehrsamkeit, Industrie, Religion und Sitten.* Vol. 4. Berlin and Stettin: n.p., 1784.

Ogesser, J. *Beschreibung der Metropolitan-Kirche zu St. Stephan in Wien, herausgegeben von einem Priester der erzbischöflichen Kur im Jahre 1779.* Vienna: Von Ghelenschen Erben, 1779.

Orel, Alfred. "Die katholische Kirchenmusik von 1600 bis 1750." In *Handbuch der Musikgeschichte.* 2 vols., 2nd edition. Ed. Guido Adler, II, 507–36. Berlin-Wilmersdorf: H. Keller, 1930. Reprint. Tutzing: Schneider, 1961.

Pass, Walter. "Josephinism and the Josephinian Reforms Concerning Haydn." In *Haydn Studies*, ed. Jens Peter Larsen, Howard Serwer, and James Webster, 168–71. New York: Norton, 1981.

Pauly, Reinhard G. "The Reforms of Church Music under Joseph II." *The Musical Quarterly* XLIII/3 (July 1957):372–82.

Paymer, Marvin E. *Giovanni Battista Pergolesi (1710–1736): A Thematic Catalogue of the Opera Omnia with an Appendix Listing Omitted Compositions.* New York: Pendragon, 1977.

Peiser, Karl. *Johann Adam Hiller: Ein Beitrag zur Musikgeschichte des 18. Jahrhunderts.* Leipzig: Gebrüder Hug & Co., 1894. Reprint. Leipzig: Zentralantiquariat der Deutschen Demokratischen Republik, 1979.

Peschek, Alfred. "Die Messen von Franz Tuma (1704–74)." Ph.D. diss., University of Vienna, 1956.

Pfannhauser, Karl. "Einführung," "Die Wiener Karmeliterkirche und Johann Georg Albrechtsberger," "Ausgaben von Johann Georg Albrechtsbergers Kirchenkompositionen," "Chronologisches Verzeichnis der Literatur über Johann Georg Albrechtsberger," and "Quellennachweis." In: Albrechtsberger, Johann Georg. *Messe in Es-dur (Missa Sancti Josephi).* Ed. Andreas Weissenbäck. Vol. 8 of *Österreichische Kirchenmusik,* ed. Karl Pfannhauser. Vienna: Doblinger, 1951.

————. "Mozarts kirchenmusikalische Studien im Spiegel seiner Zeit und Nachwelt." *Kirchenmusikalisches Jahrbuch* XLIII (1959):155–98.

————. "Wiener Kirchenmusik im Spiegel der Gesellschaftsstruktur: Eine improvisierte Historien-Betrachtung." *Österreichische Musikzeitschrift* 25 (1970):300–304.

————. "Zu Mozarts Kirchenwerken von 1768." *Mozart Jahrbuch 1954:*150–68.

Philipp, Roland. "Die Messenkomposition der Wiener Vorklassiker G. M. Monn und G. Chr. Wagenseil." Ph.D. diss., University of Vienna, 1938.

Podlaha, Antonin. *Catalogus Collectionis Operum Artis Musicae quae in Bibliotheca Capituli Metropolitani Pragensis asservantur.* Prague: Typis Typographicae Archiepiscopalis Pragae, 1926.

Pohl, Carl Ferdinand. *Denkschrift aus Anlass des hundertjährigen Bestehens der Tonkünstler-Societät, im Jahre 1862 reorganisirt als "Haydn," Witwen- und Waisen-Versorgungs-Verein der Tonkünstler in Wien.* Vienna: Carl Gerolds Sohn, 1871.

————. "Friberth, Karl F." In *Allgemeine deutsche Biographie* VII, 376. Leipzig: Duncker und Humblot, 1878.

————. *Joseph Haydn.* 2 vols. Vol. 1, Berlin: A. Sacco; Leipzig: Breitkopf & Härtel, 1878. Vol. 2, Leipzig: Breitkopf & Härtel, 1882. Reprint ed., 2 vols., Wiesbaden: Sändig, 1970–71.

————. *Joseph Haydn: Unter Benutzung der von C. F. Pohl hinterlassenen Materialien weitergeführt von Hugo Botstiber.* Vol. 3. Leipzig: Breitkopf & Härtel, 1927. Reprint. Wiesbaden: Sändig, 1971.

————. "Martines, Marianne M." *Allgemeine deutsche Biographie.* Vol. 20. Leipzig: Dunker & Humblot, 1884.

Portheimkatalog. Zettelkatalog von Max Ritter von Portheim. A bio-bibliographical file at the Stadtsbibliothek, Vienna.

Pribram, Alfred Francis, Rudolf Geyer, and Franz Goran, eds. *Materialen zur Geschichte der Preise und Löhne in Österreich.* Veröffentlichung des internationalen wissenschaftlichen Komitees für die Geschichte der Preise und Löhne. Vienna: Carl Ueberreuter, 1938.

Prohászka, Hermine. "Leopold Hofmann als Messenkomponist." Ph.D. diss., University of Vienna, 1956.

————. "Leopold Hofmann und seine Messen." *Studien zur Musikwissenschaft* XXVI (1964):79–139. (Abbreviated in text as Prohászka, "Hofmann")

Pulkert, Oldřich. *Domus Lauretana Pragensis. Catalogus collectionis operum artis musicae.* 2 vols. Catalogus Artis Musicae in Bohemia et Moravia Cultae Artis Musicae Antiquioris Catalogorum no. 1. Prague: Supraphon, 1973.

Quantz, Johann Joachim. *Versuch einer Anweisung die Flöte traversiere zu spielen* [On Playing the Flute] (Berlin, 1752). Trans. Edward R. Reilly. New York: Free Press, 1966.

Quoika, Rudolf. "Zur Geschichte der Musikkapelle des St. Veitsdomes in Prag (1619–1860)." *Kirchenmusikalisches Jahrbuch* 45 (1961):102–23.

Ratner, Leonard. *Classic Music: Expression, Form, and Style.* New York: Schirmer Books, 1980.

Raynor, Henry B. "Some Reflections upon the Viennese Mass." *The Musical Times* (Nov. 1954):592–96.

Reichert, Georg. "Mozart's 'Credo-Messen' und ihre Vorläufer." *Mozart Jahrbuch 1955:* 117–44.

———. "Zur Geschichte der Wiener Messenkomposition in der ersten Hälfte des 18. Jahrhunderts." Ph.D. diss., University of Vienna, 1935. (Abbreviated in text as Reichert, "Geschichte")

Reinhardt, Kilian. "Rubriche Generali per le Funzioni Ecclesiastiche Musicali di tutto l'Anno. Con un' Appendice in fine dell' Essenziali ad Uso, e Servizio. dell' August.^{ma} Austriaca, ed Imp.^{le} Capella . . . da Kiliano Reinharth Maestro de Concerti Musicali de dett' Aug.^{ma} Capella In Vienna d'Austria l'Anno MDCCXXVII." Autograph manuscript, Mus. Hs. 2503 in the Austrian National Library, Vienna.

Riedel, Friedrich Wilhelm. "Beiträge zur Geschichte der Musikpflege an der Stadtpfarrkirche St. Veit zu Krems." In *Festschrift 950 Jahre Pfarrei Krems,* pp. 300–341. Krems an der Donau, 1964.

———. *Kirchenmusik am Hofe Karls VI. (1711–1740): Untersuchungen zum Verhältnis von Zeremoniell und musikalischem Stil im Barockzeitalter.* Studien zur Landes- und Sozialgeschichte der Musik. Vol. 1. Munich and Salzburg: Emil Katzbichler, 1977. (Abbreviated in text as Riedel, *Karl VI*)

———. "Die Kirchenmusik im Benediktinerstift Göttweig." *Singende Kirche* 13 (1966):196–202.

———. "Liturgie und Kirchenmusik." In *Joseph Haydn in seiner Zeit,* ed. Gerda Mraz, Gottfried Mraz, and Gerald Schlag, 121–33. Eisenstadt: Kulturabteilung des Amtes der Burgenländischen Landesregierung, 1982.

———. *Das Musikarchiv im Minoritenkonvent zu Wien: Katalog des älteren Bestandes vor 1784.* Catalogus musicus no. 1. Kassel: Bärenreiter, 1963.

———. "Musikpflege bei den Augustiner-Chorherren in Herzogenburg." *Singende Kirche* 13/4 (1966):211–13.

———. ed. *Der Göttweiger thematischer Katalog von 1830.* 2 vols. Munich and Salzburg: E. Katzbichler, 1979.

Riemann, Hugo. *Musik-Lexikon.* 12th ed. 3 vols. Ed. Wilibald Gurlitt and Hans Heinrich Eggebrecht. Mainz: B. Schott's Söhne, 1959–67.

Rifkin, Joshua. "Bach's Chorus: A Preliminary Report." *Musical Times* 123 (Nov. 1982):747–54.

———. "Bach's Chorus: A Response to Robert Marshall." *Musical Times* 124 (March 1983):161–62.

———. "Bach's 'Choruses'—Less Than They Seem?" *High Fidelity* 32 (Sept. 1982):42–44.

———. "Bach's 'Choruses'—The Record Cleared." *High Fidelity* 32 (Dec. 1982):58–59.

Röhrig, Floridus. "Das religiöse Leben Wiens zwischen Barock und Aufklärung." In *Joseph Haydn in seiner Zeit,* eds. Gerda Mraz, Gottfried Mraz, and Gerald Schlag, 114–20. Eisenstadt: Kulturabteilung des Amtes der Burgenländischen Landesregierung, 1982.

Rouland, Carl. *Katalog des Musik-Archivs der St. Peters-Kirche in Wien.* Augsburg and Vienna: Böhm, 1908.

Runestad, Cornell Jesse. "The Masses of Joseph Haydn: A Stylistic Study." Ph.D. diss., University of Illinois at Urbana-Champaign, 1970.

Ryom, Peter. *Verzeichnis der Werke Antonio Vivaldi's: Kleine Ausgabe.* Leipzig: V. E. B. Deutscher Verlag für Musik, 1974.

Sadie, Stanley, ed. *The New Grove Dictionary of Music and Musicians.* 6th ed. 20 vols. London: Macmillan, 1980.

Sanders, Jr., Samuel Vernon. "The *Vesperae a due chori* of Florian Leopold Gassmann: A Study and Critical Edition." D.M.A. diss., Stanford University, 1974.

Sandgruber, Roman. "Wirtschaftsentwicklung, Einkommensverteilung und Alltagsleben zur Zeit Haydns." In *Joseph Haydn in seiner Zeit,* eds. Gerda Mraz, Gottfried Mraz, and Gerald Schlag, 72–90. Eisenstadt: Kulturabteilung des Amtes der Burgenländischen Landesregierung, 1982.

Schaefer, Jay Dee. "The Use of the Trombone in the 18th Century." *The Instrumentalist* XXII/9 (April 1968):51–53; XXII/10 (May 1968):100–102; XXII/11 (June 1968):61–63.

Scheib, Wilfried. "Die Entwicklung der Musikberichterstattung im *Wienerischen Diarium* von 1703 bis 1780, mit besonderer Berücksichtigung der Wiener Oper." Ph.D. diss., University of Vienna, 1950.

Scheibe, Johann Adolph. *Critischer Musikus.* Leipzig: B. C. Breitkopf, 1745. Reprint. Hildesheim: G. Olms and Wiesbaden: Breitkopf & Härtel, 1970.

Schenk, Erich. "Ist die Göttweiger Rorate-Messe ein Werk Joseph Haydns?" *Studien zur Musikwissenschaft* 24 (1960):87–105.

Schienerl, Alfred. "Giuseppe Bonnos Kirchenkompositionen." *Studien zur Musikwissenschaft* XV (1928):62–85. (Abbreviated in text as Schienerl, "Bonnos Kirchenkompositionen")

――――. "Die kirchlichen Kompositionen des Giuseppe Bonno." 2 vols. Ph.D. diss., University of Vienna, 1925.

Schmid, Anton. "Zwei musikalische Berühmtheiten Wiens aus dem schönen Geschlechte in der zweiten Hälfte des verflossenen [18.] Jahrhunderts." *Wiener allgemeine Musik-Zeitung,* ed. August Schmidt, VI (1846), Nr. 128 & 129, pp. 513–14, 516–18. Reprint. Hildesheim: G. Olms, 1976.

Schmitt, Eduard. "Die Kurpfälzische Kirchenmusik im 18. Jahrhundert." Ph.D. diss., University of Heidelberg, 1958.

Schneider, Constantin. "Die Kirchenmusik im St. Stephansdom zu Wien." *Musica Divina* 21 (1933):67–77.

Schnerich, Alfred. *Messe und Requiem seit Haydn und Mozart.* Vienna and Leipzig: C. W. Stern, 1909.

――――. *Wiener Kirchen und Kapellen.* Vienna, Leipzig, Zurich: Almathea, 1921.

Schnoebelen, Anne. *Padre Martini's Collection of Letters in the Civico museo bibliografico musicale in Bologna: An Annotated Index.* Annotated Reference Tools in Music no. 2. New York: Pendragon, 1979.

Schnoebelen, Sister Mary Nicole. "The Concerted Mass at San Petronio in Bologna ca. 1660–1730: A Documentary and Analytical Study." Ph.D. diss., University of Illinois at Urbana-Champaign, 1966.

Schnürl, Karl. *Das alte Musikarchiv der Pfarrkirche St. Stephan in Tulln.* Tabulae musicae Austriacae I. Vienna: Österreichische Akademie der Wissenschaften, Kommission für Musikforschung, 1964.

――――. "Josef Krottendorfer: Ein Komponistenschicksal aus der Zeit der Wiener Klassik." *Kulturberichte aus Niederösterreich* (Beilage der amtlichen Nachrichten der niederösterreichischen Landesregierung) 10 (1965):78–79.

――――. "Die Kirchenmusik im westlichen Niederösterreich bis zur Errichtung der Diözese St. Pölten." *Singende Kirche* 13 (1966):178–83.

Schönfeld, Johann Ferdinand von. *Jahrbuch der Tonkunst von Wien und Prag.* Vienna and Prague: Schönfeld, 1796. Reprint. Ed. Otto Biba, Munich and Salzburg: Emil Katzbichler, 1976.

Schröder, Dorothea. "Die geistlichen Vokalkompositionen Johann Georg Albrechtsbergers." Ph.D. diss., University of Hamburg, 1986.

Schubert, Ferdinand. *See* Hilmar, Ernst.

Schwarz, Ignaz, ed. *Wiener Strassenbilder im Zeitalter des Rokokos: die Wiener Ansichten von Schütz, Ziegler, Janscha, 1779-1798.* Prologue by Rudolf Hans Bartsch. Vienna: Gilhofer & Ranschburg, 1914.

Schwarz, Vera, ed. *Der junge Haydn: Wandel von Musikauffassung und Musikaufführung in der österreichischen Musik zwischen Barock und Klassik.* Graz: Akademische Druck- und Verlagsanstalt, 1972.

Senn, Walter. "Mehrstimmige Messe: Von 1600 bis zur Gegenwart." *Die Musik in Geschichte und Gegenwart.* 16 vols. Ed. Friedrich Blume. Kassel: Bärenreiter, 1961, IX, col. 183-218.

————. "Mozart's Kirchenmusik und die Literatur." *Mozart Jahrbuch* 1978/79:14-18.

Sherman, Charles H. "The Masses of Johann Michael Haydn: A Critical Survey of the Sources." Ph.D. diss., University of Michigan, 1967.

Spiess, Pater Meinradus. *Tractatus musicus compositorio-practicus: Das ist, Musicalischer Tractat... Opus VIII.* Augsburg: Johann Jakob Lotter seel. Erben, 1746.

Spitzer, John. "Authorship and Attribution in Western Art Music." Ph.D. diss., Cornell University, 1983.

Steblin, Rita Katherine. "Key Characteristics in the 18th and Early 19th Centuries: A Historical Approach." Ph.D. diss., University of Illinois at Urbana-Champaign, 1981. Published as: *A History of Key Characteristics in the Eighteenth and Early Nineteenth Centuries.* Ann Arbor, MI: UMI Research Press, 1983.

Stollbrock, Ludwig. "Leben und Wirken des k. k. Hofkapellmeisters und Hofkompositors Johann Georg Reuter jun." *Vierteljahrschrift für Musikwissenschaft* VIII (1892):161-203, 289-306.

Straková, Theodora. "Hudba u Brtnických Collaltů v 17. a 18. století (Musik bei Pirnitzer Collaltů in 17. und 18. Jahrhunderten)." 2 vols. Ph.D. diss., U. J. E. P., Brno, 1967.

Stute, Heinrich. "Studien über den Gebrauch der Instrumente in dem italienischen Kirchenorchester des 18. Jahrhunderts: Ein Beitrag zur Geschichte der instrumental begleiteten Messen in Italien." Ph.D. diss., University of Münster, 1928.

Sulzer, Johann Georg. *Allgemeine Theorie der schönen Künste* (Leipzig, 1771-74). 4th ed. (2nd expanded ed.) 5 vols. Leipzig: Weidmann, 1792-99. Reprint. Hildesheim: Georg Olms, 1967, 1970.

Tittel, Ernst. *Österreichische Kirchenmusik: Werden, Wachsen, Wirken.* Vienna: Herder, 1961.

————. "Die Wiener Pastoralmesse." *Musica Divina* 23/12 (1935):192-96.

Ueber die Kirchenmusik in Wien. Vienna: Sebastian Hartl, 1781. (The New York Public Library, Music Division, possesses a copy of this pamphlet.)

Unverricht, Hubert. "Die orchesterbegleitete Kirchenmusik von den Neapolitanern bis Schubert." In *Geschichte der katholischen Kirchenmusik,* ed. Karl Gustav Fellerer, vol. II, 157-72. Kassel: Bärenreiter, 1976.

Ursprung, Otto. *Die katholische Kirchenmusik.* Vol. 10 of *Handbuch der Musikwissenschaft.* 13 vols. Ed. Ernst Bücken. Wildpark-Potsdam: Athenaion, 1931.

Vogg, Herbert. "Franz Tuma (1704-1774) als Instrumentalkomponist, nebst Beiträgen zur Wiener Musikgeschichte des 18. Jahrhunderts: Die Hofkapelle der Kaiserinwitwe Elisabeth Christine." Ph.D. diss., University of Vienna, 1951.

Wagner, Hans. "Das Josephinische Wien und Mozart." *Mozart Jahrbuch* 1978/79:1-13.

Walter, Elaine Raftery. "Selected Masses of Antonio Caldara (1670-1736)." Studies in Music no. 51. Ph.D. diss., Catholic University of America, Washington, D.C., 1973.

Walther, Johann Gottfried. *Musicalisches Lexicon oder musicalische Bibliothec* (Leipzig, Wolfgang Deer, 1732). 3rd reprint. Ed. Richard Schaal. Documenta Musicologica, Series I, no. 3. Kassel: Bärenreiter, 1967.

Weber, J. F. "A Splendid Celebration of the Haydn Anniversary." *Fanfare* VI/1 (Sept./Oct. 1982):76–84, 504–5. (Discography of J. Haydn's Masses)

Weinmann, Alexander. "Musikalische Quellenforschung, beginnend mit der Zeit Joseph Haydns." *Fontes Artis Musicae* XXVI (1979):4–16.

_____. "Österreichische 'Kleinmeister' der Musik." In *Beiträge zur Musikdokumentation: Franz Grasberger zum 60. Geburtstag,* ed. Günter Brosche, 425–36. Tutzing: H. Schneider, 1975.

Weissenbäck, Andreas. "Johann Georg Albrechtsberger als Kirchenkomponist." *Studien zur Musikwissenschaft* XIV (1927):143–59.

_____. *Sacra Musica: Lexikon der katholischen Kirchenmusik.* Klosterneuburg: Augustinus Druckerei, 1937.

_____. "Thematisches Verzeichnis der Kirchenkompositionen von Johann Georg Albrechtsberger." *Jahrbuch des Stiftes Klosterneuburg* VI (1914):1–160.

Wellesz, Egon. "Giuseppe Bonno (1710–88): Sein Leben und seine dramatischen Werke," *Sammelbände der internationalen Musikgesellschaft* XI (1909–10):395–442.

Wellesz, Egon and Frederick Sternfeld, ed. *The Age of Enlightenment.* Vol. 7 of *The New Oxford History of Music,* ed. Jack Westrup et al. London: Oxford University Press, 1973.

Wienandt, Elwyn A. *Choral Music of the Church.* New York: Free Press, 1965. Reprint. New York: Da Capo, 1980.

Wiener Diarium [=*Wienerisches Diarium,* later *Wiener Zeitung*].

Wigness, C. Robert. *The Soloistic Use of the Trombone in Eighteenth-Century Vienna.* Brass Research Series, no. 2. Nashville: The Brass Press, 1978.

Wilson, David James. "Selected Masses of Johann Adolf Hasse." DMA diss., University of Illinois at Champaign-Urbana, 1973. (Includes modern edition of M. 24.)

Wurzbach, Constantin. *Biographisches Lexikon des Kaiserthums Oesterreich, enthaltend die Lebensskizzen der denkwürdigen Personen, welche seit 1750 in den österreichischen Kronländern geboren wurden oder darin gelebt und gewirkt haben.* 60 vols. Vienna: k. k. Hof- und Staatsdruckerei, 1856–91.

Zaslaw, Neal. "Mozart, Haydn, and the *Sinfonia da chiesa.*" *Journal of Musicology* I/1 (1982):95–124.

Ziffer, Agnes. *Kleinmeister zur Zeit der Wiener Klassik: Versuch einer übersichtlichen Darstellung sogenannter Kleinmeister im Umkreis von Haydn, Mozart, Beethoven und Schubert, sowie Studien zur Quellensicherung ihrer Werke.* Publikationen des Instituts für Österreichische Musikdokumentation, no. 10. Tutzing: Hans Schneider, 1984.

B. Editions of Music

Albrechtsberger, Johann Georg. *Messe in Es-dur (Missa Sancti Josephi),* ed. Andreas Weissenbäck with commentary by Karl Pfannhauser. Österreichische Kirchenmusik, vol. 8. Vienna: Doblinger, 1951. (=Weissenbäck cat. no. 78)

_____. *Messe in F-dur (Missa pro hebdomada sancta),* ed. Louis Dité. Österreichische Kirchenmusik, vol. 1. Vienna: Doblinger, 1946. (=Weissenbäck cat. no. 162; a cappella)

Caldara, Antonio. "Missa Dolorosa" (in e) in *Kirchenwerke,* ed. Eusebius Mandyczewski. Denkmäler der Tonkunst in Österreich, vol. 26 (Jg. XIII/1). Vienna: Artaria; Leipzig: Breitkopf & Haertel, 1906; reprint ed., Graz: Akademische Druck- und Verlagsanstalt, 1959.

_____. *Missa in C-dur (Missa Venerationis),* ed. Otto Drechsler. Berlin and Wiesbaden: Bote & Bock, 1962. (practical edition of this Mass of 1721)

————. *Missa in G,* ed. Wolfgang Fürlinger. Die Kantate, no. 208. Stuttgart: Hänssler, 1964. (the sixth Mass in *Chorus Musarum Divino Apollini Accinentium sive Sex Missae Selectissimae* published by Joannis Nicolai Hemmerlein in Bamberg in 1748)

Gassmann, Florian Leopold. "Missa in C" in *Kirchenwerke,* ed. Franz Kosch. Denkmäler der Tonkunst in Österreich, vol. 83 (Jg. XLV). Vienna: Universal, 1938; reprint ed., Graz: Akademische Druck- und Verlagsanstalt, 1959. (=Kosch cat. no. 3)

Hasse, Johann Adolf. *Ausgewählte geistliche Gesänge für Alt und Sopran mit Orgel- oder Klavierbegleitung,* ed. Otto Schmid. Musik am sächsischen Hofe, vol. 8. Leipzig and Dresden: Breitkopf und Haertel, 1905. ("Agnus Dei" from M. 24; "Crucifixus" from M. 23)

————. *Ausgewählte Werke von J. A. Hasse, für Klavier bearbeitet,* ed. Otto Schmid. Musik am sächsischen Hofe, vol. 2. Leipzig: Breitkopf und Haertel, 1900. ("Domine Deus" from M. 24)

Haydn, Joseph. *Harmoniemesse.* Ed. Friedrich Lippmann. Kassel: Bärenreiter, 1978. (Hob. XXII: 14)

————. *Joseph Haydn Werke.* Published by the Joseph Haydn-Institut, Cologne, under the direction of Georg Feder. Ser. XXIII: *Messen,* vol. 2–5. Munich and Duisburg: G. Henle, 1958–67.

————. *Masses Nos. 1–4.* Ed. Carl Maria Brand. The Complete Works: Critical Edition, ser. XXIII, vol. 1. Boston and Vienna: The Haydn Society, Inc., in cooperation with Breitkopf & Härtel of Leipzig-Wiesbaden, 1951. (Hob. XXII: 1, 4–6)

————. *Messe B-dur (Schöpfungs-Messe): Faksimile nach der im Eigentum der Bayerischen Staatsbibliothek befindlichen Urschrift.* Afterword by Wilhelm Virneisel. Munich and Duisburg: Henle, 1957. (Hob. XXII: 13)

————. *Missa brevis alla capella "Rorate coeli desuper."* Ed. H. C. Robbins Landon. London: Haydn-Mozart Press, 1957. (Hob. XXII: 3)

————. *Missa brevis in F (Jugendmesse).* Ed. Richard Moder. Vienna: Doblinger, 1955. (Hob. XXII: 1)

————. *Missa brevis Sti. Joannis de Deo (Kleine Orgelmesse).* Ed. H. C. Robbins Landon, Karl Heinz Füssl and Christa Landon. Kassel: Bärenreiter, 1974. (Hob. XXII: 7)

————. *Missa Cellensis (Mariazellermesse).* H. C. Robbins Landon, Karl Heinz Füssl, and Christa Landon. Kassel: Bärenreiter, 1971. (Hob. XXII: 8)

————. *Missa in Angustiis (Nelson Mass).* Ed. H. C. Robbins Landon. London, Mainz, Zürich, and New York: Eulenburg, ca. 1962. (Hob. XXII: 11)

————. *Missa Sti. Bernardi von Offida (Heiligmesse).* Ed. H. C. Robbins Landon. Kassel: Bärenreiter, 1962. (Hob. XXII: 10)

————. *Pauken Mass (Mass in Time of War).* New York: Edwin F. Kalmus [no. L-389], n.d. (Hob. XXII: 9)

————. *Theresienmesse (Theresa Mass).* Ed. Günter Thomas. Kassel: Bärenreiter, 1967. (Hob. XXII: 12)

Mozart, Wolfgang Amadeus. *Masses.* Kalmus Study Scores nos. 923–27. Melville, NY: Belwin Mills, n.d.

————. *Missa [in] C moll,* K. 427 (417^a). Ed. H. C. Robbins Landon. London, Zürich, Mainz, and New York: Eulenburg, 1956.

————. *Neue Ausgabe sämtlicher Werke.* Published by the Internationale Stiftung Mozarteum, ser. I, Werkgruppe 1, Abteilung 1: *Messen,* vol. 1–3. Ed. Walter Senn. Kassel: Bärenreiter, 1968–80.

Porpora, Niccola. *Grande Messe [in D] à Quatre Voix . . . avec Accompagnement d'Orchestre ou d'Orgue à volonté.* Paris: chez Carli, Editeur des Oeuvres de Clari, Durante, Salmi di Marcello, etc., n.d. (RISM P-5108; pl. no. 1114.R.C.)

Reutter, Georg, d.J. *Kirchenwerke.* Ed. P. Norbert Hofer. Denkmäler der Tonkunst in Österreich, vol. 88. Vienna: Österreichischer Bundesverlag, 1952. (Includes "Missa S. Caroli" = M. 49, Hofer no. 60)

Wagenseil, Georg Christoph. *Missa in A "Gratias agimus tibi."* Ed. Wolfgang Fürlinger. Süddeutsche Kirchenmusik des Barock. Vol. 3. Altötting: Alfred Coppenrath, [1973].

Index

Because the Mass itself is the main focus of study, individual parts (e.g., Kyrie, Gloria, etc.) and sections ("Christe eleison," "Gratias agimus tibi," "Qui tollis," etc.) are indexed separately in the main alphabet, *not* under Mass. Boldface indicates pages where music examples are to be found; italic indicates major discussions of a topic.